The African Philosophy Reader

Edited by

P.H. Coetzee and A.P.J. Roux

ROUTLEDGE

London and New York

First Published in the UK 1998
by Routledge
11 New Fetter Lane, London EC4P 4EE

Simultaneously published in the USA and Canada
by Routledge
29 West 35th Street, New York, NY 10001

Cover design by Collage Graphics, Gauteng, South Africa
Set in 10½ on 12 point Garamond Roman
Typesetting and reproduction by PG&A, Plumstead, Western Cape, South Africa
Printed and bound by Colorgraphic, Durban, South Africa

Library of Congress Cataloging in Publication Data
A Catalogue record for this book has been requested

British Library Cataloguing in Publication Data
A catalogue record for this book is available from the British Library

ISBN 0-415-189055

Contents

Acknowledgements

Permission given by the following copyright holders and authors is gratefully acknowledged.

S. Biko, "Some African cultural concepts", reprinted from *Frank Talk*, 1 (4), Sept./ Oct. 1984, pages 29–31, by permission of AZAPO.

K. Wiredu, "Are there cultural universals?", reprinted from *The Monist*, 78, Jan. 1995, pages 52–64, © 1995, *The Monist* La Salle, Illinois 61301. Reprinted by permission.

E.D. Prinsloo, "*Ubuntu* culture and participatory management", reprinted from an unpublished paper by permission of the author.

M. van Niekerk, "Understanding trends in 'African thinking' – a critical discussion" reprinted from *African Studies Forum*, 1, 1991 (Pretoria: HSRC), pages 125–187, by permission of the author and the publisher.

N.D. Kaphagawani, "What is African philosophy?" extracted from "The philosophical significance of Bantu nomenclature: a shot at contemporary African philosophy" from *Sage philosophy: Indigenous thinkers and modern debate on African philosophy* (Leiden: Brill, 1990), pages 181–204, reprinted by permission of the publisher.

H.O. Oruka, extracts from the introduction to *Sage philosophy: Indigenous thinkers and modern debate on African philosophy* (Leiden: Brill, 1990), pages xv–xxiv, reprinted by permission of the publisher.

K.A. Appiah, "Ethnophilosophy and its critics", from *In my father's house: Africa in the philosophy of culture* (Oxford: Oxford University Press Inc., 1992), pages 85–106, © 1992, K.A. Appiah. Reprinted by permission of the author and the publisher.

S. Gbadegesin, "*Ènìyàn:* the Yoruba concept of a person" reprinted from *African Philosophy* (New York: Peter Lang, 1991), pages 27–59, by permission of the publisher.

N.D. Kaphagawani, "African conception of personhood and intellectual identities", paper delivered at Unisa seminar, 27 August 1997, Pretoria. Reprinted by permission of the author.

G.S. Sogolo, "The concept of cause in African thought", paper delivered at Unisa, first colloqium on African philosophy, 1994. Reprinted by permission of the author.

K. Wiredu, "On decolonising African religions", paper delivered at Unisa, second colloquium on African philosophy, 1995. Reprinted by permission of the author.

G.S. Sogolo, "Logic and rationality", reprinted from *Foundations of African philosophy* (Ibadan: Ibadan University Press, 1993), pages 68–88, by permission of the author.

K. Wiredu, "The concept of truth in the Akan language", public lecture delivered at the Department of Philosophy, California State University, Los Angeles, 1980. Reprinted by permission of the author.

N.D. Kaphagawani, "Themes in a Chewa epistemology", reprinted from an unpublished paper by permission of the author.

K.A. Appiah, " Old Gods, new worlds", reprinted from *In my father's house: Africa in the philosophy of culture* (Oxford: Oxford University Press, 1992), pages 107–136, by permission of the author and the publisher.

S. Gabdegesin, "Individuality, community, and the moral order", reprinted from *African philosophy: traditional Yoruba philosophy and contemporary African realities* (New York: Peter Lang, 1991), pages 61–82, by permission of the publisher.

K. Wiredu, "The moral foundations of an African culture", reprinted from *Person and community* (CIPSH/UNESCO, 1992) pages 193–206, by permission of the author and the publisher.

K. Gyekye, "Person and community in African thought", reprinted from *Person and community: Ghanaian philosophical studies I* (CIPSH/UNESCO: Council for Research in Values and Philosophy, 1992), pages 193–206, by permission of the author and the publisher.

S. Biko, "The definition of Black Consciousness" reprinted from *Frank Talk*, 1 (1), Feb./March 1984, pages 3–4, by permission of AZAPO.

M.P. More, "Outlawing racism in philosophy: On race and philosophy", reprinted from *SA Journal of philosophy*, 16 (3), 1997, pages 124–128, by permission of the author and the publisher.

K. Wiredu, "Democracy and consensus in African traditional politics: A plea for a non-party polity", reprinted from *The Centennial Review*, 1995, pages 53–63, by permission of the author and the journal.

I.C. Onyewuenyi, "Traditional African aesthetics: A philosophical perspective", reprinted from *International philosophical quarterly*, 24, 1984, pages 237–244, by permission of IPQ.

P. English and N. Steele-Hamme, "Morality, art and African philosophy: A response to Wiredu", reprinted from *The Journal of Social Philosophy*, 27(2), 1996, pages 204–233, by permission of the author and the journal.

G. Blocker, "Is primitive art 'art'?", reprinted from *The Journal of Aesthetic Education*, 24 (4), 1991, pages 87–97, © 1991, the Board of Trustees of the University of Illinios, by permission of the author and the University of Illinios Press.

G. Blocker, "On the distinction between modern and traditional African aesthetics", reprinted from *African philosophy: Selected readings* (Englewood Cliffs: Prentice Hall, 1995), pages 428–438, by permission of the author.

L.S. Senghor, "Negritude and African socialism", from *St. Anthony's papers*, (15), 1963, pages 9–22. Also published in *Liberté II*. © Editions du Seuil, 1971. Reprinted by permission of Editions du Seuil.

List of contributors

Appiah, K.A.	Harvard University, USA
Biakolo, E.	University of Botswana
Biko, S.	Member of SASO (South Africa Students' Organisation) and generally-acknowledged intellectual leader of the Black Consciousness Movement in South Africa (†12 September 1977)
Blocker, G.	Ohio University, USA
Coetzee, P.H.	University of South Africa
English, P.	Central Connecticut State University, USA
Gbadegesin, S.	Obafemi Awolowo University, Nigeria
Gyekye, K.	University of Ghana
Kaphagawani, D.N.	University of Malawi
Malherbe, J.	University of South Africa
More, M.P.	University of Durban-Westville, RSA
Onyewuenyi, I.C.	University of Nigeria
Oruka, H.O.	University of Nairobi, Kenya
Prinsloo, E.D.	University of South Africa
Roux, A.P.J.	University of South Africa
Schutte, A.	University of Cape Town, RSA
Senghor, L.S.	African statesman, philosopher and poet; formerly president of the Republic of Senegal
Sogolo, G.	University of Ibadan, Nigeria
Steele-Hamme, N.	State University of West Georgia, USA
Teffo, J.	University of the North, RSA
Van Niekerk, M.	University of the Witwatersrand, RSA
Van Staden, C.	University of South Africa
Wilkinson, J.R.	University of South Africa
Wiredu, K.	University of South Florida, USA

Preface

This book is intended to fill a gap in the literature that is currently available to undergraduate students of African philosophy. Most texts in African philosophy are written for a professional audience – philosophers communicating with other philosophers on the nature, problems, and methods of African philosophy. Our task has been twofold: to present the professional debate to a multicultural audience in such a way that it is understandable in terms of various world-views and life-experiences, and so that it brings philosophical themes into play with existential problems.

We have set about our task with certain considerations in mind. Since there are areas in Africa where regional philosophies have grown up, notably in Ghana, Nigeria and Uganda, most of the material presented here has been drawn from these regions. The debate on the nature, problems, and methods of African philosophy is, in part, inspired by the regional contexts in which African philosophy has developed, a factor which has had considerable influence on what we have chosen to present, especially in view of the fact that each region presents its own specific existential problems. It should be pointed out here that there is no developed regional philosophy in South Africa. In South Africa philosophy has its roots largely in European traditions. Professional philosophers practise a form of neo-liberalism which draws on Western "continental" (French and German) and "analytic" (Anglo-American) prototypes. We have chosen one figure from South Africa, Steve Biko, to present something of the political philosophy in this country.

Because the philosophical geography in Africa is very fragmented, we decided to order this fragmented picture under seven categories:

1. Culture (the philosophy of)
2. Trends (ethnophilosophy, sage philosophy, ideological philosophy and professional philosophy)
3. Metaphysics (Idealism)
4. Epistemology (sociology of knowledge)
5. Ethics (communitarianism)
6. Politics (liberation ideologies and struggles)
7. Aesthetics (the status of African art as "Art")

The book begins with an introductory sketch on the problems created by European (anthropological) constructions of the African person and his/her life-world. Biakolo argues that the basis of the construction of Africa, in terms of distinctions between savage/civilised, prelogical/logical, oral/written, magical/scientific, is nothing more than European ethnocentric convention. This sets the scene for an examination of the uses of culture and cultural constructs in African contexts. An attempt is made to develop a context in which the idea of a "culture-specific" philosophy can be discussed and placed in perspective. Van Staden argues for an "articulation" concept of culture which is contrasted with a "communicalogical" concept. The articulation concept has great power to displace the communicalogical concept since it reaches beyond the cultural and ethnic frameworks to which the communicalogical idea is confined, thereby creating a context for the development of a critical discourse on culture and its uses in the African context.

The discussion of this contemporary notion of culture is essential to the main themes of the book. African philosophers argue that philosophy is a cultural enterprise and that African philosophies are culture-specific. This means that they are perspective driven. Some are ethnic perspectival models (Wiredu, Gyekye), others are non-ethnic (pan-African) models (Appiah). The specificity thesis is complemented by a diversity thesis which states that there is no single philosophical (conceptual) order for all mankind. This does not mean that cultural groups differ with respect to their capacity for cognition and rationality; it merely means that systems of reasoning are bound by the traditions within which they develop. There are cognitive as well as normative universals, but these are shaded in different colours in different cultures.

The trends in African philosophy are discussed with reference to the thesis of culture-specificity. Van Niekerk stresses the conceptual link between culture and trends. She develops this link with reference to her distinction between "Hermesian" and "Promethean" rationalities, and by applying it in a critical appraisal of ethnophilosophy and related trends.

The chapter on *Understanding Trends in "African Thinking"* connects conceptually with everything else that follows. The chapter *Metaphysical Thinking in Africa* follows the culture-specific approach which Wiredu has so aptly described as "strategic particularism". But Teffo and Roux sketch a view of metaphysics which transcends the parameters of particularity insofar as they show that the themes in African metaphysics have universal significance. This is in line with Wiredu's method of pursuing the universal through the particular, and echoes Van Staden's theme of the need to create a wider context within which particular discourses may meaningfully be examined.

In *African Epistemology* Kaphagawani and Malherbe address the question whether it makes sense to talk of an African articulation and formulation of knowledge, and find an affirmative answer in an argument pitched neatly between the relativism which attends discrete particularism and the absolutism which accompanies an uncompromising universalism. The need for a cross-cultural context and discourse is manifested in the arguments advanced for epistemic modernity, a move which again echoes Van Staden's theme.

Normative universals find a place in communitarian systems of ethics and politics. In *Particularity in Morality and its Relation to Community* Coetzee examines how Wiredu develops a notion of particularity in morals from the specifics of the kinship structures of the Akans of Ghana. Notions of the good, which specific kin groups endorse in civic contexts, generate various solidarities which find a place in civil life. The particularities of civic structures, then, find expression in the political structures of civil society.

The problem of accommodating a variety of civic perspectives in a single political unit in a multicultural state like Ghana is, in fact, a problem for all African states. South Africa is no exception. How might multicultural states accommodate different cultural and social identities within single political orders? In *The Problem of Political Self-Definition in South Africa* Coetzee argues for the need to create a political culture which accords at least an equality of regard to all cultural communities. A substantive equality may not be achieved, yet it can be approached through social programmes designed in an open forum of public debate – one which acknowledges the constraints of public reason.

In *Using and Abusing African Art* Wilkinson addresses the problem of understanding the objects of African art as *African* art, and not as re-culturised objects in the European world. She argues that the way the problem has been posed in the past has suffered from misguided attempts to be politically correct. Rather than asking how "art" should (logically) be used, we should ask how "art" has (empirically) been used in Africa and particularly in South Africa.

The book closes with Shutte's post-anthropological attempt to find a model for cross-cultural philosophical understanding. The history of Africa, Shutte claims, makes the linking between African and European philosophy unavoidable. Shutte elaborates this linking in terms of Senghor's idea of a "Civilisation of the Universal" – and in so doing develops Biakolo's theme and adds a new dimension to Van Staden's theme.

The readings which appear in Chapters 2–8 present the reader with an exposure to some genuine philosophising in Africa. They have been chosen as exemplars of the various trends, and also for the story they tell about the concerns of Africa's philosophers. Among these, a concern with cultural issues, especially the tension between tradition and modernity, which imparts a particular colour to the African experience, figures prominently. This concern with the cultural reconstruction of Africa has many facets. It raises deep critical questions about metaphysics, epistemology, ethics, politics, and, of course, the nature of African philosophy itself. And in doing so, we learn something about other tensions – between the need to conserve what is good and useful in tradition, and what is needed to modernise Africa's cultures; between preferences for traditional agrarian communities and their value structures, and the force of urbanisation which follows in the wake of technological advancement. These tensions create a need for African philosophers to engage in interdisciplinary research, for renewal requires reflection on education, government, social organisation, religious practices, and many other areas. We hope the way in which the readings are ordered in each chapter will help the reader to explore these possibilities.

The editors thank all the authors for their contributions. A very special word of thanks goes to Marinda Delport who took charge of the typing and the preparation of the manuscript, Willena Reinach who assisted her, and to Lynda Gillfillan for the language editing of the manuscript.

P.H. COETZEE
A.P.J. ROUX

CHAPTER ONE

Categories of Cross-cultural Cognition and the African Condition

EMEVWO BIAKOLO

1. INTRODUCTION

Relations between the knowing subject and its object, in any account of the epistemological process, has occupied Western philosophy from the time of Plato, but most especially since the seventeenth century, with the advent of both Cartesian rationalism and Lockean empiricism. Although in the field of philosophy the central concerns have been with the individual subject as such, it was not long before the influences of these interpretations of subject/object relations began to make themselves felt in the much younger discipline of anthropology. In consonance with the pattern of growth and development of the new science of culture, the determining factor here was race (Harris 1969:80–107). The critical question was how to *think* the non-Caucasian races, the "Other", with whom the Western world had come into increasing contact since the great exploratory journeys of the fifteenth century.

In *The invention of Africa* (1988) and *The idea of Africa* (1994) V.Y. Mudimbe has mapped out the historical course of the apprehension and description of the "Other" in Western thought from classical times until the consolidation of the African image in the power-knowledge system of colonialism and the post-colonial period. While the constancy of the ideology behind the building of the paradigm is not in doubt, it is also useful to note the variegation in its employment, the nuanced way in which it is deployed from discipline to discipline within the configuration of anthropocentric studies. It reveals an ingenuity which goes further to confirm the political project behind the Western construction of cultural paradigms of the "Other".

2. SAVAGE vs. CIVILISED

Before the publication of Lucien Lévy-Bruhl's *Les fonctions mentales dans les sociétiés inférieures* (1910) (translated as *How natives think*), when a slight shift occurred in the idiom of anthropological discourses of the "Other", the standard paradigm had been that enunciated in Lewis Henry Morgan's 1870 classic, *Systems of consanguinity and affinity of the human family.* Morgan's schemata of the developmental stages through which cultures progress was entirely unique, even among evolutionists, in its confident clarity. Neither E.B. Tylor's *Researches into the early history of mankind and the development of civilization,* published in 1865, nor his later, better-known work, *Primitive culture* (1871), matched the structural rigour and conceptual comprehensiveness of Morgan's paradigm. The latter's seven stages of development – Lower Savagery, Middle Savagery, Upper Savagery, Lower Barbarism, Middle Barbarism, Upper Barbarism, and Civilisation – were not only determined by forms of family and kinship relationships, the subsistence system and technology, they also corresponded with identifiable, that is *nameable,* societies. Of course, in this elaborate frame only Euro-American society attained the status of civilisation, typified by the possession of writing and especially of the phonetic alphabet.

The image of the African as "brutish, ignorant, idle, crafty, treacherous, bloody, thievish, mistrustful, and superstitious," (quoted in Harris 1969:89), which was current in Europe and the colonies in the eighteenth century, had a most respectable antecedent in the ethnocentricism of philosophers like David Hume, Voltaire and the French *philosophes* such as Montesquieu. This, for instance, is what Hume says:

> There never was civilized nation of any other complexion than white, nor even any individual eminent in action or speculation. No ingenious manufacturer among them, no arts, no sciences. . . . Such a uniform and constant difference could not happen, in so many countries and ages, if nature had not made an original distinction betwixt these breeds of men. (Quoted in Harris 1969:88.)

Articulated within this discourse of the "savage" or "barbaric" African, was an express cultural frame of reference. The point had a double trajectory: the absence of *any single individual* genius (as against a European milieu full of individual culture-heroes) and a *general* social context of benighted savagery. If, today, one of Europe's most celebrated philosophers sounds so ludicrous in his assertions, we have to note that this situation had as much to do with ignorance as with "a will to truth" or "power-knowledge". While travellers, traders, and explorers had since the fifteenth century provided Europeans with some knowledge of non-Western people, and though, as Mudimbe (1988) says, European artists had contemplated the "Other" in their paintings, no really systematic study of the subject had been undertaken until well into the eighteenth century.

Prior to this time, in the prehistory of anthropology, the protracted arguments between the monogenists and the polygenists, which have been amply described by Marvin Harris (1969), had less relevance as an attempt to understand the "Other" than as a disputation in biblical theology. Thus, even with the arrival of more extensive anthropological studies in the nineteenth century, the persistent paradigm until the turn of the century was that of "savagery/barbarism", of the African pitted against the "civilisation of the West". The substantive shift which occurred in this period is exemplified in the work of Lévy-Bruhl mentioned above.

3. PRELOGICAL vs. LOGICAL

The anthropology of Lévy-Bruhl marked a watershed in the understanding of the "Other". Although, like Frazer and Taylor before him, Lévy-Bruhl was an armchair anthropologist, his work departed from the evolutionary quests of his predecessors and from the social-scientific aspirations of his contemporaries, and focused instead on the psychological foundations of primitive culture. Latching on to what proved seminal in many respects, he characterised the representations of "undeveloped peoples" as evidence of, for want of a better term, a "prelogical mentality". This mentality was based on the "law of participation".

> The collective representations of primitives, therefore, differ very profoundly from our ideas or concepts, nor are they their equivalent either. On the one hand, as we shall presently discover, they have not their logical character. . . . On the other hand, they see many things there of which we are unconscious (Lévy-Bruhl 1985:37–38).

The participation mystique and prelogical mentality makes primitive reasoning "essentially synthetic", "little given to analysis", and "concrete". Thus, memory plays a much more important role in primitive mental life than in that of the civilised, European, mind. Objective validity is unknown to primitive cultures and

> the slightest mental effort involving abstract reasoning, however elementary it may be, is distasteful to them (Lévy-Bruhl 1985:86–128).

There are certain notable features in this description. Firstly, there is the mutation of the general cultural opposition, savage versus civilised, until then dominant in anthropological discourse. In its place was erected an alternative frame, "prelogical versus logical", which subsumed a host of subsidiary and associated concepts: "synthetic" versus "analytic", "concrete" versus "abstract", "particular" versus "generalising". "Prelogical" does not mean *antedating* logic, or *anti-logical* or even *alogical*, as Lévy-Bruhl (1985:78) is at pains to point out. Nevertheless, it set at nought the rules of logic as commonly known in the Western tradition, such as the law of non-contradiction and *modus ponens*. That is, primitives are "wholly indifferent" to Western logical procedures. This, for Lévy-Bruhl, was the key to understanding the difference between savage and civilised cultures, rather than the earlier futile pursuit of the evolutionary path which society had followed from one stage to another. It should, however, immediately be added that this conceptual departure did not in any way imply a repudiation or rejection of the earlier paradigm. It rather concretised and specified the sometimes nebulous meanings associated with the notions of savage and civilised.

A second feature of Lévy-Bruhl's description is that, while earlier descriptions, for example, Morgan's, had been concerned with the mode of production, or family and kinship relations of the societies in question, Lévy-Bruhl thought that these were only material expressions of the mentality of the group. Even the remarkable difference in the structure of language of primitive and civilised peoples was determined by their varying mentalities. Thus, social scientists such as Emile Durkheim might elaborate the institutions which go into the formation of the social structure, but the very foundation of these structures and processes of culture is the *form* of mind behind the operations.

The third aspect of this frame is that it posed in alternative terms what we have already seen in Hume's celebration of the superiority of European culture. Lévy-Bruhl speaks of "collective representations" of primitives, not just representations, which could imply individual creations. In the light of recent debates on ethnophilosophy among African philosophers (cf. Hountondji 1976; Wiredu 1980; Mudimbe 1988; Appiah 1992; Sogolo 1993), this idea of collective representations assumes a particular poignancy. Lévy-Bruhl speaks of them as collective, following the contemporary terminology, not because he is interested in rendering a general (collectivist) account of a culture, but because the participation mystique is at one with this collectivity. Primitive culture is participated in collectively, it is a shared reality. The idea of individual, and, by implication, dissident, grasp or assessment of reality, individual creativity, and so on, runs counter to the ethos of primitive culture. Articulated, then, together with a logic and an epistemology, were ethics.

While a vast majority of the functionalist school of anthropology (and here we include such disparate figures as Bronislaw Malinowski, Franz Boas, A.R. Radcliffe-Brown and Paul Radin) were antagonistic to the prelogical/logical frame enunciated by Lévy-Bruhl, his continued influence in cultural cognitive studies is undeniable (Scott-Littleton 1985). The thrust of this influence can be seen in two different but related directions. First of all, the *emic-etic* dispute from the sixties was articulated with critical methodological and theoretical issues concerned with the concept of cultural relativity in the new ethnography. On this basis, the functionalists' criticism of Lévy-Bruhl becomes, in effect, a validation of putative universal categories under whose suasion non-Western cultures were and could be studied.

There is a curious permutation of these ideas in the consolidation of the colonial state all over Africa. On the one hand, the French model, thoroughly convinced of the superiority of European (French) culture, in the understanding of the cognitive paradigm so clearly set out by Lévy-Bruhl, in effect created two sorts of citizens within the state – black men who had achieved honourary status as French citizens as a consequence of having acquired civilisation, and the mass of the African savage population with which the state was forced by economic and political considerations to have dealings and to protect from competitors. The British model, on the other hand, granting, as British functionalist anthropology did, some – admittedly doubtful – humanity to the African primitives, elaborated a system which permitted the natives to govern themselves after their own fashion, but within the legal and political limits set by the "Master". The cultural conquest could more systematically proceed through the religious and educational system, which, while it did not officially force anyone, became a prerequisite for the political and social advancement of any deserving native.

4.   PERCEPTUAL vs. CONCEPTUAL

From another direction comes the work of Claude Lévi-Strauss, especially his most seminal book, *The savage mind* (1966). This work was intended as a response to the arguments of Lévy-Bruhl, proposing to show the logicality of the primitive mind and the structural orderliness of its conceptual schemes. Identifying primitive knowledge-schema with magic and the civilised schema with science, Lévi-Strauss argued, however, that primitive man had a genuine scientific spirit and logical-categorial abilities, as can be seen in his nominal and classificatory systems and his myths. He admits that these modes of knowledge-acquisition are not necessarily the preserve of any one culture. Yet, fundamental differences exist between civilised and primitive cultures:

> The characteristic feature of mythical thought is that it expresses itself by means of a heterogeneous repertoire which, even if extensive, is nevertheless limited. It has to use this repertoire, however, whatever the task in hand because it has nothing else at its disposal (Lévi-Strauss 1966:17).

This mode of inquiry Lévi-Strauss characterises as "*bricolage*". In pattern of thought, the "*bricoleur*" is perceptual where the scientist is conceptual. The latter opens up new possibilities of knowledge by extension and renewal, while the former conserves knowledge by means of reorganisation of what is already known. Also, the scientist creates events by means of structures, and in this way changes the world; the "*bricoleur*", on the other hand, creates structures by means of events.

Lévi-Strauss's declaration that these two mental modes are not unique to any given culture seems to be at one with the intention of the functionalists, *contra* both Lévy-Bruhl and the evolutionists, namely, to demonstrate the similarity of all cultures in terms of their synchronic social operations, in spite of other differences. But what unites all these can be discerned by analysing some of the most important postulates of Lévi-Strauss in comparison with Lévy-Bruhl. Scientific thought, Lévi-Strauss argues, is conceptual, while mythical thought is perceptual. While his compatriot does not adopt this terminology, the conceptual is cognate with Lévy-Bruhl's "analytical", just as the perceptual shares a relation with the "synthetic". Percepts are commonly held to be integrative, while concepts on the other hand can be grasped fully only in their analytical frame, and thus belong to a higher epistemological order.

In a similar manner, scientific thought is innovative, ever-inventive of new technological forms, while mythical thought is conservative, recreating existing structures in a manipulative way, but without creating anything new. In the light of what we shall see below when we consider what Walter Ong (1977, 1981, 1982) has to say concerning his so-called "oral cultures", even Lévi-Strauss's reluctance to identify any particular cultures with a mythical or scientific spirit poses a problem, and this is not merely a moral one. What we need to ask is why the problem has to be presented in the terms employed by past theorists. If, following the structuralist thesis, all life and culture present themselves in a binary form, why would this binarism be limited only to individuals, or within cultures and not among cultures? Is not this binarism also a necessity of the conditions and possibilities of knowledge? That is to say, meta-theory in structuralism cannot be abstracted from this general binary condition, without structuralism being pressed arbitrarily into heuristic service. If the latter is the case, all forms of knowledge and their organisation and articulation within any *episteme* become binary and it is only right and fair to identify Lévi-Strauss with a binary view of racial and cultural forms of knowledge. This is in part what Jacques Derrida (1976:120–122) means when he accuses Lévi-Strauss's cultural theory of ethnocentrism masked as anti-ethnocentrism.

A further point is that if myth and science are really such dichotomous orders of knowing and knowledge, their mode of existence and mutual relationship within the individual or cultural subject is far from clear in Lévi-Strauss's explanation. Do they exist in a sub- or super-ordinate relationship with each other, or are they co-terminal, co-ordinate, homologous? Whatever the answer, myth or magic has more recently come to be seen as incommensurable with science. What is the basis of the selection of epistemes for comparative analysis? Why is myth or magic opposed to science? Why is the opposition not between myth and modern religion? Simply put, the selection of the terms of a paradigm are coloured ideologically. Lévi-Strauss works within the grid of a power-knowledge paradigm, and the supposed attempt to decontextualise this, to objectify its terms, merely serves to reinforce the paradigm in a sophisticated way.

5.   ORAL vs. WRITTEN

The change in the interpretation of the savage/civilised paradigm by the structuralists also coincided with the change in the political fortunes of imperialism. By the 1950s, the African subject was no longer content to acquire the civilisation of the "Master". He/she, too, wanted a share of the political estate. In theoretical terms, he/she could no longer be dismissed as the prelogical primitive, only now, following the Lévi-Straussian doctrine, he/she was dismissed as merely the exemplary mythical thinker. Under the new argot, everyone was adjudged to be in some way mythical, although some were indeed more mythical in thought than others. Looked at in this way, it becomes particularly significant that similar efforts to change the tune of the song without changing its sense were being undertaken from another direction at about the same time. I refer to investigations in philology and communication studies involving such a diverse collection of scholars as Milman Parry, Eric Havelock, Harold Innis, Albert Lord, Marshall McLuhan and Walter Ong. The basic argument advanced by these scholars is that civilisation – certainly Western civilisation – owes its origin to writing. With the Greek invention of the alphabet, the organisation of knowledge was radically transformed. In oral cultures the poets, sages, and thinkers depend on poetic rhythm and narrative structure to ensure the remembrance of past utterances. With the introduction of writing, this mnemonic function is most effectively served by the medium itself, making the storage and retrieval of knowledge so much easier (Havelock 1963, 1976, 1982).

The consequences of this development in the means of communication were not merely practical or mnemonic in the individual sense. What it achieved was alteration in the way the consciousness of Western men and women is organised. There was a paradigmatic shift from a time-oriented focus of communicative consciousness to a space-oriented one. Even more importantly, perhaps, there was a change in the style of knowledge-presentation, resulting in the dominance of discourses that were increasingly definitional, descriptive, and analytical (Havelock 1963, 1991; Ong 1977, 1982; Goody & Watt 1963; Goody 1977). Here was the origin of Western science and philosophy. Havelock puts it quite starkly:

> Without modern literacy, which means Greek literacy, we would not have science, philosophy, written law or literature, nor the automobile or the airplane (1991:24).

But it is Walter Ong who has provided by far the most sustained elaboration of the cultural consequences of the change in the medium of communication. For him, the transformation of the mode of codification and structuration of knowledge led to a cultural regimen which placed a greater premium on innovativeness, inventiveness, and objectivity. Discourses which emerge from such a milieu tend to be abstract, analytic, syllogistic, and definitional, and their immediate context of production is generally privatist. In contrast, oral cultures tend to be traditionalist and conservative; their members acquire knowledge and skill by personal participation and practice; also, their conceptual categories are invariably concrete and are interiorised as communal knowledge. Even the forms of social and political organisation in oral and literate cultures differ as a result of this single technological development.

Where the real challenge in this interpretation of cultures lies, and where the source of the unease it generates in many scholars (cf. Street 1984) resides, is in the question, "What valid historiographic procedure permits a causal account of culture that relies exclusively on only one technological item?". However, the problem is more complex than this. Indeed, even before addressing the epistemological issues raised, there is the elementary question of the historical validity of some of the claims made in this account. It has become a historical commonplace that we owe the phonetic alphabet to the Greeks. But this has been seriously contested by I.J. Gelb in *The study of writing* (1963). Following several authorities, Gelb contends that the Greeks borrowed their alphabetic signs from the Phoenicians. But when presented with incontrovertible evidence of this truth, some scholars have hastened to add that, even if the Greeks did not create the alphabet, it was their introduction of the vowel into the Semitic Aleph-Beth which has made the alphabet what it is today. Gelb counters the claim of these determined ethnocentrists, however:

> The Greeks did not invent a new vowel system but simply used for vowels those signs which in the various Semitic systems of writing likewise can function as vowels in form of the so-called *matres lectionis*. . . . The greatness of the Greek innovation lies, therefore, not in the invention of a new method of indicating vowels but in a methodical application of a device which the early Semites used only in an irregular and sporadic fashion. As we have seen, even the Semitic and other Near Eastern writings in the course of time developed this method of indicating vowels to such an extent that they, too, were on the way toward creating a full system of vowel signs and consequently an alphabet (1963:181–182).

But the Havelock-Ong argument has other problems as well. If literacy is responsible for Greek artistic and scientific glory, what can account for the relative low-technology of India which took over the Semitic alphabet at about the same time as Greece? In answer to this it has sometimes been argued that in India or among the Semites, literacy was restricted to the scribal class. But then, how did literacy manage to serve the commercial purpose it did with the Phoenicians? And in any case, how widespread indeed was literacy among the Greeks? The Greek city-states were not a uniform socio-political and cultural experience, and so the reliance on the Athenian model for generalisations with regard to literacy is rather problematic. To take only one brief example: the *Spartiatae* enjoyed no other but a military sort of education. Thus, to argue that Greek achievements in science and philosophy are due to the pervasiveness of literacy is to overstate the case entirely.

But even on its own grounds, the argument is difficult to sustain. Brian Street (1988) has pointed out that the formulation of the argument leaves one uncertain whether these supposed effects pertain to individuals or to sub-groups or to the entire culture. Havelock (1963) began with the description of the consequences of literacy for Plato's discourse and ended up with a large-scale generalisation for Western culture. It certainly is a questionable proceeding methodologically to generalise the findings of a subset to other subsets of a higher hierarchy. For instance, can we say that the sort of discursive virtues – rationality, objectivity, analysis, definition – associated with the academy (both Plato's and the modern one), are achieved at every instance of literate discourse? Moreover, ideologically speaking, are the virtues of the academy necessarily the virtues of all classes in the social or cultural order (cf. Street 1984)? And if the point is pressed home, it is indeed a strange sort of person who, at every discursive occasion, is without exception theoretical, objectivist, and rationalistic. But ultimately, the strongest argument against this position is that no literate mentality would have any way of knowing anything about the so-called oral mentality because, following the position of these scholars, it is already trapped in its own literate mind-cast. It has no means at all of gaining access to the oral consciousness.

One interesting aspect of the differentiation between orality and literacy is that it appears to have mastered the art of the ventriloquist, able to speak from both sides of the mouth at once. On the one hand, it is presented as a mere communicative distinction, that is, as a distinction between spoken and written forms of discourse. In such a case, it is possible to study it as a rhetorical phenomenon. On the other hand, this difference is presented as a cultural difference. There seems occasionally to be an intellectual sleight-of-hand whereby obvious communicative features are isolated, whose differences are then elaborated until an essentialist cultural paradigm is achieved. This has misled certain linguistic scholars into reposing excessive faith in the spoken/written distinction.

In the various aspects of language study – phonology, semantics, morphology, and syntax – distinctions between spoken and written language have been drawn, leading to such categorial differences as greater abstraction, elaboration, decontextualisation, explicitness, and richer vocabulary in written language (Goody 1987:264). Starting from this position, other scholars have been more concerned with specifying the discourse features of speaking and writing, that is the language production process itself (cf. Chafe 1982, 1985; Chafe & Danielewicz 1987). For instance, Chafe (1982) proposed that speaking is done in spurts of what he called "idea units" at a rate of about one in two seconds, corresponding roughly to our normal thinking rate. This can be compared to writing which is more than ten times slower, thus forcing our thoughts to get ahead of our expression. The result is that in writing

> we have time to integrate a succession of ideas into a single linguistic whole in a way that is not available in speaking (Chafe 1982:36).

Chafe (1985) and especially Chafe and Danielewicz (1987) followed up this consequence, and using as data four discourse types – dinner-table conversations, lectures, letters, and academic papers, which correspond respectively to informal spoken language, formal spoken language, informal written language, and formal written language – came to similar conclusions as Goody, using, indeed, identical terms. Spoken language, for Chafe, had greater audience involvement than written language, greater involvement of self in the speech, and greater involvement with the reality spoken about. This contrasts with the writer's detachment and his/her

> interest in ideas that are not tied to specific people, events, times or places, but which are abstract and timeless (Goody 1987:108).

Linguistic studies such as these have about them an air of "scientific" objectivity, of dealing only with "facts" and data untrammelled by the assumptions of cognitive and theoretical anthropology. In fact, in many of them (e.g. Chafe 1982, 1985) there is no evidence of any awareness of the work of Havelock, Ong or McLuhan. In this way, they mask a whole ideological apparatus. For instance, it is a commonplace of institutional pedagogy that expository and discursive writing should eschew personal references, and aim at detached forms of expression. This is an idea imparted from the earliest years of the school system. To speak of an academic norm as if it were a reality independent of its social context and discoverable by means of the empirical method is curious, to say the least (cf. Street 1984). Is it not rather the norm, however it may have come about, strengthened and safeguarded by a range of ideological operations, which gives rise to social practices that in turn enforce the normative order? To speak of these practices as objective, observable "facts" of society or culture, without adverting to their genesis and context, can only be due to wilful blindness. Fortunately, not all scholars operate in this fashion. Some, for example Deborah Tannen (1982), frankly admit that their work is based on investigating and testing the validity of the claims of cognitive anthropology. While some of their findings show divergence on certain specific features, most, however, validate these claims (cf. Olson 1977, 1988; Torrance & Olson 1985; Olson & Torrance 1991). The cumulative impression one is left with is that these scholars are getting closer to the truth.

The point can be well illustrated by the work of Tannen (1982), where she examines the processing of narrative discourse by two sets of subjects, American and Greek. Both groups are literate, but she found that Greek subjects adopted strategies "associated with orality", such as the formulaicness of language, personal/emotive involvement and internal evaluation. American subjects, on the other hand, adopted writing strategies: external evaluation, decontextualisation and novelty of expression. Tannen is clearly at pains to stress the interconnectedness of orality and literacy, as well as the limitation of her interest to these varying strategies and their fluidity in different discourse situations. But when she declares finally that "there is no point to labelling people as either oral or literate" one is at a loss as to what purpose this caveat is intended to serve. It surely cannot be very relevant to her, in the context of her discussion, whether some people are labelled one way or another. But she has a professional obligation to examine whether the constitutive terms on which she relies for the description of her research findings are reliable ones, whether there is a sufficient, rational basis for adopting them, or if they run the risk of conveying more than she intended them to do. In other words, for her to avoid the charge of blindly following those she accuses of labelling, she has a responsibility to show the propriety, not to speak of the necessity, of associating those strategies with orality and literacy. What she cannot do is to take over wholly or partially those same associations and then turn round to proclaim that she intended nothing else by them than as value-free descriptions of her research conclusions. This is especially insidious in view of her stated awareness of the ideological and cognitive dimensions of the oral-literate debate.

6. RELIGIOUS vs. SCIENTIFIC

But it is in philosophical discourses that, as the phrase goes, the chickens come home to roost. In the last three decades an ardent debate has taken place as to the degree of rationality attributable to primitive thought. Inspired mostly by the anthropological work of E. Evans-Pritchard (1937) and his later theory of religion (1980), this discourse has relied on a magic-science paradigm (Wilson 1970; Hollis & Lukes 1982). Three main positions can be isolated:

1. Primitive thought is irrational, illogical and unscientific.
2. Primitive thought is rational and logical but not scientific, or alternatively, it is rational but illogical and unscientific.
3. Primitive thought is as rational and logical as scientific thought within its own cultural context.

When presented in this manner, the rational is separated conceptually from the logical and/or scientific, but in actual practice the disputants often use these terms interchangeably.

One approach which takes account of all three positions is Robin Horton's (1970), where he provides an exposé of the methods and objectives of traditional and scientific thought. Primitive thought is, in this view, rational and logical in ways often analogous to science. Scientific thought quests for the unity, simplicity, order, and regularity which underlie apparent diversity, complexity, disorder, and anomaly in the phenomenal universe. African traditional thought also seeks this through the structure of the pantheon and the categorial relations of its spiritual forces. And, like science, it does this through causal explanations, for example in the causal connection between disease states and social conduct. Furthermore, the two forms of thought employ different levels of theory, low and high theory, to cover, respectively, narrow or wide areas of experience. Both do this by a process of abstraction, analysis, and integration. Both draw analogies between familiar and puzzling phenomena in their modelling processes.

But this does not turn African traditional thought into a species of scientific thought. For one thing, the African model is a closed system because, unlike the open scientific culture, it neither understands nor tolerates alternative thought. It has a mystical attitude to language and takes recourse to a personal idiom and a contextual basis for its discourse. In the event, African traditional thought turns out to be lacking in logic and philosophy *sensus strictu* (Horton 1970:159–160). In this way, Horton exposes finally his ambivalence about African traditional thought. But the real source of this ambivalence is not, as might well be imagined, a commonplace Western prejudice. I propose that it is to be located in the paradigmatic equation that makes all African traditional thought religious (or magical or mythical). On the other side of the paradigm is, of course, Western science. But if African traditional thought is prototypically religious, would it not then be more theoretically appropriate to compare it with Western religion, in this case, Christianity (accepting here, for the sake of the argument, that Christianity is the "traditional" religion of the Western world), given, as I have stated before, the incommensurability of magic and science?

At any rate, this should lead us to consider at some length the criteria of science. In the classical model of rationality, no scientific theory is considered valid if it is not necessary, universal, and rule-governed (Brown 1988). It is, in this sense, irrelevant whether truths have been arrived at inductively or deductively. What counts is that the results or conclusions must follow necessarily from the data or premises, that this relation be recognised as such, that the principle be applicable at every instance and in each domain, and that the entire procedure should conform to the appropriate rules. However, the question remains: on what basis are data or premises selected, and what makes them suitable and acceptable? Secondly, who makes these "appropriate rules", and how can we tell if they are really appropriate? Following these arguments, philosophers generally agree that the only propositions that can fully satisfy the fundamental conditions of rationality are *self-evident* and *self-justifying* ones, since every other conceivable proposition seems to require precedent justification, thus leading to infinite regression. Apparently, however, obtaining propositions that satisfy these two features simultaneously is impossible. When self-justifying ones are found, they are not self-evident. Their truths can only be grasped intuitively.

This untoward state of affairs has led to all sorts of speculative and critical efforts to resolve the dilemma. As a way out of the despondency of his colleagues, Karl Popper has proposed that while the truth of science cannot be proven, its falsehood can be refuted. Therefore, rationality consists not in corroboration of claims, but in our readiness to refute them, which is what empirical testing is all about. But even here, when pressed hard as to the procedural grounds for beginning this refutation at all (for example, on what rational basis we should accept Popper's "basic statements"), it turns out to be no more secure than convention. Now, if propositional foundations are lacking, we are no luckier with foundational rules. It does not seem sufficient merely to have a logical or scientific rule for testing or evaluating the rationality of any claim. We need *appropriate* rules, and therefore we need some way of judging that any given set of rules are the right ones. As we have seen, no meta-rule seems available that does not involve us in regress. In fact, not even the most traditionally incontestable laws of logic (for instance the principle of excluded middle) are indubitable, as shown by intuitionist and other recent systems of logic (Brown 1988:70–78).

If the very foundations of scientific and logical rationality turn out to be no more than intuition or convention, on what grounds can cognitivists claim some truths of culture to be irrational and others not? The position rests on pretty thin ice, as philosophers of social science now generally agree. The concern that this position might involve us in cultural and moral relativism is a genuine one, but it is not answered by evading the argument. It appears, moreover, that the only reply seems to be the position summed up by Charles Taylor. For him, even if we can find no theoretical grounds for adducing superior rationality to Western scientific and technological culture, the obvious fact of its material achievements is an irrefutable proof of its being a higher order of life than that of primitive societies:

> If one protests and asks why the theoretical order is more perspicuous transculturally, granted the admitted difference between the aims of the activities compared, and granted that the two cultures identify and distinguish the activities differently, the answer is that at least in some respects theoretical cultures score successes which command the attention of atheoretical ones, and in fact invariably have done so when they met. A case in point is the immense technological successes of one particular theoretical culture, our modern scientific one. Of course, this particular superiority commands attention in a quite non-theoretical way as well. We are reminded of the ditty about nineteeth-century British colonial forces in Africa: "Whatever happens, we have got the Gatling gun, and they have not" (Taylor 1982:104).

Indeed, confronted with a Gatling gun argument such as Taylor's, what hope of refutation have we?

7. CONCLUSION

I have attempted, in the preceding analysis, to show the intertextual connection, over a wide range of disciplines and periods, of the cross-cultural categories: savage/civilised, prelogical/logical, oral/written, magical/scientific. I have argued that the basis of the distinctions is hardly more than ethnocentric convention or intuition. Can this intuitive or conventional wisdom serve any function in the understanding of African culture and the African condition? One piece of received wisdom has it that the low state of scientific and technological knowledge in Africa is due to the intrinsic mentality of Africans, which, being mystical, illogical, and so on, is incapable of scientific pursuit. It is pointed out that the state of technology throughout Africa is proof of this. And, as an additional support, it is often stated that several Asian nationalities themselves passed through the colonial experience and underdevelopment, but have managed so far to industrialise. In sum, racial factors must have a role in scientific and technological ability. But this argument is so clearly circular that there is no way to engage it.

The other, more common, argument is historically based: for Africa to develop, the paths it must tread involve abandoning an oral, magical, prelogical past, and gradually assimilating the written, logical, scientific culture of the West. This thesis has given rise to developmental studies in anthropology, sociology, economics, and even philosophy, where pre-colonial African thought-systems, so-called ethnophilosophy, is not regarded as being philosophy because it is neither individual nor systematic and cannot show historical continuity of any kind. The implication is that only by following the epistemic path already plotted by the West can African philosophy – and other disciplines for that matter – make any progress. This argument has its own difficulties, but they need not detain us here.

For the historical thesis to be meaningful, however, it should include also the understanding that if there is no African *essence*, culturally speaking, it is because each ethnic or national formation is unique, with a unique historical and cultural experience, even within the sharedness of racial and historical experience, and therefore no general path of development can be prescribed for all African groups. As for the general underdevelopment of Africa, this is a phrase impossible to understand. It assumes either that history is already foreclosed or that in Africa development is static in a world of dynamic scientific and technological progress. But the model of history, the history of the West for instance, as one continuous upward upswing of progress, is little more than a fiction. Every national history is an uneven topography, with plains, hills, and valleys: periods of rapid material development, longer or shorter moments of stagnation, and times of more or less serious decline. The fashionable pessimism about material and societal develop-ment in Africa seems to be more part of a sustained doctrine of congenital incapacity than a serious reflection on history.

What can be made of the cross-cultural paradigms in view of the African condition? It seems, indeed, that they serve merely to obscure efforts to come to grips with the African condition. They provide no access to understanding either the past or the present of Africa. They have served great uses in the colonisation and exploitation of Africa, as Mudimbe suggests. But they provide no key to the knowledge of Africa. On the contrary, their perpetuation merely serves to repeat the outdated myth of Africa as the "white man's burden".

REFERENCES

Appiah, A.K. 1992. *In my father's house: Africa in the philosophy of culture*. Oxford: Oxford University Press.

Brown, H. 1988. *Rationality*. London: Routledge.

Chafe, W. 1982. "Integration and involvement in speaking, writing, and oral literature", in D. Tannen (ed.), 1982:35–52.

Chafe, W. 1985. "Linguistic differences produced by differences between speaking and writing", in D. Olson, N. Torrance & A. Hildyard (eds), *Literacy, language and learning*. Cambridge: Cambridge University Press, 1985:105–122.

Chafe, W. & Danielewicz, J. 1987. "Properties of spoken and written language", in R. Horowitz & J.S. Samuels (eds), *Comprehending oral and written language*. San Diego: Academic Press, 1987:83–113.

Derrida, J. 1976. *Of grammatology*. Baltimore: Johns Hopkins University Press.

Evans-Pritchard, E.E. 1976 (1937). *Witchcraft, oracles and magic among the Azande*. Oxford: Claredon Press.

Evans-Pritchard, E.E. 1980 (1965). *Theories of primitive religion*. Oxford: Clarendon.

Gelb, I.J. 1963. *The study of writing*. Chicago: University of Chicago Press.

Goody, J. 1977. *The domestication of the savage mind*. Cambridge: Cambridge University Press.

Goody, J. 1987. *The interface between the written and the oral*. Cambridge: Cambridge University Press.

Goody, J. & Watt, I. 1963. "The consequences of literacy", in J. Goody (ed.), *Literacy in traditional societies*. Cambridge: Cambridge University Press, 1968:27–68.

Harris, M. 1969. *The rise of anthropological theory*. London: Routledge & Kegan Paul.

Havelock, E. 1963. *Preface to Plato*. Oxford: Blackwell.

Havelock, E. 1976. *Origins of Western literacy*. Toronto: Toronto Institute for Studies in Education.

Havelock, E. 1982. *The literate revolution and its cultural consequences*. Princeton: Princeton University Press.

Havelock, E. 1991. "The oral-literate equation: A formula for the modern mind", in D. Olson & N. Torrance (eds), 1991:11–27.

Hollis, M. & Lukes, S. (eds) 1982. *Rationality and relativism*. Oxford: Blackwell.

Horton, R. 1970. "African traditional thought and Western science", in B.R. Wilson, 1970:131–171.

Hountondji, P.J. 1976. *Sur la 'philosophie Africaine': Critique de l'ethnophilosophie*. Paris: Maspero.

Kedourie, E. 1985. *Nationalism*. London: Hutchinson.

Lévi-Strauss, C. 1966. *The savage mind*. London: Weidenfeld & Nicolson.

Lévy-Bruhl, L. 1985 (1910). *How natives think*. Princeton: Princeton University Press.

Mudimbe, V.Y. 1988. *The invention of Africa*. Bloomington: Indiana University Press.

Mudimbe, V.Y. 1994. *The idea of Africa*. Bloomington: Indiana University Press.

Olson, D. 1977. "From utterance to text: The bias of language in speech and writing." *Harvard Educational Review*, 47(3):257–281.

Olson, D. 1988. "Mind and media: The epistemic function of literacy." *Journal of Communication*, 38(3):27–36.

Olson, D. & Torrance, N. (eds) 1991. *Literacy and orality*. Cambridge: Cambridge University Press.

Ong, W. 1977. *Interfaces of the word*. Ithaca: Cornell University Press.

Ong, W. 1981. *The presence of the word*. Minneapolis: University of Minnesota Press.

Ong, W. 1982. *Orality and literacy*. London: Methuen.

Scott-Littleton, C. 1985. "Lucien Lévy-Bruhl and the concept of cognitive relativity." Introduction to L. Lévy-Bruhl, 1985:v–viii.

Sogolo, G. 1993. *Foundations of African philosophy*. Ibadan: Ibadan University Press.

Street, B. 1984. *Literacy in theory and practice*. Cambridge: Cambridge University Press.

Street, B. 1988. "A critical look at Walter Ong and the great divide." *Literacy Research Center*, 4(1):1–5.

Tannen, D. 1982. *Spoken and written language: Exploring orality and literacy*. Norwood: Ablex.

Taylor, C. 1982. "Rationality", in M. Hollis & S. Lukes (eds), 1982:87–105.

Torrance, N. & Olson, D. 1985. "Oral and literate competencies in early school years", in D. Olson, N. Torrance & A. Hildyard (eds), *Literacy, language and learning*. Cambridge: Cambridge University Press, 1985:256–284.

Wilson, B.R. 1970. *Rationality*. Oxford: Blackwell.

Wiredu, K. 1980. *Philosophy and an African culture*. Cambridge: Cambridge University Press.

CHAPTER TWO

Using Culture in African Contexts

CHRISTO VAN STADEN

1. THE USES OF CULTURE

Culture is a Western concept with a complex and often contradictory history, and as such forms at once part of the Western discursive apparatus of modernity (and colonialism) and provides opportunities for dismantling discourses of colonialism, oppression, subjugation, and marginalisation. One might call this the double bind of the concept of culture. Therefore, any serious consideration of culture in Africa must take into account the different uses to which the concept has been put.

A multitude of definitions of culture exist in both colloquial and academic discourse. Culture is both a historical and a political concept. It is political in the sense that the concept may be used to further political enterprises or to achieve certain political effects, whether these effects are politically conservative or progressive. Thornton (1988:26) states that "there is not much point in trying to say what culture *is*", but one should rather say "what culture *does*, and how it does it". Historically, one may distinguish between two broad discursive deployments of the concept of culture. The first is anthropological, seeing "culture" not in the singular, but rather "cultures" as a category for the beliefs, practices, and systems of meaning of specific groups of people. The other considers culture in a more universalistic way as a standard of achievement, often equated to the concepts of progress and civilisation. "Universal" and "civilisation" refer here of course to Western universality, civilisation, or "modernity". Both conceptions have been harmful in the past – English colonial authorities and the South African apartheid state successfully employed both, on the one hand to distinguish between citizens with civil rights and "non-civilised" inhabitants, and on the other hand to divide the "non-civilised" inhabitants of colonial territories into tribal subjects, in order to constitute and entrench the colonial system of "indirect rule" (Mamdani 1996).

What is important here is that the notion and concept of culture has been *used*. Bennett (1993) refers to the "usefulness of culture", that is, the way in which the concept of culture is employed in certain circumstances to achieve certain effects. Culture is defined within a specific discourse, by people who have specific aims. It may be suggested that the act of defining culture is in itself a cultural act that takes place within a cultural context. This context may be that of romanticist discourse in nineteenth-century England, or it may be the academic discipline of philosophy in post-apartheid South Africa. The definition of culture that is finally adopted will be one that is informed by the philosophical discourse in which culture itself is considered.

No definition of culture is politically neutral. Thornton (1988:23) mentions that part of the problem of defining culture is "the history of the disciplines themselves" – that is, the different disciplines in which culture has been and continues to be studied. This is a significant point in post-colonial and post-independent Africa, since the various disciplines – such as anthropology, sociology, and psychology – emerged in Western modernity and are historically Eurocentric and therefore historically implicated in Western rationality. "Other" parts of the world were studied through Western eyes. Edward Said (1995) describes the development of a body of knowledge about the East within Western academe that served both to shape and contain the East – intellectuals contributed through their Western view of and "expertise" on the East to the colonial suppression of Eastern peoples.

The point is that there are several pitfalls that one needs to be careful of when attempting to define culture. Every definition of culture is already a specific use of culture as it entails certain exclusions and inclusions. Popular culture or traditional crafts may be excluded by a certain definition of culture (where culture is considered as "The Arts"). The effect is that those people who partake in or enjoy the excluded forms, or the experiences of such persons, are marginalised in a specific society. Defining an ethnic culture, and then confining certain people to that culture, may mean (as it did in South Africa) exclusion of those people from civil society and mainstream politics. Thornton (1988) mentions that culture is too often taken to be indicative of the differences between people or groups and therefore is used to exclude or exoticise, whereas people do understand each other across "cultures" and are therefore not fundamentally different.

This essay, rather than attempting to provide an all-embracing definition of culture, will consider some of the issues surrounding the use of the term culture, and suggests approaching culture through a theory of articulation or a conjunctural theory of culture. Perhaps the single most pressing issue relating to culture today is the distinction between the global and the local within an increasingly globalised economy based on the production and dissemination of, and access to, information. A conjunctural theory of culture allows one to work within local circumstances with the contradictions and tensions arising from the relationship between the local and the global.

2.   ARTICULATION AND CULTURAL FORMATIONS

What does a conjunctural theory of culture entail? With reference to the theoretical work of Stuart Hall, Grossberg (1992:156) states that "the effects of any concrete practice – its conjunctural identity – are always 'overdetermined' by the network of relations in which it is located". Conjunctural theory moves away from culturalist theory, where a cultural whole always entails "necessary correspondences", and from structuralist theory, where there are always "necessary non-correspondences" (since correspondences can always be deconstructed), towards a "middle ground" where correspondences are understood as "historically produced". Determinations are multiple and contradictory, with the effect that there can never be any guarantees relating to the deployment of cultural and other practices (Grossberg 1992:155–157).

Bell (1986:40) uses culture in the "sociological and anthropological sense to denote a process which shapes specific and distinct 'ways of life'". In this use culture refers to both artistic productions and "systems of meanings and values". This ties in with Clifford Geertz's view that systems of symbols operative within a society constitute culture. Laitin (1986:12) mentions that what "we (or a Balinese cockfighter or a Jewish shopkeeper) mean by justice, by power, by authority, by love, by change, is unavoidably symbolic".

Our daily lives are made up of certain practices in which we are guided by norms, values, beliefs, and meanings. These norms, values, beliefs, and meanings constitute systems of symbols, which may also be called networks of symbolic meanings. Symbolic, in this case, means that the meanings that one attaches to certain practices (for instance a ritual) are not given, but are ascribed to those practices. In a sense, culture is regarded as a text that can be analysed or "read"; even if culture is regarded as a process, such a process entails the production of specific, almost guaranteed meanings. In culture one finds the values, norms, beliefs, and meanings which make life within a specific community possible and *meaningful*. Thompson describes Geertz's view of culture as follows:

> He sometimes maintains that cultural analysis is concerned with texts, not simply because writing ethnography involves the production of texts, but also because the patterns of meaning that the ethnographer is seeking to grasp are themselves *constructed like a text*. Culture can be seen as "an assemblage of texts", as "acted documents", as "imaginative works built out of social materials" (Thompson 1990:134).

According to this definition, then, one would consider meaningful systems like religion, traditions, customs, political practices, economic behaviour, and so on, as subsystems of culture, as different "texts" assembled into a single culture. Laitin states:

> Cultural subsystems are those aspects of collective life which (a) are shared across classes; (b) differentiate a collectivity from other collectivities; (c) are not necessary for species survival; (d) have continuity amid social change; (e) provide significance to social events, and goals for collective action; (f) rely on the production and use of symbols; and (g) become institutionalized into "systems of patterned activity". Religion and language, as well as kinship and art, are examples of cultural subsystems (1986:13).

This is a significant adaptation of the crude Marxian notion of culture as part of the superstructure that is determined by the economic base. The economy (and economic relations) are as much determined by cultural factors as "culture" is by economic relations. Christine Okali (1983) examines, for example, the way in which kinship variables among the Akan of Ghana are related to the production of a cash crop like cocoa.

However, the problem with this conception is twofold. Firstly, as Thompson (1990:134) mentions, it "does not give sufficient attention to problems of power and social conflict". Culture is related exclusively to issues of *meaning*, but meaning is constructed within a social and political context. Meanings are not given, they are created. (The issue of power and hegemony will be discussed more fully below.)

Secondly, the fact that this conception is concerned with meaning means that it is a communicological conception of culture. Meanings are constructed and communicated between members of a group, tribe, community or society, whatever the case may be. Meaning is guaranteed, even if the meanings ascribed do differ. So, even if one does take into account the issue of power and domination in the construction of meaning, one will always find meaning where one looks for it. Moreover, domination will always be discovered to exist, without anything else really being discovered or possibilities for resistance necessarily being opened up.

As has already been mentioned, it may be more useful to consider the ways in which culture *does* things, and a useful way of doing this is to approach culture as a productive process of articulation. The above-mentioned communicological conception already entails aspects of culture as a productive process – specifically as the production of meaning. One of the characteristics of cultural sub-systems is said to be "the production and use of symbols" (Laitin 1986:13).

If, however, one focuses exclusively on the "meaningfulness" of culture, culture becomes ideological in every sense, and there may be a tendency to disregard those aspects of culture which are not in any specific sense "meaningful" as such, but are connected to materiality and affectivity.

> Cultural studies is not a study of cultures as fixed entities or essential categories, but rather a study of the articulation of cultural processes to other processes. Communicological cultural studies sees culture as communication, reducing culture to meaning, to an ideological issue. But culture is also material, which is not to say that it is in any way essential (van Staden 1996:73).

Two general conceptions of culture are criticised here. The first takes culture to be a fixed entity, that is, a complete whole that is divorced from its temporal and spatial context. The second is related to the first in that culture is endowed with certain characteristics that are independent of a specific conjuncture, that is, they are essential. If culture is reduced to issues of meaning (or ideology), such essentialising notions are unavoidable. That is, one assumes that meaning is intrinsic to cultural practices, and that meaning will manifest itself regardless of other processes such as economic processes, processes of social organisation, political processes, and so on.

The solution that is proposed to this problem is a theory of articulation. This is a rather complex theory which will not be explained fully here, though its main tenets may be highlighted. Articulation is used here in the sense that Grossberg (1992) uses it: two things are related to each other, but nothing in that relation is necessary. An example may be the way in which rock music can be articulated with rebelliousness, even though rock music is not "essentially" rebellious. The reason that it is perceived as such and often functions as such, is an effect of a productive process of articulation in which other factors, such as the social position of rock musicians or rock fans, the economic conditions in a given society in which that musical form is circulated, and so on, play a role.

One can speak of an assemblage of practices and forms that are articulated to constitute a specific cultural formation. This "cultural formation" comes into being at a specific time and place, that is, within a specific context. That is why a study of cultural formations, or of any cultural issue for that matter, can take place only contextually. Furthermore, practices and forms may be disarticulated: for example, it may happen that rock music is, for some reason or other, no longer associated with rebelliousness. Thornton states, for example, that culture is

> whole assemblages of safari-suits and tee-shirts, Zulu dance and *sakkie-sakkie*, Afrikaans, English, *gamtaal* and slang – together with all of the ways of using and expressing these and many other material and conceptual resources which our human environment presents to us (1988:25).

Different combinations of the different elements mentioned in this quotation, as well as elements from the fields of politics, the economy, and so on, can either come into being or cease to exist.

When one therefore speaks of Yoruba culture, or Akan culture or Zulu culture, one should realise that these "cultures" are not essential categories that exist regardless of historical or geographical circumstances, nor do they exist as homogeneous, undifferentiated wholes. Different practices and forms that constitute such cultures may come into play. Yoruba culture, for example, may be confronted with Christianity or Islam, as well as colonial Western culture, as well as capitalist economic practices that influence "traditional" agrarian practices. It may make more sense to speak of Yoruba cultural formations than to speak of Yoruba culture as such.

3.   THE LOCAL AND THE GLOBAL

More and more fields of social inquiry today require "culture-specific" research, which is perhaps a legacy of the increasing globalisation of economies (as these concern money, labour, culture, information, and so on), and simultaneously a recognition that such globalisation takes place within and across diverse agglomerations of peoples, "cultures", nationalities, civilisations, etc. This is at once connected to the fragmentations and dispersions that became so evident through postmodernist work (e.g. Jean-François Lyotard's insistence on the end of the grand narratives of modernity) and the spread of global capital through the rise of transnational corporations and the shift from an industrial capitalist mode of production to a capitalist mode of production centred on information. Furthermore, whereas flows of media, money, ideology, technology, and information seem to bind us together in a McLuhanesque "global village", we are paradoxically forced to abandon older centrisms and regard the notion of difference with greater care.

Hence the emergence of fields of enquiry such as "multicultural studies" and "intercultural communication", even in such diverse disciplines as organisational communication, tourism studies, business economy, telecommunications policy, literature, anthropology, and philosophy. Proto-"villages", such as the cyber-village of the Internet or the globalised community of Coke-drinkers and McDonald's-eaters, have, in a certain sense, not led to greater uniformity or homogeneity, and the pervading sense of the "not-sameness" of people provides both opportunities for, and obstacles to, the spread of global capitalism. Appadurai (1990:295) mentions that the homogenisation of culture is usually seen as Americanisation and commoditisation, and it does not take into account "indigenification" or indeed local appropriations of so-called globalised cultural forms and practices. It also, one may add, fails to take into consideration global capitalist appropriations and commoditisations of local cultural forms and practices, such as arts and crafts, dance, music, images, religious forms and practices, and so on. Moreover, the production and use of cultural practices and forms are always employed or implicated in the various hegemonic enterprises entailing nation-building, capital-accumulation, racial or ethnic exclusion, etc.

Linking "culture-specific" studies and "multicultural" studies within a globalised economy of knowledge and information is never quite innocent, and yet the notion of the "multi"-cultural in itself implies difference as a "problem" that has to be overcome in some way. Being "culture-specific" may easily become a strategy of harnessing knowledge of cultural difference to the ends of capitalist hegemony. Being "culture-specific" may then become a means of appropriating local knowledge, beliefs, feelings, and practices for global information markets, at the risk of essentialising such local information in neat packages that makes consumption easier and more attractive. Difference is not an essential feature of any local constituency. Rather, differences are invoked, constructed, and deployed in order to delimit "the local" for whatever purposes (economic, political, social, developmental, etc.). It may be said that, instead of being the opposite of the global in a neat binary pair, the local is a function of the global, as well as a condition of possibility for certain global market(ing) strategies. Local and global, rather than operating as a simple binary opposition, operate within a double articulation (Deleuze & Guattari 1988). The constitution/construction of various "loci" involves specific territorialisations and deterritorialisations (Grossberg 1992; Appadurai 1990:301–3). Indeed, Appadurai (1990:303) speaks of a cultural politics of deterritorialisation, referring to the relations between nation-states and various deterritorialised groupings. Current information globalisation processes and the economic and cultural power of transnationals have placed the nation-state under considerable strain. Hegemonic and counter-hegemonic processes take place on both a local and a global level. This is especially evident in post-colonial or third world post-independence states where there are attempts to forge nationalisms on the one hand, while participating in global economies on the other. Tomaselli and Aldridge state that

> [l]ocal cultural specificities are being jealously guarded even as large tracts of the world become a single market via the General Agreement on Trade and Tariffs (GATT), the World Trade Organization and other such regulatory bodies (1996:61).

Globalisation can be seen to pose a threat to so-called local cultural specificity, especially where the local occupies a marginal position within the global space of information capitalism.

Within "third world", "developing", "less industrialised" or indeed African contexts, cultural specificity also relates to the broad issues of a shared history of colonialism, the threat of neo-imperialism, and the exigencies of development.

Colonial strategies of government and, indeed, the philosophy of Western imperialism articulated the "dark world 'Other'" as the savage opposite of the Western civilised citizen, thereby homogenising the "Other", and also separated this "Other" into distinct tribal constituencies in order to facilitate the colonial mechanism of indirect rule (Mamdani 1996). Post-colonial theories seek to constitute "own histories" (Prakash 1990), not simply in opposition to the Western grand narratives of modernity, but as positive histories, with local agents playing positive roles in their own destinies. Local histories in the "third world" take into account the politics of both space and time (Shohat 1994:99, although she is critical of the failure within post-colonialism to address "the politics of location of the very term") and seek to acknowledge and empower the "minor" and "nomadic" discourses (Deleuze & Guattari 1988) operating in deterritorialising fashion *vis-à-vis* the major discourses of colonialism, nationalism (although nationalism may, under certain circumstances, be considered a minor discourse), globalisation, progress, etc. The "local" does not simply denote difference from the global, but positivity and the possibility of agency. If, especially within the conditions of post-coloniality, history is, in Marx's words, being made "in conditions not of our own making" (Grossberg 1992), the question is, what trajectories of empowerment are enabled by local cultural politics?

The cultural imperialism thesis, although in many respects related to theories of post-colonialism, poses its own problems. A simplified view of cultural imperialism implies the imposition of a single, homogeneous foreign culture (e.g. "American culture") on local, decentred or marginalised "cultures" (Tomlinson 1991). One often hears anxious references to the "McDonaldisation" of the world (Featherstone 1995). However, the so-called imperial culture, "American culture", is itself in no concrete way a homogeneous entity, but rather a hegemonic construction that struggles within the United States itself against such counter-hegemonic cultural forces as African-American, Latino, indigenous, and other cultural constituencies (Tomlinson 1991). Nevertheless, the discourses on cultural imperialism, regardless of their shortcomings, highlight certain issues with regard to the management of culture within conditions of information globalisation. Local cultures and, more specifically, lobbies for local culture, often insist on policies to protect indigenous or local cultural forms and practices against cheaper popular (usually American) products. Such a regulation of cultural flows across the globe, both within nation-states and from, to, and between local communities, necessitates a conception of the local and the global that provides for both the homogenising influences of globalisation and the specific articulations of "global" popular culture in local conditions. Cultural specificity, not only that of the nation-state, but also that found within the various communities of the nation-state itself, is articulated with different formations of capital, information, services, etc. Furthermore, it is articulated with issues such as nationality, politics, and ethnic or even subcultural identities; to notions of civilisation and tradition, and so on. Cultural specificity itself is articulated in various ways with specific effects, and as such its deployment may entail both discursive and material hegemonic or counter-hegemonic strategies.

The notion of "development" has in recent years been the topic of considerable controversy and debate. Whereas development within modernist discourse referred to a general project of industrialisation (progress) imposed on local, "underdeveloped" communities from above, contemporary development theory stresses the need for consultation, negotiation, and community involvement (Tomaselli & Aldridge 1996). Put differently, development in the postmodern era has become "culture-specific", and any development effort or enterprise today must take into account and respect the specific cultural environment in which such development is to take place. Tomaselli and Aldridge (1996:61) state that new development approaches "are now moving towards serious emphasis on the *cultural* and local dimension of development". In similar vein, Klitgaard states:

> In the 1990s, I believe *taking culture into account* will take centre stage in policy making and management. Today's worldwide wave of democratic and free market reforms will fail to live up to optimistic expectations. Increasingly, people from societies as different as those of Eastern and Central Europe, Africa, and Latin America will be asking for help in learning from the mistakes and successes of others, help in adapting economic and political institutions to local conditions. Africa may be a harbinger. The failures of "development" here have spawned a series of calls to take African cultures more fully into account (1993:49).

Klitgaard goes on to examine the pitfalls and potentials of such "taking culture into account", especially where change and the need for change is concerned. The danger is, once again, that the local is considered as given and timeless and the traditional as perfect. Klitgaard (1993:59) asks whether "taking the existing situation as given [is] in effect giving up on change", and goes on to enquire:

> What happens if the local cultural group, far from being the village democracy and egalitarian society Westerners tend to romanticize, is hierarchical, dictatorial, sexist, and unjust? Does one rely on its given "culturally appropriate" mechanisms for decision? Does one try to introduce change? Does one support or aid only the local cultures that are deemed appropriate, leaving the rest to fend for themselves? (1993:59).

To work, therefore, with the concept of "development", which implies change, it is necessary to take into account both the heterogeneity of cultures and the heterogeneity within a "culture". So-called "African cultures" differ significantly from "Western cultures", and even though one may argue that it is, under certain circumstances, discursively and politically useful to speak of African culture, the "cultures" of different African groups differ significantly from each other. Western development perspectives often erred by not taking into account the positive differences between a certain Western world-view and what can broadly be considered an African world-view. However, perspectives that do take into account "African world-views" run the danger of mystifying the traditional by not paying sufficient attention to internal struggle and hegemony.

Modernity, in the contemporary sense, no longer refers to the grand project of Western enlightenment, but rather to a multiplicity of modernities in different places, among different cultures, in different civilisations (Tomlinson 1991). Within the seemingly global condition of postmodernity, modernity itself is articulated in "culture-specific" ways and circumstances. Therefore, contemporary development theory does not shun "modernity" as the imposition of Western values and standards (or, indeed, embrace it as a naturalised goal of *the* Historical Dialectic), but rather seeks to examine ways in which different modernities are, or can be, articulated, manifested or mobilised in different communities, under different circumstances, in different historical conjunctures. Contemporary development theory seeks to reconcile "local cultures with global imperatives" (Tomaselli & Aldridge 1996:63) through development paradigms. This approach is not without its own difficulties, but at least, through its recognition of the temporal and spatial specificity of "modernity", more useful trajectories for "development" are enabled. This is to deny neither the global imperatives of capitalism, nor that the forces of global capital in many instances significantly shape local circumstances. However, a theory of dependency or of economic determinism would mean foreclosure, with the trajectories of change always guaranteed beforehand, so making "developmental" intervention at best a facile exercise, and at worst a significant part of the capitalist globalising enterprise which may well lead to the further marginalisation and exploitation of "less developed" communities in the third world.

Blim (1996:79) refers to the development within anthropology of "world-systems theory" on the one hand, and a "theory of sociocultural economy" on the other, in which narratives developed that "discussed economies in an idiom infused with the folk elements of local traditions" and hence the development of "a rather pluralistic theory of economies, arguing that the impact of local cultures on economic activities has produced a complicated mosaic of local capitalisms". He (1996:84) criticises these theories for their tendency to see these "cultures" as discrete and homogeneous entities, not taking into account "antagonism, struggle and difference inside; . . . hierarchy, influence or hegemony outside, i.e. between and among them". In a sense, emphases on various modernities in "developing" countries accept capitalism, in whichever form it emerges, as inevitable. Featherstone states that the

> radical implications of postmodernism and post-colonial theory are to question the very idea of the social, the unity of modernity and the metanarratives of the Western Enlightenment tradition with its belief in universalism and progress (1995:12).

Theories of post-coloniality, neo-imperialism and development are situated on the nodes between culture, politics, and the economy, and since culture cannot be regarded, in a vulgar Marxist sense, as simplistically determined by an economic base, a theory of culture is needed that considers both culture's determining and its determined aspects. Such a cultural theory will be highly contextual, and culture itself must be conceptualised within the circumstances in which it is used. Notions of what may be "high" culture and "low" culture in European or American contexts, whatever the problems with such a distinction in those contexts, may not apply at all, or in varying degrees only, in African contexts. African contexts themselves may not exclusively constitute the sites of African culture, since post-colonial/expatriate communities often articulate a so-called "black" culture. Featherstone (1995:11) notes that black people in such communities often "participate in a culture and set of collective memories which cannot be integrated with or limited to the cultures of the nation-states in which they reside". Furthermore, in formerly colonised countries the relationships between culture and concepts such as ethnicity, custom, civilisation, and tradition are all the more problematic. Culture is related to the uses to which this term is put in specific contexts, an idea that will be explored more fully in the next section of this essay.

With the contemporary emphasis in "developing", "less industrialised", and even "information-poor" countries on development, a useful way of considering culture is as a resource (Thornton 1988:24–25). This immediately shifts the focus toward a political economy of culture, and, within the current conditions of global capitalism and transnational corporate control over information (weakening the nation-state and having contradictory effects on local constituencies), highlights the tensions between the local and the global.

Thornton (1988:24–25) links culture as a resource to two issues: the fact that resources are shared (albeit in an unequal manner), and that culture is learned information. Cultural resources cannot be used up, they can only "grow, change or even disappear in use". One may add that cultural resources refer not only to information resources but also to material and affective resources, and the deployment of these resources (as well as access to them) is linked to their articulation in different circumstances. Equating "culture" with "information" designates a discursive deployment of the concept of culture that may detract from its value as an analytical term. Culture is employed across a range of formations as a resource. Laitin states, for example:

> The persistence of cultural politics in Nigeria – with Yorubas, Hausas, Igbos, and other nationality groups providing the fundamental basis for membership in party politics – demonstrates the organizational potential of groups whose members share a culture. Cultural identity becomes a political resource. Political entrepreneurs recognize that through appeals to culture they can easily attract mass followings. Individuals learn that by modifying their cultural identities they can improve their life chances. The political power inherent in shared cultural symbols is what lies behind the Machiavellian smile of culture's second face (1986:11).

The same may be true of the deployment of "Zulu culture" or the strategic use of cultural symbols in South Africa (Klopper 1989). Culture does not exist as an essential or discrete object that can be delimited without certain implications: culture and cultural practices are where their effects are, and these usually manifest on a local level. That is, the meanings that we attach to cultural forms or practices are not given or inherent in those forms or practices, but are the products of various processes of articulation and disarticulation. Cultural resources are therefore produced, circulated, or distributed and consumed, or used in conjunction with other processes of production, distribution, and consumption. This also means that sets of cultural resources are assembled together into certain formations that may at certain times be construed as "Afrikaner culture" or "Zulu culture": the cultural resources of a certain community are not just a random collection of such resources, but are assembled together with other practices and resources at a given time and place. Such assemblages or formations serve to include or to exclude, to enable or to limit access to cultural resources, and so on.

A major issue with regard to culture as a resource is that of differentiated access, and it is in this sense that one can speak of a cultural economy, and indeed of "cultural capital" (although not quite in the same sense as Bourdieu does). Access to cultural resources is linked to socio-economic and socio-political position, but once again the relation between access and position should not be seen as a guaranteed relationship (i.e. people with a certain economic status necessarily have a certain degree of access to cultural resources). Such a determinism does not explain the different investments people make in cultural resources, for example the considerable investment in "Afrikaner culture" across class barriers during the rise of the apartheid state in South Africa.

As the quotation above from Laitin shows, cultural resources are used to differentiate. Thornton (1988:24) states that "we must include our own ideas *about* culture as part of the resources that culture provides". In Africa ideas of culture with hegemonic currency related mainly to the concept of culture as a distinguishing feature of groups of people, whether these groups were races, tribes, nations or communities. Culture was, and in many instances still is, used as a marker of identity. Thornton says that while

> there are differences in the way people behave and think and live, this reflects their differing access to cultural resources, as well as their use of these resources to make statements to each other and about themselves (1988:24).

He (1988:24) goes on to say that one such statement is "the statement about identity and group membership". Claiming group membership may thus involve the employment of certain accessible cultural resources in order to substantiate such a claim. To say "I am a Zulu" may mean that one claims identification through cultural resources such as religion, traditional practices, allegiance to the king, the Zulu language, and so on. One may also, however, claim and deploy other cultural resources, for example from Christianity or Western capitalism or South African nationalism. The idea of what a "Zulu" is, is itself a cultural construct, and may mean different things to people with differing access to resources (which may include "modern" resources such as television or telecommunication technology), and who have different political affiliations, geographic constraints, historical circumstances, etc.

This means that although differences do exist, these differences are not used to explain historical or political circumstances; rather, one should regard the complex ways in which these differences and similarities are articulated with history or politics. Culture and cultural resources are used at specific times and places by specific people with certain effects.

4. THE IDEA OF "AFRICAN CULTURE"

Philosophy in Africa is considered in a culture-specific way. This means that philosophy is related to the very specific cultural context within which it is practised. If one takes culture to denote the resources through which a certain group of people delimits itself as such a group, it can include concepts such as Yoruba culture, Akan culture, or even "struggle" culture. Members of such groups draw on these cultural forms to define themselves as members of that group. Culture itself becomes the context within which specific cultures are defined.

It is therefore possible to understand the idea of "African culture" as a broad, inclusive term within the context of the struggle for liberation from colonial oppression, if one takes the imposition of Western cultural values and colonial politics as providing a context for daily life in large parts of Africa, even though this culture is in no way homogeneous. "African culture" here serves a very specific purpose, and an idea of "African culture" may provide meaning, purpose, pride, enjoyment or emotion in the daily lives of African people under colonial rule or threatened with Western (cultural) imperialism. Two points are important: African culture is distinct from Western culture; and African culture is positive and productive in itself – it is not just the opposite/"Other" of Western culture, that is, the product of a Western binary opposition.

If one studies African metaphysics or African rationality, however, this broad notion of "African culture" is of little use (though not entirely useless), even if one does take into account that there are similarities across various African "cultures". Therefore, it may be more useful to consider the ways in which certain cultural resources have congealed as specific to people with more or less the same ideas, practices, languages, and so on.

In a discussion of the issue of culture in Africa, it is impossible not to take into account the histories in Africa of colonialism in the first place, and, in the second place, Africa's current marginalised position within globalised economies.

Readings

SOME AFRICAN CULTURAL CONCEPTS
STEVE BIKO

One of the most difficult things to do these days is to talk with authority on anything to do with African culture. Somehow Africans are not expected to have any deep understanding of their own culture or even of themselves. Other people have become authorities on all aspects of African life or, to be more accurate, on BANTU life. Thus we have the thickest of volumes on some of the strangest subjects – even *The feeding habits of the urban Africans*, a publication by a fairly "liberal" group, the Institute of Race Relations.

In my opinion it is not necessary to talk with Africans about African culture. However, in the light of the above statements one realises that there is so much confusion sown, not only amongst casual non-African readers, but even amongst Africans themselves, that perhaps a sincere attempt should be made at emphasising the authentic cultural aspects of the African people by Africans themselves.

Since that unfortunate date – 1652 – we have been experiencing a process of acculturation. It is perhaps presumptuous to call it "acculturation" because this term implies a fusion of different cultures. In our case this fusion has been extremely one-sided. The two major cultures that met and "fused" were the African culture and the Anglo-Boer culture. Whereas the African culture was unsophisticated and simple, the Anglo-Boer culture had all the trappings of a colonialist culture and therefore was heavily equipped for conquest. Where they could, they conquered by persuasion, using a highly exclusive religion that denounced all other Gods and demanded a strict code of behaviour with respect to clothing, education, ritual, and custom. Where it was impossible to convert, firearms were readily available and used to advantage. Hence the Anglo-Boer culture was the more powerful culture in almost all facets. This is where the African began to lose a grip on himself and his surroundings.

Thus, in taking a look at cultural aspects of the African people one inevitably finds oneself having to compare. This is primarily because of the contempt that the "superior" culture shows towards the indigenous culture. To justify its exploitative basis the Anglo-Boer culture has at all times been directed at bestowing an inferior status on all cultural aspects of the indigenous people.

I am against the belief that African culture is time-bound, the notion that with the conquest of the African all his culture was obliterated. I am also against the belief that when one talks of African culture one is necessarily talking of the pre-van Riebeeck culture. Obviously the African culture has had to sustain severe blows and may have been battered nearly out of shape by the belligerent cultures it collided with, yet in essence even today one can easily find the fundamental aspects of the pure African culture in the present-day African. Hence in taking a look at African culture I am going to refer as well to what I have termed the modern African culture.

One of the most fundamental aspects of our culture is the importance we attach to man. Ours has always been a man-centred society. Westerners have on many occasions been surprised at the capacity we have for talking to each other – not for the sake of arriving at a particular conclusion but merely to enjoy the communication for its own sake. Intimacy is a term not exclusive to particular friends but applying to a whole group of people who find themselves together either through work or through residential requirements.

In fact in the traditional African culture, there is no such thing as two friends. Conversation groups were more or less naturally determined by age and division of labour. Thus one would find all boys whose job was to look after cattle periodically meeting at popular spots to engage in conversation about their cattle, girlfriends, parents, heroes, etc. All commonly shared their secrets, joys, and woes. No one felt unnecessarily an intruder into someone else's business. The curiosity manifested was welcome. It came out of a desire to share. This pattern one would find in all age groups. House visiting was always a feature of the elderly folk's way of life. No reason was needed as a basis for visits. It was all part of our deep concern for each other.

These are things never done in the Westerner's culture. A visitor to someone's house, with the exception of friends, is always met with the question, "What can I do for you?". This attitude of seeing people not as themselves but as agents for some particular function either to one's disadvantage or advantage is foreign to us. We are not a suspicious race. We believe in the inherent goodness of man. We enjoy man for himself. We regard our living together not as an unfortunate mishap warranting endless competition among us but as a deliberate act of God to make us a community of brothers and sisters jointly involved in the quest for a composite answer to the varied problems of life. Hence in all we do we always place man first and hence all our action is usually joint community oriented action rather than the individualism which is the hallmark of the capitalist approach. We always refrain from using people as stepping stones. Instead, we are prepared to have a much slower progress in an effort to make sure that all of us are marching to the same tune.

Nothing dramatises the eagerness of Africans to communicate with each other more than their love for song and rhythm. Music in the African culture features in all emotional states. When we go to work, we share the burdens and pleasures of the work we are doing through music. This particular facet, strangely enough, has filtered through to the present day. Tourists always watch with amazement the synchrony of music and action as Africans working at a roadside use their picks and shovels with well-timed precision to the accompaniment of a background song. Battle songs were a feature of the long march to war in the olden days. Girls and boys never played any game without using music and rhythm as its basis. In other words, with Africans, music and rhythm were not luxuries but part and parcel of our way of communication. Any suffering we experienced was made much more real by song and rhythm. There is no doubt that the so-called "Negro spirituals" sung by black slaves in the States as they toiled under oppression were indicative of their African heritage.

The major thing to note about our songs is that they never were songs for individuals. All African songs are group songs. Though many have words, this is not the most important thing about them. Tunes were adapted to suit the occasion and had the wonderful effect of making everybody read the same things from the common experience. In war the songs reassured those who were scared, highlighted the determination of the regiment to win a particular encounter, and made much more urgent the need to settle the score; in suffering, as in the case of the black slaves, they derived sustenance out of a feeling of togetherness; at work the binding rhythm makes everybody brush off the burden and hence Africans can continue for hours on end because of this added energy.

Attitudes of Africans to property again show just how un-individualistic the African is. As everybody knows, African society had the village community as its basis. Africans always believed in having many villages with a controllable number of people in each, rather than the reverse. This obviously was a requirement to suit the needs of a community-based and man-centred society. Hence most things were jointly owned by the group; for instance there was no such thing as individual land ownership. The land belonged to the people and was merely under the control of the local chief on behalf of the people. When cattle went to graze it was on an open veld and not on anybody's specific farm.

Farming and agriculture, though on individual family basis, had many characteristics of joint efforts. Each person could, by a simple request and the holding of a special ceremony, invite neighbours to come and work on his plots. This service was returned in kind and no remuneration was ever given.

Poverty was a foreign concept. This could only really be brought about to the entire community by an adverse climate during a particular season. It was never considered repugnant to ask one's neighbours for help if one was struggling. In almost all instances there was help between individuals, tribe and tribe, chief and chief, etc., even in spite of war.

Another important aspect of African culture is our mental attitude to problems presented by life in general. Whereas the Westerner is geared to use a problem-solving approach following very trenchant analyses, our approach is that of situation-experiencing. I will quote from Dr Kaunda to illustrate this point:

> The Westerner has an aggressive mentality. When he sees a problem he will not rest until he has formulated some solution to it. He cannot live with contradictory ideas in his mind; he must settle for one or the other or else evolve a third idea in his mind which harmonizes or reconciles the other two. And he is vigorously scientific in rejecting solutions for which there is no basis in logic. He draws a sharp line between the natural and the supernatural, the rational and non-rational, and more often than not, he dismisses the supernatural and non-rational as superstition. . . .
>
> Africans being a pre-scientific people do not recognize any conceptual cleavage between the natural and supernatural. They experience a situation rather than face a problem. By this I mean they allow both the rational and non-rational elements to make an impact upon them, and any action they may take could be described more as a response of the total personality to the situation than the result of some mental exercise.

This I find a most apt analysis of the essential difference in the approach to life of these two groups. We as a community are prepared to accept that nature will have its enigmas which are beyond our powers to solve. Many people have interpreted this attitude as lack of initiative and drive, yet in spite of my belief in the strong need for scientific experimentation, I cannot help feeling that more time should also be spent in teaching man and man to live together, and that perhaps the African personality with its attitude of laying less stress on power and more stress on man is well on the way to solving our confrontation problems.

All people are agreed that Africans are a deeply religious race. In the various forms of worship that one found throughout the southern part of our continent there was at least a common basis. We all accepted without any doubt the existence of a God. We had our own community of saints. We believed – and this was consistent with our views of life – that all people who died had a special place next to God. We felt that a communication with God could only be through these people. We never knew anything about hell – we do not believe that God can create people only to punish them eternally after a short period on earth.

Another aspect of religious practices was the occasion of worship. Again we did not believe that religion could be featured as a separate part of our existence on earth. It was manifest in our daily lives. We thanked God through our ancestors before we drank beer, married, worked, etc. We would obviously find it artificial to create special occasions for worship. Neither did we see it as logical to have a particular building in which all worship would be conducted. We believed that God was always in communication with us and therefore merited attention everywhere and anywhere.

It was the missionaries who confused our people with their new religion. By some strange logic, they argued that theirs was a scientific religion and ours was mere superstition in spite of the biological discrepancies so obvious in the basis of their religion. They further went on to preach a theology of the existence of hell, scaring our fathers and mothers with stories about burning in eternal flames and gnashing of teeth and grinding of bone. This cold cruel religion was strange to us but our forefathers were sufficiently scared of the unknown impending anger to believe that it was worth a try. Down went our cultural values!

Yet it is difficult to kill the African heritage. There remains, in spite of the superficial cultural similarities between the detribalised and the Westerner, a number of cultural characteristics that mark out the detribalised as an African. I am not here making a case for separation on the basis of cultural differences. I am sufficiently proud to believe that under a normal situation, Africans can comfortably stay with people of other cultures and be able to contribute to the joint cultures of the communities they have joined. However, what I want to illustrate here is that even in a pluralistic society like ours, there are still some cultural traits that we can boast of which have been able to withstand the process of deliberate bastardisation. These are aspects of the modern African culture – a culture that has used concepts from the white world to expand on inherent cultural characteristics.

Thus we see that in the area of music the African still expresses himself with conviction. The craze about jazz arises out of a conversion by the African artists of mere notes to meaningful music, expressive of real feelings. The monkey jive, soul, etc. are all aspects of a modern type of African culture that expresses the same original feelings. Solos like those of Pat Boone and Elvis Presley could never really find expression within African culture because it is not in us to listen passively to pure musical notes. Yet when soul struck with its all-engulfing rhythm it immediately caught on and set hundreds of millions of black bodies in gyration throughout the world. These were people reading in soul the real meaning – the defiant message, "Say it loud! I'm black and I'm proud." This is fast becoming our modern culture. A culture of defiance, self-assertion and group pride and solidarity. This is a culture that emanates from a situation of common experience of oppression. Just as it now finds expression in our music and our dress, it will spread to other aspects. This is the new and modern black culture to which we have made a major contribution. This is the modern black culture that is responsible for the restoration of our faith in ourselves and therefore offers a hope in the direction we are taking from here.

Thus, in its entirety African culture spells us out as people particularly close to nature. As Kaunda puts it, our people may be unlettered and their physical horizons may be limited, yet "they inhabit a larger world than the sophisticated Westerner who has magnified his physical senses through inverted gadgets at the price all too often of cutting out the dimension of the spiritual". This close proximity to nature enables the emotional component in us to be so much richer in that it makes it possible for us, without any apparent difficulty, to feel for people and to easily identify with them in any emotional situation arising out of suffering.

The advent of Western culture changed our outlook drastically. No more could we run our own affairs. We were required to fit in as people tolerated with great restraint in a Western type society. We were tolerated simply because our cheap labour is needed. Hence we are judged in terms of standards we are not responsible for. Whenever colonisation sets in with its dominant culture it devours the native culture and leaves behind a bastardised culture that can only thrive at the rate and pace allowed it by the dominant culture. This is what has happened to African culture. It is called a subculture purely because the African people in the urban complexes are mimicking the white man rather unashamedly.

In rejecting Western values, therefore, we are rejecting those things that are not only foreign to us but that seek to destroy the most cherished of our beliefs – that the corner-stone of society is man himself – not just his welfare, not his material well-being, but just man himself with all his ramifications. We reject the power-based society of the Westerner that seems to be ever concerned with perfecting their technological know-how while losing out on their spiritual dimension. We believe that in the long run the special contribution to the world by Africa will be in this field of human relationships. The great powers of the world may have done wonders in giving the world an industrial and military look, but the great gift still has to come from Africa – giving the world a more human face.

ARE THERE CULTURAL UNIVERSALS?

KWASI WIREDU

Our question is, "Are there cultural universals?" I propose a *reductio ad absurdum* proof for an affirmative answer as follows. Suppose there were no cultural universals. Then inter-cultural communication would be impossible. But there is inter-cultural communication. Therefore, there are cultural universals. Let me now try to unpack this epitome of a proof. I start with the premise that there is inter-cultural communication. This is too visible in the present-day world to be disputed; what may need arguing, however, is what it implies. But not everything regarding its implications is open to debate. For example, it is tautologically obvious that for any two persons to communicate at all they must share some common medium of communication. In turn, this implies that at some level they must share a conceptual scheme, however minimal its dimensions. Any such scheme of concepts is universal for, at least, the given participants in the communication. The question now is, "Is there any scheme of concepts which can be shared by all cultures of humankind?"

This last question is the equivalent to asking whether there is anything about which all the different cultures of the world *can* communicate. The answer, in fact, is, "Everything." But let us start with *vital* fundamentals. I use the word "vital" here to hint at the fact that, in certain respects, communication is an existential necessity. Without communication there can be no human community. Indeed, in the total absence of communication we cannot even speak of human *persons*; there could, perhaps, be lower animals, but that is another matter. A human *person* is the product of a culture. Whatever else goes into the essence of personhood, mind is a *sine qua non*. But we are not born with a mind, not even with one that is a *tabula rasa*; we are only born with the potential of a mind (in the form of a nervous system). This potential is progressively actualised in a certain way through the barrage of sensory stimulation emanating from the purely physical (i.e. non-social) environment; but the person-making attribute of mentality is not attainable without another kind of barrage, namely, the cultural or socialising barrage of sensory stimulation from kith, kin, and kindred. And this means nothing other than sundry forms of communication.

We may say, accordingly, that by and large, communication makes the mind. This, of course, is from a developmental point of view and is without prejudice to the fact that it is minds that make communication. Two basic factors are involved in communication, namely, conceptualisation and articulation. The power to conceptualise is only a development and refinement of the capacity to react to stimuli in a law-like manner which is present in even amoebic forms of life. In the more elementary forms of life, response to the environment is governed by instinctual drives for equilibrium and self-preservation. At this level of existence, instinct ensures uniformity of reaction in a species. Insofar as one can speak here of an analogue of communication, this will take the form of instinctive gestures and noises, instinctually standardised. I see in both types of uniformity the humble origins of the rules of conceptualisation and articulation which are distinctive of human communication. Human behaviour is, of course, governed by both instinct and culture. Because of the element of instinct we can be sure of a certain species-distinctive uniformity in human actions and reactions. But because of the element of culture, that is, of habit, instruction, and conscious thought, there will naturally be plenty of room for variation. The first consideration accounts for the possibility of objectivity and universality in the standards of thought and action in our species, the second for various degrees of relativity and subjectivity. The point, however, is that what unifies us is more fundamental than what differentiates us.

What is it that unifies us? The beginning, at least, of an answer is easy. It is our biologico-cultural identity as *homines sapientes*. At the very minimum this status implies that we are organisms that go beyond instinct in the drive for equilibrium and self-preservation in the following specific ways, namely, by means of reflective perception, abstraction, deduction, and induction. By reflective perception I mean a kind of awareness that involves the identification of objects and events through the conscious application of concepts and which entails, consequently, the power of recall and re-identification. Any being capable of reflective perception is already possessed of a concept of the external world. By abstraction I mean the mental procedure of bringing particulars together under general concepts and the latter themselves under still more general concepts, and so on. Both deductive and inductive capacities are already presupposed in rudimentary forms of reflective perception, for to recognise something as an X is to perceive it as an X rather than as a non-X, which implies that it is not both X and not X. Here, implicitly, is the principle of noncontradiction, which, paraconsistentism notwithstanding, is the supreme principle of deduction. Furthermore, to bring an object or event under a concept is to be able, in principle, to envisage what would obtain under certain hypothetical situations. Hypotheticals loom even larger in the context of action. To embark on an action, that is, a premeditated action, one must have some notion of the consequences of various options and, in any case, of the adjustment or maladjustment of possible means to possible ends. The power of judgement comes into play here, evidently, and with it, the power of inference.

Action, then, involves judgement and inference, but social action, an essential ingredient of human existence, involves, besides these, communication. Now, if a being is capable of judgement and inference, then, necessarily, it is capable of communication. Actually, this could be misleading as to the logical order of human mental development, if it were to give the impression that the power of judgement and inference antedates that of communication. On the contrary, however, it follows from our previous remarks about the making of mind that communication, from the point of view both of giving and taking, is present at very early stages in the development of the thinking powers of a human person. What our immediately preceding remarks were intended to do was to amplify somewhat the interconnection between thought and communication in preparation for drawing some species-wide implications. At this stage the issue may be framed as follows: "Mind presupposes communication. Granted. But communication with whom? Communication with our own kith and kin can be taken for granted, but can we guarantee the possibility of communication with people of very different climes and cultures?" This question is, in fact, anticipated in the previous paragraph. It was there noted that being a human person implies having the capacity for reflective perception, abstraction, and inference. In their basic nature these mental capacities are the same for all humans irrespective of whether they inhabit Europe, Asia or Africa, just as in their basic nature the instinctive reactions of, say, the frogs of

Europe are the same as those of the frogs of Africa. In particular, the concept of object in general is the same for all beings capable of reflective perception. The reason is because any beings that need to supplement instinct with wits in their struggle for equilibrium and self-preservation will have to have a regularised way of identifying and re-identifying items in their environment in a manner dictated both by their constitution and the impinging stimuli. On both counts there is a common human identity. The human constitution of flesh and bones quickened by electrical charges and wrapped up in variously pigmented integuments is the same everywhere, while there is only one world in which we all live, move, and have our struggles, notwithstanding such things as the vagaries of climate. These facts, which underlie the possibility of communication among kith and kin, are the same facts that underlie the possibility of communication among the various peoples of the world. The same facts make all human beings kindred.

Admittedly, communication among widely separated peoples is often more difficult than communication among people living relatively closely together. This should be easy to understand. Apart from anything else, there is the babel of languages. Widely separated groups tend to develop different symbolisms for the articulation of thought. Out of the myriad of possible phonetic articulations different peoples will use different subsets through essentially accidental circumstances. Scripts, where there are any, will also differ similarly. Nor are the differences limited to the physical aspects of symbolisation. Space and time are implicated in apparently inscrutable ways in that variegation of patterns of thought is evidenced in disparate grammars. Such disparities do quite frequently result in differences in the structure and content of particular concepts. Consider an example. English has the procedure of forming abstract nouns from "concrete" ones. Thus, for example, from "chair" we get "chairness". Adjectives can also yield abstract nouns in a similar manner: "Red", for example, gives us "redness".

On the other hand, in my own language, the Akan language spoken in parts of Ghana, the thought-transitions represented by these English grammatical transformations are handled quite disanalogically. The word for chair is *akongua*, but what corresponds to chairness is not a single word belonging to a separate grammatical category but rather a periphrasis. We would say something like "the circumstance of something being a chair" (*se bribi ye akongua*) or if it comes to that, something like, "the being a chair" (*akongua ye*). Now here is the point of this example. In a language like Akan, it is obviously going to be very hard for anybody to persuade him/herself, let alone anybody else, of the plausibility of saying something like, "Chairness is an abstract object existing over and above particular chairs." Consider what such a piece of discourse would (approximately) boil down to in such a language. One would have to say something which translates back into English as, "The circumstance of something being a chair is an abstract object over and above particular chairs." And if this sounds incongruous in English, the situation is compounded by a sizeable factor in Akan. The point is not, as is sometimes absurdly suggested, that Africans don't or can't think in abstract terms, for the phrase "the circumstance of something being a chair" is as abstract in its significance as the word "chairness". The point is, rather, that the fact that in English and languages like English in this respect, there is, in addition to the periphrastic rendering, the unitary abstract noun, is apt to incline some speakers to objectual deductions, whereas in languages like Akan there is a distinct disincentive to any such objectivisation – I do not say hypostatisation, for I do not want to beg the question in favour of the Akan language. What I want to do is to emphasise the sharpness of the present contrast between the two languages. To this purpose, one might even characterise the contrast by saying that the sentence, "Chairness is an abstract object existing over and above particular chairs", is untranslatable into Akan. One can multiply examples of differences in the conceptual suggestiveness of the grammatical patterns and lexical formations of English and Akan. As is well known, Whorf made relativistic capital out of linguistic contrasts of this sort in his comparisons of Indo-European with American Indian languages. But it is not necessary to go to Whorfian lengths in order to note that differences in languages often reflect, and are reflected in, differences of world-view and that these can exercise the most profound constraints on inter-cultural communication.

Let all the foregoing be granted. Yet no *ultimate* bar to inter-cultural communication is thereby revealed. No human language is known which non-native speakers cannot, in principle, learn as a second language. The reason underlying this fact is that language is a system of skills fundamental to being human. These are the skills of reflective perception, abstraction, and inference. By means of the first skill one can, in principle, re-identify any symbol and its possible referent; by means of the second one can, in principle, understand any semantic structures and classifications, analysing composites and synthesising units as the case may require, and by means of the third one can, in principle, map out the bearing of any given proposition on (at least some) close or remote consequences. In sum, a human being is a rule-following animal, and language is nothing but an arrangement of rules. Therefore, barring the impairment of faculties, any human being will necessarily have the capacity to understand and use a language; and if one can understand any particular language, one can understand any language. If there is any lingering doubt about this last claim, it might presumably be due to the anticipation of some contingent circumstances that might hamper the learning of a new language. Perhaps the language manual to hand is pedagogically ineffective? But, surely, one can circumvent all second-hand aids and go and live among the people concerned and, in the words of Quine (1960:47), "learn the native language directly as an infant might".

What, then, of untranslatability? In truth, the ability to perceive the untranslatability of an expression from one language into another is a mark of linguistic understanding more profound than the ability to do routine translation. The second ability involves merely moving from the one language into the other, whereas the first involves stepping above both onto a meta-platform, so to speak, an ability that has not seemed to come easily to some students of "other cultures". Untranslatability, then, can be a problem, but it does not necessarily argue unintelligibility.

But, it might be objected, if some portions of a language can be untranslatable into another, why may not the entire language be so? We shall develop our answer by elaborating on a previous remark. In essence, the answer lies in the fact that the concept of object in general is a common possession of all humans. Operating with this concept is an essential aspect of the human way of interacting with the environment. It is what gives it a cognitive dimension. And because a basic imperative of this cognitive interaction is the drive for self-preservation and equilibrium, the essential discriminations of items of the environment which the possession of the concept of object in general makes possible, will be of the same basic kind in actuality, if not necessarily in articulation, among all humankind. These essential discriminations will obviously be of the objects of direct perception. The word "direct" here does not imply the absence of conceptualisation. But at this level there is a basic similarity of conceptualisation among humans by dint of semi-instinctual constraints. For this reason, the nearer a set of items of discrimination is to direct perception, the easier it will be to correlate its elements with the different systems of symbolisation obtaining among different peoples. This is what ensures that all human languages are, *at bottom*, inter-learnable and inter-translatable.

But given this basic inter-translatability, no limits can be set to inter-cultural communication which do not also affect intra-cultural communication. The difficulties of intelligibility and translation among languages are due principally to the changes and chances to which the twin procedures of abstraction and inference are subject in this world. It is through these processes that human beings make their semantic ascents from the pedestal of direct sensible perception to the heights of sophisticated theoretical conceptions or into the clouds of conceptual obscurity and confusion. The consequent difficulties of understanding occur both across and within cultures, and they need not necessarily be, though they often are, more radical across cultures than within cultures. For example, shorn of all epistemological exaggeration, the incommensurability described by Kuhn between alternative scientific positions in certain phases of scientific thought illustrates a breakdown in communication more drastic than at least some of the difficulties that occur in inter-cultural dialogue. Nevertheless, whether the difficulty in communication occurs within one culture or between different cultures, because human beings are rule-following animals, and because we all, by and large, stand on the same cognitive pedestal of sensible perception, such difficulties can sometimes be overcome, or if not overcome, at least reduced to something less than absolute impenetrability.

It is probably needless to point out that what has to be shown is not that inter-cultural or even intra-cultural communication is always successful, but only that it need not always be unsuccessful. That conceptual understanding is possible in both theatres of discourse should be sufficiently clear from the foregoing considerations. And, as previously noted, this plainly presupposes the existence of conceptual universals. Nevertheless, it might be thought that it still remains an open question whether there are epistemic universals. It might still be wondered, in other words, whether the ways of reasoning among the different peoples of the world might not be so incommensurable as to render any cross-cultural evaluation of the truth or soundness of belief systems impossible in spite of the supposed universality of conceptual understanding. Putting it differently still, granted that there is enough mutuality of conceptual schemes for one culture to understand the intimations of another, does it follow that there must be enough commonality of cognitive criteria for the rationality of those intimations to be assessed from the point of view of an alien culture? Questions of this sort have sometimes launched some commentators on the varieties of ways of life and thought among humankind into well-intentioned flights of relativistic fancy. It is thought to be a mark of tolerance and broad-mindedness to view the allegedly disparate standards of reasoning as all equally valid within their own cultural habitats.

But in spite of the recent resurgence of sympathy for relativism, its inconsistency remains as glaring as ever. Here we are dealing with a form of cognitive relativism less sweeping than conceptual relativism, and what needs to be shown is that it is inconsistent to grant the possibility of conceptual universals and deny that of the cognitive variety. The argument is this: to understand a concept is to grasp its possibility of application; but this implies also grasping its criteria of application, that is, the conditions under which *it is true* to say that the concept holds. Two riders should, however, immediately be entered. Firstly, this argument uses a strong concept of understanding. There is, in fact, also a weaker concept of understanding by which one might speak of understanding the concept of, say, a round square without pretending to envisage the *possibility* of something being both round and square. This is a formal concept of understanding which presupposes a substantive concept of understanding at some constitutive level of the given semantic material. Thus, in the present example, one claims by implication a substantive understanding of the concepts of "round" and "square". Secondly, it should be noted that grasping the criteria of application of a concept does not necessarily amount to being able to articulate them accurately or adequately or even coherently. In fact, when the concepts in question are highly abstract and basic to a world-view, this lack of equation reveals the root of all philosophy or, at any rate, much of it.

Our argument exploits the connection, not especially recondite, between meaning and possible truth. But we can go further in linking conceptual with epistemic universals. The ground has, in fact, already been prepared for this. As previously argued, the power of conceptualisation which yields the idea of the external world involves a basic sensitivity to the principle of noncontradiction and the ability to contemplate empirical hypotheticals. The latter definitely implies the capacity to learn from experience. Let us call the principle of all learning from experience the principle of induction (without prejudging any issues about the exact nature of induction). If these two principles, of noncontradiction and induction – principles that are, by any reckoning, basic to human knowledge – are implicit in the power of conceptualisation, then it is apparent that together they unite the human activities of understanding and knowing in such a way as to make it impossible that different peoples might be able to communicate but unable to argue rationally among themselves.

So far, I have been arguing about conceptual and epistemic universals. But suppose it is objected that what is required to be proved is the existence, rather, of *cultural* universals. It would quickly emerge that the objection is founded on quite a narrow conception of culture. Culture is not just the social forms and customary beliefs and practices of a human group. These phenomena themselves depend on the existence of language, knowledge, communication, interaction, and methods of transmitting knowledge to the born and the unborn. And this is the fundamental sense of the word "culture". In this sense, one might sum up the preceding discussion by saying that the fact of language itself, i.e. the possession of one language or another by all human societies, is the cultural universal *par excellence*.

Nevertheless, conceiving of culture as the social forms and customary beliefs and practices of a human group, while not the most fundamental way of conceiving of it, is one legitimate way of doing so. Besides, it is probably the most frequent in non-philosophical discourse. From this perspective, furthermore, there is some initial plausibility in scepticism as to the existence of cultural universals. Culture, in this sense, is a patterned accumulation of contingencies of social consciousness and action in the context of a specific type of physical environment. Here, what defines culture, or to be exact, *a* culture, is the humanly contingent, not the humanly necessary. Thus, it is necessary for any human community to have *some* language, but what particular language this might be is a contingent matter. In general, it is necessary for human groups to have some customs, but contingent what specific customs they might have.

From such reflections as these, the following train of thought naturally arises. Since customs are contingent facts of particular social formations, so also must be the principles for evaluating them. It proves convenient and reasonable in this connection to view the concept of custom broadly to comprehend such things as usages, traditions, manners, conventions, grammars, vocabularies, etiquette, fashions, aesthetic standards, observances, taboos, rituals, folk-ways, and mores. All these are rules of thought and action, and to say that the basis for evaluating them is contingent is to say that there are no universally valid principles to that purpose. In more positive terms, it is to say that the rightness or wrongness of these rules is culture-relative. If we now view morality as being included under the contingent rules of good behaviour, the conclusion appears to follow that it, too, along with all other rules of conduct, is culture-relative. By this train of thought, then, we are transported not only to descriptive relativism but also to ethical relativism. It is not just the case, it would seem, that the standards of good and bad vary from people to people or culture to culture, but also that their justification consists in the fact of being adopted at a particular time and place.

Ethical relativism has often been criticised, and justly enough. But when all is said and done, it remains unclear by what criteria normative universals of human conduct are to be identified. Interestingly, the more narrow ethical or moral universals seem to be the easiest to characterise. What we need to do is to specify a principle of conduct such that without its recognition – which does not necessarily mean its invariable observance – the survival of human society *in a tolerable condition* would be inconceivable. Let us start with the following minimal premise: we assume that every human being has a concern for his or her own interests, in whatever way the concept of interest might be defined. The problem of morals arises from the fact that not everybody has a natural inclination to be concerned about the interests of others at all times in their conduct. In consideration of this, the following imperative naturally suggests itself: "Let your conduct at all times manifest a due concern for the interests of others." The question of course is, "What is *due* concern?" I propose the following criterion: a person may be said to manifest due concern for the interests of others if in contemplating the impact of his/her actions on their interests, the person puts him/herself imaginatively in their position, and having done so, is able to welcome that impact. This is obviously reminiscent of what has been called the Golden Rule. If phrased as an imperative, it might be called the "principle of sympathetic impartiality". Now, I suggest that it takes little imagina-tion to foresee that life in any society in which everyone openly avowed the contrary of this principle and acted accordingly would inevitably be "solitary, poor, nasty, *brutish*", and probably short. It is arguable – though we cannot stop to argue this here – that this principle suffices for the foundation of morality. It is easy to see, for instance, that the injection of a dose of compassion into Kant's Categorical Imperative would convert it into a principle of *sympathetic* impartiality. Certainly, whatever one may think of Kant's argumentation in basing morality on the Categorical Imperative, that effort cannot be dismissed as a triviality. And I might observe – harking back to my own background of indigenous thought – that traditional Akan ethical maxims quite demonstrably converge on some such foundation as the principle of sympathetic impartiality. It seems clear, in any case, whether or not, as a matter of philosophy, people take this principle to be the basis of all morals, that, as a fact of ethical life, it is essential to the harmonisation of human interests in society.

On these grounds it may be asserted that the principle of sympathetic impartiality is a human universal transcending cultures viewed as social forms and customary beliefs and practices. In being common to all human practice of morality, it is a universal of any non-brutish form of human life.

In retrospect one can now easily spot the error in the relativistic train of thought rehearsed earlier on. That train illicitly carried morality along with mores in the same bag of contingent rules of good behaviour. But moral rules are a class apart. Yet it is so common to confuse morality with other types of rules of conduct that, lexico-graphically, one legitimate sense of the word "morality" is "conformity to ideals of right human conduct", even thought not all such ideals are moral ideals. (Nor do the etymologies of "moral" and "ethical" provide any disincentive to the error com-plained of.) Thus people speak, for example, of the Stoic and Epicurean moralities, comparing and contrasting them as alternative models of morality. Similarly, one speaks of Christian or Islamic ethics, or even of African or European ethics. It then appears that morality itself is something that can vary from group to group.

In fact, however, in the respects in which these systems of rules and ideals of conduct differ, they are customs, that is, contingent norms of life, rather than forms of morality in the strict sense of this word. In this strict sense morality, from the standpoint of conduct, is the motivated pursuit of sympathetic impartiality. Such values as truthfulness, honesty, justice, chastity, and so on, are simply aspects of sympathetic impartiality, and do not differentiate morality from culture to culture. At best, what the contingencies of culture may do is to introduce variations of detail in the definition of some of these values. Thus the concept of chastity in a polyandrous society will accommodate more diversified sexual contacts with men on the part of a woman than in a monogamous environment. These differing constraints on definition are, of course, constraints of custom, and do not flow from sympathetic impartiality by any stretch of logical implication. This is true of customs in general, and explains why, though morality, strictly so-called, does not differ and cannot differ from place to place, custom can and does. But since strict morality, at least as precept, is a social constant – and any society will have one set of idiosyncrasies or another – what are often called alternative moralities will be found, on examination, to be composites of universal morality and contingent custom. Such, exactly, is the character of the Epicurean and Stoic moralities, for example. These systems are ratiocinative celebrations of different life-styles combined with attempts to define justice and moral virtue. A further example is the following: what is referred to as Christian ethics, is, in fact, a mixture of pure morality (e.g. "Do not steal!") and customs (e.g. "Man, you may marry only one woman!") with some taboos thrown in (e.g. "Do not work on the Sabbath!").

This insistence on a separation in thought between custom and morality does not, most assuredly, carry any suggestion that customs cannot form a basis for discriminations of the good, the bad, and the indifferent. The point is only that there are more grounds for the normative appraisal of conduct than moral merit or demerit. Neither is it implied that extra-ethical codes are not important. One has only to think of the importance of traffic rules in places like New York. And yet it can hardly be said that such a thought-experiment yields proof that traffic rules are moral principles.

Two sub-conceptions of morality are implicit in the preceding remarks. Morality has been construed, now as a set of rules, now as a pattern of conduct cognisant of those rules. Sympathetic impartiality represents a fusion of the two conceptions: the impartiality is what the moral rules embody, and the sympathy is what the moral motivation evinces. The two elements underlie a distinction in moral evaluation on which Kant was famously keen: it is one thing to act in accordance with a moral rule and quite another to act out of respect for it (or, from the sympathetic perspective, out of concern for it). Only the latter has moral worth. But here comes an objection: moral worth may be a precious thing, but it may not be a universal necessity. A society of rational egoists might conceivably get by with an exclusively prudential conformity to the moral rules. This objection does not, of course, threaten the universality of the moral rules, only the universality of the concern for them. But in picturing the rational egoists as a tribe totally bereft of human sympathy, it threatens their very status as human persons.

The objection just noted argues, in effect, that the doctrine of sympathetic impartiality says too much. There is an inverse objection to the effect that it says too little: far from sympathetic impartiality being sufficient for morality, it may be compatible with the most severe infractions of human well-being. A sadist may cause pain to others without need of special pleading. What this shows, however, is not that sympathetic impartiality is not necessary for the human community, but rather that it is not sufficient for human well-being. And this is important. Being sufficient for morality is not necessarily sufficient for all desirables. Otherwise it would not be necessary to supplement morality with custom in every society. In addition to sympathetic impartiality, human society needs various other things, including common sense and psychiatry.

An even more topical objection perceives the spectre of authoritarianism in the very idea of a cultural universal. Suggesting that some rule of conduct has universal validity seems to be interpreted as a prelude to a programme of imposition. This feeling is thanks to the history of inter-cultural oppression in which some cultures have sought, sometimes successfully, to force their ideas of good and evil, conceived as universal verities, on other cultures. The practice has, in fact, usually been doubly pernicious; for what the aggressors have pursued others with have generally been their pet customs rather than any principles of pure morality. Nevertheless, a little thought should enable one to distinguish between the universality of morality and the arbitrariness of any self-righteous pretenders to universal insight. Judicious claims of universality imply only that contending adults can, in principle, discuss their differences rationally on a basis of equality, whether inside identical cultures or across them.

But granted that moral rules are humanly universal and stand apart from all other rules of conduct, does it follow that all those others are lacking in cultural universality? No premise or rule of inference seems available for establishing any such necessary implication, but it does seem to be one of the most visible facts about human societies that customs vary greatly from one society to another and, even within the same society, from one era to another. This, indeed, is a matter of fact that we have repeatedly noted above. However, on closer examination, qualifications begin to press themselves upon our attention regarding the inscrutability of the variations. Firstly, any custom which violates a moral rule is *ipso facto* condemnable as bad, not *for* this or that society, but simple and short.

Secondly, customs often rest upon beliefs about the world. Insofar as cognitive standards are ultimately universal, as argued in the first part of this discussion, such customs are, by and large, open to cross-cultural evaluations. Thus, for example, prayer to, or in care of, the Virgin Mary is an important custom among Catholics. But, obviously, if a Catholic were, *per improbabile*, to be argued out of his/her belief in the existence of God, that custom would, barring instinctual inertia, lose its hold on him/her. And where argument is concerned, the principles of non-contradiction and induction unite all humankind. Similarly, were it, for instance, to be proven that our ancestors do not continue to exist in any shape or form, the traditional Akan custom of pouring libation to departed ancestors would be deprived of its traditional rationale. In short, so long as a custom has a rationale, it has, at least, a qualified universality via its trans-cultural intelligibility.

But – and this is our third observation – some customs do not seem to have a rationale. We exclude cases of forgotten rationale, for, logically, they belong to the class already dealt with. The relevant cases here are the ones that seem to be born of caprice or pure accident. Paradoxically, these are, perhaps, the easiest to understand trans-culturally; for caprice is caprice, and an accident is an accident everywhere. So long as the resultant modes of conduct are objectively harmless, their known variety will, at best, support only a vacuous relativism, since there is, by hypothesis, no real disparity of values. On the other hand, where they are harmful, they are, as argued above, open to cross-cultural evaluation on moral or other rational grounds. In either case, little comfort accrues to relativism, either ethical or even descriptive.

Fourthly, even in those spheres of human activity such as art (fine, literary, culinary, etc.) or music, dance, games and other recreations, where the historically well-established differences in values and sensibilities among the various peoples of the world have spawned great varieties of form and content, it is clear that increasing communication and familiarity made possible by the tremendous advances in media technology and the like are fast universalising not only appreciation but also creative assimilation. Thus, where we cannot as yet speak of actual universals we can at least anticipate potential universals.

It is apparent from all this that when, as is often the case, critics of relativism have quickly conceded descriptive relativism in their attempts at the refutation of normative relativism, they have, in fact, unwittingly passed over some quite significant anti-relativistic considerations.

We started this discussion with the question whether there are any cultural universals. We must now begin to wonder whether ultimately there are any cultural non-universals.

UBUNTU CULTURE AND PARTICIPATORY MANAGEMENT

ERASMUS D. PRINSLOO

INTRODUCTION

The focus of this essay is the application of the concept of *Ubuntu* to establish a form of participatory management in an industry. Certain activities involved in business management and the *Ubuntu* world-view will therefore also receive attention. Lovemore Mbigi is an important advocate of the *Ubuntu* style of management and I will concentrate on his attempt to link *Ubuntu* to business management.

Sound management is a basic requirement for the successful running of a business. The entrepreneur has to decide on capital structure and the type of business. A human resource policy that includes issues such as job and worker evaluation, remuneration, labour relations, and probably affirmative action also has to be addressed. All these issues and many others, including, *inter alia,* leadership and control, have to be managed. These are but a few of the activities that occur in managing most, if not all, types of businesses and service organisations. A complicating factor is that there are a variety of theoretical frameworks in terms of which such activities may be defined and evaluated. Different emphases and management approaches are possible. For example, a manager may approach a task by putting the emphasis either on the workers or on profits. An enlightened human resources policy will give rise to a humane and considerate treatment of staff, while in a capital intensive enterprise the emphasis will rather be on efficiency and obsolescence of the plant used and concomitant financial considerations. The question, then, is how these activities and their underlying considerations might be affected if a business concern were to be managed in the *Ubuntu* style.

WHAT IS *UBUNTU* ?

Thinkers such as Ruel Khoza, E.N. Chikanda, Joe Teffo, Nono Makhudu, Sisho Maphisa, and Augustine Shutte have all attempted to define *Ubuntu*. By examining their attempts I will try to establish the basic concepts which figure in *Ubuntu* discourse and which need to be considered in order to make sense of and evaluate an *Ubuntu* style of management.

Khoza's (1994) starting point is that *Ubuntu* is an African view of life and world-view; he talks of the collective consciousness of the people of Africa. He claims that Africans have their own religion, their own ethical views, and their own political ideologies (Black Consciousness, Negritude). He argues that the distinctive collective consciousness of Africans is manifested in their behaviour patterns, expressions, and spiritual self-fulfilment, in which values such as the universal brotherhood of Africans sharing and treating other people as humans are concretised. Khoza's basic idea of universal brotherhood is echoed by other African thinkers in ideas such as sensitivity towards the needs and wants of others (Chikanda), the understanding of others' frame of reference (Makhudu), and man as a social being (Teffo).

41

For Chikanda (1990), *Ubuntu,* which she sees as African Humanism, involves alms-giving, sympathy, care, sensitivity to the needs of others, respect, consideration, patience, and kindness.

The development of human potential requires, according to Makhudu (1993: 40–41), traits such as warmth, empathy, understanding, the ability to communicate, interaction, participation, sharing, reciprocation, harmony, cooperation, and a shared world-view, which collectively make up *Ubuntu* culture. Makhudu thus also relates *Ubuntu* to African Humanism, but she regards the qualities which make up the *Ubuntu* way of life, or true humaneness, as existing in every person. Makhudu particularly emphasises the values of empathy, congruence and open communication. She explains empathy (understanding the other person's frame of reference) by contrasting it to dog-eats-dog competition. Congruence or genuine-ness means, for her, that every person should be him/herself and be proud of and true to his/her own identity. Open communication involves, according to Makhudu, fearlessly establishing direct, open, and honest lines of communica-tion, which in turn involves getting in touch with oneself and admitting, *inter alia,* to one's biases and prejudices about other cultures and ethnic groups.

Teffo emphasises the human being's moral nature. Morality is acquired during a progressive process of socialisation which includes accepting obligations to others, which is the basis of morality. This social morality is manifested, for Teffo (1992: Unpublished paper), in humankind's social setting, in law, in communalism, in nature conservation, and in reconstructive development programmes. Social relations are internalised in the extended family experience and during contact with distant relatives and friends. Such groups form a closely knit social web which brings about solidarity between persons. The ultimate expression of regard for the other is to stand up (*ukusukuma*) for others by showing concern in the sense of spontaneously and voluntarily assuming a self-imposed sense of duty towards the needy, destitute or bereaved. This constitutes a consciousness of social responsibility. Nobody should be rejected or condemned as worthless. In this way African societal life accommodates all contingencies of human character and of social, economic, and political disasters.

Ubuntu, according to Teffo, thus links up with communalism and involves wealth distribution. Society is divided in terms of age and gender classes that provide a framework for orderly status distribution and social interaction. When a beast is slaughtered the carved portions are distributed according to the prescriptions of status classification. Social responsibility is expressed, for example, by harvesting only part of the crop, and leaving the rest to the less privileged, the poor, orphans, the destitute, and eventually to the birds. Nature conservation thus has a definite place in the system and is based on internal communitarian ethics. Humankind and nature are one in *Ubuntu* ethics, in contrast with the Cartesian dualism of mind and matter. Teffo argues further that social and economic reconstruction and development should include moral development as well, because without such development massive injections of capital cannot guarantee real economic and social development.

Shutte (1992:Unpublished paper) interprets *Ubuntu* in terms of the worthwhile, the good, and the valuable in human life, which means it is concerned with visions of happiness and fulfilment, and with ideas of how these might be realised. It seems that Shutte takes the African family as a model for a wider kinship system. This interpersonal character of *Ubuntu* is, according to Shutte, the source of many of its *distinctive* virtues such as patience, hospitality, loyalty, respect, conviviality, sociability, vitality, health, endurance, sympathy, and munificence. He goes on to explain the distinctiveness of some of these virtues.

The virtue of respect Shutte interprets as respect for the aged, which implies a view of personhood correlated with development – an older person is more of a person than a younger one because he/she has more to offer by way of knowledge and experience, personal influence and power. This means that the elderly played, and continue to play, an important part in *Ubuntu* societies, in contrast to the social dominance of younger people in Western societies. This means that in *Ubuntu* societies there is a strong emphasis on duties and virtues, though rights are always implied. Shutte also shows that the *Ubuntu* society emphasises that every member should visibly participate in society and not disappear in the whole. All this has a bearing on government. Officials should know the people they are serving and government should be in the service of values rooted in humanity. *Ubuntu* thus embodies a tradition of consultation with, and decision-making by, the ordinary members of society. In the sphere of work, individual creativity must go hand-in-hand with cooperation and common ownership. In education, again, personal growth and community needs must be related. The technological aspects of health care should be linked to interpersonal relations since there is a unity of mental and physical factors in human beings. Nature should be dealt with in such a way that it becomes and remains a hospitable milieu for human existence.

In summary, it may be stated that *Ubuntu* takes seriously the view that man is basically a social being. This point is made very clearly by Maphisa (1994) when he contrasts *Ubuntu* with violence in the animal world. Most *Ubuntu* thinkers therefore formulate their views in terms of "a person is a person through other persons" (Makhudu 1993:40–41), or, "I am, because you are". In this way human dignity gains a central place and seems to be related both to morality and rationality. According to *Ubuntu* thinkers, there is no dualism in this position because both rationality and morality are acquired from community life and do not follow from so-called universal categories or fixed ideologies. In this sense one can speak of communitarian morality and rationality. This is evident in Khoza's view of collective consciousness which for him involves universal brotherhood, sharing, and treating other people with respect. The sharing aspect is very important for most other thinkers on *Ubuntu*, e.g. Chikanda, Makhudu, and Teffo. As we shall see, sharing is also Mbigi's point of departure in developing his views on *Ubuntu* management.

MBIGI ON *UBUNTU* STYLE MANAGEMENT

Cooperative management

"Sharing", for Mbigi, means "participation" in the context of business management. From this notion he develops a network of concepts such as "group solidarity", "conformity", "compassion", "respect", "dignity", and "collective unity" to put across his idea of *Ubuntu* style management. This means that *Ubuntu* style management involves a departure from hierarchically structured management relations, as well as the introduction of a cooperative and supportive form of management in which the collective solidarity of the various groups employed is respected and enhanced. For Mbigi, *Ubuntu* is a social survival strategy that developed from adverse social and geographical circumstances in which people had to cooperate to survive. As such, it is part of "Africans' collective consciousness" and it should be included in management models in Africa. This means that managers will have to keep this in mind to keep up the spirit and morale of the workers, and introduce processes (e.g. "bottom-up" instead of "top-down" management) and practices (e.g. teamwork) that are in line with their workers' view of life in order to be able to achieve set goals.

But it cannot only be a matter of introducing a certain tradition. Added to this should be further training and development, which in turn have to be linked to the tradition. The workers must understand the competitive survival issues facing them, patriotism and citizenship need to be developed, technical skills should be acquired, and workers themselves must understand the organisation so as to be able to contribute to, and participate in, planning procedures and organising teams.

Key contrasts

There are two sides to Mbigi's management suggestions. On the one hand, he utilises and develops what he sees as the African view of life, the culture of *Ubuntu*. On the other, he reacts to the existing management culture and what he sees as its underlying view of life (the Western or European view), which for him differs totally from the African view. The following three contrasts should clarify his views in this regard.

Individualism

Khoza (1994:3) defines individualism as "that political and social philosophy that places high value on the freedom of the individual and generally stresses the self-directed, self-contained and comparatively unrestrained individual or ego". For him (1994:4) this implies "a value system, a theory of human nature, a general attitude or temper of belief in certain political, economic or social and religious arrangements". This value system Khoza describes as follows:

> All values are man-centred . . . the individual is an end in himself and is of supreme value, society being only a means to individual ends; and all individuals are in some sense morally equal, this quality being expressed by the proposition that no one should ever be treated solely as a means to the well-being of another person (1994:4).

This implies maximum freedom and responsibility for a person to choose his/her own objectives as well as the ways and means of obtaining them. In so doing he/she is the best judge of his/her own interests; a person can oppose authority and controls, compete, and, if sufficiently talented, go ahead of others. Khoza refers to Adam Smith to depict institutionalised economic individualism:

> Smith's "obvious and simple system of natural liberty" pictured exchange of goods and services in free and competitive markets as the ideal system of co-operation for material advantage. Such a system should maximise efficiency as well as freedom, secure for each individual participant the largest yield for his resources to be had without injury to others, and achieve a just distribution – that is, a sharing of the social product in proportion to individual contributions (Khosa 1994:5).

This means that the choices of individuals contribute to their own development and thus to the welfare of society.

In this regard Khoza (1994:10) refers to the dictum, "self-preservation is the first law of life", as a false assumption, since "we cannot preserve self without being concerned about preserving other selves. . . . The agony of the poor impoverishes the rich; the betterment of the poor enriches the rich. The manager's success at managing depends on the co-operation of the managed. . . . Whatever affects one directly, affects all indirectly."

For Khoza, individualism is not viable. It is hostile to the basic understanding of the human condition as social in nature; it has no understanding of the human being as a social being, that is, of the social nature of man. He argues:

> Man's nature, his wants, and his capacities are to a great extent the product of society and its institutions. His most effective behaviour is usually through groups and organizations, running the gamut from the family through all types of voluntary social and economically motivated associations to the state, the church, and national organizations (Khoza 1994:5).

Khoza argues that these units may promote or frustrate individualistic ideals. In short, Khoza agrees with Mbigi that communitarianism rather than individualism is characteristic of Africans.

Collectivism

Khoza (1994:6) defines collectivism as "any of several types of social organisation in which the individual is seen as being subordinate to a social collectivity such as a state, a nation, a race, a social class". He links this view of collectivism to earlier formulations such as Rousseau's idea of submission to the "general will", Hegel's idea of unqualified submission to the institutions of the nation-state, and Marx's idea of the determination of people's consciousness by their social being. He points out that we find different degrees of collectivism in twentieth-century political systems such as communism (the extreme form), socialism, fascism and social democracy (the mildest form, and one with which *Ubuntu* has a certain affinity in terms of industrious individual efforts which are lauded and rewarded as long as they are altruistic).

Although *Ubuntu* itself is a form of collectivism, Khoza (1994:9) objects to the one-sidedness and authoritarianism of Western collectivism. "*Ubuntu* would seem to be broadening respect for the individual – respect for the dignity and the rights of each person in the social unit – and purging collectivism of its negative elements." Whereas the relationship between individuals and society is thought of in hierarchical terms in Western collectivism, in *Ubuntu* culture this relationship is never seen in this way. For this reason, according to Khoza, *Ubuntu* cannot, for example, be racist, since racism is exclusivist, implying racial hatred, disunity, and painful social dislocation. The right balance between individualism and collectivism is made possible by taking people's need for dignity, self-respect, and regard for others seriously. According to Khoza, one's self-image develops out of the perception one has of oneself and the perception others have of one, which again brings in the interaction between person and community. Within organisations this involves generating an *esprit de corps* which increases productivity by reinforcing the mutually positive expectations created when people are viewed as virtuous and capable; experience shows that people are more productive when they are treated with respect.

Western Humanism

Khoza begins by examining Humanism in general, and shows the historical roots of Western Humanism by referring to Protagoras, Renaissance thought (from which Khoza believes Western Humanism mainly derives), Comte, and Nietzsche. He claims that all these views can be expressed in terms of the Protagorean dictum, "Man is the measure of all things." For Khoza, this implies the elimination of the supernatural to explain the why, what, and how of things; for this to occur, the humanist wants the human being to rely on observation, logic, and reason. For Khoza, however, this is not enough. There are indeed human achievements in science and technology, but there are also aberrations such as racism, the holocaust, and nuclear, chemical, and biological wars. This kind of Humanism is, according to him, driven by the intellect. Agreeing with Senghor, he argues that African Humanism is, in contrast, a profound spiritual/religious experience that is primarily emotional. According to this interpretation, Western Humanism is intellectual, individualistic, and atheistic, whereas *Ubuntu* is religious, expansive, transcendental, and centrifugal. Khoza points out that in *Ubuntu* culture a human being is defined dynamically (there are degrees or modifications of human nature *per se*) and in relational terms, in contrast to the Western static definition of a person (one who possesses human nature, i.e. possesses reason). Management procedures and strategies in Africa will therefore have to make provision for the religious and emotional needs of workers.

AN EXAMPLE OF *UBUNTU* STYLE MANAGEMENT

The collective consciousness advocated by *Ubuntu* thinkers involves notions such as universal brotherhood and sharing. The question is, however, how these concepts and their correlatives are to be applied in real-life issues such as labour relations. There are various examples of attempts to introduce forms of participatory management. In dealing with problems in Mpumalanga's Eastern Highlands Tea Estates, Lovemore Mbigi employed participatory management methods which I shall now examine.

When Mbigi first got involved with the labour problems of the Eastern Highlands Tea Estates, the company's financial position was precarious, industrial relations were hostile, relations with the Department of Labour were strained, there had been at least three violent strikes, and, in general, the morale of the workers was low. In short, a crisis situation had developed. Mbigi summarised the problem at hand as one of reconciling worker expectations and demands with the financial situation of the company.

Mbigi organised discussions for the workers in which they were encouraged to participate. They were requested to assess the situation critically, to air their views on what was actually going on, and to suggest how the problems were to be solved. In these discussions the existing leadership roles were played down so that anyone could take the lead on a particular occasion, and leadership thus became shared. These sessions resulted in improved morale, and a new spirit was created in the company. Sessions were then organised around specific themes relating to the situation. Speeches were made in which the workers aired their views and feelings, and the audience could react by singing, dancing, and chanting slogans. It was found that morale improved dramatically, as did productivity.

In short, Mbigi changed management strategy from one of confrontation to cooperation. Instead of being given orders which they simply had to obey, workers were given the opportunity to air their views and to make suggestions; instead of their demands simply being turned down because the company could not afford to meet them, the workers were given reports on the company's actual position which they were then invited to discuss; instead of working "blindly" they could also evaluate their role and contribution. This changed their view of their position in the company and of their joint future. Instead of views being forced on them in terms of a management strategy which imposed decisions from the top, the workers were given the opportunity to participate and thus to cooperate and to work problems out for themselves. Mbigi (1992) calls this "emergent strategy" because there is no fixed blueprint available at the outset; procedures and objectives are worked out in cooperation with the workers.

The major shift in this exercise was making room for the culture of the workers to play a role in the management of the company. The "rational" was backed up by the "emotional", and both the group and the collective consciousness were allowed to play their roles. The basic cultural attitudes of the workers were integrated into the principles of business management. In short, people's views of life, the value systems they live by, incorporate basic expectations which enable them to identify with certain ideals in terms of which life is judged as having meaning for them. Allowing these into the workplace meant, in this case, cooperation and identification with the Tea Estates' goals.

Mbigi summarises the Eastern Highlands Tea Estate experience as allowing and enabling the workers to go back to their African heritage so that they could return to their challenges at work willing and prepared to face them and to help solve them, and thus to engage in a living dialogue with the future. By utilising the tradition of caring and sharing, exclusive, legalistic, contractual relationships were changed to inclusive, enterprising, sharing relationships. By the formation of a production committee to deal with production matters and a worker's council to deal with industrial relations, that is, by introducing a culturally sensitive form of participatory management, Mbigi succeeded not only in introducing a web of intimate primary relationships which helped to create a collaborative and caring atmosphere that formed a basis for synthesising the different values involved, but also in changing the financial situation of the company, and, accordingly, of the workers themselves.

Mbigi goes even further. The model of participation is inadequate to deal with the fact of continual industrial and economic development. He quotes Henryk Skolimowski to show that something more is needed:

> Each epoch and each society is rooted in some fundamental beliefs and assumptions which are acted upon as if they were true. They justify all other things that follow from them while they themselves are accepted as faith. A change in philosophy is a change in the accepted canons of faith, whether that faith is of a religious or secular character; and conversely, when a given people, society or civilization is shaken or shattered, this calls for fresh thinking and a new philosophical basis. We shall need to create new myths to make transition in our society possible (Mbigi 1992:26).

Mbigi therefore argues for what he terms the *developmental holistic approach*. It is holistic because traditions, visions, and reality have to be synthesised – as shown in the above discussion. The notion of development is included in order to focus on the continuous growth of people and improvement of products, systems, structures, markets, productivity, quality, and performance. Mbigi (1992:26) speaks of a single-minded dedication to total development. As he sees it, unity is created in diversity, and wealth is thus optimised. Mbigi bases his model on four principles which he derives from the *Ubuntu* view of life: *morality*, which involves trust and credibility; *interdependence*, which concerns the sharing and caring aspect of relationships, that is, cooperation and participation; *spirit of man*, which refers to human dignity and mutual respect, implying that activities should be person-driven and humanness should be central; and lastly, *totality*, which pertains to the continuous improvement of everything in the organisation by every member of the organisation. This means that the values and aspirations of the workers, that is, their world-views, must be allowed to play a role in the organisation. This means that the organisation can no longer be a mere economic unit and workers mere sellers of labour. The organisation has to be changed into a holistic community in which everyone involved becomes an active member who participates in all its activities and who thus shares in its success and failures.

CRITICAL ASSESSMENT

Elimination of negativity

An aspect of the authoritarian management style is the existence of negative attitudes on the part of the workers; they experience anger, fear, bitterness, and guilt. In the *Ubuntu* system these negative feelings may be addressed during the negotiation process and are likely to be eliminated in a situation of co-responsibility. It is important to note that Mbigi's approach is not a form of Utopian thinking, but is rather based on a belief in the human need for survival. Confrontation threatens the survival of an organisation and thus the well-being of both "bosses" and workers. It may be argued that the threat to survival includes the maintenance of a resource-rich minority at the expense of a poverty-stricken majority, as well as dominating management styles and structures (which result in, or are perceived to result in, exploitation of the workers), conflicts, riots, strikes, damage to property, terror, and revolution. The aim is to avoid these and to transform strife into cooperation.

The status of *Ubuntu*

The vocabulary of *Ubuntu* is clearly not unfamiliar to Western thinking. Concepts such as "sharing", "brotherhood", "dignity", and "trust" can be found in many contexts of Western and other forms of thinking. Some of the words denoting these concepts may differ in different contexts, though still expressing the same meaning. "Comrade" in the communist context and "brother" in the context of *Ubuntu* are, when considered in isolation, examples. Differences set in when these concepts are analysed in terms of a restricted network of concepts in which they exist, that is, when they become ideologically loaded. In this sense, it may be said that communists abuse the concept "comrade" and strip it of its original meaning. A similar thing occurs with the notion of "human dignity" if it is limited to Western Humanism, and with the idea of "sharing" if it is restricted to socialism.

This has both a negative and a positive implication as far as *Ubuntu* is concerned. On the negative side it means that *Ubuntu* is not an altogether new concept – if, indeed, it is new at all; it is neither radically different nor unique. This is not, however, to dismiss *Ubuntu* since this means that *Ubuntu* shares in a world spirit and may even serve to emphasise this world spirit and to remind other cultures of its importance. This may lead to a joint application of principles of human dignity to all spheres of life in order to create relatively harmonious communities.

Practical implementation

The practical implementation of highly abstract principles, particularly value principles, is, however, a serious problem. The concepts used in the formulation of principles, despite their being "familiar" to almost all thinkers on these issues, are systematically ambiguous. We all know that a concept may be familiar in terms of its use, while being unfamiliar in terms of the criteria for its application. The concept "sharing" is a case in point. We can all understand what it means to share food, but if sharing is made a principle in terms of which we have to organise our lives, more particularly, our social, political, and economic activities, as in the case of *Ubuntu*, we are likely to experience many problems with its application in various contexts.

Consensus

The idea has been created that participatory management in terms of *Ubuntu* culture will always be consensus management because the aim is to eliminate conflict. But where people differ about important issues, consensus can be problematic. Attempting to operate with the slogan, "Don't look for differences, but look for similarities and accommodate differences", is easier said than done. A key notion here is, "the best interest of all", which is, of course, exactly what people will differ about; some may argue that a strike is in the best interests of all even if this may cause the firm to close down, while others may argue that no-one really benefits from a strike and that this should therefore not be an option. Moreover, this is the kind of difference where the vote does not solve anything since people do not change their minds simply because they are a minority.

These considerations show that the introduction of *Ubuntu* culture as such cannot solve all problems. Consensus procedures, for one, should be specifically addressed. Limited attention seems to have been devoted to this issue in the Eastern Highlands Tea Estate case. There may be two reasons for this: the problems encountered might have been uncomplicated, and secondly, the similarities among the views of the stakeholders might have been significant. These provide no guarantee for future problems, however. More difficult problems may come up in the future, or the stakeholders may differ radically among themselves on such problems. That is, consensus procedures cannot be ignored, though they are at present in their infancy. In short, the introduction of *Ubuntu* culture takes place at different social and organisational levels, and this should be recognised and the implications worked out in full.

Furthermore, cultures have to grow and to adapt to new situations; no culture can have solutions for all kinds of problems at the ready. This means that the introduction of a certain form of participatory management founded on *Ubuntu* culture can be nothing more than the beginning of a process to improve labour relations and the economic viability of the firm. Further analyses of successes and failures in dealing with labour problems are therefore necessary. Procedures and structures have to be evaluated so as to establish guidelines for handling future problems. Some of these will have general application and others will apply only to specific situations. This distinction is not drawn in Mbigi's analysis.

Ethical argumentation

Merely following tradition is no solution to an ethical dilemma. Joseph Weiss (1994:6) defines business ethics as "an area that requires reasoning and judgement based on both principles and beliefs in making choices to balance economic self-interests against social and welfare claims". The "reasoning and judgement" referred to are necessary because of the complex moral dilemmas in the field of business that have to be addressed, such as dilemmas concerning management, human resources, etc., to which there is no one right answer. Logical and ethical reasoning is therefore required to come to an understanding and to think through complex moral problems in business situations. With reference to *Ubuntu* culture this has two implications. *Ubuntu* must be analysed and described if it is to play a meaningful role in this field. Employing a tradition may work as a start, and up to a point, but in the long run more will be required because argumentation will be necessary. Apart from a description of the ethical system, a certain degree of sophistication in ethical argumentation will also be necessary. When Mbigi pleads for total development it should be realised that this is also a need. Making allowance for culture and cultural differences in the workplace is necessary, but in the long run this can have a positive influence on labour relations only if it is based on rationality.

REFERENCES

Appadurai, A. 1990. "Disjuncture and difference in the global cultural economy", in M. Featherstone (ed.), *Global culture, nationalism, globalization and modernity. A Theory Culture and Society special issue.* London: Sage in association with *Theory, Culture & Society,* 1990:295–310.

Bell, M. 1986. *Contemporary Africa: Development, culture and the state.* London: Longman.

Bennett, T. 1993. "Useful culture", in V. Blundell, J. Shepherd & I. Taylor (eds), *Relocating cultural studies: Developments in theory and research.* New York: Routledge, 1993:67–85.

Biko, S. "Some African cultural concepts." *Frank Talk,* 1(4):29–32.

Biko, S. "The definition of black consciousness." *Frank Talk,* 1(1):3–9.

Blim, M. 1996. "Cultures and the problems of capitalisms." *Critique of anthropology,* 16(1):79–93.

Boonzaier, J. & Sharp, J. (eds) 1988. *South African keywords: The uses and abuses of political concepts.* Cape Town: David Philip.

Buthelezi, M. 1992. "End of year message." *Sunday Star,* 27 December 1992.

Chikanda, E.N. 1990. "Shared values and Ubuntu". Conference paper read at HSRC conference KONTAK on Nation Building. Pretoria: Unpublished.

Deleuze, G. & Guattari, F. 1988. *A thousand plateaus: Capitalism and schizophrenia.* Minneapolis: University of Minneapolis Press.

Featherstone, M. 1991. *Globalization: Nationalism, globalization and modernity.* London: Sage.

Featherstone, M. 1995. *Undoing culture: Globalization, postmodernism and identity.* London: Sage.

Grossberg, L. 1992. *We gotta get out of this place: Popular conservatism and postmodern culture.* New York: Routledge.

Khoza, R. 1994. "Ubuntu as African humanism." Conference paper read at Ekhaya Promotions, Diepkloof Extension. Unpublished.

Klitgaard, R. 1993. "What if we knew all about cultures?" *Critical Arts,* 6(2):49–67.

Klopper, S. 1989. *Mobilizing cultural symbols in twentieth-century Zululand.* Cape Town: University of Cape Town Centre for African Studies.

Laitin, D.D. 1986. *Hegemony and culture. Politics and social change among the Yoruba.* Chicago: University of Chicago Press.

Makhudu, N. 1993. "Cultivating a climate of co-operation through Ubuntu." *Enterprise,* 68 (August 1993):40–41.

Mamdani, M. 1996. *Citizen and subject: Contemporary Africa and the legacy of late colonialism.* Princeton: Princeton University Press.

Maphisa, S. 1994. "Man in constant search of *Ubuntu* – a dramatist's obsession". Conference paper read at Ubuntu Conference (AIDSA) Pietermaritzburg, University of Natal: Unpublished.

Mbigi, L. 1992. "Unhu or Ubuntu: The basis for effective HR Management." *Peoples Dynamics,* October 1992:20–26.

Mbigi, L. & Maree, J. 1995. *Ubuntu: The spirit of African transformation management.* Randburg: Knowledge Resources.

Okali, C. 1983. *Cocoa and kinship in Ghana: The matrilineal Akan of Ghana.* London: Kegan Paul.

Prakash, G. 1990. "Writing post-Orientalist histories of the Third World: Perspectives from Indian historiography." *Comparative studies in Society and History,* 32:383–408.

Prinsloo, E.D. 1996. "The Ubuntu style of Participatory Management", in J.G. Malherbe (ed.), *Decolonizing the Mind: Proceedings of the 2nd colloquim on African philosophy held at the University of South Africa, October 1995.* Pretoria: Unisa, 1995:112–122.

Quine, W.V. 1960. *Word and object.* Cambridge, Mass.: MIT.

Said, E.W. 1995. *Orientalism: Western conceptions of the Orient.* London: Penguin.

Shaw, W.H. 1991. *Business Ethics.* Wadsworth: Belmont.

Shohat, E. 1994. *Unthinking eurocentricism: Multiculturalism and the media.* London: Routledge.

Shutte, A. 1992. "The Ubuntu project." Conference paper read at the 22nd Congress of the Philosophical Society of Southern Africa, Durban, University of Natal, July 1992: Unpublished.

Teffo, J. 1992. "African Philosophy in a human context in dialogue with Western Philosophy." Conference paper read at the 22nd Congress of the Philosophical Society of Southern Africa, Durban, University of Natal, July 1992: Unpublished.

Thompson, J.B. 1990. *Ideology and modern culture. Critical social theory in the era of mass communication.* Cambridge: Polity in association with Blackwell.

Thornton, R. 1988. "Culture: A contemporary definition", in J. Boonzaier & J. Sharp (eds), 1988:17–28.

Tomaselli, K.G. & Aldridge, M. 1996. "Cultural strategies in a changing development: Reassessing Paulo Freire in the information age." *Africa Media Review,* 10(1):54–72.

Tomlinson, J. 1991. *Cultural imperialism: A critical introduction.* London: Pinter.

Van Staden, C. 1996. "Claiming the African mind: Postcoloniality and cultural studies." *Communicatio,* 22(2):71–76.

Weiss, J.W. 1994. *Business ethics: a managerial, stakeholder approach.* Belmont: Wadsworth.

Wiredu, K. 1995. "Are there Cultural Universals?" in *The Morist.* 28(52–64).

CHAPTER 3

Understanding Trends in "African Thinking" – a Critical Discussion

MARLENE VAN NIEKERK

1. INTRODUCTION: THREE CONTEXTS

Many people are likely to raise an eyebrow at the title of this essay. Some may find the quotation marks superfluous, while others may consider them inadequate. The quotation marks have in fact been inserted to indicate that the writer is well aware of the disturbing resonance of the notion, "African Thinking".

I shall try to treat the notion in much the same way as Zora Neale Hurston (Johnson 1986) treated the question, "How does it feel to be coloured you?". She dismissed the possibility of a direct answer just as I shall dismiss the possibility of a straightforward, unwavering discussion of a matter with which nothing is supposedly "*the* matter" at all. She repeats the question: " 'How does it feel to be coloured me?' – Compared to *what?* As of *when? Who* is asking? In what context *(where)*? With what interests and presuppositions, and for what purpose *(why)*?" (emphases added).

This cluster of detective story questions (the who, the where, the why, the when, and the what of "African Thinking") determined the three contexts which I thought would justify a discussion. From the nature of these contexts it will soon be clear that by "critical discussion" I do not mean a certain type of a-historical, non-dialectical, non-materialist, and non-reflexive "analysis" – that angelic strategy employed by the voices of universal rationality when they have lowered their tone to one of subtle persuasion: the tone of scientific neutrality. The rhetoric in this article will hopefully be more obvious and less dangerous.

The first context is the context of the "crime". This is the academic context where the idea of "African Thinking" could arise as a possible field of research to complement or complete an already existing body of "world-views" and to make courses more relevant to "the South African situation". Such a notion would then play a role in the "comparison" of world-views. I shall construct the paradigm of such a "comparative" strategy as it could manifest itself in, for example, the evaluation of "animism" when compared to "civilised" world-views, rated on a classificatory scale of value determined by a basically positivist orientation.[1]

The second context will deal with the historical and political background of the "crime". This is the context of Western anthropology, taken as a history of successive strategies of othering, strategies that were (and are) at the same time rationalisations of the successive stages of imperialist expansion into, and capitalist exploitation of, non-Western territories and cultures. Projected courses on "African Thinking" are ominously prefigured in locally produced expositions of "animism". This is but one manifestation of the heroic colonialist discourse of the primitive "Other". This has as its main function the affirmation of "our" rational identity. But it is exactly the nature of this Western rationality (characterising both traditional capitalist and traditional marxist philosophy), the overbold "Promethean" rationality as it has been called (Lemaire 1976:311), that caused the chinks in the armour of Western civilisation to appear.

It is as though the crises of Western civilisation have turned into so many windows through which new, appreciative views of non-Western cultures have become possible. These "traditional" societies have become the source for the construction of a *model* of an ideal post-industrial, post-historical society – a society that will once again be "rich" without impoverishing the earth or any of its inhabitants. In such a society productivity and production will have to be moderated to such an extent that, among other things, a lasting ecological balance and a non-fragmented communal life will be possible. Such a model of an ideal society will also have a new *rationality*, a new non-Promethean philosophy of the relationship between subject and object, culture and nature, between production and natural and human resources.

Parallel to this would be a new type of anthropologist who would relate to his/her interlocutors as subjects who must be listened to instead of being used and treated as objects to be observed. A situation of coevalness (Fabian 1983:311) is called for, a sharing of the time and the activity of producing knowledge – in other words, a situation of dialogue. This co-produced knowledge will be a different product from the anthropological knowledge that was merely "gathered" or "gleaned". Therefore it will also have a different destiny: instead of being "exported" to the "mother countries" it will be used by the people themselves in the process of emancipation.

Which brings us to the third context – that of Africa beset with struggles for liberation and movements of reaction, fighting for autonomy in the wake of departed Europeans, where greedy neo-colonialist regimes are also asserting themselves. This is a place where ordinary people think and philosophise. The professional philosophers philosophise mostly in French or English about what "African Philosophy" is and what it is not. I shall analyse four of the constructs imposed on this notion by various philosophers in Africa: ethnophilosophy, philosophical sagacity, nationalistic-ideological philosophy, and professional philosophy (e.g. Diemer 1981:8). This will be done in the context of the dialectics of othering that evolved from the construction of "African Thinking" produced by a white missionary, Placide Tempels, in the service of a colonial regime. It will also be done in the context of the changing significance of tradition effected by the struggle for liberation from colonial regimes. Each of the four constructs could be understood as involving a specific mode of othering, as well as different types of evaluations of tradition.

In the light of the critique of Western rationality in Context Two, I shall try to suggest how each of these approaches to philosophical activity in Africa might be integrated into a course on "African Thinking".

To conclude this section I shall refer to an example of what I choose to label a "hermetic turn" in the self-understanding and the understanding of the locus of liberation in neo-colonial Africa. The example is of a revolutionary re-appropriation of indigenous languages as a medium of communication and a re-interpretation of tradition that makes it into a vehicle of change. The role of the intellectual in guiding such a move provides the measure for the type of committed academic needed to develop a course in "African Thinking". His/her relationship with the "Other" will need to be one of radical coevalness.

To sum up the argument: the non-Promethean philosophy positing a non-objectifying, non-exploitative attitude towards the world and nature will have to be accompanied by a new praxis of anthropology and philosophy. It will be a praxis where classical Western modes of othering as *distancing* of the "Other" will have to be replaced by taking sides, by *siding* with the "Other". Once again, as was the case in previous ways of doing anthropology, this new practical possibility is opened up by actual, concrete political developments, i.e. the rise of liberation movements in the third world. It is from this that we have to take our cue for the development of all academic courses and especially for one that deals with the "Other". This entails the inclusion in academic courses of their own history. A critique of the original "desire" for a course in "African Thinking" should be included in the eventual presentation of such a course. This critique would entail a history of the origins of such a desire. It should include Father Tempels and *La Philosophie Bantoue*. It should also include a critique of existing course structures and the desire of academics to expand them.

The prerequisites for a course in "African Thinking" would be, firstly, that the original title is maintained in quotation marks and that the course include an *analysis of the discourse* of which it is part in the present situation; secondly, that "the matter" is contextualised *historically* and *politically*, with reference to the *current self-reflection in Western anthropology*; and finally, that the course is developed with reference to the *debate* about "African Philosophy" in the rest of Africa and in a dimension of *local dialogue* and coevalness.

2.   CONTEXT ONE: "African Thinking" and the Mode of "Othering" in a Naive Positivist "Comparative" model

2.1 The notion of "African Thinking"

As a possible title for academic research and as a possible name for an academic course, "African Thinking" is problematic because it is a notion that hides its contexts and its assumptions. It assumes that there is an autonomous activity called "thinking" and that there are different modes of this autonomous activity; "African Thinking" is one mode that can, like a spade, be called by its name and be isolated for close inspection and "special treatment" because it is decidedly different and "other" and exotic. "Our" thinking, on the other hand, is so obviously normal that we don't have to refer to it as a type of thinking belonging specifically to *us*.

"African Thinking" is, furthermore, an appellation that tries to cover all its traces, the marks of its interests and the process of its selection from other possible terms that are dismissed because they do not cover the desiderata as well as the term "African Thinking" does: the encompassing *generality*, as well as the *essential* or the *typical* – *all* Africans (cf. Bodunrin 1981b:8) think the same *essentially* African thinking.

I regard the notion as an item in Eurocentric and logocentric discourse in which us/they, observer/observed, civilised/primitive, rational/irrational, in short, "the West and the Rest" dichotomies are central. It is this delirium of opposites (Fanon 1982:108) that mobilises meaning in favour of the *status quo* and its asymmetrical power relations.

2.2 "Animism" and Other "World-views": The Comparative Strategy

The paradigm informing the notion of "African Thinking" seems to be very closely related to that which informs the notion of "animism" when one encounters it in an uncritical "comparative" context. Both notions surreptitiously declare a certain attitude towards the "Other". One might suggest here that the rhetorical impact of the positivistic comparative model as a whole rests upon the following pivot of classificatory exclusion and inclusion: inclusion of "animism" to illustrate the excellence, sophistication, and intellectual progress attained in "modern" world-views; exclusion of the historical conditions of possibility and authorship of the term "animism" to support the idea of its "objective" and "given" character.

The positivist comparative model would probably depict the "animist" others as "imprecise" in their way of organising the world, as "childish" in the way they personify natural objects, as "unreliable" because of their metaphorical way of speaking about the world, as "superstitious" because of their belief in spiritual bodies. "Animism" as a world-view would probably come out of this as having little "predictive power" compared to Western science, and as "authoritarian" because of the dictates of spiritual entities. It would probably be judged as a world-view that orientates the lives of people in a simple society but that would not be intellectually satisfying to a person accustomed to contemporary Western city life.

The epistemology underlying this hypothetical model of positivist comparison is one that lacks, in the first place, a dimension of self-reflexivity. It assumes that it looks at the world with a self-sufficient gaze. And, in addition, it perceives the world as a self-revealing place and history as a conglomerate of self-labelling facts. It forgets that every observation and every text, especially ones from the field of anthropology, are part of a concrete scientific praxis in a specific cultural, historical, and political configuration that has to be *interpreted*.

Positivists tend to defend their criteria of evaluation on the basis of rationality, thus implying that the only other choices are "tradition", or more often "feeling". Accordingly, there is only one rational choice, and that is the choice for rationality, because, the argument goes, rational behaviour tends to promote survival – survival of the individual as well as the species – whereas irrational behaviour invites a quick end. It *pays* to be "rational". This argument places science in charge of survival and philosophy in charge of intellectual survival, and presupposes that the rationality of philosophy is also the rationality of science. The positivist model generally appropriates the "rationality of science" in an ambiguously appreciative gesture. Rationality is approved of as the basis of a highly influential current field of human endeavour (science). Furthermore, this rationality offers the advantage to the positivist of taking up an "externalist" view, i.e. one that allows assessment and comparison of world-views from the outside, from a distance.

As I hope to make clear at a later stage of my argument (see Context Three below), the position of "distance" adopted towards the "Other" is not as innocent as it might appear. This act of distancing objectifies the "Other" as different for a particular *reason*. The *reason*-character of this *reason* is not included in the self-understanding of scientific rationality because it would undermine the belief of the latter in its own autonomy and neutrality. The "Other" *has* to be conceived of as *different* and *distant* in order to rationalise a political praxis of exploitation and subjugation that takes place very close to home. This was the role of the type of rationalisation devised by anthropologists and philosophers alike so as to oil the workings of colonial expansion in the nineteenth century.

3.   CONTEXT TWO: Prometheus and Anthropology – A History and a Critique of Western Rationality and its "Other"

3.1 Overview

In this section I shall provide some background with regard to the roots or origin of the subject, i.e. the type of rationality that sets out for the sake of its own identity to fix the essence of the "Other" as "different" and "distant". This is the attitude of the "animist", and it is also the attitude that desires the "essence" or "nature" of "African Thinking" in the fixed and finalised form of an identifiable body of "typical" ideas.

3.2 The Promethean Image of Man

Prometheus, who stole the fire from the Gods, has always been the classical hero of Western civilisation because this civilisation bases itself on a certain set of beliefs: the heroism of progress through sleight of hand and hardship, production through labour, and the possibility of endless victories over new kinds of obstacles. The main thesis of the Promethean view, however, is that the human being can only realise him/herself through the domination of nature. He/she has to objectify, appropriate and exploit nature, which he/she constructs as basically "other" as well as adverse, in order to complete him/herself. Moreover, the Promethean image of man is one of an autonomous subject. It is only in the absolute form of master and lord that the human being can liberate himself (Lemaire 1976:199). This view of the human person has always been the hallmark of civil, industrialised society. It came to philosophical fruition in the German Idealism of Hegel, Fichte, and Feuerbach. And in Marx, it found its materialist form. In Marxism, the human being is viewed as progressively constituting itself through its labour until, ideally, it reaches a stage of complete self-possession (Lemaire 1976:393). It is this heroic self-image that accompanied the anthropological exploits of Western civilisation. It is this conqueror-mentality that pitted itself against the non-Western "Other" as a relic of its own vanquished, pre-scientific past, or as an object of its magnanimous relativist appreciation of various "exotic" cultures.

3.3 Stages in the History of Anthropology

Anthropology, when it first came into existence, understood itself to be a "naturalist *history* of culture" (Stocking 1968:79), a story of how the human species had developed itself in a cumulative process from a state of savagery to that of civilisation. This view of the father of anthropology, E.B. Tylor, is often referred to as being fairly progressive. The ruling doctrine, favoured by the Catholic Church in the early nineteenth century, was that the human being was first created as a fully civilised being. Since the time of the creation, a part of humanity degenerated into "primitives" while another part developed further to form civil society. Opposing this degenerationalism, Tylor, in *Primitive culture* (1871), posits the thesis of developmentalism: the human being is not a fallen angel but an evolving primate that has developed, in a continuing process of learning and improving, both ideas and implements, up to the present day. The story that the "history of mankind is part and parcel of the history of nature" and that civilised society evolved by natural processes from savagery to civilisation (Tylor 1913, II:2) was therefore seen as a scientific attack on theological history. Stocking (1968:102) characterises Tylor as an "empiricist, an agnostic, a rationalist and a positivist" who tries to "fill the gap between Brixham cave and European civilisation without introducing the hand of God" (1968:105–6). It must be stressed that Tylor was not interested in the scientific study of separate "primitive" societies, but solely in the relation of the "savage to civilised life" (Tylor 1913, II:21), solely in the *connection* between modern culture and the condition of the rudest savage (1913, II:159). The past was needed to explain and affirm the present in its ideas and institutions.

It is important to note that Tylor was primarily interested in the development of what Marx would refer to as the superstructure – the mental and *intellectual* evolution of the species – and not so much in the technical aspect. This focus on the development of consciousness also characterises Comte's three-phased model of development from the theological to the metaphysical to the positive scientific stage (Lemaire 1976:69). One of the assumptions of this developmental model is that the primitive cultures known at the time in America, Africa, and Australia could be compared to prehistoric primitive culture and therefore with the prehistory of contemporary Western society. Tylor finds the *proof* for continuity between lower and higher culture in the so-called "survivals". These are elements of an earlier cultural phase that continued to assert themselves through the power of habit, right up to (mainly rational) modern society.

The construct of the survival made three things possible: firstly, it made it possible to place and judge and explain the entire domain of European folklore and superstition – living testimony to an earlier evolutionary phase; secondly, it helped the rationalising civilisation to affirm its own rationality and to ascribe the failures and the imperfections of this rationality to the survival of irrational elements of tradition; thirdly, Tylor exposes these survivals not in order to appreciate them in a romantic fashion, but in order to eradicate them in favour of the values of the Enlightenment (Lemaire 1976:71–2).

The most important type of survival that reached modern civilisation is the belief that spiritual beings activate both animate and non-animate things. The largest part of Tylor's *Primitive culture* is taken up by analyses of animism and its manifestation in mythology, in metaphysics, and eventually in Christianity where the notion of the soul still ruled the day. In his reconstruction of the evolution of consciousness

Tylor takes animism to mark the first developmental stage. This roughly coincides with Comte's theological phase.

To summarise, the following three aspects of Tylor's argument may be stressed. Although he introduced the notion of primitive culture, Tylor saw this as a stage in human culture *as a whole* in a process of ever-increasing rationality. He did not use the term "culture" in the plural. A second aspect is that anthropology, being the study of this process, was constructed as a critical reformer's science – its task was to assist civilian society and mankind in general in the process of modernisation, rationalisation, and enlightenment.

> To the promoters of what is sound, and reformers of what is faulty in modern culture, ethnography has double help to give. To impress men's mind with a doctrine of development, will lead them in all honour to their ancestors to continue the progressive work of past ages, to continue it more vigorously because light has increased in the world, and where barbaric hordes groped blindly, cultured men can often move onward with clear view. It is a harsh, and at times even painful office of ethnography to expose the remains of crude old culture which have passed into harmful superstition, and to mark these out for destruction. Thus active at once in aiding progress and in removing hindrance, the science of culture is a reformer's science (Tylor 1913, II:453).

Lastly, Tylor's concept of culture is ethnocentric or Eurocentric. It is industrial European civilisation that embodies the ideal for the whole of culture, the whole of humanity, and the whole of history. Anthropology at this stage is bound to a philosophy of history and culture, and it is only later that she will be defined as a value-free and strictly empirical science of the intrinsic qualities of non-Western culture.

This is perhaps the place to note that anthropology as a science no longer deals in the "minds of others". A title such as *How natives think*[2] would be unlikely to appear today without quotation marks being employed. The fact, however, that such a title could and did appear in traditional anthropology is itself reflected upon in the process of understanding anthropology's own conditions of possibility which makes up such an important part of the current anthropological debate. Historically, the conditions of possibility of anthropology are to be fixed in civil society and its capitalist mode of production. It is the colonial expansion of this type of society that made non-Western communities economically and scientifically available to the West. Once drawn into the economic circumference of Western capitalism, the lifestyles of these peoples became scientifically objectifiable and susceptible to investigation. The fundamental historical and material fact that is irrevocably presupposed by anthropology as the science of non-Western cultures, is exactly that of the subjugation of these cultures by an expanding Western civilisation (cf. Willis 1972 & Caulfield 1972). One could offer the hypothesis that the social evolutionism of early anthropology is an ideology that offers a rationalisation and a rationale to expansionist colonialism (Lemaire 1976:174). Violent subjugation of the "Other" could be construed as an act of civilised man with an intent to civilise, to bring light into the darkness of those *minds* that had been excluded from the scientific fruits of the European Enlightenment. From the start, anthropology was involved in a relationship of the West with the non-West and with the *global* effects of modernisation. Anticipating the argument that follows, it could be said here that it is the global effect of rationalisation that has led to a renewed attempt to forge a normative philosophy of human culture *as a whole.*

But first we have to deal briefly with the dialectical antithesis of the Eurocentric evolutionism of Tylor and the Enlightenment philosophers generally, namely, cultural relativism – the school that is associated with the work of Franz Boas and his followers (e.g. Ruth Benedict and M. Herskovitz) in America. Basically, cultural anthropology of the twentieth century was a sharp empiricist reaction against the speculative philosophies of history of evolutionists who tried to reconstruct the total cultural history of the human species. The general feeling was that if anthropology wanted to become a real science it had to gather many more facts before indulging prematurely in grand theories about the laws governing the culture of the whole of humanity. The cultural relativist stand generally rejects the Eurocentrism of the evolutionist theories. Instead of taking Western civilisation as a measure of a total reconstruction, the cultural relativists try to refrain from introducing any prejudices and values from their own culture in the process of gathering true and objective knowledge from other cultures. Other cultures must ideally be studied in their own language and on their own terms. Whereas Tylor projected the self-liberation of humankind through universal Western culture, Boas stressed the culture-embeddedness of the human being. Apart from the fact that this kind of view facilitated the use of the word "culture" in the plural, as well as the relativist evaluation of all cultures as equal, it also entailed certain epistemological problems. Herskovitz developed the Boasian notion of culture-embeddedness into the theory of "enculturation" (Lemaire 1976:91). According to this theory, each person is fully determined in his/her perceptions, judgements, and general behaviour by the conditioning imposed by his/her home culture. On the basis of this, no universal judgements about cultures are possible. Cultures can and must be judged in and by themselves. Cultural relativism is viewed by Herskovitz as a value to be held up to the world so that all cultures can live peacefully together. Thus relativism, which also implies an ethical relativism, is what must be accepted interculturally.

The problem with this view, as with all radical relativisms, is, of course, that the statement of relativism itself is not relative. It is meant to be universal. A universalising statement of relativity is inherently contradictory: it means, paradoxically, that cultural relativism is the philosophy of those who have themselves transcended actual cultural relativism. If the statement of relativism is, moreover, based on a notion of scientifically *objective* and *neutral* investigations of the anthropologist, it is *science* that is not relative but universal. This means that science is the *one* element of which it is tacitly assumed that it does not bind one culture, and that it does not determine one as fully as other elements of cultural conditioning. It allows one to say something *about* other cultures, otherwise anthropology would not be possible. Surreptitiously then, the view is taken that it is only in "other" cultures that people are enculturated and imprisoned in the perceptions and judgements typical of those cultures. It is tacitly assumed and taken for granted that Western science can objectify other cultures as closed gardens of enculturation without hurting the notion of cultural relativism.

The epistemological mistake that Herskovitz makes, and that is the source of his self-contradictory position, is his assumption that the validity of judgements are bound to their genesis (Lemaire 1976:153–160), i.e. that, because judgements are always generated in, and mediated by, the context of a concrete culture, their validity is also limited to this culture. That the historical and social situation of the observer determines his/her judgement is a notion that has also governed the historicism and sociology of knowledge since the first half of this century. However, this is certainly not the belief of Marx or Hegel. For both of them, the relativism ensuing from a connection of genesis and validity can only be overcome by a philosophy of history that claims to span the history of civilisation as a whole.

The rationality of a relativist anthropological science is not founded in such a philosophy, i.e. one that would explain, for example, the superiority of science. This is exactly the type of philosophy that the relativists rejected. But this means that anthropology in this guise is not able to account for her own conditions of possibility or for her own *sense*, globally speaking. So one can say that cultural relativism is positivistic (Lemaire 1976:160–1) because it is a science that neither wants to nor is able to justify its own rationality because it does not want to adopt any "philosophy" or "metaphysics". Furthermore, it does not really represent a victory over ethnocentrism. This is because, firstly, it still implies the "advantage" that Western science offers in its ability to construct a panorama of other cultures. Secondly, in its explicit formulations, it merely serialises ethnocentrism (Lemaire 1976:162). Each culture is centred on itself and can only see the world in its own terms.

It must also be noted that however open-minded the cultural relativist stand might look, it is in fact a very conservative position. Its view of cultural determinism actually implies cultural closure. A notion such as "African Thinking" in this context would, for example, entail the proposition that "Africans always think the same typically African thinking. They won't change." Cultural relativism in fact works with a harmony model (Lemaire 1976:164–165) of culture: everybody toes the line after a successful period of enculturation – this is how the *distinctive* character of culture is maintained.

The ethical relativism inherent in cultural relativism also points to another difficulty. If it is a cultural trait of a group to be violent and intolerant of others (e.g. the exploits of the Nazis or of British imperialists), the consequence of ethical relativism is that it must be tolerated because of the absence of grounds to judge it as wrong.

The point is that cultural relativism would have been a very successful doctrine if cultures had existed next to each other like windowless monads (Lemaire 1976:163). But in a situation where all cultures are related to one another in a variety of ways, including wars and conflicts, it seems that relativism is simply an abstract and idealistic protest against Eurocentrism (Lemaire 1976:176). It is idealistic because it only criticises Western culture on the level of superstructure, the level of conscious values and ideas, and not on that of the material processes of exploitation and subjugation that are inherent in colonial capitalism. In this respect it is precisely its conservatism regarding other cultures that functions to reveal its ideological role.

As Lemaire (1976:174) puts it, if evolutionism could be said to have provided the ideology of a still-expanding colonialism, then cultural relativism could be constructed as the ideology for the phase of established colonialism. Once the subjugation of indigenous cultures was completed, it seemed necessary to promote cultural closure of the indigenous people. They had to be prevented from modernising themselves and in the process developing tendencies to emancipate themselves under the influence of liberal or socialist ideas. The subjugated peoples had to be kept under the colonial thumb, but without too much of the Western fingerprint remaining. This is why the anthropology of the day represented indigenous cultures as well-behaved, integrated cultures that had to remain as uncontaminated by Western influences as possible.

Even if the cultural relativists had had good intentions, the perspective that we now have appears to show that they in fact contributed to the fixation of an inequality between cultures, i.e. mainly the asymmetrical power relations between the West and colonised peoples.

That the cultural relativists did not themselves realise this, was the direct result of their refusal to relate their own activity as anthropologists to the concrete relationship of the West to its colonies, and to the historical effects of this relationship. Their idealistic arguments have nothing to say concerning the way in which Western influences and technologies are appropriated by the officially decolonised countries of the Third World.

With the tendency to modernisation in decolonised countries, a return of nineteenth-century philosophy was imminent. The "developing" world would once again need theories that offered a perspective as to the sense and direction of the global modernisation of mankind. This also meant a resurgence of evolutionist and Marxist thought in anthropology (Lemaire 1976:198–199) as well as an attempt to find alternatives for Marxism and evolutionism since both remained in source and content typical Western theories. The question was whether a Marxist Prometheus was to be the mascot of liberation movements – in other words, whether a philosophy that posits the total domination and ruthless exploitation of nature was a condition for the completion of the emancipation of the ex-colonies. These doubts were raised by the visibility of the terrible disasters that Western society has begun to experience as a result of unbridled industrialisation and rationalisation.

The immoderate industrial productivity of the West was seen to be destroying local and global ecosystems. The social structures imposed by the division of labour and necessitated by the production process led to a fragmentation of the diverse dimensions of social life and to the merely one-sided development, physically and psychologically, of individual human beings. The alienation wrought by the absence of a real solidarity in human community was further aggravated by a crisis of conscience due to the irrationality of globalisation that posed as a progressive rationality aimed at enveloping the world as a whole.

Such crises in post-industrial Western society acted as windows on the social and economic structures of early agrarian and post-neolithic hunter-gatherer societies. It was especially the work of the cultural ecologists (Lemaire 1976:211) that led to a revaluation by the West of these societies that had traditionally been considered to be poor, backward, and irrational. What was now recognised about these "primitive" and "illiterate" societies was that they provided a human life while maintaining a lasting ecological balance. These societies were seen in painful contrast to the industrial society that had submerged a very small section of humanity in wasteful affluence, but that had also succeeded in the two centuries of its existence to do more damage to the ecosystems of the globe than all previous cultures and generations had done together. An example of the ecological wisdom of the "primitives" is the method of shifting cultivation in some "simple" agrarian societies. With this approach the forest is not permanently uprooted to make way for the cultivation of vast monocultures. The forest is "limited" rather, for a few seasons, pushed back temporarily by cutting and burning in order to plant an assortment of edible vegetables. The original vegetation slowly creeps back again and peaceful symbiosis of cultivated land and nature ensues: the forest becomes harvestable (Geertz quoted in Lemaire 1976:215). In this way a rich (agri)culture is maintained without impoverishing the fullness of nature. These societies knew the Zen road to affluence (Lemaire 1976:20);[3] they achieved it not by impairing the means (e.g. rationalising the instruments) but by limiting the goals. This is of course diametrically opposed to bourgeois society whose economy is based on an artificial institutionalisation of scarcity: feverishly engaged in the task of satisfying infinite needs, it fights chronic poverty.

The complete irrationality of the ecological ethnocentrism of the West is highlighted by the successful adaptation of non-Western societies to nature. This success is due to a deep-seated rationality – a sense of the limits posed by nature. Ecological disasters in Europe and America can be read as the protest of nature against irrational industrial trespassing of her limits.

It is beyond the scope of this essay to investigate anthropological revaluation of other aspects of primitive life such as social integration and the adaptation of the process of production to the psychological and ethnological "nature"[4] of the human being. The point is, however, that such a revaluation of primitive cultures, which is also a critique of Western civilisation, could provide a model for an ideal future society. This model would not be used as a way of luring the nostalgic back to an impossible paradise, but would function instead as a heuristic device and as a critical measure in the economic and social planning for a future world.

In this model the ideal culture is characterised by the following:
1. Production would have to be limited and moderate for the sake of maintaining a lasting ecological balance.
2. Production would have to be organised (e.g. in its division of labour) in such a way that social life would be integrated and that a form of communal solidarity would once again become possible.
3. Its organisation would have to be such that the psychological and ethological nature of the human individual is not violated.
4. Such a cultural configuration would have to be reflected in a form of consciousness, a rationality, in short, a "philosophy" that can account for it in a conscious way. Such a philosophy would entail a "world-view" in which the dilemma between Eurocentrism and relativism would be transcended and replaced by a non-Eurocentric vision of the cultural history of humankind where the process of Westernisation and rationalisation would be understood and criticised and relativised.

In other words, the model of the ideal society as outlined above would have to find its justification in a *philosophy of cultural history* that would at the same time be a *critique of Western rationality* (Lemaire 1976:378).

Before conveying the outline of Lemaire's ideas in this respect, I want to point out the relevance of all this to the topic of "African Thinking" which is my main critical concern in this essay. A university course in "African Philosophy" would have to be developed in the context of a critical history of anthropology and a critique of Western rationality. In such a context a course in "African Philosophy" might even help facilitate the growth of an alternative rationality to the one that has informed the invasion and exploitation of the African continent. "African Philosophy" might become part of the philosophy informing an ideal society. But without such a context a course in "African Philosophy" is doomed to go off at several dangerous tangents prefigured in the historical movements of Western anthropology: Eurocentric evolutionism or positivist cultural relativism. As philosophies that "placed" the "Other" at a safe distance, both of these ultimately served the interests of a "superior" and "transcendent" Western scientific rationality, and with that the interests of Western imperialism and colonialism.

I have analysed the way in which an uncritical appropriation of Western rationality has caused a grossly distorted picture to be painted of the way in which primitive people view the world (see Context One above). I have pointed to the unquestioning affirmation of "the city" as the flower of Western civilisation in the context of the "treatment" of the "Other" as "unsophisticated". It does not seem presumptuous to predict that a course in "African Thinking" when "left to itself" would become another "tool" with which to expand the hegemony of Western rationality, a "tool" used to rationalise the relations of production and the structures of power that go with it in South Africa.

3.4 Western Rationality and its Alternatives

Lemaire argues that the current crisis experienced by Western civilisation can in fact be reduced to a crisis of Western rationality. This rationality is informed by the Promethean desire of the Western subject to gain complete control over nature and through that, complete autonomy or self-possession. The ensuing concrete process of rationalisation involving the entire world, a process still positively valued by evolutionists, was viewed with some scepticism by cultural relativists and eventually criticised by the new generation of anthropologists in a general process of revaluation of primitive societies. Their critique was also a critique of Western rationality and accordingly involved a renewed comparison with myth, the latter being the rationality or form of consciousness of primitive people.

I have also indicated how comparison in the evolutionist mode led to a devaluation of myth as belonging to an infantile way of thinking and an archaic form of consciousness, a weak prefiguration of the rationality of nineteenth-century society. Hegel sees myth as powerlessness of the spirit and a defilement of thought belonging to the "pedagogics" of humanity (Lemaire 1976:337). This rationalist optimism is somewhat inhibited by the return of myth since the nineteenth century, for example, in the idealist philosophy of Schelling, in the romantic revaluation of myth as the place of the dream and the erotic, and in the psychological theories of Freud and Jung. Still later, Ricoeur (1960:161, 327) tries to deal with myth by restoring it, not as a literal explanation of the world as it was for mythical people, but as a symbol of the holy that had been forgotten by modernity.[5]

The task is thus neither to negate and destroy myth nor to resort to a romantic glorification of it, but to understand the *connection* between myth and reason. These do in fact have the same function, i.e. to help the human being in establishing him/herself in an orderly universe and to come to terms with reality. But in doing so they employ different strategies.

What is characteristic of the mythical arrangement of the world is the personification, the anthropomorphisation and the spiritualisation of all things.

This leads to the development of a *story* about the world that is inaccessible to us and our post-mythic consciousness. The point is not that myth is rationally undeveloped, but that we no longer partake in it. We now have to relate to it in the mode of interpretive understanding. We now have to reflect on it as merely a part of the history of philosophy, part of human rationality. The most important thing about this form of human rationality is that it offers a way of making sense of a reality in which the human being has not yet pitted him/herself as an imperious subject against nature as its object. In myth, the human being affirms that he/she is only another part of nature whose power and rhythms, whose decisive events he/she accompanies in her rites and rituals. In the ritually heightened cycles of birth and death, harvesting and hoarding, feasting and fasting, the seasonal cycles of nature are repeated in the medium of culture. In all of this myth works as a story of which the mythical person deems him/herself the author.

Myth, when it *worked* as myth, did not understand itself as myth (Gusdorf 1963:17–23). But this does not mean that there is no logical consistency in the mythological arrangement of the world (Lévi-Strauss 1976:1–74). It simply means that the rationality at work here was not conscious of itself. The human being had not consciously rationalised his/her rational power over or against the power of nature. The human intelligence was at this stage at work as a function of nature itself. By this I do not imply that the mythical form of consciousness is one that is fully submerged in nature. Myth as an attempt at arranging and relating things in the world is already a sign of the discontinuity of culture and nature.

It is only with the emergence of philosophy (Gusdorf 1963:113–122) that the subject is ready to appropriate its own rationality in a conscious way. From now on the subject sees itself as the source of all interpretations and explanations of nature. From now on it will try to control the world through science. But the Greek Enlightenment does not yet lead to the total disenchantment of nature under the rule of operationalised rationality. The Greek *physis* still embodies the *logos*. The subject "reads" off and reveals the inherent objective rationality of the *logos* of nature. This substantive notion of reason is what inhibited any attempt by the subject to change nature and use it to its own full advantage. This was to be the task of the rationality that emerged in the transition from feudal to capitalist society. It was this rationality that perceived itself from the start not as contemplative with regard to nature, but as a dynamic activity of planned intervention in, and aggressive experimentation with, nature in order to subjugate it.

Nature, thus reduced to a conglomerate of meaningless, neutral, and mechanical processes, could provide the "raw material" for an economy that started to autonomise itself. All of this was seen as a process of enlightenment and emancipation of the subject. In relation to this, all non-Western cultures were judged as irrational. Marxism set out to complete the enlightenment and rationalisation of history by casting the proletariat in the role of a collective subject that would form the material condition for the emancipation of all. It was the neo-Marxists who started to point out the irrationality of Western industrialised civilisation and who started to question the total effect of the so-called progress from myth to reason.

At the risk of simplifying and of repeating views that by now have not only come to constitute a body of classical critique in social philosophy but have also sedimented in popular opinion about "alienation in a technocratic society",

I would like to summarise briefly the main tenets of the critique of the Frankfurt School.

Their main criticism was that the rationality serving Western industrial civilisation is a truncated form of rationality – an instrumental rationality that is responsible for the alienation or *Versachlichung* of humans and human relations. This rationality is deemed truncated because in the technical industrial age it understands itself as a *tool* in the service of efficient calculation of the means, while it refrains from saying anything about the value of the chosen ends. In other words, it does not serve, as reason did from Plato to Hegel, to direct the human being to his/her goals and to his/her proper place in reality. In the end, this amputation of reason leads to irrationality of the overall direction of social life. Capitalism, for one, promotes the instrumentalisation of reason to obscure the irrational desire for more and more possessions; it does this by means of a rational process of quantification and formalisation of nature and human relations.

The process of instrumentalisation (neutralisation or formalisation) of rationality leads to the autonomisation of the technical, industrial *apparatus*, the apparatus in which the instrumental reason is *objectified*. But the principle of *control* is also preserved in these tools so that the independence of the technical industrial system causes the automatisation of the dimension of *control* and *controllability*. The system in the end controls itself as well as the people who instituted it, because it has absorbed the dimension of goals into its own self-regulatory process. The technocratic rationality of this process also legitimates itself by its enormous output and the affluence that it produces. Thus the rationality of the technical order congests all other dimensions of life; the alienation resulting from this is therefore referred to as one-dimensionality. Having set out to emancipate him/herself by absolute control over nature, the human being is now imprisoned and controlled by the very instruments that he/she used to get nature under his control. The objectification of nature returns in an inverse form: the objectification of the human being by his/her own technical apparatus. It is poignantly formulated as follows by Horkheimer and Adorno (1981:29): "*Der Animismus hatte die Sache beseelt, der Industrialismus versachlicht die Seele*", and again by Marcuse (quoted in Lemaire 1976:367): "The liberating force of technology – the instrumentalisation of things – turns into a fetter of liberation: the instrumentalisation of man."

This state of affairs is not something that overcomes the process of rationalisation from the outside. It unfurls as a dialectical movement within objectifying rationality. Nature mediated by technology creates a culture that is a kind of second objective nature that dominates the human being. If one looks at the endless cycles of production and consumption, the circulation and exchange of money and goods, the merry-go-round of the people serving these cycles and repeating them, the subjugation of nature seems to have been in vain. It is not emancipation from nature, but a repetition of imprisonment, this time by a second, vengeful nature, that is the result of all of this. The process that was started by the subject consciously appropriating his/her own rationality to break through the enclosure of mythical repetition, seems to have ended in destruction.

To indicate the direction in which one must look for the formulation of an *alternative* rationality is a tall order. It implies a form of consciousness that can understand and account for both itself and instrumental rationality. As a *critique*, this philosophy must include reflection on its own conditions of possibility. This requires a *total* knowledge of the *whole* of the *real* movement of the history of culture. However, this is too much to ask from any post-Hegelian philosopher and it seems doubtful that Lemaire, as a critic of Promethean self-conscious man, can really mean this in any absolute sense. Instead, he would agree with Gadamer (1975:324ff.) who stresses the fragmented and approximate nature of our self-understanding when confronting history. At most, the idea of a total understanding of self and of history could only act as a kind of regulative idea guiding the hermeneutic exercise of fusing new and strange experiences (in this case, the projection of an ideal society) into one's already existing horizon of historical understanding. Taken as such, the alternative rationality that is able to account for the construction of an ideal culture (as outlined above) will be a utopian vision of an alternative harmonious *relationship between nature and culture*. This vision that rejects the dominating Promethean mentality characterising capitalism, includes the rejection of the immoderate Humanism of Marxism (Lemaire 1976:428). Marxism, as Lemaire understands it, is, after all, a philosophy of the infinite malleability of everything: industrial man will only rest once he has made the whole of nature into his world. Man, according to Marx, is not bound to any nature within or outside himself. He is his own measure.

As an alternative, Lemaire (1976:443) posits a materialist philosophy of the relationship between nature and culture. In this, the ultimate transcendence of nature is stressed. Nature and culture are not immediately identical. Culture is a mediated form of nature. Culture is, in fact, self-transformation and self-interiorisation of nature. Culture is a finite part of nature that tries desperately to grasp the infiniteness of nature. It is to this tension that Western civilisation owes its art, its religion, and its philosophy. To this understanding of the real relationship between nature and culture, Lemaire adds a matching attitude of the subject to nature. In this attitude, the observing, objectifying, and dominating attitude of the subject is replaced by a more passive and receptive attitude. The latter is a con-templative, imaginative, and sensuous attitude in which "harkening" and "listening" (Heidegger 1979:163–165)[6] is the mode in which one remembers the infinite ontological surplus value of nature. This is also the site of the deconstruction of the Promethean subject. It is replaced by a mystic or "hermetic" subject in which the self is decentred by a "letting go" towards a sense of the deep affinity of all beings.

3.5 Modes of Othering in Anthropology and an Alternative

It is not enough simply to place a full-stop after a critique of Western rationality and the utopian projection of the relationship between nature and culture in an ideal society. One should not end by merely suggesting the theoretical framework within which a topic like "African Thinking" might appropriately be investigated. What is needed in addition to these is a practical alternative to the mode of othering that has dominated Western rationality and guided anthropological praxis. This alternative mode of othering could also provide the practical context in which a course with the title "African Thinking" might appropriately be developed. As with Lemaire's projection of an ideal alternative culture, the ideal alternative mode of othering is one that can only be outlined dialectically, i.e. on the basis of a critique of previous modes of othering.

In the light of the concrete situations in which the theories of social evolutionism and cultural relativism were developed, it can be claimed that there is no knowledge or science of the "Other" that is not also a temporal historical and political act. Partly in order to obscure this fact, anthropology has always construed the *difference of the "Other" in terms of distance*, notably the distance of *spatialised time*. In *Time and the other: How anthropology makes its object* (1983), Johannes Fabian outlines the epistemological prejudices conditioning the traditional modes of anthropological othering. Distance, he notes, is a necessary corollary of the individual who conceives of him/herself as a subject posited in opposition to an exclusively *observed* object. As in most scientific epistemologies based on this division, the empirical presence of the object eclipses its theoretical presence (Fabian 1983:xi). To put it differently, scientistic epistemologies do not accommodate in their objectification the theoretical conditions of possibility of the constitution of the object as an object of knowledge; the objectification of the "Other" in anthropology is a case in point. The empirical presence of the "Other" eclipsed the epistemological self-reflection of the anthropologist. This reflection would have revealed both the theoretical and the practical political conditions of possibility governing the objectification of the "Other". What happened instead was that the theoretical presence of the "Other" was conjured away with an array of devices designed to keep the "Other" out of the time of anthropological praxis and out of the time of the actual politics that empowered it.

Writers on animism frequently reflect on the epistemological status of their own "use of the material", which apparently functions solely to distance the "unsophisticated" world-view from that of the "sophisticated" ones. Obviously, thought processes of selection, combination, and juxtaposition are involved. But they are not critical in the sense of "critique" – i.e. their thinkers do not reflect on their conditions of possibility in a historical and a political way. The total effect of this is that the distance of the "Other" to the reader is multiplied a few times. The naive reading, the reading in the realist mode, that governs the reader of the ethnographic material (Woolgar 1988:28)[7] and then the reader of the anthropological discourse, will also govern (in an almost impenetrable form), the reading of students who have to study texts on animism. For them the text is a neutral *medium* for conveying pre-existent facts about the "Other". They are not encouraged to problematise the text in a radical way, i.e. to question the series of agencies (ethnographers, anthropologists, encyclopedia editors, philosophy teachers) involved in the text's generation – not to mention the political and historical contexts in which these agents wrote. And so, when students write on animism in an examination, and they reproduce this type of discourse, teachers are obliged to allow them to pass.

The theoretical *presence* of the "Other" is absent from the curriculum and from the knowledge the student needs to make the grade. *Their* presence is not part of *our* time, i.e. the student's and teacher's time. *They* are perceived as having their own type of animistic time far away from us.

Parallel to Lemaire's suggestion of an alternative attitude to nature, one of cultural openness and receptivity to the experience of the affinity of all beings, Fabian (1983:31) suggests a new attitude to the "Other": one of radical contemporaneity. "Coevalness" is the word he chooses to mobilise within his critical discourse. By the choice of the term "coeval" he wants to steer between the closely related notions of synchronous/simultaneous and contemporary. The first refers to events "occurring in the same physical time", the second to "being of the same age or epoch". "Coeval" covers both meanings: occupying the same "now", (time) and being of the same epoch. The term marks the ideal quality and nature of the time of the production of anthropological knowledge. It is a knowledge co-produced by the "subject" and the *other* subject of anthropology in a co-created, closely shared time of inter-subjective communication and dialogue. Note that coeval time has to be *created*, it is not a given to be "filled up" or "whiled away" together. This is also the case for sacred time in traditional societies – it has to be *constituted* in ritual praxis. The same goes for Lemaire's receptive contemplation that is consciously cultivated.

Furthermore, one cannot as an anthropologist "grant" or "deny" coevalness to one's interlocutors. One either *submits* to the condition for co-producing knowledge or one deludes oneself into temporal distance or encyclopedic objectivity and *misses the other as subject* (Fabian 1983:32), *which ought to be the "subject" of the search.*

The distancing devices of traditional anthropology can be summed up as a denial of coevalness as a transcendental condition of knowledge. By this, Fabian (1983:34) means a "persistent and systematic tendency to place the referents of anthropology in a time other than the present of the producer of anthropological discourse". The othering engaged in by social evolutionists entailed the trick of irrevocably distancing the primitive "Other" on a *temporal slope*. This slope was seen to find its highest point in the "here and now" of industrial Victorian England and to reach down into the lower regions, the "there and then" of barbarism and savagery (Fabian 1983:27). According to Fabian, traditional anthropology always *spatialised* time in order to obscure the sometimes embarrassing actuality of present anthropological praxis. The social evolutionists had the problem that they found the naturalised time of the contemporary geological and palaeontological sciences too abstract, too neutral, and too comprehensive for their temporal scheme of things. As in the Judaeo-Christian tradition in which sacred history was time marked by great events, so, too, the time of social evolution was *marked by stages* of development. Each stage was meaningful because it led to the conclusion of a story: Western civilisation as the salvation of mankind.

This meant that the term "primitive" was a *temporal* term, it denoted a *category* of thought (Fabian 1983:18) at the time rather than an object of research. This still seems to hold for terms like "tribal" and "traditional", etc. (Fabian 1983:17). The categorical use of the term "primitive" was due to the fact that the social evolutionists thematised *time itself* as a process of development, rather than thematising any experienced reality of the "Other" as a referent of temporal discourse. This spatial fixation of time in evolutionist discourse, by which the difference of the "Other" is construed as distance, is perhaps best illustrated by reference to the fact that time is sometimes not spatialised as a chain but as a *tree* of development (Fabian 1983:15). Today one might imagine a tree, the lower branches of which carry men equipped with slingshots and bows and arrows, while the higher branches carry those equipped with cruise missiles.

Whereas in social evolutionism the time of the "Other" is distanced on a temporal slope as the category of the primitive, the problem of time is circumvented (Fabian 1983:41) by cultural relativists. The shift from social evolutionism to cultural relativism is usually construed as a shift from studying the "Other" for our sakes to studying the "Other" for their sakes, and *in* their own terms – but which is, as Fabian

(1983:39) points out, not *on* their own terms. It is upon the difference between these two propositions that the epistemological denial or affirmation of coevalness depends. Instead of involving the time that marks the confrontation in the anthropological situation of two different cultures, cultural relativism only involves the studying of time encapsulated in the other culture as an intra-systematic and synchronically present phenomenon. In other words, cultural relativists study time anti-historically. While time is held by relativists to be a cultural construction within which the enculturated "Other" is walled up, they do not realise that time is also constitutive of the process in which they study the "Other". The point is that if other people really have totally *other* conceptions of time than we have, it would not be possible for Western anthropologists to do what they patently do – i.e. communicate with the "Other" (Fabian 1983:42). Apart from the fact that cultural relativists cannot account for the actual communication taking place between the cultures, they cannot account for cultural change either. If all categories of thought are system-bound, how can one form an opinion *about* that system in order to effect a change in the system? In this context Fabian quotes Ernst Bloch's comment on Spengler's historicism to illustrate his point:

> The very process of history is broken up into Gardens of Culture or "Culture Souls". These are as unrelated to each other as they are without connection to Man and human labour (which is the pervading matter of history) or to nature. . . . Quite artfully, historical relativism is here turned into something static, it is being caught in cultural monads, that is culture souls without windows, with no links among each other, yet full of mirrors facing inside (Fabian 1983:43).

Cultural relativism circumvents the problem of common time, coeval time which constitutes the medium of inter-subjective discourse, by postulating a multiplicity of cultural gardens, which are closed gardens of cultural time. Extending the metaphor of mirrors lining the walls of windowless gardens, one could say that the cultural relativist, in observing the reflections on the inside, adjusting the mirrors so as to reveal the "thick", "coherent", "dense", and "distinctive" cultural system, also acts like a magician. He turns the mirrors in such a way that the real objects disappear – i.e. the coeval "Other" and his investigators with whom he shares time.

The point is that this circumvention of time on a theoretical level has certain possibilities on a practical level, i.e. the level where there is outright conflict between co-existing cultures. If one erects the seams between cultures as methodologically relevant walls separating them, one can rationalise political antagonism as the kind of *distance* that the anthropologist needs to form a conception of a culture as *whole* (Fabian 1983:47).

The result of this is a type of objectifying cultural holism trying to formulate the essence, the vital characteristics or the central values of a culture. This of course is useful stuff for people who must "run the show" – the colonial governors, the diplomats, the economic advisers, the agents of the state security councils (Fabian 1983:49). How *they* (the "Others"), for example, use time (unconsciously) then becomes a recipe for how they can be manipulated into serving *our* (the colonisers') interests (Fabian 1983:51). Distancing the "Other" in a closed place where *their* time counts, in fact means that the interests of "our time" are served.

Fabian (1983:67) blames the spatial distancing of the "Other" in both social evolutionism and cultural relativism on the dominance of the *visual* root metaphor in Western science. Viewing the "Other" from all sides, objectifying him/her as exhaustively as possible, ("Keep still, native!"), reducing him/her to an object, a surface, a "figure" observed in space, entails very often the eclipse of the dimension of time in which this objectification takes place, and the exclusion of time from the condition under which knowledge of an object can be gained.

We have seen that this need for an object, an obstacle, a space to survey and subjugate, is the need of the Promethean subject of Western rationality. Fabian (1983:105ff.) offers an exposé on the origin of the dominance of the *visual* and the *spatial* in Western science (originally a rhetorical device to support memory and, later, to arrange information in a memorisable way).[8]

It may suffice to quote Fabian here, in the context of a critique of the way in which knowledge of the "Other" has been traditionally represented (visually) to students. He writes:

> Concretely speaking, we must at least admit the possibility that striking images, simplified outlines, and over-wrought tables were fed to students in order to impress them with a degree of orderliness and cohesiveness which the fields of knowledge taught by these methods never possessed (Fabian 1983:122).

Fabian's (1983:155–156) alternative to anthropological praxis can be construed as running parallel to Lemaire's alternative to Western civilisation.[9] As Lemaire postulates a materialist theory of the relationship between nature and culture as an alternative to an immoderately Humanistic or "idealistic" one, so Fabian postulates a material and process-based theory of coevalness as an alternative to the objectivist and static taxonomic approach of traditional anthropology.

As Lemaire projects the totality of the movement of Western culture, its critique, and also its alternative as the framework for his discourse, so Fabian also rehabilitates the concept of totality. This differs, however, from the cultural holism of the relativists as well as from Hegel's totalising philosophy of history. As we know, the "lock nut" of Hegel's totality is the presence of the Prussian state. Against this, Fabian (1983:157) chooses with Marx the present as a context for analysis; but instead of this being a local national one, it is the co-presence of basic acts of production and re-production, eating, drinking, providing shelter and clothes. For it is, indeed, in this common conflict-ridden presence that different societies face each other.[10]

In order to preserve their common presence in the praxis of anthropology, in order not to shatter it in the distance and difference-creating stance of the subject observing the object, Fabian suggests – again parallel to the listening to nature advocated by Lemaire – the primacy of *hearing* the "Other", in a situation of inter-subjective communication.

Lastly, and again parallel to Lemaire's foregrounding of the "sense of affinity of all beings in the communion with nature", Fabian (1983:162) writes: "not solitary perception but social communication is the starting point for a materialist anthropology".

Just as Lemaire stresses that human culture is human nature transforming and interiorising itself, so Fabian stresses that communication, language, and society are not things *possessed* by the human being but things that constitute him/her *as* a human being. They mark his/her being as temporal and material and finite, and therefore as historical and political. If these tenets start to inform anthropological praxis, both the generation and the function of anthropological knowledge may change. For no longer will the observer simply glean or extract knowledge from the passive object, and no longer will he/she export it from the distant countries of "the Rest" to the markets for the "exotic" and the "different" in the West (Hymes 1972:49). Knowledge will be co-produced in coevalness as the condition for a truly dialectical confrontation between people from different societies. And this knowledge, *because* it has been created in a sphere of commitment, the sphere of real dialogue, will probably not be exported, but will remain a local product for local use by the people who produced it (cf. Anderson 1972:280), in and towards a process of emancipation. The knowledge will no longer be used only to fill the libraries and the universities of the subjugators, the rational ones who rule; it will be used to facilitate the liberation of those who are ruled,[11] among other things, by this same written knowledge about them, that has been constituted by the ruler's scientists and endorsed by teachers as suitable "prescribed material" for all.

3.6 Hermes in the stead of Prometheus?

The engagement of the anthropologist in the interests of the people he/she studies might lead to a new identity, not only politically but also epistemologically.[12] I am tempted to ask *who* must replace Prometheus as the spirit or the image to animate this new activity, this new identity.

We have seen what happens to the "Other" if he/she is reduced to an object of knowledge by an imperious subject. But in this epistemological set the subject is not unharmed either. To objectify the "Other", one is at the same time compelled to objectify the self (Diamond 1972:401). Such a subject is in fact reduced to play one role only – that of a mere operator in a one-way process of gathering objective knowledge. He/she is reduced to a warden, imprisoned by his/her own power over the "Other". Whom do we need to release this "Prometheus Bound"? Whom do we need as a figure or a symbol of emancipation to counter the image of Prometheus who is shackled by his own epistemological imperialism? Whom do we need to correct the immoderate desire, the hubris of Prometheus?

In all likelihood, this will be the same figure as that needed to assist the "Other", the former objects of Promethean knowledge, the peasants and primitives who are now "recreating themselves as subjects in the revolutionary dramas of our time" (Radin 1957:170). We need a trickster. This trickster's Greek name is Hermes.

The trickster is the exact opposite of Prometheus, the fire-stealer, the over-reacher (Radin 1957:170–247).[13] The trickster does not have to steal fire in order to gain power or to empower. He/she already lives in a blaze of reality. The trickster's fire or spirit constitutes his/her being.[14] The trickster could be taken as a mode for the reinvented anthropologist – the scientist who does not limit him/herself to the strict and univocal role of the observer, the calculator, the measurer and the weigher. The new anthropologist is not an imperious scientist wielding his tools and skills to "extract" knowledge from the "Other". He/she is partisan to redeeming his/her own and the "Other's" world that has fallen prey to the levelling spirit of instrumentalist rationality. He/she is therefore committed to the full and conflict-ridden passage of historical time, the time which also marks real dialogue with the "Other". In this dialogical time one is caught in the ambiguity and transience of life. There is no occasion to extract oneself completely and to ascend panoramic heights where the risks and failures involved in human choice can be objectified as "their problems" and "their bungling" (cf. Rombach 1983:70).

Nor does the trickster glorify the problems in which he/she chooses to take part. He/she is not a martyr. He/she ridicules everything which is regarded with immoderate reverence. He/she is the refusal, the burlesque of identity (Diamond 1969:182). It is the high-serious reduction of the self to a fully self-possessed subject, and of the "Other" to a fully-controlled object that he/she rejects. He/she plays tricks on those who desire things and people to be fixed and stable and always recognisable as "the same". He/she is a debunker of what I have called the "realist mode". The trickster says things are not what they are: *"lees maar er staat niet wat er staat"* (Nijhof 1964:216). He/she is a clown and a fool. And, as we know with both of these, their ridicule of both identity and the "realist mode" has an important function. In a paradoxical way their behaviour is a welcome reminder of the fact that to forgive and accept oneself for being "only human" (i.e. a finite, material, and political being) is not a weakness but a grace. Prometheus is more than human and Western "man" has, as suggested, modelled himself on this image, overreaching himself repeatedly until, in the end, he burns his fingers in the fire of technology with which he has set the world alight (Rombach 1983:97).

The new anthropologist is the artist of the dialogue, the skilful conversationalist – not one that manipulates, but one that engages without reserve in the "play" of conversation (Gadamer 1975:464ff.). Only in this play can the truth be co-produced. But this is a practical truth, a truth that "happens" to *work*: it is, indeed, one that can fail, that can be suppressed or inherited – an incomplete truth.

As Fabian (1983:161) has pointed out, the disembodied consciousness observing and classifying his object has been replaced with the sensuous and subjective activity of embodied consciousness hearing and producing meaningful sounds in communion with the "Other". But this does not mean that the anthropological conversation is mere "talking across differences". It means rather the ability to *be* with the "Other" and to *share* with the "Other", which Fabian marks out as the real meaning of coevalness. In this type of conversation things "may work out" in any way. Nothing can be predicted where interlocutors choose to be radically present to each other.

This face-to-face quality of the conversation marks another hermetic aspect: the concern with boundaries, the standing on the threshold, the transgression of limits, and the regression into "known territory". Being coeval does not mean that the anthropologist *forgets* his/her own world in order to *participate* in another. It means rather that a fusion of worlds is allowed and facilitated. It means holding onto the old while entertaining the new. It is in this tension that a new co-created meaning can be produced *between* worlds.

We have seen how this dialectic has informed Lemaire's reconstruction of the history of anthropology: the revaluation of the non-Western "Other" is inextricably bound to the self-critique of the West. In this context Fabian writes about anthropology's "peculiar position":

> It patrols, so to speak, the frontiers of western culture. In fact, it has always been a *Grenzwissenschaft*, concerned with boundaries: those of one race against another, those between one culture and another, and finally those between culture and nature. These liminal concerns have prevented anthropology from settling down in any one of the accepted domains of knowledge other than the residual field of "social science" (1983:117).

Now, once the anthropologist *engages* in conversation, it is not unthinkable that he/she will "get involved". Conversational engagement might lead to the anthropologist getting involved in the emancipatory programmes of liberation movements. In his/her new role of partisan translator, interpreter, messenger, the anthropologist is also the guide of "lost souls". I shall return to this at the end of the next section where there is reference to the role of the organic intellectual in liberation movements (cf. Gramsci 1978:133).

The not-so-organic intellectual has also, however, a truly hermetic task to fulfil, and that is to dismantle the realist readings of texts and to reveal the agencies involved in their production, to reveal their interests, their pedagogical assumptions, their self-image, and above all the spirits that animate their works – the gods of their machinery. That this activity will have to retreat behind the wings and into "the basement dressing rooms" is, at the present conjuncture, not unthinkable.

4. CONTEXT THREE: "African Philosophy" – the Debate and Some Suggestions for Course Development

4.1 From Ethnophilosophy to Negritude: the Ironies of Othering

In the light of the history of anthropology and its modes of othering – which constitute a rationalisation for the phases of colonial oppression – it ought not to be surprising at all that the debate about the term "African Philosophy" is an ongoing affair.[15] It is debated precisely because it also denotes an instance of essentialist or typological othering: it is a term that assumes "that there is a way of thinking or a conceptual frame-work that is *uniquely* African and which is at the same time radically unEuropean" (original emphasis) (Oruka 1981:1). This is how Odera Oruka formulated the problem of essentialist or typological othering in a paper delivered at the 1978 symposium on "Philosophy in the Present Situation of Africa". That the term continues to be fiercely criticised is a sign that the time is long past that the "Other" and "their thinking" could be "arrested" and "held up" by the West as objects of study. It is also a sign that the process of (re)forging an identity in the wake of the *deculturation* (Caulfield 1972:201) effected by colonialism is still in full force. It is a sign that the philosophers of Africa are even today working at the deconstruction of their objectification by whites, that they are involved in the analysis and critique of what happened to the people of Africa as a result of the desire of the West for an "Other" as object. This work is parallel to the work of self-critique in the West, especially in the current self-reflection of anthropologists and in continental philosophy generally – in this work it is the Promethean subject that is deconstructed.

The terms "African Thinking" and "African Philosophy" would certainly not have had such a negative resonance if they did not have a history. To cite an example of how the rejection of the term is linked with a rejection of the whole history of European colonialist exploitation, I shall quote Paulin Hountondji on the notorious book by the Belgian missionary, Placide Tempels, originally entitled *La philosophie Bantoue*:

> Being a European's discourse, addressed to other Europeans, an exhibit in a debate in which the Bantus have no part to play and appear only as an object or pretext, *Bantu Philosophy* is cut to its public's size. In a dual motion that is contradictory only in appearance, it aims on the one hand at facilitating what it calls Europe's "mission to civilise" (by which we understand:

practical mastery by the coloniser of the black man's psychological wellsprings) and, on the other hand, at warning Europe itself against the abuses of its own technocratic and ultra-materialistic civilisation, by offering her, at the cost of a few rash generalisations, an image of the fine spirituality of the primitive Bantu. It is a double problematic, that of the "mission to civilise" and the "heightening of the soul"; neither can be separated from the other. The colonisers "civilise", but only on the condition that they rehumanise themselves and recover their soul. The theoretical objective of *Bantu Philosophy* is entirely contained in this double problematic which itself finds its meaning solely in the ideological problematic of triumphant imperialism. This one has to accept: every such theoretical project, every attempt at systematising the world-view of a dominated people is necessarily destined for a foreign public and intended to fuel an ideological debate which is centered *elsewhere* [original emphasis] – in the ruling classes of the dominant society (Hountondji 1983b:49).

According to Hountondji this book by Tempels was the trendsetter for a

deluge of works which aimed to reconstruct a specific world-view commonly attributed to all Africans, abstracted from history and change and claiming to be *philosophical* [original emphasis], through an interpretation of the customs and traditions, proverbs and institutions . . . concerning the cultural life of African people (Hountondji 1983b:34).

To illustrate the us/them principle that underlies this type of discourse about the "Other", i.e. the other-for-us principle, consider this passage from Tempels:

We have seen that the Bantu soul hankers after life and force. The fundamental notion under which being is conceived lies within the category of forces. . . . We can conceive the transcendental notion of "being" by separating it from its attribute "Force", but the Bantu cannot! Where we see concrete beings, they see concrete forces. When we say that "beings" are differentiated by their essence or nature, Bantu say that "forces" differ in their essence or nature (1969:49–53).

Hountondji (1983b:39, 49–50) goes on to show how this "ethnophilosophy", as he calls it, was taken over and elaborated on not only by European Africanists but also by African intellectuals themselves: the common goal was to "reveal" the immutable collective unconsciousness and utterly unanimous philosophy common to all Africans. A case in point is the work of Alexis Kagamé who produced a text typically entitled: *La philosophie Bantu-rwandaise de l'être*. This ethnophilosophy produced by African philosophers is nothing but a kind of Eurocentrism in reverse, or put differently, a serialisation of the ethnocentrism instituted by the Europeans. It appears as though, in a poignant but dialectically understandable reversal, the African intellectual "others" himself, objectifies himself into the shape of a product that he has seen proven fit for the export market – the distinctive shape of the ethno-mind.

Hountondji's observations on the ethnophilosophers bear repeating:

[They] have this in common with him [Tempels]: that they have chosen to address themselves primarily to a European public. This choice largely explains the context of their discourses. Their objective has been to describe the main features of African civilisation for the benefit of their European counterparts, to secure their respect for African cultural originality – but on Europe's own terms. In the circumstances it was inevitable that they should have ended up by inventing as a foil to European philosophy an African "philosophy" concocted from extra-philosophical material consisting of tales, legends, dynastic poems, etc., by aggressively interpreting these cultural data, grinding them down to extract their supposedly "substantive marrow", turning them over, again and again, in order to derive from them what they could not, cannot and never will yield: a genuine philosophy (1983b:50).

One could – and should, of course – take issue with Hountondji here about the nature of the "extra-philosophical", and about the interpretation of traditional legends as an integral part of philosophical reflection. To start with I could mention Heidegger's (1979:196–199) use of a myth to develop his notion of *Sorge*,[16] especially when one reads what Hountondji himself considers to be "genuine philosophy": "In the strict(er) sense of the word . . . philosophy, like chemistry, physics or mathematics, is a specific theoretical discipline with its exigency and methodological rules" (Hountondji 1983b:47). But this is not my focus at this point. I want to emphasise the political and historical genesis of the notion of ethnophilosophy and its strange career in the self-objectification of the African ethnophilosophers. Perhaps the most poignant example of this is the adage of Senghor's Negritude, a poeticised radicalisation of ethnophilosophy: "Emotion is negro as reason is hellenic" (quoted by Irele in Hountondji 1983b:18).

This is the type of sentence that could be used as a heuristic device in a lecturing situation to launch an introduction of the notion of ethnophilosophy. And if it is going to be studied, it must be studied *as* ethnophilosophy and not naively as "information" on how Africans "think", "ontologise", "spiritualise" or "move" or "dream" or "spit" or whatever. If it is going to be studied it must be studied in the context of its historical genesis and of its backwash effects on what Fanon (1982:73) calls the "*experience vécue*" of the black person in a world dominated by whites. A critique *by* a black person on the appropriation by black people of an othering originally projected onto blacks themselves by Westerners in order to satisfy a desire for the "exotic" and the "wild" and the "wildness that pleases"[17] would be indispensable for any university course on "African Thinking". Without it the study of the "roots" of philosophical activity on this continent would remain a "topic": ethnophilosophy cut off from its original historical context as export product of the colonies would *remain* an "export product" in education as well – it would be deposited in the heads of students, a corpus of fixed and petrified facts about an "other mind", also fixed and petrified. Thus deposited as a permanent investment it would yield a meagre interest and accumulate other Loch Ness-type stories about "racial mentality". It should rather, indeed, be presented in such a way as to become of real value in a concrete dialogical process of self-understanding of students, both black and white. If this does not happen, the black person, as Hountondji (1983b:34) puts it, would continue to be the "opposite of an interlocutor" and remain "a voiceless face under private investigation, an object to be defined and not the subject of a possible discourse".

Examples from Fanon's critique of Negritude would clarify my meaning. His pointed remarks would be the best catalyst to open up a lively discussion on ethnophilosophy. Fanon talks of the black person's psychological assimilation of the "biological history" that white racists have constructed for him. In a test conducted by Fanon and some white friends (who were used as "controls"), whites generally responded as follows when asked what their associations were with the word negro: "biological", "sexual", "strong", "potent", "sportsman", "boxer", "Joe Louis", "Jesse Owens", "Sengalese soldier", "wild", "animal", "devil", "sin", "cannibal" (Fanon 1982:80, 108).

Transformed and sentimentalised, these notions return in the impassioned poetics of self-affirmation by, for example, Léopold Senghor and Aimé Césaire, of the essence of their Africanness which is the opposite of Europeanness. "Rhythm", for instance, is considered by Senghor to be the most vital element of black art. It is the first sign and determining factor of negro art, it belongs to sculpture as breathing belongs to life, it is the attitude of abandonment (Fanon 1982:82). One by one, Fanon isolates the elements of the poetic mythologising of being other than the whites, or blacker than the other – the sublimated backwash of radical prejudice. First there is the figure of the "bitter brotherhood" of those who have not invented gunpowder, the compass, steam or electricity, then the "band of oldest sons of the world", those who did not want to rule but only to play with the holy fire of the world, descending into the red flesh of the earth, ascending into the burning flesh of heaven (Fanon 1982:83). Rhythm, mystical closeness to the fertile earth mother, occult coital rites, rousing drums, black magic, primitive mentality, animism, and excessive eroticism are the figures of blackness lined up by Fanon in an analysis of the strange coincidence of white othering and black "self-ing". "Our writers," he says ironically in the course of quoting Senghor on "feeling", "help me to convince your white civilisation that they neglect a costly treasure, feeling" (Fanon 1982:84).

The point that he makes is that this mechanism is a kind of self-justification and self-appreciation on the part of the black person who does not fully understand its dialectical relation to white othering: "You are different and distant" (said by the white person) is transformed by the black person into something like, "I am different and distant because I have something that you don't have and can never have. Be jealous and desire me." In this way, the difference that the white racist subject originally constitutes between him/herself and the black object is transformed into a mutually defining mechanism reproducing difference as an ideology of picturesque exoticism – ideology because the difference can act as a *diversion*. It can divert attention from the fundamental political contradictions by fixing it on the level of poetically wrought differences of "essence".

Thus Negritude represents a dialectically later version of the dissimulation started by Tempels. According to Césaire, Tempels's *Bantu philosophy* (in which the highly appreciated "spiritual values" of blacks are recommended as a universal remedy for all the ills of the then Belgian Congo), acts as a diversion from the burning reality of colonial exploitation. Césaire's irony is biting:

> Since Bantu thought is ontological, the Bantu only ask for satisfaction of an ontological nature. Decent wages?! Comfortable housing?! Food?! These Bantu are pure spirits, I tell you (1972:38).

He goes on to quote from Tempels:

> What they desire first of all and above all is not the improvement of their economic or material situation, but the white man's recognition of and respect for their dignity as men, their full human value (Césaire 1972:38).

Césaire resumes:

> In short, you tip your hat to the Bantu life force, you give a wink to the immortal Bantu soul. And that's all it costs you! You have to admit you're getting off cheap (1972:38).

Césaire goes on to quote Tempels, who notes with obvious satisfaction that the Bantu viewed the white man from the only point of view that was possible for them, that of their Bantu philosophy. They "integrated the whites in their hierarchy of life forces at a very high level" (Césaire 1972:39). In this way Tempels forged a mechanism prohibiting the black man from rising against his oppressors, because the black man has institutionalised the white in his own "philosophy" as a ruling force (cf. Césaire 1972:38–39).

In Negritude something similar happens, but in an inverse form. The black intellectual launches him/herself through rhetorical means high into the "wildest dreams" entertained about him/her by whites. Once up there the admiration of the whites diffuses any attempt of the black to come down from the clouds, to demystify the inverse mechanism of othering, i.e. of fulfilling someone else's dream to earn a feeling of one's own personal worth (Miller 1986:292).[18]

I have now but touched upon three moves in the dialectics of othering: white ethnophilosophy, black ethnophilosophy, and Negritude. What should not be overlooked and what is very important for the understanding of this dialectic is that the critique of these different stages is made by people – and quoted *as* critique by a person – who are themselves part of this dialectic in different historical and political situations. I have quoted the critique of a black professional philosopher (originally published in French in 1976) on black and white ethnophilosophy. I have quoted the critique of one of the founders of Negritude (Césaire, educated at the *École Normale Supérieure* in Paris) on white ethnophilosophy, and I have quoted Fanon's critique of Negritude – being one of the Africans of the diaspora, as Hountondji calls him (Fanon studied and published in France and later joined the Algerians as a doctor in their war of liberation against France). These are obvious and perhaps even superfluous remarks. But they are made for two reasons: firstly to stress the extremely limited "beginner's choice" of "voices", and secondly to stress the complexity, the poignance, and the opacity – even within this small "sample" – of the epistemological situation governing this type of exercise, the extent and significance of which are only beginning to emerge. Without constructing yet another outlandish mystique of the mazes of self-reflexivity, I think that an awareness of this tendency should be constantly operative as well as explicitly thematised in the teaching of a course on "African Thinking". We (but who are we?) think about how others think about others who thought about "difference" and "identity". This awareness could, I think, help to facilitate an "openness to strangeness" in a situation where the "closed shop" attitude – if not irrevocably ingrained by school education – has become the safest option, both for the angry and the anxious.

With these remarks in mind, I now – somewhat apprehensively – resume my argument. Negritude was a literary and philosophical movement forged by a black intellectual elite in the 1930s in the Latin Quarter of Paris. It was plugged into the anthropological discourse of Leo Frobenius, a German anthropologist of the first half of the twentieth century, and of whom Senghor writes, "no one better than Frobenius revealed Africa to the world and to Africans themselves" (Miller 1986:289). As with Tempels's philosophy, Africans themselves are "*subject* to and even subjugated by an essence discovered by an outsider" of which they might have been wholly unaware (Miller 1986:290). What they were aware of was their programme, i.e. to create a missing African "Great Tradition". They did it from the outside and from above "through refined synthetic restatement of indigenous cultural materials" (Caulfield 1972:206).

As Fanon (1982:119) made clear, this amounts to a kind of literary mythology. It conjures up a pre-colonial mythical golden age of the "black Orpheus", mystifying rather than verbalising the actual political hopes and aspirations of the people for the future. The dialectics set off by white othering does not end with Negritude. It could be said, however, to be a kind of prefiguration of what Caulfield (1972:203) calls an eventual qualitative leap in consciousness, i.e. from "boundary maintaining mechanisms" to positive affirmation of cultural and racial worth and dignity. This announces a definite step in the dialectics of othering and in the course of liberation struggles. One might argue that this has also been the work of the Black Consciousness Movement. In *I write what I like*, Steve Biko comes close to some of Senghor's formulations when, for example, he refers to the difference between the Western and the African mentality and to the rhythmical sense that is "in us" (Biko 1984:44, 45). However, unlike the literary formulations of Negritude, these new formulations of culture are not bound to a distant and glorious past, but are meant to constitute a thoroughfare to the future. It is a culture of defiance, self-assertion, group pride and solidarity, and it is seen as offering "a hope in the direction we are taking from here" (Biko 1984:46).

This merits an extensive citation from Fanon who stresses a relationship of solidarity between culture and the liberation struggle, rather than one of "embellishment":

> The native intellectual nevertheless sooner or later will realize that you do not show proof of your nation from its culture but that you substantiate its existence in the fight which the people wage against the forces of occupation. No colonial system draws its justification from the fact that the territories it dominates are culturally non-existent. You will never make colonialism blush for shame by spreading out little-known cultural treasures under its eyes (1982: 179–180).

Fanon goes on to say that the native intellectual, in the decisive stages of the struggle, might try to cultivate a national culture in all possible ways. Apart from establishing exotic Negritudes, he might try to grasp the essence of the actual culture of the people, even using a dialect to get as close as possible to what lives in their hearts. This, however, would be a mere "clutching at outer garments", because the visible aspects are merely reflections of a "hidden life, teeming and perpetually in motion" (Fanon 1982:180). Fanon seems to be saying that the visible conventions of outwardness which characterise a people in a time of political mobilisation are like "old skins" (1982:180) cast off from something that is freshly emerging at every moment. He speaks of the

> inert, already forsaken result of frequent and not always very coherent adaptations *of a much more fundamental substance which itself is constantly renewed.* . . . When a people undertakes an armed struggle or even a political struggle against a relentless colonialism, *the significance of tradition changes.* . . . During the period of struggle *traditions are fundamentally unstable* and are shot through by centrifugal tendencies (my emphases) (Fanon 1982:180).

4.2 Sages and Ideologues

The nature, the circumstances, and the effects of major "changes of the significance of tradition", both for the colonisers and for the colonised (and, indeed, for the writer of such a story), would of course demand a major historical study. For the moment, I simply want to point out that this is what must be stressed in a teaching situation. Briefly, I would also like to illustrate some of the implications that this might have for a South African teaching situation when "philosophical sagacity" and "nationalist ideologies" are investigated as areas of philosophical interest. These areas, distinguished by Oruka during the symposium referred to above, represent a reaction to the idea of a collective or communal thinking held by members of the ethnophilosophical trend.

"African Philosophy" understood as philosophical sagacity would denote, as the locus of philosophical activity, the company of sages in a traditional African community. According to this view, these sages are critical and independent thinkers who "know their own minds" and who maintain a critical distance from the authority of communal consensus. They are looked to for comment and evaluation of communal opinion on decisive matters. The advocates of traditional sagacity as a source of philosophy stress that literacy is not a necessary condition for philosophical reflection and exposition. The philosophy offered by traditional philosophers, it is claimed, does not come in an elaborate form, but is in most cases expressed in enthymematic form. An enthymeme is a short-cut logical argument of which the full logical argument can easily be uncoiled (Oruka 1981:3–4).

The inclusion of investigations into philosophical sagacity in a course on "African Thinking" would ideally entail that students do some supervised anthropological fieldwork. Of course, the requirements for this would be a praxis of radical coevalness in Fabian's sense of the word. Only on that basis could "the real stories" come out in any case. Because the early traditions of black communities in South Africa have been sorely corroded by the colonial machinery, it would more than likely be the "constant renewals", the "instabilities", and the "centrifugal tendencies" which would be encountered by students doing fieldwork. It is not unlikely that students would come home with tape-recordings that might include interpretations of actual political problems grafted onto older traditions. This might be a fine counterpart to the naive portrayal of the "Great Spirit" and his relationship with the people in animist texts. To illustrate, let us examine a quote from the vision of the *kikmongwi* or traditional wise man of Hotaville, a Hopie village in a Red Indian reservation in the United States of America:

> The Hopi have, in following the Life Pattern ever since the Great Spirit gave it to us, obtained many prophecies. One of the things that was told to us was that the white man will come and be a very intelligent man, bringing to us many things that he will invent . . . that there would be a road in the sky. How could anyone build a road in the sky? we wondered. But when we see airplanes going back and forth over us we know what they were talking about. . . . These signs tell us that we are nearing the end of our Life Patterns, that we will soon have to be judged. . . . [On] Purification Day . . . [t]he Hopi, for instance, will identify many people who have beaten us up, put us into jail, taken our land, starved us. Those people will of course be punished. If, when [the Purifier] comes, it will be found that the white man has done the best he can to right the wrongs he has committed, some of the white people in the US may be saved. If . . . not . . . it will be doubtful if the white race will be allowed to live on any of this land after Purification Day. This is as it was told by our forefathers (Clemmer 1972:233–234).

Another way in which the "significance of tradition" can change is exemplified by "nationalistic-ideological philosophies", as Oruka describes them. These would include, for example, Kwame Nkrumah's "Consciencism", Julius Nyerere's "*Ujamaa*" and Kenneth Kaunda's "Zambian Humanism".[19] These philosophies were formulated "as a response to a specific need arising out of the prevailing historical circumstances of decolonisation" (Bwalya 1987:31). While it would be beyond the scope of this essay to give an exposition of these philosophies, it could be suggested that they arose from a need for redemption (Bwalya 1987:32) or restoration. What needed to be restored were the traditions of pre-colonial communal Africa, to which all three laid claim as part of their "roots". The redemption is not only an intellectual exercise – these philosophies all try to provide *practical applications* in trying to restore some of their heritage to the post-colonial societies. An example of this would be the way in which Nyerere's concept of "*Ujamaa*" ("familyhood") finds application in the Tanzanian educational system where the school is developed as a self-supporting family. If included in a course on "African Thinking" in a South African university, there must be reference to, for example, Es'kia Mphahlele's African Humanism and its philosophical and political implications (cf. de Kock 1987:35–48).

4.3 The "Professional" (philosopher) and the Liberator

If it is true that we can criticise the present and project the future only in the name of an ideal which acquires its content from the creative appropriation of traditions (Ricoeur 1981:97), two more moves in the dialectics of othering need to be engaged. These two moves also appear to indicate two alternative ways in which the theoretical bias and the practical organisation of a course in "African Thinking" might be set up. The one is what Oruka (1981:5) calls "professional philosophy"; the other remains, at this point, nameless. Its name will reveal itself to us when we find it. It is a critique and a self-critique that leads us to an emancipatory praxis on the basis of a remembered and revitalised tradition. It is an interpretation of the traditional world that leads to changing the present world – a combination of hermeneutics and critique of ideology.

But first of all, let us examine the notion of "professional philosophy". P.O. Bodunrin, contributing to the same symposium as Oruka, states that philosophy, professionally speaking, must have "the same meaning in all cultures" (i.e. the so-called "universalist" view of philosophy which actually boils down to Western philosophy), but, he adds:

> the subjects that receive priority and perhaps the method dealing with them may be dictated by cultural biases and the existential situation in a society within which the philosopher operates. The present debate in Africa as to what really constitutes philosophy . . . is a case in point (Bodunrin 1981b:9).

A course in "African Thinking" will most certainly have to deal with this debate. It is essential that polemics between authors be read and reconstructed. Hountondji's (1983) definition of African Philosophy as a "set of texts" produced on the continent is acceptable insofar as it would enable students to become involved in the "internal discords of the literature".

But this will not suffice. Texts have to be selected. And the selection will show a bias. Which "cultural bias" and which "existential situation" are likely to dictate priorities in a course on "African Thinking" in South Africa or in the United States of America? It would appear that the advocates of "professional philosophers"[20] in Africa do share a bias. It is the belief that "a way of life which made it possible for our ancestors to be subjugated by a handful of Europeans cannot be described as totally glorious" (Bodunrin 1981b:14). Wiredu formulates it almost identically. He speaks of the "pervasive trait" (i.e. the pre-scientific, spiritistic, and superstitious nature) of African culture that enabled "sparse groups of Europeans to subjugate large masses of African populations and keep them in colonial subjection for many long years and which even now makes them a prey to neo-colonialism" (Wiredu 1977:169).

Hountondji (quoted in Miller 1986:297) advocates that "we must at all costs liberate our thought from the Africanist ghetto where some have sought to lock it up". Marcien Towa goes straight to the heart of "the matter":

> The will to be ourselves . . . brings us face to face with the necessity to transform ourselves profoundly, to negate our inner being in order to become the other. In order to appropriate for ourselves Europe's secret, that is, this new and foreign spirit, we must revolutionise our own spirit completely; in so doing, we will assuredly become like the European (1986:297).

For Towa, to be different is to be a slave.

What is implied in all of this is that "Africa's failure to resist European conquest is a sign of almost ontological, certainly philosophical weakness" (Towa 1986:297). Bodunrin (1981b:14) is explicit about this. He recommends, with Wiredu, an examination "of features of our thought system and our society that made this possible". Philosophical strength, they appear to say, is what constitutes the strength of the West, the strength of science. This philosophical secret of the West is the one that permitted it to conquer the world. Philosophy in Africa must therefore model itself on the scientific rationality of the West (cf. Hountondji 1983b:98–99).

The point has often enough been made that the "success" and "progress" offered by this truncated scientific rationality is a "myth" and a "superstition" – that it leads to the destruction of the human being and of nature on a scale that myth and ritual, as unconscious products of rationality, could never have achieved. Mytho-logical arrangements of production, of society, of the relationship to nature, might contain a "secret" which could restore to the entire modern and modernising world a "measure" and a "direction". Africa might need "science" desperately, as Hountondji says, but it need not be had under the guidance of a scientistic and positivistic philosophy, a philosophy that concerns itself only with the means (technology) and not with the ends (its effects). Wiredu (1977:167) somewhat dubiously calls the logical positivist movement "one of the most influential and fruitful movements in recent western philosophy", especially because it helped articulate criteria with which to distinguish between "pre-scientific, spiritualistic and modern scientific thought". The colonisation and exploitation of Africa could not have occurred without the West's Promethean instrumentalist rationality. Neither could Europe's chemical waste have been dumped on Africa without the objectification of this rationality in "sophisticated" technology. It is for this reason that, together with a critique of instrumental rationality, a text such as Schumacher's *Small is beautiful* should be prescribed, for instance, in a first-year course in "African Thinking".

The last move in the dialectics of othering that I shall refer to may be seen as an example of the reaction against the racism of universalism,[21] or the "Westernism" of the neo-colonial "professional" intellectual. By a stretch of the imagination this can be seen as a "hermetic" turn. It *withdraws* into a position of strength. It refuses to be part of the Western "public eye", it does not constitute its image at "symposia", it has stopped using French or English. It has cut its ties with the ruling class and their intellectual yes-men. At the same time it is intensely creative, fully community-centred, with an emancipatory praxis.

I am referring to an account of an "experiment" in theatre by Ngugi wa Thiong'o (1987:xi), in *Decolonising the mind*, the last book he will write in English. The rationality of this project is rich in suggestions for both the theoretical bias and the practical business of putting together a course in "African Thinking".

The event that started it all and that ended in a neo-colonial jail and finally exile (wa Thiong'o 1987:62) was Ngugi wa Thiong'o's decision to wrest himself loose, after seventeen years of producing Afro-European literature, from what Achebe once described as the "fatalistic logic of the unassailable position of English in our literature" (quoted in wa Thiong'o 1987:7). The return to the Gikuyu language meant the return of the university lecturer to his people – it also meant the restoration of tradition to redeem the present. Writing in one's mother tongue, he says (wa Thiong'o 1987:28), represents the most authentic commitment to the anti-imperialist struggle. Likewise also community-based theatre when it is conceived of as a reappropriation of pre-colonial traditional ritual. Rites and rituals linked peasant production processes to the decisive events of human life and to the seasons of the earth. They mediated and moderated social conflict. Together, they were a symbolic praxis integrating members of a society and affirming its attitude of companionship rather than mastership towards nature. Small wonder, then, that colonial rule could tolerate neither them nor, especially, the "empty spaces" in the middle of the villages needed for the performance of these rituals. School halls and churches were built to fill these spaces. And community halls were erected where West-end comedies and saccharine musicals were presented to make Africans laugh and forget "this business of Mau-Mau, Freedom and all that" (wa Thiong'o 1987:36–38).

Freedom was not really freedom when it came, however. In Kamiruthu, a township of Limuru in Kenya, the open-air theatre of the oppressed factory workers and peasants was first banned and then razed to the ground by armed policemen of the neo-colonial regime (wa Thiong'o 1987:59). One of the main reasons for this was that the hidden was revealed and the revealed was hidden – a strategy characteristic of hermetic praxis. What was always hidden by bourgeois education, i.e. the sources and the agencies involved in the production of knowledge, were revealed. "Knowledge and hence reality was demystified" (wa Thiong'o 1987:57). People rehearsed in the open and argued in the open, they compared experiences and came to agreements in the open. The finished product, the actual performance of the play, was not an imperious surface inhibiting and threatening the people with its "objectivity" and definiteness. The people knew where it came from and they recognised their real and actual concerns in it. They did not all have expertise with regard to the *means* to get the thing going – i.e. the technical skills, the talent, the practical know-how, but nobody was excluded when it came to designing the *ends*. A rationality of consensus about the goals governed the process.

But what was revealed was also hidden by the "hermetic" closure, the close solidarity engendered by a shared creative process: the latter was the shared experience *created* by the community that consequently inspired a series of creative communities, set up by people who had a part in the original project (wa Thiong'o 1987:61–62). Rombach's words are apt here: "I cannot tell you what it was like. We must do it again and then you'll know" (1983:80–81).

I thought it necessary to tell this story because of its exemplary nature. It gives a clue as to what the guiding rationality should be in the development and the teaching of a course in "African Thinking". *Ideally* it would involve an interdisciplinary work community with "real" as opposed to "academic" interests in the project. It would also involve, and hopefully be guided by, African intellectuals who share the sentiments of Ngugi wa Thiong'o. Participation in the project would depend on a demonstrable willingness on the part of those members who do not know an African language, to learn one.

5.   CONCLUSION

I conclude in the hope that nothing has been closed off – nothing, that is, except the "realist" possibility of concealing the operative political and historical "conditions of production" involved in preparing "study material" on "African Thinking". I hope, however, that I have indicated the kind of theoretical "opening" that will keep "the matter" of "African Thinking" open. Provisionally, I shall call this opening "the dialectics of othering in the history of 'African Thinking' ", and this of course will have to be worked out and refined in far more detail than I have done here – that is to say, as far as it has not been done already. It would be the actual *process* of producing the theory and its praxis that would have to save it from closure, from degenerating, for example, into some outlandish metaphysic. The possibility is not excluded that the whole exercise might end up in a sensational totalising system that fixes the mechanisms of othering in an elegant and inevitable sequence that leads to an elaborate abstract "synthesis". That would be very dangerous. For it would make a mere "piece of thought" from the thinking that I would like to call, after Cornelis Verhoeven (1982), "vulnerable" thinking. In the South African context, the latter would refer to thinking that *dares* to think *through* the strident us/them swivel that currently articulates, to varying degrees, the consciousness of people.

This "vulnerable" thinking, (swivelling vigorously to "feel the rub" and understand it) would be rendered all the more vulnerable when thought *aloud*, articulated *aloud* by the philosophers. Ideally, of course, this should happen in the form of a real coeval dialogue or *Auseinandersetzung* involving as many people from as many interest groups as possible. The ideal is that the philosophers get out of their distance control tower and go and talk to the people, forging with them "open spaces in the village" (approximations of ideal speech situations) or requesting to participate with them in existing spaces. This, I think, is the only possibility of getting out of the "fixes" of othering in a context of a-symmetrical and racist power-relations.

This is a naive and idealistic projection – probably a dead give-away of how the greed of the fathers (who observed, objectified, and exploited the "Other") is being revisited upon their over-fed children who only long to listen and respond to the "Other" when it is too late. The only function of the projection here is to open up a *possibility* (as the extreme opposite of a likelihood, a *probability*), i.e. that an attempt will be made to construct an "African world-view", or to identify a system of "typical" African beliefs, or to extract an "essentially African" conceptual scheme, and include it in a list of world-views or in an exposition of different ways of finding "meaning in life". But this would boil down to a reproduction of the partitioning that separated us all into "us" and "them" in the first place. It would entail the "separate development" (or the "federated state" or the "canton" or whatever euphemism may be fashionable at the time) of "African Thinking".

It would entail its "forced removal" from the historical and political context in which it was "called forth" by white missionaries. It would be made into a "self-governing state" (of mind), watched over like hawks by the philosophers of Western decorum: "African thinker, know your place." This must be avoided. Because *we* are the occupiers.

6.   NOTES

1. I believe that this construction is not unfounded and that further research could come up with many examples of university study material containing naive Eurocentric treatments of traditional cultures.

2. L. Lévy-Bruhl (1926). In this work a distinction is drawn between Western logical and primitive (prelogical) mentalities. A characteristic of the latter is that they do not function according to the principles of identity and noncontradiction. These principles are replaced by the principle of participation – everything participates in the essence of everything else. The mystical and the cosmic unity of all things dominates the primitive conception of the world. Primitives think like children and pathological adults in the West. At the end of his life Lévy-Bruhl changed his views as to the absolute difference between Western and primitive minds.

3. Lemaire (1976:220) here quotes M. Sahlins, *Stone age economics* (1972).

4. See Lemaire (1976:236–280 & 281–334) for evaluations of social integration in primitive societies (Lévi-Strauss, Mauss, Marx, Durkheim) and for theories of "human nature" (Freud, Marcuse, Fromm, Lorenz, Marx).

5. Ricoeur refers to the interpretative reappropriation of myth as the post-critical equivalent of the pre-critical revelation of the holy.

6. Heidegger's appreciation of listening and hearing as the first and authentic mode of openness to one's own possibilities is taken over here by Lemaire (1976:373), presumably because he also finds the Heideggerian distinction between "*Rede*" and "*Sprache*" sympathetic. "*Rede*" is the pre-articulation of "*Sprache*". It is the ontological basis of "*Sprache*" and therefore precedes speaking as its condition of possibility. This is why "listening to" is seen as a more fundamental attitude to the world than "speaking about".

7. In this context such a reading seems to have been operative in the author's reading of whatever text he read about animism. "The habits involved in this type of reading encourages the unproblematic and unhesitant singular interpretation of text, the unreflexive perception of a reported reality . . . and the essentially uninteresting character of the agency involved in the report's generation. In the realistic genre, the text is a neutral medium for conveying pre-existing facts about the world. The epistemological commitment here, is that subjects of study appear exotic by virtue of their inherent qualities rather than as a result of *their construction in the text*. An important corollary of this position is that the text's neutrality exempts it from consideration as a species of social/cultural activity. The text is thought to operate at a different level from the world 'about which' it reports" (Woolgar 1988:28, emphasis added).

8. Fabian refers to the work of Frances Yates, *The art of memory* (1966), and Walter J. Ong, *Ramus: Method and the decay of dialogue* (1958), to support his thesis of the spatialisation of time and the removal of the "Other" to a position of observed object.

9. The doubts expressed here as to the viability of a Marxist anthropology also constitute a parallel to Lemaire's remarks. According to Fabian, Marxists "share" with bourgeois positivist anthropology certain fundamental assumptions concerning the nature of ethnographic data and the use of "objective" methods. Apart from this he doubts the integrity of the "allochronic periodisations of human history" that play such an important role in Marxist analyses. In the context of imperialism Fabian points out that communist countries "have built analogous spheres of colonial expansion and . . . of foreign aid and

development". He adds the question: "Does the routinised world revolution construe a different other than the capitalist world market?" (Fabian 1983:155–156).

10. This is essentially the view taken by Hymes (1972:35–36).

11. Hymes (1972:52): "I would hope to see the consensual ethos of anthropology move from a liberal humanism, defending the powerless, to a socialist humanism, confronting the powerful and seeking to transform the structure of power."

12. See Stanley Diamond (1972:426): "Clearly the study of man can reconstitute itself only in the struggle against the civilised objectification of man, in our own society and elsewhere. Anthropologists who recognise this may now decide to turn to the arena in which the generality of men, notably peasants and primitives, the conventional 'objects' of study, are now re-creating themselves as subjects in the revolutionary dramas of our time. In accordance with their competence, these anthropologists are likely to declare themselves partisans in the movements for 1) national liberation, the nation being the ground for culture, and 2) social reconstruction, which begins with socialism, the name for the rights and possibilities of man. If fieldwork remains possible for them, it will not be in the pursuit of their careers, but independently, as amateurs, in order to learn, not to 'examine', in dynamic and possibly revolutionary circumstances."

13. Here the relationship between a *moderate form of life* and a *tragic* (rather than heroic) *sense of life* is explicated.

14. See Kurt H. Wolff (1972:113). The revaluation of "primitive" forms of life sometimes leads to a nostalgic desire to recover what is lost in terms of a sense of life: "We have traded our 'worth/mana/power/pnema'. . . for compulsive domination, for an indifferent or cynical or hypocritical play with life and death. . . . We must emerge from this condition into such 'innocence' as man is capable of, through whatever 'opening the back' human and political radicalism can jointly discover."

15. Bodunrin (1981a:9): "It has been the theme of most conferences held in Africa to date."

16. Here the pre-ontological self-understanding of *Dasein* is used to support the notion that care is one of the ultimate ontological constituents of human existence. See also Mulang (1987).

17. See Christopher Thacker (1983:73–76) for references to pleasing ideas of wildness ("cannibalism") incorporated into the behaviour of literary characters in romantic literature.

18. Miller (1986:292) quotes from Stansislas Adotevi's *Négritude et Negrologues*: "Négritude is a notion of reflexive consciousness, the intellectual alienation of the Negro. . . . You can't stand at the window and watch yourself go by in the street. . . . Négritude is the last-born child of an ideology of domination . . . it's the black way of being white. . . . It is the end product of many decades of ethnology. . . . Négritude is to politics what *Bantu Philosophy* is to ideology for Africa. Senghor is Father Tempels on the field of action, for the same cause and in the same misadventure."

19. Kwame Nkrumah, *Consciencism: Philosophy and ideology*, (1978); J.K. Nyerere, *Ujamaa: Essays in socialism*, (1968). See R.M.K. Bwalya (1987:31–38) on Kaunda.

20. Bodunrin (1981b:9) includes himself, Kwasi Wiredu, Paulin Hountondji, and H.O. Oruka in this group.

21. See Miller (1986:282) quoting Wole Soyinka: "We black Africans have been blandly invited to submit ourselves to a second epoch of colonisation – this time by a universal-humanoid abstraction defined and conducted by individuals whose theories and prescriptions are derived from the apprehension of *their* world and *their* history, *their* social neuroses and *their* value systems" (original emphases). One might advise that this "universalism" is also propagated by African humanists (of whom Mphahlele is one): "a humanism that draws on ultimately bourgeois conceptions of cultural value" (cf. de Kock 1987:35–48).

Readings

WHAT IS AFRICAN PHILOSOPHY?

DIDIER N. KAPHAGAWANI

INTRODUCTION

Though "gathering momentum" as Kwasi Wiredu (1980:14) happily and hopefully observes, African philosophy is, as accepted by philosophers in Africa, still in its embryonic stage. As such, it has yet to establish not only a tradition, as some scholars in Africa as well as elsewhere would have us believe, but seemingly *several* such traditions. Odera Oruka (1983:384) has this proliferation of traditions in African philosophy in mind when, in remarking on the general lines along which African philosophy is to proceed, he encourages the attitude of "letting one hundred flowers to bloom [*sic*]" so as not only to create traditions, but also to promote debates, critical analyses, and self-criticism when grappling with the numerous issues in contemporary Africa which are amenable to philosophic solutions.

It is in the interests of almost all scholars seriously engaged in research that is of potential or immediate relevance to Africa, that a good number of traditions in African philosophy should emerge so as to make possible debates and critical and constructive analyses; this is in order to eschew the three evils, as pointed out by Wiredu (1980:1–6), that are currently tormenting, or about to bedevil, most, if not all, African cultures and nationalities. These are: *authoritarianism*, permanent control of all aspects of life, politics included, that ensues in people doing things against their will; *anachronism*, systems or principles outliving their suitability and utility; *supernaturalism*, the tendency to establish supernatural foundations for a natural code of conduct.

It is to a general critique of African philosophy that we now turn.

THE QUESTION OF AFRICAN PHILOSOPHY

Why the question about African philosophy?

The question, "What is African philosophy?" has preoccupied scholars in Africa for several decades now for basically two reasons. Firstly, the attempt to falsify certain anthropological theses, Lévy-Bruhlian theses in particular, which denied Africans south of the Sahara properties of ratiocination and its cognates due to the apparent primitiveness of these peoples' mentality. As Oruka observes, anthropologists of a Lévy-Bruhlian persuasion presented Africans as incapable of evolving a "scientific and reason-oriented culture":

> for them, the situation was that of unphilosophy rather than prephilosophy. What they claimed to have established in Africa were (1) the impossibility for a philosophic dialogue and (2) an obvious non-existence of a tradition of organized philosophical systems (Oruka 1983:383).

That was the anthropological factor which resuscitated or motivated, for good or ill, philosophers in Africa to ask the question, "What is African philosophy?"

Secondly, the political factor is also quite significant here. It is a palpable fact that almost all Africa was at some point in history a colony of some Western nation or other. When the process of decolonisation, mental as well as physical, gathered momentum, it led to the post-colonial quest for an African identity. A combination of these factors inevitably compelled scholars in Africa to face the question of what African philosophy is. But, to the present day, philosophers are so divided in their answers to this question that, as Wiredu (1980) observes, tremendous amounts of time, energy, and effort are wasted by philosophers in Africa on discussions *about* what would constitute African philosophy instead of actually *doing* African philosophy.

It is, however, appropriate at this juncture to point out that although Wiredu holds "the quest for an African identity" as solely responsible for this protracted dispute, one other reason lies in the very nature of the discipline of philosophy itself. It is a long-standing tradition in philosophy, or at least a tendency, for philosophers to define all the basic material, be they concepts, words or phrases, before actually philosophising. And philosophers in Africa, particularly those who have been heavily exposed to the analytic tradition in philosophy, are no exception.

Two conceptions of African philosophy

Philosophers in Africa seem to subscribe to, or tend to vacillate between, the following two conceptions of African philosophy. The first conceives of African philosophy as merely consisting in "collecting, interpreting and disseminating African proverbs, folktales, myths, and other traditional material of a philosophical tendency" (Wiredu 1980:3–4). The second underscores and takes cognisance of modern developments in knowledge and techniques in reflection. This conceives of African philosophy as a joint venture and product of traditional as well as modern trained philosophers, philosophers of different perspectives and holding divergent world outlooks and who employ different methods of philosophising in debates and research of philosophic virtue and of relevance to the cultures and nationalities of Africa.

The first definition has of late fallen into disrepute among philosophers in Africa for reasons to be discussed below when considering the so-called ethnophilosophical approach to African philosophy. But those philosophers who subscribe to the second conception insist, in a frighteningly fanatical way at times, that rationality, rigour, objectivity, and self-criticism be properties of the African philosophy they have in mind. Paulin Hountondji (1976) as well as Oruka no doubt champion this position. But demanding that African philosophy bow to all these conditions confines the conception of philosophy to just one aspect. And although Wiredu can rightly be said to belong to this camp, he is quick to point out the adverse implications of overly strict adherence to these demands:

> if we demand that a philosophy has to have all these attributes by definition, then we are debarred from pointing out, what is a well known fact, that some philosophies are unrigorous or unsystematic or dogmatic or irrational or even antirational (1980:6).

Obviously the history of Western philosophy has instantiations of Hountondji's view of African philosophy as discussed in Anne Seller's review of his book, *African philosophy: Myth and reality* (originally published in French in 1976 and again in English in 1983). In her review, Seller remarks:

Hountondji insists on a conception of philosophy as coherent discourse subject to rules of logic and reflective about the aims of science. Yet that in itself is not merely a European concept, but one belonging to a specific period in Europe's history – roughly from Descartes to Wittgenstein (1984:12).

Both definitions no doubt have their shortcomings, as all definitions do in philosophy. Nevertheless, with these definitions in the background, four approaches have either emerged or are in the process of doing so in African philosophy. Oruka (1983:384) claims, as he has often done in his earlier work, that the four trends are: *ethnophilosophy, philosophic sagacity, nationalistic-ideological philosophy*, and *professional philosophy*. The philosophic arena in Africa is currently dominated by debates on this Orukan framework, inevitably shifting the emphasis from the question of what African philosophy is, to questions of what *ethnophilosophy*, or *philosophic sagacity*, or *nationalistic-ideological philosophy*, or *professional philosophy*, is. Here again, as in all philosophic discourses, divisions among philosophers are quite pronounced.

Types of philosophies or methods of philosophising?

What is striking about this categorisation of African philosophy into four schemata is that it is amenable to misconception in the sense that this classification might be misconceived as representing four independent *types* of African philosophy, as opposed to seeing them as four *methods* used in African philosophy. But it should be borne in mind that although it makes perfect sense to talk of *ethnophilosophy, nationalistic-ideological philosophy*, and *professional philosophy* as *types* of philosophy, this is not the case with *philosophic sagacity* since this is, if anything, more of an inborn or presumably acquired skill or talent than anything else. Nevertheless, the classification could still be preserved by conceiving of the finished product of this skill as a philosophy distinct from the other three. Then *ethnophilosophy, philosophic sagacity, nationalistic-ideological philosophy*, and *professional philosophy* turn out to be bivalent: they represent types of African philosophy on the one hand, and methods of philosophising in Africa on the other.

Regardless of function, these four should not be taken as rigid, with fine lines distinguishing one type or method from the other; for they criss-cross or flow into one another at various levels and with insensible degrees. Some aspects of *philosophical sagacity* can quite rightly qualify, and have been classified – by Oruka (1983:385–386), for instance – as *ethnophilosophy;* some *professional philosophy* as *nationalistic-ideological philosophy;* and some *professional philosophy* as *ethnophilosophy*. Needless to say, some contemporary African philosophers who consider their works to be contributions to *professional philosophy* tend to resist attempts to refer to those discourses as nothing but *ethnophilosophy*. This problem is not of their making; it is due rather to the unjustifiable disrepute into which *ethnophilosophy* has fallen.

This four-rung Orukan framework introduced into African philosophy has, as a matter of interest, some affinities with the framework introduced to the subject of African oral literature by Okpewho, and as alluded to by Anthony Nazombe (1983:45–36). The indebtedness to Nazombe's rendition is quite apparent.

Okpewho (1990 & 1992) classifies African oral literature into four categories. The first is what Nazombe (1983) has termed "tradition-preserved"; it comprises the literature of writers who have merely "translated indigenous tales into modern

European language or structured the tale into what they consider a more representative mode" (Nazombe 1983). This category or approach has much in common with what in contemporary African philosophy has been termed *ethnophilosophy*.

The second category or approach is what Nazombe (1983) has termed "tradition-observed". This consists of works of writers "who have simply woven the themes and techniques of the oral narrative tradition around the experiences of their characters" (Nazombe 1983). This is what in African philosophy qualifies as products of *philosophic sagacity*, as is soon to be observed.

The third approach is termed "tradition refined". This is an approach which abandons the old forms of tales, but preserves their "enduring essences" (Nazombe 1983) which are then applied to the socio-political circumstances contemporaneous with the writer. In the Orukan framework this would fall under *nationalistic-ideological philosophy*.

The fourth approach is "tradition revised". The literature in this category underscores not so much "the cultural outlook defined by a known setting" as a "culture yet to be evolved or in the process of evolving" (Nazombe 1983). Is not this what philosophers in Africa would want to call *professional philosophy*? I think it is.

The "twin-framework" operative in African oral literature demonstrates the fact that, although useful and perhaps indispensable to contemporary African philosophy, the Orukan framework is by no means to be considered sacrosanct and esoteric to contemporary African philosophy; for similar frameworks are at work in other disciplines of which African oral literature is but one. So much for observation, however. It is to the evaluation and analysis of each of the four approaches to, or types of, African philosophy that we now turn.

APPROACHES IN AFRICAN PHILOSOPHY

Ethnophilosophy

The term ethnophilosophy, for etymological interests, was coined by francophone African philosophers. It is an approach which has a large following, for it is heavily subscribed to by anthropologists, sociologists, ethnologists, and some philosophers. This approach conceives of African philosophy as a description and as "communal thought . . . [as] opposed to seeing [it] as a body of logically argued thoughts of individuals" (Bodunrin 1981a:161). Ethnophilosophy is premised on the assumption that "there is a metaphysical system, and an ideology, embodied in the traditional wisdom, the institutions and the languages of Africa". It aims at thrashing out from the myths, folktales, beliefs, proverbs, and languages, "the quintessential African approach to the world" (Seller 1984:21). The chief representatives of this approach are: Placide Tempels (1959), John Mbiti (1969) and Alexis Kagamé (1971).

Anthropologists have been attracted to this approach mainly because of conceptual problems in their home discipline, particularly that of defining and making distinctions between ethnography, ethnology, anthropology, and sociology. Some anthropologists define ethnography as "observation, description, and fieldwork", while ethnology is defined as a subject amenable to more general conclusions, one in which not much emphasis is laid on first-hand information; finally, anthropology is defined as a subject in which all knowledge accruing from human sciences is synthesised. So, the distinction between these branches of human science turns out to be that of difference in perspectives. But the most telling question looms large when the relationship between ethnology and anthropology on the one hand, and sociology on the other, is considered. If a difference in subject-matter is asserted, then, as Marc Augé (1982:80) quite rightly observes, "taken to its logical conclusion, ethnology would . . . be a science of observers, observing others, and sociology that of observers observing themselves".

All these definitional problems notwithstanding, anthropologists are convinced that there exists an extraneous relationship between philosophy and ethnology (or cultural anthropology), but are not unaware of the considerable differences in methods and objectives in these differing disciplines. Ethnophilosophy and ethnology, it is argued, interilluminate in mainly two respects:

1. Some issues of ethnological value are best understood by acknowledging their philosophical significance. As such, cultural anthropology, or ethnology in other words, though empirical, must recognise the philosophical implications of some of its statements.

2. Cultural anthropology provides a perspective from which philosophers can benefit, particularly in their quest for "understanding culture as a reality" (Dupré 1975:1–2).

Cultural anthropologists, particularly ethnographers, have ever been faced with a contradiction arising from their continuous lamentation of the gradual extinction of primitive societies. Although primitive societies were announced to be waning as early as the turn of this century, ethnographers

> have continued quite happily . . . and not just they, but the generation trained by them, and then the following generation trained by the previous one. . . . In short they [ethnographers] are still with us (Augé 1982:87).

This is testimony to the fact that ethnology distorts the picture of reality by disregarding the present conditions of the object of study and the tendency to "particularise its object, to allow itself ideal conditions for analysis, quite regardless of any concrete factors, and to reconstitute lost states, which are really phantom ones" (Augé 1982:89). This is the problem ethnologists have, inadvertently or not, left behind, presumably to be solved through the ethnophilosophical approach.

Some African evangelists, John Mbiti and Alexis Kagamé, for instance, also subscribed to the ethnophilosophical approach, and produced works paraded as *the* African philosophy for several decades in many intellectual circles, because they were concerned with "a psychological and cultural basis for planting the Christian message in the African mind, without betraying either the one or the other" (Augé 1982:8). This group misconceived the form and function of philosophy in assuming that philosophical models are isomorphic to religion models, and by implication thought of philosophy as being "a permanent and stable system of beliefs, allowing of no evolution, always identical to itself, impermeable to time and to history" (Augé 1982:8).

This sin was, however, not only committed by African evangelists, but also by those lay persons whose main objective was, as pointed out earlier in this discussion, to search for an identity denied by the colonisers, but with the underlying idea that one of the elements of cultural identity is indeed "philosophy", the idea that all culture rests on a particular, permanent and unalterable metaphysical substratum (Augé 1982:85).

Ethnophilosophy has come under a lot of criticism. It has been charged with conflating philosophy, mysticism, and religion, and hence paying lip-service to reason and critical analysis. This has resulted in a distorted picture of an African philosophy in which everyone is in unison with everyone else, and it has also presented a picture of African culture in which the collective opinion is highly cherished while the individual is not given due consideration. Thus conceived, Hountondji (1976:1) insists that African philosophy is a myth and not a reality. Furthermore, ethnophilosophy has been criticised for conflating two senses of the word "philosophy" when used in the phrase "African philosophy". These two senses are: the ideological sense, used when making reference to a group or people's slogan; and, secondly, the technical sense in which philosophy is conceived as a product of systematic and ratiocinative methods. For, as boldly expressed by Augé (1982:84), "no society can produce philosophy without knowing it". Critics claim that the word "philosophy" has been carelessly used in all ethnophilosophical literature, and in their view "conceptual impotence" and "intellectual colonialism" are to be held responsible for the abuse. Philosophers of a Hountondjian persuasion therefore argue for the extinction of the term "ethnophilosophy". They claim it has outlived its time and defines, as noted earlier in the discussion, non-existent objects. "Practical ideology" should, they argue, be substituted for "ethnophilosophy"; for the former is simply a constitution of "both schemes of conduct and schemes of thought (not a philosophy)" (Augé 1982:86).

The most damaging criticisms of the ethnophilosophical approach are the following. Firstly, it propagates a holistic approach to the analysis and exposition of world outlooks implicit in most, if not all, African cultures. Secondly, this approach does not take account of individualised philosophies also prevalent in these cultures. But critics in this camp have gone to the other extreme, namely, the non-holistic approach which in itself is not without fault, for it cannot account for what Oruka terms "culture philosophy". No justice can be done to any philosophy of culture unless that culture is, as far as possible, taken as one distinct whole. And in Africa the problem is compounded by the presence of long-standing oral traditions which have maintained quite accurate ideas of communal thought but virtually no accounts of the thoughts of individuals. As far as culture philosophy is concerned the much maligned ethnophilosophical approach is, in my opinion, quite appropriate.

Nevertheless, ethnophilosophy is still confronted with two recalcitrant problems, namely, the problem of *authenticity* – of whatever literature is realised from reflections on, and analyses of, cultures with incomparable levels of oral traditions – and the problem of *differences* which distinguish one African culture from another, which calls for specific studies of those particular cultures. This is the contradiction which faces most of the philosophers in Africa, particularly those who still think that ethnophilosophy is the only way to African philosophy. For they seem to operate simultaneously on the assumptions that differences between African cultures cannot be resolved, and that generalisations on certain aspects of African cultures are possible. As pointed out by Augé (1982:81) these assumptions are doomed to face an intellectual contradiction. But, as Gordon Hunnings (1972:15) observes, "human beings have again and again shown their preference for comfortable confusion rather than disquieting clarity."

Critics of ethnophilosophy seem to thrive on these problems of authenticity and of difference. Commenting on both Tempels's book and that of Kagamé, Hountondji highlights the problem of authenticity in ethnophilosophical literature, remarking that

> the Bantu philosophy presented by Tempels is certainly not the philosophy of the Bantu, but the philosophy of Tempels himself. [Similarly] the "Bantu-Rwandese philosophy of Being" is not the philosophy of the Rwandese, but rather the philosophy of Kagamé himself (Hountondji 1976:8).

Hountondji, unlike for instance Wiredu and Oruka, quite obviously conceives of this collective philosophy – or culture philosophy, to use Oruka's terminology – as absolutely unknowable for the simple reason of "it mostly being a creation of 'anthropologists who pride themselves in philosophizing'" (Hountondji 1976:8).

This unsympathetic view of Hountondji on ethnophilosophy ensues from his conception of African philosophy. According to him, philosophy is African only if it is produced by Africans: "[it is] a kind of literature produced by Africans and dealing with philosophical problems" (Hountondji 1976:9). In this case then, African philosophy is African by geographical accident, and all non-Africans cannot, by definition, contribute to African philosophy, but are at best eavesdroppers. To define African philosophy in such a way is to offer too narrow a perspective; for non-Africans can and have made contributions as invaluable to philosophical issues of current relevance to Africa as the contributions of Africans themselves; for instance, Francis Gillies (1980:16–30) and John Parratt (1976:65–68). That Hountondji's definition calls for rethinking has been argued at length by Kwasi Wiredu (1980:2–6).

That culture philosophies are theoretically possible and knowable need not be belaboured here. Suffice to say that African philosophers cannot be severed from their differing cultures which, to say the least, influence them in various ways. "[The] ethnic tradition is bound to affect the emergent African philosopher whether he seeks to expound and interpret it or whether he seeks to renounce it" (Parratt 1976). The question of authenticity is a problem which any attempt to formulate a culture philosophy has to face. It should not be considered as calling for an urgent solution, but rather as a *caveat* against taking things for granted. That is the way ethnophilosophy should proceed, given that most cultural data are provided through oral tradition.

The criticism that ethnophilosophy emphasises communal thought and not the thoughts of individuals turns out to be less damaging if the following points are borne in mind. Firstly, despite attempts by philosophers in Africa to model African philosophy along the lines of contemporary Western philosophy which is notoriously individualised, we must not be blinded to the fact that this philosophy also originated from communal thought. Secondly, African philosophy, as pointed out by Parratt (1976:66), need not necessarily follow the same paths Western philosophy has trod; for African philosophy has certain resemblances to Eastern philosophies. For example, in Brahminism or Upanishadic thought the names of sages appear in the recorded accounts of these philosophies. Parratt argues that these philosophies were not the works of individual sages; rather, they represented a movement. This point should not, however, be overwrought since there are differences between Oriental and African cultures, particularly with respect to oral tradition.

Ethnophilosophy cannot simply be jettisoned, because both sage philosophers and professional African philosophers are indebted to it. The relationship between ethnophilosophy, sage philosophy, and professional philosophy is clearly outlined by Wiredu as follows:

> there is an intimate relation between the thought of the individual sage-philosophers and the communal world outlooks of their people. It is the communal thought which provides a point of departure of the sage-philosopher. It provides, in fact, his philosophical education and must in many ways determine his theoretical options. On the other hand . . . the communal thought itself is the pooling together of those elements of the thought of individual philosophers of the community that remain stuck in the common imagination (Wiredu 1980:7).

Since this is certainly the case, ethnophilosophy has a lot to offer to contemporary African philosophy; and African philosophers should admit, as Oruka does, their indebtedness, be it positively or negatively, to ethnophilosophy. "I believe that even those of us in Africa who currently claim to be on the right track on the question of African philosophy have been helped in no mean way in adopting this position by provocation of ethnophilosophy" (Oruka 1983:390).

Philosophic sagacity

Admittedly, philosophic sagacity, as an approach to African philosophy other than ethnophilosophy, is still quite new and known in few intellectual circles. One feature characteristic of this approach is that it makes an assumption which is logically opposite to that of ethnophilosophy. Ethnophilosophy is holistic; it lays emphasis on the dimension of communal thought, but philosophic sagacity is non-holistic; it underscores the thoughts of individuals in a community. So, ethnophilosophy and philosophic sagacity are polar approaches. As such, Oruka (1983:384) argues that, unlike professional philosophy and nationalistic-ideological philosophy, sage philosophy "is the only trend that . . . can give an all acceptable decisive blow to the position of ethnophilosophy". But, as this discussion will reveal, it is not a question of *either* this approach *or* that one which should preoccupy African philosophers, but a question of *both* this *and* that, and so on. In other words, a reconciliation of all approaches to African philosophy is more beneficial and productive than an attempt to consider these approaches as mutually exclusive and antagonistic.

Despite Oruka's disagreement, the main task of philosophic sagacity is, in Bodunrin's words,

> to identify men in the society who are reputed for their wisdom with the view of demonstrating that literacy is not a necessary condition for philosophical reflection and exposition; and that there exists in Africa critical and independent thinkers who guide their thoughts and judgements by their power of reason and inborn insight rather than by authority of communal consensus (1981a:162).

Oruka (1983:392) is in disagreement with Bodunrin, not particularly on what philosophic sagacity is, but rather on the implications of Bodunrin's definition of philosophy in general, and African philosophy in particular. It is Bodunrin's conviction that literacy is a necessary condition for any philosophy to get off the ground. Since most African cultures are inundated with oral traditions, Bodunrin argues that Africa has a late start in philosophy. That is why Bodunrin conceives of philosophic sagacity as an approach which ultimately refutes his own conception of philosophy in general, and of African philosophy in particular.

Because it is a new terminology and an approach relatively new to African philosophy, Oruka (1983) has distinguished two senses of philosophic sagacity. He makes distinctions between sage-philosophers who only produce what he terms "culture philosophy" or a philosophy of a culture, and those sage-philosophers who, aware of the paraded culture philosophy, transcend it and attain a philosophic capacity; the latter "are rationally critical and they opt for or recommend only those aspects of beliefs and wisdoms which satisfy their rational scrutiny" (Oruka 1983:383). This distinction having been made, Oruka confines the use of the phrase philosophic sagacity to the latter group of sage-philosophers. The former, he claims, merely parade conventional wisdom "known to almost every average person within the culture" (Oruka 1983:386).

The difference between philosophic sagacity and culture philosophy is that the latter is mainly an exposition of the basic principles, regarded as absolutes, which preserve and justify a particular culture; the former is essentially the attempt to expose these basic cultural principles to ratiocination, the product of which is an independent "system within a system, and order within an order" (Oruka 1983:393). Culture philosophy is, in this case, the first order system with its dogmatic truth claims and absolute ideas, whereas philosophic sagacity is a second order system, a metaculture philosophy which analyses critically the validity of the truth claims made in the first order system – culture philosophy – and is as such "generally openminded and rationalistic" (Oruka 1983:386).

According to philosophers of an Orukan persuasion, a philosophy is second order if it is not only representative of a particular culture's world outlook, but also reflectively critical about it. Anything merely championing a representative world outlook of a people is nothing but a culture philosophy; it is certainly not philosophic sagacity. The question is whether this culture philosophy is not identical to ethnophilosophy.

That philosophic sagacity, as an approach to African philosophy, is modelled on the Alfred Tarskian framework is quite evident from the way Oruka (1983:386–387) presents it. If it admits of the Tarskian categorisation, as it seems to do, then so-called culture philosophy turns out to be nothing more than the much ridiculed ethnophilosophy. What is said to hold for culture philosophy, particularly the claim that it provides a picture as representative of a culture as theoretically possible, is also true of ethnophilosophy. Philosophic sagacity, in this case, becomes therefore a second order system of ethnophilosophy, a meta-ethnophilosophy, analytical and critical – as are all metasystems – of ethnophilosophy. If this is conceded, then philosophic sagacity cannot survive in the absence of ethnophilosophy, just as it is impossible, according to Tarski's theory, to have a second order system or language without a first order one. Therefore, philosophic sagacity is, I am persuaded to believe, not antagonistic to ethnophilosophy; it seems, rather, to be complementary to ethnophilosophy or culture philosophy. The fundamental difference, however, lies in the difference in assumptions; ethnophilosophy is premised on the holistic assumption whereas philosophic sagacity sets out from the assumption of non-holism.

Philosophic sagacity as an approach to African philosophy is, in Bodunrin's view, confronted with two problems; the first is methodological, and the second, definitional. The methodological problem is that of authorship. In Bodunrin's view, when a trained, professional philosopher interviews a sage who in the end fleshes out his otherwise implicit philosophical ideas, the product is "a new creation out of their reflections on the beliefs previously held by them. But the philosopher and the sage are 'doing their own thing' " (Bodunrin 1981a:168). In this case, as is also noted by Oruka, the final product is neither wholly the sage's nor wholly the philosopher's. Oruka (1983:389) grants this with equanimity, but proceeds to point out that, in rummaging through the history of philosophy, "nearly all philosophers including even the professional ones such as Moore and Russell hold their philosophies as joint works with those philosophers who initially inspired or provoked them." This also holds for the final product of philosophic sagacity. The professional philosopher is at best a midwife providing necessary and sufficient assistance to a sage who in the end gives birth to a philosophic child. On this point I concur with Oruka to the extent that the professional philosopher merely assists in the process of creation, obviously through the formulation of his/her questions, but does not determine the sort of philosophic child ultimately borne by the sage. In a way this highlights the problem of authenticity discussed earlier on, an enigma which should not be seen as requiring an urgent solution, but to be viewed, rather, as a *caveat* against naivety when dealing with works of a philosophic but sagacious nature.

The second objection amounts to denying Africa any type of philosophy whatsoever due to the virtual absence of *written*, systematic philosophical reflections by Africans themselves (Bodunrin 1981a). And since written African philosophy is still in the offing, Bodunrin argues, Africa must admit to a late start in philosophy (Bodunrin 1981a). Needless to say, all contemporary African philosophy is written philosophy. And if by "African philosophy" Bodunrin wishes to refer only to this present philosophy which addresses itself to issues arising from the vicissitudes of the present African situation, then it would surely be granted by all African philosophers that this philosophy is still in its infancy. There is no denying that the new African situation, as rightly remarked on by Bodunrin (1981a:166), is in no way radically different in complexity and sophistication from the corresponding traditional way of life: governments, for instance, changing leadership overnight or resisting change until God knows when; or governments signing treaties of all sorts with neighbouring governments that they would not previously have considered doing; people having to live in conditions so hostile and unpredictable as to change from one extreme, say a severe drought, to the other extreme, say, drowning as a result of a cyclone.

Yet, if Bodunrin denies Africa any type of philosophical tradition at all because of its lack of written works and the presence only of a recalcitrant oral tradition, then, as Oruka rightly argues (1983:392), Bodunrin urgently needs to multiply his original definitional matrix with its inverse, for he seems to have put the cart before the horse, as it were. It is indeed the case that "writing cannot be a precondition for philosophical *thinking*, for one must think a thought before writing it down" (Wiredu 1980:6).

Nationalistic-ideological philosophy

Nationalistic-ideological philosophy in Africa is basically those works realised from attempts "to evolve a new and, if possible, unique political theory based on the traditional African socialism and familyhood" (Bodunrin 1981a:162). Some of the chief representatives of this view are Kwame Nkrumah, Julius Nyerere and Léopold Senghor. Certain claims, commonplace in the parlance of some African leaders, such as that their governments are neither capitalist nor socialist nor communist, but are *African,* are no doubt testimony to the existence of this conception of African political philosophy, an amorphous political philosophy believed to be uniquely African and with a unique political theory. As to what these writers mean by "African" is still not quite clear.

These nationalistic-ideological philosophers, though fully aware of the difference between the present African social context and the traditional way of life, still assume that the traditional political system is a good point of departure. According to Bodunrin (1981a:166) this procedure confronts them with some methodological problems. To use Bodunrin's example, a non-money economy has been superseded by a money economy, thus rendering African communalism obsolete – a view with which I am in total disagreement. Urbanisation, which has brought together different peoples in one locale, has, he argues, been a threat not only to African communalism (which worked due to familyhood) but also to the security of the traditional setting.

Bodunrin's objections are, to my mind, quite amiss. Familyhood is not the essential factor in the equation of African communalism; it is rather, at least in part, "living in one locale" which keeps African communalism going. Given the difference in complexity and sophistication between traditional Africa and modern Africa, African communalism is still possible if it is granted that the disposition to share is not a property of a *class* of individuals, say, a family, be it extended or not, but is rather a property of the *individuals* of any African class or group one cares to consider. This explains the presence of African communalism in modern Africa. Regardless of origin, people living in one street in a location in some urban area, say Zingwangwa in Blantyre (Malawi), still have in common an amazing number of basic items: for example, mortars, pestles, or drums for brewing *masese* or *kabanga* (traditional maize beers). African socialism is therefore possible even in a money economy. It is not necessarily the money that is shared, but the basic items bought by that money.

What is more important, nationalistic-ideological philosophers who contend that Africa can progress only from a *unique* political theory are saddled with a problem similar to that of ethnophilosophers who claim that Africa has a unique and distinct philosophy. The African political arena is inundated with diverse political systems which, presumably, are amenable to different and possibly incompatible solutions provided by different political theories. In this sense a philosopher in Africa has, theoretically, a political role to play. According to Wiredu (1980:52) the role of an African philosopher is that of assuming a leading position in the questions of the best options, befitting Africa's divergent or different conditions, of social and political organisation, and the re-examination and re-appraisal of traditional culture in the hope of identifying and preserving what is useful and worth developing from what is obsolete and fit for the dustbin. As far as the analysis of traditional culture is concerned, I am in consonance with Wiredu that philosophers can and should be in the forefront, bearing in mind that philosophic discourses are well known for being notoriously abstract and, in ordinary parlance, obscure – a feature which inevitably alienates philosophers in Africa from their societies. Wiredu (1980:61) is, however, not unaware of this problem and attempts to get round it by suggesting serious communication between the philosophers and the people with whom they hope to communicate; this could occur through the urban population which, he claims, would not feel as remote from the philosophers as the rural population would, owing to the number of thinking, educated people now living in urbanised areas in Africa. It is my view, however, that Wiredu is too optimistic on this point.

But as far as social and political issues are concerned, it is doubly difficult for any philosopher in Africa to take a leading position due to social and political constraints – limitations which have, lamentably, provoked many African intellectuals to write obscurely and indirectly. Felix Munthali's (1980:124) poem, "Iran 1979", clearly expresses this plight:

Airborne by an earth-shaking whirlwind
it pays to speak in riddles
so that marooned on a precipice
by one of your doctrines
you can switch on
anyone of your thousand and one meanings
which the people of Iran
may have forgotten –
who has ever won a battle
against an oracle?

. . . .

You had better speak in riddles
for the agonies of dawn
are altogether too real
for the rainbow
in your mind.

These are the feelings of a poet; below are the words of a philosopher:

If we want our countries to adopt it [science] one day, then it behoves us to create a human milieu there in which and by which the most diverse problems can be freely worked out, and where these discussions may be no less freely taken down, diffused by virtue of the written word, to be submitted to appreciation by all and transmitted to future generations, who, one can be sure, will do much better than we. . . . . All this presupposes freedom of expression. This is a liberty which so many political regimes these days do their best to stifle, in varying degrees (Hountondji 1970:130).

As a matter of interest, Bertrand Russell (1950:13) lodges a similar sort of complaint. This is indicative of the fact that, contrary to Hountondji (1970:130) who argues that philosophical discussion is impossible without political freedom, political freedom is not a necessary condition for philosophising. I am therefore inclined to the view that African philosophy can develop in the absence of political freedom.

Professional philosophy

What qualifies as professional philosophy in Africa is actually the finished product of trained, African philosophers whose definition and conception of African philosophy is:

the philosophy done by African philosophers whether it be in the area of logic, metaphysics, ethics or history of philosophy. It is desirable that the works be set in some African context, but it is not necessary that they be so (Bodunrin 1981a:162).

According to this approach, what passes as philosophy is that only which is "engrained with argument and criticism". This school of thought is represented chiefly by Wiredu, Hountondji, Bodunrin, and Oruka.

Despite the overall acceptability of the definition, the attempt to confine the phrase "professional African philosophy" to those works produced by trained *African* philosophers only has yet to be defended; for the works of some non-African philosophers who are currently working, or who have at some point in time worked in Africa, should, in my view, qualify as African professional philosophy – for instance the work of Francis Gillies (1980) and Gordon Hunnings (1972). Professional philosophy has been defined differently by different African philosophers, and Wiredu (1980:2–6) feels somewhat uncomfortable with the way in which Bodunrin defines African professional philosophy. But for the purposes of this discussion Bodunrin's definition quoted above is quite adequate.

Professional philosophy in Africa has its own limitations, as Oruka (1983:384) observes. The first is that contemporary African professional philosophy is too preoccupied with questions relating to what constitutes philosophy in general, and African philosophy in particular. As such, the literature realised is basically a metaphilosophy with no actual bearing on the African continent.

Secondly, professional African philosophy, it is argued, is mainly a critique of ethnophilosophy, has no history, and hence lacks a literature of its own. So, the only hope for progress in professional African philosophy lies in switching from predominantly protest-researches against ethnophilosophy to the study of "specific philosophical issues and concepts". However, this plea for redirection by Oruka seems to beg the very metaphilosophical question of what "issues and concepts" are philosophical. To study certain issues and concepts is to assume that these are indeed philosophical. But are not almost all concepts philosophical? Some issues, needless to say, are, while others are not philosophical at all.

CONCLUSION

To wind up the discussion, I concur with Wiredu that ultimately the question, "What is African philosophy?" should not be considered as requiring an immediate answer, though it should be provided with one in the concluding remarks of a philosophic research programme:

> Thus the question "What is African philosophy?" is at this juncture of our history at bottom, one to be answered not with a definition *per genus et differentia*, but rather with a programme (Wiredu 1980:14).

African philosophy is, as all philosophers in Africa admit, still in the process of becoming, and has yet to give birth to philosophic traditions from which definitions can be formulated as to what, in each particular tradition, constitutes African philosophy. This would obviously depend on the basic principles underpinning the various philosophic research programmes. Needless to say, since even Western philosophers define philosophy in different ways, there is no reason why African philosophers should all define African philosophy in the same way. So much, then, for the question of African philosophy.

SAGE PHILOSOPHY
HENRY O. ORUKA

ON THREE NEGATIVE CLAIMS

A major objective of this essay is to introduce the issue of research concerning the sagacious and philosophical thinking of indigenous native Africans whose lives are rooted in the cultural milieu of traditional Africa. What emerges from a dialogue with these thinkers provides an interesting and useful contrast with certain current trends in philosophical claims.

PHILOSOPHICAL UNANIMITY

The first claim is that of *ethnophilosophy*. This is the claim that traditional Africa is a place of philosophical unanimity allowing no room whatsoever for a Socrates or Descartes. This means that no indigenous African person had the frame of mind, let alone the inclination, to detach him/herself from prevailing established beliefs and taboos and offer a critical assessment or ratiocinative rejection of such beliefs. The practice of critique, it is claimed, is *Western* not *African*. And so it is in order, for example, that most current governments in Africa are based on a one-party system since an opposition party would be a *critique*. This claim is both false and absurd: it is false because traditional African thinkers are as diverse in their views as it is possible for any system of thinkers to be, and it is absurd because its application makes African politics totalitarian and African philosophy static.

Thinkers are not always rulers. Let us not forget the failure of Plato's *Republic*. Rulers everywhere demand unanimity, where thinkers crave for dialogue. If, then, traditional Africa had no opposition, this was at the level of rulers, not of thinkers.

PHILOSOPHY AND THE ART OF WRITING

The second philosophical claim with which the contents of this article is in contrast is the claim that philosophy is, and can only be, a "written" enterprise, and, accordingly, that a tradition without writing is incapable of philosophy. Therefore, a claim that there is philosophy (even when termed "sagacity") in illiterate Africa is regarded as a non-scientific, mythological claim. But this claim is also false, as we shall shortly show.

BLACK ATHENA

The third claim is that the sayings of the numerous Greek sages such as Thales, Anaximander, Heraclitus, Parmenides, and Socrates are "philosophical" while those of traditional African sages are anything but philosophical. This arises from the implicit belief that philosophy is an activity of some races and civilisations but not of others. Philosophy is "Greek" or "European" – it is white. Strictly speaking, it is "white-male". Since this claim is also false, however, it is part of the objective of this study to expose this falsehood too.

Some of the Greek sages are known and regarded as philosophers for having made only one or two utterances. Thales, for example, is known to have said that everything is made of water, while Heraclitus stated that strife is the truth of all life. Such sayings have been repeated and commented upon in numerous books, giving their utterers the prestigious status of philosophers. Now what reasonable proof do we have to believe that traditional Africa lacked any such sayings? We have no proof other than the claim that traditional African sages did not write their thoughts down. But neither did Thales and Socrates write down their sayings. That was a function carried out by others, and we have no idea how much of the distinction was made in the original oracles themselves.

Sage philosophy should be treated as one of the important trends in the development of philosophical thought in Africa. This can be seen in two aspects: firstly, the thoughts of the given and named individual sages express and defend themselves as philosophical counsellings on various issues of nature and human life. Anybody concerned with looking for answers or advice on fundamental moral and metaphysical questions will find much material in the thoughts of the sages. Secondly, their thoughts form significant raw data for technical philosophical reflections by professionals.

AREAS AND PERSONS OF THE RESEARCH

One significant question in our study relates to who is really a sage and how one goes about contacting and carrying out a dialogue with a person believed to be a sage. There is a general attitude harboured even in learned circles that a sage is one wise person in an illiterate or technologically undeveloped community whose residents depend much on the oracular sayings of seers to keep up with the mysteries and surprises of life.

Two points need to be mentioned here concerning this erroneous view of a sage. Firstly, it confuses a sage with a prophet. A sage may be a prophet and a prophet can be a sage, but the two are not identical. Secondly, the view mistakenly associates sagacity exclusively with illiteracy and frees literate and technologically developed societies from having any need or capability for sagacity.

A prophet makes predictions to his/her community about the future. Some prophets do this as a result of a flash of insight or revelation which they may not always be able to repeat. Others predict the future based on their insightful experience of past and present, and they skilfully extrapolate the future in a systematic sagacious reflection. In traditional Kenya, among the most famous of the prophets were Mugo wa Kibiru in Kikuyuland, Elija Masinde of the Luhyia community, and Sakawa of the Gusii in Nyanza. Almost every sage we interviewed in Kikuyuland knew something about Mugo wa Kibiru. Of Elija Masinde, who died as recently as 1987, much is known indeed. Thirty years before *uhuru*, he predicted the disappearance of white colonialists from positions of power in Kenya and the emergence of black power and the triumph of black culture and religion.

However, a prophet or anybody else is not a sage just because he/she has a flair for predicting the future. A person is a sage in the philosophic sense only to the extent that he/she is consistently concerned with the fundamental ethical and empirical issues and questions relevant to the society, and has the ability to offer insightful solutions to some of those issues. An instant and one-time only visionary may be a prophet, but not a sage. This is not to say that of these two individuals one is better or greater than the other. It is a question of recognising their non-identity.

In Africa, we have looked for sages among the non-literate masses. But this is not to demonstrate that *sagacity* is possible only in an illiterate culture. It is merely because we were not immediately interested in contacting sages from among

Africans endowed with the achievements of Western education. However, sages exist in all cultures and classes no matter whether a culture is literate or non-literate and technologically advanced or technologically underdeveloped. Indeed, sages are among the custodians of the survival of their respective societies. A society without its sages would easily get swallowed up as an undignified appendage of another. All societies use their sages or, at least, the ideas of their sages to defend and maintain their existence in the rough world of inter-societal conflict and exploitation. And it does not matter that such sages may not bear the name "sages" but rather the name "philosophers", "statesmen", or "warriors". So a sage may be a Gandhi, a Lenin, a Nyerere, or a John Rawls.

All this boils down to the fact that there is no special area or community where we must look for sages. There are sages in all societies and in the various aspects and classes of society. The one difference, however, is that some societies feel a need for a sage more than others. A society in which most people think the libraries, books, and museums are the real sources of what they need to know, will feel it has less need for a living sage than a society which lacks the good fortune of having numerous libraries, books, and museums.

When it comes to the question of who qualifies as a sage, the best judge must be the community from which the person hails. The researcher should follow up on the guidance provided by the community. However, the researcher must also be capable of assessing those alleged to be sages and dismissing others from the qualification for the trade, for a community may be misled in treating certain persons as sages. This is not strange, since following from the sayings of sage Stephen M. Kithanje, there are three kinds of wise persons:
1. those wise in service of their stomachs,
2. those wise for having learnt from the wisdom of the wise, and
3. those wise because they were born wise.

Those wise "in the service of their stomachs" may be too clever to make the community realise it has misjudged them as wise. It should be the function of the sage philosopher researcher to help detect such pseudo-sages.

A WORD TO CRITICS

The six trends

A number of years ago I described four trends in the development of African philosophy: ethnophilosophy, professional philosophy, nationalist-ideological philosophy, and philosophic sagacity. To this list, we probably need to add two more: the hermeneutic trend and the artistic or literary trend. The former consists of the philosophical analysis of concepts in a given African language to help clarify meaning and logical implications arising from the use of such concepts. Kwasi Wiredu, for example, is already doing this with useful results from an analysis of the Akan language. And studies by Kwame Gyekye, *An essay on African philosophical thought: The Akan conceptual scheme* (1987), and Barry Hallen and J.O. Sodipo, *Knowledge, belief and witchcraft* (1986), are, in my view, at best exercises in hermeneutic African philosophy. The two, however, tend to claim that they are reports of the philosophies and wisdom of indigenous traditional thinkers rather than the unhindered conceptual analysis of the language of their informants by the researchers. I will have something more to say about these two schemes shortly.

The artistic or literary trend consists of what Richard Bell, in elucidating Wamba dia Wamba and Wole Soyinka, refers to as the *narrative* element in African philosophy. Parallel to the philosophical trend created by African nationalists coming forward to offer philosophical or quasi-philosophical texts, which, to date, we have witnessed in such texts as Kwame Nkrumah's *Consciencism,* Julius Nyerere's *Ujamaa,* Léopold Senghor's *Nationhood and the African road to socialism,* Ali Mazrui's *The African condition,* Frantz Fanon's *The wretched of the earth,* Oginga Odinga's *Not yet uhuru,* and Daniel Arap Moi's *Nyayo philosophy* , we have a trend emanating from African literary intellectuals such as Chinua Achebe, Wole Soyinka, Ngugi wa Thiong'o, Okot p'Bitek, Taban Lo Lo Liyong, and many others. Does this then mean that there is philosophy in everything? Yes, it means, after all, that almost every subject can be studied to the highest level, i.e. that termed the level of "Doctorate in Philosophy". But if this is so, are professional philosophers not then redundant? They are not, for they alone are best equipped to help explicate the philosophical underpinnings in the texts and sayings of non-professional philosophers. Plato was professional, Socrates was not. And Plato helped to make Socrates explicit. Professional philosophers are to philosophy what linguists are to a language.

The issue concerning African philosophy is not really that it is now wide enough to embrace various kinds of intellectual approach to knowledge and life. The issue is that some scholars either explicitly or implicitly denied to African philosophy what they saw as the "Western mode" of philosophy. And this, as I have already mentioned, has been the idea that conceptual and critical analysis is "Western", and therefore foreign to the African mind. But why should this be so when Egyptian thought was not foreign to the Greek *logos?*

For many years now, it has occurred to me that one way of looking for traces of African philosophy is to wear the uniform of anthropological field work and use dialogical techniques to pass through anthropological fogs to the philosophical ground. The ethnophilosophers tried to do this, but were not able to pass through the fogs and instead came to rest contented with the fogs as the definition of African philosophy. This eventuality was inevitable since the ethnophilosophers started with the strong assumption that African philosophy and Western philosophy must and can only be different. But the assumption was a fallacy. In any case, how can you assume that that which you do not yet know must be different from that which you already know, unless you have already defined the *unknown* in opposition to the *known?*

Peter Bodunrin and Lansana Keita

Bodunrin objected to my project. The position of Bodunrin is similar to that of Hountondji, who, within our ranks, is associated with the remark that philosophy cannot develop fully unless it "writes its memoir" or "keeps a diary" (quoted in Oruka 1990b:xxii).

We should not make a great issue about writing. Writing is a good way to store thought and so to store philosophy. But writing is not thinking, and philosophy is thinking, and one can think even if one is incapable of, or has no facilities for, writing. In his article, "Narrative in African Philosophy", Richard Bell offers a good answer to the position of Hountondji and Bodunrin. Bell writes:

When Hountondji said, "truth is the very act of looking for truth, of enunciating propositions and trying to justify and found them", he concisely stated a Socratic vision of philosophy. What he failed to accept, however, and what his first criterion disallows, is that Socrates himself is a philosopher, an oral and sagacious philosopher! Though we certainly must accept the notion that without Plato, Socrates would be at best a faint memory, we can also construct from the early Platonic dialogues, a picture of Socrates's philosophy which had some autonomy from Plato's philosophy (1989:371).

Lansana Keita's (1985) main objection against the claim of philosophic sagacity is that it purports to be "unwritten". And if unwritten, how can its advocates demonstrate its existence except through writing, and if through writing then writing is (*à la* Bodunrin) a necessity for philosophy. Keita needs to be reminded that Socrates's philosophy, for example, did not exist just because Plato and others gave birth to it through their pens. Plato and others wrote it down (even if they distorted much of it) because it existed in the first place. And such is the case with sage philosophy in Africa. It exists independently of Odera Oruka or anybody else, so we search for it and write it down as this is the modern practice for recording thought. But this is not to discredit the philosophic merit of unwritten thought; the "unwritten" can be written, and vice versa. There is no mutual exclusivity between the unwritten and the written – what is *written* can be reported orally, and what is *oral* can be expressed in writing.

D. N. Kaphagawani

Kaphagawani's judgement is that "philosophic sagacity" is a kind of second order philosophy to ethnophilosophy and hence could not exist without the latter. This is correct, provided we equate ethnophilosophy with what I have called "culture philosophy", as Kaphagawani does. The two, however, are not quite the same. Culture philosophy consists of the beliefs, practices, myths, taboos, and general values of a people which govern their everyday life and are usually expressed and stored in their oral vocabulary. Ethnophilosophy, on the other hand, as we have come to understand it following Hountondji's popularisation of the same, is a written work of some scholar claiming to offer an objective description of the culture philosophy of a people. As a trend, ethnophilosophy is much more recent than culture philosophy which dates back to the days of the first ancients. In historical order philosophic sagacity antedates ethnophilosophy but is second order to culture philosophy. Thus, although ethnophilosophy can produce its own philosophic sagacity, which it has now done through the works of some of its professional critiques, philosophic sagacity can exist and has existed without it.

A Vienna Circle in African Philosophy?

The Nigerian philosopher, Campbell Momoh (1989 and 1991), is currently engaged in a harsh critique of the African philosophers he classifies as "Neo-logical positivists", among whom he regards Bodunrin, Hountondji, and Oruka as the hard core. However, Bodunrin's "The question of African philosophy" (1981a), which Momoh enjoys flogging, disappointed my interest in sage philosophy and I therefore replied to it in "Sagacity in African philosophy" (1983). Bodunrin was obliquely defended by Keita (1985), whose argument I have attempted to answer.

Interestingly, when it comes to suggesting what should constitute authentic African philosophy, Momoh offers no answer other than to fall back on sage philosophy. He does so apparently unaware of my own position and research on the subject.

Momoh's main concern is that those who demand that African philosophy must not shy away from employing logic, rigour, and critical analysis, deny by this demand the existence of "African Philosophy". And so they are *European-*influenced, particularly by the attitude of the "Vienna Circle" in Western philosophy.

To suggest that African philosophy should not abandon the use of logic and critical analysis is not to deny that there is African philosophy. Indeed, it is the person who thinks that such demands deny the existence of African philosophy that takes African philosophy to be free of logic, critique, and analysis, i.e. merely a matter of "unexamined" belief and attitude about life – a culture philosophy. And if this innocence of critique is what we see as a special characteristic of African philosophy, we should be reminded that it is nothing special to Africa: most Europeans and Americans also harbour unexamined beliefs and attitudes, for example, "the world and life are no more than what my community and ancestors left for me to believe." In America such an attitude may be expressed as follows: "I am a free person in a free world created by the wisdom of the founding fathers." This kind of attitude arises purely from a culture philosophy, it is self-praising and ideologically hostile or indifferent to values outside itself.

Postulating that logic, science, critique, and so on are un-African and typically *accidental* is an unconscious way of advancing imperialism, albeit a different form of imperialism, namely, academic and intellectual imperialism.

PHILOSOPHY AND CLASS IDEOLOGY
G.R. Hoffman

G.R. Hoffman, arguing from the standpoint of a limited orthodox Marxism, claims that my sage philosophy project is a bourgeois reflection which tends to isolate philosophy from ideology. To him, philosophy and ideology are identical and there can be no philosophy in a society without classes. Hence, to the extent that "sage philosophy" is a philosophy rooted in a classless peasant Africa, it cannot be a "philosophy" but is rather some form of "peasant storytelling". He admits ancient Greece had a philosophy, but then, he argues, ancient Greece was already a class society.

Philosophy is, I believe, among other things, a human reflection on life and nature, and on what there is and what could be. Such reflection takes place in every human society no matter whether the society has classes or is classless. Should we believe that in the predicted classless communist paradise, philosophy too will wither away? Even in the communist paradise people will seek to evaluate and reflect on the alternative choices facing them in life. For example, one living in such a paradise would still reflect on whether the material abundance inspires or stagnates human creative efforts.

I have already mentioned the tendency to treat a Greek sage such as Heraclitus as a philosopher while denying the label to an African sage such as Mbuya Akoko. The African sage is seen as a mere "peasant storyteller". Well, there are many routes to philosophy. Some may employ stories, poetry or oracles to philosophise. Indeed, those same Greek "philosophers" such as Heraclitus, the dialectician, and

Parmenides, the founder of abstract logic in the West, expressed their philosophies using oracular epigram, epic poem, and storytelling. In *The philosophers of Greece*, Robert Brumbaugh has the following to say about Heraclitus and Parmenides:

> A poet, rather than an engineer or mathematician, Heraclitus expressed in oracular epigrams the tension between the changeless, general ideas of philosophy and the transient concrete facts of life and death, of flow, of restless change (1981:43).

And again:

> Parmenides presented his ideas in an epic poem, a form that had been used by orphic poets for recording revelations. . . . The poem opens with a prologue, in which Parmenides journeys to the palace of the sun, where a goddess greets him and instructs him (Brumbaugh 1981:50).

Parmenides then begins telling the story of his journey and reception by the goddess:

> The goddess greeted me, taking my right hand in hers and spoke thus to me: Oh youth, whom immortal charioteers have brought, with their horses, here to my home: Greeting! (Brumbaugh 1981:50, quoted in Oruka 1990b:xxv)

Hoffmann appears to pour scorn on peasant storytelling, but the above passages are no less storytelling than the stories told by folk sages in rural Africa. Yet he takes the ancient Greek sages to be philosophers and denies the title to modern African sages.

PHILOSOPHICAL ANTHROPOLOGY

Recently, two studies conducted by professional philosophers in West Africa making use of anthropological generality to advance philosophical points have emerged. These are Barry Hallen and J.O. Sodipo's *Knowledge, belief and witchcraft: Analytic experiments in African philosophy* (1986), and Kwame Gyekye's *An essay on African philosophical thought: The Akan conceptual scheme* (1987).

These studies appear to resemble our project in Kenya. But the Kenya Project has one very significant difference. The concepts and issues discussed in the two studies are communalised, i.e. they are attributed to a community as represented by its *unanimous* thinkers. Emphasis is on the analysis of Yoruba language or Akan language in order to assemble, for example, what is to be seen as the Yoruba concept of "knowledge" or the Akan concept of "person". Gyekye (1987:ix) writes: "Philosophical concepts . . . can be found embedded in African proverbs, linguistic expressions, myths and folktales." But then why are the wise men or women (the *onisegun* in Yoruba) not mentioned by name? Hallen and Sodipo (1986:14) have an excuse: they agreed with the "informants" that their names would be kept secret. Also, during the course of their research, they could not cross-check their findings by mentioning the name of one informant to another. Every point was a matter only between the individual *onisegun* and the researchers. And the main reason is because the *onisegun* are masters of medicine who want to keep their trade secret and known only to themselves.

What emerges from such studies as these is an expert philosophical analysis of the ethnographical beliefs and conceptions of a select number of persons, with the analyst eager to stress in particular the common points between the informants.

The ideas presented are named Yoruba or Akan instead of being directly associated with the particular individual sages, as we have done in Kenya. Thus, the researchers are still trapped in anthropological mists.

Hallen and Sodipo even shy away from treating their informants as sages, conceiving instead of sagacity, as Hoffman does, as a "peasant storytelling". They write:

> Some of our colleagues in philosophy in Africa have already arrived at an assessment of our approach . . . on the basis of previous methodological and research publications arising from this same project. This assessment differs in several ways from our own understanding of what we are doing. In this assessment, our approach has been awarded the rather unpalatable (euphoniously, at least) appellation of "philosophic sagacity" (Hallen & Sodipo 1986:121).

The authors go on to suggest that their *onisegun* are neither philosophers nor sages:

> We have never claimed that this role entitles them to be acclaimed philosophers, in the professional, academic sense. . . . To return to "philosophic sagacity" the terms "philosophy" and "sage" are not, to our mind, compatible. The connotation of "sage" is that of a wise man, but wise in the archaic ("traditional") sense of being knowledgeable about his people's beliefs, and not particularly or deliberately critical of them. If the philosopher's task is to analyze/ criticize, there is then an element of inconsistency in conjoining the two (Hallen & Sodipo 1986:123).

Earlier in this article, I referred to the habit of associating sages with "primitive" societies only, and philosophers with civilised, developed societies. This is, however, a mistaken tendency. The philosopher's task is not just to "analyze/ criticize" (for there may be nothing to analyse or criticise). The philosopher must also intuit and postulate insights. And this latter role is one in which the sage usually earns high marks. It is also the role which differentiates great philosophers, even in the West, from the common run of the mill philosophers who start and end their careers in analysis. I have argued this point at length in "Cultural fundamentals in philosophy" (1990a).

The tendency in academic circles in the West has been to draw a dichotomy between reason or rationality, and intuition, and to claim that intuition is a primitive or mystical means of understanding and judgement. Rational persons are then regarded as incompatible with those governed by intuition. This is, I believe, a false notion.

In his biography of Winston Churchill, *The last lion*, William Manchester treats Churchill and Hitler as men of intuition rather than reason: "The inescapable fact is that Hitler and Churchill both were ruled not by reason but by intuition" (1988:351), and again, "Churchill was never a rational man . . . in moments of crisis he sought guidance not by reasoning but by intuition" (1988:664).

To return to the question of the relation between sage and philosopher: in a strict sense, a sage has at least two abilities, insight and ethical inspiration. So, a sage is wise, he/she has insight, but employs this for the ethical betterment of his/her community. A philosopher may be a sage, and vice versa. But many philosophers lack the ethical commitment and inspiration found in the sage. Indeed, the first teachers of Western philosophy, the sophists, were mercenaries who taught people how to twist ideas to win arguments regardless of the issue of truth. A sage proper is usually the friend of truth and wisdom. A sage may suppress truth, but only because wisdom dictates, and not because of some instrumental gain. Indeed, Pythagoras's definition of a philosopher as "the lover of wisdom" should have been reserved for a sage, since the sophists were the grave-diggers of wisdom and truth. Socrates was wrongly labelled a "philosopher"; for he was, first and foremost, a sage. Socrates used philosophy only as a means to advance his sagacity and expose the hypocrisies of his time. But after all this has been said, we still need to emphasise that sagacity and philosophy are not incompatible, as Hallen and Sodipo believe.

Hallen and Sodipo write that their *onisegun* were not just informants, they were far more elevated than this. The *onisegun* and the researchers, they claim, collaborated in the analysis:

> By the word "collaborative" we mean to emphasize the fact that the onisegun explicitly, deliberately, and without being "led" participate in the piecemeal analysis of their conceptual and thought system. . . . They are men of keen intellect as well as of extraordinary practical skills. This is the basis upon which we work with them, and this is the sense in which we refer to them as our traditional colleagues (Hallen & Sodipo 1986:124).

It must be the case that the *onisegun* – all of them – hold a common conceptual understanding of all the concepts analysed. For if they do not, and as they are not to know of one another, the researchers cannot easily arrive at a conclusion as to what philosophical meaning to derive from a given concept. If, however, the *onisegun* are in consensus, then what we have here is "anthropology" and not a "philosophy".

For their findings to constitute a philosophy, the researchers should stop over-emphasising that the *onisegun* collaborated with them in analysis. The *onisegun* probably supplied the raw data, i.e. the common Yoruba meanings of the concepts in question, and the researchers carried out a hermeneutical philosophical treatment of the data. The result is a contribution to a trend in African philosophy which I have already referred to as the "hermeneutical trend".

Onisegun, it is claimed, are not just "informants"; they are not "philosophers" in an academic or intellectual sense, and they are not "sages". Then what are they? It was Bodunrin who branded Hallen and Sodipo's project, and the Nairobi Project that I am involved in, as dealing with "philosophic sagacity". I pointed out the error of this view in my 1983 reply to Bodunrin, and I took time to emphasise the methodological difference between our Nairobi project and the "Sodipo-Hallen" approach.

One last word: I do not mean to draw an iron curtain between philosophy and anthropology. Indeed, as I mentioned earlier, one way to search for African philosophy is to pass through anthropology. A collaboration between philosophers and anthropologists can be very useful, especially if the two groups are conscious of what they know and do not know about each other.

At a Smithsonian Institute Seminar, I replied to D.A. Masoto (see Oruka 1990b:xxviii), who, in his paper "A half century of philosophy", had objected to my treatment of sages such as Paul Mbuya Akoko as philosophers. Masoto's objection was framed in the question, "Is one a philosopher just because one does make [sic] statements which are witty or non-mediocre?" (quoted in Oruka 1990b:xxviii–xxix). Masoto said that he found statements such as those attributed to Mbuya to be both "witty" and "non-mediocre". But he wondered if this was sufficient for them to qualify as philosophy.

Indeed, this may not be sufficient at all. There are many other factors in the sayings of Mbuya and sages of his type which contribute to making such sayings both sagacious and philosophical. One such factor is that the sayings are concerned with the most fundamental issues of human life. Another is that the sayings are accompanied by reflective insight. And there are other factors besides. It is my hope that researchers such as Masoto will in future look carefully and closely for such factors.

LINK+

Hold

St. Jean, Francine

patron name

SEP 2 5 2003

Remove Date

PLEASE NOTE

Fines are $1.00 per book,
per day overdue
and
replacement cost for
a lost Link+
book is $115.00.

ETHNOPHILOSOPHY AND ITS CRITICS

KWAME A. APPIAH

> By "African philosophy" I mean a set of texts, specifically the set of texts written by Africans themselves and described as philosophical by their authors themselves (Hountondji 1983b:33).

My epigraph is a definition proposed by the Beninois philosopher Paulin Hountondji – a definition that knowingly sidesteps what has been one of the cruces of philosophical debate in post-colonial black Africa. As we have puzzled over whether philosophers who happen to share a continent should for that reason be classified together, we have wondered, too, what sorts of intellectual activity should be called "philosophy". And, despite Hountondji, we know that not just any answer whatever to that question will do. If Sir Isaac Newton had lived in Africa, *Principia* would be, by this criterion, a work of African philosophy: for Newton called this, the first great text of modern theoretical physics, a work of natural philosophy. And thousands of books published each year in the United States on astrology or bogus Hindu mysticism would count by an analogous criterion as American philosophy.

Yet there is something to be said for Hountondji's strategy. While philosophers in Africa are seeking a role for themselves – or wondering, perhaps, whether they have any role at all – it may be as well not to rely too much on restrictive definitions. The worst that can be said, after all, against someone who calls a cookbook a contribution to the philosophy of cooking is, perhaps, that *philosophy* is a rather grandiose word.

We do well to be especially careful in applying definitions borrowed from the European philosophical traditions in which contemporary African university philosophers have been trained, because even within these traditions there is a notoriously wide range of opinion about the tasks and the topics of philosophy. And the disagreements within the Western academy about the character of philosophy pale into insignificance when we seek to give a unitary explanation of what makes both Confucius and Plato philosophers, or of what makes certain Indian and Chinese and Latin writings all *philosophical* texts.

So that, though we *could* try to approach the question of African philosophy by the method of definitions, asking what "philosophy" means and what it means to be African, settling the issue by definitional fiat is unlikely to be productive. A cookbook might better not be called "the philosophy of cooking", but it might be a good cookbook nevertheless. I suggest we start instead by examining the range of things that have come to be called "African philosophy" and asking which activities are worthwhile or interesting, and in what ways.

Since I do not wish to prejudge the issue of what should count as philosophy, I shall not assume, as Hountondji does, that it has to be written. There is something to be said for, and a good deal to be said against, a view of written African philosophy as continuous with earlier preliterate forms of intellectual activity. But my concern is primarily the situation of African intellectuals. And because the training of African university philosophers has been in the traditions of the West, we may begin here as elsewhere in the characterisation of African intellectual life – by relating the situation of the contemporary African intellectual to the cultures of their former colonisers. Provided we keep open minds, that need not blind us to the way that philosophy in Africa grows also out of her own indigenous traditions.

Western academic philosophy may have a hard time agreeing on its own definition, but any definition must be responsible to certain facts about the application of the concept. In the Euro-American tradition nothing can count as philosophy, for example, if it does not discuss problems that have a family resemblance to those problems that have centrally concerned those we call "philosophers". And nothing that does address itself to such problems but does so in ways that bear no family resemblance to traditional philosophical methods ought to count either. And the Wittgensteinian notion of family resemblance, here, is especially appropriate because a tradition, like a family, is something that changes from one generation to the next. Just as there may be no way of seeing me as especially like my remote ancestors, even though there are substantial similarities between the members of succeeding generations, so we are likely to be able to see the continuities between Plato and Frege only if we trace the steps in between. Contemporary philosophical discourse in the West is, like all discourse, the product of a history, and it is that history that explains why its many styles and problems hang together.

It would be difficult to give an exhaustive list of the problems that have come to be at the core of the Western tradition. But they can all, I think, be seen as growing out of a history of systematic reflection on widespread, pre-reflective beliefs about the nature of humankind, about the purposes, and about our knowledge of, and our place in, the cosmos. When these beliefs are not subjected to systematic and critical analysis we speak of "folk philosophy". But in Western academic philosophy, by contrast, for example, with anthropology or the history of ideas, what is required is not just a concern with the issues that are the topic of folk philosophy, but a critical discourse in which reason and argument play a central role.

We cannot, however, characterise philosophy simply as the discourse that applies to our folk beliefs the techniques of logic and reason. Not only because others – in physics and sociology and literary theory – make such arguments too, but because academic philosophy has come to be defined by a canon of subjects as well as by its argumentative method. If we understand "philosophy" as the tradition to which Plato and Aristotle, Descartes and Hume, Kant and Hegel belong, then at least the following concepts are bound to be regarded as central to that canon: beauty, being, causation, evil, God, gods, good, illusion, justice, knowledge, life, meaning, mind, person, reality, reason, right, truth, understanding, and wrong.

No doubt, not all cultures have exactly these concepts, but all of them will probably have concepts that bear a family resemblance to them. No human being could think about action who did not have a concept like our concept of causation; or think about why things happen in the world without such a concept. No one could have social norms without concepts at least something like *good, evil, right,* and *wrong* and a society without norms could hardly exist – not simply because the concept of a society is connected with the idea of shared norms, but because without common norms it is difficult to conceive of any collective action. Similarly, every culture has had views about what it is to have something like a mind, and of its relationship to the body; almost every culture has had a concept that plays some of the roles of concepts of divinity. And even if there were a human culture where nothing like any of these concepts was present, it is hard to make sense of the idea of a culture that did not have *any* crucial organising concepts.

There is, then, in every culture a folk philosophy, and implicit in that folk philosophy are all (or many) of the concepts that academic philosophers have made central to their study in the West. Of course, there might not be in every society people who pursued a systematic critical conceptual inquiry, but at least in every culture there is work for a philosopher, should one come along, to do.

There are many reasons for supposing that the task might be difficult, and many besides for doubting that every society would come, without exogenous intervention, to take up the project. But in the actual world, there *has* been an exogenous intervention, and it has left people with Western philosophical training in Africa. Because they are Africans rooted at least to some degree in their traditional cultures, and, at the same time, intellectuals trained in the traditions of the West, they face a special situation. They may choose to borrow the tools of Western philosophy for their work. But if they wish to pursue such conceptual inquiries in the thought worlds of their own traditions, they are bound to do so with a highly developed awareness of the challenges of Western ideas.

They are bound also to have to make choices within Western traditions. Not only is there a considerable difference in the styles of philosophy in France and in Germany, on the one hand, and in the anglophone world, on the other, but there is in Britain and in North America a wide divergence between the practice – and the metaphilosophical theory – of the dominant Anglo-American tradition, and the theory and practice of those whose work is conceived as closer to the traditions that remain strong in France and Germany. That the work of these latter philosophers is often referred to as "Continental" philosophy is a reflection of the essentially English origins of this dichotomisation.

When, in the first decades of this century, Frege began to replace Hegel as the tutelary spirit of English philosophy, the ethos of Continental historicist modes of thought was gradually eliminated from the philosophy faculties of English (though, curiously, not from Scottish) universities. In England the most influential body of philosophical practice through the mid-century derived from the transfer, through such figures as Ludwig Wittgenstein and Alfred Ayer, of the logical positivism of the Vienna circle to Oxford and Cambridge, into the context provided by the critique of idealism that had been begun by G.E. Moore and Bertrand Russell. The tradition that resulted came to be known as *analytical philosophy*.

This wind from Austria blew less vigorously in the United States, where pragmatism provided an indigenous alternative to the influences of the Vienna circle. But W.V.O. Quine, one of the most potent influences in the formation of the modern idiom of American philosophy, had been influenced, like Alfred Ayer, by his contacts with the Viennese school, even if, as he acknowledged, pragmatism was another of his major influences. While Wittgenstein brought the gospel to Cambridge, the influence of Moritz Schlick – a central figure in the organisation of the circle – and, above all, of Rudolf Carnap – from one perspective, the greatest systematic philosopher of the century – also left their impress on American academic philosophy.

For the many who resisted these strains of thought in the United States, the founding figure of their tradition remained not Frege, but Hegel, and the most influential of the moderns were not Wittgenstein and Carnap but Husserl and Heidegger. Those in this tradition felt at ease with Sartre, who had introduced into French philosophy the influence of the German phenomenologists, and turned it, as he claimed, to good existentialist use. They continued to read Schopenhauer. They rediscovered Nietzsche – decontaminated of his Nazi associations – after the Second World War. The analytical philosophers, meanwhile, were reading Russell and Moore and the early Wittgenstein – and later on Carnap and the later Wittgenstein and Quine – and spending more and more of their time on something called the *philosophy of language.*

Far more striking to the casual observer than the differences in doctrines of these groups – for neither "Continental" nor "analytical" philosophy is easily characterised by a creed – are their differences in method and idiom. They share, of course, a vocabulary of key words that belongs to the language of the Western philosophical tradition – *truth* and *meaning*, for example, being familiar lexical presences for each – but they often put these shared words to radically different uses; and words like *being* (for the analyticals), and *reference* (for the Continentals), which were important for the other tradition, became for a period virtually taboo.

For an outsider this fuss may seem simply preposterous: what is at stake, after all, is only the right to the label "philosophy". Why should it matter to anyone (analytic or Continental) whether someone else (Continental or analytic) cares to call what they are doing by this label? But the answer is simple: "philosophy" is the highest-status label of Western Humanism. The claim to philosophy is the claim to what is most important, most difficult, most fundamental in the Western tradition. And the enduring power of that claim is reflected in the commonest response from the inquisitive French or British or American stranger who asks what I do: "Philosophy?" Pause. "You must be very clever." To admit to a Western audience that philosophers, like all intellectuals, can be witless as well as smart; and that the questions we ask and answer are hard, but no harder than the questions in physics or literary theory; to admit *that* – our darkest secret – would be to throw away a couple of millennia of cultural capital.

We can characterise the divided house of anglophone academic philosophy not only by its double idiom but also by a double self-image. Analytical philosophers think of themselves as on the side of logic, science, and method against superstition; on the side of a modest and careful search for truth against bombast. For them philosophy is often a technical subject, and a grasp of these technicalities is a condition of professional competence. Continentals believe that the issues they deal with are difficult and important and that their tradition is continuous with the best and deepest of the Western tradition of humanistic scholarship. They are likely to see philosophy as continuous not with the sciences but with literature and the arts. If they complain about the analyticals, they complain that their work is shallow, cold, dry, inconsequential; that they evade the difficulty of the central philosophical questions by reducing them to trivial, often semantic, debates; that they lack a sense of the historical development of the life of reason. And, in return, the analyticals are likely to object that Continentals mistake obscurantism for profundity.

These self- (and other) images are, I suppose, stereotypes. Few, on either "side", express themselves as clearly and strongly as this; most analytical philosophers will agree that there is some interest in, say, Sartre's moral psychology, and most Continentals will agree that analytical philosophy of logic and language, while not nearly as important as it is supposed to be, is often the work of subtle and gifted minds. But though these images are stereotypes, they are not, in my view, caricatures. Bernard Williams, a leading British analytical philosopher, has written recently that analytical philosophy "has no distinctive subject matter":

> What distinguishes analytical philosophy from other contemporary philosophy (though not from much philosophy of other times) is a certain way of going on, which involves argument, distinctions, and, so far as it remembers to try to achieve it and succeeds, moderately plain speech. As an alternative to plain speech, it distinguishes sharply between obscurity and technicality. It always rejects the first, but the second it sometimes finds a necessity. This feature peculiarly enrages some of its enemies. Wanting philosophy to be at once profound and accessible, they resent technicality but are comforted by obscurity (1985:6).

"A certain way of going on": no choice of phrasing could more vividly display the laid-back tone of much analytical philosophising, the sense that we shall go further, faster, if we do not make too much fuss. The "enemies" are bound to be enraged by someone who speaks of "a certain way of going on", when what is at issue is philosophical methodology, not least because this conversational tone attempts to claim as natural and uncomplicated what is often, from another point of view, a profoundly challenging philosophical claim. For anyone who has watched the Anglo-American philosophical scene, even from afar, it will not be hard to guess who these "enemies" are.

In the United States this discourse of mutual incomprehension and distaste has become more complicated in recent years. Many younger philosophers see little point in the labels. There is a tendency more and more to speak – as Williams does here – of differences of idiom and to hope for some sort of common ground. But in the academy, as in politics, true detente requires more than the regular expression of a desire for rapprochement.

The Continentals in the United States, though drawing on the canon of academic philosophy in France and Germany, differed from their literally European cousins in one major respect. For political philosophy, and in particular, various readings of and reactions to Marxism, have never had the central place in the American tradition that they have had in Europe. In Europe, figures such as Althusser and Sartre in France, or Adorno or Habermas in Germany, have developed a philosophical reflection on politics that takes Marxism seriously, however much it is criticised.

Recent rapprochements made the work of European philosophers increasingly familiar to Anglo-American philosophers, but there is also in Europe a growing interest in the work of the British, North American, and Australian philosophers who constitute the canon of analytical philosophy. Nevertheless, we must recognise, in the first twenty-five years of the post-war era, two powerful and powerfully distinct philosophical traditions in the West. And it was in those decades that the philosophy departments of anglophone and francophone Africa were established.

Philosophers in African philosophy departments inherited, then, the two warring Western traditions, and one thing that we can say with certainty is that if we accept Hountondji's proposal we shall, as a result, have to count as African philosophy many texts whose connection with Africa is no more (and, one should say, no less) profound than the nationality of their authors. This is a consequence Hountondji (1983b:66) accepts. His definition, with which I began, is intended to restore the simple, obvious truth that Africa is above all a continent and the concept of Africa an empirical, geographical concept and not a metaphysical one (Hountondji 1983b:66).

But the important questions for an African scholar about his/her involvement with Western academic philosophy are not to be settled by facts of geography. For the scholar will want to ask, firstly, if there is anything distinctive he/she can bring to the Western tradition from his/her history, culture, language, and traditions and, secondly, what, in Africa, the teaching and writing of Western-style philosophy is for.

Now many contemporary philosophers in the West would treat the question as to what philosophy is *for* with the special disdain reserved for philistinism. Of course, they have their reasons for doing philosophy, and most believe that the fact that philosophy is studied in their universities is a positive good for their culture. But they are inclined to regard as a complex question what positive good it is. And, since the practice of philosophy is not seriously threatened, however tight the purse strings of the academy are drawn, they do not spend much time on answering it. Granted that philosophy serves some purpose, the task is not to justify it, but to do it.

In Africa the question of the usefulness of philosophy is not so easily put aside. Universities compete with other areas of national life for the scarce resources of development. For the politicians, for the populace generally, it is easy to see why it is worth having doctors, engineers, economists, even lawyers; it is easy, too, to believe that the theoretical sciences, from physics to jurisprudence, are inextricably bound up with the applied ones. But the humanities, and above all, philosophy, are not so easily valued. For philosophy as it is practised in the university is peculiarly remote from the thoughts of ordinary individuals, in Africa as elsewhere, about truth and reason, gods and good, matter and mind.

The worth of any formal philosophy is especially hard to see outside the Islamised regions, because there is no indigenous formal tradition. Muslims have a long history of philosophical writing, much of it written in Africa, so that the study of philosophy can be seen as traditional (and therefore holy) and endogenous (and therefore nationalistic). But in much of black Africa there is no Islamic tradition, indeed no written tradition at all. The sense in which there is a philosophical tradition is, as I suggested earlier, that there is an oral folk philosophy, whose authority lies largely in its purported antiquity, not in the quality of the reasoning – or the evidence – that sustains it, and which is usually unable to treat critical activity as disinterested. Given the not-unreasonable post-colonial scepticism about everything foreign, it is natural that there should be a growing literature, written by Africans trained in Western philosophy, that asks what African philosophy is for. Not only is this natural, it is surely also salutary – even if this means that much time is taken up, in the words of the Ghanaian philosopher Kwasi Wiredu (1980:xi), "talking *about* African philosophy as distinct from actually doing it".

In Wiredu's conception, which grows out of the Anglo-American tradition, African philosophy may borrow and refine the methods of Western philosophy and apply them to the analysis of the conceptual problems of African life. To do this, in his view, it is necessary first to develop a sympathetic reflective understanding of traditional modes of thought. And, to a large extent, our modes of thought remain (as I shall argue later) much closer to traditional ideas than many are willing to acknowledge. Since the specific ideas of different African cultures vary, each philosopher must speak from within some specific tradition; the project is African only because the philosopher is, say, Akan, and the Akan are geographically African.

But others have sought to make their philosophy African in a different way. They have asked the question, "Is there an African philosophy?" and answered it in the affirmative. Since *philosophy* is so equivocal a word, however, there are a number of ways in which the question might be taken.

If it means, "Is there folk philosophy in Africa?" the answer is: "Africa has living people and cultures and therefore, of necessity, folk philosophies." But if *African* in *African philosophy* is meant to distinguish a natural kind, there seems to be no terribly good reason for supposing that the answer should be yes. Why should the Zulu, the Azande, the Hausa, and the Asante have the same concepts or the same beliefs about those matters which the concepts are used to think about and discuss? Indeed, it seems they do not. If similarities are expected, it should be on the basis of the similarities between the economies and social structures of traditional societies or as the result of cultural exchanges; but the cultural exchange across the continent at the level of ideas has been limited by the absence of writing, and the socioeconomic similarities are often exaggerated. Many African societies have as much in common with traditional societies that are not African as they do with each other.

The question may, however, be intended as one about philosophy in the sense of the Western academic canon: the sense in which Socrates or Thales is reputed to be the first Western philosopher. And in this sense the question is more difficult. Certainly the elders of many African societies discuss questions about right and wrong, life and death, the person and immortality. They even discuss the question whether an argument is a good argument or a consideration a weighty consideration.

And this is at least the beginning of philosophy as a reflective activity. But often difficult problems are put aside by appealing to "what the ancestors have said" in a way that is reminiscent of argument from authority in the Middle Ages in Europe. And just as those philosophers in the scholastic tradition who argued that something must be so because "the Philosopher" – Aristotle – had said it was so, were arguing badly, so it seems to me that the elders who argue this way are simply making bad arguments. But the idea of a discourse free from the constraints of the authority of tradition is an extraordinarily modern conception in Europe – and it should not be a matter of shame and reproach that those elders who have faced the question whether the ancestors might have been wrong have been, in all probability, quite few. Creative, critical philosophers have been few in the history of the West, and their bravery has often been made easier by their access to a written critical tradition. Oral traditions have a habit of transmitting only the consensus, the accepted view: those who are in intellectual rebellion (and European anthropologists and missionaries have met plenty of these) often have to begin in each generation all over again.

I have already said that there is no reason to think that the folk philosophies of Africa are uniform. What account can we give, then, of the belief that there is a role for something that is importantly African to be done in philosophy? Part of the explanation must lie, as we have seen, in racialism: what more natural reaction to a European culture that claims – with Hume and Hegel – that the intellect is the property of men with white skins, than to insist there is something important in the sphere of the intellect that belongs to black men? If there is white philosophy, why not also black philosophy? The origins of the argument are intelligible – and it is somehow healthier than the view of the apostles of Negritude, that black men should give the intellect over to whites and explore the affective realm that is their special property. Unlike Césaire (1971:117), we need not say, "Eia for those who never invented anything."

But black philosophy must be rejected, for its defence depends on the essentially racist presuppositions of the white philosophy whose antithesis it is. Ethnocentrism – which is an unimaginative attitude to one's own culture – is in danger of falling into racism, which is an absurd attitude to the colour of someone else's skin.

So that if the argument for an African philosophy is not to be racist, then some claim must be substantiated to the effect that there are important problems of morals or epistemology or ontology that are common in the situation of those on the African continent. And the source of that common problematic, if it cannot be racial, must lie in the African environment or in African history.

Now you might say that I have just *assumed* that an argument for an African philosophy must be an argument that there are problems in philosophy that are either crucially or uniquely raised in the African situation, and that I have assumed this even though it is clear that differences in styles of philosophy are often, as I have said, not so much differences in manner as in method. But these assumptions are surely quite unreasonable. For what reasons could there be in the African situation for supposing that we must deal with philosophy in a particular way? The most that can be said is that what our problems are will determine what methods are appropriate – and perhaps the problems that concern us now are so different from European philosophical problems that we will have to develop a radically different methodology. If, however, African philosophy shares neither the problems nor the methods of Western philosophy, one is bound to wonder what the point is of calling the activity "philosophy" at all. There is, surely, no more reason to suppose that every intellectual activity in the West should have an African twin than there is to suppose that we must have African harpsichords or African sonnets.

But, of course, I have left something out of account. "Philosophy", as I said earlier, is the highest-status label of Western Humanism. The urge to find something in Africa that "lives up to" the label is, in part, a question of wanting to find something in Africa that *deserves* the dignity; that warrants the respect that we have been taught (in our Western or Westernised schools and colleges) is due to Plato and Aristotle, Kant and Hegel. And part of a proper response to this impulse is to demystify that canonical respect; something that requires only, surely, that we acknowledge the preposterous foundations upon which it is established.

Our textbook histories of Western culture may insist that Plato and Aristotle are at the root of its central insights. But if we ask ourselves what is most valuable in Euro-American culture, we shall surely want to mention, for example, democracy, to which Plato and Aristotle – and, for that matter, Kant and Hegel – were opposed; applied science and technology, to which Plato contributed nothing and Aristotle provided a long false start whose overthrow in the Renaissance finally made possible the scientific revolution; and a literary culture that refers back to Plato and Aristotle almost exclusively in moments of Christian religiosity (which they would have repudiated) or snobbism or hocus-pocus. The point is not that these are authors we should not read – reading them has provided me, as it has provided many others, with some of the greatest pleasures of my reading life – but rather that we should not read them as repositories of forgotten truth or sources of timeless value. Plato and Aristotle are often interesting because they are wicked and wrong; because they provide us with access to worlds of thought that are alien, stretching our conception of the range of human thought; because we can trace, in tracing the history of reflection on their work, a single fascinating strand in the history of the mental life of our species.

Even if the philosophical canon *were* the *fons et origo* of all value in Western culture – and even if there were nothing to match up to it in Africa – what, more than a moment's regret that we can share pride in it only as human beings and not as Africans, would hang on it? Surely not that we would thereby be deprived of some rights against the West? There is no reason to accept the astonishing hyperbole that what is most of value to Westerners (or to anyone else) in their culture – what will justify it at the Last Judgment – is to be found in a few-score philosophical works written over a couple of millennia by a small company of Western European men. It is not as members of the national (or racial or intellectual) community from which these writers sprang that Europeans deserve equality of respect or claim their rights under the United Nations Declaration of Human Rights – and not to belong to that community is, in consequence, no bar to claiming those rights for the rest of us.

If we want to find a place for philosophy in Africa, let us begin with a sense of proportion about its significance; I am all in favour of keeping my job, but not at the price of an ignoble lie.

What projects, then, *should* philosophers concerned with the intellectual health of the continent pursue? Richard Wright has provided an accurate survey of the answers to this question that are currently on offer:

> (1) The thought of the African people is intrinsically valuable and should be studied for that reason, if for no other; (2) it is important to the history of ideas that we discover and understand the relation between (or influence of) African thought and the thought of the Western world. For, if Western civilization had its origin on the African continent . . . the correct pattern of intellectual development . . . will become clear only as we begin to understand the basis and direction of that development . . . (3) it is important in understanding practical affairs that we clearly delineate their underlying philosophical motivation (1979:26–27).

The first of these options leads swiftly to what Hountondji calls "ethnophilosophy", the attempt to explore and systematise the conceptual world of Africa's traditional cultures. It amounts, in effect, to adopting the approach of a folklorist: doing the natural history of traditional folk thought about the central issues of human life.

The founding text of ethnophilosophy is *La philosophie bantoue*, a book in which the Belgian missionary, Father Placide Tempels, sought to characterise the essential features of the thought of the Bantu-speaking peoples of central and southern Africa. Tempels argued that the Bantu way of thought had at its centre a notion of "force", a notion that occupied the position of privilege of the notion of "being" in Western (by which, as a Catholic, he meant Thomist) thought. I do not myself believe that this way of formulating his claim has been helpful. But Tempels's influential formulation can at least be seen as registering the crucial role played by concepts of agency in many traditional African cultures, in places where the West has come to see only efficient – that is, impersonal – causation.

Though much ethnophilosophical material is indeed very interesting – at least where it is not, as it too often is, woefully inaccurate – we should go carefully in discussing how to put it to philosophical use. For though anthropology (like travel) may broaden the mind, the kind of analytical work that needs to be done on these concepts is not something that is easily done second-hand, and most anthropological reports – though not, perhaps, the best ones – are pretty philosophically naive. This would be mere carping (there is, after all, too little written about Africa that is philosophically serious) were it not for the fact that the view that African philosophy is just ethnophilosophy has been largely assumed by those who have thought about what African philosophers should study.

Now the description of someone else's folk philosophy, without any serious analysis of its concepts or any critical reflection on how understanding the world with those concepts allows us to appreciate what may not be appreciated in other conceptual schemes, is surely a mere curiosity. It might, I suppose, lead to intellectual tolerance, but it might just as easily lead to chauvinism or total incomprehension: "So they believe all that; so what? They're wrong, aren't they?"

Of course, where the beliefs are those of our *own* cultures, we cannot make this response. You cannot intelligibly say: "We believe all that; so what? We're wrong, aren't we?" But the fact is that philosophers in Africa are bound, by their position as intellectuals educated in the shadow of the West, to adopt an essentially comparative perspective. Even if it is their own traditions they are analysing, they are bound to see them in the context of European (and often Islamic) as well as other African cultures. No one can be happy celebrating his/her own tradition in the knowledge that it makes claims inconsistent with other systems, without beginning to wonder which system is right about which issues. A cosy celebration of one's own conceptual and theoretical resources is a simple impossibility. For one has to live one's life through concepts, and, despite the fact that people everywhere constantly inhabit inconsistent presuppositions, in one life at one time there can sometimes be space for only one system. That system does not have to be either "Western" or "traditional": it can take elements of each and create new ones of its own. But the life of reason requires the integration of elements: if elements in different systems or within the same system are incompatible, something has to go.

Most existing ethnophilosophy is predicated on two major assumptions. The first, which Hountondji has dubbed "unanimism", is the factual assumption, which I have already rejected, that there is some central body of ideas that is shared by black Africans quite generally. The second is the evaluative assumption that the recovery of this tradition is worthwhile.

Against the dominant stream of ethnophilosophy runs a current of recent work, which explicitly denies one or both of the presuppositions of ethnophilosophy. Hountondji's *African philosophy: Myth and reality* – originally published in French, with the subtitle, "a critique of ethnophilosophy", in 1976 – and Marcien Towa's 1971 *Essai sur la problématique philosophique dans l'Afrique actuelle*, in francophone Africa, and Wiredu's 1980 *Philosophy and an African culture*, in anglophone Africa, are the major texts of this second tradition.

Towa and Wiredu have made a sustained assault on the evaluative assumption: Wiredu, by arguing persuasively that there is no philosophical interest in a recovery and preservation of traditional ideas that is not critical; Towa in suggesting, following Césaire, that the mere accumulation of traditions is a diversion from engagement with the real political issues facing Africa, issues her philosophers ought to articulate and address. Hountondji endorses both these lines of attack, but he combines them with a sustained attack on the unanimism that undergirds the project of ethnophilosophy. I shall return to the work of Hountondji and Wiredu at the end of this essay. But we can examine both the prospects and the pitfalls of ethnophilosophy by examining some representative work in this tradition.

If there is one question, above all, that is almost never satisfactorily addressed by such work, it is what the *point* is of this cataloguing of thought worlds. Wiredu has argued that it serves no *philosophical* purpose: what other purposes could it serve? Consider a couple of the papers Richard Wright has collected in *African philosophy: An introduction* – John Ayoade's (1979) discussion of "Time in Yoruba thought", and Helaine Minkus's (1979) essay, apropos of Ghana, on "Causal theory in Akwapim Akan philosophy" – and ask the question as sharply as it can be phrased: since, in Hountondji's (1983b:161) words, "African traditions are no more homogeneous than those of any other continent", why should anyone who is neither from Akwapim nor from Yorubaland take an interest in these papers?

This question is raised particularly urgently for me because the Twi-speaking peoples of Akwapim share most of the concepts and the language of Asante, my home. At the points of divergence between Akwapim beliefs (as reported by Minkus) and Asante beliefs, even an unphilosophical Asante might wish to raise the question Minkus never addresses, the question whether what the Akwapim Akan believe is *true*. Minkus (1979:127) has a paragraph of discussion of the fact that Akan thought – like natural science, Christianity, Islam, and the quantum theory – has features that "insulate it from attack and doubt", in effect observing that this way of looking at the world has the properties that the great French philosopher-physicist, Pierre Duhem, noticed in physical theory. But what conclusions are we supposed to draw from this – the only critical observation Minkus makes?

The applicability of Duhem's thesis to traditional religion is a mark of certain underlying similarities of Western and traditional – in short, of human – modes of thought. But here I want simply to make the point that since, as I have argued, the African philosopher is bound to adopt an essentially comparative perspective, Minkus, in adopting an essentially descriptive enterprise, stops precisely at the point where the questions that are urgent for us begin.

The beginnings of a more comparative analysis *are* to be found in an interesting paper of Ben Oguah's: "African and Western philosophy: A comparative study" (1979). Oguah argues that the materials for reflecting on certain perennial problems of Western philosophy are available in the Fanti conceptual vocabulary. Thus he shows convincingly (as I, at least, would expect) that the concepts necessary to discuss the nature of the person, of other minds, of freedom of the will, of immortality, of rationalism and empiricism – in short, of the whole gamut of philosophical questions familiar in the West – exist in the Fanti vocabulary. To organise these concepts and their relations into a coherent system is the task of what the English philosopher Peter Strawson (1959) – one of Oguah's teachers – has called "descriptive metaphysics". But, as many philosophers have observed in discussing Strawson's work, though this sort of careful conceptual analysis is indeed a helpful preliminary to the philosophical project, it is surely only a preliminary to the "revisionary metaphysics" that seeks to assess our most general concepts and beliefs, to look for system in them, to evaluate them critically, and, where necessary, to propose and develop new ways of thinking about the world.

More than this, the systematisation of what exists prior to the sort of organised, written collaborative discourse that academic philosophy represents inevitably changes the character of our ideas. The image of philosophy presented by British conceptual analysis in the 1950s and 1960s as an activity that takes as its material the raw stuff of everyday conceptual life, merely organising and articulating it, is false to the experience of doing philosophy. We may agree with J.L. Austin that the structure of the concepts with which people ordinarily operate is highly complex and subtly nuanced, without agreeing that the process of making the implicit explicit leaves the pre-reflective texture of our thought unchanged.

A simple example will make the point for me. If we were reporting, as ethnographers, the views of rural French men and women, we should have to accept that many of them believe that something of themselves – their spirit, as we might say – survives the death of their bodies. But to systematise this sort of view, we should have to decide whether this entity has a location in the ordinary world of space and time. Many of these people, if asked, would be likely, if they took any view of the matter at all, to answer that it does not. We can imagine that, for them, the idea of disembodied existence is essentially subjectively conceived as the having of experiences without the possession of a body. But philosophical reflection stretching back through Wittgenstein to Descartes has led many of us to conclude that this notion is just incoherent. And since anyone with a Western philosophical training knows that there are grounds for thinking it incoherent, there is something less than sane in the intellectual project of recovering this notion without at least considering whether, in the end, it makes sense.

We know there are mystical traditions, in Catholicism or Buddhism, for example, that have at their core a belief in the ultimate unintelligibility of the deepest truths about our human situation; each believes that there are "mysteries in the strict sense". John Skorupski summarises the Catholic position thus:

> In a nutshell, a "mystery" is a doctrine whose truth cannot be demonstrated but must be taken on faith; a mystery "in the strict sense" is a doctrine such that not merely the fact that it is true, but also the fact that it has definite coherent sense must be taken on faith (1976:218).

But even in these traditions the class of such mysteries is restricted, and their truth and intelligibility have the sanction not of evidence and argument, it is true, but, in the one case, of divine revelation and, in the other, of a certain kind of contemplative experience.

There is one other crucial example of an acceptance of unintelligibility, which is of importance to an understanding of Western intellectual life, namely, the quantum theory. Here the acceptance of indeterminism requires us also to accept the ultimate inexplicability of certain events – they are simply and irreducibly random – and thus to give up the Laplacean vision of a world whose motions are completely predictable and determined by intelligible laws. But there is a tremendous resistance – epitomised in Einstein's pained exclamation that God does not play dice with the world – to accepting this. And if the ultimate unintelligibility of some aspects of the world is accepted, it is accepted only reluctantly and in the face of very powerful evidence. If science accepts unintelligibility, it is in the name of truth.

In the Catholic tradition, too, there is no question but that the truth of the mysteries is conceived of as the source of their importance. Perhaps the Western Catholic, in religious moments, can accept this restricted domain of doctrines beyond our capacity for interpretation, but an intellectual, a university woman or man, formed at least in part in the Western tradition, cannot allow the proliferation of unintelligibility. If the Buddhist sage really does simply accept the unknowability of the world, it is an acceptance that most African intellectuals will find as hard as most European ones to share.

Because the issues of truth and intelligibility are thus bound to be central to any intellectual project conceived of by someone with a Western conception of a reflective life, Oguah (1979) faces, as a result, the following dilemma. If, on the one hand, his view is that European and Fanti concepts are the same but their beliefs are different, a crucial question, which he hardly raises, is, "Who is right?". And if, on the other hand, the concepts are different, the interesting question is whether the Fanti concepts are more appropriate to the world than European ones, or, if not, at least more appropriate to the problems and form of life of the Fanti. In either case, to refuse to go beyond mere description of the conceptual situation seems at best eccentric, at worst simply irresponsible.

These problems are, of course, problems in the natural and biological sciences or in anthropology or comparative thought. But a philosopher, with a philosopher's training, is at least in a better position to see and say what Fanti concepts are, and how they work, than many social scientists – in particular if that philosopher is, like Oguah, a Fanti. And, at all events, in the present African situation this preliminary work must be done by somebody, if the inescapable task of deciding who is right – and therefore whether or not to give up traditional Fanti modes of thought – is to be rationally accomplished. Not to address this issue is to leave the outcome in the hands not of reason but of chance; or, perhaps, to leave the intellectual future of the Fanti-speaking peoples, and that of other Africans, to be decided by the fact of the technological superiority of the already hegemonic cultures of the metropolitan world.

There is, therefore, in my view, no possibility of not bringing a Western philosophical training to bear. What we must be careful of is simply projecting Western ideas, along with these Western-derived methods, onto the indigenous conceptual framework, and Oguah seems to me not to have successfully negotiated this problem. I want to consider this issue in the context of his interesting discussion of Fanti philosophy of mind, but for reasons that will become clear, I shall begin by saying a little about the philosophical psychology of the Asante people, whose culture and language belong to the same Akan culture area as the Fanti.

According to most traditional Asante people, a person consists of a body (*nipadua*) made from the blood of the mother (the *mogya*); the *sunsum*, which is the main bearer of one's personality; and a third entity, the *okra*. The *sunsum* derives from the father at conception. The *okra*, a sort of life force, departs the body only at the person's last breath; it is sometimes, as with the Greeks and Hebrews, identified with breath and is often said to be sent to a person at birth, as the bearer of one's *nkrabea*, or destiny, from God. The *sunsum*, unlike the *okra*, may leave the body during life and does so, for example, in sleep – dreams being thought to be the perceptions of a person's *sunsum* on its nightly peregrinations. Since the *sunsum* is a real entity, dreaming that you have committed an offence is evidence that you have committed it, and, for example, a man who dreams that he has had sexual intercourse with another man's wife is liable for the adultery fees that are paid for daytime offences.

Since Asante-Twi and Fanti-Twi are largely mutually intelligible, it is reasonable, I think, to consider Oguah's account in the light of these Asante conceptions. Oguah asserts that the Fanti conceptual scheme is dualist – in fact, Cartesian. But at least three caveats need to be entered about this claim. Firstly, since Fanti is an Akan language and the word *okra*, which Oguah translates as soul is, of course, the same as the word for what, in Asante, I identified not with the mind but with the life force, we might wonder why there is no mention, in Oguah, of the *sunsum*. There is, of course, no reason why the Fanti should have precisely the tripartite system we find among the Asante (and other Akan peoples in, for example, Akwapim), and there is some tendency among modern Asante speakers as well to use the words *okra* and *sunsum* almost interchangeably, even while insisting, when asked, on the distinctness of their referents. But Oguah's access, as a contemporary native speaker of Fanti-Twi, is to these terms as mediated by the many Christian influences that have settled in the coastal regions of Ghana, after four centuries of trade and missions from Europe, and over a century of an extensive British cultural presence in the Gold Coast colony. Even if, therefore, there is, for the Fanti, no *sunsum,* we are not free to infer that this is a fact about unadulterated Fanti traditions: it might be the result of Christianisation.

I emphatically do not wish to imply that Christian beliefs are *in se* un-African. But the Fanti live on the coast of modern Ghana, and this case allows us to focus on the question whether, in cultures that have exchanged goods, people, and ideas with each other and with Europe (or, in East Africa, with the Middle and Far East) for many centuries, it makes sense to insist on the possibility of identifying some pre-colonial system of ideas as *the* Fanti tradition. Of course, for a Fanti speaker today the beliefs of his/her ancestors are surely not intrinsically more valuable than the beliefs of his/her contemporaries, and it is perfectly reasonable for Oguah to treat the concepts as he finds them – now – in his own culture. But the fact that there is reason to suppose that these beliefs are the product of a history of cultural exchanges, that they are probably not, as the elders sometimes claim, the unadulterated legacy of immemorial tradition, *does* bring into sharp relief the question why these particular beliefs should be granted a special status. If our ancestors believed differently, why should not our descendants? Such reflection is bound to make especially compelling the demand, to which I have returned again and again, for African intellectuals to give a critical – which does *not* mean an unsympathetic – reading of the modes of thought of their less Western influenced sisters and brothers.

Secondly, however, and putting aside the question whether this reportage is, by itself, what is needed, the evidence that the Fanti are now dualists, and Cartesian dualists at that, is surely not very compelling. For a Cartesian dualist, mind and body are separate substances, and this doctrine which I admit to finding less than easy to understand is not one I would expect to find among the Fanti. The Fanti, for example, according to Oguah's (1979:170) own account, hold that "what happens to the *okra* takes effect in the *honam*" – that is, the body. And Oguah offers no evidence that they find this idea at all problematic. But if that is so, their dualism must be at least in some respects different from Descartes's, since, for a Cartesian, the relation of mind and body *is* felt as problematic.

More than this, there is, as Kwame Gyekye – another distinguished Twi-speaking philosopher – has pointed out (1995:85–103), a good deal of evidence that the Akan regard the psychic component of the person as having many rather physical-sounding properties. So that even if there were not these problems with the general notion of the Fanti as Cartesian interactionists, Oguah's (1979:177) insistence that the "*okra*, like the Cartesian soul, is not spatially identifiable", looks to me like a projection of Western ideas. For if, as I suspect, my Fanti step-grandmother would have agreed that the *okra* leaves the body at death, then there is no doubt that at least sometimes – namely, as it leaves the body – it is thought of as having a spatial location; even if, most of the time, it would be thought strange to ask where it was since the answer, for a living person, is obvious – in the body; and for a dead person this is likely to be regarded as speculative at best.

But, thirdly, it seems to me that the imputation of philosophical doctrines as specific as Cartesian dualism to a whole people by virtue of their possession of a notion that has some of the characteristics of a Cartesian mind is intrinsically not very plausible. Were Descartes's peasant contemporaries dualists because they used such words as *penser*? Oguah offers evidence on these issues in the form of proverbs, and this is part of an established tradition in African ethno-philosophy.

I do not myself believe that any of Ghana's Akan peoples are dualist. But I do not think that it makes sense to say they are monists either: like most Westerners – all Westerners, in fact, without a philosophical training – most simply do not have a view about the issue at all. For, as I have argued already, the examination and systematisation of concepts may require us to face questions that, prior to reflection, simply have not been addressed. What the Fanti have is a concept – *okra* – ripe for philosophical work. What is needed is someone who does for this concept the sort of work that Descartes did for the concept of the mind, and, in doing this, like Descartes, this Fanti philosopher will be covering new territory.

Ethnophilosophy, then, strikes me as a useful beginning: a point from which to strike out in the direction of negotiating the conceptual lives – which is, in a sense, to say the lives *tout court* – of contemporary Africans. But, as I have argued, without an impetus toward such interventions (or, worse, as a substitute for them), it is merely a distraction.

In the catalogue I cited from the philosopher Richard Wright, both the first option (studying African conceptual systems for their own sake) and the third (studying them because in "understanding practical affairs" we need to "delineate their underlying philosophical motivation") can lead naturally to ethnophilosophy (though, as I shall argue at the end of this article, the latter argument can also lead in other directions). Nevertheless, ethnophilosophy is, as Wright's account suggests, only one of the options that have engaged African philosophers. And his second option – or, more precisely, its rationale – strikes me as even more dubious than the project of an uncritical ethnophilosophy.

Consider the passage once more:

> it is important to the history of ideas that we discover and understand the relation between (or influence of) African thought and the thought of the Western world. For, if Western civilization had its origin on the African continent . . . the correct pattern of intellectual development . . . will become clear only as we begin to understand the basis and direction of that development.

It is, of course, crucial, as I have argued myself, that we understand (as the second option proposes) "the relation between (or influence of) African thought and the thought of the Western world". But Wright, like numerous others, takes this as a reason for raising the question whether Egyptian philosophy, as the genuine prehistory of philosophy in Africa, should not be studied in African philosophy departments.

> For, if Western civilization had its origin on the African continent . . . the correct pattern of intellectual development . . . will become clear only as we begin to understand the basis and direction of that development.

I object to this argument not only because I think it is answers, not histories of answers, that matter, but also because it is absurd to argue that because a thought is African, and the prehistory of European thought lies in Africa, that thought will help us to understand Western thought. Should we conduct a study of Italian peasantry in the twentieth century as a preliminary to the study of Cicero? Or go to the mayor of Athens for an understanding of Plato's *Republic?*

The importance of ancient Egyptian philosophy for contemporary African intellectual life has been argued with most vigour in the writings of the Senegalese man of letters, Cheikh Anta Diop, whose work makes clear, I think, the motivations of the school. In *The African origins of civilization,* Diop (1974:xiv–xvi) summarises his claims: "Ancient Egypt was a Negro civilization. . . . The moral fruit of their civilization is to be counted among the assets of the Black world." Because "[a]nthropologically and culturally speaking, the Semitic world was born during protohistoric times from the mixture of white-skinned and dark-skinned people in Western Asia . . . [and] all races descended from the Black race" (Diop 1974:xiv–xvi), it followed that the first great human civilisation – one from which the Greeks, among others, borrowed much – was a black civilisation. Since Diop (1959) had also argued in *L'Unité culturelle de l'Afrique noire* for the existence of "features common to Negro African civilization", Diop exhibits, in our own day, the essential elements of the romantic racialism of Crummell and Blyden and Du Bois, and he makes quite explicit the connections between claims about Egyptian philosophy and the projects of Pan African nationalism. For it is, of course, the historical depth of the alleged tradition, along with its putative Negritude, that makes Egyptian thought a suitable vehicle for contemporary racial pride. And since philosophers have succeeded in persuading many in the West that philosophical ideas are central to any culture – a trick that depends on an equivocation between "philosophy", the formal discipline, and "folk philosophy" – and since these men are Western-trained intellectuals, it is natural that they should see in Egyptian philosophy the continent's proudest achievement.

Yet it seems to me that Diop – whose work is clearly among the best in this tradition – offers little evidence that Egyptian philosophy is more than a systematised but fairly uncritical folk philosophy; he makes no argument that the Egyptian problematic is that of the contemporary African, and he allows for a hovering, if inexplicit, suggestion that the Egyptians are important because the originators of the Pharaonic dynasties were black.

I have never seen any particular point in *requiring* European and American philosophers – *qua* philosophers – to study the pre-Socratics: their work is a mixture of early "science", poetry, and myth, and if it is important for modern philosophy at all it is important partly because it creates the world of texts in which Plato began – or, should we say, took the first faltering steps toward – the business of systematically reflecting on and arguing about the concepts of folk philosophy, and partly because it has been the subject of sustained attention from philosophers in the Western tradition. No analogous argument exists for the study of ancient Egyptian thought in contemporary Africa: there are no founding texts, there is no direct or continuous tradition.

Even what we might call the historicist view that understanding a concept involves understanding its history does not justify the study of either Greek or Egyptian "philosophy": for the transformations that the conceptual world of Africa and Europe have undergone since, respectively, the fifth century B.C. and the eighteenth dynasty are so great, and our forms of life so different, that the level of understanding to be gleaned by historical research is surely very limited. The understanding of the prehistory of a concept is helpful in present conceptual inquiries only if the prehistory is genuinely and deeply understood. And the distance and the paucity of data from ancient Greece or Egypt are enough to preclude any deep historical understanding, certainly if the study of that history is regarded merely as a propaedeutic. Besides which, the historicist claim is only plausible where there are important social and intellectual continuities between the various stages of society in which a concept is studied. And I deny that this condition is satisfied in the relationship between ancient Egypt and modern Africa, or ancient Greece and modern Europe. Even if I am wrong, I find nothing in Diop to persuade me otherwise.

If Diop and his followers – a group we might call the "Egyptianists" – are right, then ancient Egypt deserves a more central place than it currently has in the study of ancient thought: and if they are right, then it should be studied intensely in Africa and Europe and America and Australasia – wherever there is an interest in the ancient world. If European or American or Australasian intellectuals are too blinkered or too deeply chauvinistic to accept this, then maybe these matters will only be studied in Africa. But that would be a matter for regret.

The only paper in Wright's collection that exemplifies the critical analysis that characterises the best philosophy – the only paper that seems to me to offer a standard for African philosophy to aim at – is Kwasi Wiredu's "How not to compare African thought with Western thought". In essence, what he argues is that the common view that there is something particularly puzzling about African thought relating to "spirits" derives from a failure to notice that these beliefs are very like beliefs widely held in the European past. His presupposition that what makes a concept interesting is not whose it is but what it is and how it deals with the realities that face those whose concept it is, is one that I find thoroughly sympathetic. We can put the issue between Wiredu and the ethnophilosophers simply enough: analysis and exposition are necessary preliminaries to the critique of concepts, but without the critique the analysis is Othello without the Moor of Venice.

With the exception of Hountondji and Diop, the works I have discussed so far come from the anglophone tradition. And in discussing the structure of African philosophical debate, we have, as I have said, to distinguish the two major distinct traditions of modern philosophical work on the African continent. But I do not think that, so far as the issues that I am discussing are concerned, this divide is now of the same significance, say, as the (diminishing) intellectual gap between London and Paris. African philosophers are now significantly aware of each other across the anglophone-francophone divide. There is a great deal of ethnophilosophy published in French, for example, in the francophone *Cahiers des religions Africaines* as in the bilingual *Africa,* and it provides material for philosophical reflection. But without the further step of critical reflection on the ethnophilosophical material, this is, as Hountondji (a francophone from Benin) and Wiredu (an anglophone from Ghana) have both insisted, of no direct interest to *philosophy,* in that sense of "philosophy" that distinguishes those who pursue philosophy in the university. And uncritical ethnophilosophy fails in the end, as I have argued, to face the truly urgent questions that would be faced by a critical tradition.

I do not, however, wish to minimise the importance or deny the intelligibility of one important motivation for the work of the ethnophilosophers: namely, the desire to recover for Africa a history in philosophy, to deny Robin Horton's (1967:159) claim that logic and philosophy are absent from the continent's traditional thought. But the objection to this strategy has been well stated by Towa:

> Le concept de philosophie ainsi élargi est coextensif à celui de culture. Il est obtenu par opposition au comportement animal. Il se differencie donc d'un tel comportement mais demeure indiscernible de n'importe quelle forme culturelle: mythe, religion, poésie, art, science, etc. (1971:26).[1]

To make a case for "philosophy" by eliminating what is distinctive in philosophical thinking is to fight for a word only. Yet, it seems to me, there *are* reasons for philosophers in Africa to continue to analyse the nature of the pre-colonial conceptual worlds of our cultures – reasons essentially captured in Wright's (1979:27) formulation of the third option: "It is important in understanding practical affairs that we clearly delineate their underlying philosophical motivation." For some of the common features that there *are* in many of the traditional conceptual worlds of Africa plainly persist in the thinking of most Africans, even after modern schooling in secondary schools and universities. They provide the basis for a common set of African philosophical problems: for where we differ from the West, only a careful examination of the merits of our own traditions can allow us to escape the complementary dangers of adopting too little and too much of the intellectual baggage of our former colonisers. Wiredu and Hountondji share this belief; in exploring Africa's current philosophical options, it is right to return to them.

Wiredu's rejection of ethnophilosophy reflects his opposition to the claim that for philosophy to be acceptably African, its subject matter or its claims or its methods, or all three, must differ from those of philosophy in the cultures that colonised Africa. Others have often assumed, where they have not asserted, that the distinctive features of philosophy in Africa will be African and not Kikuyu or, say, Yoruba – reflecting a continental (or a racial) metaphysical community.

As a believer in the universality of reason, Wiredu holds the relevance of his being African to his philosophy to be both, in one sense, more global and, in another, more local; more local in that, as his title implies, he speaks as a Ghanaian for *an* African culture, more global in that he asks what it is that the particularity of his Ghanaian experience can offer to the philosophical community outside Africa. For Wiredu there are no African truths, only truths – some of them about Africa.

It is with these assumptions that Wiredu (1980:ix) asks "what a contemporary African philosopher is to make of his background". If his reply to this question has a central theme, it is that modernisation, the central project of black Africa, is essentially a philosophical project. Development, Wiredu (1980:43) argues, is to be measured by the "degree to which rational methods have penetrated through habits". For Wiredu (1980:43) "the quest for development . . . should be viewed as a continuing world-historical process in which all peoples, Western and non-Western alike, are engaged." Looked at this way, modernisation is not "unthinkingly jettisoning" traditional ways of thought and adopting foreign habits, rather it is a process in which "Africans, along with all other peoples, seek to attain a specifically human destiny" (Wiredu 1980:43).

Wiredu's tone in this book is strongly Humanist – morally serious but not moralistic. He criticises the apostles of Negritude, observing that people die daily in Ghana because they prefer traditional herbal remedies to Western medicines, so that "any inclination to glorify the unanalytical cast of mind is not just retrograde; it is tragic." He articulates and endorses the communalism of traditional society while deploring the authoritarianism that seems to go with it, saying that "it is important . . . to see what contribution philosophical thinking can make" to the question whether the former can be preserved without the latter.

Wiredu makes explicit the connection between an understanding of tradition and his concern for the possibilities of modernisation:

> Obviously it is of prime philosophical importance to distinguish between traditional, pre-scientific thought and modern, scientific thought by means of a clearly articulated criterion or set of criteria (1980:38).

While sharing the view that traditional thought involves literal belief in quasi-material agents – Wiredu (1980:38) remarks upon the "ubiquity of references to gods and all sorts of spirits" – he thinks it helpful to take the "folk thought" of the West as a model (1980:37). For, as he claims, what is distinctive in African traditional thought is that it is traditional; there is nothing especially African about it. Wiredu (1980:38–41) argues that what is called the "traditional" mode of thought is not especially African, and he is highly critical of its rationality. Wiredu says, for example, in *Philosophy and an African culture*:

> Many traditional African institutions and cultural practices . . . are based on superstition. By "superstition" I mean a rationally unsupported belief in entities of any sort. . . . Folk thought can be comprehensive and interesting on its own account, but its non-discursiveness remains a drawback (1980:41,47).

The problem is not with the contents of the beliefs expressed, however, or even whether they are comprehensive, but that they are held superstitiously (Wiredu 1980:41, 47): "The attribute of being superstitious attaches not to the content of a belief but to its relation to other beliefs." It is this lack of an interest in reasons, with the appeal to "what our ancestors said", which is part of the "authoritarianism" of traditional thought, that differentiates traditional from scientific thought. So this critique gives rise to an urgent call for the

> cultivation of rational enquiry. One illuminating (because fundamental) way of approaching the concept of "development" is to measure it by the degree to which rational methods have penetrated thought habits (Wiredu 1980:43).

Wiredu's book is, as I have said, most often seen as belonging with Hountondji's *African philosophy: Myth and reality,* a book that collects the major papers in which Hountondji has pursued his attack on ethnophilosophy.

Hountondji makes his major objections to ethnophilosophy in the first three essays, which appear in their original order of publication. Beginning with a recapitulation of Césaire's political critique of Tempels as a "diversion", he moves on to discuss the work of Kagamé, Tempels's major African follower, whose *La philosophie Bantou-rwandaise de l'etre*

> expressly and from the outset, establishes its point of view in relation to Tempels's work as an attempt by an autochthonous Bantu African to "verify the validity of the theory advanced by this excellent missionary" (Hountondji 1983b:39).

While endorsing some of Kagamé's specific criticisms of Tempels, Hountondji objects to their shared unanimism.

It is in these objections to Kagamé that Hountondji's argument seems weakest. For Kagamé explicitly roots his analysis in *language.* And though it is indeed odd to suppose, with some unanimists, that a people should share the same beliefs on all the major issues in their lives, it is not at all odd to suppose that people who speak the same language should share concepts, and thus those a priori beliefs whose possession is constitutive of a grasp of concepts. If this view – which was just the official theory of ordinary language philosophy and is the unofficial assumption of a great deal of conceptual analysis – is wrong, it cannot be refuted by Hountondji's arguments, which show only that a whole people is unlikely to share all their important a posteriori beliefs.

Along with his attack on ethnophilosophy, Hountondji (1983b:45) has a plausible and unflattering analysis of its motivations. Ethnophilosophy, he alleges, exists "for a European public". It is an attempt to cope with feelings of cultural inferiority by redefining folklore as "philosophy", so as to be able to lay claim to an autochthonous philosophical tradition.

The most original of Hountondji's objections to the ethnophilosophers derives from an essentially Althusserian view of the place of philosophy. The appeal to Althusser – which contrasts rather strikingly with Wiredu's appeals to Dewey – reflects the distinction between francophone and anglophone traditions with which I began. Hountondji (1983b:97) cites a passage from *Lenin and philosophy* where Althusser says that philosophy "has been observed only in places where there is also what is called a science or sciences – in the strict sense of theoretical discipline, i.e. ideating and demonstrative, not an aggregate of empirical results", and then goes on to argue himself that if

> the development of philosophy is in some way a function of the development of the sciences, then . . . we shall never have, in Africa, a philosophy in the strict sense, until we have produced a history of science (Hountondji 1983b:98).

Hountondji then develops in Althusserian language a version of Wiredu's insistence on the development of that critical tradition, which literacy for the first time makes possible.

This explicit Marxism differentiates Hountondji from Wiredu. For when Wiredu discusses the relationship between philosophical reflection on politics and political life, he is concerned above all to challenge the hegemony of Marxists in African political philosophy. But I take this no doubt significant difference between them to be less fundamental for my purposes here than their agreement about what is special about the African philosopher's position.

Hountondji's critique of method and motivation leads naturally on to his prescriptions. His primary prescription is that we should think of African philosophy as being African not (as the ethnophilosophers claim) because it is *about* African concepts or problems, but because (and here he agrees with Wiredu) it is that part of the universal discourse of philosophy that is carried on by Africans. Indeed, this claim is announced in the first – extremely well-known – sentence of the first essay, the sentence with which I began myself:

> By "African philosophy" I mean a set of texts, specifically the set of texts written by Africans themselves and described as philosophical by their authors themselves (Hountondji 1983b:33).

This sentence foreshadows the full burden of much of his argument. The definition of African philosophy as simply philosophy written by Africans is the first step in an argument for a discourse in African languages addressed to Africans. And the stress on "texts" with "authors" anticipates Hountondji's objection both to the idea of ethnophilosophy as the property of whole communities and to the possibility of an oral tradition of philosophy. Orality is inconsistent with the demands of what Althusser calls "science": writing liberates the individual mind "to make innovations that may shake established ideas and even overthrow them completely" (Hountondji 1983b:104).

In rejecting the possibility that there are specifically African topics and concepts that deserve philosophical study, Hountondji seems to me to draw too radical a conclusion from his critique of ethnophilosophy. For if philosophers are to contribute at the conceptual level to the solution of Africa's real problems, then they need to begin with a deep understanding of the traditional conceptual worlds the vast majority of their fellow nationals inhabit. In this, I believe, it is Wiredu who is right: what is wrong with the ethnophilosophers is that they have never gone beyond this essentially preliminary step. The test, Wiredu says,

> of a contemporary African philosopher's conception of African philosophy is whether it enables him to engage fruitfully in the activity of modern philosophising with an African conscience (1980:10).

Going beyond the descriptive project of ethnophilosophy is the real challenge of philosophers engaged with the problems of contemporary Africa; like Wiredu – and Hountondji – I aspire to a more truly critical discourse.

NOTE

1. The concept of philosophy thus enlarged is coextensive with that of culture. It is obtained by opposition with animal behaviour but remains indiscernible from any cultural form: myth, religion, poetry, art, science, etc.

(Translated by Norman Strike, Dept. of Romance Languages, Unisa.)

REFERENCES

Anderson, Jr, E.N. 1972. *The life of culture in Ethiopia*, in D. Hymes (ed.), 1972:264–283.

Appiah, K.A. 1992. "Ethnophilosophy and its critics" in K.A. Appiah, *In my father's house: Africa in the philosophy of culture*, Oxford: Oxford University Press.

Augé, M. 1982. *Anthropological circle*. Cambridge: Cambridge University Press.

Ayoade, J.A.A. 1979. "Time in Yoruba thought", in R. Wright (ed.), 1979:71–90.

Bell, R. 1989. "Narrative in African philosophy." *Philosophy*, 64:363–379.

Bernal. M. 1987. *Black Athena: The Afroasiatic roots of classical civilization.* Vol. 2. *The fabrication of ancient Greece* 1785–1985. New Brunswick: Rutgers University Press.

Biko, S. 1984 (1978). *I write what I like.* London: Heinemann Educational.

Bodunrin, P.O. 1981a. "The question of African philosophy." *Philosophy*, 56:161–179.

Bodunrin, P.O. 1981b. "Which kind of philosophy for Africa?", in A. Diemer (ed.), 1981:8–22.

Brumbaugh, R.S. 1981. *The philosophers of Greece.* Albany: State University of New York Press.

Bwalya, R.M.K. 1987. "On Kaundaism." *Quest: An International African Journal of Philosophy*, 1:31–38.

Caulfield, M.D. 1972. "Culture and imperialism: Proposing a new dialectic", in D. Hymes (ed.), 1972:182–212.

Césaire, A. 1971. *Cahier d'un retour au pays natal.* Paris: Présence Africaine.

Césaire, A. 1972 (1955). *Discourse on colonialism.* Tr. Joan Pinkham. New York: Monthly Review Press.

Clemmer, R.O. 1972. "Resistance and the revitalisation of anthropologists", in D. Hymes (ed.), 1972:213–247.

De Kock, L. 1987. "Literature, politics and universalism: A debate between Es'kia Mphahlele and J.M. Coetzee." *Journal of Literary Studies*, 3(4):35–48.

Diamond, S. (ed.) 1969 (1960). *Primitive views of the world.* New York: Columbia University Press.

Diamond, S. 1972. "Anthropology in question", in D. Hymes (ed.), 1972:401–429.

Diemer, A. (ed.) 1981 (1978). *Symposium on philosophy in the present situation of Africa: Wednesday August 30 1978.* Wiesbaden: Franz Steiner Verlag, 1981:8–22.

Diop, C.A. 1959. *The cultural unity of Negro Africa.* Paris: Présence Africaine.

Diop, C.A. 1974. *The African origins of civilization: Myth or reality.* New York: Lawrence Hill.

Dupré, W. 1975. *Religion in primitive cultures: A study in ethnophilosophy.* The Hague/Paris: Mouton.

Evans-Pritchard., E.E. 1976 (1937). *Witchcraft, oracles and magic among the Azande.* Oxford: Claredon Press.

Fabian, J. 1983. *Time and the other: How anthropology makes its objects.* New York: Columbia University Press.

Fanon, F. 1982 (1967). *The wretched of the earth.* Tr. C. Farrington. Harmondsworth: Penguin.

Fanon, F. 1983 (1952). *Zwarte huid, blanke maskers.* Tr. E. van Leuwen. Amsterdam: Van Gennep.

Finnegan, R. 1973. "Literacy vs non-literacy: The great divide?", in R. Horton & R. Finnegan (eds), *Modes of thought*, London: Faber & Faber, 1973:112–144.

Gadamer, H-G. 1975 (1960). *Wahrheit und Methode.* Tübingen: J.C.B. Mohr.

Gates, Jr. H.L. (ed.) 1986. *"Race," writing and difference.* Chicago: University of Chicago Press.

Gillies, F. 1980. "The Bantu concept of time." *Religion*, 10 (Spring): 16–30.

Gramsci, A. 1978. *Marxisme als filosofie van de praxis*. Amsterdam: Van Gennep.

Gusdorf, G. 1963. *Mythe en metafisica*. Tr. S. Schilstra. Utrecht: Bijleveld.

Gyekye, K. 1995 (1987). *An essay on African philosophical thought: The Akan conceptual scheme*. Philadelphia: Temple University Press.

Hallen, B. & Sodipo, J.O. 1986. *Knowledge, belief and witchraft: Analytic experiments in African philosophy*. London: Ethnographica.

Heidegger, M. 1979 (1963). *Sein und Zeit*. Tübingen: Niemeyer.

Horkheimer, M. & Adorno, T. 1981 (1955). *Dialektik der Aufklärung*. Frankfurt: Fischer Taschenbuch Verlag.

Horton, R. 1967. "African traditional thought and Western science." *Africa*, 37 (1,2):50–71.

Hountondji, P.J. 1970. "Comments on contemporary African philosophy." *Diogenes*, 71(Fall 1970):109–130.

Hountondji, P.J. 1976. *Sur la "philosophie Africaine": Critique de l'ethnophilosophie*. Paris: Maspero.

Hountondji, P.J. 1983a. "Reason and tradition", in H.O. Oruka & D.A. Masolo (eds), *Philosophy and cultures: Proceedings of the 2nd Afro-Asian philosophy conference, October/November, 1983*. Nairobi: Bookwise, 1983.

Hountondji, P.J. 1983b (1976). *African philosophy: Myth and reality*. Tr. H. Evans and J. Rée. London: Hutchinson.

Hunnings, G. 1972. "African traditions and scientific creativity." *Malawi Journal of Social Science*, l.

Hymes, D.N. (ed.) 1972 (1969). *Reinventing anthropology*. New York: Pantheon.

Johnson, B. 1986. "Thresholds of difference: Structures of address", in H.L. Gates, Jr (ed.), 1986:319–324.

Kagamé, A. 1971 (1968). "L'Ethnophilosophie des Bantu", in R. Klibansky (ed.), *Contemporary philosophy: A survey*. Vol. 4. Firenze: La Nuova Italia, 1971:589–612.

Kaphagwani, D.N. 1987. "The philosophical significance of Bantu nomenclature: a shot at contemporary philosophy" in H. Odera Oruka (ed.) *Sage philosophy*. Leiden: Brill, 1987: 181–204.

Keita, L. 1985. "Contemporary African philosophy: The search for a method." *Diogenes*, 130:105–125. Reprinted in *Praxis International*, 5:145–161.

Lemaire, T. 1976. *Over de waarde van kulturen*. Baarn: Ambo.

Lévy-Bruhl, L. 1926. *How natives think*. London: Allen & Unwin.

Lévi-Strauss, C. 1962. *La Pensee Savauge*. Paris: Plon.

Lévi-Strauss, C. 1976 (1962). *The savage mind*. Tr. G. Weidenfeld. London: Weidenfeld & Nicholson.

Manchester, W. 1988. *The last lion: Winston Spencer Churchill*. Boston: Little, Brown.

Mazrui, A. 1980. *The African condition*. London: Heinemann.

Mbiti, J.S. 1969. *African religions and philosophy*. London: Heinemann.

Miller, C.L. 1986. "Theories of Africans: The question of literary anthropology", in H.L. Gates, Jr (ed.), 1986:281–300.

Minkus, H. 1979. "Causal theory in Akwapim Akan philosophy", in R. Wright (ed.), 1979:91–132.

Mitchell, J.C. 1976. "A note on African conception of causality." *The Nyasaland Journal*, 5(2):51–58.

Moi, D.A. 1986. *Kenya African nationalism: Nyayo philosophy and principles*. London: Macmillan.

Momoh, C. 1989. *Substance of African philosophy*. Auchi: Nigeria African Philosophical Projects.

Momoh, C. 1991. *Philosophy of a new past and an old future*. Auchi: African Philosophy Projects.

Mulang, I.I. 1987. "Mythe et philosophie: Résponse a Elungu, Towa et autres." *Quest: An International Journal of Philosophy*, 1:13–22.

Mnthali, F. 1980. *When sunset comes to Sapitwa*. Harlow: Longman.

Nazombe, A. 1983. *Malawian poetry from 1970 to the present day: A study of myth and socio-political change in the works of Steve Chimombe, Jack Mapanje, Frank Chipasula and Felix Mwthali.* Unpublished Ph.D thesis, University of Sheffield.

Nijhof, M. 1964. *Verzamelde Gedichten.* Amsterdam: Bert Bakker.

Nkrumah, K. 1978. *Consciencism.* London: Panaf.

Nyerere, J.K. 1968. *Ujamaa: essays in socialism.* Oxford: Oxford University Press.

Odinga, O. 1967. *Not yet Uhuru.* London: Heinemann.

Oguah, B. 1979. "African and Western philosophy: A comparative study", in R. Wright (ed.), 1979:195–214.

Okpewho, I. 1990. *The oral performance in Africa.* Ibadan: Spectrum.

Okpewho, I. 1992. *African oral literature – backgrounds, character, and continuity.* Bloomington: Indiana University Press.

Olela, H. 1981. "From ancient Africa to ancient Greece", in E.F. Collins, *From ancient Africa to ancient Greece: An introduction to the history of philosophy.* Atlanta: Black Heritage/Selected.

Ong, W.J. 1958: *Ramus: Method and the decay of dialogue.* Cambridge, Mass.: Harvard University Press.

Oruka, H.O. 1981. "Four trends in current African philosophy", in A. Diemer (ed.), 1981:1–7.

Oruka, H.O. 1983. "Sagacity in African philosophy." *International Philosophical Quarterly,* 23:383–393.

Oruka, H.O. (ed.) 1990. *Sage Philosophy: Indigenous thinkers and modern debate on African philosophy.* Leiden: Brill.

Oruka, H.O. 1990a. "Cultural fundamentals in philosophy." *Philosophy and Theology,* 90:19–37.

Oruka, H.O. (ed.) 1990b. *Sage philosophy: Indigenous thinkers and modern debate on African philosophy.* Leiden: Brill.

Parratt, J. 1976. "Ethnophilosophy – facts or fiction?" *Malawi Journal of Social Science,* 5:65–68.

Radin, P. 1957 (1927). *Primitive man as philosopher.* New York: Dover.

Ricoeur P. 1960. *Finitude et culpabilité.* Vol. 2. *La symbolique du mal.* Paris: Aubier Editions Montaigne.

Ricoeur, P. 1981. "Hermeneutics and the critique of ideology", in J.B. Thompson (ed.), 1981a: 63–100.

Rombach, H. 1983. *Welt und Gegenwelt.* Basel: Verlag Herder.

Ross, M.G. 1984. *Leibniz.* Oxford: Oxford University Press.

Russell, B. 1950. *Unpopular essays.* London: Allen & Unwin.

Sahlins, M. 1972. *Stone age economics.* Chicago: Aldine-Atherton.

Schopenhauer, A. 1970 (1851). "On Women", in A. Schopenhauer (ed.), *Essays and aphorisms (Parerga and Paralipomena).* Berlin: Penguin.

Schumacher, E.F. 1973. *Hou het klein: Een economische studie waarbij de mens weer meetelt.* Baarn: Ambo.

Seller, A. 1984. Review of Hountondji's African philosophy: Myth and reality. *Third World Review,* 1(1):1–21.

Skorupski, J. 1976. *Symbol and theory: A philosophical study of theories of religion in social anthropology.* Cambridge: Cambridge University Press.

Stocking, Jr, G.W. 1968. *Race, culture and evolution: Essays in the history of anthropology.* New York: The Free Press.

Strawson, P.F. 1959. *Individuals: An essay in descriptive metaphysics.* London: Methuen.

Tempels, P. 1959 (1945). *Bantu philosophy.* Tr. A. Rubbens. Paris: Présence Africaine. [French version: *La philosophie Bantoue,* Elizabethville: Lovania.]

Tempels, P. 1969 (1959). *Bantu philosophy.* Paris: Présence Africaine.

Thacker, C. 1983. *The wildness pleases: The origins of romanticism.* London: Croom Helm.

Thompson, J.B. (ed.) 1981a. *Hermeneutics and the human sciences.* Cambridge: Cambridge University Press.

Thompson, J.B. 1981b. *Critical hermeneutics*. Cambridge: Cambridge University Press.

Towa, M. 1971. *Essai sur la problématique philosophique dans l'Afrique actuelle*. Yaoundé: CLE.

Towa, M. 1986. "A reply to Harold Fromm", in H.L. Gates, Jr (ed.), *"Race", writing and difference*. Chicago: University of Chicago Press.

Tylor, E.B. 1913 (1871). *Primitive culture: Researches into the development of mythology, philosophy, religion, language, art, and custom*. Vols 1 & 2. London: John Murray.

Verhoeven, C. 1982. *Weerloos denken: Beschouwingen over de inval en het oeuvre*. Baarn: Ambo.

Wa Thiong'o, N. 1987 (1981). *Decolonising the mind: The politics of language in African literature*. Harare: Zimbabwe Publishing House.

Williams, B. 1985. *Ethics and the limits of philosophy*. London: Fontana.

Willis, Jr, W.S. 1972. "Skeletons in the anthropological closet", in D. Hymes (ed.), 1972:121–152.

Wiredu, K. 1979. "How not to compare African thought with Western thought", in R. Wright (ed.), 2nd ed. 1979:133–147.

Wiredu, K. 1980. *Philosophy and an African culture*. Cambridge: Cambridge University Press.

Wolff, K.H. 1972. "This is the time for radical philosophy", in D. Hymes (ed.), 1972:99–118.

Woolgar, S. (ed.) 1988. *Knowledge and reflexivity. New frontiers in the sociology of knowledge*. London: Sage.

Wright, R. (ed.) 1979. *African philosophy: An introduction*. 2nd ed. Washington: University Press of America.

Yates, F. 1984 (1966). *The art of memory*. London: Ark.

CHAPTER 4

Metaphysical Thinking in Africa

LESIBA J. TEFFO and ABRAHAM P.J. ROUX

1. METAPHYSICAL THINKING

Why does lightning kill people and destroy property? Why are some people successful whereas others, despite their efforts, fail? Why do innocent and good people become ill and die? These and other similar questions show humankind's need to understand the world they are living in; to make sense of the kind of reality they find themselves in. People differ about the validity of these questions. In some communities they are seriously asked and answered. In others they are rejected as non-questions, as meaningless. Why is this? Because people have different conceptions of reality and of the interrelations between aspects of their world. People who ask the above questions have a teleological conception of reality, that is, reality hangs together because of aims, and it is driven by aims; there are no blind happenings but only planned action. Those who reject these questions as meaningless think of reality in mechanical terms, in terms of mechanical causation. That a house or a person was struck by lightning, has, according to them, to be understood in scientific terms, in terms of mechanical causation and not in terms of some or other aim behind it. Such thinking about reality, that is, such attempts to fathom what is real and what is not and what the ultimate nature of reality is, is metaphysical thinking. "Metaphysics is that branch of philosophy concerned with the most fundamental questions: existence, essence, space and time, the nature of universals, cause and effect, etc." (Sparkes 1991:207).

There are people who think that our perception of reality is an objective, almost mechanical affair; that what we see, taste, hear, and smell must be exactly the same for all. This view has long been rejected both on the basis of experience and with reference to the way in which we use our concepts. Our perceptions are influenced by our expectations, beliefs, and emotions, but also by our conceptual schemes, our histories and social circumstances, and the language we talk. That is to say, the conception of the nature of reality varies from culture to culture, almost suggesting that different cultural communities live in different worlds.[1]

The above exposition leaves us with two serious problems:

1. If we are dealing with different conceptions of the world, is it possible for a person to know and to discuss other conceptions or are we totally fenced in by our own conceptions? And if it is possible to know and discuss other conceptions, can this be of any use? Is it possible to change or even to replace a "given" way of conceiving of reality?
2. Is it necessary to spend time on conceptions which we believe are wrong because they clash with what is scientifically accepted?

We cannot go into these questions in depth but they take us to an important reason for making an issue of African philosophy. We shall therefore deal with them albeit in a rather indirect and superficial way.

A dominant feature of philosophy, which until recently meant Western or European philosophy, is its theory of rationality. Rationality has been seen as a universal inherent ability of humankind to determine *the* truth. According to this theory, rationality is based upon logical deduction and strict rules of evidence; the distorting tendencies of affect must be avoided at all costs. This provides a method of investigation in which correct answers are thought to be rationally determined, that is, true. Rationality, therefore, is seen as the only avenue toward reliable knowledge, and also as being certain of success in yielding correct, final answers if its methods are promptly followed. This view has been severely criticised in recent times and it can now only be viewed with scepticism. Rationality is now (in post-modernity, as it is called) seen by many as a social process, i.e.

> reason is neither necessary nor universal, but nor is it arbitrary, for it emerges in plural conversations, in which people together inquire, disagree, explain, or argue their views in the pursuit of a *consensual outcome*. Such an outcome is one that the participants, after careful deliberation of different opinions and alternative perspectives, are satisfied with for that moment in time (Higgs 1997:7).

The only condition for such a discussion is the possibility of communication. Communication can never be guaranteed – even among people with the same conceptual scheme. Miscommunication, and thus explanation and correction, is always possible. If the will to communicate is there, it is possible to cross even conceptual divides. Given this view of rationality and the logical possibility of open communication, such discussion – and particularly cross-cultural discussion – is possible, but what is important is that it is essential, because no one can claim that he/she is in possession of *the truth*.

Against this background Nordenbo has developed a pluralistic approach to cultures and frameworks, which he calls "alternativism". He accepts that there are different cultures with different questions, answers, values, etc. and that it is possible to understand and communicate with other cultures. This then implies that for every position there are substantiated alternatives. Such alternatives thus have to be evaluated. He concludes:

> this . . . means that dangers of cultural chauvinism are avoided. Alternativism does not imply that a definite . . . belief is more sacrosanct than a[nother] view . . . only a test of the views can substantiate their validity. Alternativism, in fact, implies a more modest ambition with regard to the possibility of creating an all-embracing cosmology. The recognition that alternatives can always be thought of with regard to the prevailing view liberates us from orthodox restraint on

the one hand, but at the same time places us – intellectually speaking – in a little boat in the open sea with no safe harbour in sight (Nordenbo 1995:42).

2. IS THERE AN AFRICAN METAPHYSICS?

There have been many attempts to show that there is one set of ideas which are common to the whole African continent and which may be termed "African philosophy".[2] In terms of this approach there must then also be a particular African metaphysics. As we saw in Chapter 3, this is only one of many different approaches to, or trends in, African philosophy. In fact, this approach has come in for severe criticism (see Neugebauer 1988, Withaar 1986, Van Niekerk 1991, & More 1996). In present-day philosophical activity on the continent there is a strong tendency to approach philosophy in a culture-specific way, that is, not to try to come up with views which are supposed to apply to all groups on the continent, but rather to describe and discuss the views of specific cultural groups such as the Akan, the Igbo, the Yoruba or the Zulus, as for example in the analyses of the Akan/Yoruba conception of a person. People became wary of the vastness of the continent; what is the case in West Africa need not be the case in East or Southern Africa.

The question of the approach that should be followed is the theme of intense ongoing debate among African philosophers. We can say, however, that the culture-specific approach has much in its favour. For example, philosophical thinking in Africa is not fully documented and described, and it is dangerous to generalise at this early stage. Furthermore, as was pointed out earlier, truth is a social construction. No person and no group can assume that the final word about any problem has been spoken. Any contribution which may help to further our understanding of reality should get a hearing. Wiredu (cf. 1996a:169–177 & 1996b:178), for one, is strongly in favour of this approach which he calls "strategic particularism". It thus seems risky to opt for *an* African metaphysics at this stage.

These considerations immediately reflect on the methodology of this article. In spite of the above arguments, we do not outline the metaphysical ideas of one cultural group nor do we work comparatively in this introduction. In fact, our approach reveals much regarding ethnophilosophy as a trend – a particular and separate *African* approach to problems concerning reality. Moreover, there are also traces of the traditional approach, that is, the emphasis is on ideas which are seen as part of traditional Africa. We argue that, generally speaking, metaphysical thinking in Africa has features which make it a particular way of conceptualising reality. Facets of this conceptual scheme are discussed with reference mostly to specific cultural groups. There is no denying that people who believe in witchcraft or a supreme being have particular conceptions of reality which include aspects such as causality, personality and responsibility, the nature of matter, and so forth. It is clear, and in the exposition we often show, that views which are called "traditional" still play a role, indeed an important role, in the lives of Africans. Such views cannot be ignored because they also come into play when issues such as development, education, government, and legislation are discussed.

A further consideration is in place here. There is no reason why all peoples on a continent, or even all members of a cultural group, should think the same about metaphysical matters. In so-called Western philosophy there is no prevailing tradition of presenting and practising philosophy along ethnic or geographical lines. Although there is talk of Greek, British, French or German philosophy, the assumption is that these are aspects of a common activity and parts of an ongoing tradition. An ethnic or geographic classification such as this is then made for very specific reasons which are seldom of a true philosophical nature. One of the reasons is that in philosophy we are concerned with general or universal matters. Epistemologists want to account for knowledge as such, not British or French knowledge, but knowledge in general. The moral philosopher wants to know about morality in general. Even if the outcome of the analysis is a moral relativism, it is not seen as relative in any way but as applying to all moral systems. In the case of metaphysics, the same principle applies. Talk about causality, God, personal identity, etc. is not supposed to apply only to Europe or Africa, or only to the British or the French or the Xhosa. The conclusions are supposed to be general in application. Even though the starting-point may be particular, because of different cultures, languages, and customs, the outcome will be regarded as general. A generalised approach as such is therefore not out of order; even if a generalisation is wrong, it can stimulate attempts to correct it.

Claims to a common African philosophy are made here although we know that this is dangerous. A great deal of descriptive work still has to be done. One of our aims is to stimulate such descriptive research. Furthermore, given what has been said about the general nature of philosophical reasoning, the latter often works with possible conceptualisations. Descartes did not describe and reflect on a factual situation. In this sense, views held in Africa about metaphysical issues should be dealt with like any other views. What this means is that African views should be raised in general philosophical debates as possible views about these matters, and as based on arguments which should be considered as arguments. Irrespective of the factual correctness of the ascription of certain views to Africans in general, these views can and should be evaluated critically. This then is a further aim, to draw the readers into the ongoing metaphysical debate. This is what most writers about African metaphysics see as their aim, and a younger African philosopher such as Appiah (see, for example, Appiah 1992) is definitely pushing African philosophy in this direction.[3]

When we talk of the views of the Akan or the Yoruba this is not to be taken literally as meaning that every member of that group holds these beliefs or accepts these views. As with any group, we are dealing with general or majority trends. There will be people who reject such beliefs or who believe otherwise. Intra-cultural debates also take place, however.

In summary, then, we may say that we aim at providing information about metaphysical thinking in Africa, and we believe that we are outlining and discussing views which are alive in a fairly large part of Africa and which can serve as representative of metaphysical thinking in Africa. We realise, however, that we are dealing with a vast continent and with many cultural groups and that it is dangerous to talk of African metaphysics and to ascribe views to all cultural groups. However, given the nature of philosophy, we do not see this as a problem. According to the literature the views discussed do have currency in Africa and they are views which need to be addressed in a discussion of metaphysical thinking.

Metaphysical discourse in Africa must be based on the African perception of reality as determined by a history, geographical circumstances, and such cultural phenomena as religion, thought systems, and linguistic conventions entrenched in the African world-view. This implies that most metaphysical discourses on the continent have certain common features. Central to African metaphysics are religious beliefs relating to the African conception of God, the universe, and their interrelations. Further notions such as spirit, causality, person, space and time, and reality, in their various conceptions, play a significant role in the life of Africans as they grapple with existential realities through phenomena such as religion, ancestral veneration, witchcraft, magic, etc.

Furthermore, African metaphysics is holistic in nature. Reality is seen as a closed system so that everything hangs together and is affected by any change in the system. Withaar (1986:169) echoes Tempels (cf. More 1996:152) in arguing that African metaphysics is organised around a number of principles and laws which control so-called vital forces. There is a principle concerning the interaction of forces, that is, between God and humankind, between different people, between humankind and animals, and between humankind and material things. These forces are hierarchically placed, they form a "chain of being". In this hierarchy God, the creator and source of all vital forces, is at the apex. Then follow the ancestors, then humankind, and then the lower forces, animals, plants, and matter. This system of vital forces constitutes a closed universe. When one element gains in force another has to lose it. For example, when someone gets ill, this means that he/she loses vital force, which has been taken from him/her in some or other way by someone/ something else. In this way disasters such as illness and death are explained ontologically (metaphysically). Withaar (1986:169) emphasises that this system shows an almost unbreakable interrelation between God, the dead, the living, and nature, but, as will become clear, the living person takes a central place in this system. The "vital or life force" metaphysics put forward here is strongly questioned by More and Kaphagawani (More 1996:152 and Kaphagawani, in this volume), but the hierarchic structure and thus the holistic feature of African metaphysics are not.

To take up a question which was posed earlier, it should be noted that this kind of explanation is more fundamental than scientific explanations and the latter cannot replace the first unless there is a change in the way in which reality is conceived. That is, scientific questions arise and answers to them are looked for in terms of a more basic perspective.

Since metaphysical discourse is generally about non-physical aspects of phenomena that transcend space and time, the bulk of the subject matter of African metaphysics falls under the category that is traditionally described in Western metaphysics as "supernatural". Two considerations are important here. On the one hand, as will be emphasised repeatedly, dualisms which are the stock-in-trade of Western metaphysics, such as that between the natural and the supernatural, and others such as those between matter and mind/soul/spirit, do not appear in African metaphysics. On the other hand, the possible misconception that life in traditional African culture is wholly enmeshed in metaphysical or magico-religious speculations has to be corrected. Much of the African way of life and day-to-day activities are based on empirically verifiable facts, independent of "supernatural" influence. In fact, a feature of African metaphysics is that it has a strong empirical (i.e. based on experience) flavour. However, in seeking to come to terms with existential realities, and in an effort to understand the universe, African cultures draw on explanatory models that may appear to be at variance with perceptual experience and the familiar principles of science. We can say that the African realises the enormous complexity of the universe, and is aware that mankind and its world constitute an "environment" much deeper than what the human senses can perceive. The essence of African metaphysics, then, is the search for meaning and ultimate reality in the complex relationship between the human person and his/her total environment.

Causality plays an important part in metaphysical thinking. What it is for A to cause B, how we can be certain that A is the cause of B, how to find true causes of given events, are all standard metaphysical questions. Such questions gain a place in metaphysical thinking when they are asked about reality as such, for example, asking about the origin (cause) of the world or of morality, which leads to the proposition that God is such a first cause. The same happens when we ask about the base (cause) of personal identity or of free will or of action, and then refer to the mind or the soul as such a cause. In African metaphysical thinking cause also plays a pivotal role. In fact, African philosophers such as Wiredu, Sogolo, and Appiah see an understanding of the African view on cause as the key to understanding African metaphysics. These writers point out that there is a difference between the Western view of causality which according to them is mechanistic, and the African view which is in general more teleologically inclined. Appiah's explanation shows that this links up with a basic feature of African metaphysics – the rejection of chance:

> what is most striking about the "unscientific" explanations that most pre-colonial African cultures offer is not just that they appeal to agency but that they are addressed to the question "Why?" understood as asking what the event in question was for. Evans-Pritchard in his account of Zande belief insists that the Azande do not think that "unfortunate events" ever happen by chance; their frequent appeal to witchcraft – in the absence of other acceptable explanations of misfortune – demonstrates their unwillingness to accept the existence of contingency. But to reject the possibility of the contingent is exactly to insist that everything that happens serves some purpose: a view familiar in Christian tradition . . . or in the deep need people feel . . . for answers to the question "Why do bad things happen to good people?" Zande witchcraft beliefs depend on an assumption that the universe is in a certain sort of evaluative balance . . . (1992:171–172).

This leads Sogolo to distinguish between what he terms primary and secondary causality. What he terms "secondary causality" is what Westerners usually understand as cause, that which brings about an event or a change, such as "a petrol bomb caused the fire". By calling these causes "secondary", Sogolo indicates that they are not of primary concern to the African. The petrol bomb and the resulting fire are, so to speak, expressions of an aim which interrelates event (world) and person. Sogolo says:

> Primary causes . . . are those predisposing factors not directly explicable in physical terms. Some of these take the form of supernatural entities such as deities, spirits, witches; others are stress-induced either as a result of the victim's contravention of communal morality or his strained relationship with other persons within his community (1994:215).

We shall return to this view of causality later.

This account of causality points at another feature of African metaphysical thinking: it is social in nature. In fact, as will become clear in the discussion, it is difficult to distinguish metaphysics, social theory, and morality in African thinking because all philosophising is communitarian in nature. This comes out very clearly in More's criticism of Shutte's use of the idea of vital force to characterise African metaphysical thinking. More asserts that:

Seriti in Sesotho [which Shutte translates as force, which More rejects] is not so much a metaphysical but a moral and social concept that has to do with observable behaviour patterns and human relationships (1996:152–154).

This also takes us back to the point made earlier that African metaphysics is basically empirical in nature.

3.   THEMES
3.1   God
3.1.1 God in African life

In the past, various judgements – some of them contradictory – were made about the place of religion in the lives of Africans. According to Wiredu (1996b:178), who made an intensive study of religion in Africa and particularly of conceptions of God or a supreme being, Africans are now seen as deeply religious with a strong belief in the existence of a supreme being. Wiredu (1995:313) argues that the approach is, generally speaking, empirical. He also shows the danger of rash generalisation by pointing out that

> some African peoples, such as the Luo of East Africa, do not seem to have any place for such a concept [the concept of God] in their (highly sophisticated) traditional thought. Significantly, the reason for the a-theism . . . is cognate with the conceptual orientation underlying the particular conceptions of the supreme being held by those African peoples who make such a postulation in their communal philosophies. That cast of thought is preeminently empirical (Wiredu 1995:313).

3.1.2 God as supreme being

In spite of a strong sense of the goodwill of God, Africans do not accept *ad hoc* interventions by God in the order of nature. They have a strong commitment to the universal reign of law in all spheres of existence (Wiredu 1995:314). God is not apart from the world. Together with the world, God constitutes the spatio-temporal "totality" of existence. As we saw earlier, the natural-supernatural dichotomy has no place in the African conceptualisation of the universe. The thinking is hierarchical, with God at the apex and extra-human beings and forces, humans, the lower animals, vegetation, and the inanimate world, in this order, as integral parts of one single totality of existence.

3.1.3 God as creator

God is seen as creator of the world but, because God is not outside the world, this cannot mean that he created the world out of nothing. God is seen as a kind of cosmic architect, "a fashioner of the world out of a preexisting manifold of indeterminacy" (Wiredu 1995:313). This raises the question of the origin of the material which was necessary to fashion the world. Wiredu points out that for the Akan people, to which he belongs, this is a meaningless question:

> The absolute nothingness entailed in the notion of creation out of nothing . . . scorns any . . . context. This abolition of context effectively abolishes intelligibility, as far as the Akan language is concerned (1996b:179).

More is involved here than just the peculiarity of a particular language. A point of general metaphysical interest is at stake here which also shows why and how African philosophy is part of philosophical reflection in general. Wiredu argues as follows:

if a concept is incoherent within a given language, it does not necessarily mean that there is anything wrong with it, for it may be that the language in question is expressively inadequate. In the case of the concept of creation out of nothing, however, its coherence, even within English, is severely questionable. In English, the concept of "there is" – note the "there" – which is equivalent to "exists", is quite clearly spatial. It is because the word "exists" does not bear its spatiality on its face, that it has been possible in English to speak as if existence were not necessarily spatial without prohibitive implausibility. Besides, the maxim that *Ex nihilo nihil fit* (Out of nothing nothing comes), which, ironically, is championed by Christian philosophers such as Descartes, conflicts sharply with the notion of creation out of nothing. That nothing can come out of nothing is not an empirical insight; it is a conceptual necessity, just like the fact that two and two cannot add up to fifty. Thus to say that some being could make something come out of nothing is of the same order of incoherence as saying that some being could make two and two add up to fifty. Besides, . . . the causal connotation of creation is incompatible with the circumstance or rather, non-circumstance, of absolute nothingness. Causation makes sense only when it is, in principle, possible to distinguish between *post hoc* and *propter hoc* (i.e. between mere sequence and causal sequence). If there were one being and absolutely nothing besides him, then logically, that distinction would be impossible. If so, the notion of causation collapses and with it that of creation (1996b:179–180).

This is not the place to discuss these views in any great depth. It should, however, be pointed out that the views about God as they are summarised here are problematic in various ways. We do not experience God in the normal way – we do not see God. That God exists, how God exists, and how God interacts with the world are all problems that need looking into.

3.2 Ancestors

We have seen that the distinction between the natural and the supernatural does not exist for the African metaphysician. Another dichotomy which plays an important part in Western reflection, the distinction between the material and the spiritual, has no place either in African thinking. When it comes to immortality, at no stage does mortal life or immortal survival involve absolute immateriality. The ancestors interact with mortals, and because the world of the ancestors is ontologically both analogous and contiguous to that of mortals, that is, there is no difference in kind between these worlds (as was pointed out, it is all one and the same world); there is no logical problem with this interaction; category problems do not arise; the actions of the ancestors are believed to be within the regular pattern of events. The immortals merely happen to occupy a higher status in the order of things than mortals.

Metaphysical thinking in the African context starts from social and moral considerations. In the attempt to account for social interaction or the breakdown of such interaction metaphysical ideas are developed. The ancestors are a striking example. Immortality is conceived in pragmatic terms. Survival is of no particular personal value. What is important, however, is that the deceased can assist the living sections of their families and provide and exercise moral leadership among them. The ancestors thus have to do with group solidarity and tradition and in this way help to guarantee moral consistency.

How does communication between the living and the ancestors take place? It occurs through ritual and other similar practices. The ancestors are often discussed as part of African religion in terms of ancestor worship. It is, however, not a matter of worship but of veneration; the ancestors are integrated into ordinary life situations and their guidance in such situations is accepted as part of ordinary life.

The social, and particularly the moral importance of ancestor veneration, and with this the possession of ancestral land, is well illustrated by the Kikuyu or Mau Mau uprising in Kenya in the 1950s. Basil Davidson discusses this in a review of two books on this "anti-colonial rebellion". Davidson shows that the Kikuyu lost little land to settler expropriation:

> But what they crucially did loose [sic] was all assurance of control over ancestral forests and fields that had been theirs from "time out of mind"; they lost, it could be said, their environment. . . . The name that the forest fighters gave themselves was the Land and Freedom Army, the army of *ithaka na wiathi. Wiathi* emerges as the symbol of a strong inner compulsion, standing . . . for the moral agency that legitimises or at any rate sponsors maturity and self-respect, in line with Kikuyu ancestral concepts of the difference between good and evil, between success and failure, eventually between life and death. . . . Rather than "atavistic" beliefs or superstitions [the way in which the colonists and the colonial government saw the motives of the rebels], or the brash claims of the nationalist agenda, it was *wiathi* that could challenge Kikuyu degradation and despair (1994:12).

Davidson concludes:

> this sense of degradation, the product of dispossession, is the nearest we will get to an explanation of phenomena such as Mau Mau. As was the case among other subjected peoples, colonial dispossession led to a more or less complete disjuncture from previous Kikuyu history. With a contemptuously dismissive hand, the ancestors were banished to realms of impotence and anonymity from which there seemed no way of recalling them, and so, for "the living and the yet unborn", there was no way of conserving the notion of community as these peoples had learned to understand it (1994:12).

This then meant "moral dislocation". We can clearly see here how African thinking is community centred, and thus how closely together metaphysics, morality, and social theory are knit.

There is nothing wrong with honouring one's ancestors and using their lives and decisions as guidelines. But, in the end, a decision is something personal which has to be taken with reference to the particular context and the relevant facts and for which relevant reasons have to be given. There are also situations in which a break with tradition and existing beliefs and practices may be necessary. The "revolution" in South Africa is a case in point where tradition and traditional ways of doing and judging had to be changed or at least critically evaluated. Moreover, the theory of immortality on which this veneration rests can be questioned from at least two sides. What is it for an individual to be immortal? How can he/she be and remain the same in such a state? Can a person be a person and remain the same person without reference to ordinary situations and experiences? The believers try to meet this criticism by playing down the difference between the material and the spiritual, and saying that the ancestors have what the Westerner would call a material existence, and that this is still part of life as long as the ancestors have offspring and are remembered by them. Only after this does existence move to a different realm. Only then will it be necessary to explain what is meant by the phrase "remain part of life", because the ordinary ways of knowing of such participation and interaction, those of observation, direct discussion, and physical acts are not possible.

3.3 Witchcraft

Witchcraft, magic, sorcery, and other such phenomena are normally not considered as objects of scientific study because they are not based on empirical observation. Indeed, by scientific criteria these powers are rejected as unreal and belief in them is generally classified as irrational, if not outright unintelligible. Yet, the history of every human society shows evidence of such beliefs and practices, whether in the past or in contemporary times. The point then is that these paranormal activities are not an African peculiarity, although their strength and spread among African communities deserves special attention. In South Africa, particularly in the Northern Province, the authorities are concerned about the phenomenon of witchcraft, and two investigations into it have been conducted, one by a commission of inquiry appointed by the government of the Northern Province, and the other by a research team appointed by the Human Sciences Research Council. The Provincial Commission of Inquiry found that most people in the province believe in the existence of witches and in witchcraft (Ralushai *et al.* 1996:12); they go even further:

> it is quite clear that witchcraft as a phenomenon is still a factor to be reckoned with in other regions of South Africa . . . witchcraft beliefs occur among people of all levels (Ralushai *et al.* 1996:57).

They found that executions of witches without formal trials by members of the community have increased dramatically over the past ten years. Communities believe that witches destroy people's possessions and cause misfortune such as illness and death to their friends, enemies, and neighbours. "Trials" and the resultant executions of witches often take place in the event of "untimely death", for example in the case of a child. When someone is killed by lightning (as often happens in the Northern Province) it is also seen as untimely death and thus as the result of witchcraft. We can safely say that the belief in witchcraft is intense in most African societies and that people conduct their daily activities under tension, suspicion, and fears of bewitchment.

There are issues of genuine philosophical interest about the status and possibility of events attributed to witchcraft. The possibility of such acts, of course, presupposes that witches exist. But, first, we need to know the kind of entity that witches are supposed to be. Generally – and granting the possibility of local variations – the conception of witchcraft in Africa is that witches are normal human beings who operate mainly within the domain of their own extended family. Thus the suspected witch is usually a close or distant family member who is believed to harbour ill-feelings against her victims. Witches possess the extraordinary capacity of transforming themselves into disembodied forms or into animals. In their incarnates, and with their real bodies left behind, they can fly and move instantaneously from one point to another. And with these powers, they cause the death of people, make men impotent and women barren, and cause failure in all forms of human endeavour.

The actions of witchcraft are usually couched in a language well-nigh indistinguishable from the actions of normal persons. For instance, it is claimed that witches hold assemblies, prey on human bodies or suck the blood of their victims – claims that are obviously not intended to convey literal meanings. But to the believer, claims about witches and witchcraft are neither metaphorical nor mere symbolic representations. They are as real to the traditional African as scientific claims are to the modern scientist.

Sogolo thinks that to understand this phenomenon we have to refer to primary causes because a combination of the different categories of causes will provide a fuller explanation of this and other phenomena in African life. The kind of problem to which witchcraft is supposed to provide a solution draws on human relations, and it has thus to be understood in a meaningful cultural context. But then the question still remains: why link the misfortune to a specific person as the cause who has then to be executed for the alleged deed? What Sogolo (1994:205) calls "a combination of the categories of causes" seems rather to be a confusion of the teleological and mechanical categories. The starting-point is teleological: why did this happen to me/at this stage/in this way? Why did the lightning strike her? Why this death? These are attempts at integrating events at a higher level, to make sense of the event. This then changes to straightforward "mechanical" causation: A killed my son/A is the cause of my failure/A caused the lightning to kill B. This can be linked with killings to get hold of *muti* (medicine) which functions within the "mechanical" frame of causality: business people often ask for a human skull to build into the foundation of a new shop to guarantee (i.e. to cause) good business; warm blood, it is believed, gives instant strength, and "fresh" genitals cause fertility. In other words, the quest for understanding is simply swapped for a desire to sniff out the cause.

Because we have to do, in the case of witchcraft, with perceptions based on a logical error (that making sense of an event is the same as finding the cause), neither the provision of facts (e.g. scientific schooling) nor punishment will change the situation. That is why the commission of the Northern Province recommended (Ralushai *et al.* 1996:61–2, 64–86) that rather than talk of the "suppression" of witchcraft, for example in legislation, to change to "management/managing" of the practice. Furthermore, medicine people should be encouraged to accept and comply with a code of conduct and to register with the Council for Traditional Healers. The Commission further recommended that the government start an intensive education programme "to free the inhabitants of the province from this belief" (Ralushai *et al.* 1996:60). In this the Commission was right, but again such a programme will have to be carefully planned so as to deal with the real problems: the first is a logical one about confusing different kinds of questions, while the second is about human relations and the settlement of differences. The new school subject "Guidance and life skills" could be of value here because it should also address the problem of the meaning of life; what kind of question this is and how we are to handle it; that is, to see questions regarding so-called primary causes for what they are, to understand how we can try to answer them and what the status of proposed answers is.[4]

3.4 Personhood

What is a person? Different answers have been given to this question. One of the best known is perhaps the answer of the French philosopher, René Descartes (1591–1650), that a person is a combination of two radically different substances, matter (i.e. a body) which is extended in space, and mind with thinking as its essential characteristic and which does not occupy space. This theory brought a whole range of problems in its wake such as that of the interaction between these two radically different substances (to account for human action for example), and that of other minds – how we can ever be sure of the other bodies we meet being "inhabited" by minds. In general this is an unacceptable account of the nature of a person. Menkiti (1984:172) sees this as a reduction of the person to "some isolated static quality of rationality, will or memory".

In line with Wiredu's suggestion of "strategic particularisation", the stratification of the person has received a lot of attention in African metaphysical thinking. A striking feature of these analyses is the differences between them. There are even contradictions between accounts of conceptions of the same cultural group. For example, Wiredu (1987b:318) argues that thinking is not part of the spiritual aspect of a person. He even remarks that this insight prevented the Akan from committing the category mistake of confusing concept and entity, as happened in the case of Western philosophy. Gyekye (1978:378) specifically makes thinking part of the spiritual aspect of a person. In spite of such differences, however, there are a few general points which can be made here.

3.4.1 The relational basis of selfhood

In Western philosophy the starting-point for an account of personhood is usually epistemological and psychological. Knowledge is the "possession" of a particular individual and the question then becomes how this knowledge can be accounted for, how the knower sees him/herself from the inside. In African thinking the starting-point is social relations – selfhood is seen and accounted for from this relational perspective. Kuckertz puts it like this:

> African thought and philosophy on personhood and selfhood is that the "I" belongs to the I-You-correspondence as a stream of lived experience without which it could not be thought and would not exist (1996:62).

Although the community plays an important part, Raditlhalo states, for example:

> A child is held to be the property of the community, and it is the community who are going to see to it that the individual child becomes a significant member of the community, an asset to all (1996:123).

In similar vein, Kuckertz emphasises the following:

> Certainly African thought appears to have greater ease of access to the relational existence of selfhood of human beings, without reducing them to mere products of any kind of collective or community . . . (1996:62).

3.4.2 Empirical considerations

There are two issues of interest here. A lot of metaphysical thinking has to do with a lack of scientific knowledge. In other words, we have proto-theories to account for events in the world for which there is no generally accepted explanation. There is something of this in African accounts of the person. With more knowledge of anatomy, and particularly neurology, these views will change or simply vanish. However, this knowledge actually plays a negligible part here. What is at stake here again is the way of conceptualising, of understanding human reality. As we saw in the previous paragraph, the approach in African thinking is from the standpoint of interpersonal relations.

These interpersonal relations presuppose an empirical reality. In African thinking this plays an important role. Personal relations presuppose living people in interaction. What is it to be alive? There is a clear difference between living things and dead matter. There is a difference between a living and a dead person. Even among living things there are marked differences. What then is the cause of such differences? Africans postulate a life principle, a "spiritual" (quasi-material) entity, which brings about life and which is responsible for the particular kind of life, to account for these differences.

A problem with this is that it leads to an infinite regress, however. To ensure life this entity itself must be alive, so a further entity is needed to account for its life and so on *ad infinitum.*

People have different personalities and character traits. Even though they are members of the same family or community and are raised in more or less the same way, individuals differ and they may differ radically. Why is this so? According to African thinkers this is because of another "spiritual" aspect of the person. Often this is linked to God; it is said that this part of the person is placed there by God and is the basis of a person's immortality.

3.4.3 Dualism

Although there are differences with reference to the constituting parts of a person, there is agreement that the person consists basically of a material aspect and a "spiritual" aspect or aspects. We thus have a dualism with the resulting question of how these different aspects function together. According to Wiredu (1987b:318), the question of interaction is not dealt with, but he also points out that we do not have the same kind of problem here as in the case of Descartes. Here it is stated from the start that these spiritual entities have material qualities; there is no radical or categorical difference between the spiritual and the material. This, however, raises other problems such as the true nature of the spiritual and the necessity of postulating such entities if they are not really different; are there different kinds of matter?

More (1996:153), perhaps, shows the way out of this difficulty. According to him (at least in the case of the Sotho people) the spiritual is not thought of as "some inner force, a mysterious or ghost-like inner power or hidden operations of an occult power which governs the individual's various general behaviour". His interpretation is behaviouristic in nature – not the postulation of entities in terms of metaphysical speculation, but what concepts refer to in actual communication. He says:

> When we describe a person as being ambitious, generous, or even as having a "good" or "bad" character or personality . . . it is to refer to certain types of tendencies manifested by certain kinds of behaviour pattern which allow us to anticipate, with a reasonable amount of assurance, the individual's actions and reactions to a variety of circumstances and possible contingencies (More 1996:153).

This kind of interpretation is more in line with the so-called quest for primary causes, that is, an attempt to understand and integrate events into wider patterns. It is, however, not without problems. There is talk here of "tendencies" and "anticipa[tion]". These must in turn be descriptions of behaviour that ascribes tendencies. This means that we do not have an explanation but only a theory about meaning. We know that this does not satisfy the metaphysically inclined.

3.4.4 Destiny

An important aspect of the African conception of a person is destiny, whose "choice" or "imposition" pre-determines for the person what he/she will be in life. A person's destiny determines his/her success or failure, his/her personality, luck or ill-luck. The available literature on the subject varies as to how an individual's destiny is allotted, whether it is a result of the person's own choice or through an imposition by another being.

The possibility that destiny could be an outcome of a person's own choice raises a fundamental problem. To be able to make a choice, one must have adequate information as well as a preference for the rational. All this certainly makes it most unlikely that an individual would opt for a destiny that is undesirable. On the other hand, if a person's destiny is an imposition, it has serious implications in matters of moral responsibility. Why should a person be held morally responsible for his/her actions if he/she had no choice in the making of his/her character and personality?

A greater conceptual problem arises from the issue of the alterability or otherwise of a person's destiny. If, indeed, the causes of our actions have been pre-ordained such that what will be will be, then why do we make efforts to alter pending misfortunes? One possible explanation has been that destiny does not amount to fatalism in which the person resigns him/herself to fate with respect to future situations. Among the Yoruba, for instance, it is believed that in certain conditions a person's destiny can be altered on earth, either for good or for bad. This sounds contradictory, but the main point of emphasis is on a person's moral character in the sense that destiny co-exists with freedom, morality, and responsibility. In Africa, the poverty of a lazy person is not blamed on destiny, nor is an offender spared punishment on account of his/her destiny. Some, in fact, argue that destiny among the Yoruba is conceived as a mere potentiality whose actualisation depends on a person's human qualities. Others claim that a person's destiny merely determines the broad outline of his/her life and not the minute details. To that extent, the concept of destiny may be understood as a version of soft determinism.

Gbadegesin (1991:360–368) discusses all these problems in connection with, and also as possible interpretations of, the idea of destiny. He concludes that destiny has two aspects, the individual's character and the influence of society, but in the end it is the influence and the demands of society that are really at stake:

> Persons are what they are in virtue of what they are destined to be, their character and the communal influence on them. . . . A person whose existence and personality is dependent on the community is expected in turn to contribute to the continued existence of the community. . . . The meaning of one's life is therefore measured by one's commitment to social ideals and communal existence (Gbadegesin 1991:367).

4. CONCLUDING REMARKS

Henk Withaar (1986:164) identifies the problem of political and cultural identity in black Africa as the central problem of African intellectuals. This is an impossible enterprise without a serious reflection on basic metaphysical thinking. Henri Maurier hits the nail on the head when he says:

> The awakening to a properly African conceptual framework will enable us to escape the "imperialism" of Western thought, as the politicians might say. We will be better able to locate our concrete problems. The West has used an individualistic and objectivist framework, and

that has given it a civilization where the individual is powerful, where liberty is a good that is absolute, where there is room for the play of free enterprise, where scientific and technological progress covers the world with its achievements. In Africa things are quite otherwise, since African civilization is characterised above all by solidarity, communitarianism, traditionalism, participation (1979:12, quoted in Withaar 1986:167).

This difference in perspective in thinking about reality poses both an internal and an external challenge. It is not enough for Africans to state that their perspective is a social or communitarian one; the views have to be explained, substantiated, and the implications for metaphysical thinking of such an approach have to be worked out. But the debate between African philosophers and philosophers belonging to other traditions or cultures is as important – no culture and particularly no philosophical perspective can develop in isolation. Such communication poses the challenge to other traditions and particularly to European (Western) philosophers to note the differences in perspective and to take the trouble to understand them. To interpret concepts such as God, spirit, cause, personality, immortality, etc. in the traditional Western way when dealing with African thinking must result in miscommunication. Both these challenges need to be taken up to further the discussion and understanding of ourselves, our world, and our relation to the world.

NOTES

1. Two of the most renowned thinkers who accepted such cultural relativism were the philosopher, Hegel, and the anthropologist, Lévi-Strauss. Hegel claimed:
   > for, culture does not allow us to be judged from the outside with foreign yardsticks. Conceived as a way of life and a specific language game, every culture is closed in on itself (quoted in Nordenbo 1995:39).

   Lévi-Strauss puts it even more strongly:
   > We . . . perceive our own identity as bound up with our culture. . . . A meeting between two cultures resembles . . . two trains passing one another – they travel in their own directions, at their own pace. A person who sits in one of the trains is able to go into another compartment and talk with his fellow travellers but can get only a glimpse of the travellers in the other train (quoted in Nordenbo 1995:40).

   Ironically both Hegel and Lévi-Strauss studied other cultures in great depth and used their findings in their respective historical and anthropological theorising.
2. For example, Placide Tempels's *Bantu Philosophy* (1959), Alexis Kagamé's *La philosophie Bantu-rwandaise de l'être* (1956), Léopold Senghor's *Les fondements de l'Africanité* (1967), John Mbiti's *African religions and philosophy* (1969).
3. Paulin Hountondji in an argument against ethnophilosophy proposes another idea:
   > it is urgent for African thought – in order to assure its own progress, its relevance to the problems of our societies – to remove itself from the Western philosophical debate in which it is submerged at present. It should stop languishing in the vertical dialogue of every African philosopher with his European counterpart, in order to shift from now on, following a horizontal axis to an internal debate in our societies concerning real philosophical problems, strictly geared to our actual preoccupations . . . we must from now on think for ourselves . . . and produce by so doing, new problem-fields, rooted in the concrete soil of our history of today (1989:13).
4. Hountondji would probably say that witchcraft must become the subject of philosophical analysis and debate. For him, to take folklore and popular modes of thinking seriously does not mean their blind acceptance; it should lead to a project of critical study
   > destined to show, among other things, what in those cultural forms must be overcome in view of the real emancipation of the people (Hountondji 1989:20).

Readings

ÈNÌYÀN: THE YORUBA CONCEPT OF A PERSON
SEGUN GBADEGESIN

In this chapter, we are concerned with the issue of human existence. I would like to address the question, "What is a person?" Deriving either from introspective reflections or from observations of life, this question is a crucial one which any rational human being is bound to raise at some point. That some traditional thinkers in African cultures must have raised such a question should be obvious from an examination of the traditional conceptual schemes. I will limit myself here to Yoruba traditional thought, while exposing similarities and differences through comparison with the Akan conceptual scheme. The reason for this should be obvious. Being a Yoruba, I may claim to have an intuitive understanding of the Yoruba language; and this makes it easier for me to investigate the conceptual scheme derived from it. Secondly, the problem created by generalisation for all traditional African societies has been demonstrated by several studies, and should be avoided. However, a comparison of the Yoruba and Akan views on these issues is perfectly in order, fortunately because there are philosophical studies of the Akan conceptual schemes on the same subject.

The Yoruba word for person is *ènìyàn*. However, *ènìyàn* has a normative dimension as well as an ordinary meaning. Thus it is not unusual when referring to a human being for an observer to say, "*Ki i se ènìyàn*" (He/she is not an *ènìyàn*). Such a comment is a judgement of the moral standing of the human being who is thus determined as falling short of what it takes to be recognised as such. I will come back later to the requirements of being, morally speaking, an *ènìyàn*. In the Yoruba language greater emphasis is placed on this normative dimension of *ènìyàn* than is perhaps placed on the concept of person in the English language. For now, however, I would like to address the issue of the structural components of the human person.

Among the terms that feature in discussions of the Yoruba concept of *ènìyàn*, the following are prominent: *ara, okàn, èmí, orí*, though there is a lot of confusion about what each of these means and what relationship exists among them. One way to avoid or at least minimise confusion is not to start with English equivalents of these terms, but rather to describe their usages among the Yoruba and to relate them to each other in terms of their functional interdependencies. Besides helping us to avoid inadequate prejudgements concerning resemblances between English-language and Yoruba-language philosophical discourses, this approach will also help throw light on the distinctiveness of Yoruba philosophical language.

Ara is the physico-material part of the human being. It includes the external and internal components: flesh, bone, heart, intestine, etc. It is described in physical terms: heavy/light, strong/weak, hot/cold, etc. Of course, sometimes its usage seems to suggest that it refers to the whole of the person, as when it is said:

Ara re lo mò (She knows herself only – She is selfish). In such a usage, however, we can be sure that the intention is to convey the message that the person referred to is judged as having concern for his/her own body – without caring for others or even for his/her own real self. *Imotara-eni-nikan* is the Yoruba word for selfishness. The idea is that a selfish person is concerned with the well-being of his/her body only (as opposed to the spirit). This suggests that if human beings were to be concerned with their spirits, they would not be selfish. It is ignorance of what is required for true well-being that makes people selfish. The body is like a case which houses the senses, which also constitute its most important elements. It is also the window to the world. Through the senses, a person is acquainted with the external world. There is, indeed, no serious controversy on the nature of the body. It is also significant that the question whether a human person is all body or something else is not seriously raised by typical Yoruba thinkers because it appears too obvious to them that there is more to a person than the body.

However, reference to *ara* as a material frame does not do justice to its conception as the totality of the physical organs. Furthermore, and perhaps resulting from this, because different human beings have different bodily constitutions, they naturally adapt differently to different situations. A heavily built person will absorb external pressures differently to a lightly built person. Illness and health are functions of bodily constitution, and this is an important consideration in the traditional diagnosis of illness and counselling. Traditional healers take account of the physico-chemical constituents of the human body.

Internal organs of the body are conceived as having their roles in the proper functioning of the person. For instance, the intestine plays a role in the physical strength of a person. A weak person is described as having only one *ìfun* (intestine) or none at all. This is on the basis of an understanding that the intestine has an important role in building strength through its part in the metabolic activity of the body. A weak person is thus one whose intestine is not functioning well or who has none. In the same way, *opolo* is recognised as the life-line of logical reasoning and ratiocinative activities. Located in the head, *opolo* controls the mental activities of human beings. A person who misbehaves is described as having no *opolo* or a malfunctioning *opolo*. A mentally retarded person is one whose *opolo* is not complete, while the insane is one whose *opolo* is disrupted. *Opolo* is thus a material component and the functions and activities it performs are carried out and recognised on the physical plane. It can also be located in the head, and traditional psychiatrists generally identify a disruption in its functioning as a physical cause of mental illness. This, of course, does not rule out their also looking for extra-natural causes for such illness if, after a period of medication based on the theory of physical cause, the patient does not improve.

Okàn is another element in the structure of the human person. In the Yoruba language it appears to have a dual character. On the one hand, it is acknowledged as the physical organ responsible for the circulation of blood, and it can be thus identified. On the other hand, however, it is also conceived as the source of emotional and psychic reactions. To encourage a person, one is asked to *kíí lókàn* (strengthen his/her heart). A person who is easily upset is described as having no *okàn*; and when a person is sad, it is said that his/her *okàn* is disrupted. In this usage, then, it appears that the emotional states of persons are taken as functions of the state of their *okàn*. Is *okàn*, the seat or centre of conscious identity, then equivalent to the English concept of "mind"? This is a difficult question for the reason that the Western concept of mind is itself ambiguous.

If we attend to the non-technical conception of mind, it means "that which feels, perceives, wills, thinks"; or that from which thought originates. This is how *Webster's new international dictionary* defines it, reserving the technical sense for "the conscious element in the universe (contrasted with matter)". In the non-technical sense, the mind may be an entity but not necessarily in the Cartesian sense of "that entity whose essence is thought". That which is "the subject of consciousness" may be a material entity. The dictionary does not give any clue as to its nature. On the other hand, the philosophic sense of mind which contrasts it with matter makes it more of an immaterial entity whose essence is thought. Since we are interested here in the question whether the Yoruba language entertains the concept of mind, we should attend to the non-technical sense. The question then is whether *okàn* is construed as "that from which thought originates" in the language. This is an especially pertinent question since *okàn* is recognised as a material component of the body. So is it just that *okàn* is a material component whose activities have consequences for the psychic, emotional, and thinking states of a person, and is therefore responsible for them? Or is it that beyond the physical and visible *okàn* there is something invisible and perhaps non-physical which is responsible for all forms of conscious identity?

It appears to me that something of the latter is involved. The Yoruba word *okàn* translates as heart. Following the former suggestion, it would mean that the pumping and circulation of blood by the physical heart is construed as so crucial that its results are connected with the state of a person's thoughts and emotions at any point in time, and that, therefore, between *opolo* (brain) and *okàn* (heart), conceived in physical terms, we may account for the mental activities and emotional states of persons. Though reasonable, I think this is a far-fetched hypothesis for understanding the Yoruba views on the matter. The reason is as follows. Drawing this kind of connection between the activity and/or state of the physical heart and the mental states of persons requires more than an intuitive understanding, and this requires adequate scientific knowledge which is not available to everyone, whether Africans or Westerners. This accounts for the non-physical conception of heart in the English language. Thus, after entering a technical zoological definition such as, "a hollow muscular organ which keeps up the blood circulation", *Webster's new international dictionary* gives the following, among others: "the heart regarded as the seat of spiritual or conscious life; consciousness, soul, spirit. Hence, a faculty or phase of consciousness or its seat." This suggests that beyond the physical organ there is a source of conscious identity which is construed to be invisible and more or less spiritual.

In the Yoruba language, *igboiyà* (bravery), *èrù* (fear), *ìfé* (love), *ìkórira* (hate), *ayò* (joy), *ìbànújé* (sadness), *ojora* (cowardice) are different manifestations of the state of the person and the *okàn* is identified as the basis for such conditions. A coward is an *aláèlókàn* (a person without a heart). But this cannot be taken literally as "a person without the physical organ". A stubborn person is *olókàn líle* (a hard-hearted person). In these cases, the reference is to the state of the person's conscious feelings, which is not identified with the functioning of the physical heart. Of course, the reference may not also be identified with a spiritual entity beyond the physical organ. There is no necessity about such identification, and reference to *okàn* in such statements may just be a manner of speaking, a metaphorical twist on language.

Yet there appears to be even stronger evidence for suggesting that, in Yoruba language and thought, *okàn* is conceived as the source of thought, and that it therefore makes sense to speak of something like an invisible source of thought and emotions which is quite distinct from the physical heart. To refer again to *Webster's new international dictionary's* definition of mind in the non-technical (non-philosophical) sense, mind is "that from which thought originates", "the subject of consciousness", "that which feels, perceives, wills, thinks". Interestingly, Webster's adds the following: "formerly conceived as an entity residing in the individual", which seems to suggest that it is no longer conceived as such. For the technical (philosophical) sense, the following is given: "the conscious element in the universe (in contrast to matter)". If we focus on the non-technical sense, it would appear that mind refers to something which is the source of thought in a broad sense. Since the existence of thought in this sense is recognised in the Yoruba language, it would appear that we may indeed locate its source too.

The Yoruba word for thought is *èrò*. To think is to *ronú*; thinking is *ìrònú*. Etymologically, to *rò* is to stir; and *inú* is the inside. Thus to *ronú* is to stir the inside of a person; and *ìrònú* is, literally, stirring the inside. But this does not make sense unless we identify the inside as the receptacle for the various organs and therefore thought as an activity that belongs to the totality of the organs. This runs against the Yoruba view of the matter, however, and it means that an appeal to etymology will not help here. The question, *Kíni èrò e?*, means, "What are your thoughts?", and this compares with *Kíni ó wà lókàn re?* which means, literally, "What is in your *okàn*?" or "What are your thoughts?". This seems to suggest that the seat (or source) of *èrò* (thought) is somewhere close to, if not identical with, *okàn*. But, as we have seen, *okàn* translates as physical heart; and in view of the Yoruba understanding of the heart as the organ for pumping and circulation of blood, they are not likely to see it as the seat of conscious thought. There would seem, therefore, to be some other source for such activities, though perhaps closely related to the heart. This is where the postulation of a double nature for the heart appears to make sense. For it appears, from an examination of the language, that while *okàn* (as physical heart) is recognised as responsible for blood circulation, it also has an invisible counterpart which is the seat of such conscious activities. It would seem that this invisible counterpart is the equivalent of the mind in English.

This of course raises a further problem. If *okàn* is thus taken as the seat of thought, what function is performed by *opolo* (brain)? *Erò* as it occurs in *okàn* seems to refer to a wider range of processes than what the *opolo* does. These include willing, desiring, wishing, hoping, worrying, believing, etc. When a person is described as an *aláèlókàn* (one with no *okàn*), it means that the person lacks the capacity for endurance. However, there is a class of activities which *opolo* seems to be particularly responsible for: ratiocinative activities. Thus a person who is incapable of simple logical reasoning is described as *aláèlópolo* (a person without a brain). It is a misuse of language to refer to a hard-hearted person as *olópolo líle* (one with a hard brain), just as it is incorrect to describe a mentally ill person as *olókàn dídàrú* (one with a disturbed *okàn*). Rather, the right description for such a person is *aláèlópolo*. In short, *opolo* seems to be recognised as the source of logical reasoning, while *okàn* is the source of all consciousness and emotional response.

The foregoing has centred on *ara* and *okàn* as parts of the make-up of a person. *Ara* (body) is physical, while *okàn* (heart) seems to have a dual nature with both physical and mental functions. But even if *okàn* is given only a physical meaning, its combination with *ara* still does not exhaust the components of the person. There is *èmí* which is another element different from *ara* and which is nonphysical. *Èmí* has been variously translated as soul, spirit, etc., but I think such translations confuse more than they clarify. The way *èmí* is conceived in the language and by the thinkers is better approached by attending to how it comes into the body, and this cannot be separated from the religious aspect of Yoruba thought on the matter.

Ènìyàn is made by the combined effort of *Olódùmarè*, the supreme deity, and some subordinates. The body is constructed by *Orìsà-nlá*, the arch-divinity. The deity then supplies *èmí* which activates the lifeless body. *Èmí* is thus construed as the active principle of life, the life-giving element put in place by the deity. It is also construed as part of the divine breath. But it is to be distinguished from *èémí* (breath) which is physically identifiable. *Èémí* is construed as a manifestation of the continued presence of *èmí*. In other words, once the body is supplied with *èmí* through divine action of the deity, *ara* (body) now has *èémí* (breath) and begins to *mí* (breathe). The presence of *èmí* ensures that the human body, previously lifeless, now becomes a human being – a being that exists. Since *èmí* is part of the divine breath, it will continue as the principle of life for a particular human being at the pleasure of the deity. When it is recalled, the human being ceases to exist. So *èmí* is more the determinant and guarantor of existence. It is the breathing spirit put in a human body by the deity to turn it into a human being. Having *èmí* thus makes one a child of the deity and therefore worthy of protection from harm. Reference to one as an *elèmí* is an indirect warning against being maltreated. It is interesting that this usage is also extended to other creatures, including insects, because they are believed to come into being by the creative activity of the deity.

Èmí, as the active element of life, is thus a component common to all human beings. It not only activates the body by supplying the means of life and existence, it also guarantees such conscious existence as long as it remains in force. As an affirmation of life, it also brings hope and makes desires realisable. Two claims have been made about the nature of *èmí*: it is spiritual, and it has an independent existence. Both claims are subject to philosophical dispute. Firstly, it has been contested that *èmí* cannot be spiritual while it at the same time occupies space by being embodied. Secondly, the question of independent existence is disputed on the ground that it is not an entity but a force, and as such cannot have an independent existence. So we must address the question whether *èmí* is conceived as spiritual by the Yoruba, and, if so, whether such a conception is incoherent.

Frankly, attending to language alone by attempting to translate "spiritual" into Yoruba is not of much help to the objector. The Yoruba dictionary translates spirit as *èmí*, spiritual as *ti èmí*, matter as *ohunkóhun tí a fi ojú rí, tí a sì fi owó kàn* (i.e. whatever we see with our eyes and touch with our hands), and material as *nkan ti ara* (that which pertains to the body). Furthermore, however, it seems clear that the Yoruba understand *èmí* as the lifeline of human existence. They understand it as a portion of *Olódùmarè's* divine breath. But since *Olódùmarè* is also understood as spiritual, that portion of this source of being which is given to the human being must also be spiritual. It is also recognised that it is the possession of *èmí* that makes humans children of *Olódùmarè*. It is the logic of the source of *èmí*, therefore, that suggests its nature as spiritual. Unless we deny the spirituality of *Olódùmarè*, we cannot deny, without inconsistency, the spiritual nature of *èmí*.

Now, we have to address the other question regarding the incoherence of the belief: how can a spirit occupy space and still remain a spirit? It must be remarked that this is not an issue which engaged the attention of the traditional thinker. Yet I think there are two approaches to the issue. Firstly, we may understand the reference to *èmí* as spiritual as in fact reference to an invisible entity and nothing more than that. The dictionary meanings cited above confirm this. On this showing, it may very well be that *èmí*, as a spiritual entity, is only invisible to the ordinary eyes and may contain quasi-physical attributes which make the idea of its occupation of space coherent. Indeed, this is how people understand free spirit (*iwin, òrò*) that features in fairy tales. Also, the *èmí* of a witch is understood in this way: it can fly away at night to attend meetings with fellow witches. For this to be an adequate resolution of the issue, however, it has to be the case that the spiritual nature of the supreme deity is also understood in such a quasi-physical sense since, as we have noted, *èmí* is a portion of *Olódùmarè*. A second approach is to brush off the apparent inconsistency. On this showing, one may just understand *èmí* as the spiritual entity which, by virtue of this, has the capacity to change forms, unlike a material entity. So it could assume a physical nature when there is need for it, and revert to the spiritual nature thereafter. This would make it neither physical nor quasi-physical. It would just be that, by virtue of its spiritual nature (which presumably endows it with the power of changeability), it is capable of changing form. Again, this is how other free spirits are construed. And though *Olódùmarè* is sometimes presented as having transactions with human beings (in *Ifá* divination poetry), this is also understood it terms of the deity's spiritual nature. Indeed the traditionally acknowledged ability of some special human beings to "see" and "communicate" with spirits does not suggest that such spirits have physical properties since they are supposed to operate beyond ordinary space.

Finally, there is the question of the independent existence of *èmí*. Thus, it has been suggested that if *èmí* is like a force injected into the body by the deity, then it can have no independent existence, and should be construed as just a principle or force which activates but which is not itself an entity. I think this is too far-fetched, however. As I remarked above, if we attend to the language, there is a difference between *èmí* and *èémí*. The latter is identifiable empirically. But when the Yoruba say *èmí wa* (there is *èmí*), they mean more than "there is breath". It is also important constantly to bear in mind the religious aspect of this conception of a person. If the deity is believed to be spiritual and to have an independent existence, what difficulty is there in conceiving the independent existence of an *èmí* outside the bodily frame? Furthermore, if it is the *èmí* that is thought of as activating the human body, there also appears to be no problem conceiving its consciousness outside the body. If we do not deny consciousness to the deity, which is construed as spiritual (and therefore not in bodily existence), then having no body cannot be a basis for denying the consciousness of *èmí* which, again, is just an aspect of the deity.

Orí is another element in the make-up of the human person. *Orí* has a dual character. On the one hand, it refers to the physical head and, given the acknowledged significance of the head *vis-à-vis* the rest of the body, *orí* is considered vital even in its physical character. It is the seat of the brain and, from what we observed earlier on about this, its importance cannot be over-emphasised. The postulation of a spiritual *orí* beyond this physical *orí* is in recognition of this. In any case, there is the conception of an *orí* which is recognised as the bearer of the person's destiny as well as the determinant of personality. How does this element come into the picture? Earlier on, I referred to the creative process of the human being as a combined effort of the deity and some subordinates. I mentioned only *Orìsà-nlá* as the crafter of the body. The other is *Ajàlá,* the "potter of *orí*". The idea is that after *èmí* has been put in place, the newly created human being proceeds to the next stage – the house of *Ajàlá* – for the "choice" of an *orí*. The *orí* is, as it were, the "case" in which individual destinies are wound up. Each newly created being picks up his/her preferred "case" without knowing what is stored there. But whatever is stored therein will determine the life-course of the individual in the world. It is thus the *orí* so chosen that, as the bearer of the individual's destiny, determines his/her personality.

There are conflicting accounts of the process of the choice of *orí* or, indeed, of its nature. Some accounts indicate that the *orí* itself, as a fully conscious personality-component of the person, kneels down to pick the destiny. Others, however, suggest that *orí* is chosen by the individual after he/she is animated by the deity with the supply of *èmí*. Both seem to be coherent accounts, and may be made sense of by appeal to the language. Thus, the latter account may be defended on the grounds that it is derived from oral tradition as recorded in the Ifa divination poetry. Secondly, it appears to capture more clearly the idea behind the linguistic expression of the choice of destiny. For in the language, the process is described as the choice of *orí*, and *orí* is construed as an entity in which destiny is encased. That is, it is the *orí* that is chosen. The picture one gets from this latter account is that of numerous *orí's* with different destinies or portions already wound up in them, and the individuals (*ara* + *èmí*) going to make a choice of any *orí* that appeals to them without knowing the destiny wound up in them.

The other account suggests that it is the *orí* itself, as a full personality, that kneels down to make the choice of destiny. This does not take into consideration the fact that a personality is not determined before the choice of destiny. It is the destiny or portion that is chosen that forms a personality. On the other hand, one way of reconciling the two positions is to reconstruct the former position which claims that it is the *ara* + *èmí* that does the choice of *orí*. To do this one may allow that what is meant by the choice of *orí* here is that the individual (*ara* + *èmí*) kneels down before *Olódùmarè* to choose, by verbal declaration, what he/she would be or do in the world. In other words, to choose one's *orí* simply means choosing one's destiny. In this case, there is no entity in any form, physical, quasi-physical or spiritual, which is picked up by the individual. He/she just speaks the words of destiny and these words are approved by the deity. This account looks a lot more coherent. For one thing, it allows us to avoid the problem of how an *orí*, whether physically or quasi-physically construed, can enter into the physical structure of the person so as to become part of his/her component. But though it avoids this problem, it raises a number of others. Firstly, it leaves no room for the deity that figures in the Yoruba account, namely *Ajàlá,* the potter of human *orí*. Secondly, it does not account for the fact that the Yoruba regard *orí* as a spiritual component of personality which is in fact raised to the level of a personal divinity. Finally, if *orí*, as understood by the Yoruba, merely refers to the words of destiny as declared by individuals, then their constant reference to *orí* in supplications and the offerings of sacrifices to it should be judged a mistake. Yet the fact remains that if it is a mistake, it is one which a typical Yoruba would prefer to make. The idea of *orí* as a spiritual component chosen by the individual and having the power of a guardian and protector over him/her, seems too deep-rooted in the Yoruba world-view to be given up.

It is thus the *orí* so chosen, with destiny wound up in it, that determines the personality of the individual. And though the *orí* is symbolised by the physical head, it is not identical with it. For the *orí* is construed as the inner – or spiritual – head (*orí-inú*). And as Abimbola (1971:80) has pointed out, "*Orí* is regarded as an individual's personal divinity who caters for their personal interests." As such, sacrifices are offered to it. This raises the question whether it is (or should be) regarded also as a component of the human person. I think it should indeed be regarded as a spiritual component of the person. To regard *orí* as a personal divinity is to underscore its primacy *vis-à-vis* the divinities. This is already indicated by what it means. As the bearer of one's destiny, it has the key to one's future success or failure, in which case it is indeed more important than the divinities. The saying, "*Orí l'à bá bo, a bá f'òrìsà sílè*" (We thought to offer sacrifices to our *orí*, laying aside the *orìsà's*) is indicative of the importance of a personality-determinant which means more to us than the divinities. Therefore, as the personality-determining element of the individual, *orí* is a spiritual component of his/her make-up. This way of putting the matter should take care of any puzzles that may arise from regarding the *orí* as a constituent of the human being. For instance, if destiny is the pattern of events that will unfold in a person's life history, how can any constituent of that human personality be said to bear it? The answer to this is that, as has been mentioned above, though *orí* is construed as a component of the person, it is also construed as a divinity, in which capacity it is spiritual. It is in this respect that it is said to bear the destiny of the person. Indeed, this is also the meaning of its spiritual nature. If you perform an autopsy on a person, you are not going to be able to locate *orí* in addition to the physical head. So the *orí* that bears destiny is at once the personality component of the person (in the sense that it determines that personality), as well as a divinity, in which capacity it is more or less the guardian spirit of the person. Another term for it in the language is *enìkejì* (the partner or double).

There are further problems with the concept. For instance, if the *ara* is physical body, how can it be available before birth to choose an *orí*? Or if the pre-natal *ara* is not the physical body, is it quasi-physical? Is the *èmí* that is involved in this combination of *ara* and *èmí* spiritual or physical? Firstly, the time frame here is pre-natal. Activities like choosing an *orí* go on in the spirit world where the divinities and prospective human beings are construed as engaging in all kinds of relationships and exchanges. In this world, anything is conceivable. Indeed, it will be recalled that a divinity (*Òrìsà-nlá*) is postulated as responsible for moulding the human body. So it could be the physical body that is involved. Also there are images of physical activities presented: the newly formed *ara* with its associated deity-given *èmí* moves to the "house" of *Ajàlá*, the "potter of heads" who is responsible for the *orí*. It seems clear, however, that it is a combination of conceptualisation and imagination that is brought into play here. On the one hand, there is a conception of a spirit world in which anything can happen. On the other land, some of the things that can happen there are imagined on the basis of what is experienced in the physical world and are therefore endowed with its attributes. We may choose to impose the idea of a quasi-physical *ara* on this basis, and we may perhaps thus succeed in making the account look more coherent to us. However, we should note that such a reconstruction may fail to do full justice to the ideas as understood in the language.

We should next address the issue of the relationship between the so-far identified components of the person; *ara, okàn, èmí,* and *orí.* From what has been said thus far, the following seems clear. Firstly, these components may be grouped into two: physico-material and mental-spiritual. *Ara* belongs to the first, *èmí* to the second, and *orí* and *okàn* have physical and mental aspects. Secondly, a mentalistic conception of *okàn* is postulated to account for the phenomenon of thought. Perhaps there is no need for such a postulation, but there is no doubt that it exists. We have seen that it also exists in the ordinary use of the heart in the English language. Thirdly, *orí* is also postulated as a spiritual entity (in addition to its meaning as physical head) to account for the phenomenon of destiny. There is no parallel to this postulation in the English language, and I consider it the distinctive aspect of the Yoruba concept of a person. Even when *okàn* is postulated to account for the phenomenon of thought, whatever it has to do with this and with the emotional state of a person cannot be separated from the *orí* as the bearer of her destiny. Therefore, *okàn,* as source of conscious thought and emotions, could be regarded as a subsequent (post-natal) expression of the destiny portion encased pre-natally in the *orí.* This may be explained as follows: *orí* determines the personality of the individual. The emotional states, on the other hand, are reflections and good indicators of the personality. *Okàn,* as the source of post-natal consciousness and emotions, therefore only reflects that which had been encased in the *orí* originally. In other words, *okàn* may be regarded as one of the avenues through which destiny unfolds in the post-natal existence of the person.

The symbolic representation of *orí* by the physical head is indeed indicative of how its importance is construed. As the location of *opolo* (brain), the physical head is the seat of intelligence. The introduction of *orí* (inner-head and bearer of destiny) as a spiritual element is to suggest that there is more to what is seen to be going on, and this is the spiritual direction of the *orí.* Hence the idea of currying its favour.

Orí is therefore the determinant of the personality of the individual. The *èmí,* as the active life force supplied by the deity, is a common denominator. Though it guarantees existence and activates the lifeless body into consciousness, it cannot be the basis for identifying persons as individual selves because it is common to all. Furthermore, that *èmí* activates the lifeless body does not make it the locus of conscious identity because an individual may have *èmí* (as an activating life principle) and still not be conscious of his/her existence as a self. On the other hand, *orí* is identified with each person; it is an essential component of human personality. However, this does not make it the locus of conscious identity. Because of its spiritual dimension, *orí* functions as a remote controller of the person's fundamental activities, including thinking; but it is not itself the centre or seat of thought. The very thought of appealing to one's *orí* through sacrifice already presupposes the existence of the *orí* which is, in that case, the object of the thought. The subject of conscious identity responsible for the phenomenon of thinking, feeling, willing, and desiring is, in the Yoruba language, *okàn,* which would seem to correspond to the concept of the mind in English. The relationship, with directions of functional control may be represented as follows:

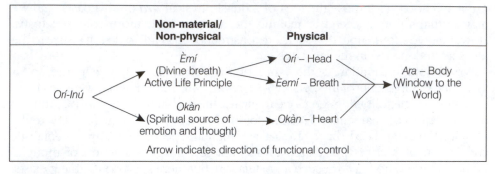

COMPARISON WITH THE AKAN CONCEPT OF THE PERSON

The purpose of this comparison is to explore the similarities and differences between the Yoruba and Akan concepts of the person. For the most part, I adopt Kwame Gyekye's analysis of the Akan conception for this purpose with references to Kwasi Wiredu's as necessary. I note also some major disagreements between the two Akan authors.

For the most part, there appear to be more similarities than differences between the two conceptions. The major difference is in the Akan conception of *okra* which is also regarded as the active life principle supplied by the deity, but which is, in addition, the bearer of destiny. It will be recalled that in the Yoruba conception *èmí*, which is the equivalent of Akan *okra*, is not the bearer of destiny. Something else, *orí*, is postulated for that. Furthermore, according to Gyekye, *okra* and *sunsum* (an immaterial entity responsible for thought) constitute a spiritual unity but they are not identical. There is a disagreement between Gyekye and Wiredu on the latter's account of the *okra* as "quasi-physical" and his denial that *okra* is postulated to account for thought. Gyekye's point, which seems to indicate a correspondence between Yoruba and Akan thinking on the matter, is that *okra* is believed by the Akans to be spiritual and not quasi-physical. But Wiredu has argued that the Akan *okra* is construed as quasi-physical and one reason he gives is that

> highly developed medicine men are claimed to be able to enter into communication with an *okra,* and those that have eyes with medicinally heightened perception are said to be capable of seeing such things (1983:119–120).

My own initial reaction to this argument is that the fact that medicine-men enter into communication with *okra* should not suggest its having a quasi-physical nature because, after all, medicine-men are generally believed to have the ability to operate in the spiritual realm. However, in a private correspondence with me, Wiredu has further clarified his position on the matter. His point is this:

> The eye is a sense organ and the concept of seeing is bound up with spatiality. However heightened the powers of an eye may become, if it *sees* something, that thing will have to be in space. In regard to any claim to see something, it must make sense to ask, 'Where is it?' (private exchange between myself and Wiredu).

He takes this to be a conceptual point. While I understand this conceptual point, it seems to me to miss the crucial point of the dispute which is that the herbalists, in such contexts, operate outside ordinary space and time and that stories of paraphysical sightings cannot be taken as evidence of a physical existence of the sighted beings. This is what the idea of extra-sensory perception is all about. If the concept of "seeing" is involved, it is not ordinary seeing and is therefore not bound up with ordinary spatiality. Of course, scientists may deny the reality of such occurrences for the reason that there are no scientific proofs for them, but as Albert Mosley has observed, the

> idea that each individual has an aspect of his being that defies description in terms of the classical concepts of space, time, and matter, which is non-physical, but which can nonetheless affect physical manifestations, is an essential metaphysical assumption under-lying the beliefs and practices of traditional magic (1978:12).

On the other issue, it seems again that Wiredu's account of thought, which he uses to deny that *okra* is distinguishable from soul, needs to be broadened. While I grant that the concept of soul, as it features in Christian and Western philosophy, is problematic in the context of African thought, it is not clear to me that, on the basis of the shared assumptions between Wiredu and Gyekye, they could not agree on the idea of an equivalence of *okra* and soul. For if thought refers to consciousness, and *okra* is the principle of consciousness, then it could be taken as the equivalent of soul. There seems to be a confusion, though, arising from Gyekye's account of a spiritual unity of *okra* and *sunsum*. On the one hand, *sunsum* is responsible for thought in the narrow sense – as ratiocination (Gyekye 1987:87) – and at the same time it is the "activating principle in the person" (Gyekye 1987:88). On the other hand, however, Gyekye also says that *okra* "is the principle of life of a person" (Gyekye 1987:97). What *sunsum* does as the "activating principle" is unclear since *okra* is also regarded as the "principle of life". In the Yoruba conception, *èmí* as the activating principle brings the body to conscious existence and (as in the case of *okra*) its departure from the human being is death.

Again from the characterisation of the *okra* as the bearer of destiny, it would appear that it (and not *sunsum*) should be regarded as the component on which "one's health, worldly power, position, influence, success, etc. would depend" (Gyekye 1987:98). This is how *orí* (as bearer of destiny) is conceived in Yoruba thought. If *sunsum* is "that which thinks, desires, feels", then it performs functions similar to that attributed to *okàn* by the Yoruba. But again, the Yoruba do not regard *okàn* as the determinant of health, worldly power, position, etc. Insofar as these various components go, then, the following seems to me to be the picture from this comparison:

1. *Okra* seems the equivalent of *Èmí*, but while *okra* is postulated as the bearer of destiny, *èmí* is not.
2. *Sunsum* (as that which thinks, feels, etc.) seems the equivalent of Yoruba *okàn*, but while *sunsum* is postulated as the determinant of power, success, and wealth, *okàn is* not.
3. *Okra* (in Akan) is postulated as responsible for activities for which the Yoruba postulate two parts *(Èmí* and *Orí).*

I wish to conclude this section with a few observations on Gyekye's argument to demonstrate the nature of *sunsum* as an immaterial element. To do this, Gyekye examines and attempts to debunk some anthropological accounts of *sunsum*. It is in this exercise that I find some of Gyekye's arguments unconvincing. It may very well be that the anthropologists are wrong in their accounts, but Gyekye's arguments fail to show this, at least in some cases.

. The first position that Gyekye (1987:89) takes up is that which characterises *sunsum* as "something that perishes with the body". What is interesting here is that Gyekye does not conclude his argument against Danquah. He gives us only one premise in the form of a conditional: "now, if the *sunsum* perishes along with the body, a physical object, then it follows that it is also something physical or material." He goes on to show that this seems to be Danquah's position. And yet, he does nothing more to show the incorrectness of this position.

Next, Gyekye argues that

1. The functions or activities attributed to the *sunsum* indicate that it is neither material nor mortal nor derived from the father.
   a. *sunsum* moulds the child's personality (Busia 1954)
   b. *sunsum* constitutes or determines a person's personality and character (Danquah 1944), etc.
2. Personality involves such characteristics as courage, thoughts, feelings, actions, etc.
3. Such qualities (courage, jealousy, gentleness, forcefulness) are psychological, not sensible.

Therefore:

4. If *sunsum* is what constitutes the basis of an individual's personality, it cannot be a physical thing.

I sympathise with this argument, but it is not convincing to ground the position that a "material conception of *sunsum* is logically impossible". For, suppose the function of *sunsum* is the development of personality, nothing prevents it from performing this function as a physical thing. Courage can be connected with a solid constitution of the physical *sunsum* which strengthens the psyche. To press his point here, I think Gyekye has to rely on how religious concepts filter into the people's understanding of these relationships. Just as I argued in the case of the Yoruba *okàn*, it seems to me that a purely physical concept of *sunsum* is not logically inconceivable even on Gyekye's grounds, unless it is argued that *sunsum*, like *okra*, is an aspect of the deity; and since the deity is spirit, *sunsum* must also be spirit. This may, in fact, be Gyekye's argument as the following seem to suggest:

1. Busia (1954) and others (e.g. Danquah 1944) claim that *sunsum* derives from the father and that it is therefore mortal.
2. But *sunsum* derives from the supreme being.

Therefore:

3. It must be divine and immortal.
4. After all, trees, plants and other objects also have *sunsum*.
5. But if *sunsum* derives from the father, these natural objects cannot have it.
6. Therefore *sunsum* does not derive from the father.

This argument could have nailed the point down at premise 3. Gyekye could simply have added that since *sunsum*, following its source, is divine and immortal, it must therefore be spiritual too. But Gyekye goes on to premise 4 which suggests that since trees and animals have *sunsum*, it could not derive from the father, apparently because trees and plants do not have fathers. But must trees have human fathers for their *sunsum* to be passed on to them? One would think that the reproductive activities of trees and animals are sufficient to pass on their *sunsum* to their offspring.

THE CONCEPT OF DESTINY

As we have seen, the belief in predestination, expressed in the concept of *orí*, seems to suggest that the Yoruba have some anxiety about human helplessness in certain situations. However, it also expresses the people's conviction that human existence has meaning. It suggests, for instance, that human beings are not on a purposeless mission in this world, that they have a mission to fulfil, a message to deliver – which is the meaning of their existence – and that this mission has been fully endorsed by the creator. Whatever is (or is not) done by them should therefore be explained by appeal to this original mission. The concept of *orí* expresses this idea.

However, like most common cultural beliefs, there are a number of philosophical puzzles connected with this concept. Firstly, the relationship between *orí* and the concept of destiny has been variously conceived. There is need for clarification. Secondly, there is a problem with regard to the relationship between the beliefs in predestination, immortality, and reincarnation. Thirdly, there is the problem of the apparent contradiction between the belief in predestination and the attribution of responsibility for actions to human beings. I shall take up these problems in turn.

Orí literally means head, as has been seen above. Ordinarily, the physical head, in addition to its other functions, is used to carry things. It is the bearer of goods and commodities. Before the development of machines and vehicles, human portage was the mode of movement. Farm products were carried on heads to market centres or homes. The head therefore served an economic function. But more than this, the head is the location of important parts of the human body: the eyes, regarded by the Yoruba as *oba-ara* (king of the body), are located there; so is the brain, which controls intelligence and sanity. Perhaps this special nature of the physical head suggests to the Yoruba the idea that it must also have a spiritual dimension. Thus, the physical head is believed to symbolise or represent an inner head which is the bearer of a person's destiny and which therefore is the remote controller of one's endeavours in the world. It is this inner head which is referred to as *orí-inu,* or simply, *orí*. Therefore *orí* is not identical with destiny, though it is its bearer.

Destiny refers to the pre-ordained portion of life wound and sealed up in an *orí*. Human beings have an allotment of this destiny which then determines what they will be in life – whether a success or a failure. Destiny determines the general course of life, and since *orí* is the receptacle and bearer of destiny it is also regarded as its controller. Hence the idea of appealing to one's *orí* to lead one aright. But how does an actual destiny get affixed to a particular human being? The procedure has been variously conceived, giving rise to three models of destiny. Firstly, there is the idea that the portion gets allocated to individuals as a result of their own "choice", or rather, the "choice" of their own *orí*. Hence the idea of destiny as *àkúnlèyàn* (that which one kneels down to choose). Secondly, there is the conception of destiny as the position which is affixed to an individual, not necessarily by his/her own choice. In this model, the individual kneels to receive the pre-ordained portion from the creator. Hence the idea of destiny as *àkúnlègbà* (that which one kneels to receive). Thirdly, there is the conception of destiny which seems to stand between the previous two. In this conception, though there is the idea of choice, the identity of the choice-maker is not clear – whether it is the individual or some other being making the choice for him or her. In addition, there is the idea of a fixation of the portion on the individual. This is the idea of destiny as *àyànmó* (an affixed choice).

In all these conceptions, there is a common thread; namely, the fact that the individual is either the choice-maker or the passive receiver or the one for whom the choice is made and affixed. On the other hand, what is chosen – the portion of life – is wound up in the *orí* which is its bearer and therefore the object of choice or allocation. There is thus a close relationship between *orí*, the bearer, and *kádàrá* (destiny) the portion of life that is borne. This has led to the idea of speaking of *orí* as if it were the portion itself, or as if it had a great deal of influence on shaping the course of the destiny it is supposed to bear. Thus appeals and supplications are made to *orí* to either help win a particular battle, or succeed in a particular endeavour. It is believed that if one's *orí* is against one, there is no question of success. Perhaps there is a justification for this belief in the efficacy of *orí* to influence the course of destiny. After all, in the three variants of the conception of destiny discussed above, *orí* plays the role of bearer of destiny.

A word should be added here with regard to the question of the choice of destiny as explicitly conceived in one of the variants discussed above. A Yoruba song expresses the idea of choice of *orí* as bearer of destiny thus:

> *Èmí 'o mo ibi ol'orí nyan orí o*
> *Mbá lò yan t'èmí*
> *Ibi kan náà l'ati nyan orí o*
> *Kádàrá kò papò ni.*

> (I do not know where people with good *orí* choose their *orí*,
> I would have gone to choose mine there;
> But no! We choose our *orí* from the same source;
> It's only that our destinies are not identical.)

Again, this is a song expressing anguish. But the point that I want to make now is with regard to the element of choice referred to in the song. It has been argued that, strictly speaking, an individual cannot be said to have chosen a destiny. This is because, for there to be a choice, there has to be adequate information and rational preference; and, as some have argued, none of this is present in the conceptualisation of the choice of *orí*.

Let us look at the problem more closely. The three procedures which have been identified as the manner in which *orí* and destiny get attached to a person are:

1. *àkúnlèyàn* (chosen while kneeling down)
2. *àkúnlègbà* (received while kneeling down)
3. *àyànmó* (affixed choice).

Of these, it is clearly the first that suggests the idea of an individual really making a choice. The second clearly does not since it portrays the idea of an individual receiving the portion by receiving an *orí* (this is the version that agrees with the Akan concept of destiny). The third also does not clearly represent the individual as making a choice; it may be made by someone else and then affixed to him/her.

If we focus on the first version – *àkúnlèyàn* – we may now raise the question whether indeed there is a genuine choice. Firstly, let us have a picture of the individual who is to make the "choice". As we have observed before, the making of the human being is a collective effort of *Olódùmarè*, *Orìsà-nlá* and *Ajàlá*. *Orìsà-nlá* makes the body (complete), after which *Olódùmarè* supplies the *èmí* (active life principle – divine breath). Then, this body plus life-principle, who is now a quasi-conscious individual, moves to the house of *Ajàlá* who is the maker of *orí*. The mission is to have his/her portion of life. The individual portions of life are wound up in the various *orís* in different shades and colours, some over-burnt, some not properly done. Some of the *orí* look beautiful outside, but inside are full of "worms". Some of them look ugly, but inside are solid and neat. The insides are not accessible to the individual, but the outsides are. So, depending on the "taste" of each "body-life principle", that is the quasi-conscious individual, one of the *orís* is picked up. After picking it up, the conscious individual is ready to proceed to the gate-keeper of heaven. There the *orí* just picked starts automatically to replay the wound-up information about what its owner will be; after which it is sealed again and the individual proceeds on his/her journey to the earth, on the way crossing the river of forgetfulness, which makes it impossible to remember what the *orí* had relayed at the gate.

We may now ask: is this a real choice? Obviously, if we are concerned with what is wound up inside the *orí*, the individual does not have adequate information. However, the question may be raised as to why we should be so concerned with what is wound up inside the *orí* if we agree that in the choice of a particular *orí*, the individual makes a choice on the basis of his/her taste. That this turns out to be harbouring a bad destiny, it may be urged, does not detract from the fact that *orí*, the bearer of this destiny, was chosen from among others. To press this argument, we may be asked to consider the analogous case of a game of lottery. You are presented with fifty-four numbers out of which six will be the winning numbers. On your own, you pick six numbers that appeal to you. Of course, you have no idea which numbers will win. But you happen to prefer the numbers you pick. If this is a blind choice, it remains your choice nonetheless. You did not choose to lose; you chose the numbers which you hoped would win. This may appear to be similar to what goes on in the choice of *orí*. A similar situation of choice is in the case of a spouse. Let us assume that we all make our choices on the basis of our taste, after some reflection. But it is also true that in most cases we do not reflect at all, or at least not enough. Otherwise, the adage that love is blind would not make sense. Shall we say that in such cases we cannot be said to know every detail about our spouse and have therefore not made a choice in the real sense. It may be argued then that the important criteria are consciousness of the alternatives (in the case of destiny, the various *orís*) and one's own judgement as to the preferable alternative.

This is an interesting argument, but I do not think that it succeeds without further assumptions. It is true that if one is conscious of what one is choosing, then one cannot complain. And in a sense, it may also be true that the individual, at the point where the *èmí* is implanted, is conscious. However, there are problems. Firstly, it is not clear that the concept of taste is applicable here since the personality of a person plays a crucial role in his/her taste. Yet it is the *orí* itself that determines the kind of personality a person will have. Therefore one cannot be expected to have taste before one has made that "choice" of *orí*. The choice is therefore blind in this respect. Secondly, it is not the *orí* in itself that is desired, if the concept of desire can even be applied here. Rather it is what is inside it. So, if what is inside is not known and there is no information about it, strictly there can be no choice. In other words, since the real object of choice is the destiny (life-portion) and not just the *orí* (as the carrier), we should expect more information on the former. Perhaps the important point about this concept is that the various destinies represent the various missions to be accomplished in the world, and the messages are to be borne by different individuals. The most that can be done is to seal them up in various receptacles which may then be "chosen" so that there is no question of favouritism, and all the messages get delivered. But if the receptacles – *orí* as bearers of the destinies – are "chosen" on the basis of the "tastes" of individuals who make the "choice", whatever is inside should be construed as having been "chosen". As should be clear, this way of putting it does not remove the fact of the blindness of the choice of destiny. More important is the fact that the analogy with the game of lottery will not work for one obvious reason. With regard to lottery, an individual may choose not to choose, but this is not the case with destiny. You cannot refuse to choose an *orí* and this makes it a matter of forced choice in addition to its being a blind one.

The second problem I want to address is that of the relationship between beliefs in predestination, immortality, and reincarnation. The Yoruba believe that earthly death is not the end of life and that a person who has reached maturity before death will reincarnate in a different form in a later life. This is why dead ancestors are not forgotten and why newborn children may be named after a recently deceased older member of the family. With respect to the belief in destiny, this raises the question whether the original destiny allotted to the individual governs his/her later life or whether a new portion has to be allotted each time the *èmí* is about to reincarnate. There seems to be not much reflection on this problem in traditional thought. The problem is this. In addition to the belief in destiny and reincarnation, there is the belief in divine sanctions in the after-life. Thus any individual who has grossly misbehaved while on earth will be punished at death and the *èmí* of such a person may be made to inhabit the body of an animal to become a beast of burden in later life. In such a situation, the question arises whether the reincarnated *èmí* will be expected to have a new portion (destiny) allotted to him/her or whether such a punishment will have been wound up in the original destiny. If the former is the case, it is quite possible that the new destiny so chosen may be a good one so that the reincarnated *èmí* escapes the kind of punishment envisaged for such a wicked life, unless there is a way of teleguiding a reincarnated *èmí* to pick the deserved destiny. Here, the idea of *àkúnlégbà* (that which is received while kneeling down) will seem to make sense. In other words, the second time around, it may have to be imposed as deserved. On the other hand, if the second alternative above is the case – subsequent punishment or reward for the first life is bound up with the original destiny – it follows that the individual has no chance of escaping the consequences of the original portion of his/her destiny. This may seem unfair; however, it is not even clear that we should consider it as punishment. For the suffering that the person now goes through in a subsequent life has already been included in the portion allotted to him/her originally, and it is this original portion for the first life that is responsible for the behaviour that warrants the subsequent life's suffering.

There is, in addition to the above, the problem of the apparent contradiction between a belief in destiny and the practice of attributing responsibility to human agents, and the consequent apportioning of praise and blame. If a person is predestined to be a certain sort of person, can we at the same time hold him/her responsible for his/her actions? The problem is the subject of Ola Rotimi's *The Gods are not to blame* (1971), a Yoruba adaptation of Sophocles's *Oedipus Rex*. The main character of the play, *Odéwálé*, is predestined to kill his father (the King) and marry his mother (the Queen). This was the voice of the oracle as the child was born and given names. To avoid this unspeakable tragedy, the parents were advised to get rid of the child. They did not disagree. He was handed over to the palace messenger to take to the forest and kill. The messenger, on his own initiative, decided against killing the child. He gave him to a hunter from a far-away village where he could be raised without interacting with his real parents. However, the theme of an unchangeable destiny continued to sound as the boy grew. One day, he was informed by a soothsayer that he would kill his father and marry his mother. Thinking that he was living with his real parents, he voluntarily decided to leave home to avoid this kind of tragedy befalling him. On his way, he was confronted by a group of people from another village in what looked like a royal tour. They were rude to him to the point of ridiculing his parentage. He was annoyed, drew the sword, and killed the leader of the team, the King. This was his real father. He went on his way until he got to his real place of birth. Meanwhile, the town was thrown into mourning for the loss of their King. They were also troubled by some marauders who had taken advantage of their being without a King. *Odéwálé*, the "stranger", helped them to get rid of the marauders and to get their lives together again. Indeed, he was a symbol of struggle, an optimistic human being who would not resign himself to fate:

> Crossing seven waters
> I, a son of the tribe of
> *Ijèkùn Yemoja,*
> found my way,
> to this strange land
> of *Kútújè.* I came
> to see suffering,
> and I felt suffering.
> "Get up,
> Get up," I said
> to them; "not to do something
> is to be crippled fast. Up, up,
> all of you;
> to lie down resigned to fate is madness. Up, up, struggle: the world is
> struggle" (Rotimi 1971:6).

He struggled against destiny. But did he succeed? For a while, it seemed he triumphed. As a reward for his help, he was made King of *Kútújè*. But he had to inherit the former King's widow, who was his real mother. In no time, things began to turn sour for the town. There was famine, pestilence, and death. The oracle had to speak and it spoke the unspeakable: the King was married to his mother. Now, who is to blame? The boy, the parents, or the gods? The title of the play provides the answer – it is not the gods who are to blame. Is it then the helpless victims of an unwanted destiny who tried their utmost to prevent it? This is the problem.

The tendency is for us to try to make sense of this belief by drawing a distinction between fatalism and predestination on the one hand, and between strong destiny and weak destiny on the other. While fatalism (or strong destiny) presents the picture of a cut-and-dried portion of life, predestination (or weak destiny) leaves room for manoeuvers within the context of a general allotment of destiny. Thus, an individual destined to be rich cannot fold his/her arms every day and expect such a destiny to be fulfilled. Also, a person destined to be poor can turn things round by using his/her legs and brain, the symbols of industry and intellect. Again, there is the belief that the character of a person may influence the fulfilment of his/her destiny, and if this happens, he/she is sure to be held responsible.

Though there is some sense in this reconciliation, it does not seem to me to solve the real problem. Indeed, one would expect that such factors as character, industry or the lack of it, and mischief by others, can provide adequate explanation for significant events in a person's life, thus diminishing the importance of predestination as an explanatory model. But apparently the average Yoruba, like most Africans, is not satisfied with such explanations. After all, such factors may be present in other cases of other persons and different consequences may follow. It is especially in pathetic situations where a person cannot be wholly blamed for his/her misfortune that the Yoruba mind makes final recourse to explanation in terms of destiny: what is the case is what has to be since it has been so predestined. The difference between fatalism and predestination does not seem to be noticed in practice in such situations.

But these are only grave situations in which a person is known to have tried his/her human best to avoid misfortune. Thus, the poverty of a lazy person is not blamed on destiny, nor is a notorious robber spared punishment on account of destiny. This is where the question, "Why hold people responsible?", becomes legitimate. If a lazy person has chosen a destiny which makes him/her lazy, is it his/her fault? One way to make sense of this is to suggest that blame or punishment is not imposed by the community on their own; it is already included in the destiny chosen by the lazy person or the robber. That is, in the act of choosing the life of a robber, he/she must have chosen along with it the punishment that goes with such a way of life. On the other hand, if we go back to the original choice of *orí* which bears the different destinies, and we come to terms with the argument that, even if a choice of *orí* may be said to be made, the choice of a particular destiny has not been made, then it would seem to follow that the individual cannot also be said to have made a choice of the punishment that goes along with his/her way of life.

A final problem with regard to this issue of destiny is the question of its changeability. Perhaps if destiny is changeable, then the responsibility belongs to the individual to make efforts to change a bad destiny. If he/she does not make such efforts, then he/she deserves the blame for any lapses. Is this the way the matter is expressed in the language? As we have discussed above, destiny is itself not easily appealed to. It comes into explanations when all else seems to have failed in spite of efforts. Thus a person avoids being killed in an automobile accident involving a mechanical fault only to be killed when being conveyed to the hospital. How do we explain this but by saying that the person was destined to die that way. It was, after all, not his/her fault. Could events have been changed? This is where the religious belief which feeds the concept of destiny creeps in. Before embarking on any important venture, a person is expected to consult with the god of divination to find out what will be the outcome. If the prediction is terrible, it will usually come with directions as to the kind of sacrifice to offer, and it is believed that a bad destiny may be changed if such a sacrifice is offered. If a person therefore refuses to find out what is in store for him/her, or to perform the necessary sacrifice, he/she cannot blame everything on destiny. This is one way in which it is believed destiny may be changed.

Another means involves the character of the person. A good destiny may become bad as a result of a person's own character. It seems then that destiny expresses only a potentiality which may fail to be realised. This seems to account also for the belief in *esè* (leg) as an important element in human personality. *Esè* is the symbol of movement. If a person has a good destiny but is not dynamic, the destiny may not come to fruition. So individual destinies express the potentialities of becoming something, of accomplishing a task. If we look at the matter this way, the whole problem of responsibility and changeability appears to be resolved. But then the further question that emerges is this: what is the role of the concept of destiny? If character, industry, sacrifice, and dynamism are essential to success, why may the concept of destiny not be eliminated? Again, this is the crux of the problem, but one that cannot be resolved easily. While this last point is understood by many Yoruba, they are not prepared to let go the concept of destiny. For, in the final analysis, neither good character nor dynamism nor industry guarantees success that is not encased in one's destiny.

COMPARISON WITH THE AKAN CONCEPTION

The Akan conception of destiny, as presented by Gyekye (1987:104–128), seems to avoid these problems, though it has some of its own. For in this conception, it is not the individual who chooses a destiny. Rather, it is *Onyame,* the supreme deity, that imposes destiny, and the deity always imposes good destiny, which is unchangeable. If so, then there is no problem of apportioning blame or responsibility. But, as will be obvious, this hardly resolves the other problems. The following are the essentials of this concept:

1. God imposes destiny.
2. Destiny is always good.
3. Destiny is unchangeable.

Given these three facts, one then needs to have a way of accounting for the existence of wickedness in Akan society unless Gyekye is going to deny this exists. For if Onyame never imposes bad destiny, and destiny is unchangeable, from where do bad things come into the world? For Gyekye (1987:16) there is no need for anyone to change their destiny since it is good, and "talk of changing destiny really refers to the attempt to better one's condition". One may need to do this if one's path is "strewn with failures, either because of his or her own actions, desires, decisions, and intentions or because of the activities of some supposed evil forces". What is crucial here is the recognition, firstly, that there may exist failures (which I suppose is bad, but not included in the message of destiny); secondly, such failures may be caused by oneself (actions, intentions, desires, etc.), which seems to suggest that such things may cause a change in a good destiny; or, thirdly, that failures may be caused by certain evil forces. Are these evil forces human or natural? If human, and their nature is to cause misfortune for others, can we say that this is their own allotted destiny (in which case, there is bad destiny), or that their allotted good destiny has been thwarted (in which case destiny may be changed).

It appears to me that all three features that Gyekye attributes to the Akan conception of destiny can co-exist without tension only if there is no evil or wickedness in society. And this appears to me to be contrary to the facts of life. It is also no use treating such evils as accidents, for this begs the question. If the premature death of a decent young man at the hands of a habitual hoodlum is an accident, which is not included in the destiny of either the young man or the hoodlum, the question of what the concept of destiny itself is supposed to account for has yet to be resolved, especially if we also believe in a good destiny which pertains to the key events of a person's life and is unchangeable. Obviously death is a key event, just as murder on the part of the hoodlum is.

THE NORMATIVE MEANING OF *ÈNÌYÀN*

As can be seen from the foregoing, the concept of destiny is crucial in understanding the thought and practice of Africans in general. I have focused here on the Yoruba conception and it is clear that there is much in it that requires clarification and analysis. I would like to end this chapter with a brief note on the normative understanding of *èníyàn*.

As has been seen, destiny is construed as the meaning of a person – the purpose for which the individual exists as chosen by the other self and sealed by the deity. However, this purpose, though personal to him/her, cannot be separated from the social reality of which he/she is just a part. It is here that the limit of individualism may be found. The purpose of individual existence is intricately linked with the purpose of social existence, and cannot be adequately grasped outside it. Though destiny confirms the individual's personality, it also joins him/her to the community, and individuality and community thus become intertwined. Personality is rendered meaningful by appeal to destiny and community. This is because the individual is nurtured by the community, and the idea of destiny itself emanates from communal experience. It is a community-concept.

Persons are what they are by virtue of what they are designed to be, their character, and the communal influence on them. It is a combination of these elements that constitutes human personality. The "I" is just a "we" from another perspective, and persons are therefore not construed as atomic individuals. A person whose existence and personality are dependent on the community is expected in turn to contribute to the continued existence of the community. This is the normative dimension of the concept of *èníyàn*. The crown of personal life is to be useful to one's community. The meaning of one's life is therefore measured by one's commitment to social ideals and communal existence. The question, "What is your existence for?" (*Kíni o wà fún?*) is not always posed. It is posed when a person has been judged to be useless to his/her community. It is therefore a challenge, a call to serve. It presupposes a conception of human existence which sees it as purposeful, and the purpose is to contribute to the totality of the good in the universe. This is achieved by a life of selfless devotion and sacrifice to the communal welfare. Here selfishness and individualism are abhorred and are expected to be superseded by a developed sense of community. But does this mean that the individual is therefore crushed under the heavy weight of the community and its moral order?

AFRICAN CONCEPTIONS OF PERSONHOOD AND INTELLECTUAL IDENTITIES

DIDIER N. KAPHAGAWANI

INTRODUCTION

The concept of person or personhood has at one time or another occupied centre stage in Western as well as African philosophy. In fact, in Western philosophy the problems of person and personal identity were labyrinths where philosophers' minds tended to reach an impasse. Hume, for instance, is quite explicit in describing his bewilderment whenever he attempts to consider these problems. He remarks:

> Most philosophers seem inclined to think that personal identity arises from consciousness; and consciousness is nothing but a reflected thought or perception. The present philosophy, therefore, has so far a promising aspect. But all my hopes vanish when I come to explain the principles that unite our successive perceptions in our thought or consciousness. I cannot discover any theory which gives me satisfaction on this head (1974:635–636).

Although Hume admits dissatisfaction with any theory, he propounds what is known as the causal theory of personal identity, whose main thrust is that a person is what he/she is because "distinct perceptions bear a certain relation of resemblance or causation to another" (Perry 1975:26). This is also regarded as the unity argument in that it addresses the question of what it is that unites a succession of experiences, rendering them the same person's experiences (Vesey 1974:38).

Locke, on the other hand, propounds the memory theory in which the unity and identity of a person are guaranteed by virtue of remembering things done in the past. For Locke, a person is

> a thinking intelligent being, that has reason and reflection, and can consider itself as itself, the same thinking thing, in different times and places (1947:39).

Thus, the ability and power to reflect and meditate is, for Locke, a feature unique to human beings; and the fact that persons remember past actions and events is sufficient evidence for the identity of the person doing the remembering.

At this juncture it should be pointed out that although the problem of the conception of person is usually discussed in tandem with that of personal identity, the two problems are distinct; the problem of personal identity is logically posterior to that of what it is that makes a person a person. Yet the problem of personal identity presupposes as resolved the issue of what qualifies as a person and what does not, and is rather concerned with the issue of what distinguishes one human being from another.

It should, however, be admitted that making reference to only Hume and Locke, as this paper has done, might be misconstrued as regarding earlier or later attempts at explicating the notions of person and personhood as of no significance. Humean and Lockean theories of person have indeed been preceded, as well as followed by, theories of no less significance. Both essentialist and causal theories of personhood have not only undergone reformulations and modifications, but they have also been superseded by theories which are a synthesis of what Jackson and

169

Karp (1990:18) have called the sociocentric and egocentric conceptions of personhood. Hume and Locke have been referred to not because of the significance of their theories as such, but because of the significance of the problem of person and personhood in philosophy in general.

Now, this paper is more concerned with the question of personhood than that of personal identity, concentrating on the analysis of some conceptions of person propounded by philosophers in African philosophy, particularly those proffered as employing evidence from Central and Southern African cultures. These conceptions are presented in this paper as theses; namely, the Force thesis by Tempels; the Communalism thesis by Mbiti; and the Shadow thesis by Kagamé. I have limited my analysis to these three formulations of African conceptions of person for two reasons: these theses have a direct bearing on the Chewa culture (a culture in which I was born and bred) insofar as the Chewa culture is a Bantu culture; and secondly, the language and thought of the Chewa seems to contain evidence for and against some of the theses so far presented on the conceptions of person in Africa.

However, using evidence from some aspects of Chewa culture the way this paper intends to do immediately raises a number of methodological criticisms; namely, that in indulging in the conceptual analysis of a number of Chewa terms, phrases, and expressions, the paper merely underscores the significance of some central Chewa cultural concepts and ignores, as do all discourse analyses of a substantial bias, the social, historical, and cultural context in which these expressions feature; and hence, the analysis completely ignores the processual, situational, and historical aspects of the Chewa culture. That this paper only considers one aspect of social discourse – that of analysing some central cultural notions and expressions – is indeed a limitation of this paper; for the paper attempts to evaluate several conceptions of person by providing evidence, for or against, from Chewa phrases and expressions. But it does not follow that such an evaluation is therefore biased towards presenting a static or essentialist conception of personhood; it is not an exposition of a Chewa conception of person; rather, it is an appraisal of some expositions of Bantu conceptions of person. Moreover, the doctrines considered in this paper are divided between the static and the dynamic conceptions of person. It is to the analysis and appraisal of these theses that the discussion turns.

THE FORCE THESIS

What I have termed the Force Thesis was first propounded by Placide Tempels (1959) who strongly believed in a radical conceptual difference between Africans and non-Africans on the essential nature of beings and entities in general, and human beings in particular. Africans, or the Bantu in particular, conceive of entities or beings, claims Tempels, as nothing more than essential energies or vital forces. Using Bantu – or Luba, to be precise – expressions of greeting, sympathy, and hunger, Tempels (1959:45) concludes that every Bantu language contains "words or phrases denoting a *force*, which is not used in an exclusively bodily sense of the integrity of our whole being". He goes on to claim that those words or phrases, *kufwa* and *kufwididila* in Luba, and *kufa* and *kufadi* in Chichewa, for instance, indicating different degrees of loss of vital force, "the superlative of which signifies total paralysis of the power to live", should not be translated in English as "to die" and "to die entirely" (1959:47) precisely because, for Tempels, Westerners "hold a *static* conception of 'being', [and Africans] a dynamic [one]" (1959:51). Indeed, according to Tempels, for a Bantu " 'Force' in his thought is a necessary element in 'being', and the concept 'force' is inseparable from the definition of 'being' . . . without the element of 'force', 'being' cannot be conceived" (1959:50–51).

What needs to be pointed out immediately is that by claiming, as Tempels does in the passage above, that force is an essential property of being, he is, by implication, stating that although "force" is a necessary attribute of "being", it is nevertheless not a sufficient condition, the consequence of which is that "being" possesses some properties or attributes other than that of force. However, the picture becomes clearer soon after when Tempels (1959:51) insists that force is not only a necessary attribute of being, but *is* being in Bantu thought: "Force is not for [the Bantu] an adventitious, accidental reality. Force is even more than a necessary attribute of being: *Force is the nature of being, force is being, being is force*".

A number of questions immediately arise in the Tempelsian Force Thesis. Significantly, the thesis seems to beg the question; for, given that being has been defined in terms of force, the question arises as to what force is in Bantu languages and thoughts. And Chichewa, one of the Bantu languages, provides us with no clue as to how the word force is to be comprehended in Chewa thought and language. Even Tempels himself does not give an example of the possible translation and conception of force in the Luba language.

Secondly, I find it quite baffling that Tempels regards it a mistake to translate *kufa* as "to die" and *kufadi* as "to die indeed"; for if there are words and phrases which admit of the easiest translation, *kufa* and *kufadi* are some such words. To say X *akufa* in Chichewa is no more to regard death or dying as process as when in English it is said: "X is dying." Similarly, to say X *akufadi* in Chichewa is not so much to ascertain the ultimate degree of loss of life as to demonstrate one's certainty about X's eventual death. And to regard these terminologies as expressions of degrees and intensities of force is to take too literally a mode of expression or matter of speech.

Thirdly, in the same vein, Tempels (1959:55) insists on the distinction between "man" and "person", and claims, rather surprisingly, that *munthu* in Chichewa, for example, should not be translated as "man", but rather as "person", because " 'Muntu' signifies [the] vital force endowed with intelligence and will". However, one cannot help but ask what the term "human" means if it does not denote entities in possession of intelligence and will. On this, Tempels leaves us in the dark as if there are humans (*wanthu* in Chichewa) who do not possess intelligence and will. On this point, Chichewa has counter-evidence: " 'munthu' denotes as much a 'human being' as it does a 'person' " (Tempels 1959:57).

However, this point has to be made with a qualification. In Chichewa it is held and said, *Azungu siwanthu*. In literal translation this statement means "Whites are not human", which would seem to indicate that the Chewa deny humanness to whites. Yet with a little analysis it becomes clear that this statement is not uttered to assert the non-humanity of whites; rather it denies that whites are persons insofar as their looks and behaviour are at variance with that of the Chewa. Thus, this statement should not be translated as "Whites are not human", but rather as "Whites are not persons." And to this extent, Tempels is quite right in advising against translating *munthu* as "human", but rather as "person".

But certain situations warrant translating *munthu* as "human". For example, to say *Achewa ndi wanthu* is more to assert the humanness of the Chewa than their personhood; similarly for *Azungu ndi wanthu*, meaning that whites are just as human as the Chewa except for pigmentation differences. Here *munthu* refers to the species of human beings and has universal applicability, whereas when this word is translated as "person" it involves a sociocentric view of personhood which varies from one culture to another and from one time to another due to the dynamic nature of culture and society.

Fourthly, although Tempels tries to steer away from the Western conception of being, he surreptitiously reverts to the very distinctions employed in Western philosophy to distinguish humans from other entities. He claims that in Bantu thought humans are beings distinct from other beings by their properties of reason and volition. Thus, on the Tempelsian thesis of being as force, it should have been possible to distinguish between rational and non-rational forces, and voluntary and non-voluntary forces. For, according to the Force Thesis of beings as forces, there must be a radical difference between vital forces that have intelligence and those that do not. But as to what it means for a vital force to have intelligence and will or, for that matter, what an intelligent vital force or a voluntary vital force is, cannot be accounted for in the Tempelsian framework. In any case, the properties of intelligence and will are precisely what in Western philosophy are taken to be properties distinguishing the genus "humans" from the species "animals". These are some of the problems bedevilling the Force Thesis. So much, therefore, for the Force Thesis.

THE COMMUNALISM THESIS

This thesis has Tempelsian origins, although Mbiti is these days closely associated with it. In *Bantu Philosophy*, Tempels is quite explicit in claiming that in Bantu thought, persons or humans are defined and individuated communally:

> This concept of separate beings, of substance . . . which find themselves side by side, entirely independent one of another, is foreign to Bantu thought. Bantu hold that created beings preserve a bond one with another, an intimate ontological relationship, comparable with the causal tie which binds creature with Creator. For the Bantu there is interaction of being with being, that is to say, of force with force (1959:58).

And a few pages later it is remarked that the

> child, even the adult, remains always for the Bantu a man, a force, *in causal dependence and ontological subordination* to the forces which are his father and mother. The older force ever dominates the younger (Tempels 1959:60).

In the same vein, Mbiti writes:

> In traditional life, the individual does not and cannot exist alone except corporately. He owes his existence to other people, including those of past generations and his contemporaries. He is simply part of the whole. The community must therefore make, create, or produce the individual; for the individual depends on the corporate group. . . . Whatever happens to the individual happens to the whole group, and whatever happens to the whole group happens to the individual. The individual can only say: "I am, because we are; and since we are therefore I am". This is a cardinal point in the understanding of the African view of man (1969:108–109).

That Mbiti is propagating a sociocentric view of personhood, in which the status of an individual is determined through cultural criteria, is quite evident from the assertion that a society "makes, creates or produces the individual". And although Mbiti does not spell out any of the criteria societies use, Shaw and Parkinson (in Jackson & Karp 1990) provide some examples: personhood as dependent on the number of secrets an individual keeps, among the Temne; and personhood as a function of Islamic and cultural knowledge, among the Swahili.

As with the Force Thesis, this thesis is also confronted with a number of problems. Firstly, it should be conceded that in putting this thesis in a form reminiscent of the Cartesian *cogito* argument, namely that in Africa *we are* therefore *I am*, Mbiti aims at underscoring the extent to which communal life is esteemed in Africa.

However, and this is the second point, the validity of Mbiti's argument is questionable. Although the *cogito* argument could have pretensions of validity when provided with "Whatever thinks, exists" as a suppressed premise, I find it difficult to imagine quite what suppressed premise would render Mbiti's argument valid.

Thirdly, to assert African communalism is not in any way to imply the denial of recognition of individual human beings *qua* individuals. African communalism in fact takes cognisance of ontological pluralism; and to assert, as Mbiti does, that *we are*, presumes prior recognition of the individuality of those making up the *we*. For although it is mathematically possible to imagine a set which happens to be empty, it seems impossible to imagine the existence of an empty human society. And to claim, "whatever happens to the individual happens to the whole group", and vice versa, is no doubt to forget the difference between individuals on the one hand, and *sets* of individuals on the other. For Africans, certainly the Chewa, are aware of this important difference as exemplified by the following expressions: *Chaona mnzako chapita mawa chili paiwe* (What your neighbour has experienced is gone, tomorrow it will be your turn); *Mvula ikakuona litsiro siikata* (When the rain has seen that you are dirty it does not stop pouring); and *Wanthu ndi mchenga saundika* (Human beings are like sand out of which one cannot make a mountain). All these proverbs and expressions reflect the Chewa's cognisance of the individuality of human beings, their fates, predicaments, and experiences.

Fourthly, it is indeed the case that the elders tended to have an epistemological monopoly over the young. But to concede this point is not to assert an ontological distinction between the elders and the young; rather, it is merely to point out an epistemological difference; the young are not ontologically less human than the elders. Furthermore, although African cultures in general, and the Chewa culture in particular, contain expressions extolling the elders as the seat of wisdom, for instance, *Mau wa akuluakulu akoma atagonela* (The elders' words are sweet after a year), there is also evidence demonstrating the rebellious tendencies of the young. To such a proverb, they would retort: *Tsobola wakale sawawa* (Old pepper is never hot), meaning that what held sway before need not necessarily hold sway now or in the future; and that the elders' advice is most likely to be obsolete and irrelevant on that count. Thus, the most serious problem of the Communalism Thesis is that it conflates the epistemological status of a human being with the ontological status.

However, one advantage of this doctrine is that it underscores the processual nature of personhood, the constant and gradual remaking of persons through, *inter alia*, the acquisition and mastery of both cultural and esoteric knowledge. And to acquire such knowledge, "the ontological priority of the collectivity" is indeed emphasised, and "the ontological uniqueness" of each individual recognised though not underscored. Though different, these two perspectives are complementary; for "the integrity and perpetuation of every *collective* order depends on the last analysis in [*sic*] the initiatives and actions of *individual* persons" (Jackson & Karp 1990:27–28).

THE SHADOW THESIS

The Shadow doctrine has been proffered by Alexis Kagamé who claims, in certain respects quite rightly, as is to be shown below, that for the Bantu a human being is both a *complete* animal and a being endowed with *intelligence*; complete, because he/she possesses "the vital principle of animality known as shadow"; and he/she has intelligence insofar as he/she "is animated by a second vital principle which is immortal and in which are anchored the intelligent operations proper to man" (Kagamé 1989:35).

However, Kagamé points out other considerations which clearly demarcate humanity from animality in general. The Bantu, he claims, not only possess intelligence, but also "the heart". With the intelligence, the human being is not only capable of reflecting and meditating "upon the data of his senses", but also able to "compare the facts of the knowledge he has acquired", and "*to invent* something new by combining previously acquired knowledge" (Kagamé 1989:36). All these operations are open to a human being by virtue of being in possession of the faculty of reason or intelligence.

But as regards the "heart", Kagamé (1989:36) claims that it "integrates all that the interior man is; it harmonises the operations and acquisitions of intelligence, by adding to them the acts which other cultures attribute to the will". Kagamé's remark is, as it stands, quite misleading because physiologically humans cannot be said to be more in possession of a heart than, say, pigs. However, precisely because he claims that the Bantu regard this human "heart" as being in charge of the operations of the intelligence, then pigs definitely do not possess such a "heart".

Now, what exactly is this "heart"? In almost all Bantu cultures in general, and certainly in Chewa culture, by "heart" is meant the *personality* of an individual human being; "in the heart lies the *personality* of man"; "it is that by which this man is himself and not another" (Nothomb quoted in Kagamé 1989:36). Thus, the "heart" understood as personality is what characterises human beings, and is one of the criteria for distinguishing one person from another. And in this, Kagamé is quite right; his observations are in unison with the expressions and practices extant in Central and Southern African cultures in general, and in the Chewa culture in particular.

One advantage of Kagamé's thesis, particularly with regard to the significance of the personality of a human being, is that it is a move towards the resolution of the problem of personal identity; for an individual person would, in Bantu languages and thought, be distinguished from another *at least* because of his/her personality and behaviour.

But problems arise with regard to Kagamé's claim that human beings are *complete* animals; for a cow would be said to be as complete in itself as a goat.

Thus, the question arises as to what could possibly be meant by "*complete* animal". On this issue, Kagamé leaves us in the dark. Instead of tackling this question, he raises the question regarding the point at which a person becomes a complete animal. In response, Kagamé receives such varied answers as: "from the moment he exists in his mother's womb" (East Africa); "when a name has been given him" (West Africa) (1989:30); and "from the moment he puts reason to good use" (Southern Africa) (1989:37).

What should be noted is that it is not a question of *when* an individual becomes human or a person. Phrasing the question in this way automatically demands an answer with time as a significant factor, and this may vary from one culture to another, as the examples above demonstrate. Rather, it is what constitutes the completeness of humanhood which it is important to extract from the various cultures, and to analyse (see Wright 1984:153 & Floistad 1987:180).

True, the significance of naming an individual has been emphasised by a number of scholars in Africa. But what should be borne in mind is that the acquisition of a name is of cultural significance, not of ontological significance. And to say that a child is "fully a man only when a name is given him" (Kagamé 1989:36) is no doubt to underscore the cultural significance at the expense of the ontological status. For, before an individual is given a name he/she is an existent human being who happens to be nameless; the significance of the name has more to do, *inter alia*, with what the society expects, or wishes a person to be; before receiving a name a person is not any the less human; he/she is endowed with feelings and senses, and an intellect which has yet to be put to some use.

Kagamé, it should be acknowledged, fails to define what he means by the "completeness" and the "shadow" of human beings. And the picture is further complicated by his remarks on what the Bantu believe happens to a person at death. He claims that, to the Bantu, death marks the dissolution of the union between the "shadow" and the "intelligence" of a person, and that after death the "shadow" completely disappears (see Onwuanibe 1984:185ff.). Indeed, it is still believed among the Chewa that a dead person is devoid of a "shadow", even when exposed to the light of the sun. But how to comprehend exactly what "shadow" means seems to be somewhat difficult.

However, what seems incontestable is that the Chewa do not mean literally that a dead person has no physical shadow; rather, what seems to be meant is a symbolic or metaphorical shadow. This symbolic shadow presumably refers to the departure or absence, at death, of an individual's personality and individuality. Insofar as personhood is not static, but a dynamic, gradual, and persistent process, death marks the end of this process of personhood creation and thus signals the absence of shadow creation insofar as personhood is as elusive as a shadow. And among the Chewa, as is the case among the Bantu of the Lower Congo, the "shadow of a person is a perfect symbol of individual identity" (Jackson & Karp 1990:18); and individual identity is as problematic to pinpoint as is personhood. Thus, ascribing a metaphorical meaning to "shadow" seems to lead to the conclusion that the Chewa in particular, and possibly the Bantu in general, regard personhood more as a process than as an essence, whereas rendering a literal meaning of "shadow" does not seem to lead us anywhere. But the Shadow Thesis, its problems notwithstanding, seems to hold some promise in reflecting on the thoughts of the Chewa.

AFRICAN INTELLECTUAL IDENTITIES

To discuss the question of African intellectual identities is to presume, among other things, an answer to the question of who or what an African is. From the foregoing discussion of some African conceptions of personhood, it seems quite apparent that an African acquires an identity not in an instant, but through a process. And to talk of African intellectual identities is to presuppose intellectual identities which are distinctively African. A person is African not only for geographical reasons or accidents, but also for being born and bred in the African environment, one of whose fundamental elements is culture. Now, just as there are a plurality of African cultures, there should also be as many African intellectual identities, traditions, and methodologies. What should not be lost sight of is the disquieting fact that in any particular culture variations in intellectual articulation and disposition abound.

Now, the question arises as to what, in general, an intellectual is. This question has been aptly handled both by Gouldner and Hollander. Gouldner defines intellectuals as

> those who are readier to engage in a critique of conventional knowledge and knowledge-generating institutions, including those paradigms that are the consensual ideals of scholarly communities. . . . Scholars and scientists are intellectuals insofar as they adopt the standpoint of "critique" to the *paradigms* and elaborated speech variants of their respective domains of scholarship and science. In *that* special sense, intellectuals may adopt . . . an "adversary" relationship to their society in general and to knowledge paradigms in particular (1975/76:23).

In the same vein, Hollander defines intellectuals as those

> preoccupied with ideas that have broad cultural, social or political relevance. They like to explain and interpret the world for others and for their own satisfaction. Intellectuals . . . reflect, raise difficult questions, and pontificate on the great private and public issues of life and death, the character of human beings, the ends of life, relationships between individual and society, and social institutions and organisations (1987:546).

An intellectual, therefore, not only has to be acquainted with "conventional knowledge and knowledge-generating institutions", he/she must also be able to reflect upon, analyse, and raise questions – whether difficult or not is another matter – on conventional epistemologies and wisdoms as well as on various socio-cultural issues. In this regard, the role and identity of an African intellectual becomes quite apparent; he/she has not only to know the African epistemologies, but also to evaluate them in accordance with the African socio-cultural milieu and in terms of their cogency and consistency.

African intellectuals, in my view, acquire identities when their analyses, critiques, and reflections are on issues and problems specific to Africa, and distinctively African. In this regard, scholars like Tempels, Mbiti, Kagamé, Wiredu, Oruka, Masolo, Mudimbe, Hountondji, and Appiah, for example, are African intellectuals insofar as they have articulated fundamental problems in African cultures; however, their identities may vary owing to differences, *inter alia*, in philosophical inclinations, dispositions, and methodologies. One would not be surprised, therefore, to find a Tempelsian or Wireduan or Orukan or Hountondjian tradition in Africa. Indeed, this goes for all the disciplines which embrace Africa at heart. But it behoves all African intellectuals to be "mindful of the ultimate implications of the thought that one way of being and only that is desirable for all peoples" (Owomoyela 1996:36).

THE CONCEPT OF CAUSE IN AFRICAN THOUGHT

GODWIN S. SOGOLO

One of the puzzles yet unresolved by scholars seeking to understand traditional African belief-systems is how, in the explanation of observable events, disembodied or non-extended entities (spirits, witches, ghosts, gods, etc. existing beyond the confines of space) can possibly be invoked as causes. The problem arises mainly due to the widespread mechanistic view of causality in which when C is said to be the cause of E, a necessary connection is assumed to exist between C and E in accordance with certain scientific principles subsumed under a general law. The literature on causality has appreciably expanded since Hume substituted his "constant conjunction" for "necessary connection", thereby denying cause and effect that connective power thought to exist between them.

I do not intend here to go into a philosophical excursus of all this, neither about what counts as a cause or an effect, nor about what constitutes a causal explanation in the scientific sense. Those concerned with these technical analyses would agree that the notion of causality is now so loose and varied in meaning that what counts as a causal explanation of an event would depend on factors such as, for example:

1. The nature of the event to be explained.
2. Our interest in the event.
3. Whether the event has one cause or a multiplicity of necessary causes.
4. Whether, when the causes are more than one, they can be compatibly invoked.
5. Whether some of the causes are sufficient such that the others become unnecessary and superfluous, etc.

One other possibility is to conceive of a causal explanation as the sum total of the variety of possible causes (which, in some cases, are indefinite). In all, what seems obvious is that there are different conceptions of what constitutes a causal explanation.

In this discussion, I examine the nature and function of the varying explanatory models in traditional African thought. Based on a distinction drawn between two basic notions of causality, the primary (non-mechanistic) and the secondary (mechanistic), I analyse the corresponding features of two explanatory models which, quite often, appear to be mutually exclusive. I then attempt to show that the two kinds of explanation perform different functions which are complementary and non-mutually exclusive. With specific examples drawn from an African approach to the explanation of diseases, I then show how a combination of both the mechanistic and the non-mechanistic explanatory models provides a fuller, more comprehensive understanding than the exclusive use of either.

At first it would appear that claims in traditional African thought do not fall within the category of explanations generally associated with science-oriented thought systems. The reason for this is obvious. In seeking to understand events, as Horton (1970) points out, the prevalent explanatory models adopted by a given culture are determined by the peculiarities of that culture. Horton's main interest is to compare the forms of explanation in traditional African thought with those of Western science. His comparison is based on what he observes as essential similarities between the two thought systems. One essential similarity is that in both models one finds two "distinct" but "complementary" levels of thought and discourse, which Horton (1970:171) labels the "commonsense" and the "theoretical" – or "primary theory" and "secondary theory" (Horton 1982:228). More specifically, what Horton regards as fundamental similarities in the explanatory models of the two systems are, firstly, that both are primarily concerned with explanation, prediction, and control of natural phenomena, and secondly, that in doing so, they invoke theoretical entities, albeit of different kinds. Horton, however, points out what he regards as a superficial differential based on the idiom or expression as derived from the cultural contexts – that science involves impersonal theoretical entities, while traditional thought draws on personal theoretical entities.

Our concern here is not with Horton's general points of similarity and difference between traditional African thought and Western thought. His ideas have been severally criticised and it is difficult to say who is right, Horton or his opponents. Surely, however, Horton is not wrong in his observation that all human societies, traditional or modern, have two levels of discourse, that of primary theory and that of secondary theory. He is also right about the basic characteristics he assigns to these levels of thought. As Horton (1982:229) explains, "the entities and processes of primary theory are thought of as directly 'given' to the human observer while those of secondary theory are thought of as somehow hidden". He also thinks that primary theory lacks the "'push-pull' causal vision" largely associated with secondary theory. In all, Horton's distinction boils down to nothing but the difference between commonsense explanation involving the use of material-object language and theoretical explanation involving hidden mechanisms not susceptible to observation language.

The layman's explanation of day-to-day events both in traditional Africa and in the modern West stands for Horton's primary theory (although it is not clear why the term "theory" is appropriate at this level). At the level of secondary theory, Horton thinks that traditional African religious explanations occupy the position which scientific explanations occupy in the West. His main concern, therefore, is to compare and contrast the two modes of thought at the secondary level. And as far as doing this is concerned, Horton's enterprise appears harmless, although it could be argued that any reason one might have for comparing traditional African religious thought with Western science should also serve as a reason for comparing Western religious thought (traditional or modern) with Western science, since, by Horton's own classification, all religious forms are to be seen as secondary theoretical schemes. What is of substance to us here in relation to Horton's comparative analysis, is the claim he makes that although traditional thought and Western science are concerned with the explanation, prediction, and control of natural phenomena, the former is more successful in achieving these objectives than the latter.

Surely, the question of success or failure depends here on the function(s) assigned to the two modes of thought. Horton's assumption is that both traditional African thought and Western science are concerned with explanation, prediction, and control of natural phenomena. But part of this basic premise is questionable. It is true that traditional African thought seeks to explain events and create order and regularity where there seems to be discord and irregularity, as Horton would put it. From this, we may also agree that both share in common the goal of prediction since knowledge of past and present events may serve as a basis for predicting future ones.

But, we may understand past and present events, and be able to predict future ones without any interest or motivation directed at control. By their nature, traditional African explanatory models, unlike those of science, are not intended for the control of natural phenomena. One is tempted, no doubt, for example, to interpret oracular practices and belief in divination as efforts by traditional African practitioners to change the order of nature. This is mistaken. The practitioner claims to be able to foretell the course of future events and his prescription to a client is mainly one of how to avert such events. The practitioner does not attempt to change, stop or control the normal course of events. The order of nature is believed to be laid down and it is not subject to change by mortals. However, it is believed that any human being adequately informed about such events can avert them by moving beyond their reach.

By way of analogy, what the African diviner aims at is similar to the objectives of modern preventive medicine. In orthodox preventive medicine, the practitioner merely seeks to protect his client from being afflicted by certain diseases. The practitioner knows that his client could catch malaria when bitten by the appropriate parasite-carrying mosquito. What he does, therefore, when he prescribes a weekly dose of chloroquine, is not to stop the parasite from causing malaria but to ensure that his client is not predisposed to this disease. In the same way, the traditional African diviner claims to know that events of misfortune will always occur. He cannot stop them from occurring, but he claims to be able to ensure that his client is not predisposed to such events. When the practice of divination in traditional Africa is seen in this way, it is clear, *contra* Horton, that traditional explanatory models are not intended for control of natural phenomena.

The more crucial point about the issue of success or failure of an explanatory model depends, as we said earlier, on the nature of the event to be explained and our interest in that event. In particular, the interest one has in an event influences and determines what one would regard as its cause – which makes it possible for a given event to be given a variety of causal explanations that are not necessarily mutually exclusive of one another. E.A. Troxell and W.S. Snyder (1976:54–59) have provided an interesting example of how a single event could attract different causal explanations. They take an imaginary incident of fire breaking out which has caused considerable damage and whose cause is to be determined. Troxell and Snyder make us imagine that in the course of investigating the cause of the fire, fire fighters found that little children were playing with matches in the garage and that one of them, Bobby Jones, confessed to having lit a match which led to the fire breaking out. Now, according to Troxell and Snyder, the fire fighters in writing their report on the incident would say "children playing with matches" *caused* the fire. Their primary interest in the matter (as people whose profession it is to prevent the occurrence of fire breaking out) is to find out the kinds of human action that led to the fire, whether it was a case of arson, careless acts of drunken adults, children playing with matches, etc.

It is supposed, further, that a physicist was involved in the investigation. According to the authors, the physicist's explanation of the cause of the fire would not only be different in kind but would include details which were of no interest to the fire fighters. The physicist's report might say, for instance, that the fire was caused by a match being placed very close to some old newspaper which was, in turn, next to some cardboard boxes. He/she might even go further to explain the physical compositions of the materials involved – how their combustion was aided by the flow of certain gases and why fire had to spread in certain directions and not others, etc. It is not that fire fighters are ignorant of these details. These are simply not matters of interest to them, just as the aspect of the incident that has to do with human action is not of interest to the physicist.

So, in providing an explanation for the fire, we could say that for the fire fighters the "cause" was "children playing with matches", while for the physicist the "cause" was the ignited match. But as Troxell and Snyder rightly point out, the fire fighters' explanation and that of the physicist are not in conflict. They simply complement each other in providing more details in the explanation of the fire outbreak. However, let us suppose further, say the authors, that a psychologist or a social worker was interested in the fire. The psychologist might be interested in the factors that could have led the children, particularly Bobby Jones, to the habit of playing with matches – she might find out that Bobby Jones's parents used to entertain him with match tricks. Or a social worker might look into the domestic circumstances that might possibly have led to these children being left alone – he could find out that their parents were so poor that material pursuit took so much of their time that the children were ignored. Both the psychologist and the social worker are thus likely to say that the parents were indeed the "cause" of the fire. Troxell and Snyder even extend the example with more interesting elaborations – the anti-smoking campaigner who (believing that smokers are in the habit of leaving matches around that children then play with) could explain that smoking was the "cause" of the fire. They even refer to the apparently remotest of possible causes, the position that a fundamentalist preacher might take, namely, that the birth of the children is the "cause" of the fire since if they had not been born in the first place, the incident would not have occurred.

Our interest in the details of the fire example is two-fold. Firstly, it shows the almost infinite kinds of "causal" explanation that can be given for a single event. And because the explanations are of different sorts, the question of the superiority of one over the other is misplaced. The explanations provided by the fire fighters, the psychologist, social worker, anti-smoking campaigner, and the fundamentalist preacher, might appear to be out of tune with what, in scientific terms, is accepted as a causal explanation, but this is so only from the point of interest of the scientist. Besides, there is no consensus among scientists about the notion of causality or what should count as an adequate causal explanation.

The second crucial point about the example we have chosen is that the different explanations are complementary and non-mutually exclusive. In some sense, the chain of causes that led to the fire could be traced to the birth of the children, such that there is plausibility in saying that the birth of the children "caused" the fire. And if it were true, as the psychologist or social worker would claim, that the children's habit of playing with the fire was acquired due to faults in their upbringing – faults caused by the parents – then, there is also a sense in which the parents could be said to be the "cause" of the fire. All these causes do not exclude the fact that the children and the match are also the causes of the fire. This way, the causes of the fire number as many as the interests of those who seek to provide an explanation for it.

And where causes do not exclude one another, we might say that when put together they constitute an adequate or complete explanation of the fire incident.

However, normally no problems would arise if the different explanations, causal or otherwise, of a given event or phenomenon were to share this complementary relationship. Problems arise when, as we said earlier, multiple causes are invoked as explanations, with some either incompatible with, or rendering others superfluous. The history of science is replete with instances of phenomena that were at one time explained in supernatural terms but which at the dawn of experimental science had their scientific principles fully uncovered by scientists. In such instances, one could say that their scientific explanations either mutually exclude their supernatural interpretations or that the former have rendered the latter superfluous. This is what the growth of knowledge means – a gradual process of explaining phenomena that were at one time either inexplicable or inadequately explained. Within a given culture, it is generally assumed that the new explanations are true while those they replace are false, or that the new ones are superior to the old ones. But, as we have just seen, this is misleading since the explanations – although different in kind – may not necessarily stand as incompatible alternatives. In fact, the question of comparative truth-value or superiority of some over others does not arise because of the difference in their explanatory functions.

In traditional African thought, this non-commensurability in explanatory functions is most clearly manifest in the people's mode of explaining the causes of illness. Of course, in every culture, what counts as an acceptable explanation of illness is tied to the people's general conception of health and disease. To a great extent, it is dependent on their overall world-view. The firm assumption has always been that African cultures hold a *holistic* conception of disease or illness – a man is considered ill if he displays a state of unusual feeling, suffering pain or incapacitation or being in danger of death or mutilation. Once his day-to-day life activities (e.g. the ability to work or to perform other social duties) are affected by this general feeling, such a man is said to be ill, whether or not the causes are traceable to specific structural changes in the cells of the body. This holistic conception of health and illness – which may be considered unorthodox in modern medical practice – is firmly held among the Yoruba community of Nigeria. The Yoruba word *alafia*, which translates as health, according to Ademuwagun (1978:89) "embraces the totality of an individual's physical, social, psychological and spiritual well-being in his total environmental setting". Contrary to the claim by Lewis (1953:111) that "it is the presence of disease that can be recognized, not the presence of health", the Yoruba believe that both states are recognisable, and in a negative terminology, they conceive of illness as *aisan*, which translates as the absence of health. Again, their holistic conception of health and sickness is reinforced when the Yoruba speak of the former state as when *ara* (body) is "strong and active", and of the latter as when *ara* (body) is "broken down" (Ademuwagun 1978:90). The main indicator of health or disease in Yoruba thought is thus the ability or inability to perform one's routine work, or adequate or inadequate performance.

An important aspect of the African conception of health and illness is that it is the whole human body – not merely certain parts of the body – that is considered either well or in a state of disease. Unlike in the West, where a patient consulting a physician often hints as to what part of the body he/she thinks is afflicted, the traditional African (except in the case of easily identifiable anatomical parts of the body or where there are external injuries due to an accident) is generally non-specific as to the part of the body afflicted by disease. And the healer who is consulted does not press for such specific information. This non-specificity in associating diseases with parts of the body is clear from the fact that, generally, traditional healers do not start their diagnosis of illness by a physical examination of the patient's body. Their primary concern is with the patient's background in socio-cultural and in divine/supernatural relations. Thus a given illness or disease is generally explained by reference to several causes, some of which, in modern scientific thought, appear to be logically incompatible. An African healer may attribute a disease to a scientific/natural cause – not too dissimilar to the germ theory of modern medicine. Yet the healer may also believe that the same disease is "caused" by supernatural forces, and would then proceed to cure the disease in these two seemingly incompatible ways.

Normally, any such conception of illness that appeals to supernatural forces, deities, spirits, witchcraft, etc., is classified as a form of animism, which, in fact, is common in the history of every society. For example, early medical practice in Scotland took this form where, according to Clough (1981:183), "healing lay in propitiating the powers (supernatural) against which the patient might have offended." Such supernatural factors play an important role in almost all pre-literate (ancient and contemporary) societies of the world. It is common for modern scientific thinkers to read irrationality into this supernatural approach to medical healing. However, in relation to the African conception of health and illness this impression is misleading. Although apparently animistic in outlook, the traditional African conception of disease or illness conforms, at least in part, with the basic norms of modern medical practice. I shall return to this point shortly.

Basically, the causes of illness in traditional African thought fall into two major categories, the primary and the secondary. Care must be taken here not to confuse these two arms of explanation with Horton's broad distinction between levels of theoretical discourse. For clarity and ease of analysis, our primary and secondary causes are to be seen as a sub-division within Horton's category of secondary theory. Primary causes of illness are those predisposing factors not directly explicable in physical terms. Some of these take the form of supernatural entities such as deities, spirits, and witches; others are stress-induced either as a result of the victim's contravention of communal morality or his/her strained relationships with other persons within the community. Secondary causes, on the other hand, involve direct causal connections similar to the cause-effect relations of the germ theory in orthodox modern medicine. If, for instance, a person is suffering from stomach ache, acute diarrhoea, and vomiting, that person is suspected of having eaten "poisoned" food. It has been reported that in Yoruba, *ete* (leprosy) is spread either by spiders or through chewing sticks on which flies have landed or by drinking "local gin" (Maclean 1971:87). The Yoruba concept, *kokoro*, synonymous with "germ" in English, suggests that there are in the culture non-metaphysical/causal explanations of disease. Such explanations may lack the theoretical details of modern medicine but they are, in principle, similar to diagnoses in modern medicine – their truth or falsity being irrelevant. Our main concern here is with primary causes of illness and their relationship with secondary causes.

Normally, any explanation that draws on supernatural forces is regarded as incompatible with the principles of science upon which modern medicine rests. In fact, the scientist would see such an explanation as a direct violation of the principles of science. The connection between the two is always missed. Yet modern medical practitioners would find the connection difficult to deny. They would agree, for instance, that stress reduces the natural resistance of the body against certain diseases such that people in a state of stress are more susceptible to their affliction than those not socially disturbed. It is perhaps important to distinguish the African conception of stress from the way it is conceived in the West. A business executive in the West could suffer from stress if his/her business were on the verge of collapse; a heavy day's work without rest could lead him/her into such a state. Or, anxiety over possible contingencies could make the executive suffer from stress. In traditional Africa, stress is mainly due to a strained relationship either with one's spiritual agents or with other persons within one's community. It could also be due to a feeling of guilt arising from a breach of communal norms. For example, in some African groups, if a man were involved in an adulterous act with his brother's wife – whether or not this act were detected – the person would undergo stress, having disturbed his social harmony. If he cheated his neighbour, was cruel to his family or had offended his community, the anxiety that followed could take the form of phobias, either of "bewitchment" or of the affliction of diseases. Such a person would feel vulnerable and this feeling alone could result in real vulnerability.

The parallel to this in modern orthodox medicine is the practice whereby medical scientists explain certain diseases by a conjunction of the germ theory and the patient's reduced resistance due to stress. The possible difference between this and the corresponding primary and secondary explanations of traditional African thought is that Western medical science has at its disposal a well systematised body of theories to follow, while the African system operates on a piecemeal basis of trial and error. It should be noted, however, that not all orthodox medical physicians are theoreticians in the scientific sense of the word. There are many whose practice is based on trial and error – they follow the germ theory without knowing or being able to articulate its mechanisms. In the same way, it could be said that the traditional African healer follows certain principles although he/she is unable to say exactly what these principles are. Unlike the modern physician who has to rely almost entirely on the pharmacological efficacy of drugs, cure for the traditional African healer is directed towards the two targets of primary and secondary causes. The healer may be confident of the pharmacological activities of his/her herbs, but that is not all. The herbs are efficacious, the healer believes, only if the primary causes have been taken care of. The herbalist is thus also a diviner, which gives his/her profession a metaphysical outlook. But, again, this could be misleading. The point is that the primary causes result in the weakening of the defence mechanisms of the body. Cure in this respect simply means restoring the body to a state of increased capacity to heal itself, a state in which the pharmacological efficacy of the drugs is maximised.

Again, there is a parallel with this kind of integrated approach in modern medical practice. The well known *placebo* effect in orthodox medicine, in which confidence and positive belief – on the part either of the physician or the patient – produce a favourable effect, is well-nigh indistinguishable from the dual-approach of the

African healer. Belief, here, must be distinguished from the mere unquestioning faith of the religious type. It has a psychological overtone which leads to physically effective results. Both in African and modern medicine, the patient's belief that the physician is competent, and that the drug works, helps to restore his/her body to a state of harmony with the applied drug.

Psychological states, attitudes, and beliefs have been known to play significant roles in traditional African medicine; they now provide acceptable explanations for some of the ailments that have in the past been attributed mainly to supernatural forces. J.C. Carothers claims that anxiety, for instance, which in Africa is believed to be an outcome of bewitchment, leads to phobias

> whose physical symptoms take predominantly the forms of gastric and cardiac neuroses and of impotence. Anorexia nervosa or something akin to this, from time to time may be fatal. Fears that the food is poisoned may initiate the syndrome, but its continuance is governed by a feeling (a disguised depression) that the unusual struggle has been lost and the time has come to die (1953:121).

It is clear from this why the diagnostic method is such that the primary cause (in this case, bewitchment, believed to be the cause of anxiety) must be counteracted first or simultaneously with the secondary cause.

This, however, is not to say that the beliefs which inform the primary explanations are true, meaningful or even rational. The important point is that the beliefs are, as a matter of fact, held; also that they play an important role in the diagnosis of illness, and that they affect the pharmacological activities of drugs. Dorothy Rowe stresses the importance of such beliefs in her critique of the orthodox approach in the psychiatric administration of psychotropic drugs. According to her, it can be established

> that if a person believes that he has a good reason to be anxious or depressed (this "reason" may not be rational or even expressible in words) the drug does not change his belief and the effect of the belief overrides the effect of the drug (Rowe 1980:110).

Psychotropic drugs, she contends, are like aspirin which takes away the pain of toothache without healing the tooth.

There are conceptual difficulties with any such account which draws simultaneously on both natural and non-natural forces. Where the non-natural forces are social or psychological factors, the problems may adequately be handled by a psychoanalyst. But in Africa, where the causes of illness are a blend of supernatural forces (gods, deities, spirits, etc.) and natural forces (germs, parasites, *kokoro,* etc.) the apparent difficulty that emerges is similar to the body/mind problem, a sub-species of the general issue of how a non-physical entity can possibly interact with a physical entity.

I have argued elsewhere (cf. Sogolo 1989:119–130) that a clear dichotomy between the natural and supernatural does not exist in African thought. Even if it does, the apparent conflict in people's explanations of illness may still be resolved by invoking the difference in principle between primary causes and secondary causes. It could be said that a healer in tropical Africa, attending to a patient suffering from, say, severe cerebral malaria, is aware (if only vaguely) that the patient's ailment is caused by a parasite (secondary cause). But in a culture where almost everybody suffers repeatedly from bouts of malaria, and where the disease is normally not severe, it is obvious why the patient's consultation is bound to move beyond the "how" question to the "why" question: "Why such a severe attack and why me and not someone else?". These are quests for primary causes beyond the level of the physical. Note that in searching for answers to these questions, unlike in Western cultures, the concept of chance hardly plays any significant role (cf. Sodipo 1973:40–69).

The issues raised at the level of primary causes cannot be resolved by applying the canons of scientific reasoning. Indeed, viewed from the paradigm of science, some of the claims made are likely to sound meaningless, irrational, and false (if these terms are ever applicable). The crux of the matter is that the seeming conflict that exists between primary and secondary causes can be shown to be unreal, which is to say that there is no absurdity involved in an integrated diagnostic process which blends the natural with the supernatural nor in a curative process involving the pharmacological activities of herbs and the appeasement of supernatural entities.

The whole point of this excursus into the two-dimensional approach to causal explanation in African thought is to provide a parallel to the example of the fire cited earlier. In both cases, what stands as an acceptable explanation depends on our interests in the matter. Just as the conjunction of the explanations by the fire fighters, the physicist, the psychologist, etc. provides a fuller explanation of the cause of the fire, so would the various ailments mentioned in Maclean's examples provide a fuller comprehension of the pharmacological powers of the drug.

ON DECOLONISING AFRICAN RELIGIONS

KWASI WIREDU

As might be expected from my advocacy of strategic particularism, my focus will principally be on Akan religion as an example of African religions. I invite others to compare and contrast (where appropriate) their own perceptions of their indigenous religions. Religion is, indeed, an area in which there is a super-abundance of characterisations of African thought in terms of inappropriate or, at best, only half-appropriate concepts. I shall examine concepts like creation out of nothing, omnipotence and eternity, and categorial contrasts such as the natural versus the supernatural, and the physical versus the spiritual.

Africans are nowadays frequently said, not only by themselves but also by foreign students of their culture, to be a profoundly religious people. This was not always so. Some of the early anthropologists felt that the concept of God, for example, was too sublime for the African understanding – assuming that Africans had any understanding at all. The present situation in which indigenes as well as foreigners vie with one another to testify to the piety of the African mind is a remarkable reversal of earlier attitudes and prepossessions. There is virtual unanimity, in particular on the report that Africans have a strong belief in the existence of God.

On virtually all sides, it seems to be assumed that it speaks well of the mental capabilities of a people if they can be shown to have a belief in God, especially a God of a Christian likeness. Accordingly, the literature on African religions is replete with generalisations about African beliefs in the Almighty. In this discussion I want to start with a fairly extended look at the concept of God in the thought of the Akans of Ghana. Since this is the group to which I belong and in which I was raised, I hope I may be excused some show of confidence, though, of course, not dogmatism, in making some conceptual suggestions about their thought. I will also try, more briefly, to draw some contrasts between Akan thought and the thought of certain other African peoples on the question of belief in God, though this time more tentatively. It will emerge that not all African peoples entertain a belief in God, and that this is, nevertheless, without prejudice to their mental powers.

To start with the Akans, then: any cursory study of the thought and language of the Akans will, indeed, reveal a belief in a supreme being. This being is known by various names. I will mention just a few here. *Nyame* is the word most often used for this being. It means something like "absolute satisfier". Another of his names is *Onyankopon*, which means, literally, "He who is alone great", a notion that reminds one of St. Anselm's "that than which a greater cannot be conceived", though this is not to assume conceptual congruence in other respects. There is also the name *Twediampon* ("He upon whom you lean and do not fall"). Cosmologically, perhaps, the most important name is *Oboade*, which, for the time being, I will translate as Creator. Frequently, the word *Nana* is added to either of the first two names. The word means grandparent or ruler or, in a more general sense, honoured personage. In this context, all these meanings are available, but often it is the grandfatherly connotation that is uppermost in the consciousness of people invoking the name.

Indeed, in literature this grandfatherly appellation of God has often been emphasised by indigenous writers because some early European writers had suggested that the Akan (and, more generally, the African) God was an aloof God, indifferent to the fate of his creatures. These foreign observers even had the impression that this attitude of the supreme being was reciprocated by the Akans when they (the visitors) found among them no evidence of the worship of God, institutional or otherwise. In fact, however, the Akan have a strong sense of the goodwill of God; only this sentiment is not supposed, cosmologically speaking, to be manifested through *ad hoc* interventions in the order of nature.

The word "nature" is, perhaps, misleading in this context, insofar as it may suggest the complementary contrast of supernature. Here, we come, in fact, face to face with an important aspect of the cosmology of the Akans. God is the creator of the world, but God is not apart from the universe: together with the world, God constitutes the spatio-temporal "totality" of existence. In the deepest sense, therefore, the ontological chasm indicated by the natural/supernatural distinction does not exist within Akan cosmology. When, then, God is spoken of as creator we must remind ourselves that words can mislead. Creation is often thought of, at least in run-of-the-mill Christianity, as the bringing into existence of things out of nothing. Now, the Akan God is, certainly, not thought of as such a creator. The notion of creation out of nothing does not make sense in the Akan language. The idea of nothing can only be expressed by some such phrase as *se whee nni ho*, which means something like "the circumstance of there not being something there". The word *ho* (there, at some place) is very important in the phrase; it indicates a spatial context. That of which there is a lack in the given location is always relative to a universe of discourse implicitly defined by the particular thought or communication. Thus, beholding a large expanse of desolate desert, an Akan might say *whee nni ho*. The meaning would be that there is a lack there of the broad class of things that one expects to find on a land surface of that magnitude. The absolute nothingness entailed in the notion of creation out of nothing, however, scorns any such context. This abolition of context effectively abolishes intelligibility, as far as the Akan language is concerned.

But, it might be asked, does it not occur to the Akan that if God created the world, as he/she supposes, then prior to the act of creation there must have been nothing, in quite a strict sense? The answer is that it depends at least on what one means by "create". In the most usual sense, creation presupposes raw materials. A carpenter creates a chair out of wood and a novelist creates fiction out of words, ideas. If God is conceived as a kind of cosmic architect who fashions the world order out of an indeterminate raw material, the idea of absolute nothingness would seem to be avoidable. And this is, in fact, how the Akan metaphysicians seem to have conceived the matter (cf. Wiredu 1992/3:41ff.). Moreover, *Oboade*, the Akan word that I provisionally translated as "creator", means the maker of things. *Bo* means to make and *ade* means thing. But in Akan to *bo ade* is unambiguously instrumental, you only make something with something.

The almost automatic reaction from many people to such an idea is: if the "divine architect" fashioned the world out of some pre-existing raw material, then, however indeterminate it may have been, surely somebody must have created it. But this takes it for granted that the concept of creation out of absolute nothingness makes sense. Since this is the question at issue, the reaction just begs the question. If the concept of nothing in Akan is relative in the way explained, then obviously the notion of absolute nothingness will not make sense. The fundamental reason for this semantical situation in Akan is that in that language existence is necessarily spatial. To exist is to *wo ho*, be at some location (cf. Gyekye 1987:179). So if God exists, he is *somewhere*. If nothingness excludes space, it has no accommodation in the Akan conceptual framework. On the other hand, if nothingness accommodates space, it is no longer absolute.

Of course, if a concept is incoherent within a given language, it does not necessarily mean that there is anything wrong with it, for it may be that the language in question is expressively inadequate. In the case of the concept of creation out of nothing, however, its coherence, even within English, is questionable. In English, the concept of "there is" – note the "there" – which is equivalent to "exists", is quite clearly spatial. It is because the word "exists" does not bear its spatiality on its face, that it has been possible in English to speak as if existence were not necessarily spatial, without prohibitive implausibility. Besides, the maxim, *Ex nihilo nihil fit* (Out of nothing nothing comes), which, ironically, is championed by Christian philosophers such as Descartes (1951:39), conflicts sharply with the notion of creation out of nothing. That nothing can come out of nothing is not an empirical insight; it is a conceptual necessity, just like the fact that two and two cannot add up to fifty. Thus, to say that some being could make something come out of nothing is of the same order of incoherence as saying that some being could make two and two add up to fifty. Besides, as I have pointed out elsewhere (Wiredu 1992/3:44), the causal connotation of creation is incompatible with the circumstance or, rather, non-circumstance, of absolute nothingness. Causation makes sense only when it is, *in principle*, possible to distinguish between *post hoc* and *propter hoc* (i.e. between mere sequence and causal sequence). If there were one being and absolutely nothing besides this being, then logically, that distinction would be impossible. If so, the notion of causation collapses, and with it that of creation.

So the notion of creation out of nothing would seem to be incoherent not only in Akan, but also absolutely. At least, the last reason given in evidence of its incoherence was an independent consideration in the sense that it was independent of the peculiarities of Akan or English. It appealed only to a general logical principle. In fact, the conceptual difficulties in creation out of nothing have not been lost on religious thinkers, which accounts for the fact that it is not very unusual to find a sophisticated Christian metaphysician substituting some such rarefied notion as "the transcendental ground of existence" for the literal idea of creation, even while cooperating with the generality of pious Christians in speaking of God as the creator. Another escape from the paradoxes of *ex nihilo* creation by some religious sophisticates, going far back into history, has been by way of emanationism. It might be worth remembering also in this connection that Plato's *demiurge* was an idea innocent of *ex nihilo* pretensions.

Be that as it may, it seems clear that the Akan supreme being is thought of as a cosmic architect rather than a creator out of nothing. The world resulting from the process of divine fashioning is conceived as containing all the potential for its development and bears all the marks of God's goodwill once and for all. In this scheme there are postulated various orders of beings. At the top of this hierarchy is God. Immediately below God are a host of extra-human beings and forces. Then come human beings, the lower animals, vegetation, and the inanimate world, in that order. All these orders of being are believed to be subject to the universal reign of (cosmic) law. And the absence of any notion of creation out of nothing reflects the Akan sense of the ontological homogeneity of that hierarchy of existence.

Since I have mentioned inanimate things, I ought, perhaps, to dispose quickly of the allegation, often heard, that Africans believe that everything has life. The Akans, at least, are a counter-example. Some objects, such as particular rocks or rivers, may be thought to house an extra-human force, but it is not supposed that every rock or stone has life. Among the Akans a piece of dead wood, for example, is regarded as absolutely dead and is the humorous paradigm of absolute lifelessness. A more serious paradigm of the same thing is a dead body. Thus, the automatic attributions of animism to Africans manifest little empirical or conceptual wisdom.

I shall now return to the subject of order. The strength of the Akan sense of order may be gauged from the following cosmological drum text:

> Odomankoma
> He created the thing
> "Hewer out" Creator
> He created the thing
> What did he create?
> He created Order
> He created Knowledge
> He created Death
> As its quintessence (Danquah 1968:70).

The translation is Danquah's, and though it incorporates some interpretation, it is, I think, accurate. What we need particularly to note is that to the Akan metaphysician, order comes first, cosmologically speaking. The stanza is a statement, above all else, to quote Danquah (1968:72) again, of "the primordial orderliness of creation".

This sense of order in phenomena is manifested at another level in the strong belief in the law of universal causation. There is an Akan saying to the effect that if nothing had touched the palm nut branches they would not have rattled. (*Se biribi ankoka papa a anka erenye kredede.*) This is often quoted by writers on Akan thought as the Akan statement of universal causation (cf. Oquah 1984:217 & Minkus 1984:115). It is right as far as it goes, but there are more explicit formulations of the principle, such as one quoted by Gyekye (1987:77): *Asem biara wo ne farebae*, which literally means, everything has what brought it about. There is another formulation which, in addition to being more literal and explicit, is also more comprehensive. It says simply that everything has its explanation (*Biribiara wo nenkyerease*). The advantage of this is that it discourages any impression that the sense of order under study is only conversant with mechanical causation. In Akan thought this kind of causation corresponds to only one kind of explanation, though there are other kinds of explanation that are taken to evince the orderliness of creation (understanding creation, of course, in a quasi-demiurgic sense). These include psychological, rational, and quasi-physical explanations with various combinations of these. As one might expect, they correspond to the orders of being postulated in the Akan world-view.

To illustrate with a case which combines all these: suppose that an illness is interpreted as punishment from the ancestors for wrong conduct. There is here a cosmological dimension. The ancestors are conceived to be the departed "spirits" of erstwhile elders of our societies who live in a world analogous and contiguous to ours, and work for the good of the living while watching over their morals. On this showing, they are both like and unlike the living. Like the living, they have an interest in morality, of which they are indeed recognised as, in some ways, guardians. Moreover, insofar as any imagery is annexed to the conception of the ancestors, it is person-like. But, unlike persons, they are not normally perceivable to the naked eye, and they can affect human life in super-human ways for good or, in exceptional cases, as by the present hypothesis, for ill. The explanation involved here, then, is at once psychological, rational, mechanical, and quasi-physical. It is psychological because it is supposed that the hypothetical misconduct incurs the displeasure of the ancestors, which is a matter of mental dynamics. It is also rational in conception, for the imagined punishment is viewed as a reformatory and deterrent measure, which, in principle, is a reasonable objective in the enforcement of morals. It has a mechanical aspect in that the illness being explained involves a physiological condition that will in many ways exhibit scenarios of physical causality. And finally, it is quasi-physical because, as pointed out, although the ancestors are psycho-physical in imagery, the manner of their operation is not fully constrained by the dynamical and associated laws familiar in day-to-day experience.

That the activities of beings such as the ancestors are not supposed to be completely amenable to "physical" laws is not to be taken to imply that they are regarded as contradicting them. What in Western thought are called physical laws are, in the Akan world-view, understood to govern the phenomena of one sphere of existence. But that understanding, as explained, also postulates another sphere of existence which is believed to be governed, both internally and in interaction with the human sphere of existence, by laws different in some respects from physical or psychological laws, and supplementary to them. Though the generality of Akans do not pretend to understand many aspects of the *modus operandi* of the beings and forces belonging to the super-human sphere, they still view them as regular denizens of the cosmos. Moreover, there is no lack of "specialists" in Akan (and other African) societies who are supposed to have uncommon insights into the operations of such beings, and to enjoy expertise in communicating with them. So the idea of the ancestors punishing misbehaviour evokes no sense of cosmological irregularity. On the contrary, it is perceived as exactly the kind of thing that might happen if people misbehave in certain ways.

Certain conceptual consequences flow immediately from these last considerations. To begin with, since all the orders of being are conceived as interacting in a law-like manner, the natural/supernatural dichotomy has no place in the Akan world-view, which reinforces our earlier remark on this issue made in a slightly different connection. Furthermore, the notion of a miracle does not make sense in this context, if a miracle is something that is supposed to happen contrary to the laws of "nature". Strange things may happen, of course, but in this system of thought, if they cannot be accounted for on the basis of the laws of the familiar world, they will be assumed to be accountable on some quasi-physical laws. This cosmological orientation seems to be not at all uncommon in Africa.

Yet, in the literature on African religions, there are profuse references to the supposed African belief in the supernatural, which is frequently inspired by such things as ancestral veneration, almost standardly misdescribed as "ancestor-worship". Obviously, these misconceptions are the result of that superimposition of Western categories upon Akan thought-formations that is the quintessence of conceptual colonisation. Through education in colonial or neo-colonial circumstances, many Africans have come to assimilate these modes of thought and, in some cases, have internalised them so completely that they can apparently take great pride in propagating stories of the ubiquity of the supernatural in African thought. Perhaps none of us Africans can claim total freedom from this kind of assimilation, but at least we can consciously initiate the struggle for conceptual self-exorcism.

Other aspects of conceptual superimposition need to be noted. The beings I have, by implication, described as super-human (and not supernatural) are often called spirits. If the notion of spirits is understood in a quasi-physical sense, as it sometimes is in narratives of ghostly apparitions even in Western thought, there is no problem of conceptual incongruity. But if the word "spirit" is construed, as so often happens, in a Cartesian sense, to designate an immaterial substance, no such category can be fitted into the conceptual framework of Akan thought. The fundamental reason for this is to be found in the spatial connotation of the Akan concept of existence. Given the necessary spatiality of all existents, little reflection is required to see that the absolute ontological cleavage between the material and the immaterial will not exist in Akan metaphysics. Again, that Africans are constantly said to believe in spiritual entities in the immaterial sense can be put down to the conceptual impositions in the colonising accounts of African thought in colonial times, and their post-colonial aftermath.

It is, of course, an independent question whether the notion of an immaterial entity is intellectually viable. I will not pursue that question here (cf. Wiredu 1990:98ff. for such a discussion). What is urgent here and now is to note certain further dimensions of the conceptual misdescriptions of African religions. One of the most entrenched orthodoxies in the literature is the idea that Africans believe in a whole host of "lesser gods" or "lesser deities". That many Akans have accepted this story of a pantheon of "lesser gods" in their traditional religion must be due to a consistent forgetfulness of their own language when thinking about such matters. There is no natural way of translating the phrase "lesser gods" into Akan. In Akan, none of the names, as distinct from descriptions, for God has a plural. In any case, it is very misleading to call the super-human beings and forces gods. Since the notion of a god, however diminutive, is intimately connected with religion, the use of that word in this context encourages the description of African attitudes to those entities as religious. Then, since Africans do often regard themselves as being in relationship with them, the stage is set for the inference that their life is completely pervaded by religion. African scholars have not left it to foreigners alone to proclaim this image of African thought. Some of them have assumed eminent responsibility in that direction. Thus, John Mbiti, for example, in his *African religions and philosophy*, has said things like, "Wherever the African is, there is his religion: he carries it to the fields where he is sowing seeds or harvesting a new crop; he takes it with him to the beer party or to attend a funeral ceremony", or "African peoples do not know how to exist without religion" (1990:2), or "religion is their whole system of being" (1990:3). At work here, certainly, is an assimilation of African thought to Western categories.

As far at least as the Akans are concerned, it can be said that their attitude to those extra-human beings generally called minor gods in the literature is not really religious. On the contrary, it is utilitarian for the most part. The powers in question are, as previously noted, a regular part of the resources of the world. If human beings understand how these powers function, and are able to establish satisfactory relations with them, they can exploit their powers to their advantage. One has, of course, to be circumspect, because falling foul of them could be dangerous. The way of establishing satisfactory relations with them is through those procedures that are often called rituals. But these are not regarded as anything other than a method of making use of the super-human resources of the world. Because the powers that are called lesser gods are conceived to be, in some ways, person-like, the "rituals" often have a communicative component heavily laden with flattery. But the tactical character of the procedure is manifest in the fact that a so-called god who is judged inefficient, by reason, for example, of persistent inability to render help at the right time in the right place, is consigned to obsolescence by the permanent averting of attention. An attitude of genuine religious devotion cannot be conditional. Accordingly, it would seem inappropriate to call the "rituals" in question religious. Nor, for the same reason, can the procedures be called acts of *worship* unless the word is used in so broad a sense as to make the concept of worship no longer inseparably bound up with a religious attitude. That the attitude under discussion is not religious or that the procedures do not amount to worship does not imply a judgement that the people concerned fall short of some creditable practice; it simply means that the concepts of religion and worship have been misapplied to aspects of the given culture on the basis of less than rigorous analogies of foreign inspiration. It would, in any case, be hasty to assume that there is anything necessarily meritorious about religious activities.

The Akans, in common with most other African peoples, nevertheless do have a religious aspect to their culture. The question is its proper characterisation. I would say that Akan religion consists solely in the unconditional veneration of God, and trust in God's power and goodness – in a word, in God's perfection. This religion is, most assuredly, not an institutional religion, and there is nothing that can be called the worship of God in it. The insistence that any genuine belief in God must be accompanied by a practice of God-worship is simply an arbitrary universalisation of the habits of religionists of a different culture. It is difficult, in fact, to see how a perfect being could welcome or approve of such things as the singing of his/her praises. Another significant contrast with other religions, particularly certain influential forms of Christianity, is that although God is held to be all-good, morality is not defined in Akan thought in terms of the will of God, but rather in terms of human interests. Neither are procedures for the promotion of morality attached to Akan religion; they belong primarily to the home.

The inclusion of the attitudes and practices associated with the Akan belief in various super-human beings and forces within the scope of the Akan religion, is an adulteration of the traditional religion that has exposed it quite severely to unconsidered judgement. It has helped to eclipse the religion in certain layers of the consciousness of the average educated Akan. The movement of thought has been as follows. When this overly-inclusive view is taken of Akan religion, the supposed worship of the supposed gods looms so large in it that the whole religion becomes more or less identified with it. Thus it is that in Christian translation Akan religion is called *Abosomsom*, that is, the worship of stones. The same system of pious translation, by the way, called Christianity *Anyamesom*, that is, the worship of God. When, therefore, ordinary educated Akans brought up in Christianity come to think that they have shed belief in the "lesser gods", they automatically see themselves as too enlightened for the traditional religion. Actually, the shedding of the traditional mind-cast is often superficial only. But let that pass. We are only concerned here to illustrate one of the things that the uncritical assimilation of African categories to Western ones has done to an African self-image.

But let us return to the Akan God. An important question is how the Akans suppose that knowledge of God is obtained. In this connection there is an extremely interesting Akan saying to the effect that no one teaches God to a child. (*Obi nkyere akwadaa Nyame.*) This is sometimes interpreted to mean that knowledge of God is inborn and not the fruit of argumentation. But this is inconsistent with the implications of some of the names for or descriptions of God in Akan. One designation calls God *Ananse Kokroko*, meaning, the Stupendous Spider. Now, the spider is associated with ingenuity in designing, and the designation is clearly a metaphorical articulation of the notion of God as the Great Designer. Citing an Akan designation which calls God the Great Planner, Oguah also comments that we have here a hint of the argument which in Western philosophy is called the teleological argument. Oguah is, I think, right, and this shows that the Akans do think that reasoning is involved in the acquisition of the knowledge of the existence of God. If so, the maxim cited at the beginning of this paragraph is unlikely to be one that seeks to rule out the relevance of argument. Its most plausible interpretation is that the reasons for the belief in God are so obvious that even a child can appreciate them unaided.

In my own experience the interpretation last suggested has tallied best with the reactions of those Akans not steeped in foreign philosophies, that I have accosted from time to time on the justification of the belief in God. They have never refused the invitation to reason, though they have tended to be surprised that so obvious a point should be the object of ernest inquiry. The following type of argument has often been proffered:

> Surely, somebody must be responsible for the world. Were you not brought forth into this world by your parents? And were they not, in turn, by their parents, and so on? Must there not, therefore, be somebody who was responsible for everything?

Another type of argumentation that I have been supplied with is this:

> Every household has a father, and every town or country a king. Surely, there must be someone who rules the whole universe.

In this last connection a very common Akan saying comes to mind, namely, "God is King" (*Onyame ne hene*).

Regarding these arguments, no one can, or should, pretend that they are cogent pieces of reasoning, especially the last one. It is relevant to note that these arguments were deliberately solicited from ordinary Akans, not from their metaphysicians. But two points can be made, the second of which has especial significance for our discussion. Firstly, if these arguments were sound, they would prove the conclusions advertised or something very close. They would, that is, prove that there is a cosmic architect or ruler of the universe or something like that. This is very much more than can be said for almost all the principal arguments for the existence of God in Western philosophy. These arguments are also such that, if they were sound, they would only prove some such being as a cosmic architect or governor. Yet, as a rule, there is, at the concluding point, an inconceivable leap to the affirmation of an *ex nihilo* Creator-God. On this point Hume's words should have been the last. He pointed out, with particular reference to the teleological argument, otherwise known as the argument from design, that even if granted valid, it would only prove a designer, not a creator (*ex nihilo*). But faith, even when it pretends to argue, is apparently stronger than logic, and the concluding unphilosophical leap remains a favourite exercise for some philosophers.

Secondly, and more importantly, the fact that even ordinary Akans are so willing to reason about the basic proposition of their religion demonstrates a rational attitude to religion which contrasts with the attitude which fundamentalist Christianity brought to many parts of Africa through the missionaries. Their key idea in this regard seems to have been that faith as belief is inaccessible to rational discussion. Many Africans have taken the idea to heart and have, in some cases, even been born again. If you ask them for the reason behind their preference for the new religion over the traditional one, the standard reply is that it is a matter of faith, not reason. The foregoing enables us to show also that this irrationality is uncharacteristic of the traditional outlook on religion. In fact, the notion of faith as belief without, and inaccessible to, reason is untranslatable into Akan except by an unflattering paraphrase. *Gyidi hunu*, literally, useless belief, is probably all that is available, unless one preferred a more prolix circumlocution, which would be something like *Gyidi a enni nkyerease*, that is, again literally, belief without explanation. The pejorative connotation of the latter periphrasis, however, does not come through in the English version. Thus, within Akan semantics one would be hard put to sell the idea of faith inhospitable to reason. In this circumstance one must admire the simplicity of the Christian solution to the problem of translating faith (in the non-rational sense) into Akan. They say simply *Gyidi*, which in genuine Akan means, simply, belief. Since this is patently inadequate, one must assume that the translators may have put their faith in *ad hoc* evangelical glosses. But it is also simple to see that decolonised thinking in religion must make short work of the evangelical talk of faith.

Let us return once more to the concept of God. Oguah (1984:216) advances the interesting claim that the Akan concept of God as the one who is alone great (*Onyankopon*) is the same as the concept of the greatest conceivable being or that than which nothing greater can be conceived, which forms the basis of Saint Anselm's ontological argument for the existence of God. In a formal sense this is correct, for an Akan believer cannot consistently concede the possibility of any being greater than or even equal to God. However, this formal identity pales into insignificance when it is recalled that the Akan God is a cosmic architect, while Anselm's is an *ex nihilo* creator. These two concepts are so different that the chances are that the ingenious saint would have considered the Akan concept quite atheistic. Accordingly, when we use the word God to translate *Nyame*, we must bear the disparity in connotation between this and the orthodox Christian concept of God firmly in mind.

This is particularly worth stressing in view of the tendency of many African writers on African religions, proud of their African identity, to suggest that their peoples recognise the same God as the Christians, since God is one. The origin of this tendency seems to me to be the following. Almost all these writers have themselves been Christians, in most cases divines. Being scandalised by the opinion of some of the early European visitors to Africa that the African was too primitive to attain to belief in God unaided, they have sought to demonstrate that Africans discovered God by their own lights before ever a European or any foreigner, for that matter, set foot in Africa. But, since they themselves have been brought up to think that the Christian God is the one true God, it has been natural for them to believe that the God of their ancestors is, in fact, the same as the God of Christianity. In this way also they have been able to satisfy themselves that, in taking to Christianity, they have not fundamentally forsaken the religion of their ancestors. (Incidentally, in this respect, many African specialists in religious studies have differed from average African Christians, who, if they are Akans, would probably, at least verbally, declare traditional religion to be just *abosomsom*, the worship of stones.) Consider what one very famous African authority on African religions says:

> There is no being like "the African God" except in the imagination of those who use the term, be they Africans or Europeans . . . there is only one God, and while there may be various concepts of God, according to each people's spiritual perception, it is wrong to limit God with an adjective formed from the name of any race.

The writer is Bolaji Idowu and the passage occurs in his *African traditional religion: A definition* (1973:146). Idowu was for many years Professor of Religions at the University of Ibadan, and was in his retirement the Patriarch of the Methodist Church of Nigeria for some years. He is the author of perhaps the most famous book on the religion of the Yorubas, *Olodumare: God in Yoruba belief* (1962). The Yoruba have a concept of God that is substantially similar to that of the Akans. This is confirmed by Idowu's study of the direct descriptions of the Yoruba concept of God. In both cases what we have is a cosmic architect. But if this is so, it is extremely implausible to suggest that either the Yoruba or the Akan conception of God is just a different way of conceiving one and the same being as the God of Christianity. To see the fallacy clearly, consider that it is conceivable that God as a cosmic architect exists, while an *ex nihilo* creator-God does not or cannot exist. Or, since Idowu's thesis is quite general, imagine that Spinoza, on the verge of ex-communication from his synagogue on account of his view that God and nature are one, had sought to placate the authorities by proleptically taking a leaf out of Idowu's book and assuring them that God is one and that therefore they were all, after all, talking of the same being. The inevitable aggravation of tempers would, surely, have been blameable on no one but Spinoza himself. As it happened, the gentle metaphysician knew better than to attempt any such misadventure. But in pure logic, when Idowu tries to serve both Olodumare and the God of Christianity, he is embarking on a similar misadventure. Put frankly, he is trying to have his cake and eat it. But it is not given to even an ex-Patriarch to prosper logically in such an enterprise. The obvious lesson is that African thinkers will have to make a critical review of those conceptions and choose one or none, but not both. Otherwise, colonised thinking must be admitted to retain its hold.

Since, by the present account, God is the beginning and the end of Akan religion, it may be useful to probe still further the Akan doctrine of God. And in so doing, it will be important to bear the point made at the end of the last paragraph securely in mind. What, then, are the attributes of the Akan God? There are Akan expressions used of God that warrant saying that God is conceived to be omnipotent, omnibenevolent, omniscient, all-wise, and eternal. But these attributes, especially omnipotence and eternity, must be understood only in a sense applicable to the type of being that a cosmic architect is. For example, the eternity of this being means simply that he has always existed and will always exist. The pressure that some Christian thinkers have felt to say that God is eternal in the sense of being timeless, that is, of not existing in time, is absent from the Akan mind. This pressure acts on some Christian minds because, if God created everything out of nothing, then it might conceivably be asked whether he did not create time also (however time may be conceived). And if God did, he can hardly be said himself to have been existing in time. It is well-known that Saint Augustine held that God created time along with everything else. (This great divine was, by the way, an African, but his mind was soaked in classical Roman culture. It has, indeed, been speculated that his thought was not totally untouched by his African origins. But, if so, this particular doctrine was not one of the ways in which that may have manifested itself.)

Again, if we take the concept of omnipotence, we notice the same absence of the pressure to push it to transcendental proportions. The Akan God is omnipotent in the sense that he is thought capable of accomplishing any conceptually *well-defined* project. Thus, for example, he will not be supposed capable of creating a person who is at once six foot tall and not six foot tall, going by identical conventions of measurements. And this will not be taken to disclose a limitation on God's powers because the task description discloses no well-defined project. Perhaps, to many people, this sounds unremarkable. But consider the following. It is apparent from one of the most famous Akan metaphysical drum texts that God is not supposed to be capable of reversing the laws of the cosmos (cf. Wiredu 1992/3:41ff.). The question is whether the project is a coherent one. The answer is: "Of course not!" from the point of view of the metaphysics in question. Here, then, is another illustration of formal identity amidst substantive disparities. Formally, both the Akan and the Christian may subscribe to the same definition of omnipotence as follows: "A being is omnipotent if and only if he, she or it can accomplish any well-defined project." Substantive differences, however, emerge when information is volunteered on both sides regarding the sorts of things that are or are not taken to be well-defined projects. It is interesting to note, in the particular case of omnipotence, that even this formal identity evaporates in the face of certain Christian interpretations of the concept. Omnipotence, for some Christian thinkers, means that God can do absolutely anything, including (as in the example mentioned above) creating a person who is both six foot tall and not six foot tall at the same time. On this showing, omnipotence implies the power to do even self-contradictory things. So powerful a Western Christian mind as that of Descartes was apparently attracted to this idea (cf. Wilson 1978:121–131).

To be sure, the Akans are innocent of such a solecism. But they are not free from the intellectual difficulties that have plagued the Christian doctrine of omniscience, omnibenevolence, omnipotence, and unlimited wisdom. If God has all these qualities, couldn't he/she have prevented the abundance of evil in the world? And ought God not to have done so? This is "the problem of evil". In discussing it, one thing that will become clear is that the communal philosophy of a traditional society need not always display unanimity, contrary to the impression fostered by certain colonial-type studies of African life and thought.

It is sometimes suggested that the problem does not really arise in Akan thought. Helaine Minkus, an American researcher who lived among the Akwapim Akans and learnt their language and studied their philosophy, advances a view of this sort in her "Causal theory in Akwapim Akan philosophy":

> God's attribute of transcendence and the concomitant belief that he has delegated power to the other agents that more directly interact with human beings pragmatically diminish His omnipotence. The other agents are treated in practice as if endowed with an independent ability to act. . . . The postulation of a great number of beings empowered to affect events, joined with the acceptance of evil as necessarily co-existing with good from creation obviates the problem of evil so burdensome to those monotheistic theologians who define the Supreme Being as both omnipotent and totally benevolent and attempt a reconciliation of these qualities with the existence of evil (Minkus 1984:116).

Minkus talks here of the pragmatic diminution of God's omnipotence. But this represents a dilemma rather than a dissolution. If the diminution of omnipotence is only "pragmatic", God as the ultimate source of the powers delegated to the "other agents" remains ultimately in charge, and the original problem ultimately also remains. If, on the other hand, the diminution is real, this contradicts the well-attested postulate of omnipotence in Akan cosmology. Is the contradiction a feature of Minkus's exposition or of the Akan system expounded? I shall return to this question below.

Interestingly, in an earlier exposition of Akan thought Busia shifted the responsibility for evil from God to the "other agents", not pragmatically, but positively. He remarks:

> the problem of evil so often discussed in Western philosophy and Christian theology does not arise in the African concept of deity. It is when a God who is not only all-powerful and omniscient but also perfect and loving is postulated that the problem of the existence of evil becomes a philosophical hurdle. The Supreme Being of the African is the Creator, the source of life, but between him and man lie many powers and principalities good and bad, gods, spirits, magical forces, witches to account for the strange happenings in the world (Busia 1965).

Gyekye (1987) quotes this passage and points out that if God is omnipotent, the question still arises why he does not control the "lesser spirits". This, he rightly concludes, shows that the problem of evil is not obviated. Gyekye's own account of the Akan solution of the problem of evil, which for him is a real problem in Akan philosophy, is that

> [t]he Akan thinkers, although recognizing the existence of moral evil in the world, generally do not believe that this fact is inconsistent with the assertion that God is omnipotent and wholly good. Evil, according to them, is the result of the exercise by humans of their freedom of the will with which they were endowed by the Creator, *Oboade* (1987:128).

In Gyekye's account, the Akan thinkers in question advocated a solution to the problem of evil which is also canvassed by some Western thinkers and is known as the "free-will defence". Gyekye is certainly right in seeing this solution in Akan thought. But Akan sources also reveal other solutions. Before considering some of them, let us quickly note two things with regard to the free-will defence as it relates to moral evil. Firstly, it does not provide a satisfactory answer to the question why God does not intervene to stop or forestall evil acts when they are planned. This is, of course, different from the idea that God could have guaranteed *ab initio* that human beings made only right choices. The usual reply to the suggested intervention is that it would destroy the free will of humans. But this reply does not appear to be plausible. Even human beings are sometimes able to intervene by force or by persuasion to stop the evil designs of others, without affecting their free will. In the abstract, countless smooth ways are conceivable by which God might forestall, counteract or neutralise the evil acts that humans might use their free will to contemplate. Possibly, there might be something wrong with this hypothesis; but clearly, it would not be because of any threat to free will. Secondly, this solution does not begin to deal with physical evil.

However, the problem of physical evil might, theoretically, be tackled by Akan advocates of the free-will defence with only a little elaboration on the remark of Busia quoted above. They might simply argue that the "principalities, good and bad, spirits, gods" etc., rather than God, are responsible for physical evil – in Busia's (1965) phrase – for "the strange happenings in the world". On this supposition, these happenings would be the result of the exercise, by those beings, of the free will "with which they were endowed by the Creator". In Western philosophy, by the way, the same idea occurred to Saint Augustine, who debited Satan and his cohorts with much of the physical evil in the world, a manoeuvre which has recently been exploited by some highly sophisticated apologists (cf. Davis 1983:105ff.). In the face of a claim of this sort, one can but await probative evidence.

Meanwhile, we may usefully note another Akan angle on the question of evil which is evident in the quotation from Minkus above, but which she does not separate from her theory (on behalf of the Akans) of the pragmatic diminution of God's omnipotence. She attributes to the Akans "the acceptance of evil as necessarily co-existing with good from creation". What is proposed here is not just the semantic point that you cannot talk of good if the possibility of the contrast with evil does not exist, but rather the substantive cosmological claim that the components of existence which we describe as good could not possibly exist without those components we call evil. That the Akans do actually entertain this thought is attested to by a common saying among them. It is, indeed, one of the commonest sayings of the Akans. "If something does not go wrong," they say, "something does not go right" (*Se biribi ansee a, biribi nye yie*).

However, even if it is granted that good cannot exist without evil, that still does not amount to a theodicy, for it does not follow that the quantity of evil in the world does not go beyond the call of necessity. But there is another Akan saying that seems to suggest exactly this. The Akans delight in crediting their maxims to animals, and in this instance the epigrammatic surrogate is the hawk. It is said: "The hawk says that all that God created is good" (*Osansa se nea Onyame yee biara ye*). The sense here is not that all is good to a degree that could conceivably be exceeded, but rather that all is maximally good. Again, the hawk is not trying to fly in the face of the palpable facts of evil in the world; what it is saying is that the evil, though it is evil, is unavoidably involved in the good and is ultimately for the best – a sentiment that would have warmed the heart of Leibniz, author, in Western philosophy, of the maxim that this is the best of all possible worlds (Leibniz 1951:12).

But how do we know this? Possibly because of the difficulty of this question, the Akans, or at any rate, some of them, do not seem to have sustained this cosmic optimism indefinitely, and there is evidence of another approach to the problem of evil which seeks to dissolve it by foregoing the claim of the total omnipotence of God. This brings us back to the pragmatic diminution of omnipotence spoken of by Minkus (1984:94). But this time the diminution is real, not pragmatic. So, too, is the possibility of inconsistency in the traditional thought of the Akans on this subject. Though in the context of cosmological reflection they maintain a doctrine of unqualified omnipotence, in connection with issues having a direct bearing on the fate of humankind on this earth, such as the problem of evil, they seem to operate with a notion of the power of God implying rather less than absolute omnipotence. That power is still unique in its extent, but it is conceptually not altogether unlike that of a human potentate. Indeed, correspondingly, God himself comes to be thought of on the model of a father who has laid well-intentioned plans for his children which are, however, sometimes impeded not only by their refractory wills but also by the grossness of the raw materials he has to work with. In conformity with this way of seeing God, a popular Akan lyric cries: "God descend, descend and come and take care of your children" (*Onyame sane, sane behwe wo mma*). The apparent inconsistency in this dual conception of God and his powers in the Akan communal philosophy may possibly be due to its diversity of authorship; but, on the other hand, it may well be a real inconsistency harboured in identical Akan minds. Actually, a similar inconsistency is evident in some Christian thinking on the same problem.

Be that as it may, the position in question is approvingly expounded by Danquah as *the* Akan solution to the problem of evil. I quote from Danquah *in extenso*:

> What, then, is the Akan solution to the fact of physical pain in man's animate experience? On the Akan view [sic], we could only regard this as a difficulty if we lost sight of the fundamental basis of their thought, namely, that Deity does not stand over against his own creation, but is involved in it. He is, if we may be frank, "of it". If we postulate, as the Christians do, that the principle that makes for good "in this world", Nyame or God, stands over against the community . . . and if we postulate again that the aforementioned principle is omnipotent, and is also responsible as creator of this world, the existence of physical evil or pain . . . becomes an insoluble mystery. . . . It is quite otherwise if we deny that the principle is omnipotent but is itself a "a spirit striving in the world of experience with the inherent conditions of its own growth and mastering them" at the cost of the physical pain and evil as well as the moral pain or disharmony that stain the pages of human effort. . . . That is to say, in Akan language, where the Nana, the principle that makes for good, is himself or itself a participant in the life of the whole . . . physical pain and evil are revealed as natural forces which the Nana, in common with others of the group, have to master, dominate, sublimate or eliminate (1968:88–89).

This reminds one of John Stuart Mill (1875:116–117), who was constrained by the problem of evil to resort to the concept of a limited God.

Danquah is not quite right in seeming to think that the view just noted is the one and only solution to the problem of evil in Akan thought. Whether by way of inconsistency or doctrinal fecundity among Akan thinkers, there is, as shown above, a diversity of thought on the problem. This discussion, then, demonstrates a vitality of philosophical thought in an African traditional society that the generality of colonial studies of African thought, intending to give the impression of monolithic unanimity, has tended to obscure. In addition, in view of the repeated examples of philosophical convergences, it shows that although it is the hallmark of decolonised thinking to be critically cognisant of the differences between African thought and its Western counterpart in its various forms, this is without prejudice to the possibilities of parallels in intellectual concerns and even doctrinal persuasion. This, it need hardly be added, can be a basis for fruitful interchange between African and Western (and presumably also Oriental) philosophy.

The reference to philosophical diversity above is worth exploring at least briefly. The multiplicity of philosophic options is in evidence not only within the Akan tradition but also across the African continent. Thus, it is not to be taken for granted that the Akan doctrine of a basically demi-urgic God is universal in Africa. On the evidence of studies such as Harry Sawyer's *God: Ancestor or creator?* (1970) and Kofi Asare Opoku's *West African traditional religion* (1978), it might be conjectured that this doctrine is widespread in West Africa. On the other hand, if Mbiti is right, this does not apply to certain other parts of Africa. The latter observes that the

> concept of creation *ex nihilo* is . . . reported among the Nuer, Banyarwanda and Shona, and undoubtedly a careful search for it elsewhere is likely to show that there are other peoples who incorporate it into their cosmologies (Mbiti 1990:39).

As regards the Banyarwanda, Maquet has written as follows:

> The world in which men are placed and which they know through their senses was created *ex nihilo* by *Imana*. The Ruanda word *kurema*, means to produce, to make. It is here rendered "to create" because our informants say that there was nothing before *Imana* made the world. This belief concerning the origin of the material world is universal and clear. To any question on this point, the answer is ready (1954:166).

This account, if it is correct, together with our previous findings, shows that not all traditional Africans think alike about God. It would seem that the Banyarwanda think more like orthodox Christians than like the traditional Akans. In fact, however, Maquet's (1954:166) account is not unproblematic. He says, for example, that *Imana*, the God of the Banyarwanda, "is non-material. His action influences the whole world; but Ruanda is his home where he comes to spend the night." But how does a non-material being spend the night, and in physical environs, such as Ruanda? Presumably, the idea is that a non-material being can sometimes materialise itself, i.e. manifest itself in a material guise. But this involves a category mistake not unlike that of supposing that the square root of minus one might be able to dance calypso from time to time. Moreover, it is as full-blooded a logical inconsistency as ever there was. Is the present incarnation of this inconsistency Maquet's or the Banyarwanda's? While the question remains open, confidence in Maquet's report of the belief in *ex nihilo* creation among the Banyarwanda cannot be limitless, but neither can it be discounted out of hand.

In vast contrast to the religious thought of both the Akans and the Banyarwanda is that of the Luo of Uganda, if we may go by Okot p'Bitek. According to him, the Central Luo do not entertain any belief in a supreme, or, as he phrases it, High God. They do not even have truck with the concept of such a being, nor does the notion of creating or even moulding the world make sense within their conceptual framework. In two books, namely, *African religions in Western scholarship* and *Religion of the Central Luo*, he argues with intriguing illustrations that "the idea of a high God among the Central Luo was a creation of the missionaries" (p'Bitek 1970:50). If truth be told, p'Bitek was the true pioneer of conceptual decolonisation in African philosophy. His *African religions in Western scholarship* might well have been sub-titled "The decolonisation of African religions". He is an interesting exception to the practice among African writers of endeavouring to prove to the world that Africans had, by their own efforts, reached a concept of God essentially identical with the God of Christianity before the arrival of the missionaries. The general assumption among these writers, as I pointed out earlier, has been that it is a glorious achievement for a culture to be able to arrive, without outside help, at the belief in a God who created the world out of nothing. p'Bitek had no such assumption. He was a sceptic, and found nothing necessarily creditable in such a belief. He thus had no special joy at the prospect of it being demonstrated that the Central Luo were original true believers. It is, of course, open to his critics to argue that, in writing as he did, he was foisting his own unbelief upon his people. There is, certainly, no substitute for an objective and conceptually critical examination of his account of Luo religion. That would, in itself, be an admirable exercise in conceptual decolonisation. For my part, given the ease and frequency with which Western categories of thought have been superimposed on African thought, I am inclined to suspect him innocent until proven guilty.

According to p'Bitek, then, the Central Luo believe in a whole host of forces or powers called, in their language, *jogi* (plural of *jok*), each independent of the rest. These *jogi* are regarded as responsible for particular types or patterns of happenings. Some of them are chiefdom *jogi* who are supposed to see to the welfare of particular groups of people. Others are hostile. For example, *jok kulu* causes miscarriage, *jok rubanga* causes tuberculosis of the spine, etc. Even the supposed power of a witch to cause harm is called a *jok*. Some *joks* may be used against other *joks*, but no one *jok* dominates all. This is a far cry, indeed, from the Christian religious ontology which postulates an omnipotent creator *ex nihilo*, and also from the Akan system with its divine architect who is "alone great".

In substantiation of his assertion that the idea of a high God among the Luo was the invention of the Christian missionaries, p'Bitek recounts the following incident. I have quoted it elsewhere (cf. Wiredu 1992:301–302) in a similar connection, but I cannot forebear to quote it again in the present context, as it furnishes a perfect paradigm of conceptual imposition in perfect drama:

> In 1911, Italian Catholic priests put before a group of Acholi elders the question "Who created you?"; and because the Luo language does not have an independent concept of *create* or *creation*, the question was rendered to mean "Who moulded you?" But this was still meaningless, because human beings are born of their mothers. The elders told the visitors that they did not know. But we are told that this reply was unsatisfactory, and the missionaries insisted that a satisfactory answer must be given. One of the elders remembered that, although a person may be born normally, when he is afflicted with tuberculosis of the spine, then he loses his normal figure, he gets "moulded". So he said "Rubanga is the one who moulds people." This is the name of the hostile spirit which the Acholi believe causes the hunch or hump back. And instead of exorcising the hostile spirits and sending them among pigs, the representatives of Jesus Christ began to preach that Rubanga was the Holy Father who created the Acholi (p'Bitek 1971:62).

Disentangling African frameworks of thought from colonial impositions such as this is an urgent task facing African thinkers, especially philosophers, at this historical juncture. Clarifying African religious concepts should be high on the agenda of this kind of decolonisation.

REFERENCES

Abimbola, W. 1971. "The Yoruba concept of human personality", in *La notion de personne en Afrique Noire*. Paris: Centre National de la Récherche Scientifique, 1971:73–89.

Abimbola, W. 1975. *Sixteen great poems of Ifa*. Centre d'Études Linguistique et Historique pour Tradition Orale. Niamey: Unesco.

Ademuwagun, Z.A. 1978. "Alafia – Yoruba concept of health: Implications for health education." *International Journal of Health Education*, XXI(2):89–97.

Annobil, J.A. 1971. *Mmebusem nkyekyeremy (Proverbs and their explanations)*. Cape Coast.

Antubam, K. 1963. *Ghana's heritage of culture*. Leipzig: Koehler & Amelang.

Appiah, K.A. 1992. "The myth of an African world", "Ethnophilosophy and its critics", "Old Gods, new worlds", from *In my father's house: Africa in the philosophy of culture*, in P.H. Coetzee & M.E.S. van den Berg (eds), 1995:1–13, 79–101, 154–184.

Bolaji, I. 1962. *Olodumare: God in Yoruba belief*. London: Longman.

Bolaji, I. 1973. *African traditional religion: A definition*. London: SCM.

Burke, F.G. 1964. "Tanganyika: The search for Ujamaa", in W.H. Friedland & C.G. Rosbert, *African socialism*. Stanford: Stanford University Press, 1964:194–219.

Busia, K.A. 1954. "The Ashanti of the Gold Coast", in D. Forde (ed.), *African world: Studies in cosmological ideas and the social values of African peoples*. Oxford. Oxford University Press, 1954:190–209.

Busia, K.A. 1965. "The African world view". *Présence Africaine*, 4:16–23.

Carothers, J.C. 1953. *The African mind in health and disease: A study in ethnopsychiatry*. Geneva: WHO. Monograph Series, 17.

Clough, M. 1981. "Early healing", in R. Passmore (ed.), *Proceedings of tercentenary congress on 6–11 September 1981*, Edinburgh: Royal College of Physicians, 1981:183.

Coetzee, P.H. & Van den Berg, M.E.S. (eds), 1995. *An introduction to African Philosophy*. Pretoria: Unisa.

Cureau, A.L. 1915. *Savage man in central Africa: A study of primitive races in the French Congo*. London: Unwin.

Danquah, J.B. 1968 (1944). *The Akan doctrine of God: A fragment of Gold Coast ethics and religions*. 2nd ed. London: Frank Cass.

Danto, A.C. 1980. *Nietzsche as philosopher*. New York: Colombia University Press.

Davidson, B. 1994. "The motives of Mau Mau." *London Review of Books*, 24 February 1994, 12.

Davis, S.T. 1983. *Logic and the nature of God*. Grand Rapids, Mich.: Eerdmans.

Descartes, R. 1951. *Meditations of first philosophy*. Tr. L. Lafleur. New York: Macmillan.

Floistad, G. 1987. *Contemporary philosophy*. Dordrecht: Nijhoff.

Gbadegesin, S. 1991. "Ènìyàn: The Yoruba concept of a person", in P.H. Coetzee & M.E.S. van den Berg (eds), 1995:335–368.

Gbadegesin, S. 1991. "Ènìyàn: The Yoruba concept of a person", in S. Gbadegesin, *African philosophy*. New York: Peter Lang, 1991:27–59.

Gouldner, A.W. 1975/76. "Prologue to a theory of revolutionary intellectuals." *Telos*, 26: 3–36.

Gwengwe, J.W. 1970. *Kukula ndi mwambo*. Limbe: Malawi Publications of Literature Bureau.

Gyekye, K. 1978. "The Akan concept of a person", in P.H. Coetzee & M.E.S. van den Berg (eds), *An introduction to African philosophy*. Pretoria: Unisa, 1995:369–380.

Gyekye, K. 1984. "The Akan concept of a person", in R.A. Wright (ed.), 1984:199–212.

Gyekye, K. 1987. *An essay on African philosophical thought: The Akan conceptual scheme*. New York: Cambridge University Press.

Higgs, P. 1997. "A re-vision of philosophy of education in South African education." Conference paper read at Faculty of Education seminar, Unisa: Pretoria. Unpublished.

Hollander, P. 1987. "Intellectuals and conformity in American society." *The World and I*, January 1987.

Horton, R. 1970. "African traditional thought and Western science", in B.R. Wilson (ed.), *Rationality*. Oxford: Blackwell, 1970:130–171.

Horton, R. 1982. "Tradition and modernity revisited", in M. Hollis & S. Lukes (eds), *Rationality and relativism*. Oxford: Blackwell, 1982:201–260.

Hountondji, P.J. & Zegeye, A. 1989. *Religion, magic and witchcraft: Structures of belief in everyday life*. Oxford: Hans Zeller.

Hume, D. 1974. *A treatise of human nature*. London: Dent.

Idowu, E.B. 1962. *Olodumare: God in Yoruba belief*. Lagos: Longmans.

Idowu, E.B. 1973. *African traditional religion: A definition*. New York: Orbis.

Jackson, M. & Karp, I. (eds) 1990. *Personhood and agency*. Washington: Smithsonian Institute.

Kagamé, A. 1956. *La philosophie Bantu-rwandaise de l'être*. Brussels: Johnson.

Kagamé, A. 1989. "The problem of 'Man' in Bantu Philosophy." *Journal of African Religion and Philosophy*, 1.

Kuckertz, H. 1996. "Selfhood and its reason to be", in J.G. Malherbe (ed.), 1996:57–66.

Kumakanga, S. 1970. *Nzeru zakale*. Nairobi: Longman.

Leibniz, G.W. 1970 (1951). "Monadology", in *Philosophical writings by Leibniz*. Tr. M. Morris. London: Dent, 1970:3–20.

Lewis, A. 1953. "Health as a social concept." *The British Journal of Sociology*, 4(2):109–124.

Locke, J. 1947. *Essay concerning human understanding*. London: Dent.

Maclean, U. 1971. *Magical medicine: A Nigerian case study*. Harmondsworth: Penguin.

Makinde, M. 1983. "Immortality of the soul and the Yoruba theory of seven heavens (Orun Meje)." *Journal of Cultures and Ideas*, 1(1):31–59.

Makinde, M. 1985. "A philosophical analysis of the Yoruba concepts of Ori and human destiny." *International studies in philosophy*, XVII(1):53–69.

Malherbe, J.G. (ed.) 1996. *Decolonizing the mind. Proceedings of the second colloquium on African philosophy*. Pretoria: Department of Philosophy, Unisa.

Maquet, J.J. 1954. "The kingdom of Ruanda", in D. Forde (ed.), *African worlds*. Oxford: Oxford University Press, 1954:164–189.

Maurier, H. 1979. "Do we have an African philosophy", in R.A. Wright (ed.), 1979:1–17.

Mbiti, J.S. 1990 (1969). *African religions and philosophy*. 2nd ed. London: Heinemann.

Menkiti, I.A. 1984. "Person and community in African traditional thought", in R.A. Wright (ed.), 1984:171–181.

Mill, J.S. 1875. "On Nature", in *Three essays on religion*. London: Longman, 1875.

Minkus, H. 1984. "Causal theory in Akwapim Akan philosophy", in R.A. Wright (ed.), 3rd ed. 1984:113–147.

More, M.P. 1996. Review of A. Shutte, "Philosophy in Africa". *South African Journal of Philosophy*, 15(4):152–154.

Mosley, A. 1978. "The metaphysics of magic: Practical and philosophical implications." *Second Order*, VII(1,2):3–19.

Neugebauer, C. 1988. "Die 'Akan-Philosophie' – Ihre Diskussion in der akademischen Philosophie in Ghana seit 1970." *Conceptus*, 22(56):93–107.

Nkrumah, K. 1978 (1964). *Consciencism: Philosophy and ideology for decolonization and development with particular reference to the African revolution*. London: Panaf.

Nordenbo, S.E. 1995. "What is implied by a 'European Curriculum'? Issues of Eurocentrism, rationality and education." *Oxford Review of Education*, 21(1):37–46.

Nothomb, D. 1965. *Un Humanisme Africaine: Valeurs et pierres d'attente*. Brussels: Lumen Vitae.

Oguah, B.E. 1984. "African and Western philosophy: A comparative study", in R.A, Wright (ed.), 1984:213–226.

Onwuanibe, R. 1984. "The human person and immorality in Ibgo metaphysics", in R.A. Wright (ed.), 1984:183–198.

Opoku, K.A. 1978. *West African traditional religion*. London: F&P International.

Owomoyela, O. 1996. *The African difference: Discourses in Africanity and the relativity of cultures*. Johannesburg: Witwatersrand University Press.

p'Bitek, O. 1970. *Religion of the Central Luo*. Nairobi: East African Literature Bureau.

p'Bitek, O. 1971. *African religions in Western scholarship.* Nairobi: East African Literature Bureau.

Perry, J. 1975. *Personal identity.* Berkeley: University of California Press.

Raditlhalo, S.I. 1996. " 'Kenosi: I am alone'. Philosophical imperatives of African names", in J.G. Malherbe (ed.), 1996:123–127.

Ralushai, N.V. *et al.* 1996. *Report of the commission of inquiry into witchcraft violence and ritual murders in the Northern Province of the Republic of South Africa.* Pretoria: HSRC.

Rotimi, O. 1971. *The Gods are not to blame.* London: Oxford University Press.

Rowe, D. 1980. "Philosophy and psychiatry." *Philosophy,* 55, (January 1980):109–112.

Sawyer, H. 1970. *God: Ancestor or creator?* London: Longman.

Schacht, R. 1983. *Nietzsche.* London: Routledge.

Senghor, L.S. 1964. *On African socialism.* New York: Pall Mall.

Senghor, L.S. 1967. *Les fondements de l'africanité.* Paris: Présence Africaine.

Sodipo, J.O. 1973. "Notes on the concept of cause and chance in Yoruba traditional thought." *Second order,* 11(2):40–69.

Sogolo, G.S. 1989. "Doctrinal oppositions and religious conversion: The African experience." *Ibadan Journal of Religious Studies,* XXI:119–130.

Sogolo, G.S. 1993. *Foundations of African philosophy: a definitive analysis of conceptual issues in African thought.* Ibadan: Ibadan University Press.

Sogolo, G.S. 1994. "The concept of cause in African thought", in P.H. Coetzee & M.E.S. van den Berg (eds), 1996:203–221.

Sono, T. 1994. *Dilemmas of African intellectuals in South Africa.* Pretoria: Unisa Press.

Sparkes, A.W. 1991. *Talking philosophy: A wordbook.* London: Routledge.

Tempels, P. 1959. *Bantu philosophy.* Paris: Présence Africaine.

Troxell, E.A. & Snyder, W.S. 1976. *Making sense of things: An introduction to philosophy.* New York: Martin's.

Van Niekerk, M. 1991. " 'African thinking' – A critical discussion", in R. Hill, M. Muller & M. Trump (eds), *African studies forum.* Pretoria: HSRC, 1991:125–191.

Vesey, G. 1974. *Personal identity.* London: Macmillan.

Webster's new international dictionary. Springfield: Merriam.

Wilson, M.D. 1978. *Descartes.* New York: Routledge and Kegal Paul.

Wiredu, K. 1983. "The Akan concept of mind." *Ibadan Journal of Humanistic Studies,* 3:113–134.

Wiredu, K. 1987a. "The concept of mind with particular reference to the language and thought of the Akans", in G. Floistad, 1987: 153–179.

Wiredu, K. 1987b. "The Akan concept of mind", in P.H. Coetzee & M.E.S. van den Berg (eds), 1995: 307–334.

Wiredu, K. 1990. "Universalism and particularism in religion from an African perspective." *Journal of humanism and ethical religion,* 3(1):85–108.

Wiredu, K. 1992. "Formulating modern thought in African languages: Some theoretical considerations", in V.Y. Mudimbe (ed.), *The surreptitious speech.* Chicago: University of Chicago Press, 1992:301–332.

Wiredu, K. 1992/3. "African philosophical tradition: A case study of the Akans." *The Philosophical Forum,* XXIV(1–3), Fall/Spring:35–62.

Wiredu, K. 1995. "Metaphysics in Africa", in J. Kim & E. Sosa (eds), *A companion to metaphysics.* Oxford: Blackwell, 1995:312–315.

Wiredu, K. 1996a. "Particularistic studies of African philosophies as an aid to decolonization", in J.G. Malherbe (ed.), 1996:169–177.

Wiredu, K. 1996b. "On decolonizing African religions", in J.G. Malherbe (ed.), 1996:178–193.

Withaar, H. 1986. "Wat is Afrikaanse filosofie?" *Algemeen Nederlands Tijdschrift voor Wijsbegeerte,* 78(3):163–188.

Wright, R. (ed.) 1979. *African philosophy: An introduction.* 2nd ed. Lanham: University Press of America.

Wright, R.A. (ed.) 1984. *African philosophy: An introduction.* 3rd ed. Lanham: University Press of America.

CHAPTER 5

African Epistemology

DIDIER N. KAPHAGAWANI and JEANETTE G. MALHERBE

1. THE QUESTION OF AFRICAN EPISTEMOLOGY

The question whether or not there is an African epistemology cannot be addressed without taking due cognisance of the answer to the question whether or not an African philosophy exists. A negative answer to the latter would imply a negative answer to the former. Similarly, to assert the existence of an African philosophy is also to imply the existence of an African epistemology, to the extent that an African epistemology is a subset of African philosophy. The question whether African philosophy exists has been discussed and debated for several decades in various forums by different scholars. The general trend of thought has been that there is indeed such a thing as African philosophy. And since African philosophy encompasses all forms and types of philosophising, it therefore follows that it does make sense to talk of an African epistemology, just as it is sensible to talk of African ethics, aesthetics, and metaphysics, for instance.

Having once decided that there is such an animal as African philosophy, one is naturally inclined to ask what it is like and how it differs from others of the breed. There have been roughly four answers to the question of what the character of African philosophy is. These answers have been formulated as the "standard positions" of ethnophilosophy, philosophic sagacity, politico-ideological philosophy, and professional philosophy (Oruka 1983:384). The conception of African philosophy that one favours from among these four will have a decided influence on what one takes an African epistemology to be. The ethnophilosopher, for instance, examines features of a culture like language and religious ceremonies for clues to its philosophical systems, and so, too, its epistemology. The student of philosophic sagacity will find answers to questions about knowledge in what the wise elders of the tribe have to say about it; the politico-ideological philosopher typically has some social goal in mind in his/her theory of knowledge; the professional philosopher will want to study the international epistemological literature and keep abreast of the current academic debate on knowledge. Because the professional philosopher engages in a world-wide debate, his/her task is minimally contextualised and has hardly any specific cultural character. So an

African philosophy and epistemology will have to be constructed with the possibilities for cultural contextualisation that the other three positions offer. We shall be concentrating here on the ethnophilosophical approach.

Now, there are two questions which need our attention: "What is epistemology?" and "What does it mean to call an epistemology *African*?" (We will look more closely at the first question in section 2 below, and then concentrate on the second question in the remaining sections.) Epistemology is the study of theories about the nature and scope of knowledge, the evaluation of the presuppositions and bases of knowledge, and the scrutiny of knowledge claims. In short, epistemology is a branch of philosophy whose main focus is to analyse and evaluate claims of knowledge. And to the extent that all humans have the capacity to know, epistemology is universal regardless of culture, tribe or race. However (and this is part of the answer to the second question), the means to, presuppositions, and bases of knowledge claims vary from culture to culture. The ways in which an African comes to know, or claims to know, that something is the case might differ from the ways in which a Chinese or European, for instance, would arrive at and assert his/her knowledge claim.

In other words, although epistemology as the study of knowledge is universal, the ways of acquiring knowledge vary according to the socio-cultural contexts within which knowledge claims are formulated and articulated. It is from such considerations that one can sensibly talk of an *African articulation and formulation of knowledge*, and hence of an African epistemology. The phrase "African epistemology", we should note, is used in the generic sense in which the term "African philosophy" is normally used, which does not deny that there are significant variations among the many cultures in Africa. But, before coming to the specific question of what makes up the features of *African* epistemology, we need to consider what may reasonably be taken as the generic features of knowledge, and so, as the common framework of any epistemology.

A fundamental question is what Africans mean and understand when they say that they know something. An analysis of some specific aspects of African cultures, including language (the meanings of philosophically important words, sentence structures, linguistic habits like proverbs and adages), and social convention (traditional ways of settling conflicts, educating the young, finding out about the world, using that knowledge) would no doubt assist us in coming up with some answers to this all-important epistemological question.

There are those who take a strong universalist line and deny that there *are* any distinctive cognitive principles belonging only to this society or that one. Their claim is that knowledge cannot differ from one society to the next. If we call something "knowledge", then it is true for all people, anywhere, at any time. After all, say the universalists, aren't the criteria by which we decide the truth or falsity of a claim like, "It's raining", the same across all cultural contexts? And if this is so, then the epistemological character of all cultures is basically the same. There may well be ways in which communities differ with regard to the institution of knowledge, but these are not *epistemologically* important. Epistemology, wherever it is practised, is the same, and just as one does not find a distinctively Chinese or American or African mathematics, so, too there is no such thing as a distinctively African epistemology, except insofar as it might be epistemological studies done on the continent of Africa.

On the other hand, there are those who take a strong relativist line, claiming that every different ethnic group's knowledge is absolutely unique, and so its analysis of that knowledge, or epistemology, will be unique too. The study of each group's way of knowing will have its own appropriate terms and concepts, and a framework tailored exactly to that way of knowing, and so the epistemology of each cultural community will not be applicable to any other group or even recognisable to someone from another culture. It is actually misleading to speak of "epistemology" as "the study of knowledge" when there is no such single branch of study. So where the universalist denies that an *African* epistemology is possible, the relativist suggests that an African *epistemology* is just an empty term.

In what follows, i.e. in the practical project of discussing and exemplifying what an African epistemology actually is, we adopt a position midway between the two. To the degree that this project is successful, we shall see that there is both some universality to the phenomenon of knowledge as well as local variations in it which different cultural contexts generate.

2.   THE NETWORK OF EPISTEMOLOGICAL CONCEPTS

In any epistemological study one is bound to come across claims having to do with knowledge, justification, truth, belief, theory, ideas and intentions, explanation, understanding, experience, and human action. They may all be grouped loosely together under the heading of rationality. Rationality is that quality which enables us to achieve our goals and act successfully; it helps us to negotiate the immediate physical environment; it is the means by which we are able to form a reasonably accurate picture of our world; it is the framework within which we interpret and understand the behaviour of others. It is a highly desirable quality. To say of persons or actions that they are rational is usually to be complimentary; conversely, the term "irrational" normally expresses a negative judgement. This evaluative aspect of the concept of rationality is very important. It means that *the rational* is a kind of ideal representing the highest excellence in intellectual and epistemological matters. Because it is an ideal, we may not always be able to find it in the real world, or in actual behaviour and thinking, though we may recognise it as being present to a greater or lesser degree in particular cases, and we tend to make judgements that one theory or action or belief or religion or custom or science or even culture, is more (or less) rational than another. Essentially, rationality is a goal which we strive to attain; it is a regulative ideal which directs our thinking and provides the standards by which we measure intellectual things of a certain kind as good or bad.

Rationality is closely connected to knowledge. Unless we have a true and reliable picture of how things are in the world around us – unless, that is, we have knowledge of the world – we are unlikely to have much success in acting. Knowledge is the means by which we direct our behaviour to achieve our ends most efficiently and successfully. Rationality of the kind which we humans strive for, is epistemic rationality, or rationality which aims at the truth and is based on knowledge.

Rationality is also closely connected to the idea of justification. If someone is rational in a belief or action or assertion, then that person is able *to say why* he or she acts in a certain way or believes or states what he or she does. To say why is to give one's reasons or justification. If one believes or does or says something for no reason at all – if, on reflection, one cannot find any reason to explain why one believes or acts or speaks as one does, then one will know that one's belief or behaviour is irrational.

It needs to be pointed out that there are many kinds of thoughts other than beliefs, thoughts which do not need reasonable grounds to justify your having them. You may be daydreaming, and a series of pleasant images of yourself as a TV star, or scoring the winning goal in the Africa Cup Final, drift about in your mind. If someone were to ask you on what grounds you were thinking these things, you would probably find it hard to answer because these are not beliefs about how you are or the world actually is; they are imaginings about how things might be. They are not factual thoughts and they do not make any claim to truth. A great deal of our mental life is taken up by other-than-true thoughts. Wishes, fears, hopes, imaginings, guesses, suppositions – all these are kinds of thoughts which carry no implication of aiming at the truth. If someone says: "I wish I were a TV star!" it makes little sense to reply, "That's not true."

But beliefs are different. They do have at least an implication of truth; if you believe something, then you believe it to be true. If someone believes that she is a TV star, then we will be able to find out whether her belief is true or false; we will be able quite properly to ask her why she believes this. If she states: "I am a TV star", it will make sense to say: "Yes, you truly are" or "No, that's not the case", depending on whether she is one or not. We can also ask her on what grounds she believes this, and her justification for the belief, if it is good justification, will consist in giving us the evidence that there is for the truth of her claim. She has starred in a TV soap opera, say; her picture appears regularly in popular magazines; she was nominated for an acting award. It is in the nature of belief to aim at the truth, and when people say they believe something then they are committing themselves to the truth of whatever they believe. And when we are very sure that we have got a belief right and that it is true, we claim to *know* that something is the case. Two further concepts which are closely related to the concepts of knowledge and rationality, therefore, are the concepts of belief and truth.

3.   THE AFRICAN EPISTEMOLOGIST'S TASK

Social epistemology, that is, epistemology deliberately situated in a particular cultural context, as African epistemology is, has an active role to play with regard to rationality. It is up to the philosopher to develop and exercise the concept of rationality appropriate to his/her society, to have a critical awareness of the intellectual and cognitive traditions of both his/her own society and of other societies. (It is important to note that the term "critical awareness" does not *only* mean negative appraisal. It includes the appreciation and positive evaluation of whatever is good in the tradition.) It is necessary that we be able to do this so that we can construct a sound intellectual identity for our society, one that meets the particular demands of our unique cultural context. It is also important so that we can hand on what is best in the tradition to our cognitive heirs in succeeding generations. Just as we are the recipients of the long-developed, ancient customs and beliefs of our ancestors, so our descendants will receive whatever tradition we hand on to them. We want to make sure it is a good legacy that will serve them well in the future. So our situation in the historical context, as both inheritors and transmitters of an intellectual tradition, makes it necessary for us to consider well what we commend as "rational".

This duty becomes all the more urgent in our present circumstances in Africa, where cultural evaluation is intensified by what we might call "the C^4 factor": the "Contemporary Confluence of Cultures on the Continent". The availability of a variety of options from other cultures provides a stimulus for discarding, from one's own culture, those practices, ideas, and traditions which have outlived their usefulness. It also means that the distinctive character of a particular ethnic group may come under threat, as people are seduced by fashions outside their own culture. If we are to shape a distinctive social and ethnic identity, we must resist the pull towards cultural assimilation (usually the assimilation of all others by one dominant culture), that C^4 brings with it. On the other hand, we must ensure that our African cultures are alive and progressive, renewing themselves by discarding outworn practices and ideas, taking what they need from other cultures to adapt to changing circumstances.

There are hosts of different cultures from every corner of the globe milling about at present on the continent of Africa, along with all the indigenous cultures. For our purposes, however, that is, for a broad consideration of African epistemology, it is possible to oversimplify this diversity, and look only at "African traditional culture" and "modern Western culture" as the two significant mainstreams. And with regard to the issue of cultural assimilation between these two, it should be noted that the answer which we give to the question of whether knowledge, rationality, and their associated concepts are relative to various communities or common to all human beings (see section 1), is of crucial importance to everyone on the continent of Africa. If we deny, along with the relativist, that our ethnic group's way of knowing has anything in common with other groups, then we cannot look to other cultures for revisionary ideas, comparisons or assessments of our intellectual life, and we will instead have to struggle along on our own. If, on the other hand, we take up a universalist stance, then we will want to discard all traces of ethnic and cultural character as soon as possible – which is also undesirable. This is something we must be conscious of in deciding "whether – and if so, how – our cultures are to become modern" (Appiah 1992:105).

4. EPISTEMOLOGY AND CULTURAL CONTEXT

So far, we have been discussing rationality and its associated concepts in a perfectly general and unqualified way, as if they applied to all people at all times and places. And in one way, they do. To be human is to be rational; to act is necessarily to aim at achieving some goal; to experience the world is to try to make sense of it and to try to acquire an accurate representation of it; to believe something is necessarily to accept its truth. In perceiving the immediate environment, for instance, nobody would deliberately set out to acquire false beliefs. Our eyes, ears, sense of smell, etc. are set up in such a way that they tell us (when they are working properly) how things in fact are. This is the case whatever continent we are on, no matter what language we use to express our experiences, and whatever the behavioural codes our society has taught us.

Similarly, to understand or explain a phenomenon in any cultural context is to bring it under a rational framework of some sort, whether the thing to be explained is a drought or the depression of a family member, and whether the explanatory framework is drawn from modern meteorology, from traditional or contemporary religion, or from current psychological theory.

The way in which epistemic rationality and its related concepts are instantiated, "filled out" as it were, the concrete content that they are given in terms of linguistic descriptions and social customs, varies a great deal from one cultural context to another. What counts as a good theory, or a widely accepted concept, or a satisfactory explanation, is different in contemporary industrialised Asia, say, from what it was in a rural community in Biblical Israel. The set of established facts accepted as true within the society (the so-called "body of knowledge") will be vastly different in the two cases; the methods by which the knowledge is acquired will be different; and the ways in which it is certified as reliable fact (that is, its reasonable justification), will also be different.

The *social* philosopher works in the framework of societies and their characteristics. The things of interest here are the habits and customs, the religions, languages, belief systems, values, interests, preferred occupations, divisions of labour, in a particular culture. The social *epistemologist* or philosopher of knowledge, is concerned with the rational practices, values, institutions, etc. of a culture. What exactly are these things? You will get a more concrete idea of them from the articles accompanying this chapter, but for the moment it is useful to think of them as a collection of:

1. The well-established general beliefs, concepts and theories of any particular people, in various fields such as medical science, religion, child-rearing, agriculture, psychology, education, etc.
2. The favoured ways, usually institutionalised in the society, of acquiring new knowledge and evaluating accepted fact, science being a prime example of such an institution.
3. The accumulated wisdom which is passed on to the youth in the form of proverbs, revered traditions, myths and folktales.
4. The language of an ethnic group, the single most important repository of a society's accumulated knowledge.
5. Customs and practices in the areas of religion and judicial procedure.
6. The accepted authorities (whether people, institutions or texts) in matters of knowledge and belief.

All these can be regarded as the epistemic threads in the fabric of a culture.

The question that faces us here is: how are we to decide what is rational in the context of African culture? How are we to understand and apply the principles of rationality in an African context, so that we will have some yardstick by which to sort the rational from the irrational? How are we to assess the beliefs, theories, and explanations of traditional and contemporary African cultures? What are we to make of the practices, guiding principles, and social institutions that make up the epistemic threads in the fabric of a characteristically African society?

A word of warning: to speak of "*African* culture" or "a characteristically *African* society", is to make a huge generalisation. Africa includes so many diverse peoples from such different backgrounds, that any generalisation is bound to be an over-simplification. If we make claims about "African" beliefs or religion or customs or knowledge, then those claims should, strictly speaking, be equally applicable to a community of Bedouin tribesmen in the Sahara, to Ghanaian businessmen in Accra, to the Khoisan people of the Kalahari, to Ethiopian shepherds. It is obviously going to be very difficult to find general definitions that will cover this variety of cases.

There will almost always be a counter-example to be found, to disprove the general claim. If the *only* thing that these various peoples and cultures have in common is that they occur on the continent of Africa, if all that they share is a (very broad) geographical location, then it will not be possible to speak generally of African philosophy or rationality or religion or traditional lifestyle.

The assumption is usually made in contemporary philosophical writing that we can be tolerant of differences on this point, and continue to speak of things African without having in mind an absolutely precise definition of what it means to be "African". One good reason for tolerating this vagueness is that the criteria for what is characteristically African (in the various fields of philosophy), is just what is being debated. The central question is: "What is *African* philosophy?" It does not do, therefore, to press too hard for exact criteria of Africanness before we enter the debate. It will be better to rely on an intuitive understanding, a roughly acceptable meaning of the term "African" as we go along, and see if, at the end of our considerations, we are in a better position to say what is characteristically African in epistemology, rationality, and philosophy in general.

The use of the term to cover different ethnic groups indigenous to the continent, for instance those listed above, is at any rate not a *contentious* generalisation. It becomes contentious when people want to apply or withhold the description "African" for political reasons, as when people or customs originating in cultures which are not indigenous lay claim to being African, or when alien innovations are advocated as being preferable for the modern African to the traditional ways of his/her people.

Because of the sensitive nature of this issue, and the deeply-held values it involves, it is very important to keep an open mind on the question of what counts as an African culture/philosophy/religion, etc. It is also, and for the same reasons, very easy to harbour unnoticed assumptions on the point. The stand which you take on it marks your position in the traditionalist/modernist debate in African philosophy.

Roughly speaking, traditionalists say that only those cultures which were on the continent before the arrival of European colonisers can properly speaking be called "African". Everything else is, by definition, an invasive alien influence which can only debase the purity, and destroy the pristine unity, of African traditional thinking, lifestyles, and values. The modernists, on the other hand, stress that the question of what counts as African is being asked *now*, and they believe that the C^4 factor cannot be ignored. The presence of alien cultures, whether for good or bad, is a fact that we must make the best of, say the modernists.

The traditionalist is essentially backward-looking and the modernist essentially forward-looking. This affects one's answer to the question of whether the culture of people from different continents, now living here, counts as African. Of course, there is a clear sense in which people of European or Asian origin are not Africans, simply because they are Europeans and Asians. This is the sense reflected in the ordinary use of language. We do not without qualification call someone from Liverpool or New York an African, unless perhaps that person is black, and then we would think of him/her as Afro-English or Afro-American. This way of classifying people is traditionalist insofar as it looks to their *past*, at the historical traditions and cultural backgrounds from which they have come, for clues as to who they are. It is from this perspective that we see the people on the continent of Africa as *various*, as Chinese, Indians, Hollanders, Lebanese, English, Portuguese, Thais, Germans, etc. and from which we remark on the confluence of so many different cultures in Africa today. The modernist, however, looking to the future, will tend to say that anyone who has a commitment to living in Africa and so to contributing to the ongoing construction of African identity, has some grounds for claiming to be African. According to this viewpoint, African culture is already "modernised" with admixtures of Western and Asian cultures.

When it comes to the question of a contemporary African philosophy and epistemology, the modernist will tend towards a professional view, while the traditionalist will favour the methods of sage philosophy or ethnophilosophy. Because the aim of this text is to sketch a characteristically African epistemology, and the modernist/professional view tends to deny that there is a unique African character, we shall answer the question of African epistemology in terms that are basically ethnophilosophical.

5. PROBLEMS OF AFRICAN EPISTEMOLOGY

African epistemology faces a number of problems. Firstly, if it is to be an epistemology worth the name, then African epistemology has to take into serious consideration both the similarities and differences in the varying conceptions of knowledge and truth in disparate African cultures. One possible way of solving this problem of specificity versus generality is suggested in the texts of Wiredu and Kaphagawani which examine an important epistemological concept as it appears in two different African languages. What emerges from these two is that the concept of truth is generally recognisable across different cultures (as are many other words in philosophical usage). That this is so is proven by the fact that we have no difficulty in translating the English word truth into various African languages, or in saying that *truth, nokware,* and *zoona* all mean roughly the same thing, all refer roughly to the same concept. But there is only a rough similarity of meaning. There are differences and local peculiarities which make each of the three terms unique, and this is the value of "particularistic" studies of philosophical concepts: they show up subtle variations in old philosophical concepts.

A second problem is that if African epistemology is to be of relevance to contemporary Africa, it has to cope with and assimilate whatever is assimilable from the advancements in science and technology of the West. Thirdly, there is in general among traditional African communities an emphasis on age as a necessary condition for knowledge and wisdom, as illustrated by Kaphagawani in "*Themes in a Chewa epistemology*". Such an emphasis denies epistemological authority to the young and able. It provides an epistemological monopoly to the old, a monopoly which might have been justified in traditional Africa, but is not necessarily tenable in contemporary Africa. The lines of the modernist/traditionalist debate are clearly revealed in these last two problems and they are indeed inextricably intertwined around the central issue of cognitive cultural assessment and revision. Let us see how African epistemologists at present set about dealing with this issue.

6. UNDERSTANDING THE EPISTEMOLOGY OF TRADITIONAL COMMUNITIES

We asked above whether African culture is *in fact* suffused with a spiritistic character or not. The issue becomes rather different when we ask – as Wiredu

(1995) does – questions like: "*Should* African culture ideally be suffused with a spiritistic quality or not?" To what degree should supernatural entities like ghosts, witches, and spirits be present in contemporary African thinking? Are beliefs in such things compatible with modernisation? On the other hand, is the wholesale revision of traditional thinking compatible with maintaining our African identity? What do we lose when we give up the time-honoured traditions of our ancestors? When questions like these are posed, the need for some kind of rational appreciation and assessment of customary magico-religious beliefs arises.

The factual question of whether African culture is essentially magico-religious in character might be thought to be the work of scholars other than philosophers anyway. It is surely up to psychologists to examine the thinking patterns of a representative sample of Africans, or anthropologists to give detailed descriptions of ethnic cultural patterns, and then in the light of this evidence to decide the matter. The philosopher's work is not *scientific* or *empirical*; it does not seek to investigate situations or establish facts. It is rather conceptual and argumentative in nature.

Furthermore, the objection might be made that the whole question is rather out of date. Surely in most African countries, and certainly in South Africa in the last years of the twentieth century, there are very few people left who are still completely convinced of the power of traditional spirits. People are modern, it might be said; they know all about the latest technologies. They work in a world of computers, cars, and cell-phones and they relax in a world of CD's, TV and jet travel. Any remnants of customary thinking in their lives are just colourful and well-liked reminders of where they have come from.

There is no doubt that the average African in South Africa today is more or less modernised in the sense that he/she is familiar with most, or at least a good many, of the trappings of modern Western technological society. There is, thus, knowledge of Western culture on the part of contemporary Africans. But this is not a particularly interesting or significant fact. It is possible for someone to have knowledge of a culture, to live according to its norms and practices, and yet at the same time to reject that culture. In urban East London, in South Africa, there were (and maybe still are) two distinct groups of amaXhosa, rural people of the Xhosa tribe who came to work in the city (Mayer 1972). The one group, known as the "red Xhosa", clung to traditional ways, and though they knew everything they needed to know about European ways, they practised them only as far as they were obliged to and returned to tribal ways whenever they could. The other group, known as the "school Xhosa", were just the opposite in that they adopted European ways enthusiastically, and showed no preference for traditional customs. They continued to wear Western-style clothes and to eat Western food even when they returned to their homes in the country. The conclusion to be drawn from this is that a person may have a thorough knowledge of a culture, even live within it, and yet assess it as undesirable and unacceptable; which brings us back to the philosophical question of how we should assess cultures, what criteria of judgement we should apply.

Notice that this need for rational appreciation does not usually arise for those people who have grown up and who live their lives within the boundaries of a particular culture. In a sense, they understand it very well, since their culture is intimately well-*known* to them. The outside observer from another culture can never know it as the insiders do. In another sense, however, the people brought up in a certain tradition can never see it. They are blind to it just because it is, for them, the only way things could possibly be.

Consider a simple analogy. The people living in Durban are so used to a warm, humid climate that they do not notice it. For them, a visitor's remark that the day is unbearably muggy and hot may be surprising, since it appears to those used to local conditions to be a fairly crisp and cool day. The Durbanite assesses particular weather conditions against the background of the general weather conditions in Durban, not some other place, as the visitor does. If you were to ask the Durbanite what the general weather conditions there are like, he/she would be inclined to reply: "They're just the weather here." To characterise them as hot and humid, he/she would have to have some wider standard against which to measure them. It is only in the context of national weather conditions, say, or Gauteng's weather conditions, where the temperature and humidity averages are moderate, that Durban by comparison appears hot and humid.

This notion of acclimatisation works in the cultural context as well. People who have never experienced a culture other than their own have no wider standard or more general background against which to think about and appreciate their own traditions. ("Appreciate" does not mean only to think uncritically that something is wonderful. It means to have a fair, full, and conscious knowledge of both the good and bad points of a thing. Appreciation of the thought systems of a culture is the first condition for cognitive revision and renewal.) Suppose you were to ask a traditional witchdoctor from a remote rural community without any elements of contemporary urban life, a man thoroughly immersed in the lore of his calling, the question that we considered in the last section, viz., "Is traditional thought essentially marked by belief in the supernatural?" You would probably be met with blank incomprehension. After all, from the witchdoctor's point of view, what other kind of thought *is* there, or *could* there be?

So critical apprehension of one's own ingrained cultural background is not easy. Nevertheless, epistemological revision of cultural traditions does take place, and when it does, there is usually one (or both) of these two factors at work: intellectual exploration or cross-culturation.

Who are the intellectual explorers, the intellectual adventurers – the cognitive revisionists whose inner gaze is so clear and persuasive that people follow them against their habit? Obviously they will be the sages of a community, the so-called "epistemic authorities" of a society to whom we referred earlier. These are the people to whom others turn for knowledge and advice, and to find out what the tradition says on any question that needs answering. Epistemic authorities in the West tend to be the philosophers, historians, scientists, doctors, engineers, and lawyers; in the East, they would include the gurus, astrologers, shamans, swamis, ayurvedic doctors, and scientists. But it takes more than just sagacity to engage in critical reflection on a tradition; not all sages are philosophic sages, and it is only the philosophic sages who are "intellectually adventurous".

In Africa, the sages are the elders of the tribe, people whose wisdom and knowledge of the traditions, the folklore, the values, customs, history, habits, likes and dislikes, character, and thought of their people is very great. Sages are the mouthpieces of a culture. They are applied to by ordinary folk for authoritative judgements and decisions on various matters. The sages of African traditional society are a rich source of philosophical insights – the raw material of much work by professional African philosophers who aim at systematising the folk philosophy of particular African societies, linguistic communities or ethnic groups. Marcel Griaule's *Conversations with Ogotemmeli* (1965) was an early recording of the thoughts of this remarkable Dogon hunter/sage. Odera Oruka (1983) recorded his conversations with the sages of Kenya to provide a body of traditional thought which could serve as the basis for philosophical analysis and reflection, and sometimes he came upon a philosophical sage. Indeed, as Oruka writes:

> My real purpose in this project was to help substantiate or invalidate the claim that traditional African people were innocent of logical and critical thinking. Was traditional Africa a place where no persons had the room or mind to think independently and at times even critically of the communal consensus? If this claim were true, then it must follow that it is not possible to discover individuals in traditional Africa who can demonstrate their ability and practice in critical thinking. And whoever is considered a thinker or a wise man must simply be, at best, a good narrator of traditionally imposed wisdom and myths (1987:51–52).

Oruka found among the sages of Kenya many intellectually adventurous thinkers who not only know traditional thought thoroughly, but are able to suggest revisions of it. There are such individuals in every community now and again, and it is their thinking which moves the epistemological traditions of their culture forward.

A society rich in such individuals will have a vital and progressive epistemology with a tradition of evaluation and renewal. Contemporary African philosophers like Kwame Appiah, Odera Oruka, Godwin Sogolo, Kwasi Wiredu and many more, are such thinkers. They engage in sifting the wisdom out of their traditional culture: its linguistic usages, habits, proverbs, etc. Consider how Wiredu ("The concept of truth in the Akan language") undertakes a philosophico-conceptual study of truth in the particular context of the Akan culture. He examines an important epistemic theme in his own culture. It is work which requires an insider's intimate knowledge of the culture. Much of the work of these African philosophers, however, also involves comparative analyses of Western or European, and African concepts, as Wiredu's work on the Akan concept of truth once again shows. This brings us to the second factor which stimulates cognitive evaluation and revision within a culture, our old friend C^4, or cross-culturation.

When different cultures meet and mingle, people automatically become aware of different sets of values and customs, of different conceptual possibilities. Their own cultural background is no longer the only one available to them. In terms of the weather-conditions analogy, when the Durbanite has lived in Gauteng for a while, she, too, may come to realise that Durban's weather is hot and humid. In a situation of cross-culturation, people can, if they choose, step into a different framework and look at their own culture from a radically different viewpoint. This makes a fully-conscious appreciation of one's own culture possible for everyone, not only philosophical sages.

Appiah (1992:120–127) discusses Horton's characterisation of traditional cultures as "closed", that is, cultures "in which there is no developed awareness of alternatives to the established body of theoretical tenets" (Appiah 1992:127). Appiah is critical of it, because according to him, even in pre-colonial African society there was a fair amount of interaction by way of trade, wars, and invasion between different cultures. Note, however, that the *availability* of different viewpoints does not always ensure that use is made of them. A society may even be closed in a situation like C^4.

For instance, there is much justification for saying that Western society, represented by colonial enclaves of the imperialistic European powers, was truly closed. The colonial administrators and adventurers who found themselves in Africa were careful to cocoon themselves in European culture. They wore European clothes (often in great discomfort), imported European foods, furniture, art, music, etc. They never lost sight of the fact that England/France/Italy/Germany was home, and also the source of that "civilisation" which it was their duty to uphold before the indigenous peoples of Africa. They almost never learned African languages. Their interest in those parts of Africa they occupied was limited to the exploitable natural resources found there; they showed interest in the people of Africa chiefly insofar as they were relevant to that exploitation.

Colonial society, even though Western, deliberately shut itself off from the possibility of perceiving or experiencing cultural alternatives, and if this is the mark of a "closed" society, then it was shut up tight. Horton claims that in "scientifically-oriented cultures" such as those of Western Europe, such an awareness is "highly developed" (quoted in Appiah 1992:125). Western society – by contrast with the colonial manifestation – was "open", while traditional African society was "closed". It is difficult to understand such a remark from an African point of view.

Today, as a result of C^4, there must be very few pockets of traditional culture on the continent that are totally untouched by foreign influences, and wholly unaware of the existence and general character of alien cultures – European, Middle Eastern, American, Indian, etc. It has been a feature of cultural interaction on the African continent that indigenous cultures have been quicker to react – either to absorb or reject foreign influences – than the invasive cultures which, as we noted, made a point of being impervious to African culture. If we can say that Africa is now in a post-colonial period of history, it is because indigenous culture has come back into its own. European culture, so far as it is still in evidence, has lost its continental hegemony and is developing here, not Eurocentrically but Afrocentrically, that is, in response to African rather than European influences.

Readings

LOGIC AND RATIONALITY
GODWIN S. SOGOLO

There are several philosophical conceptions of man. One such conception, which remains vague, is that man is a rational being. It points to a basic quality which all humans are thought to share in common. Not only are they all assumed to be rational, it is believed that their thought processes are essentially governed by the same principles. It is further believed that in some cultures these principles have been well systematised and expressly stated; that the individuals internalise them, and that a few even preoccupy themselves with the business of thinking about these thought processes themselves.

Logic is one of the core areas of philosophy. Over the years it has been assumed that the ability to reason logically and to draw valid inferences is an essential characteristic of all human races. Philosophers, ancient and modern, have always worked with this presumption, and in the comparative study of cultures the main aim of the student is to satisfy him/herself that all cultures operate within the framework of these logical principles. When confronted with a belief or some aspect of a people's thought, the student is expected to test whether or not such cultural items conform with the canons of logic.

Aristotle was the first philosopher to systematise all forms of positive thinking about thought, the result of which was the invention of formal logic. Since then, formal logic has had no rival except for the introduction of dialectic logic in Western Europe in the sixteenth to nineteenth centuries. Even then, with this challenge and the radical idea that there are two forms of thought, the general belief remains that formal logic is indispensable for correct thinking; some would say it is the only way to correct thinking. Formal logic has thus been described as the systematic formulation of the instinctive logic of common sense.

There are three interrelated fundamental laws in formal logic. The first and most important of them is the law of identity which simply states that a thing is always equal to or identical with itself (A equals A). The second law of formal logic is the law of contradiction which strictly speaking is a negative formulation of the first law. The law of contradiction states that a thing cannot be unequal to or different from itself (A is not non-A). The third law, referred to as the law of the excluded middle, combines the first and the second. The law of the excluded middle states that if a thing is equal to itself it cannot be unequal to or different from itself (if A equals A it cannot equal non-A). By their formulations these laws imply absolute difference and absolute identity in which things are mutually exclusive. A thing cannot be two different and mutually exclusive things at one and the same time.

The example which Aristotle used in illustrating the principles of formal logic is of great relevance to our discussion. According to him,

[a] man cannot simultaneously apprehend first, that man is essentially animal, i.e. cannot be other than animal, and secondly, that man is not essentially animal, that is, that he is other than

animal. That is to say, a man is essentially a man and can never be or be thought of as not being a man (Aristotle quoted in Novack 1975:21).

The reasoning seems self-evident and this indeed is the essence of formal logic. For thousands of years mankind has thought and acted in obedience to these laws even before they were systematically formulated. The reason is that they fit readily into our perception of the interrelationship of things in the universe.

Our conceptual experience compels us to accept the law of identity that definite objects and traits of things persist, that they maintain recognisable similarities despite the phenomenon of change. Common sense experience tells us that essential continuity exists in nature and that the human mind has no choice but to reckon with this perceived continuity. The significance of formalising our reasoning process is clear from what Novack says of the law of identity:

> The law of identity directs us to recognize likeness amidst diversity, permanence amidst changes, to single out the basic similarities between separated and apparently different instances and entities, to uncover the real bonds of unity between them, to trace the connections between different and consecutive phases of the same phenomena. That is why the discovery and the amplification of this law was so epoch-making in the history of scientific thought and why we continue to honour Aristotle for grasping its extraordinary significance. That is also why mankind continues to act and to think in accordance with this basic law of formal logic (1975:24–25).

The appeal of formal logic to common sense has been so overwhelming that for a long time it was thought that logical principles were prior to all experience and that they constituted "the a priori order of the universe".

It should now be clear why scholars of different ages and orientations have always felt the inclination to insist that for any form of thought or action to be judged intelligible or rational it has to conform to the rules of formal logic. Contemporary literature on human societies abounds with theories whose basic assumption is that there are these ineluctable logical principles by which all human experience must be assessed. In particular, the works of classical anthropologists dating back to the intellectualist school pioneered by Tylor and sociologists such as Lévy-Bruhl and Durkheim, are clear manifestations of this assumption. For them, there is only one way of judging the intelligibility of any thought system and that is to see whether or not it conforms to the rules of formal logic.

Lévy-Bruhl (1923:21) seems to be more heavily influenced by this idea than his contemporaries in his general classification of human societies into two categories, those with a "primitive mentality" and those with a "civilized mentality". Africans in this broad division fall into the former category. But what is it, in Lévy-Bruhl's conception, that distinguishes the "primitive" from the "civilized"? The answer, according to him, is that the former is characterised by a prelogical mode of thought while the latter is marked by logical thought. Lévy-Bruhl describes prelogical thought as one that is unscientific and uncritical, containing evident contradictions. People with such thought differ not in degree but in quality from those with logical minds.

It is not too clear what Lévy-Bruhl means by prelogical. He is quoted as having denied the equation of prelogical either with alogical or with anti-logical:

> Prelogical does not mean alogical or anti-logical. Prelogical, applied to primitive mentality, means simply that it does not go out of its way, as we do, to avoid contradiction. It does not always present the same logical requirements (Lévy-Bruhl 1923:21).

By this, Lévy-Bruhl seems to grant that these thoughts have their own logical principles, albeit of a different sort – what he calls the laws of "mystical participation" (1923:21). He does not seem to insist too firmly on the qualitative peculiarities of these modes of thought. One possible interpretation is that the logic or reason Lévy-Bruhl finds in these thought systems is still in its rudimentary form, still infantile, so to speak.

It should be noted that Lévy-Bruhl was writing in an era when the notion of evolution had its strongest grip on the minds of intellectuals – when almost everything, animal, man, and even thought, was placed in some position within the evolutionary hierarchy. Lévy-Bruhl possibly saw his comparative analysis of societies and their modes of thought as parallel to Darwin's theory of organic matter. The other possible reason why Lévy-Bruhl had to concede that there is some rudimentary form of logic among traditional people might be that he entertained some doubt as to how a people totally devoid of reason or who perpetually live in a "dream world" could have survived for so long.

However, no matter what concessions or modifications Lévy-Bruhl made, the fact is that he studied traditional thought purely as a formal logician. It is from this viewpoint that he finds contradictions in assertions such as when the Nuer says "twins are birds" or "crocodiles are spirits". As Evans-Pritchard (1976) explains, the Nuer is not saying that twins are like birds, but that they are birds; he is not saying that crocodiles symbolise spirits but that they are spirits. From Lévy-Bruhl's point of view, this is a clear violation of the rules of logic which do not permit a thing to be itself and yet another thing. The Nuer is therefore involved in contradiction by saying that a twin is a twin (A is A) and at the same time that a twin is a bird (A is non-A).

Now, Lévy-Bruhl's suggestion is that such thought is intelligible only to a mind that applies the law of mystical participation. One is tempted to ignore Lévy-Bruhl as an obsolete thinker or simply as unhelpful in our bid to understand traditional modes of thought. But unfortunately, his notion of the law of mystical participation has been strongly echoed by Senghor, one of the greatest thinkers Africa has produced. For Senghor, the traditional man does not differentiate between the organic and the inorganic, between the subject and the object, between himself and the land he inhabits. Like Lévy-Bruhl, Senghor attributes some form of reason to traditional man. Both insist that traditional man's reasoning is of a different sort because it is determined by mystical representations. So, what Lévy-Bruhl calls the "logic of sentiments" Senghor describes as "intuitive reason".

There is not much to hang onto in these unargued bold assertions of Lévy-Bruhl and Senghor. They do, however, provide us with a very significant lead by insisting that the peculiar features of traditional thought which they describe are not biologically or psychologically imposed, but socially acquired. They are an inherent part of the social milieu into which individuals are born and which they leave behind when they die. To say that these modes of thought are superimposed on the minds of the individual is to evade our main concern, which is with the structure of the mind that entertains such thoughts. However, recognising the potency of society in moulding the mind of the individual, one is inclined to look at the matter via the social structure involved.

A number of attempts have been made to free traditional thought from the charge of irrationality. Of these, the most forceful is the argument that different forms of life call for different paradigms of discourse. Following Wittgenstein's claim that the logic of our reasoning resides in the language we speak, Winch (1958) rejects any attempt to assess the rationality of the logic of science. Science, according to him, operates with its own concept of reality which is determined by a set of paradigms. In a different form of life such a language of discourse is inapplicable. Winch thus rejects Evans-Pritchard's view in which reality is seen as an independent standard of measure. Holding to this relativist position, Winch (1958) also rejects the claim by Lévy-Bruhl that there are some universal principles of reasoning by which any given thought system can be judged to be logical or illogical.

In Winch's view, there are different forms of life and each has its own criteria of assessing what is logically intelligible and what is not. He defines a form of life as a set of linguistic rules and practices with specific procedures for judging the validity or otherwise of given claims. In direct opposition to Lévy-Bruhl, Winch states his position:

> criteria of logic are not a direct gift of God, but arise out of, and are only intelligible in the context of, ways of living or modes of social life. It follows that one cannot apply criteria of logic to modes of social life as such. For instance, science is one such mode and religion is another; and each has criteria of intelligibility peculiar to itself. So within science or religion actions can be logical or illogical: in science, for example, it would be illogical to refuse to be bound by the results of a properly carried out experiment; in religion it would be illogical to suppose that one could pit one's own strength against God's; and so on. But we cannot sensibly say that either the practice of science itself or that of religion is either illogical or logical; both are non-logical (1958:100–101).

Here, Winch is speaking strictly about two forms of life, that of science and that of religion, and he is challenging the idea that the paradigm of the former is applicable to the latter. Also, he does not see any independent universe of discourse which can be applied in assessing the two forms of life.

In relation to traditional thought, Winch (1958:113ff.) thinks that claims involving magic and witchcraft cannot be assessed in terms of either scientific conceptions or scientific standards of rationality. All such magico-religious beliefs have their own language of discourse and they can only be said to be intelligible or unintelligible when analysed in the context in which they are held. Also, these claims are not to be seen as truth-propositions since they do not attempt to provide some quasi-scientific understanding of the world. In other words, the Western scientist and the Azande witch-doctor, for instance, do not make truth-claims *vis-à-vis* the same notion of reality.

This way of contrasting forms of life could, however, be misleading, particularly when used as a means of differentiating between two cultures. Although from Evans-Pritchard's account we are inclined to see the Azande system as typifying a magico-religious form of life, the truth is that the Azande – indeed all traditional systems – also have a non-magico-religious form. They provide descriptions of objects and explanations of events in theoretical categories not tied to magical or religious beliefs. The Azande have principles and beliefs about how to grow crops and how to hunt for animals. They know the kind of soil that will produce harvests and the place where, or season when, hunting is most successful. They have knowledge of nutritional techniques, the food that nourishes and that which does not, that which is poisonous and that which is not. It would, therefore, be a mistake to suggest that in each of these areas of their daily activities the Azande always resort to magical or religious explanations. The point is often made that the principles they apply are not always expressly articulated in theoretical forms. But the same may be said of Western societies – most Westerners go about their daily life applying principles which they do not consciously articulate.

The point being established is not merely that traditional cultures have more than one form of life and, therefore, more than one paradigm of discourse. It is that all cultures do. The world of the so-called scientific cultures has its own share of the forms that exist in traditional societies. This point has been emphasised by Wiredu:

> Even Western scientists, fully convinced of the universal reign of law in natural phenomena, may pray to a supernatural being for rain and a good harvest. Those who are tempted to see in such a thing as witchcraft the key to specifically *African* thought – there is no lack of such people elsewhere as well as in Africa – ought to be reminded that there are numbers of white men in London today who proudly proclaim themselves to be witches (1980:42).

It is thus clear that in every society people employ both scientific and non-scientific explanatory models in accounting for their world of common sense. Whatever contradictions there may be in the models applied should be seen as internal contradictions within a given culture rather than features for distinguishing between one culture and another. This is not to suggest, however, that it is unenlightening to embark on cross-cultural comparison. It is simply that whatever can be derived from such an exercise can also be got from comparing modes of thought within one given culture.

At whatever level the comparison is done, Winch's (1958:40–42) insistence on the incommensurability of different forms of life still holds. His position is that the magico-religious form predominantly associated with traditional cultures has its own universe of discourse, its own conception of reality and criteria of rationality, all different from those of the scientific form of life. Winch (1958:100ff.) sees each as a distinct form of social life whose practices and beliefs are intelligible only in the context in which they are held. This position has been criticised on several grounds, one of which is that it is too relativistic and that it makes impossible any kind of communication across cultures. Some of these issues will be examined in our discussion of cross-cultural rationality.

However, whatever the weaknesses of Winch's thesis may be, it is a caution to those neo-Lévy-Bruhleans and followers of Senghor in Africa who are eagerly seeking to revive the idea that the mind of the African is so intellectually malstructured that it does not accord with some presumed universal principles of reasoning. For such principles do not exist. The mind of the African is not structurally different from that of the Westerner. Also, the contextual contrast between Western thought and traditional African thought, which considers only the former as suitable material for philosophical reflection, rests on false premises. The truth is that both are similarly marked by the same basic features of the human species. The difference lies in the ways the two societies conceive of reality and explain objects and events. This is so because they live different forms of life. And it is for this reason alone that an intelligible analysis of African thought demands the application of its own universe of discourse, its own logic, and its own criteria of rationality. The primary task of the African philosopher is to fashion these unique working tools with which to unearth the complexities of the social form that confronts him/her.

The analysis of the ontological status of claims in traditional African thought involves matters of logic and forms of reasoning. Some philosophers argue, just as they do for truth and reality, that all people, irrespective of their cultural differences, share in certain common minimum criteria of logic, and that in their reasoning they find such criteria compelling. Steven Lukes (1970) and Martin Hollis (1970) belong to this class of philosophers. They argue for the universality of certain logical rules and methods of drawing inference. For instance, they think that all rational persons should recognise and follow the law of identity and noncontradiction – that nobody can afford not to see that the truth of p excludes the truth of its denial. This involves the principle of *noncontradiction* in which two contradictory propositions cannot both be true. But, as we argued earlier in our discussion of the limitations of formal logic, this principle is mistaken.

In recent times, logicians have argued for a many-valued logic that recognises more than two values. More importantly, it is clear from the familiar locutions we adopt in our ordinary discourse that these formal logical rules are freely violated while the intelligibility of our meaning remains unassaulted. Don't we normally say in answer to a question, "yes and no"; don't we say that "the statement is both true and not true"; that "one statement is nearer the truth than another"; or that "one proof is better than another"? Surely, when all these are put in the context of our discussion, the meanings remain consistent and coherent such that no serious charge of logical contradiction can be raised.

However, Hollis's (1970) claim concerning inference goes beyond the simple violation of formal rules. His position is that there are certain patterns of inference which all rational humans of necessity follow. Hollis instantiates his point by using the logical form, "If p and if p implies q, then q." In his view, this *modus ponens* with {p.(p ⊃ q)}⊃ q (see Glossary) has a compelling force on all reasoning minds. It is one of the patterns of inference which is not context-dependent, and as such all people are disposed to follow it whether or not they are able to articulate or provide an exposition of the principles involved.

Not only is it claimed that these basic patterns of logical inference are shared in common by humankind, it is also expected that whenever their premises are presented in a syllogistic form of argument all people must, of necessity, accept the conclusion that follows. By the nature of the logical rules, the steps involved in arriving at the conclusion have no alternatives. Take the following: when you have "p ⊃ q" and "p" you must conclude "q". The point Hollis (1970) is making is that given "p ⊃ q" and "p" every rational person is compelled to conclude "q". He thinks that in studying the beliefs of an alien culture, the student and members of the community being studied do follow this pattern of inference since if they do not, cross-cultural understanding would be impossible.

In the context of Hollis's argument these compelling rules of logic and universal modes of inference are sufficient grounds for rejecting Winch's theory of relativism. Hollis postulates a common game whose rules are context-free and which all men play. Two important questions seem to arise from this. How did these rules come about? What happens if one of the parties involved refuses to obey the rules of the game? It is implicit from Hollis's universalist position that he would not concede the suggestion that his so-called universal rules of logic were socially acquired since that would open the possibility that people in some cultures simply did not acquire them. The only alternative left for Hollis is to suggest that people adhere to the rule because it is part of their nature to do so; that people are biologically constituted in such a way that their brain is structured to follow given logical rules and patterns of inference. It is obvious, however, that Hollis would not dare to make this suggestion for the simple reason that there is no way of establishing if it is right or wrong. Besides, it has not been possible for scientists, natural or social, to present a clear taxonomy of which of our qualities are biologically acquired and which are socially learned.

The issue of what happens if we refuse to follow the suggested rules of inference does not even arise considering the general problems that result from the justification of deduction. In Lewis Carroll's (1895) "What the tortoise said to Achilles", the compelling force of *modus ponens*, which Hollis uses as an example, turns out to be questionable. In Carroll's analysis (cf. Winch 1958:55–57), Achilles presented the tortoise with premises of the form "p ⊃ q" and "p" but the tortoise refused to conclude "q". Instead, the tortoise turned the tables on Achilles by demanding why, in the first instance, he should accept Achilles's rule. Of course, Achilles could not provide an acceptable answer since he found himself justifying his rule by applying the very rule he was asked to justify. The point, as Barnes and Bloor (1982:41) put it, is that "justifications of deduction themselves presuppose deduction. They are circular because they appeal to the very principles of inference that are in question."

So, Hollis's universals of logic and reason are not *of necessity* acceptable after all. It is true that logic presents us with a systematic framework, a pattern of reasoning that is accepted as intelligible. However, logical rules, like other conventional rules, are drawn up for those who wish to play the logician's game to learn and apply. Since they govern most of our experimental world, as we argued earlier, they cannot have a compelling force on all people. In fact, logical concepts and terms have assigned meanings and roles different from their usage in ordinary discourse. Logical connectives such as "and", "or", and terms such as "if", "then", "entailment", "implication", etc. are assigned technical meanings which deviate from their ordinary usage. To that extent, it is right to define logic as "a learned body of scholarly lores . . . a mass of conventional routines, decisions, expedient restrictions, dicta, maxims, and ad hoc rules" (Barnes & Bloor 1982:41). There can be nothing universal about any drawn-up rules intended for reasoning in a given pattern; such rules cannot be compelling to all people. Hollis's claim about the universality of logical rules and modes of reasoning seems to be a relic of the traditional efforts by rationalists to justify faith in what they believe to be the supremacy of reason.

EPISTEMOLOGICAL ISSUES: KNOWLEDGE AND BELIEF

In ordinary discourse, whether in traditional societies or in modern science-oriented ones, we normally make claims applying "know" and "believe" without paying attention to any possible epistemological difference that may exist between the two concepts. So, if you ask a traditional African why he/she thinks that witches exist, you are likely to get two answers purported to convey the same meaning: either "because I know that witches exist" or "because I believe that witches exist". This "or" is an inclusive injunction, suggesting that he/she is either prepared to substitute one of the answers for the other or to hold both together without any change in meaning. The traditional African is, therefore, claiming to know and to believe the same thing at the same time. But this is not in accord with the epistemological doctrine which claims that we cannot know and believe the same thing at the same time. If I know p is q, I cannot at the same time believe that p is q and if I believe it, I cannot at the same time know it. The only possibility, according to this view, is that we can believe something at one time and know it at another time – that is to say, that we move progressively from belief to knowledge.

It would appear therefore that the traditional African who simultaneously claims to know and to believe that witches exist, has either not critically reflected on the matter so as to see that, having moved to the point of knowledge, his/her belief claim stands redundant, or that his/her peculiar state of mind or the nature of his/her object of reference allows for both knowledge and belief to be simultaneously entertained. Note how viciously circular the answers are. In the strict sense the question, "Why do you think X?" is not satisfactorily answered by, "Because I know X" or "Because I believe X". Such an answer would be considered inadequate in the normal English linguistic convention. It is true that every linguistic convention has a way of accommodating vagaries of this sort. Still, it is possible that the problem we associate with knowing and believing the same thing at the same time is one that is peculiar to the conventional rules of the English language and, therefore, nonexistent in other linguistic conventions. In the Western philosophical tradition one of the dominant views, which in fact derives from common usage, is that knowledge is justified belief. An Englishman, therefore, who receives the answer from the traditional African that witches exist because he knows/believes that they exist would be inclined to regard it as lax, if not muddled.

The grounds upon which in normal English usage belief is held to be distinct from knowledge is that the former lacks the element of certitude associated with the latter. But Pritchard denies that the difference is one of degree. They are, according to him, different kinds of activity:

> Knowing and believing differ in kind. . . . To know is not to have a belief of a special kind, differing from beliefs of other kinds; and no improvement in a belief and no increase in the feeling of conviction which it implies will convert it into knowledge (1967:62).

Despite his claim of categorial difference between believing and knowing, Pritchard (1967:62) still grants that "believing presupposes knowing" and that "believing is a stage we sometimes reach in the endeavour to attain knowledge".

He however makes the important point that truth or falsity should not be the criterion for distinguishing between knowledge and belief since truth and falsity only apply to belief and not to knowledge. His second point for holding to the distinction between belief and knowledge is that we recognise whichever one we entertain whenever it is entertained:

> When we know something we . . . know that our condition is one of knowing that thing, while when we believe something we . . . *know* that our condition is one of believing and not of knowing: so we cannot mistake belief for knowledge or vice versa (Pritchard 1967:63).

(Pritchard intends the italicised "know" to mean consciously recognise.) Even when Pritchard's distinction is restricted to the English linguistic convention his arguments are difficult to sustain: outside that convention they seem to fall flat. To say that no improvement in a belief can convert it into knowledge is to presuppose that no belief ever turns out to be true. But this assaults the very concept of belief, namely, that it is either true or false. Without implying that "belief" is of the same genre as "knowledge", it is obvious that each of the two species belongs to different levels marked off by varying degrees of conviction. Take the following propositions expressing different degrees of belief and knowledge:

1. I think I believe X.
2. I am almost sure I believe X.
3. I surely believe X.
4. I think I know X.
5. I am almost sure I know X.
6. I surely know X.

Pritchard seems to think that no amount of pull can connect the surest belief, "I surely believe X", with the least certain knowledge, "I think I know X". And this is where he goes wrong.

The factors that improve the certainty of my belief from (1) to (3) may, although not necessarily, be the same or similar to those that improve on my knowledge from (4) to (6). Where the factors are the same or similar, it is possible to improve on the surest level of belief (3) and elevate it, at least, to the level of the least sure knowledge (4). Or, to reverse the argument, it should be possible, where the influencing factors are the same or similar, to relegate (where the factors backing a knowledge claim are weak) the least sure knowledge (4) to the surest level of belief (3). Briefly, the point is that once the grounds upon which we move from one level to another are the same in the two spectra, the same grounds should break the boundary between the two: it should be possible to move from (3) to (4), from belief to knowledge and vice versa. That possibility, it may be argued, depends on the influencing factors, whether they are ever the same in matters of belief and knowledge.

There are a variety of factors that sustain credulity or even strengthen our knowledge claims and beliefs. For this, numerous considerations are taken into account. In some cases the belief we hold or the knowledge we claim to have is expected to be supported by our perceptual experience. In others, all that is needed is that the believer or knower has sufficiently good reasons for whatever he/she claims to believe or know. Here, "good reason" may simply mean empirical evidence (direct or through testimony) or even some a priori logically deduced inference. In all, the main presupposition is that the belief or knowledge is rational or true. The point Pritchard seems to ignore in his distinction between belief and truth is that the considerations that support our belief could also be the same that lend support to our knowledge.

One thing that is clear about the relationship between knowledge and belief is that the former entails the later. A man cannot without absurdity claim to disbelieve what he knows to be true. The converse of this may not be straightforward, but there is an important sense in which belief is accompanied by some form of knowledge although the belief itself is not construed as knowledge. Price's analysis of belief clearly illustrates this. "Believing p", according to Price (1967:47), means:

1. Entertaining p together with one or more alternative propositions q and r.
2. Knowing a fact (or set of facts) F, which is relevant to p, q and r.

3. Knowing that F makes p more likely than q or r, i.e. having more evidence for p than q or r.
4. Assenting to p; which in turn includes
   a. the preference of p to q and r;
   b. the feeling of a certain degree of confidence with regard to p.

Here, our believing p derives from our knowledge of some facts F, which we consider to lend more support to p than q and r. Although F is not enough to convert p to knowledge, the situation is conceivable where F1 F2 F3 . . . Fn are overwhelming enough for p to be considered knowledge. The sense in which we can justifiably claim to know rather than merely believe p is that there is overwhelming evidence for our claim.

Pritchard's (1967:51) second claim is more problematic. He thinks that we can distinguish between knowledge and belief by consciously identifying which is which. When we know something, "we know that our condition is one of knowing that thing", and when we believe something, "we can know that our condition is one of believing and not of knowing". It is true that we do regard certain conditions as those of knowing and others as those of believing but we are never sure of the correctness of our classification. If we were, the question of degrees of conviction and the doubt we entertain as to whether we truly believe what we claim to believe or whether we truly know what we claim to know, would not arise.

One crucial objection to Pritchard's claim is that we hold to certain beliefs which we never formulate to ourselves or even bring to consciousness. The critical examination of concepts such as belief, knowledge, truth, etc. is only done under peculiar circumstances such as when we embark on the kind of philosophical enterprise we are now doing. Normally, men have a great amount of unquestioning attitude to the norms, beliefs, and the principles they live by. We may grant that this general lack of scrutiny of concepts and notions varies from culture to culture, but that it is a basic human trait is beyond doubt. The impression, therefore, that through some form of continuous introspective reflection we always know whether our attitude is one of knowledge or of mere belief is mistaken.

Besides, even if it were true, as Pritchard (1967:47) suggests, that people always undertake this kind of second-order thought, the process is susceptible to the error of taking belief for knowledge or knowledge for belief. Price (1967:51) provides an illustration of this possibility by citing the knowledge claim of the Middle Ages about the earth being flat. Going by Pritchard's view, this knowledge claim was expected to be accompanied by the conscious recognition by people of the Middle Ages that what they entertained was knowledge and not belief. But it has since been proved that, as a matter of fact, the earth is not flat. It is clear, therefore, that people in the Middle Ages did not know that the earth was flat. They merely believed that it was flat, but they mistook this belief for knowledge. For them to have known that the earth was flat, it has to be true that it is flat.

This example establishes several points: that we cannot through introspection distinguish between knowledge and belief; that it could lead to the error of taking belief for knowledge and vice versa. More importantly, the example shows the limitations of our knowledge claims – that most of what we claim to know may turn out to be mere belief. In saying this, of course, we may exclude certain kinds of knowledge, knowledge by immediate sense perception and their images, knowledge of our mental processes, and perhaps also knowledge of mathematical and logical truths. The rest of our knowledge, it would seem, is liable to the kind of problem faced by the claim by people of the Middle Ages about the earth being flat. However, if this stretches the example beyond acceptable limits, it undoubtedly shows that the distance between knowledge and belief is not as wide as is sometimes presented. It also shows that the traditional African who interchangeably uses knowledge and belief or simultaneously adopts both in his/her claims is not as muddled as he/she appears.

There are important reasons why the distinction between knowledge and belief need not be pursued further here. As hinted earlier, it may simply be a peculiar feature of the English linguistic convention. And more importantly, the distinction does not seem to be stressed in the context of African thought. For the African, the most important concern seems to be whether a statement (be it knowledge claim or belief claim) is true or false. There was a surface brush on this in our discussion of the possibility of cross-cultural rationality. Although the issue of rationality is a matter of validity and logical inference, not of truth and falsity of propositions, Winch's (1958) theory of relativism spreads through both areas. Under what conditions can we say of a statement or claim that it is true or false? In traditional epistemological discourse, answers to this question would involve stating a variety of theories of knowledge, each depending on what we take truth to mean.

I.C. Jarvie summarises Winch's thesis on truth as follows:

Whether a statement is true or false will depend upon what it means. What it means, in Winch's view, will depend upon how it is being used, how it functions as part of the form of life it belongs to. The notion then, of translating one form of life into the terms, concepts, preconceptions of another, does not make much sense. The way belief operates in a form of life is peculiar to that form of life. In particular, there is no reason to suppose that a statement true-to-them is translatable into a statement true-to-us; but if it is translatable into a statement true-to-us that does not show that it is false-to-them. One way or another, it makes no sense to talk of true or false *tout court* (Jarvie 1972:44).

This is the form of relativism in which what is true or false is culture dependent, one in which what is real or unreal depends on the paradigms and the linguistic conventions of the culture in which the concepts are used. In other words, Winch is denying the concept of truth or falsity which is extra-linguistic and universal. This is what he regards as the "senselessness" of trying to translate the truth propositions of one culture from the standpoint of another.

The most common example often used to illustrate Winch's doctrine is the Azande claim that witches exist. Whether or not this claim is true, says Winch (1958:100–101), the proof can only be established within the context of the Azande culture, applying their conception of truth and what the people mean when they say of a statement that it is true. According to him, it would be an error for an English speaking investigator on the matter to analyse such a statement applying the English conception of truth, and what it means in the English linguistic convention to say that a statement is true. This, according to Jarvie, is what Winch means by saying that "it makes no sense to talk of true or false *tout court*" (1972:44). There are no independent standards or criteria of truth applicable to all cultures. Winch is not saying that the Azande do not apply any standards; he is merely claiming that their standards are non-comparable.

In arguing for this position, Winch points to the difficulties that would arise if the truth or falsity of Azande statements were to be analysed from the point of view of scientific paradigms. To start with, our first assumption would be that Azande claims, like the claims of science, can be established to be true or false by scientific methods; that through experimentation and the logic of scientific reasoning they can be shown to be true or false. This, according to Winch (1958), is an erroneous assumption since the Azande claims are neither scientific hypotheses nor parasitic on scientific principles. They are therefore not verifiable or refutable by scientific methods. Azande magic and claims about witchcraft are metaphysical, and metaphysical claims are irrefutable by science (Otubanjo 1983).

Furthermore, Winch (1958) sees Azande beliefs as being tied to a whole form of life and, as such, they cannot be disputed in isolation of the totality of the form of which they are an integral part. It is not certain whether Winch is right on this point. It should be possible to appraise any part of a given form of life insofar as we understand its relations to the other parts and to the whole. At least, this is done within the realm of science. Known scientific principles are used in ascertaining the validity or otherwise of novel claims. But Winch would be right if all he meant is that we cannot declare part of a people's way of life false without relating it to other parts or to its totality. His main emphasis is that the appraisal of whatever we do should not be conducted by applying part of an alien form of life. So, if part of the Azande form of life is to be judged true or false, this can only be done from within the culture itself. It is the culture that is to appraise the truth or falsity of its own parts.

Anthropological literature, until recently, has given the impression that this process of internal assessment is absent in traditional thought; but, on the contrary, a lot of it does go on. Evans-Pritchard (1976) claims that traditional people show no theoretical interest in exposing and extirpating inconsistencies in their beliefs. But his own report on the Azande shows that the people do make conscious efforts at resolving conflicting claims. Although we said earlier that these claims are not scientific hypotheses to be proved true or false, Evans-Pritchard's account shows that when Azande pronouncements turn out to be false they embark on elaborate measures to explain why. The failure of their *benge* (poison) is followed by series of *ad hoc* explanations, either that the substance used was bad, that the operator failed to follow the procedure or that the whole ritual had been influenced by sorcery. It is not therefore correct to say that there is a total absence of theoretical interest or that traditional people do not make efforts to resolve inconsistencies. The adoption of *ad hoc* devices for explaining failures and contradictions is, in fact, common even in science-oriented cultures.

However, Winch's relativist theory about the incommensurability of truth claims and reality across cultures has been strongly criticised from different standpoints. Jarvie (1972), who gives Winch's ideas the most lucid exposition, and who even claims to have expanded on them, thinks that the ideas have major unacceptable implications. Firstly, Jarvie (1972:46–54) argues that Winch is wrong in his claim that there are no universal standards either of rationality or of truth claims. In his view, there are such standards, and every culture (including traditional ones) possesses and applies such universal standards. Secondly, Jarvie objects to Winch's view that a culture can successfully appraise itself internally. In his view, the best interpretation of a culture is most likely to be given from outside that culture.

One of the major objections Jarvie (1972) seems to have against Winch is the latter's claim that Azande magic is central to Azande forms of life and therefore not parasitic on some other principles by which it can be appraised. In Winch's argument, religion in the West is parasitic on science so that the former can be judged by the principles of the latter. He does not see this kind of relationship among the Azande. But Jarvie (1972) thinks that if Winch had looked closely enough, the relationship he found in English culture would have been seen among the Azande also. The Azande, according to Jarvie, have magic but they also have technology (which he equates with Western science) and it could be said (just as we say of Western religion) that Azande magic is parasitic on Azande technology. And although Jarvie thinks that there is a conceptual problem about some principles being regarded as parasitic on others, his main point is that we can use the standards of Azande technology in appraising Azande magic. This, it seems, would be acceptable to Winch since the appraisal is still done within the Azande context. But, Jarvie's final point would be that there is no essential difference between the principles of Azande technology and those of science, so that if the former can be used in appraising Azande magic, the latter are also appropriate. He does not therefore see any reason why Winch should think that Azande magic cannot be analysed applying the principles of science.

Jarvie reinforces his disagreement with Winch on the same point with another argument. To say that traditional beliefs cannot be analysed with scientific concepts, argues Jarvie (1972:53), is to imply that there is no empirical content to traditional beliefs, and this is false. Here, Jarvie betrays a certain predisposition to realism by claiming that "the reality of the world is extra-linguistic", for "if reality (or the world) shows itself *in the sense that language has,* then there is no such thing as a truth independent of the ideas and wishes of men." It is clear from this that Jarvie accepts the correspondence theory of truth. But more specifically, what he is saying is that traditional people, like people in other societies, make factual claims which are intended to reflect the actual world of existing things, and they believe that their claims can be true or false in the same sense in which statements are true or false outside their culture. "Truth and consistency," says Jarvie (1972:53), "are qualities we attribute to statements apropos their relationship to this 'external world' . . . true statements are true of this world; false statements are false of this world." For Jarvie, therefore, concepts such as truth, falsity, reality, etc. have universal standards of measure and they are not culture bound, as Winch claims.

Some of Winch's critics are more moderate. Steven Lukes (1970:208–213), for instance, concedes that certain criteria for appraising the truth of belief claims are context dependent. He, however, thinks that there are others which are universal. Lukes thus makes the distinction between "criteria 1", which he describes as universal, and "criteria 2", those that are culture bound. On the former, Lukes's argument is that the existence of a common reality is a precondition for the understanding of any alien language. By this he means that any statement of truth in one language is translatable into another and vice versa. Lukes points out that a culture must have the distinction between truth and falsity if we are to understand its language. Without this distinction we would not even be able to agree on the definition of our immediate objects of perception. Lukes (1970:208) supports this universal conception of reality by pointing out that any culture that engages in prediction must presuppose a given reality. He thinks that all cultures do predict, and, more importantly, that traditional and modern people "predict in roughly the same way". It is for this reason that they can learn each other's language – because they share the same concept of reality. And in doing so, says Lukes, the criteria used must correspond to this independent reality.

Following almost a similar argument, Martin Hollis (1970:221–239) supports Lukes's universal conception of truth and reality. Across cultures, argues Hollis (1970:231), there is what he calls a "common core" or "rational bridgehead", the existence of which must be assumed a priori if communication between cultures is to be made possible. He describes this core or bridgehead as the basic assumption that in simple perceptual situations, people of different cultures perceive the same reality. From this they adopt standard meanings which make trans-cultural understanding possible. And, like Lukes's "criteria 2", Hollis (1970) allows for ambiguous situations which may lie outside the bridgehead situations in which supernatural, metaphysical or ritual beliefs are expressed. But he thinks that the bridgehead even provides for some limited understanding and clarification of these ambiguous situations.

Lukes thus tends more to Winch than to Hollis. His "criteria 2" refers to situations in which beliefs held may be such that they violate the laws of logic. He describes such beliefs as "mysterious" but admits the possibility of their having context dependent criteria of truth. Lukes uses the example of the Nuer statement that "twins are birds" and asks what criteria we can possibly apply in appraising the truth status of such a statement. His answer is that the criteria to be applied are different from those of "criteria 1", because the statement does not correspond to any reality. The criteria to be used "are *in principle* neither directly verifiable nor directly falsifiable by empirical means. (They may, of course, be said to relate to 'reality' in another sense; alternatively they may be analysed in terms of the coherent or pragmatist theories of truth)" (Lukes 1970:211). So, Lukes accepts that there are contextually given criteria by which beliefs (not only in traditional societies but in all societies) can be classified as "true" or "false". But note the caution with which Lukes uses true and false in quotes in his "criteria 2".

All in all, Winch's various critics seem to concede to him as much as they reject in his thesis. One thing, however, remains obvious, namely, that Winch's most violent critics are adherents of the correspondence theory of truth, the view that conceives of truth as "the perceived and assured correspondence of thought to a reality independent of that thought". This is no place to examine the merit of this theory. All that needs to be said is that it is no longer as compelling in philosophical circles as it was when it first appeared. In fact, one major reason why we need not discuss the correspondence theory of truth here is that it is parasitic on some preconceived notion of reality as understood in the context of Western philosophy.

But whether we judge Winch to be right and his opponents wrong or vice versa, the question of the truth or falsity of beliefs in traditional societies remains an internal problem – internal, that is to say, to the traditional person who lives by and confronts a world guided by these beliefs. Earlier, we conceded the possibility that traditional people may not engage in constant reflection to see whether or not their beliefs truly reflect reality. That, as we said, is not peculiar to traditional people. Human beings generally do not engage in this kind of reflection as a matter of routine. They do so only when the need arises. But it might immediately be pointed out that there is always the need for such conscious reflection to avoid the danger of living by false beliefs. The obvious answer is that all people, no matter what their level of intellectual sophistication may be, still hold to certain false beliefs. It is true that some false beliefs are destructive to life, while others are merely harmless. Any wise person ought to minimise those beliefs that are dangerous. This is not to suggest that traditional beliefs are false but harmless. It is merely to speculate that if these beliefs were indeed false and destructive to life, most traditional societies would not have survived for so long.

Now, the nature of the belief we hold is mainly determined by its source or origin which incorporates the kind of evidence that sustains it. Epistemologists have identified four such basic sources: perception, self-consciousness, memory, and testimony. The first three are first-hand sources while the last is second-hand. By far, most of the beliefs that attract the greatest doubt and scepticism are those based on testimony. It happens to be the case that the bulk of traditional African beliefs whose rationality and truth status are disputed derive from testimony. It has been argued earlier that there are beliefs derived from second-hand testimony whose credibility ranks even higher than those of first-hand sources. That it is so depends on several factors: the nature of the belief, the kind of evidence that is required to justify it, and what Price describes as "volitional and emotional factors" (Price 1967:48–49). In relation to traditional thought, the beliefs in question are mainly metaphysical and, as we pointed out, there are problems about the kind of evidence that is required to justify them.

The important thing about the volitional and emotional factors of our beliefs is that they sometimes lead to a certain kind of attitude which throws overboard issues of evidence and justification. This attitude takes the form of unquestioning acceptance in which, according to Price (1967:47–48), "we are not aware of the possibility that we may be mistaken" about the belief we entertain, a state of mind describable in several phrases, as "taking for granted or acceptance", "being under an impression that" or "thinking without question". Price labels this attitude "acceptance" and thinks that although it is a genre of belief, it is distinct from belief proper. In "acceptance" we do not feel any doubt and we entertain the attitude without questioning:

> We just surrender ourselves to the proposition in a childlike and effortless way. Accordingly, we are unaware of the fact that the proposition may after all not be true. And if it turns out false, we feel a particularly disconcerting and painful shock, quite different from the mild surprise and disappointment which results from the unmasking of an ordinary false belief. It is like the shock of being suddenly waked from a dream (Price 1967:47–48).

The basis of the distinction between acceptance and belief, according to Price, is that the former is conceived as unreasoned absence of dissent while the latter is reasoned assent to an entertained proposition: "There is deciding to act as if p was true, and there is the merely acting as if p was true from habit or possibly from instinct" (Price 1967:50).

Now, acting from habit or instinct is not distinct from acting according to tradition or the acquired norms of society. The attitude involved in all this is such that the concept of evidence or justification seems to play very little role. Surely, there could be some sense in which one might call for evidence in the genre of belief called "acceptance", but the kind of evidence involved is different from that usually given for a reasoned belief. Our perceptive experience may lead to the acceptance that p is true. But, as Price argues, we may not recognise that it is the experience that makes us accept p to be true. According to him, where this recognition is present, and although we also recognise that p may be false, our attitude is one of belief:

> Thus it is not true that in acceptance (or taking for granted) we have no evidence for what we accept; though we could have it, if we aroused ourselves from our unquestioning state of mind and consider critically what we are already conscious of (Price 1967:50).

The central proposition here is that beliefs in traditional cultures are predominantly of the kind Price calls acceptance. Their main sources are custom and tradition which the believers assimilate and adopt unquestioningly and some of which their personal experience may have to reinforce. If the traditional person is pressed for evidence or justification, he/she may conjecture some possible reasons why his/her society has held to these beliefs, but these reasons are normally not regarded as a satisfactory explanation. Or it may simply be pointed out that they are part of a culture which he/she has no choice but to adopt. Beyond that, there seems to be no other way of justifying these kinds of belief.

It is perhaps important to stress that this category of belief is not peculiar to traditional cultures although we may accept their greater predominance in these cultures. In science-oriented cultures, as Mounce (1973:147–162) points out, similar kinds of belief are entertained. Mounce's explanation of how such beliefs may be acquired is more psychological than social, akin to the way traditional people pick up similar beliefs through personal experience. Mounce (1973) illustrates this with two examples. The first is based on the general belief among the English that the loss of a wedding ring is a bad omen for a married couple. This belief, says Mounce, is seen by some as absurd. But he makes us imagine a situation in which a couple has just lost a wedding ring. We should suppose, according to him, that soon after the loss the couple begins to experience unusual events which subsequently lead to the breakup of their marriage. Mounce thinks that the couple will find it difficult to resist the feeling of acceptance that the loss of a wedding ring is a bad sign. The second example used by Mounce is a belief that is usually associated with traditional people, the belief that one could harm one's enemy through what one does to his/her image or likeness. Mounce imagines an instance in which a modern science-oriented person could sincerely accept this belief which normally he would consider false. Mounce then supposes a situation in which a person is asked to stick a pin on a sheet of paper imprinted with an excellent portrait of his mother. The person does so aiming at the right eye. Let us suppose, according to Mounce, that soon after this, the person is informed that his mother developed an affliction in the right eye exactly at the time he did the sticking. In Mounce's view, that person would find it difficult to resist the feeling of acceptance that there is a connection between his sticking a pin on the portrait and the actual affliction in the eye.

The crux of the matter here is that in both examples, the belief adopted or reinforced may not be rational; it may not even be true that the loss of a wedding ring leads to the breakup of marriages or that sticking a pin on a portrait causes physical injury. Yet we are led to accept the connections because that is the way our minds work. Human beings are endowed with an emotional attitude which allows for the unquestioning acceptance of certain kinds of belief which are either assimilated from their cultures or based on the association of ideas. This acceptance is normally reinforced by the individual's psychological reaction to his/her personal experiences. This is not to be taken as a psychological deficiency. It is part of what makes us human.

To come back to traditional African thought, it should be realised that when beliefs of this sort are picked from one's culture or acquired through personal experience, what counts as evidence or justification becomes difficult to determine. Take the Yoruba adage: "There was the cry of the witch yesterday; and the child died this morning; who does not know that the witch caused the death of the child?". Implied in this adage is the belief that a witch can cause the death of a child. If one were to demand from a Yoruba person evidence for this belief, the answer would possibly be that in Yoruba culture the cry of a witch is associated with imminent misfortune. Inquiring further why this belief is adopted is like asking why the person must accept the Yoruba culture to which he/she belongs. To take Mounce's example of the man who stuck a pin on his mother's portrait, the Yoruba person might cite possible personal experiences which he/she has had, to explain how these reinforced the belief that witches can cause people's deaths. Now, anybody who understood the source and emotional content of this kind of belief would hesitate to press for further evidence.

Finally, it is clear how complex the question of the truth or falsity of beliefs is, particularly across cultures. In any culture, people believe not just what is mistaken or foolish, but even what is absurd and unintelligible. For this reason, the tempting alternative is to abandon all questions about the possibility of any universal criteria for the truth of people's beliefs. But this can only be done at great cost. There is a need for communication between cultures, and this in turn calls for some standards, no matter how loose, by which people of one culture might understand people of another culture.

It is for this reason that in recent times some thinkers have appealed to the so-called Principle of Charity. What this means is that in judging the truth-status of beliefs outside one's culture, one should be maximally charitable. One should assume that a belief-claim coming from a culture one does not understand accords with the standards of one's culture, and one should assume further that it is consistent and correct. Davidson thinks that we have no choice but to make these assumptions in our attempt to understand the beliefs of other cultures. The Principle of Charity is "forced on us; whether we like it or not, if we want to understand others, we must count them right in most matters" (Davidson quoted in Lukes 1982:263). It should be noted, however, that this principle has a normative character which tends to weaken its intellectual merit.

We might want to understand the truth of claims in cultures other than ours, but many would insist that we can only be charitable to the truth of belief-claims when an initial foundation of confidence and trust has been built. There is charity in accepting novel claims in science because we are able to count on previous claims. Where no such foundation has been laid, there could be danger in applying the Principle of Charity. Besides, we can only be charitable in accepting the truth of a person's claim if it is logically possible thereafter to investigate further whether what the person claims is truly so. But since we must accept the possibility of Winch's claim that we are never in a position to conduct such an investigation, the point of granting initial charity no longer arises.

THE CONCEPT OF TRUTH IN THE AKAN LANGUAGE

KWASI WIREDU

Ask any ordinary Akan who speaks English what the Akan word for truth is, and unless he/she has made a special study of the matter, the chances are that the answer will be *nokware*. In a certain sense this would be right. A little reflection, however, discloses a complication. The opposite of *nokware* is *nkontompo* which means lies. But the opposite of truth is falsity, not lies.

What seems to have happened is that the Akan has correlated the word truth with a primarily moral rather than cognitive concept of truth in the Akan language. There are three reasons why this occurred. Firstly, the main preoccupation with truth in traditional Akan society was moral. Secondly, the moral concept of truth presupposes the cognitive concept of truth, and thirdly, the English word truth itself is ambiguous. When high-minded publicists wax eloquent in praise of the eternal verities of Truth, Beauty, and Goodness, what they have in mind in this reference to truth is truthfulness rather than truth. And it is not only in particularly high-minded contexts that truth is used as a synonym for truthfulness; it is quite a common usage. So we have to say that our non-too-sophisticated Akan had some excuse for his/her translation.

It emerges, then, that *nokware* translates as truthfulness rather than truth in the cognitive sense. Naturally we must go on to show how the latter, i.e. the cognitive concept of truth, translates into Akan. But before this, let us note one or two things about *nokware*. This word is made up of two words: *ano*, meaning mouth and *koro*, meaning one. *Nokware*, then, means literally being of one mouth. Less literally, it means being of one voice. It is sometimes suggested that this oneness of voice refers to communal unanimity, so that the truth is that which is agreed to by the community. Obviously, the authors of this suggestion have failed to distinguish between *nokware* and the purely cognitive concept of truth. It is intelligible, though extremely implausible, to suggest that truth in the cognitive sense is constituted by communal agreement, but it is not intelligible at all to make the same suggestion about truthfulness. Truthfulness has to do with the relation between what one thinks and what one says. To be truthful is to let one's speech reflect one's thoughts. In this, what others think or say has no particular role to play. And this was not lost upon the traditional Akan. One may conceive of thinking as a kind of talking to oneself without embracing behaviourism; all that is needed is a little flight of metaphor. It then becomes possible to see truthfulness as saying unto others what one would say unto oneself. This is the oneness of voice that is etymologically involved in the word *nokware*.

The idea that truth (cognitive truth) consists in agreement among the members of a community is, in fact, far from the traditional Akan mind, for there is a sharp awareness of the disparity between the cognitive capabilities of the wise persons of the community (*anyansafo*) and the populace (*akwasafo*). No elitist contempt for the populace is implied here. The Akan are communally oriented people, and consensus is one of their most prized values. Nevertheless, to make communal agreement the essence of truth is an epistemological aberration that cannot be imputed to the Akan.

Of course, truth has something to do with agreement, which is evident in the fact that to say of something that someone has said it is true implies agreeing with him/her. This is agreement between two points of view which does not necessarily involve a whole community. But community-wide or not, agreement cannot be the essence of truth in the primary sense, for when there is agreement in cognition it is about something being so; the agreement is that something is so, i.e. that it is the case. It is this notion of something being so that connects agreement with truth at all. It is, indeed, a notion that will loom large in our discussion of the concept of truth in Akan.

It is important to note that *nokware* (truthfulness) involves the concept of truth. To say that somebody is speaking truthfully is to say that the person genuinely believes what he/she is saying to be *true*. Moreover, it also implies that it is in fact true. Apparent counter-examples are easily accommodated. If, for example, a man speaking sincerely says that there is a cat on the mat when there is, in fact, no cat on the mat, there is a sense in which he speaks truthfully. Certainly, we would not say that he was telling lies. But it would be misleading to say simply that he spoke truthfully when he said that there was a cat on the mat. The most that can be said is that he was being truthful in conveying the impression that he believed that the cat was on the mat.

It is the connection between truthfulness and truth which makes the ambiguity of the English word truth so confusing when it comes to translating it into Akan. To say that an *asem* (statement) is *nokware* implies that it is true (cognitively). And so long as one is preoccupied with the affirmative, one might be tempted to think that this is all it means. As soon, however, as one considers the negative, i.e. the case in which we say that something someone has said is not *nokware*, it becomes clear that there is also an element of moral comment in the use of *nokware*. There are a couple of words in Akan which have the same significance as *nokware*, for example, *ampa* and *ewom*. *Ampa* implies truth but it has the same excess of meaning over truth that truthfulness has. The word is a unification of the phrase *eye asem pa*, literally "it is a good piece of discourse". *Ewom* literally means "it is in it".

We shall now consider the Akan rendition of truth, in its purely cognitive sense. And here we meet with the remarkable fact that there is no one word in Akan for truth. To say that something is true, the Akan say simply that it is so, and truth is rendered as what is so. No undue sophistication is required to understand that although the Akan do not have a single word for truth, they do have the concept of truth. This concept they express by the phrase *nea ete saa* (a proposition which is so). The word *nea* means "that which", *ete* which is a form of "to", which is the verb "to be" in Akan, means "is", and *saa* means "so". *Asem* is an all-purpose word which means, in the present context, statement or proposition.

Notice that in the case of the adjective "true", the Akan have a single word *saa* which provides a simple translation. (*Saa*, you will recall, means "so".) But in English one has both "is true" and "is so", whereas in Akan one has only *te saa* (is so). This obviously does not indicate any insufficiency in the Akan language, for if "is true" means the same as "is so", then one can get along as well with either one of them as with both, as far as the making of truth claims (i.e. "is-so" claims) is concerned.

Another linguistic contrast between Akan and English is that there is no word in Akan for the English word "fact". A fact in Akan is simply that which is so (*nea ete saa*). Again no insufficiency is indicated; whatever can be said about the world in English using the word "fact" can be said in Akan using the notion of what is so.

These linguistic contrasts have some very interesting consequences for the theory of truth. Consider the correspondence theory of truth. This is supposed to assert something like this: "p is true" means "p corresponds to a fact". What does this come to in Akan? Simply that "p *te saa*", which in truth is nothing more than saying that "p *te saa*" means "p *te saa*". In other words, the correspondence definition amounts to a tautology in Akan. In a certain sense, this might be taken as a verification of the correspondence theory, for it might be said that being a tautology is an especially splendid way of being true. Be that as it may, one thing that cannot be pretended in Akan is that the correspondence theory offers any enlightenment about the notion of being so.

This comes out even more clearly in connection with the following variant of the correspondence theory. Some proponents of the theory sometimes formulate it by saying that a proposition is true if, and only if, things are as they are said to be in the proposition. Now, as pointed out above, in Akan "p *te saa*" translates as "p is so", and this obviously is an abbreviation of "what the proposition p says things are is as they are". Accordingly, the theory reduces to tautology that things are as a proposition says they are if and only if things are as they are said to be in the proposition.

Aristotle's famous dictum about truth and falsity which provided Tarski's (1956) intuitive motivation in his semantic conception of truth is a close approximation to the formulation commented upon in the last paragraph. Aristotle says in his *Metaphysics,* "To say of what is that it is not, or of what is not that it is, is false, while to say of what is that it is, or of what is not that it is not, is true."

This is very compressed phrasing indeed. "What is", in Aristotle's context, is of course short for "what is so". Translating into Akan then yields: "To say of what is so that it is not so, or of what is not so that it is so, is (to say what is) not so, while to say of what is so that it is so, or of what is not so that it is not so, is (to say what is) so." One might perhaps derive some lesson about double negation from this piece of discourse, but certainly no insight into the notion of something being so.

It seems, then, that there are some apparently important issues that can be formulated in English but not in Akan. Such, for example, is the question, "How are true propositions related to facts?" Since this is not because of any insufficiency in the Akan language it might be tempting, at least to an Akan philosopher, to suggest that the issues in question are not really philosophical issues but narrowly linguistic ones due to the character of the vocabulary of English. Now, although it is, I think, correct to say that a problem like the one about the relation between truth and fact arises out of the nature of the vocabulary of English, it does not follow that it is not a genuine philosophical issue in English. The concepts of truth and fact are among the most fundamental concepts of human thought. Without the notion of something being a fact or of a proposition being true, thinking is inconceivable unless it be a mere succession of ideas, and even that can be doubted. It seems obvious then that the relation between the terms truth and fact is a philosophical issue; for, of course, one cannot give a fundamental clarification of either of these foundational concepts in English without relating them one to the other. Yet, since these terms need not both be present in all natural languages, as the case of Akan shows, this task is not inescapable for the human mind. From which it follows that some philosophical problems are not universal. Of course, there must be others that are universal. It must, for example, be apparent from a remark just made that the clarification of the notion of something being so is a universal philosophical problem.

As the point that a problem may be genuinely philosophical and yet dependent on some contingent features of a particular natural language may possibly be controversial, I shall endeavour to reinforce it by analogy with a simple illustration still involving a linguistic contrast between English and Akan. In the English language there occur both the statement forms "p is equivalent to q" and "p if and only if q". It seems obvious that any natural language should have the means of expressing the idea of equivalence; and, indeed, in Akan we have a way of doing so, albeit somewhat circuitously. We say of two equivalent statements that they have the same destination: *ne nyinaa kosi faako*, or, more literally, "they both reach the same place". Since equivalence is distinct from identity of meaning, we might note parenthetically that we have a different way of expressing the latter. We say *nsem no mienu ye baako*, "the two pieces of discourse are one". The point now is that in Akan we have no such statement form as might be rendered as "p if and only if q". We can, of course, assert "if p then q" *(se* p *a ende* q) and "only if p then q" *(se* p *nkoara a na* q), and the conjunction of these two forms is equivalent to "p if and only if q". But the conjunction is not the same form as the biconditional. If we now assert that the statement form "p if and only if q" is equivalent to "(if p then q) and (if q then p)" we are obviously asserting a logical truth in English, but no such logical truth exists in Akan. There is nothing necessary about the form "p if and only if q", so that it might be thought obligatory that Akan should have a phrase literally corresponding to it. Whatever can be expressed by means of that form can be expressed by the Akan way of expressing equivalence as indicated above. It follows that the question whether the relation between "p if and only if q" and "[(if p then q) and (if q then p)]" is really one of equivalence is a genuine logical issue in English which is, nevertheless, not universal.

The analogy with the question of the relation between truth and fact is quite complete. Just as the relation between "p if and only if q" and "[(if p then q) and (if q then p)]" is a genuinely logical question which is dependent on a contingent feature of English vocabulary (and that of any similar language), so is the relation between truth and fact a genuine philosophical issue dependent on the English language. And just as any reasoner in English, whether he/she be a native speaker or not, will have to be conversant with the logic of the two statement forms, so anybody essaying a theory of truth in the medium of the English language will have to give some attention to the relation between truth and fact. It is probably the case that there are ontological pitfalls for native as well as non-native speakers of English in their thought about this relation.

There is a fairly obvious lesson that can be drawn from the foregoing observations. If some philosophical and logical problems – for logical problems are philosophical problems – are relative to particular natural languages, then they cannot be as fundamental as those that are universal to all natural languages. Take, for example, the concept of implication. Any natural language will have to be capable of expressing this concept. Furthermore, if we use the term "entailment" to refer to the relation between the premises and conclusion of a valid argument, then we can raise the question whether and how entailment can be defined in terms of implication. Such a question would be universal to all natural languages in the sense that it can be posed for any intuitively workable logic that may be constructed in any natural language. In comparison with this, the question of the relation between "p if and only if q" and "[(if p then q) and (if q then p)]" is of very much less moment for the analysis of human reasoning.

Consider now the issue of the relation between fact and truth on the one hand, and the problem of clarifying the notion of something being so, on the other. Since, as I have suggested above, no cogent thinking is possible without the notion of something being so, but one can reason to one's heart's content in Akan without any recourse to any word or phrase separately standing for *fact* (that is, in addition to the term expressing the idea of being so), it follows that the second problem (that is, concerning being so), is more fundamental than the first (that is, as to the relation to truth of fact).

Suppose the problem of relating truth to fact is solved in the English language. Still, if there is a problem of truth in the Akan language at all – and there surely is – the position would be that the question has not even begun to be raised. In Akan the question would correspond to: "What is meant by saying that a statement is so, that is, what is meant by saying that things are as a statement says they are?" It is here obvious that certain versions of the correspondence theory of truth can at best only be part of the fundamental problem of truth, not part of its solution. The correspondence theory begins to shape up as an attempted solution at all when a certain account of the nature of facts is offered. Some accounts, whether correct or incorrect, will not satisfy this requirement. For example, defining "fact" simply as "true proposition" may be correct, but it would leave us exactly where we started in the matter of the more fundamental problem of truth. On the other hand, an ontological interpretation of "fact" may take us somewhere, though not necessarily in a desirable direction. Suppose, for example, that facts are construed as interconnected objects of a certain sort, then to say that a statement corresponds to fact would mean claiming a certain relation between the statement and the interconnected objects in question. From the point of view of the Akan language this could be interpreted as saying that being so is a relation between a statement and a certain configuration of objects.

In the following passage taken from his *Philosophical essays*, Russell seems to be advancing a theory of this sort:

> When we judge that Charles I died on the scaffold, we have before us, (not one object but) several objects, namely, Charles I and dying and the scaffold. Similarly, when we judge that Charles I died in his bed, we have before us Charles I, dying and his bed. . . . Thus in this view judgement is a relation of the mind to several other terms: when these other terms have *inter se* a "corresponding" relation, the judgement is true; when not, it is false (1966:153).

(Note that since Charles I died many years ago, the objects which one is supposed to have before one's mind when one makes a judgement now to that effect must be of a rather unearthly nature.) Russell gave a somewhat more refined formulation of the correspondence theory in later life (cf. Russell 1948:170). However, refined or not, it seems to me that when the correspondence theory is fleshed out in an ontological fashion it becomes open to fatal objections.

But it is not my intention to discuss the merits or demerits of the correspondence theory. I merely wish to make a metadoctrinal point which reflection on the Akan language enables us to see, which is that a theory of truth is not of any real universal significance unless it offers some account of the notion of being so. This some correspondence theories fail to do.

Let me in this connection make one or two comments about Tarski's (1956) semantic conception of truth since it is closely related to the correspondence theory of truth and is, besides, of great independent interest. The apparent intuition which motivates Tarski's theory is the same as that which underlies the correspondence theory at the level at which, as I have tried to show, it has a philosophical interest only relative to the English language and kindred languages. (Recall, in this regard, our comment on Aristotle's dictum.) Still, Tarski's theory – or a part of it – has the merit of providing a logically precise formulation of the idea of a statement being so, that is, the idea of things being as a statement says they are. A Tarskian "T" sentence to the effect that "Snow is white" is true if and only if "Snow is white" may be taken as a logically precise instantiation of the idea that to say that a statement is true is to say that things are as they are said to be in the statement. In Akan, since "is true" is *te saa* which means "is so", that is, "is how things are", the Tarski sentence becomes " 'Snow is white' is as things are if and only if snow is white." In this form the sentence sounds trivially truistic, and is indeed so if it is intended even as a partial theory of truth.

But it can acquire a more substantial significance if it is made the starting point of an inquiry into the status of the second "snow is white" in the Tarski equivalence. This component gives a "concrete" instantiation of the idea of something being so. If, as I suggest, the puzzle about truth is a puzzle about the notion of something being so, then the use of Tarski's equivalence (in this connection) can only be to provide us in its second component with a vivid instantiation of our abstract notion of something being so. Such presentation can concentrate the mind and possibly lead to an illuminating elucidation. However, in itself, Tarski's "T" sentence, even as completed by the rest of the theory, can only provide a possible starting point in the solution of the problem of truth.

The other main theories of truth, namely the pragmatic and coherence theories, do not suffer any trivialisation on being translated into Akan, but they do take on a new look if they are measured against the task of elucidating the notion of something being so, which reflection on the concept of truth in the Akan language presses on our mind.

THEMES IN A CHEWA EPISTEMOLOGY

DIDIER N. KAPHAGAWANI

NOTIONS OF TRUTH

To know that something is the case is to assert that the thing is true. Knowledge presupposes truth; and that this is the case can be defended universally, irrespective of cultural or environmental contexts. However, differences arise when the question of what constitutes truth is addressed. In Western philosophy for instance, at least three theories of truth have been propounded: the correspondence theory, which claims that a statement is true if it corresponds to a fact out there in reality; the coherence theory, emphasising that a statement is true if it is consistent with, or can be true together with, other statements; and the pragmatic theory, which claims that a statement is true if it serves some useful purpose. These theories provide differing answers to the issue of what constitutes truth.

Now the question which looms large at this juncture is: "What constitutes truth in African epistemology?" I cannot pretend to possess one answer to this all-important question because to do so would be to presume, rather mistakenly, that all African cultures conceive of truth in the same way. Kwasi Wiredu has discussed and analysed an Akan conception of truth (see "The concept of truth in the Akan language"), and one hopes that many more such studies in specific cultures will be conducted. I therefore confine my discussion to the Chewa culture because, being born and bred a Chewa, I feel competent to discuss and analyse Chewa notions of truth, knowledge, and wisdom.

A CHEWA NOTION OF TRUTH

There are a number of ways in which issues of truth are discussed among the Chewa. But in their language, Chichewa, the word which stands out as the Chewa equivalent of truth is *zoona*. This word literally means "the seen" because it is a derivative of the verb *kuona*, meaning "to see" with *ku-* as the infinitive particle "to" and *-ona* as the verb stem "see".

Here I should hasten to point out that the passive of the verb *kuona* is *kuonedwa* with *kuonewa* and *kuoneka* as its variants. Thus if linguistic rules are to be applied strictly, then "the seen" or "the visible" should be translated as *zoonedwa* or *zoonewa* or *zooneka*. But on issues of truth claims these passives are not used in the Chewa language. What is employed seems, in my opinion, to be a truncated form of *zoonedwa*, namely *zoona*, where the letters *-edw-* have been deleted. In fact, one could as well argue that *zoona* is a truncated derivative of *zoziona*, meaning "things that have been seen or visualised". In my view the passivity of the verb *kuona* seems to be implied in both forms of expression.

However, another word in the Chewa language for "true" is *zedi*. This word is used interchangeably with *zoona* in Chewa conversation and discussion. For instance, if a Chewa is asked: "Kodi ndi*zoona* kuti ku Malawi kuli njala?" (Is it true that Malawi is famine-stricken?), "Ndi*zoona*" or "Ndl*zedi*" would do as an answer if indeed it were the case that Malawi were in such a situation. Otherwise, "Si*zoona*" or "Si*zedi*" would be the response. Notice that the prefix "si-" in "Si*zoona*" and "Si*zedi*" is the mark of negation in Chichewa, clearly showing that truths are negations of falsehoods.

Unlike the word *zoona* which is translatable as "the seen" in English, *zedi* does not seem to have an English equivalent. But since it means the same as *zoona*, I will dwell on *zoona* in this discussion, leaving *zedi* aside for the moment.

Now, what is true among the Chewa is what is seen. And since seeing is experiencing visually, it follows that what is true is what is experienced. At this point one would be inclined to conclude that the Chewa people treasure experiential knowledge rather than non-experiential knowledge, implying that their notion of truth is empirical rather than non-empirical or rational. But that is not the case because, as I should hasten to point out, what has so far been presented is the literal meaning of *zoona*. The general connotations of this word also include perception, extending the notion of truth past that which is only *seen*, to all that is perceived in a general way. This has to be said because the Chewa do engage in talk about such things as wizardry, witchcraft and sorcery, for instance, issues which are more cognitive than seen or experienced visually. Similarly, hypothetical discussions which require imagination rather than visual experience are not a rarity in Chewa culture, particularly in juridical matters.

To come back to the point, it could be said that the general idea of seeing or perceiving is fundamental to the notion of truth among the Chewa. Notice, however, the passive voice of *zoona*, "the seen". What is true is what is seen. And to the question: "Seen by whom?", this notion is silent. It therefore allows us to conclude that truth is seen or perceived by either an individual or a collection of individuals. Whatever is seen, perceived or experienced individually or collectively is, for the Chewa, the truth from the point of view of that specific individual's or group's experience.

A CHEWA EPISTEMOLOGY

Chichewa, the language spoken by the Chewa people, is littered with proverbs, the messages of which are indicative of the Chewa conception of knowledge. The first and foremost is *Akuluakulu ndi m'dambo mozimila moto*, which means, literally, "The elders are rivers where fire is extinguished". The message of this proverb is that the elders have most, if not all, solutions to any kind of problem; they are live encyclopaedias to which reference can be made for the answers to troublesome questions. At this stage, however, the concept of knowledge does not surface unless a further question is posed as to why the elders are held in such high esteem. The answer is not far to seek. It is this: the elders have had more experience than most other people; they have lived through famine, war, peace, and so on. From these, it is assumed, they have learnt both from their own mistakes and successes as well as those of others. They know that some things are the case; they also know how to do what, what to do when, and when to do what, and how.

Now the concept of knowledge starts to come to light. It is something along the lines of "maximum cumulative experience", not for its own sake, but rather for practical purposes. Ideally, if this interpretation is not wrong, a Chewa would love to be in possession of as much experience as possible to gain authority and respect from people prepared to construct and shape their world outlooks and habits on what is asserted by the wise.

An examination of more proverbs suggests a further division of experience, "temporal" experience on the one hand, and "spatial" experience on the other. The proverb quoted above emphasises the former type of experience. But, consider the proverb, *Galu wamkota sakandira pachabe*, which means, literally, "A mother-dog never scratches or digs in an empty hole" (there are several other similar proverbs). This proverb compares and contrasts old with young hunting dogs and puts across the idea that whereas young dogs might scratch or dig in a hole in which there are no mice, old dogs would not. They would always sniff first, and attempt to dig in a hole which contained at least one mouse. (Note that the Chewa are a mice-eating society.) "Temporal" experience is what determines the correct action in such cases; for it must have taken a lot of time for the mother-dog to distinguish rewarding from unrewarding holes.

But the following proverb suggests a different kind of experience, namely spatial experience: *Mlendo ndiye adza n'kalumo kakuthwa* which means, literally, "A visitor is the bringer of sharp razor blades." The message this proverb puts across is that more often than not, visitors or those new to a society are carriers and introducers of novel ideas, which may either be the solutions to some vexing problems or phenomena, or may contribute very positively towards the search for solutions. What is particularly interesting about this kind of experience is that it is not restricted to the elders; the young may also have access to it. And this feature inevitably leads one into thinking that the two types of experience are in some way separable and possibly independent of each other. But that is not to rule out the possibility of the two occurring at the same time in a particular person.

Other proverbs may apparently destroy the epistemology so far constructed. *Mwala wogubuduzika-wogubuduzika sumela ndele* is one such proverb, which means "A rolling stone gathers no moss." It could be argued that the proverb completely discourages "spatial" experience. Such an argument does not hold, however, because it mistakes the literal meaning for the actual message the proverb has in store for us. Although it makes reference to "rolling", it does not necessarily imply a change of place. It may very well mean change of occupation or profession, for example, from a basketmaker to a carver or medicine-man; and it is conceivable that one could change professions without actually effecting a change in place. That aside, this particular proverb still stresses the importance of experience as knowledge. And again, even if one were to take the proverb literally, it could still be pointed out that although the stone gathers no moss, it collects tremendous amounts of rolling experience. Such experience would be both temporal and spatial. But of course that is stretching the argument too far.

Now if "cumulative experience" is what the Chewa aspire to possess, then one cannot resist the temptation of pointing out that such a conception of knowledge totally neglects creativity and imagination as other possible sources of knowledge, and hence it is shallow and restrictive. In such a case the epistemological picture so far constructed would have to undergo revision.

To the extent that experience is considered or construed as knowledge among the Chewa, such criticisms are justified, but examination of some aspects of the Chewa culture, namely their aesthetics, indicates the presence of creativity and imagination. Although experience is the overriding factor in the determination of the status of a carver, potter or basketmaker, creativity and imagination are also important criteria, and to that extent Chewa society takes account of non-experiential aspects. It does, nevertheless, tend to lay a lot of emphasis on experience. This claim is further testified to by such proverbs as *M'chiuno mwamwana simufa nkhuku*, and *Nkhwangwa sithwela pachipala*. Respectively, these two literally mean "The loins of a child are not worth a chicken", and "No axe gets sharp in a blacksmith's workshop." The former refers to dancing and claims that no matter how well an amateur may dance, a chicken (given in appreciation of the excellent performance) goes to the one who taught the young person how to dance. The second proverb uses the analogy of an axe which is in general blunt when newly made at the blacksmith's workshop or blastfurnace, but which gets sharpened in the course of felling trees. Clearly these two proverbs have one message, namely that experience and authority determine who is worthy of praise and who is to be held in high esteem. So far the Chewa could be construed as holders of the view that people accumulate wisdom (knowledge) through experience; they accumulate it not for its own sake as was done by the Greeks, but for certain ends and also for the adoption of certain means to some well-defined ends.

"Do the Chewa have a concept of knowledge or of wisdom or of both?" is the question which looms large at this point. An examination of certain words in Chichewa, namely *kudziwa* and *nzeru*, seems to suggest an absence of the knowledge/wisdom distinction. In Chichewa the verb "to know" may be translated as *kudziwa*. However, whereas the noun "knowledge" is derived from the verb "to know" in English, no noun is derivable from the verb *kudziwa* in Chichewa. Instead there is a totally different word, namely *nzeru*, which seems to serve two purposes, and could be translated as "wisdom" in English. The question is whether or not there exists a knowledge/wisdom distinction in the Chewa language and culture. Let us for the moment not assert the absence of such a distinction too hastily; there may be other ways round this.

The claim that knowledge is distinguishable from wisdom presupposes prior acquaintance with what wisdom as opposed to knowledge is. Wisdom is defined as

> sound and serene judgements regarding the conduct of life. It may be accompanied by a broad range of knowledge, by intellectual acuteness, and by speculative depth, but it is not to be identified with any of these and may appear in their absence. It involves intellectual grasp or insight but is concerned not so much with the ascertainment of fact or the elaboration of theories as with the means and ends of life (Blanshard 1967:322).

Wisdom has two elements, namely reflection and judgement. Reflection is the tendency to analyse or examine events in terms of their grounds and implications, and after all these have been apprehended and considered, a judgement is passed.

An interesting feature of wisdom is that it is always invested with authority. No argument can gainsay a wise person's judgement; it is always assumed that a wise person's judgement is more correct than anybody else's. In actual fact,

> [t]he decisions of a wise judge may be freighted with experience and reflection. Experience, even when forgotten beyond recall, leaves its deposits, and where this is the deposit of long trial and error, of much reflection and of wide exposure in fact or imagination to the human lot, the judgement based on it may be more significant than any or all the judge could adduce for it. This is why age is accredited with wisdom; years supply a means to it whether or not the means are consciously used (Blanshard 1967:324).

Now, since age is credited with wisdom, and wisdom with authority and respect, then it follows that age is credited with authority and respect. There is a distinction in the Chewa culture between knowledge and wisdom, despite a claim to the contrary which the analysis of *kudziwa* ("to know") and *nzeru* ("wisdom") has suggested. Knowledge is cumulative experience whereas wisdom is a product of experience, making the acquisition of wisdom a second-order activity, and of knowledge a first-order one. The *kudziwa/nzeru* analysis is not indicative of an absence of the knowledge/wisdom distinction; it demonstrates *inter alia* the semantic and grammatical differences between English and Chichewa. Although there is no noun in Chichewa for knowledge, it is possible to say of some person that he/she knows how to do certain things but deny him/her wisdom. People do make such assertions, and this indicates the existence of the knowledge/wisdom distinction in the Chewa culture. In conclusion, we could say that the elders in the Chewa culture have most knowledge because they have more experience than anybody else; but not all are wise. Only some are. The elders have an aura of respect and authority mainly because of their knowledge, not their wisdom; for if the latter were the determinant for respect, some elders would not be respected – yet all elders are indeed respected.

OLD GODS, NEW WORLDS
KWAME A. APPIAH

In coming to terms with what it means to be modern, Western and African intellectuals have interests they should share. For, the nature and meaning of modernity is a topos that recurs in the modern Western imagination. Whether in reactionary romanticisms or in futurist celebrations of the new, whether in a confident optimism in the ameliorative capacities of modern science or a nostalgic longing for the unalienated, unhurried – and, by now, unfamiliar – traditional sense of community, much of Western thought about intellectual and social life is predicated upon an understanding of what it is to be modern, and on reactions, whether positive or negative, to the fact of modernity.

For the African intellectual, of course, the problem is whether – and, if so, how – our cultures are to *become* modern. What is for the West a *fait accompli* – indeed, we might define modernity as the characteristic intellectual and social formation of the industrialised world – offers most Africans at best vistas of hope, at worst prospects to fear. But, plainly, the question of what it is to be modern is one that Africans and Westerners may ask together. And, as I shall suggest, neither of us will understand what modernity is until we understand each other.

Since I am a philosopher – and, in consequence, intellectually perverse – I will begin by trying to understand the modern through its antithesis, the traditional. I want to try to expose some natural errors in our thinking about the traditional/ modern polarity, and thus help toward an understanding of some of the changes in progress in Africa, and the ways in which they have – and have not – made her more like the West. I want to examine some aspects of traditional culture – understanding this simply to mean culture before the European empires – as it manifested itself in one place in Africa, and then to look at some of the ways in which the experience of colonisation and extended interaction with the West has produced a culture in transition from tradition to modernity, a culture that, for want of a better word I shall call "non-traditional".

But I propose to begin in a place whose strangeness for most Europeans and Americans, and whose naturalness for many Africans, is a measure of the distance between Nairobi and New York – namely, with what, with some unhappiness, I shall call "religion". For, one of the marks of traditional life is the extent to which beliefs, activities, habits of mind, and behaviour in general are shot through with what Europeans and Americans would call "religion". Indeed, it is because understanding traditional religion is so central to the conceptual issues that modernisation raises that philosophical discussion of the status of traditional religion has been so central in recent African philosophy. And the urgency and the relevance of the issue to central questions of public policy is one of the reasons why there is greater excitement to be found in philosophical discussion of religion in Africa than in the philosophy of religion in the West.

If I am reluctant to use the term *religion* without qualification, it is because religion in the contemporary West is, by and large, so different from what it is in traditional life that to report it in Western categories is as much to invite mis-understanding as to offer insight. But the examples I want to discuss should help make this point for me. Let us begin, then, with an account of a traditional ceremony.

The place is somewhere in rural Asante. The time is the ethnographic present – which is to say, the past. As we arrive, a male figure dressed in a fibre skirt and with charms about his neck is dancing to the accompaniment of drumming and singing. Suddenly he leaps into a nearby stream and emerges clasping something to his breast. This he places in a brass pan and pounds with clay (which we later discover comes from the sacred river Tano) and the leaves or bark of various plants, some gold dust, and an aggrey bead.

During the pounding, the figure utters words, which we may translate as follows:

God, Kwame, Upon-whom-men-lean-and-do-not-fall; Earth Goddess, Yaa; Leopard and all beasts and plants of the forest, today is sacred Friday: and you, Ta Kwesi, we are installing you, we are placing you, so that we may have life, that we may not die, that we may not become impotent. To the village head of this village, life; to the young men of the village, life; to those who bear children, life; to the children of the village, life.

Spirits of the trees, we call upon you all, to let you come here now, and let all that is in our heads be placed in this shrine.

When we call upon you in darkness, when we call upon you in the day, if we say to you, "Do this for us", that will be what you will do.

And these are the rules that we are placing here for you, God of ours: if a king comes from somewhere and comes to us or our children or our grandchildren, and says he is going to war, and he comes to tell you; and if he is going to fight and will not have a victory, it is necessary that you should tell us; and if he is going and he will have a victory, tell the truth also.

The peroration continues, and the spirit is asked repeatedly to tell the truth about the sources of the evil that makes men ill. The priest ends by saying:

We have taken sheep and a chicken, we have taken palm-wine, which we are about to give you that you may reside in this village and preserve its life. . . .

Perhaps on some tomorrow the King of Asante may come and say, "My child So-and-so is sick", or perhaps, "Some elder is sick"; or he may send a messenger to ask you to go with him; and in such a case you may go and we will not think you are fleeing from us.

The mouths of all of us speak these things together.

Then the sacrifices of the animals are made, and their blood is allowed to flow into the brass pan. While this is going on, perhaps some other priest will go into trance and sing the song of some other minor local spirit.

This account is a rough paraphrase of one that R.S. Rattray (1955:147–149) published in the 1920s and, with few modifications, you could find just such a ceremony at the installation of a spirit – an *obosom* – in a shrine today.

Perhaps there is nothing puzzling in the ritual I have described. I have tried deliberately to give an account of a series of actions that people outside the culture are unlikely to believe could possibly succeed, but that all of us could surely at least imagine believing in. Yet this ritual is part of a religious world that is typical of the many traditional cultures whose modes of thought have struck Western ethnography and philosophy as puzzling.

We can begin to see why, if we ask ourselves not what it is that is believed by these actors, but how they could have come to believe it. Most intellectuals outside Asante think they know, after all, that there are no such spirits, that, for all the requests in the priest's prayer, no unseen agent will come to inhabit the shrine; no one will answer the questions, "What made this person ill?" or "Would we win if we went to war?" or "How should we cure the king's elder?" Yet here is a culture where, for at least several hundred years, people have been setting up just such shrines and asking them just such questions and asking the spirits they believe are in them to perform just such tasks. Surely by now they should know, if they are rational, that it won't work?

Now it is the appeal to a notion of rationality in this last question that will lead us into characteristically philosophical territory; and it is, in part, because of what it tells us about rationality, about the proper scope and function of reason, that these rituals are of philosophical significance. And if we press the question of how these beliefs can be sustained in the face of a falsity that is obvious, at least to us, we shall return in the end to the question whether we have really understood what is going on.

It is as well, however, to begin with some distinctions. I have already made what is the first crucial distinction: between understanding the content of the beliefs involved in the actions in a religious performance on the one hand, and understanding how those beliefs became established in the culture on the other. But we shall need more distinctions than this. For we need, I think, to bear in mind at least these three separate types of understanding: firstly, understanding the ritual and the beliefs that underlie it; secondly, understanding the historical sources of both ritual and belief; and thirdly, understanding what sustains them.

One of the advantages of making such distinctions – exactly the sort of distinction that is often held up as typical of the trivial logic chopping that makes academic philosophy so unpleasing to those who do not practise it – is that it allows us to set some questions to one side. So we can say, to begin with, that to understand these ritual acts, what is necessary is what is necessary in the understanding of any acts: namely, to understand what beliefs and intentions underlie them, so that we know what the actors think they are doing, what they are trying to do. Indeed if we cannot do this we cannot even say what the ritual is. To say that what is going on here is that these people are inviting a spirit to take up its place in a shrine is already to say something about their beliefs and their intentions. It is to say, for example, that they believe that there is a spirit, Ta Kwesi, and believe, too, that asking the spirit to do something is a way of getting that spirit to do it; it is to say that they want the spirit to inhabit the shrine.

Perhaps this is obvious; perhaps there are no behaviourists left in the world, or at least in the little portion of it that might read this book. So perhaps I do not need to say that it is not just the performance of certain bodily movements by the priest and the other villagers that makes up this ritual. But it is important to remember that you and I could carry out these very movements in order to demonstrate the form of the ritual, and that if *we* did it in *that* spirit, we should not be inviting anyone – least of all Ta Kwesi – to do anything. It is thus precisely because we think these particular Asante acts are intended in a certain way that we know what is going on is a religious act. What makes it religious is what the people are trying to do.

Any theoretical account of this ritual must begin by trying to understand, therefore, what the beliefs and intentions are that inform it. But that is not, of course, all there is to understanding the ritual. For there are certainly features of it – the use of gold dust and the aggrey bead in making up the contents of the brass pan, for example – that may still remain in need of explanation. We may well discover that, though the priest means to put the gold dust into the pot, he does so only because this is, as he might say, part of "how the ancestors called a spirit" – that is, he might have no special reason of his own for using the gold dust.

What does it mean to say that this still needs explaining? The priest does many things in the performance of the ritual for no special reason of his own. He waves a stick up and down as he dances, and he does so deliberately: it is part of his intention in dancing to wave the stick up and down. Yet we may find nothing to explain in this.

I think the first step in answering the question, "Why does the gold dust need explaining?" is to distinguish between two kinds of things that the priest does in the performance of the ritual. On the one hand, there are such things as the addition of the gold dust, which the priest believes are an essential part of what he is doing. To leave out the gold dust would be to fail to do something that is essential if the performance is to succeed in bringing the spirit to its new shrine. These essential components of the ritual are to be contrasted with what we may call the "accidental" components. Maybe the priest wipes the sweat off his nose as the dancing rises in crescendo, and, when asked, he tells us that this is, of course, something that the ritual could have done without. If the waving of the stick and the wiping of the sweat are accidental to the performance, then this is why we do not need to explain them to understand the ritual. So that part of why the gold dust needs explaining is that it is essential to the ritual action.

Now, in saying that the gold dust is essential, we have already given part of its explanation. It is there because without it the act is believed to be less efficacious, perhaps not efficacious at all. But a question remains. Why does adding it make a difference? After all, all of us probably have ancestors, great-grandmothers, for example, who had remedies for the common cold, of which we take little or no notice. Why should the priest think that this piece of ancestral lore is worth holding onto, especially if he has no idea why the ancestors thought it an essential part of calling a spirit?

Here, I think, many cultural anthropologists will be disposed to say that the gold dust attracts our attention because it plainly symbolises something. We can make up our own stories. Let us suppose, for the sake of argument, that what it symbolises is the giving of riches to the spirit, a sort of spiritual sweetener for the contract between village and spirit that is in the making. The plausibility of this suggestion should not distract us from what is problematic in it, however. For if this *is* why the gold dust is there, why doesn't the priest know it? The obvious answer is that he doesn't know it because he is only carrying out the prescribed form. The people who designed the ritual, the people the priest calls the ancestors, knew why the gold dust was there. They put it there because they thought that part of a proper invitation to a powerful spirit was to give it some of your riches. For to do this is to do what you would do when asking any powerful person for a favour. It is true that spirits have no use for money – the spiritual economy is greased by something other than gold – but in handing over this gold dust you are treating the spirit as you would treat a human being you respect. For these ancestors, then, the handing over of the gold dust is an act whose efficacy depends upon the spirit's recognition that it is an expression of respect.

I do not know if anything like this is true; it would be a hard thing to find out simply because "the ancestors" are not around to ask. But notice that this explanation of the presence of the gold dust as symbolic takes us out of the arena of understanding the ritual acts themselves into examining their origins. This resort to origins is not, however, what makes it true that the gold dust functions symbolically. Our priest might himself have been aware that the gold dust functions symbolically in this way. And I shall try in a moment to say a little more about what this means. But it is important to see that treating an element of a ritual as symbolic requires that there be someone who treats it symbolically – and that this someone be either the actor him/herself, or the originator of the form of ritual action. Finding that the priest does not see the act as symbolic, we needed to look for someone who did. There are more and less sophisticated versions of this sort of symbolist treatment. Durkheim (quoted in Skorupski 1976), for example, appears to have thought that religious practices can symbolise social reality because, though the agent is not consciously aware of what they symbolise, he/she may be unconsciously aware of it. Lévi-Strauss (quoted in Skorupski 1976) seems to believe something similar. In my opinion this belief is mistaken, but whether or not Durkheim was right, he recognised at least that a symbol is always somebody's symbol: it is something that means something to someone.

But what is it exactly to use the gold dust as a symbol of respect? We are so familiar with this sort of symbolic act that we do not often reflect upon it. Here again, it is useful to make a distinction. Some symbols, of which words are the paradigm, are purely conventional. It is because there exists a complex interaction of beliefs and intentions between speakers of the same language that it is possible for us to use our words to express our thoughts to each other. This complex background makes it possible for us to refer to objects, and thus to use words to stand for those objects symbolically. But words are not the only purely conventional symbols, and speaking is not the only purely conventional act. In saluting a superior officer, a soldier expresses his recognition of the officer's superiority. And it is only because such a convention exists that the act of saluting has the meaning it has.

Now the gold dust is not a purely conventional symbol. It is possible to use the gold dust in this context as a symbol of respect, because in other contexts the giving of gold dust is a sign of respect. After all, the reason that giving gold dust to a powerful figure in Asante is a sign of respect is not that there is a convention to this effect. People give gold dust to powerful people because gold dust is money, and money is something that powerful people, like others, have a use for. To give someone money when you need him/her to do something for you is to seek to influence a person's acts, and thus to acknowledge that the person has it in his/her power to do something for you. The person knows that you think he/she has that power because you both know that you would not be giving the money otherwise. If the giving of gold dust along with a request occurs regularly in contexts where people require something of someone with powers they do not themselves have, and if, as in Asante, to ask someone in a position of power to do something for you is to show respect, then offering gold dust in conjunction with a request becomes a sign of respect – in the simple sense that it is something whose presence gives evidence that the giver respects the receiver.

It is thus not *arbitrary* that the ancestors in my story chose gold dust as a symbol of respect, even though they realised that in placing the gold dust in the pan they were not in fact giving the spirit something that it could use. Many symbolic ritual acts have this character. They are not arbitrary signs, like words or salutes; they are acts that draw their meaning from the non-ritual significance of relevantly similar performances. What makes them symbolic is the recognition by the agents that these acts in ritual contexts do not work in the standard way. The spirit comes not because we have given it some money but because we have done something that shows respect, and giving the gold dust shows respect because outside these ritual contexts the giving of gold dust is generally accompanied by respect.

I have spent some time discussing the role of this symbol in this ritual because to many it has seemed that it is the distinguishing character of these religious acts that they are symbolic. Clifford Geertz (1973:90) has famously remarked that religion is "a system of symbols". Now it is, of course, an impressive fact about many religious practices and beliefs that they have symbolic elements: the Eucharist is loaded with symbolism, and so is the Passover meal. But I want to argue that the symbolism arises out of the fundamental nature of religious beliefs, and that these fundamental beliefs are not themselves symbolic.

All my life, I have seen and heard ceremonies like the one with which I began. This public, ritual appeal to unseen spirits on a ceremonial occasion is part of a form of life in which such appeals are regularly made in private. When a man opens a bottle of gin, he will pour a little on the earth, asking his ancestors to drink a little and to protect the family and its doings. This act is without ceremony, without the excitement of the public installation of an *obosom* in a new shrine, yet it inhabits the same world. Indeed, it is tempting to say that, just as the public installation of a spirit is like the public installation of a chief, the private libation is like the private pouring of a drink for a relative. The element of the ceremonial is not what is essential; what is essential is the ontology of invisible beings. So that in the wider context of Asante life it seems absurd to claim that what was happening when my father casually poured a few drops from the top of a newly opened bottle of Scotch onto the carpet involved anything other than a literal belief in the ancestors. The pouring of the drink may have been symbolic: there is no general assumption in Asante that the dead like whisky. But for the gesture of offering them a portion of a valued drink to make sense, the ancestors who are thus symbolically acknowledged must exist.

It is true, as Kwasi Wiredu (1980:42) has expressed the matter, that the proposition "that our departed ancestors continue to hover around in some rarefied form ready now and then to take a sip of the ceremonial schnapps is . . . [one] that [he has] never heard rationally defended". But that it is never rationally defended is not, perhaps, so surprising: it is, after all, not usually rationally *attacked*. (Nor, as I say, do we need to suppose that a literal sip is at stake.) The proposition that there are planets hovering around the sun, larger than the earth, however small they may appear as we ponder the night sky, is not in the usual course of things rationally defended in Europe or America. It is not rationally defended, not because anyone thinks there could be no rational defence, but because it is taken, now, to be obviously true. And, in traditional Asante culture, the existence of disembodied departed spirits is equally uncontroversial. I shall return to this issue later.

If I am right, and it is – as Tylor (1924) claims – a commitment to disembodied agency that crucially defines the religious beliefs that underlie rituals like the one I have described, then there is, of course, an important question that needs to be answered, namely, why in many such rituals symbolism plays so important a part. And the answer is implicit in the account I gave earlier of the relationship between the installation of a chief and the installation of a spirit.

For, as any Asante could tell you, symbolism is a major feature of both of these ceremonies. And though there is a religious component in the installation of a chief, as there is in any public ceremony in Asante, that does not make the installation an essentially religious act. Symbolism is in fact a feature of all major ceremonial occasions in any culture, and the presence of symbolism in religious ceremonials derives from its nature as ceremonial and not from its nature as religious. In private and less ceremonial religious acts in a traditional culture (such as, for example, an appeal at a household shrine to the ancestors), there is still, of course, an element of symbolism. But it is important to recall here that in Asante culture relations with *living* elders where a request is being made in private are also ceremonious. All important contacts between individuals in traditional cultures are ceremonious. When Rattray (1955) reported a seance at the Tano shrine in the early part of this century, he described how, when the priest with the shrine "containing" the spirit on his head entered the trance in which he would speak for the spirit, the assembled priests and elders said, "*Nana, ma akye*" (Sir, good morning), as they would have done if a chief (or an elder) had entered. The formality of the response is somehow less striking to me than its naturalness, the sense it gives that the Tano spirit is simply a being among beings addressed with ceremony for its status or its power and not because the scene is set apart from the everyday.

And once we have seen that the ritual setting is ceremonial, we need only the further premise that all ceremony has elements of symbolism to complete a syllogism: ritual entails symbolism. I do not myself have theories as to why human beings so closely bind together ceremony and symbolism. It is something many of us begin to do in our play as children, and it is surely as much a part of our natural history as, say, language. But that the prevalence of symbolism in religious ritual in Asante derives from the conception of relations between people and spirits as relations between persons seems to me, in the light of these facts, hard to deny. Case by case, the same claim can be made for religion in most non-literate cultures – in Africa and elsewhere.

If the emphasis in Western theory on the distinctively symbolic character of traditional religious thought and practice is misleading, it is worth taking a moment to consider why it should have been so pervasive. And the answer lies, I think, in the character of religion in the industrial cultures in which this theorising about religion takes place.

Christianity is a religion that defines itself by doctrine; heresy, paganism, and atheism have been, as a result, at various times central *topoi* of Christian reflection. In this respect Christianity is not, of course, unique; Islam, too, is defined by its doctrine and, like Christianity, its Book. Islamic evangelists have sometimes held that the simple acceptance of two items of doctrine – that God is one, and that Muhammad is his prophet – was sufficient to constitute conversion, though Christian missionaries have usually insisted on at least token assent to a somewhat more complex credo. But these differences seem relatively unimportant when we come to contrast Christianity and Islam, on the one hand, with many of the other systems of ritual, practice, and belief that we call religions. Never has the contrast been more sharply drawn than in a remark made by Chinua Achebe (1982:209): "I can't imagine Igbos travelling four thousand miles to tell anybody their worship was wrong!"

The extraordinary importance attached to doctrine in the Christian churches is not a modern phenomenon; growing up between Roman and Hellenistic paganism on the one side, and Judaism on the other, and divided bitterly and regularly from the very beginning on topics that may seem to us wonderfully abstruse, the history of the church is, to a great extent, the history of doctrines. But, though doctrine is indeed central to Christianity in this way, it is important to remember what this means. Doctrine does not mean, precisely, beliefs (for it is easy to show, as Keith Thomas (1971) does in his marvellous *Religion and the decline of magic,* that the character of the actual propositions believed by Christians has changed radically in the last two millennia); rather, it means the verbal formulae that express belief. And this has proved something of an embarrassment for many Christians in the world since the scientific revolution.

It is a familiar theme in the history of theology that Christianity has followed in some measure Oscar Wilde's (1982:418) epigram: "Religions die when they are proved true. Science is the record of dead religions." One powerful reaction among Christian intellectuals has been to retreat in the face of science into the demythologisation of the doctrines whose central place in the definition of religious tradition they cannot escape. And – as I think the work of Keith Thomas (1971), among others, shows – it is correct to say that the effect of demythologisation has been to treat doctrines that were once taken literally as metaphorical or, to return to my theme, symbolic. This has led us, if I may caricature recent theological history, to the position where the statement that "God is love" can be claimed by serious men – Paul Tillich (cf. 1951) for example – to mean something like "Love is tremendously important", and to treating the traditional doctrine of the triumph of the kingdom of God as a "symbolic" way of expressing a confidence that "love will win in the end". And similar demythologising tendencies can be detected in liberal (or otherwise counternormative) Jewish theology (certainly they are found in Martin Buber (cf. 1958)). It is not my business to say whether this is a healthy development, though it will no doubt be clear which way my sympathies lie. But even if, as I doubt, this is consistent with the main traditions of Christianity or Judaism, to treat the religious beliefs of traditional cultures as likewise symbolic is radically to misrepresent their character.

The intellectual reformulation of Christianity coexists with a change in the character of Christian lay life, at least insofar as it concerns intellectuals. For educated Christians in Europe prior to the scientific revolution and the growth of industrial capitalism, the belief in spiritual beings – saints, angels, principalities, and powers – had in many respects just the character I claim for traditional Asante religion. Through acts at shrines that Westerners would call magical in Asante, the faithful sought cures for their ills, answers to their questions, guidance in their acts. As technological solutions to illness and a scientific understanding of it have developed, many people (and, especially, many intellectuals) have turned away from this aspect of religion, though, as we should expect, it remains an important part of Christianity in the non-industrial world and in those (significant) parts of the industrial world where the scientific world-view remains ungrasped.

But in the industrial world, the religious life of intellectuals has turned more and more toward the contemplative, conceived of as spiritual intercourse with God. If God's answer is sought to any questions of a technical character, it is those questions that have remained recalcitrant to scientific management (questions about one's relations with others) and questions that could not even in principle be addressed by science (questions of value). This is itself a very interesting development, but it has driven a great wedge between the religion of the industrial world and the religion of traditional cultures.

There is a further change in the nature of contemplative religion in the West. It connects with the observation I made earlier that symbolism characterises the ceremonious, and that social relations of importance require ceremony in traditional cultures. As our relations with each other have become less ceremonious, so have our private religious acts. Prayer has become for many like an intimate conversation. But so it is also for Asante tradition. It is just that the understanding of intimacy is different.

I have largely been addressing the first group of questions I posed about religious ritual: those about the nature of the ritual and the beliefs that underlie it. I have said little about the origins of these beliefs; in predominantly non-literate cultures, such questions often cannot be answered because the evidence is lacking. For Christianity or Judaism it is possible to discuss such questions because we have records of the councils of Nicea and Chalcedon, or because we have the extensive traditions of literate Jewish reflection. But if we are to face the question of the rationality of traditional belief we must turn, finally, to my third set of questions: those about what keeps these beliefs, which outsiders judge so obviously false, alive.

It is in asking these questions that some have been led by another route to treat religion symbolically. The British anthropologist John Beattie, for example, has developed a "symbolist" view of Africa's traditional religions, whose "central tenet", as Robin Horton (1972:31) (a philosopher-anthropologist, who is a British subject and a longtime Nigerian resident) puts it, "is that traditional religious thought is basically different from and incommensurable with Western scientific thought"; so that the symbolists avoid "comparisons with science and turn instead to comparisons with symbolism and art".

The basic symbolist thought is neatly (if ironically) captured in this formulation of the Cameroonian philosopher, M. Hegba:

> *Une première approche des phénomènes de la magie et de la sorcellerie serait de supposer que nous nous trouvons là en face d'un langage symbolique. . . . Un homme qui vole dans les airs, qui se transforme en animal, ou qui se rend invisible à volonté . . . pourraient n'être alors qu'un langage codé dont nous devrions simplement découvrir la clef. Nous serions alors rassurés* (1979: 219).[1]

Simply put, the symbolists are able to treat traditional believers as reassuringly rational only because they deny that traditional people mean what they say. Now, Robin Horton has objected – correctly – that this tale leaves completely unexplained the fact that traditional people regularly appeal to the invisible agencies of their religions in their explanations of events in what we would call the natural world. Horton could usefully have drawn attention here to a fact that Hegba (1979:219) observes, when he moves from characterising symbolism to criticising it, namely that *"le langage symbolique et ésoterique est fort en honneur en notre société"*. It is peculiarly unsatisfactory to treat a system of propositions as symbolic when those whose propositions they are appear to treat them literally *and* display, in other contexts, a clear grasp of the notion of symbolic representation.

I have referred to Durkheim (quoted in Skorupski 1976) once already, and it is in his work that we find the clearest statement of the connection between the urge to treat religion as symbolic and the question why such patently false beliefs survive. For Durkheim (quoted in Skorupski 1976) cannot allow that religious beliefs are false, because he thinks that false beliefs could not survive. Since if they are false they would not have survived, it follows that they must be true: and since they are not literally true, they must be symbolically true. This argument is based on a misunderstanding of the relationship between the rationality of beliefs, their utility, and their truth; it is important to say why.

Rationality is best conceived of as an ideal, both in the sense that it is something worth aiming for and in the sense that it is something we are incapable of realising. It is an ideal that bears an important internal relation to that other great cognitive ideal, truth. And, I suggest, we might say that rationality in belief consists in being disposed so to react to evidence and reflection that you change your beliefs in ways that make it more likely that they are true. If this is right, then we can see at once why inconsistency in belief is a sign of irrationality: for having a pair of inconsistent beliefs *guarantees* that you have at least one false belief, as inconsistent beliefs are precisely beliefs that cannot all be true. But we can also see that consistency, as an ideal, is not enough. For someone could have a perfectly consistent set of beliefs about the world, almost every one of which was not only false but obviously false. It is *consistent* to hold with Descartes in one of his sceptical moments, that all my experiences are caused by a wicked demon, and, to dress the fantasy in modern garb, there is no inconsistency in supporting the paranoid fantasy that the world is "really" a cube containing only my brain in a bath, a lot of wires, and a wicked scientist. But, though consistent, this belief is not rational: we are all, I hope, agreed that reacting to sensory evidence in *this* way does not increase the likelihood that one's beliefs will be true.

Now the question of the utility, the survival value, of a set of beliefs is quite separate from that of both their truth and their reasonableness, thus conceived. Anyone who has read Evans-Pritchard's (1976) elegant discussion of Zande witchcraft beliefs – to which I shall return later – will remember how easy it is to make sense of the idea that a whole set of false beliefs could nevertheless be part of what holds a community together. But the point does not need labouring: since Freud we can all understand why, for example, it might be more useful to believe that one loves someone than to recognise that one does not.

With such an account of reasonableness, we can see why the apparently obvious falsehood of the beliefs of the Asante priest might be regarded as evidence of his unreasonableness. For how could he have acquired and maintained such beliefs if he was following the prescription always to try to change his beliefs in ways that made it more likely that they were true? The answer is simple. The priest acquired his beliefs in the way we all acquire the bulk of our beliefs: by being told things as he grew up. As Evans-Pritchard (1976:202) says of the Zande people, they are "born into a culture with readymade patterns of belief which have the weight of tradition behind them". And so, of course, are we. On the whole, little has happened in the priest's life to suggest his beliefs are not true. So, too, in our lives.

Now it may seem strange to suggest that accepting beliefs from one's culture and holding onto them in the absence of countervailing evidence can be reasonable, if this can lead to having beliefs that are, from the point of view of Western intellectuals, so wildly false. And this is especially so if one views reasonableness as a matter of trying to develop habits of belief acquisition that make it likely that one will react to evidence and reflection in ways that have a tendency to produce truth. But to think otherwise is to mistake the relatively deplorable nature of our epistemic position in the universe. It is just fundamentally correct that there is no requirement other than consistency that we can place on our beliefs in advance, in order to increase their likelihood of being true; and that a person who starts with a consistent set of beliefs can arrive, by way of reasonable principles of evidence, at the most fantastic untruths. The wisdom of epistemological modesty is, surely, one of the lessons of the history of natural science; indeed, if there is one great lesson of the failure of positivism as a methodology of the sciences, it is surely, as Richard Miller (1987) has recently argued, that there are no a priori rules that will guarantee us true theories. The success of what we call "empirical method" seems, in retrospect, to have been, like evolution, the result of capitalising on a series of lucky chances. If the priest's theory is wrong, we should see this as largely a matter of bad luck, rather than of his having failed culpably to observe the proper rules of an a priori method.

We may also fail to see how reasonable the priest's views should seem, because, in assessing the religious beliefs of other cultures, we start, as is natural enough, from our own. But it is precisely the absence of this, our alien, alternative point of view in traditional culture, that makes it reasonable to adopt the "traditional" world-view. The evidence that spirits exist is obvious: priests go into trance, people get better after the application of spiritual remedies, people die regularly from the action of inimical spirits. The reinterpretation of this evidence, in terms of medical-scientific theories or of psychology, requires that there be such alternative theories and that people have some reason to believe in them; but, again and again, and especially in the area of mental and social life, the traditional view is likely to be confirmed. We have theories explaining some of this, the theory of suggestion and suggestibility, for example, and if we were to persuade traditional thinkers of these theories, they might become sceptical of the theories held in their own culture. But we cannot *begin* by asking them to assume that their beliefs are false, for they can always make numerous moves in reasonable defence of their beliefs. It is this fact that entitles us to oppose the thesis that traditional beliefs are simply unreasonable.

The classical account of this process of defence in the ethnography of African traditional thought is Evans-Pritchard's *Witchcraft, oracles and magic among the Azande*. Toward the end of the book he says (1976:201): "It may be asked why Azande do not perceive the futility of their magic. It would be easy to write at great length in answer to this question, but I will content myself with suggesting as shortly as possible a number of reasons." He then lists twenty-two such reasons. He mentions, for example, that since "magic is very largely employed against mystical powers . . . its action transcends experience" and thus "cannot easily be contradicted by experience" (1976:201), reinforcing a point made a few pages earlier: "We shall not understand Zande magic . . . unless we realize that its main purpose is to combat other mystical powers rather than to produce changes favourable to man in the objective world" (1976:199). He says that the practices of witchcraft, oracles, and magic presuppose a coherent system of mutually supporting beliefs:

> Death is proof of witchcraft. It is avenged by magic. The accuracy of the poison oracle is determined by the king's oracle, which is above suspicion. . . . The results which magic is supposed to produce actually happen after the rites are performed. . . . Magic is only made to

produce events which are likely to happen in any case . . . [and] is seldom asked to produce a result by itself but is associated with empirical action that does in fact produce it – e.g. a prince gives food to attract followers and does not rely on magic alone (Evans-Pritchard 1976: 201–203).

And, though he acknowledges that the Azande notice failures of their witchcraft, he shows, too, how they have many ways of explaining this failure: there may have been an error in executing the spell, there may be an unknown and countervailing magic, and so on.

It is the fact that it is possible to make exactly these sorts of moves in defence of traditional religious beliefs that has led some to draw the conclusion that traditional religious belief should be interpreted as having the same purposes as those of modern natural science, which are summarised in the slogan, "explanation, prediction, and control". For, when scientific procedures fail, scientists do not normally react – as I once heard a distinguished physicist react after an hour in a lab with the allegedly parapsychological phenomena produced by Uri Geller – by saying that we must "begin physics all over again". Rather, they offer explanations as to how the failure could have occurred that are consistent with the theory. Biochemists regularly ignore negative results, assuming that test tubes are dirty, or that samples are contaminated, or that in preparing the sample they have failed to take some precaution that is necessary to prevent the action of those enzymes that are always released when a cell is damaged. A sceptical Zande could well make the same sorts of observation about these procedures as Evans-Pritchard makes about Azande magic: "The perception of error in one mystical notion in a particular situation merely proves the correctness of another and equally mystical notion."

Philosophers of science have names for this: they say that theory is "underdetermined" by observation, and that observation is "theory-laden". And they mean by underdetermination what the French philosopher-physicist Pierre Duhem noticed in the early part of this century: that the application of theory to particular cases relies on a whole host of other beliefs, not all of which can be checked at once. By the theory-ladenness of observation, relatedly, they mean that our theories both contribute to forming our experience and give meaning to the language we use for reporting it. Karl Popper's (1972) claim that science should proceed by attempts at falsification, as we all know after reading Thomas Kuhn (1970), is incorrect. If we gave up every time an experiment failed, scientific theory would get nowhere. The underdetermination of our theories by our experience means that we are left even by the most unsuccessful experiment with room to manoeuver. The trick is not to give up too soon or go on too long. In science, as everywhere else, there are babies and there is bathwater.

I have suggested we might assimilate the theories that underlie traditional religion and magic to those that are engendered in the natural sciences because both are explanatory systems of belief that share the problem of underdetermination. But there are other routes to this assimilation, and if we are to explore the plausibility of this idea, it will help if we assemble a few more pieces of the evidence.

For the sake of comparison with the ceremony with which I began this chapter, let me describe another ceremony in which I participated some years ago in Kumasi. It was, as it happens, my sister's wedding, and the legal ceremony occurred in a Methodist church, in the context of a service in the language of the old

English Book of Prayer. "Dearly Beloved," it began, "we are gathered here together in the sight of God." In the front row sat the King of Asante, his wife, the Queen Mother, and the King's son, Nana Akyempemhene, as grand a collection of the Asante traditional aristocracy as one could wish for. Afterwards, we went back to the private residence of the King, and there we had a party, with the Queen Mother's drummers playing, and hundreds of members of the royal household present.

But, not long after we began, the Catholic archbishop of Kumasi (remember, this is after a *Methodist* ceremony) said prayers, and this was followed (and remember, this was a *Catholic* archbishop) by the pouring of libations to my family ancestors, carried out by one of the King's senior linguists. The words addressed to those ancestors were couched in the same idiom as the words of the priest that Rattray had heard. And the King of Asante is an Anglican and a member of the English bar; his son, a lawyer then in the Ghanaian Diplomatic Service, has a Ph.D from Tufts; and the bride and groom met at Sussex University in England (each had another degree as well) and were, respectively, a medical sociologist and a Nigerian merchant banker. These, then, are modern Africans, not merely in the sense that they are alive now, but that they have that essential credential of the modern man or woman – a university's letters after one's name. I shall argue, in a moment, that these letters are of more than metaphorical importance.

What are we to make of all of this? Or rather, what are Europeans and Americans to make of it, since it is all so familiar to me – as it is to most contemporary Africans – that I find it hard to recover the sense of contradiction between the elements of this no-doubt remarkable "syncretism".

These ceremonies are what I want to call "non-traditional" – they are not traditional because they coexist both with some degree of belief in the Christianity that came with the colonials on the one hand, and with some familiarity with the vision of the natural sciences on the other. But they are not "modern" either – because the meanings attached to these acts are not those of the purely symbolic Eucharist of extreme liberal theology. The question, of course, is how all these elements can coexist, what it is that makes this conceptual melée not a source of intellectual tension and unease but a resource for a tremendous range of cultural activity.

The key to this question is, I think, to be found in following up the idea that we were led to earlier, the idea that traditional religious theory is in certain respects more like modern science than modern religion – in particular, that it shares the purposes of modern natural science, which we may summarise in the slogan, "explanation, prediction, and control". It is his systematic development of the analogy between natural science and traditional religion that has made the work of Robin Horton so important in the philosophy of African traditional religions, and it will be useful to begin with him.

Horton's (1967) basic point is just the one I made earlier: the fundamental character of these religious systems is that the practices arise from the belief, literal and not symbolic, in the powers of invisible agents. Horton argues persuasively, and I believe correctly, that spirits and such function in explanation, prediction, and control much as do other theoretical entities: they differ from those of natural science in being persons and not material forces and powers, but the logic of their function in explanation and prediction is the same.

Horton's view, then, is that the religious beliefs of traditional peoples constitute explanatory theories and that traditional religious actions are reasonable attempts to pursue goals in the light of these beliefs – attempts, in other words, at prediction and control of the world. In these respects, Horton argues, traditional religious belief and action are like theory in the natural sciences and the actions based on it. As Hegba in the francophone African tradition says:

> *Sans méconnaître ses limites ni freiner la marche vers le progrès, la science et la libération, il faut admettre que l'explication africaine des phénomènes de la magie et de la sorcellerie est rationelle. Nos croyances populaires sont déconcertantes certes, parfois fausses, mais ne serait-ce pas une faute méthodologique grave que de postuler l'irrationnel au point de départ de l'etude d'une sociét?* (1979:267).[2]

Horton's thesis is not that traditional religion is a kind of science, but that theories in the two domains are similar in these crucial respects. The major *difference* in the contents of the theories, he argues, is that traditional religious theory is couched in terms of personal forces, while natural scientific theory is couched in terms of impersonal forces. The basic claim strikes me as immensely plausible.

Yet there is in the analogy between natural science and traditional religion much to mislead also. The first way in which the assimilation risks being deceptive emerges when we remind ourselves that most of us are quite vague about the theoretical underpinnings of the medical theories that guide our doctors and the physical theories that are used to make and mend our radios. In this we are, of course, like the average nineteenth-century Asante, who was, presumably, quite vague about the bases on which herbalists and priests practised their arts. In application, in use by non-specialists in everyday life, our theories about how the world works are often relied on in general outline in a practical way, without much articulation and without any deep investment in the details. In much contemporary African religious practice (and this includes the ceremony I have described), there is (within each community of practice, each sect or cult or community) a great deal more consensus on the proper forms of ritual and liturgical action than there is as to what justifies it; in this, religious practice in Africa differs little from religious practice in the contemporary industrialised world. Though the extent of literal belief in invisible agency may be somewhat greater in Africa than in the United States (and is probably much greater than in, say, Britain or Norway), there is both there and here a sense in which religious life can continue and be participated in with little curiosity about the literal beliefs of fellow participants, and little theoretical commitment on our own parts. In insisting on the role of *theory* here, one is bound, as a result, to seem to be focusing on something that is far from central for those whose religious practices we are discussing, and thus to be distorting their experience in order to draw the analogy with natural science. But provided we bear in mind that no claim is being made beyond the claim that these religious practices operate on the assumption of a certain theory – that there are spiritual agencies of various kinds – and that this theory allows for explanation and prediction in the sort of way that scientific theories do, I do not think we need be led into misjudging the relative importance of theory and practice in traditional religion in this way.

Still, this worry comes close to a second difficulty with the assimilation of traditional religion and natural science, one Wiredu has pointed out, namely, that it is, *prima facie*, very odd to equate traditional religious belief in West Africa with modern Western scientific theory when the obvious analogue is traditional Western religious belief. I think it will be obvious from what I have already said that it seems to me that there need be no contest here: for the explanatory function of religious beliefs in traditional Europe seems to me to be identical in its logic with that of scientific theory also.

What *is* misleading is not the assimilation of the logic of explanation of theories from religion and science, but the assimilation of traditional religion and natural science as institutions. This is, first of all, misleading because of the sorts of changes that I have sketched in Western religious life. For the modern Westerner, as I have shown, to call something "religious" is to connote a great deal that is lacking in traditional religion and not to connote much that is present. But there is a much more fundamental reason why the equation of religion and science is misleading. And it is to do with the totally different social organisation of enquiry in traditional and modern cultures. I shall return to this issue.

Horton (1967) himself is, of course, aware that traditional religious beliefs are certainly unlike those of natural science in at least two important respects. First of all, as I have already insisted, he points out that the theoretical entities invoked are agents and not material forces. And he offers an account of why this is so. He suggests that this difference arises out of the fundamental nature of explanation as the reduction of the unfamiliar to the familiar. In traditional cultures, nature, the wild, is untamed, alien, and a source of puzzlement and fear. Social relations and persons are, on the contrary, familiar and well understood. Explaining the behaviour of nature in terms of agency is thus reducing the unfamiliar forces of the wild to the familiar explanatory categories of personal relations.

In the industrial world, on the other hand, industrialisation and urbanisation have made social relations puzzling and problematic. We move between social environments – the rural and the urban, the workplace and the home – in which different conventions operate; in the new, urban, factory, market environment we deal with people whom we know only through our common productive projects. As a result, the social is relatively unfamiliar. On the other hand, our relations with objects in the city are relations that remain relatively stable across all these differing social relations. Indeed, if factory workers move between factories, the skills they take with them are precisely those that depend on a familiarity, not with other people, but with the workings of material things. It is no longer natural to try to understand nature through social relations; rather, we understand it through machines, through matter whose workings we find comfortably familiar. It is well known that the understanding of gases in the nineteenth century was modelled on the behaviour of miniature billiard balls, for nineteenth-century scientists in Europe knew the billiard table better than they knew, for example, their servants. Alienation is widely held to be the characteristic state of modern man. The point can be overstated, but it cannot be denied:

> In complex, rapidly changing industrial societies, the human scene is in flux. Order, regularity, predictability, simplicity, all these seem lamentably absent. It is in the world of inanimate things that such qualities are most readily seen. And this . . . I suggest, is why the mind in quest of explanatory analogies turns most readily to the inanimate. In the traditional societies of Africa we find the situation reversed. The human scene is the locus *par excellence* of order, predictability, regularity. In the world of the inanimate, these qualities are far less evident . . .

here, the mind in quest of explanatory analogies turns naturally to people and their relations (Horton 1967:64).

Horton relies here on a picture of the function of scientific theory as essentially concerned to develop models of the unified, simple, ordered, regular underlying features of reality in order to account for the diversity, complexity, disorder, and apparent lawlessness of ordinary experience (1967:51). His story works so well that it is hard not to feel that there is *something* right about it; it would indeed explain the preference for agency over matter, the first of the major differences Horton acknowledges between traditional religion and science.

And yet this cannot be quite right. All cultures – in modest mood, I might say, all the cultures I have knowledge of – have the conceptual resources for at least two fundamental sorts of explanation. On the one hand, all have some sort of notion of what Aristotle called "efficient" causation: the causality of push and pull through which we understand the everyday interactions of material objects and forces. On the other hand, each has a notion of explanation that applies paradigmatically to human action, the notion that the American philosopher Daniel Dennett (1987) has characterised as involving the "intentional stance". This sort of explanation relates actions to beliefs, desires, intentions, fears, and so on – the so-called propositional attitudes – and is fundamental (in ways I suggested earlier) to folk psychology. We might say, analogously, that efficient causality is central to what cognitive psychologists now call "naive" or "folk physics".

These kinds of explanation are, of course, interconnected: when I explain the death of the elephant by talking of your need for food, your hunt, your firing the gun, there are elements of folk physics and of folk psychology involved in each stage of this narrative. To say that mechanical explanation is unfamiliar to pre-industrial peoples is, of course, to say something true. Mechanical explanation is explanation in terms of machines, which are, of course, exactly what pre-industrial cultures do not have. But mechanical explanation is by no means the only kind of non-intentional explanation: there is more to folk physics than a view of machines. And the fact is that the stability of the causal relations of objects in the pre-industrial world is surely quite substantial: not only do people make tools and utensils, using the concepts of efficient causation, but their regular physical interactions with the world – in digging, hunting, walking, dancing – are as stable and as well understood as their familial relations. More than this, pre-industrial *Homo* is already *Homo faber,* and the making of pots and of jewellery, for example, involves intimate knowledge of physical things and an expectation of regularity in their behaviour. Pots and rings and necklaces break, of course, and they often do so unpredictably. But in this they are not obviously less reliable than people, who, after all, are notoriously difficult to predict also.

What we need to bring back into view here is the kind of explanation that is missing from Horton's story, namely, functional explanation, which we find centrally (but by no means uniquely) in what we might call "folk biology". Functional explanation is the sort of explanation that we give when we say that the flower is there to attract the bee that pollinates it; that the liver is there to purify the blood; that the rain falls to water the crops.

This sort of explanation is missing from Horton's story for a very good reason, namely, that the positivist philosophy of science on which Horton relies sought either to eradicate functional explanation or to reduce it to other sorts of explanation, in large part because it reeked of teleology – of the sort of Aristotelian "final" causation that positivism took to have been shown to be hopeless by the failure of vitalism in nineteenth-century biology. And, surely, what is most striking about the "unscientific" explanations that most pre-colonial African cultures offer is not just that they appeal to agency, but that they are addressed to the question, "Why?" understood as asking what the event in question was *for*. Evans-Pritchard (1976) in his account of Zande belief insists that the Azande do not think that "unfortunate events" ever happen by chance: their frequent appeal to witchcraft – the absence of other acceptable explanations of misfortune – demonstrates their unwillingness to accept the existence of contingency. But to reject the possibility of the contingent is exactly to insist that everything that happens serves some purpose. This is a view familiar in Christian tradition in such formulas as, "And we know that all things work together for good to them that love God" (Rom. 8:28), or in the deep need people feel – in Europe and America as in Africa – for answers to the question, "Why do bad things happen to good people?" Zande witchcraft beliefs depend on an assumption that the universe is in a certain sort of evaluative balance; in short, on the sort of assumption that leads monotheistic theologians to develop theodicies.

What Zande people will not accept, as Evans-Pritchard's account makes clear, is not that "unfortunate events" have no explanation – the granary falls because the termites have eaten through the stilts that support it – but that they are meaningless; that there is no deeper reason why the person sitting in the shade of the granary was injured. And in that sense they share an attitude that we find in Christian theodicy from Irenaeus to Augustine to Karl Barth: the attitude that the cosmos works to a plan. Pre-colonial African cultures, pre- and nonscientific thinkers everywhere, are inclined to suppose that events in the world have meaning; they worry about the possibility, not of the unexplained (what has no efficient cause or agent explanation), but of the meaningless (what has no function, no point). And this marks those who accept the scientific world-view – a minority, of course, even in the industrialised world – from almost all other humans throughout history. For it is a distinctive feature of that scientific world-view that it *accepts* that not everything that happens has a human meaning.

To explain this difference between scientific and nonscientific visions we need, I think, to begin with the fact that the world, as the sciences conceive of it, extends so hugely far beyond the human horizon, in time as in space. As Alexandre Koyre (1980) indicated in the title of his well-known study of the birth of modern celestial physics, the Newtonian revolution took the intellectual path *From the closed world to the infinite universe,* and the Victorian dispute between science and religion had at its centre a debate about the age of the earth, with geology insisting that the biblical time scale of thousands of years since the creation radically underestimated the age of our planet. Copernicus turned European scientists away from a geocentric to a heliocentric view of the universe and began a process, which Darwin continued, that inevitably displaced humankind from the centre of the natural sciences. A recognition that the universe does not seem to have been made simply for us is the basis of the radically non-anthropocentric character of scientific theories of the world. This non-anthropocentrism is part of the change in view that develops with the growth of capitalism, of science, and of the modern state, the change to which, for example, Weber's account of modernisation was addressed;

it also contributes profoundly to the sense of the universe as disenchanted that Weberians have taken to be so central a feature of modernity (a claim that makes more sense as a claim about the life of professional intellectuals than as one about the culture as a whole).

But Horton in his original work made, as I said, a second important claim for difference: he summarised it by calling the cognitive world of traditional cultures "closed" and that of modern cultures "open". "What I take to be the key difference is a very simple one," he writes, "[i]t is that in traditional cultures there is no developed awareness of alternatives to the established body of theoretical tenets; whereas in scientifically oriented cultures, such an awareness is highly developed" (quoted in Wilson 1970:153). And it is here, when we turn from questions about the content and logic of traditional and scientific explanation to the social contexts in which those theories are constructed and mobilised, that Horton's account begins to seem less adequate.

We should begin, however, by agreeing that there clearly are important differences between the social contexts of theory formation and development in pre-colonial Africa on the one hand, and post-Renaissance Europe on the other. Modern science began in Europe just when her peoples were beginning to be exposed to the hitherto unknown cultures of the Orient, Africa, and the Americas. The first vernacular scientific works – Galileo's dialogues, for example – were written in Italy at a time when the Italian trading cities had been for some time at the centre of commerce between the Mediterranean, the Near and Far East, the New World, and Africa. In such a climate, it is natural to ask whether the certainties of your ancestors are correct, faced with cultures such as the China Marco Polo described, whose technical ingenuity was combined with totally alien theories of nature.

This challenge to traditional Western beliefs occurs not only in terms of the theory of nature but also recapitulates Greek discussions of the ways in which matters of value seem to vary from place to place – discussions that lead very naturally to moral as well as scientific scepticism of exactly the kind that we find in the early modern empiricists. And it seems no coincidence that those earlier Greek discussions were prompted by an awareness of the existence of alternative African and Asian world-views, an awareness to be found in the first historians, such as Herodotus. (Herodotus's account of the Persian Wars begins with an extended discussion of the variety of religious and social customs found within the Persian empire.) It is, in other words, the availability of alternative theories of morals and nature that gives rise to the systematic investigation of nature, to the growth of speculation, and to the development of that crucial element that distinguishes the open society – namely, organised challenges to prevailing theory.

Remember the answer the priest gave to the question about the gold dust: "We do it because the ancestors did it." In the open society this will no longer do as a reason. The early modern natural scientists, the natural philosophers of the Renaissance, stressed often the unreasonableness of appeals to authority. And if modern scholarship suggests that they overstressed the extent to which their predecessors were bound by a hidebound traditionalism, it is still true that there *is* a difference – if only in degree – in the extent to which modernity celebrates distance from our predecessors, while the traditional world celebrates cognitive continuity.

Now, Horton's account of the sense in which the traditional world-view is closed has – rightly – been challenged. The complexities of war and trade, dominance and clientship, migration and diplomacy in much of pre-colonial Africa are simply not consistent with the image of peoples unaware that there is a world elsewhere. As Catherine Coquery-Vidrovitch, a leading French historian of Africa, has pointed out:

> In fact, these reputedly stable societies rarely enjoyed the lovely equilibrium presumed to have been disrupted by the impact of colonialism. West Africa, for example, had been seething with activity even since the eighteenth-century waves of Fulani conquest and well before the creation of units of resistance to European influence. . . . The Congolese basin was the site of still more profound upheavals linked to commercial penetration. In such cases the revolution in production rocked the very foundations of the political structure. As for South Africa, the rise of the Zulus and their expansion had repercussions up into central Africa. How far back do we have to go to find the stability alleged to be "characteristic" of the precolonial period: before the Portuguese conquest, before the Islamic invasion, before the Bantu expansion? Each of these great turning points marked the reversal of long-term trends, within which a whole series of shorter cycles might in turn be identified, as, for example, the succession of Sudanic empires, or even such shorter cycles as the periods of recession (1724–1740, 1767–1782, 1795–1811, and so on) and the upswing of the slave-trade economy of Dahomey. In short, the static concept of "traditional" society cannot withstand the historian's analysis (1976:91).

In particular – as Horton (1967) himself has insisted in "A hundred years of change in Kalabari religion" – African historians can trace changes in religious and other beliefs in many places long before the advent of Christian missionaries and colonial educators. The Yoruba were aware of Islam before they were aware of England, of Dahomey before they heard of Britain. But Yoruba religion has many of the features that Horton proposed to explain by reference to a lack of awareness of just such alternatives.

It is also possible to find first-rate speculative thinkers in traditional societies whose individual openness is not to be denied. I think here of Ogotemmeli, whose cosmology Griaule (1970) has captured in *Dieu d'eau,* and Barry Hallen (1977:82) who has provided evidence from Nigerian sources of the existence, within African traditional modes of thought, of styles of reasoning that are open neither to Wiredu's stern strictures nor to Horton's milder ones. To begin with, Hallen says, when Yoruba people answer the question, "Why do you believe x?" by saying, "This is what the forefathers said" in the way that Wiredu objects to and Horton also takes to be typical, they are not trying to offer a reasoned justification for believing x. Rather they are

> taking the question as one about the origin of a belief or custom. They are giving the same sort of response Westerners would be likely to if asked how they came to believe in shaving the hair off their faces. However, if one goes further and asks a Yoruba to explain what a belief "means" a more sophisticated response is often forthcoming (Wiredu 1980:82).

And, Hallen (1977:82) goes on to argue, in Yoruba culture this more sophisticated response often meets standards of being critical and reflective. Hallen takes as a model Karl Popper's characterisation of critical reflection on tradition, a gesture all the more significant given the Popperian provenance of the open-closed dichotomy. This requires:

1. Identifying the tradition *as* a tradition;
2. Displaying an awareness of its consequences; *and*

3. Being aware of at least one alternative and, on some critical basis, choosing to affirm or to reject it.

By this test the Yoruba *babalawo* – the diviner and healer – whom Hallen (1977) cites, *is* critically appreciative of the tradition he believes in.

Hallen is right, then, to challenge the structure of Horton's original dichotomy of the open and the closed. On the one hand, as I said earlier, there is in post-Kuhnian history and sociology of science a good deal of evidence that these Popperian desiderata are hardly met in physics, the heartland of Western theory. On the other hand, Horton's original stress on the "closed" nature of traditional modes of thought looks less adequate in the face of Africa's complex history of cultural exchanges and of Hallen's *babalawo,* or in the presence of the extraordinary metaphysical synthesis of the Dogon elder, Ogotemmeli. In a recent book – co-written with the Nigerian philosopher J.O. Sodipo – Hallen (1986) insists on the presence among Yoruba doctors of theories of witchcraft rather different from those of their fellow countrymen. Here, then, among the doctors, speculation inconsistent with ordinary folk belief occurs, and there is no reason to doubt that this aspect of contemporary Yoruba culture is, in *this* respect, like many pre-colonial cultures.

But in rejecting altogether Horton's characterisation of the traditional world as "closed", we risk losing sight of something important. Such thinkers as Ogotemmeli are individuals – individuals like Thales and the other early pre-Socratics in the Western tradition – and there is little evidence that their views have a wide currency or impact (indeed, it seems clear that the *babalawos* of Hallen and Sodipo's acquaintance are not especially concerned to *share* or to *spread* their speculations). If "traditional" thought is more aware of alternatives and contains more moments of individual speculation than Horton's original picture suggested, it is also true that it differs from the thought of both theorists and ordinary folk in the industrialised world in its responses to those alternatives and its incorporation of these speculations.

Horton has recently come – in response, in part, to Hallen's critique – to speak not of the closedness of traditional belief systems but, borrowing a term from Wole Soyinka, of their being "accommodative". He discusses work by students of Evans-Pritchard that not only addresses the kind of static body of belief that is captured in Evans-Pritchard's picture of the Azande thought world but also stresses the dynamic and – as Horton admits – "open" way in which they "devise explanations for novel elements in . . . experience", and "their capacity to borrow, re-work and integrate alien ideas in the course of elaborating such explanations". "Indeed," he continues, "it is this 'open-ness' that has given the traditional cosmologies such tremendous durability in the face of immense changes that the twentieth century has brought to the African scene." Horton then contrasts this accommodative style with the "adversary" style of scientific theory, which is characterised by the way in which the main stimulus to change of belief is not "novel experience but rival theory".

And it seems to me that this change from the Popperian terminology of "open" and "closed" allows Horton to capture something important about the difference between traditional religion and science – something to do not with individual cognitive strategies but with social ones. If we want to understand the significance of social organisation in differentiating traditional religion and natural science, we can do no better than to begin with Evans-Pritchard's answers to the question why the Azande do not see the falsity of their magic beliefs that mention social facts about the organisation of those beliefs. Evans-Pritchard writes:

> Scepticism, far from being smothered, is recognized, even inculcated. But it is only about certain medicines and certain magicians. By contrast it tends to support other medicines and other magicians. . . .
>
> Each man and each kinship group acts without cognizance of the actions of others. People do not pool their ritual experiences. . . .
>
> They are not experimentally inclined. . . . Not being experimentally inclined, they do not test the efficacy of their medicines. . . .
>
> Zande beliefs are generally vaguely formulated. A belief, to be easily contradicted by experience . . . must be clearly shared and intellectually developed" (1976:202–204).

Whatever the practices of imperfect scientists are actually like, none of these things is supposed to be true of natural science. In our official picture of the sciences, scepticism is encouraged even about foundational questions – indeed, that is where the best students are supposed to be directed. Scientific researchers conceive of themselves as a community that cuts across political boundaries as divisive as the (late and unlamented) cold war Iron Curtain, since results, "experiences", are shared. The scientific community is experimentally inclined, and scientific theory is formulated as precisely as possible in order that those experiments can be carried out in a controlled fashion.

That, of course, is the only *official* view. Three decades of work in the history and sociology of science since Thomas Kuhn's iconoclastic *The structure of scientific revolutions* has left us with a picture of science as much more messy and muddled – in short, as a more human business. Yet while this work has had the effect of revising (one is inclined to say "tarnishing") our image of the institutions of scientific research, it has not revised the fundamental recognition that the production of scientific knowledge is organised around competing theoretical positions, and that the demand for publication to establish the success of laboratories and individual scientists exposes each competing theory to review by ambitious counter-theorists from other laboratories, with other positions. What we have learned, however (though it should have been obvious all along), is that there are serious limits placed on the range of positions that may be entertained. In 1981, for example, when Rupert Sheldrake's *A new science of life* was published, a correspondent in *Nature* suggested it might usefully be burned; this was inconsistent with official ideology because Sheldrake, a former research fellow of the Royal Society who had studied the philosophy of science, had constructed a proposal which, though provocative, was deliberately couched in terms that made it subject to potential experimental test. Still, it outraged many biologists (and physicists), and if there had not been a challenge from the *New scientist* magazine to design experiments, his proposal, like most of those regarded as in one way or another the work of a "crank", would probably simply have been ignored by his peers. (There is some conclusion to be drawn from the fact that the copy of Sheldrake's book listed in the catalogue at Duke University appears to be in the Divinity School library!) The development of science is not a free-for-all with all the participants cheering each other on with the cry: "And may the best theory win!" But science is, crucially, adversarial, and the norms of publication and reproducibility of results, even though only imperfectly adhered to, are explicitly intended to lay theories and experimental claims open to attack by one's peers, and thus make competition from the adventurous "young Turk" possible.

More important than the hugely oversimplified contrast between an experimental, sceptical science and an unexperimental, "dogmatic" traditional mode of thought is the difference in images of knowledge that are represented in the differences in the social organisation of inquiry in modern as opposed to "traditional" societies. Scientists, like the rest of us, hold onto theories longer than they may be entitled to, suppress – unconsciously or half consciously – evidence they do not know how to handle, lie a little; in pre-colonial societies there were, we can be sure, individual doubters who kept their own counsel, resisters against the local dogma. But what is interesting about modern modes of theorising is that they are organised around an image of constant change: we expect new theories, we reward and encourage the search for them, we believe that today's best theories will be revised beyond recognition if the enterprise of science survives. My ancestors in Asante never organised a specialised activity that was based around this thought. They knew that some people know more than others, and that there are things to be found out. But they did not seem to have thought it necessary to invest social effort in working out new theories of how the world works – not for some practical end (this they did constantly) but, as we say, for its own sake.

The differences between traditional religious theory and the theories of the sciences reside in the social organisation of inquiry, as a systematic business, and it is differences in social organisation that account both for the difference we feel in the character of natural scientific and traditional religious theory – they are the products of different kinds of social process – and for the spectacular expansion of the domain of successful prediction and control, an expansion that characterises natural science but is notably absent in traditional society. Experimentation, the publication and reproduction of results, the systematic development of alternative theories in precise terms – all these ideals, however imperfectly they are realised in scientific practice, are intelligible only in an organised social enterprise of knowledge.

But what can have prompted this radically different approach to knowledge? Why have the practitioners of traditional religion, even the priests, who are the professionals, never developed the organised "adversarial" methods of the sciences? There are, no doubt, many historical sources. A few, familiar suggestions strike one immediately. Social mobility leads to political individualism of a kind that is rare in the traditional polity: political individualism allows cognitive authority to shift, also, from priest and king to commoner; and social mobility is a feature of industrial societies.

Or, in traditional societies, accommodating conflicting theoretical views is part of the general process of accommodation necessary for those who are bound to each other as neighbours for life. I remember once discussing differences in cultural style between Ghana and America with a fellow Ghanaian and an American. The American student asked what had struck us both as the most important cultural difference between Ghana and the United States when we first arrived. "You are so aggressive," said my Ghanaian friend, "in Ghana, we would not think that very good manners." Of course, what he had noticed was not aggression, but simply a different conversational style. In Ghana, but not in America, it is impolite to disagree, to argue, to confute. And this accommodating approach to conversation is part of the same range of attitudes that leads to theoretical accommodations.

We could mention more differences in social, economic, and ecological background, which together might help to account for this difference in approach to theory. But it seems to me that there is one other major fundamental difference between traditional West African culture and the culture of the industrial world, and that it plays a fundamental role in explaining why the adversarial style never established itself in West Africa. It is that these cultures were largely non-literate.

Now literacy has, as Jack Goody (1971) points out in his influential book *The domestication of the savage mind*, important consequences; among them is the fact that it permits a kind of consistency that oral culture cannot and does not demand. Write down a sentence and it is there, in principle, forever; that means that if you write down another sentence inconsistent with it, you can be caught out. It is this fact that is at the root of the possibility of the adversarial style. How often have we seen Perry Mason – on television in Ghana or the United States or England (for television, at least, there is only one world) – ask the stenographer to read back from the record? In traditional culture the answer can only be: "What record?" In the absence of written records, it is not possible to compare the ancestor's theories in their actual words with ours; nor, given the limitations of quantity imposed by oral transmission, do we have a detailed knowledge of what those theories were. We know more about the thought of Isaac Newton on one or two subjects than we know about the entire population of his Asante contemporaries.

The accommodative style is possible because orality makes it hard to discover discrepancies. And so it is possible to have an image of knowledge as unchanging lore, handed down from the ancestors. It is no wonder, with this image of knowledge, that there is no systematic research: nobody need ever notice that the way that traditional theory is used requires inconsistent interpretations. It is literacy that makes possible the precise formulation of questions that we have just noted as being one of the characteristics of scientific theory, and it is precise formulation that points up inconsistency. This explanation, which we owe to Horton, is surely very plausible.

Given the orality of traditional culture, it is possible to see how the accommodative approach is maintained. With widespread literacy, the image of knowledge as a body of truths always already given cannot survive. But the recognition of the failures of consistency of the traditional world-view does not automatically lead to science; there are, as I have already observed, many other contributing factors. Without widespread literacy it is hard to see how science could have got started: it is not a sufficient condition for science, but it certainly seems necessary. What else, apart from a lot of luck, accounts for the beginnings of modern science? So many things: the Reformation, itself dependent not merely on literacy but also on printing and the wider dissemination of the Bible and other religious writings, with its transfer of cognitive authority from the Church to the individual; the experience of mechanisation, of machinery, in agriculture and warfare; the development of universities. My claim is not that literacy explains modern science (China is a standing refutation of that claim); it is that it was crucial to its possibility. And the very low level of its literacy shaped the intellectual possibilities of pre-colonial Africa.

For literacy has other significant consequences. Those of us who read and write learn very quickly how different in style written communication is from oral; we learn it so early and so well that we need to be reminded of some of the differences – reminded, in fact, of the differences that are really important. Here is one, whose consequences for the intellectual life of literate peoples are, I think, considerable. Suppose you found a scrap of paper, which contained the following words: "On Sundays here, we often do what Joe is doing over there. But it is not normal to do it on *this* day. I asked the priest whether it was permissible to do it today and he just did this." A reasonable assumption would be that you were reading a transcription of words someone had spoken. And why? Because all these words – *here, there, this, today,* and even *Joe* and *the priest* – are what logicians call *indexicals.* You need the context in which the sentence is uttered to know what they are referring to.

Every English speaker knows that "I" refers to the speaker, "you" to his/her audience; that *here* and *now* refer to the place and time of the utterance. And when we hear someone speak we are usually in a position to identify speaker and audience, place and time. But when we write we have to fill in much of what the context provides when we speak. We have to do this not only so that we avoid the uncertainty of indexicals, but because we cannot assume that our readers will share our knowledge of our situation, and because, if they do not, they cannot ask us. But thinking about this – and trying to rephrase speech into writing to meet these demands – is bound to move you toward the abstract and the universal, and away from the concrete and the particular.

To see why literacy moves you toward universality in your language, consider the difference between the judgements of a traditional oracle and those of experts in a written tradition. A traditional thinker can get away with saying that if three oracles have answered that Kwame has engaged in adultery, then he has. But in a written tradition, all sorts of problems can arise. After all, everybody knows of cases where the oracles have been wrong three times because they were interfered with by witchcraft. To escape this problem, the literate theorist has to formulate principles not just for the particular case, but more generally. Rather than saying, "Three oracles have spoken: it is so" – or, as the Akan proverb has it, *Obosom anim, yeko no mprensa* (One consults a spirit three times) – he/she will have to say something like the following: "Three oracles constitute good *prima facie* evidence that something is so; but they may have been interfered with by witchcraft. This is to be revealed by such and such means. If they have been interfered with by witchcraft, it is necessary first to purify the oracle" – and so on, listing those qualifying clauses that we recognise as the mark of written scholarship.

And to see why literacy moves you toward abstraction in your language, listen to traditional proverbs, orally transmitted. Take the Akan proverb, *Abe a eto nyinaa na efifiri a, anka obi rennya dua ase kwan,* which means (literally), "If all seeds that fall were to grow, then no one could follow the path under the trees." Its message is (usually) that if everyone were prosperous, no one would work. But it talks of seeds, trees, and paths through the forest. The message is abstract, but the wording is concrete. The concreteness makes the proverb memorable – and in oral tradition all that is carried on is carried on in memory; there are, as I said, no records. But it also means that to understand the message – as I am sure only Twi-speaking people did before I explained it – you have to share with the speaker a knowledge of his/her background assumptions to a fairly specific extent. The proverb works because, in traditional societies, you talk largely with people you know; all the assumptions that are needed to unpack a proverb are shared. And it is because they are shared that the language of oral exchange can be indexical, metaphorical, context-dependent.

Write, then, and the demands imposed by the distant, unknown reader require more universality, more abstraction. Because our reader may not share the cultural assumptions necessary to understand them, in contexts where the communication of information is central, our written language becomes less figurative. And so another nail is hammered into the coffin of the inconsistencies of our informal thought.

For if we speak figuratively, then what we say can be taken and reinterpreted in a new context; the same proverb, precisely because its message is not fixed, can be used again and again. And if we can use it again and again with different messages, we may fail to notice that the messages are inconsistent with each other. After all, the proverb is being used *now* in *this* situation, so why should we think of those other occasions of its use *here* and *now?*

The impulse to abstract and universal and away from figurative language, and the recognition of the failures of consistency of the traditional world-view do not automatically lead to science; there are, as I have already observed, many other contributing factors. But, like literacy itself, these traits of literate cultures, while not sufficient to make for science, are ones it is hard to imagine science doing without.

In characterising the possibilities of literacy, there is, as we have seen in many of the attempts to oppose tradition and modernity, a risk of overstating the case; our modernity, indeed, consists in part in our wishing to see ourselves as different from our ancestors. The communities of specialised knowledge that produce new physics and new ecology and new chemistry are small worlds of their own, with complex codes and practices into which *ephebes* (novices) are inducted, not merely by the transmission of writings. Literate culture is still the culture of people who speak, and the mark of the autodidact, the person who has only book learning, is an unfamiliarity with the context of conversation needed to make a sound professional judgement. Physics textbooks do not tell you how to operate in the sociology and politics of the lab, and nowhere will you find it written exactly what it is about the major theorists in a field that makes their work important. More than this, the kind of checking for consistency that writing (and, now, the computer) makes possible is no guarantee that this possibility will be actualised or that, once inconsistencies are identified (as they seem to have been at the heart of the quantum theory), it will be clear what to do about them.

On the other hand, there are many devices for supporting the transmission of a complex and nuanced body of practice and belief without writing. In Asante, for example, the figurative brass weights used for weighing gold dust are associated with proverbs that they represent in ways that mean that the daily conduct of trade offered reminders of ideas of society and nature; and the same sorts of cultural coding are found in the patterns imprinted on the *Adinkra* cloth, or carved into our stools.

Still, intellectual style in cultures without widely distributed literacy was for that reason radically different from the style of contemporary literate cultures. And, complex as the real story is, the sorts of differences I have been discussing are real and have been important. Literacy, then, makes possible the "modern" image of knowledge as something that is constantly being remade; what drives the culture to take up this possibility is, I believe, the economic logic of modernity.

Once it *did* start, scientific activity followed the pattern of all other activity in industrial society: it became subject to the division of labour. Firstly, a class of scientists; then of biologists, then of zoologists, then of embryologists, in an endless hierarchy of proliferating species. This differentiation has its own important consequences for the nature of science and those theories that are its product. The division of labour in the West is so highly developed that, as Hilary Putnam has pointed out, we even leave the task of understanding some parts of our language to experts: it is because words like *electron* have precise meanings for physicists that I, who have no very good grasp of their meaning, can use them, and the same goes for the word *contract* with regard to lawyers. These words, as my tools, only do their business for me because their meanings are sharpened by others.

The literacy of the period immediately preceding the scientific revolution in Europe differed in at least one crucial respect from that of the High Middle Ages and of antiquity: it was beginning to be widespread. Through printing it had become possible for people other than clerics and the very rich to own books. There are many factors – some of which I have already mentioned – that made possible the breakdown of the cognitive authority of the Church in the Reformation, but for the purposes of a comparison with contemporary Africa, indeed with the contemporary developing world, printing, and the independence of mind that it breeds, is crucial.

We all know of the significance of printing in the spread of the Bible – it based Protestantism in the European Reformation, but the importance of widespread literacy for modern Africa was anticipated in nineteenth-century Asante. Some at the Asante court in the late nineteenth century were opposed to the transcription of their language, in part because they were able, in a nation without literacy, to maintain, as they thought, greater control of the flow of information. When they did want to send written messages, they used the literate Islamic scholars who were to be found in the major towns of the West African interior, relying on translation from Twi into Arabic or Hausa, and then back into the language of their correspondents. Now, only a hundred or so years later, a significant majority of the children of Kumasi can write in English and (to a lesser extent) in Twi. And they can read books from libraries and newspapers and pamphlets on the street, which effectively make it impossible for the authority of Asante tradition to remain unchallenged.

Let me say, finally, why I think that the gap between educated Africans and Westerners may not be so wide for much longer, and why all of us will soon find it hard to know, from within, the nature of the traditional. The answer is simple enough: we now have a few generations of literate African intellectuals, and they have begun the process of examining our traditions. They are aided in this by the availability of Western traditions, their access to which, through writing, is no different from that of Westerners. This process of analysis will produce new, unpredictable fusions. Sometimes, something will have to give. What it will be, I cannot predict, though I have my suspicions, and you will be able to guess what they are if I say that it seems to me that the overwhelming political and economic domination of the third world by the industrialised world will play its part.

The fact that our culture's future has the chance of being guided by a theoretical grasp of our situation is an extraordinary opportunity. In 1882 William Lecky, an English scholar, published his *History of the rise and influence of the spirit of rationalism in Europe*. Lecky writes:

> If we ask why it is that the world has rejected what was once so universally and intensely believed, why a narrative of an old woman who had been seen riding on a broomstick, or who was proved to have transformed herself into a wolf, and to have devoured the flocks of her neighbours, is deemed so entirely incredible, most persons would probably be unable to give a very definite answer to the question. It is not always because we have examined the evidence and found it insufficient (1914:8–9).

When I first came across this passage it struck me at once as wonderfully apt to the situation of African intellectuals today. This paragraph records a sense that the intellectual secularisation of Lecky's culture – the "growth of rationalism" – occurred without a proper examination of the evidence. I have enough faith in the life of reason to believe that Africans will have better prospects if we do not follow that example. And we have the great advantage of having before us the European and American – and the Asian and Latin American – experiments with modernity to ponder as we make our choices.

Why should the issues I have discussed be thought important? There are, for me, two reasons: a practical one (for us Africans), and a moral one (for everybody). The moral one is simple: unless all of us understand each other, and understand each other as reasonable, we shall not treat each other with the proper respect. Concentrating on the non-cognitive features of traditional religions not only misrepresents them but also leads to an underestimation of the role of reason in the life of traditional cultures.

The practical reason is this. Most Africans, now, whether converted to Islam or Christianity or not, still share the beliefs of their ancestors in an ontology of invisible beings. (This is, of course, true of many Europeans and Americans as well.) There is a story – probably apocryphal – of some missionaries in northern Nigeria who were worried about the level of infant mortality due to stomach infections transmitted in drinking water. They explained to "converts" at the mission that the deaths were due to tiny animals in the water, and that these animals would be killed only if they boiled the water before giving it to the children. Talk of invisible animals produced only a tolerant scepticism: the babies went on dying. Finally a visiting anthropologist suggested a remedy. There were, he said, evil spirits in the water; boil the water and you could see them going away, bubbling out to escape the heat. This time the message worked. These people were "converts"; for the missionaries' appeal to spirits was an appeal to demons, to what the New Testament calls "principalities and powers". For the "converts", the Christian message was from the High God they had known existed (there is a king in every kingdom, then why not among the spirits?), and the injunction to abjure other spirits was a reflection only of the usual jealousy of the priests of one god toward those of another.

It is this belief in the plurality of invisible spiritual forces that makes possible the – to Western eyes – extraordinary spectacle of a Catholic bishop praying at a Methodist wedding in tandem with traditional royal appeal to the ancestors. For most of the participants at the wedding, God can be addressed in different styles – Methodist, Catholic, Anglican, Moslem, traditional – and the ancestors can be addressed also. Details about the exact nature of the Eucharist, about any theological issues, are unimportant: these are theoretical questions, and theory is unimportant when the practical issue is getting God on one's side. After all, who needs a theory about who it is that one is talking to, if one hears a voice speak?

These beliefs in invisible agents mean that most Africans cannot fully accept those scientific theories in the West that are inconsistent with it. I do not believe, despite what many appear to think, that this is a reason for shame or embarrassment. But it *is* something to think about. If modernisation is conceived of, in part, as the acceptance of science, we have to decide whether we think the evidence obliges us to give up the invisible ontology. We can easily be misled here by the accommodation between science and religion that has occurred among educated people in the industrialised world in general, and in the United States in particular. For this has involved a considerable limitation of the domains in which it is permissible for intellectuals to invoke spiritual agency. The question regarding how much of the world of the spirits we intellectuals must give up (or transform into something ceremonial without the old literal ontology) is one we must face; and I do not think the answer is obvious.

The narrator of Ake Loba's *Kocoumbo, l'etudiant noir* says:

> *Tout Africain qui voulait faire quelque chose de positif devait commencer par détruire toutes ces vieilles croyances qui consistent à creer le merveilleux là où il n'y a que phénomène natural: volcan, forêt vierge, foudre, soleil,* etc. (1980:141).[3]

But even if we agreed that all our old beliefs were superstitions, we should need principles to guide our choices of new ones. Furthermore, there is evidence that the practical successes of technology, associated with the methods and motives of inquiry that I have suggested, are largely absent in traditional culture. The question whether we ought to adopt these methods is not a purely technical one. We cannot avoid the issue of whether it is possible to adopt adversarial, individualistic cognitive styles, and keep, as we might want to, accommodative, communitarian morals. Cultures and peoples have often not been capable of maintaining such double standards (and I use the term non-pejoratively, for perhaps we need different standards for different purposes), so that if we are going to try, we must face up to these difficulties. Scientific method may lead to progress in our understanding of the world, but one does not have to be a Thoreauvian to wonder if it has led to progress only in the pursuit of all our human purposes. In this area we can learn together with other cultures – including, for example, the Japanese culture, which has apparently managed a certain segregation of moral-political and cognitive spheres. In this respect, it seems to me obvious that the Ghanaian philosopher Kwasi Wiredu is right. We will only solve our problems if we see them as human problems arising out of a special situation, and we shall not solve them if we see them as African problems, generated by our being somehow unlike others.

NOTES

1. A first approach to the phenomena of magic and witchcraft would be to suppose that we are faced with symbolic language. . . . A man flying through the air, who transforms himself into an animal, or makes himself invisible whenever he wants to . . . could be nothing more than a coded language of which we would simply have to find the key. We would thus be reassured.

2. Without forgetting its limits, or halting the march of progress, science, and liberation, one has to admit that the African explanation of the phenomena of magic and witchcraft is rational. Our popular beliefs are undeniably disconcerting, sometimes false, but would it not be a serious methodological error to postulate the irrational from the outset when studying a society?
    (Translated by Norman Strike, Department of Romance Languages, Unisa.)
3. Any African who wanted to do something positive had to start by destroying all these old beliefs which consisted in creating marvels where there was only a natural phenomenon, a volcano, virgin forest, thunder, sun, etc.
    (Translated by Thomas Tschiggfrey, Department of Romance Languages, Unisa.)

REFERENCES

Achebe, C. 1982. "Interview with Anthony Appiah", in D.A.N. Jones & J. Ryle, *Times Literary Supplement*, 26 February 1982: 209.

Appiah, K.A. 1992. *In my father's house: Africa in the philosophy of culture*. New York: Oxford University Press.

Aristotle. 1975. *Posterior analytics*. Book 1. Oxford: Clarendon.

Barnes, B. & Bloor, D. 1982. "Relativism, nationalism, sociology of knowledge", in M. Hollis and S. Lukes (eds), *Rationality and relativism*. Oxford: Blackwell 1982:21–47.

Blanshard B. 1967. "Wisdom", in P. Edwards (ed.), *Encyclopedia of philosophy*. Vol. 8. London: Macmillan, 1967:322–324.

Buber, M. 1958. *I and Thou*. Tr. R.G. Smith. New York: Scribner.

Carroll, L. 1995 (1895) "What the tortoise said to Achilles." *Mind*, 104(416):691–693.

Coquery-Vidrovitch, C. 1976. "The political economy of the African peasantry and modes of production", in P.C.W. Gutkind & I. Wallerstein (eds), *The political economy of contemporary Africa*. Beverly Hills: Sage, 1976:94–116.

Davidson, D. 1982. "On the very idea of a conceptual scheme." *Proceedings of the American Philosophical Association*, 1982:47:5–20.

Davidson, D. 1982. "On the very idea of a conceptual scheme", in M. Hollis and S. Lukes (eds), *Rationality and relativism*. Oxford: Blackwell.

Dennett, D.C. 1987. *The intentional stance*. Cambridge: Bradford.

Evans-Pritchard, E.E. 1976. *Witchcraft, oracles and magic among the Azande*. Oxford: Oxford University Press.

Geertz, C. 1973. *The interpretation of cultures*. New York: Basic Books.

Goody, J. 1971. *The domestication of the savage mind*. Cambridge: Cambridge University Press.

Griaule, M. 1965. *Conversations with Ogotemmeli*. Oxford: Oxford University Press.

Griaule, M. 1970. *Dieu d'eau: Entretiens avec Ogotemmeli*. Frankfurt: Herder.

Hallen, B. 1977. "Robin Horton on critical philosophy and traditional thought." *Second order*, 6:81–92.

Hallen, B. & Sodipo, J. 1986. *Knowledge, belief and witchcraft*. London: Ethnographica.

Hegba, M.P. 1979. *Sorcellereie: Chimère dangereuse . . .?* Abidjan: Inades.

Hollis, M. 1970. "Reason and rituals", in B.R. Wilson (ed.), 1970:231–239.

Horton, R. n.d. *Traditional thought and the emerging African philosophy department: A reply to Dr Hallen*. Unpublished manuscript.

Horton, R. 1967. "African traditional religion and Western science." *Africa*, 37(1):50–71 & (2):155–187.

Horton, R. 1972. "Spiritual beings and elementary particles – a reply to Mr Pratt." *Second order*, 1:21–33.

Jarvie, I.C. 1972. *Concepts and society*. London: Routledge & Kegan Paul.

Koyre, A. 1980. *From the closed world to the infinite universe*. Frankfurt am Main: Sührkamp.

Kuhn, T.S. 1970. *The structure of scientific revolutions*. Chicago: University of Chicago Press.

Lecky, W. 1914. History of the rise and influence of the spirit of rationalism in Europe. Vol. 1. New York: Appleton.

Lévy-Bruhl, L. 1923. *Primitive mentality.* London: Allen & Unwin.

Loba, A. 1980. *Kocoumbo, l'étudiant noir.* Paris: Flammarion.

Lukes, S. 1970. "Some problems about rationality", in B.R. Wilson (ed.), 1970:208–213.

Lukes, S. 1982. "Relativism in its place", in M. Hollis & S. Lukes (eds), *Rationality and relativism.* Oxford: Blackwell, 1982:261–305.

Mayer, P. 1972. *Townsmen and tribesmen.* Cape Town: Cambridge University Press.

Miller, R. 1987. *Fact and method.* Princeton: Princeton University Press.

Mounce, H.O. 1973. "Understanding a primitive society." *Philosophy*, 48(186):147–162.

Novack, G. 1975. *An introduction to the logic of Marxism.* New York: Pathfinder.

Oruka, O. 1983. "Sagacity in African philosophy." *International Philosophical Quarterly*, 22(4):383–393.

Oruka, O. 1987. "African philosophy: A brief personal history and current debate", in G. Floistad, *Contemporary philosophy: A new survey.* Vol. 5. *African philosophy.* Dordrecht: Nijhoff, 1987:45–77.

Otubanjo, F. 1983. "Rationality and irrationality in anthropoligical theories of religion." *Ibadan Journal of humanistic studies.* 3:99–112.

Popper, K. 1972. *Conjectures and refutations.* London: Routledge.

Price, H.H. 1967. "Some considerations about belief", in Griffiths (ed.), *Knowledge and belief.* Oxford: Oxford University Press, 1967:41–59.

Pritchard, H.A. 1967. "Knowing and believing", in A.P. Griffiths (ed.), *Knowledge and belief.* Oxford: Oxford University Press, 1967:60–68.

Rattray, R.S. 1955. *Ashanti.* London: Oxford University Press.

Russell, B. 1948. *Human knowledge: Its scope and limits.* London: Allen & Unwin.

Russell, B. 1966. *Philosophical essays.* London: Allen & Unwin.

Sheldrake, R. 1981. *A new science of life: The hypothesis of formative causation.* London: Paladin. New Editions.

Skorupski, J. 1976. *Symbol and theory.* Cambridge: Cambridge University Press.

Sogolo, G. 1993. *Foundations of African philosophy.* Ibadan: Ibadan University Press.

Tarski, A. 1956. *Logic, semantics, metamathematics.* Oxford: Clarendon.

Thomas, K. 1971. *Religion and the decline of magic.* London: Weidenfeld & Nicolson.

Tillich, P. 1951. *Systematic theology.* Vol. 1. Chicago: University of Chicago Press.

Tylor, E.B. 1924. *Primitive culture.* New York: Brentano's.

Wilde, O. 1982. "Phrases and philosophies for the use of the young", in H.M. Hyde (ed.), *The annotated Oscar Wilde.* New York: Clarkson N. Potter, 1982:418–419.

Wilson, B.R. (ed.) 1970. *Rationality.* Oxford: Blackwell.

Winch, P. 1958. *The idea of a social science and its relation to philosophy.* New York: Routledge & Kegan Paul.

Wiredu, K. 1980. *Philosophy and an African culture.* Cambridge: Cambridge University Press.

Wiredu, K. 1995. "The need for conceptual decolonization in African philosophy", in O. Oladipo (ed.), *Conceptual decolonization in African philosophy.* Ibadan: Hope, 1995:22–32.

CHAPTER SIX

Particularity in Morality and its Relation to Community

PIETER H. COETZEE

1. INTRODUCTION

Usually moral controversies are addressed from a particular standpoint within one of two broad approaches. The first takes the concrete circumstances of moral agents to be decisive, thus offering decision procedures which run on such particularist contingencies as ethnicity, race, gender, culture, and language. The second approach abstracts from these circumstances in an attempt to find a universal standpoint, one that operates with a minimal definition of what is morally relevant, such as rationality or human nature or the common factors in our understanding of moral problems.

The second of these broad approaches disclaims the possibility of particularism, though there are at least three possible ways in which its attempts to give substance to universalism may be understood. According to one line of argument, rationality is the only attribute of human cognition which has moral relevance. Humans are simply systems of rationality and nothing more; all social and cultural particularities are mere morally irrelevant contingency. The right answers to moral controversies are the ones which rational agents in a given description of circumstances would endorse, not only for themselves, but for all other rational agents situated as they are (in relevantly similar circumstances) – simply on grounds of their common rationality. Another line of argument proceeds on the premise that moral questions are resolvable with reference to the notion of "the human condition", which is generally defended as empirically established commonalities with regard to the beings we are – "facts" about our common human nature. The fulfilment of certain basic needs (e.g. health, happiness, etc.) are treated as necessary conditions for humans to flourish, thus offering a cross-cultural grounding for morality, one which transcends whatever is accorded highest value in actual historical or cultural communities. Yet another line of argument attempts to root a form of universalism in the convergence of our common understanding of core moral propositions – propositions which prohibit things like murder, deception, betrayal, cruelty, torture, etc. It is possible – so it is argued – to extract a core of universal moral principles from this "common understanding" and to ground a trans-cultural morality on it.

The first of our broad approaches places morality on a particularist footing, and treats moral theory as perspective driven. In the African context the idea of a perspectival model is ascendant. Perspectival models fragment the moral geography, making moral philosophy radically pluralistic and heterogeneous. This fragmentation is reflected in two poles of opposition – between attempts to construct ethnic and non-ethnic perspectival models and between "left" and "right" interpretations of moral (communitarian) theory.

2.   SOME NECESSARY DEFINITIONS

The possibility of constructing perspectival models assumes the truth of two theses:
1. Philosophy (in Africa) is culture-specific (there is no African philosophy which is not a product of cultural construction).
2. The moral domain admits a multiplicity of moral orders (there is no single moral order for all human beings).

A proper understanding of what these theses entail requires that we begin with definitions of concepts we must know to understand the idea of a perspectival model. At bottom, the notion of a perspectival model turns on other notions: culture, community, tradition, and the all-important idea of self-understanding.

The preferred and most useful definition of *culture* in the context of African philosophy is one which treats culture as a resource. Culture is an open-ended resource of social meanings upon which members of a community draw to mediate the contingencies of their everyday lives.[1] A culture denotes the resources of a community's material and moral[2] worlds. It is through these resources that a certain group of people delimits itself as a cultural group. Delimitation implies drawing a boundary between members and strangers. Drawing a boundary implies a recognition that members owe certain things to each other which they do not owe to strangers (or do not owe strangers to the same degree). They owe to each other mutual provision of all those things for the sake of which they have separated themselves from everyone else and joined forces in the particular community which they in fact make up.[3]

The idea of mutual provision suggests the following definition of *community*: a community is an ongoing association of men and women who have a special commitment to one another and a developed (distinct) sense of their common life. The *common life* is any public discursive space which members construct through action-in-concert. It is constituted by a particular set of social meanings – i.e. shared understandings and interpretations of events to which members have access through their participation in the creation of their commonality. A communal or social identity is the community's characteristic way of life, one which members have sustained over some considerable period of time as an integrated cultural whole and to which members stand in a dialogical relation.

A *dialogical relation* supplies an interactive context which serves two purposes: first and foremost it is the context in and through which members actualise their social identity. The history of a person's life is the story of his/her transactions with the community's material and moral worlds, which, in effect, is the story of his/her relations with particular sets of social goods. Goods acquire social meaning from actual patterns of distribution,[4] and their meanings regulate social relations, which implies that the common life is a function of the distributive patterns and the social meanings of social goods. Secondly, an interactive context of the kind we have just considered is not only a determinant of (social) identity; it is also a determinant of choice.[5] Since the goods available to members are all goods *internal* to particular social structures, choice is ultimately informed by the accumulated cultural capital. It is only within a culturally specified range of options that persons make decisions, for example about life-plans. If all this is correct, identity and choice have cash-value for members with reference to particular sets of social meanings.

Choice and identity are informed by a community's accumulated cultural capital through the agency of a *tradition*. A tradition is a historically extended socially embedded narrative about the systems of thought (moral, political, epistemological, etc.) and social practices of a specific community.[6] The idea of a historically extended narrative stresses the role of traditions in contemporary community which lies in the possibility traditions create for interpretative continuity: the possibility of reinterpretation of exemplars from history connects contemporary events with the past, which means that the social meaning of any particular tradition is always open-ended. According to one moral tradition to which we shall pay attention, a society is just if its social life is lived in accordance with its own self-understanding.[7] Such a tradition links justice to culture, thus yielding a cultural account of morality.

Traditions embody standards of excellence. We shall treat the idea of a commonality as a substantive conception of the good which defines a community's way of life. We shall accordingly treat the standards of a tradition as constitutive – in a substantive sense – of moral and political precepts. If this is correct members cannot be said to know their good prior to social interaction, and experience their good as constitutively bound to the good of the community. It follows that they look to community to understand their ends, and this is an appeal to the *self-*understanding of a community. Self-understanding is the logical product of shared understandings. Shared understandings are the bedrock of a community's cultural capital, providing at any given time in history

1.   an interpretative framework for the generation of social meaning;
2.   a marker for the boundaries of social and moral identity; and
3.   a conception of the social processes by which material and moral goods are produced and distributed.

The integrated sum of these things we shall call a community's self-understanding.

3.   THE PARTICULARITY OF A COMMUNITARIAN PERSPECTIVAL MODEL

Our typification of a communitarian morality will proceed in terms of the idea of social meanings rather than in terms of the moral codes specified by customary law.

This way of proceeding will help us to establish two central lines of thought, one centring on the idea of a social practice, the other on practical reason:

1. a community's moral life is lived in conformity to established practices; and
2. models of the good life can be contested through culturally generated forms of criticism.

3.1 Social conditions which unite a community's social and moral identity

The particularity of one kind of communitarian model is perhaps best exemplified by examining some of the essential social conditions which unite a community's *social* and *moral* identity[8].

3.1.1 The social thesis

It is a major assumption of the approach adopted here that the capacity for moral choice and development can only be exercised in a cultural setting which makes provision for its growth. Let us call this the social thesis. The social thesis describes the *self*-understanding of one kind of community and, as formulated below, shows one sense of the social meaning of a communitarian standpoint. According to the social thesis, an individual's choice of way of life is a choice constrained by the community's pursuit of shared ends. This pursuit of the common good is the primary goal of the political community and always takes precedence over the pursuit of individually chosen ends. Communal ends cannot – all other things being equal – be overridden or vetoed because shared ends have much greater weight (value) in the life of the community than other ends. The common good is conceived of as a good which fits the patterns of preferences of individual members; it is not a single good, but many goods, each fitting a sphere of social life and resting on a consensus (agreement) about its value. The common good, then, defines substantive conceptions about the good life – identified for application in specific social contexts. The good life for an individual is conceived of as coinciding with the good of the community, and a person's choice is highly or lowly ranked according to whether it contributes to or detracts from the common good.[9]

3.1.2 The role of language

The social thesis describes a linguistic community. A linguistic community has a history and various traditions (of morality and reasoning) which inform the narratives of individuals' lives and link them to those of their ancestors. Languages embody distinctive ways of experiencing the world and so play a crucial role in defining the experiences of a community as *their* particular experiences. Since language is a determinant of a particular outlook, it is one significant factor that shapes a way of life. Speakers communicate with each other about their common history and have access to the significance of events in it in a way not communicable to non-speakers, or in other languages. This means that language is never just a neutral medium for communication or for identifying the contents of actions – rather language itself is content, a value-laden reference for communal loyalties and animosities[10].

3.1.3 Dialogical relation

The social thesis also describes a community of mutuality, one in which each member stands in a dialogical relation to other members, i.e. a relation which requires the recognition of reciprocal obligations. In a community of mutuality members recognise that since the (personal) projects they pursue – through which they give meaning to their lives – are projects made available by a cultural structure, they have – all other things being equal – a duty to sustain these structures. Insofar as the recognition of the need to preserve a cultural context is the prerequisite of a meaningful life, it derives from the social meaning of a socially embedded notion of obligation. We are here interested in two kinds of socially embedded obligation. Primary obligations are owed to people connected through kinship relations. The boundaries of kinship structures mark the boundaries of a member's (primary) moral obligations (who owes what to whom). Moral differentiations are embedded in social meanings: primary obligations, as distinct from secondary obligations (which are owed only to strangers), rest on a correlation between distributive patterns of social goods and filial relations which determine that distribution proceeds in accordance with what kin and kinship groups owe one another (loyalty, respect, honour, etc.)[11].

3.1.4 *The community is the locus of deontology*

According to the social thesis the community (and not individual members) is the locus of deontology[12]. Argument about morality and reason takes place within traditions. A major assumption of this attempt to contextualise argument is that beliefs about morality and reason cannot successfully be justified outside of actual ways of life and the social meanings embodied in them. We cannot, for example, understand Akan beliefs about human rights without seeing how their conception is linked to their understanding of the relationship between the ontology of the human person and a system of entitlements; differentiation in the distribution of rights is rooted in differentiation in the ontological make-up of humans, a differentiation that ultimately stems from kinship relations in the Akan social structure[13]. Nor, for example, can we understand Akan beliefs about justice without first seeing their understanding of the relationship between practical reason and the social meaning of consensus. It is only within a system of agreements, making possible agreed actions without agreed notions, that rational questioning in moral and political traditions takes place[14]. A moral/political tradition will include an account of what (moral/political) reasonable belief and good reasoning is. There is no single African perspective on the problem of conflict resolution in this context. But Akan social meanings give recognition to a central idea: tension between tradition and critical reasoning must be looked at from a perspective which gives weight to social practice and to practical reason[15]. The tension at issue here is a familiar one: the longer a particular interpretation of a social practice goes back in time, the greater its historical significance. Traditions embody many years of communal effort and thought, and it is unlikely that a deeply held view will have failed to get something right regarding truth. But though deeply held views have historical depth in the sense just outlined, they are open to reinterpretation. Open-endedness is a general feature of African traditions, so there is in principle no difficulty with reinterpreting the notion of "deeply held" to mean what is currently of great importance or significance for a community (even if this conflicts with the commitments of a community's ancestors).

3.2 Practical reason for self-in-community

So, what is this perspective which balances reason against practice in the social meanings of Akan culture? The social thesis sketched above must now be amplified. We begin by noting that membership of Akan society informs attempts at self-understanding and shapes self-identity insofar as personhood is something that has to be acquired (by becoming a member of society). According to this view – called the "processual" view of the self – the concept of a person is a social concept[16]. Humans (Akans) undergo a process of social transformation until they attain full status as persons, and during this process of attainment the community plays the vital role of catalyst – of the prescriber of ends. Achieving the status of personhood is conditional on social achievements which contribute to the common good. For instance, the pursuit of a life of confirmed celibacy is regarded as failing in respect of perpetuation of the lineage (unless due to impotence), and so as deserving of moral condemnation. Similarly, any adult male who fails amply to provide for his household fails to make a contribution to his lineage and so is subject to moral disapprobation. These failures are treated as instances of a general failure to live up to a moral precept which enjoins that all action ought to be directed at the harmonisation of the interests of community members, which precept governs all interpersonal relations.

Not all humans (Akans) become persons in the normative sense just outlined. The potential to acquire personhood is given biologically. So the normative meaning of being a person has an ontological basis which is the same for everyone, and which is the ground for assigning rights and their corresponding obligations. A human is born from the union of a man and a woman. The woman contributes the *mogya* (the blood) and the man the *ntora* (the semen). These biological constituents of a person have social significance, the *mogya* being the basis of lineage identity and the *ntora* the basis of membership of a kinship group. The unity of social and moral identity is reflected in the fact that lineage identities and kinship groupings are the loci of sets of rights and obligations. We may picture the lineage as a series of concentric circles of (matrilineal) kinship relations, each circle being a set of rights and obligations and connected to other circles through the "blood" ties of kinship, the whole being (or representing) various levels of relationships between lineage members.

Once integrated into a social structure, a person becomes the bearer of rights. The specifics of the structure determine his/her rights (and the corresponding obligations). The rights in question are all "role"-rights[17]. For example, to be a rights bearer requires a place in a social structure, and so rights can only be awarded to, and exercised by, persons occupying specific social roles. In this context rights are understood as justified entitlements: they are akin to statutes determining appropriate actions with respect to the distribution and reception of the material and moral goods of Akan society (who receives what from whom, and who owes what to someone else). They are justified with reference to the communal welfare, which is the final court of appeal in cases of conflict, the idea being that the harmonisation of the interests of the community best secures optimal utility in respect of the overall welfare.

The social meaning of a "role"-right is a pattern of distribution of a social good within a social structure which determines the entitlements of the inhabitant of a structured role. Two examples (see Wiredu 1992a:84 & Wiredu 1992b:107) may help to illuminate this point. Kinship is the highest value in Akan culture and lineage the most significant kinship grouping (because Akan society is matrilineal). But infants also have a social link to a patrilineal kinship group, which is acquired through the *ntora*, and which entitles the child during adolescence to receive sexual education from the father's sister. Similarly, by virtue of internal constitution, this time through the *mogya*, which secures membership of a lineage, every adult male has a right to land. Exercising this right devolves on performing duties: to sustain a household and make contributions to the welfare of the lineage through the products of his labour, i.e. conforming to an appropriate pattern of behaviour.

The force of the idea of an appropriate pattern of behaviour, implicit in exercising a "role"-right, comes to this[18]: there is a connection between the good of a person *qua* aunt, father, educator, provider, etc. and his/her good *qua* specific pattern of behaviour and/or action of educating, providing, etc. – a connection such that were an aunt not to educate, or a father not to provide, he or she would either

1. be denying that educating or providing was for his/her good *qua* aunt or father, or
2. be acting as a person who does not care about his/her good *qua* member of the lineage.

The connection is given by a social meaning which inheres in a structured role and which defines the good of the person *qua* inhabitor of that role, or *qua* member of the lineage. If (1), an appeal to the self-understanding of the community and to consistency (i.e. to attempts within the community to make practice conform to professed ideals) will settle the issue. If (2), an appeal to custom is called for (such persons are customarily designated *onye onipa* (non-persons)). The connection, given by a social meaning, helps us to recognise the necessity for rational action by someone inhabiting a structured role in which the material and moral goods of practice are distributed in accordance with the provisions of a rights-role. The imperative for rationality in the provisions of rights-roles are also the imperatives for rationality in the wider social picture. This is a matter of extrapolation – a rationality contextualised in the specifics of social life presents a picture of how the rational social life is conceptualised. We shall return to this shortly (see 3.3.2).

Social practice can hold rationality to a context, or to be more specific, to a tradition understood as a coherent system of thought. A successfully justified moral belief is one which rests on the unity of social and moral identity and therefore is one that brings together moral conviction and rationality. But though practical reason is tied to social practice, it is not the slave of practice, for practical reason can modify practice. This means that for the traditions within which reason displays itself to be good, they must supply the tools to meet the confrontations and challenges which their encounters with other traditions bring about.

How does reason modify practice? Earlier on we noted that justice is mediated through the relationship between practical reason and the social meaning of consensus. As we shall see, when we examine how rationality tests are generated, this relationship reduces the potential for conflict that may arise between the distributive patterns of specific social goods and the concomitant inconsistency in social practices. Justice – like any other social good – is best approached by examining the social structure within which it is produced and distributed. And the structures that matter here are the ones that make consensus possible[19]. A consensus denotes an agreement about the status of certain kinds of expectations and treatment as *rights.*

In other words, the cash-value of a consensus depends on three interrelated considerations: the consensus must be dominant (i.e. reflect the considered judgement of the collective); it must be in step with the requirements of a communal good; members must affirm that it is constitutive of (and not in conflict with) their moral identity. These considerations determine that consensus as agreement does not require unanimity, but simply a willingness to suspend disagreement, making possible common (political) action. The idea is to make possible "agreed actions without necessarily agreed [substantive] notions" (Oladipo 1995:54). How is it possible that participation in power triumphs over its appropriation? Earlier on we noted that a successfully justified moral belief is one that rests on the unity of social and moral identity and is therefore one that unites moral conviction and rationality. This is possible in a tradition which ranks kinship as its highest value[20]. Traditions which rank kinship highly make it a requirement of a consensus that it must affirm the moral identity of a people. Any agreement which denies moral identity, thereby also denying social identity, is in conflict with established social meanings, and for that reason cannot become a consensus. What does this entail for justice? Justice, it would seem, is the proper (appropriate) ordering of social goods in accordance with the meanings generated by role-structured actions within kinship groupings. And rights fit neatly into this context: they are the expectations of certain treatments which the occupier of a role may claim, and which he/she accords another occupier of a role.

The point made illustrates one sense in which justice is a harmony of social arrangements. But harmony is not given; it has to be worked, i.e. argued, for. Argument is shaped by the relationship between practical reason and consensus, which is informed by an ideological perspective relating to the Akan conception of justice. The form of reasoning employed in consensus bargaining serves a moral, and ultimately a social, end. This end is "the harmonization of the interests of the individual with the interests of others in society" (Oladipo 1995:38) and requires, in the psychology of every rational agent, the motive of sympathetic identification. Wiredu (in Oladipo 1995:36) describes this motive as "a frame of mind which facilitates the mind's ability to contemplate with equanimity the possible abridgement of one's own interests in deference to the interests of others."

Harmonisation as a social end is common to all societies, and morality has to that extent a cross-cultural or non-relativised standard. This standard pushes practical reason into a teleological direction and generates rationality tests[21] which show how consensus works. If there is a conflict between social goods or between their distributive patterns, it has to be shown that a transition from one position to another represents a gain towards the harmonisation of interests (which is a gain in moral understanding).

A gain has been made if the ascendant position can explain how to solve problems that have arisen in the traditional position, and how it can accommodate or incorporate everything in this position which survives scrutiny by critical reasoning. This kind of reasoning or rational questioning goes on in the context of a fixed system of agreements which is a broad consensus about the practical value of reasoning aimed at uniting social and moral identity. The rational strength of a good argument is its persuasiveness to secure actual agreement in this regard. The central experience of morality is then a developed sense of communal unity and harmony. Reason shapes practice by balancing conflicting experiences against interests common to all, thus creating a sphere of shared experience. This area of shared experience forms the basis or the heart of consensus, which is the possibility of common action without agreed notions.

If critical questioning takes place within a fixed system of agreements, then what is moral argument about? Persons inhabiting structured roles, which form the social foundation of their moral and material rights and obligations, are interpreters of the social meanings they inherit. Interpretation itself allows for disagreement and dissent, and this creates the critical space needed for debate about social meanings. Wiredu (Oladipo 1995:33–52) identifies custom as the domain of contested dialogue over prescriptions and proscriptions regarding birth and death, work and leisure time, reward and punishment, relationships between the sexes and the generations[22]. Since moral judgements are relative to lifestyles, the domain of custom admits a relativism of judgements[23] rooted in a multiplicity of perspectives reflecting power differentials or status in the community. Such a relativism of judgements admits differing perspectives from which moral precepts may be interpreted or reinterpreted. For instance, in keeping with contemporary movements, Akan women view the world as members of an oppressed sex, through the lenses of a traditional culture in which they are the unequal partner in a (marriage) relationship – unequal in the sense that their perspective has been defined for them by men. Attempts to define their own perspective requires a reconstruction of the social meaning of the marriage custom, with concomitant attitudinal changes towards birth control, abortion, sterilisation, consensual sex, etc. Reconstructing social meanings introduces new or modified rights, articulated within the framework of a form of moral reasoning which accepts as a constant factor the idea of moral agency conceptualised as a structured role. This keeps moral agency within a definition of the good in terms of the harmonisation of human interests, a notion driven by a community centred focus in which no schism arises between the good of the individual and the good of the community, and no inconsistency arises between distributive patterns of social goods and social practices.

3.3   Interpreting particularity

3.3.1 *Particularity vs. relativism*

Any attempt to sketch a picture of difference and diversity in morality, and to present a view of an ethnic perspectival model, raises the problem of universals. Particularity separates group from group, yielding a multiplicity of perspectives. Wiredu's particularity, however, does not separate, without also linking, all moral particularisms to a single defining characteristic of human existence as *social* existence. There is a source of normative values that is not relative *only* to the Akan culture in which they contingently reside. Common to all, and serving as the basis of a cross-cultural critique of moral practice, is the idea that morality is concerned with the harmonisation of human interests or, more precisely, of the members of particular communities. A morally defensible culture will have this characteristic, though it will be variously understood and implemented in different cultures:

"Different peoples, groups . . . understand morality in different ways" (Flack & Pellegrino 1992:80). This must not, however, be read as a defence of a *cultural* relativism of moral standards. Wiredu (1995g) allows for the legitimacy of differing perspectives, in particular, differing *ethnic* perspectives, thereby accepting only a relativism of judgements. With this in mind, particularity must be understood in terms of the factors that determine how things will look to a percipient situated within the standpoint of Akan ethics. For, the factors shaping the particular Akan standpoint impart a determinate content, which is simply the view from the standpoint in question.

First and foremost among these factors sits a substantive value which, in the Akan hierarchy, yields a determinate content for all other values[24]. This is that

1. Kinship is the highest value.

    Kinship is both a biological and a social category, so it is not surprising to find that the social dimensions of the Akan ethic are rooted in biological relationships (parental, filial). (1) focuses attention on ethnic particularism and would raise a problem were it not for an earlier observation: particularism must transcend its particularity at some point in order to bring a critical commentary to bear on society. The ethos of harmonisation outlined above brings a valid critique to bear on (1), a critique which has universal significance as one of the moral misuses of the cultural constraints of role-structured obligations.

A second, but almost equally significant factor, is a characteristic of a tradition which values familial and community links over the (bare) individual in moral importance. This is that

2. To have a moral identity is to be morally constituted through another.

    (2) is a premise relating to the metaphysics of the moral self, but, like the biological premise underlying (1), (2) also has a significant moral-social spin-off: persons in structured roles can have moral responsibility which they have not chosen by virtue of the obligations which attach to a role. But (1) alleviates the pain of (2): filial attachments set an ideal for particular roles, and a set of priorities with reference to the ideal which enable the inhabitor of the role to rank-order obligations, and carry them out accordingly. So the unity of social and moral identity, which brings together moral conviction and rationality, is preserved.

Thirdly, the phenomenon of moral affirmation requires

3. Reciprocity.

    Reciprocity is required as a functional requirement of role-structured obligations and ultimately as a value. As a social good, reciprocity is a value for autonomous agents. But autonomy is conceptualised in a context that shapes how persons are constructed as moral agents. The significant premise to which appeal has been made is that choice is a function of the self-understanding of a community and constrained by the social goods internal to its cultural structure. The good one has as an autonomous agent is presented in a context which determines how beneficial autonomy is to one, *qua* moral agent: one's autonomy has a high utility function within the moral requirements of one's role, if exercised in accordance with those requirements. Constrained choice is a typical feature of moral choice in any moral system. Thus, to describe choice-making activities as being subject to constraints does not mean that agents have no choice. Autonomous choices are the choices made by independent and authentic agents – independent in the sense that their choice accords with what they would choose if their roles themselves were "freely" chosen, and authentic in the sense that their choice accords with their status as constructed or shaped by a given context. As such, choices are honoured and agents respected.

Fourthly, non-reciprocal actions are actions that fall outside the scope of choice under the given specified conditions, and so reciprocity requires
4. Autonomy.

By implication, reciprocity also requires
5. Honour and respect.

It requires these specifically as functional requirements, and, ultimately, as values.

3.3.2 Fluid and fixed constitution

The picture that is emerging is one of an ethic shaped by cultural presuppositions which admit a diverse set of relevant conditions (rather than a specific set of necessary and sufficient conditions) of the moral. Cultural presuppositions constitute moral agents and their precepts: they are embedded in a cultural matrix that encodes them with meaning. The dynamics of a cultural matrix has great formative power over moral agents, specifically insofar as a way of life specifies the content of social relations, thereby specifying the moral precepts appropriate to role-structured agency. But, it is precisely because of this that we need a critique of social constitution – a way of deconstructing a formative force which, particularly under conditions of cultural ossification, tends to render autonomy and other dependent values functionally ineffective. So, how might we develop a social critique without losing what is characteristic of the ethic that constitution generates?

Societies particularise by making use of a range of informal interpersonal practices, created through conflict between the needs of agents to pursue local goals – which require spaces between families and kingroups on the one hand and society at large on the other – and a communal need for basic collective solidarity. We shall refer to these spaces collectively as civil society, and to all individuated public spaces as civic society[25]. Civic society permits the growth of various solidarities among kingroups, usually in opposition to an established solidarity which is experienced as too distant and detached to maintain sociability in the realms where individuals interact. Civil society is best understood as an institutionalised correlate of political authority and cannot be defined in terms which express opposition to the state. Civic society, by contrast, is a form of social organisation embedded within civil society and acting as a counterbalancing force to civil society and to the state.

Civic society is the proper forum of renewal, and the arena in which autonomy and kinship values engage in a dialectic, and converge in a "bottom-up" strategy for cultural and moral regeneration. Since civic society is managed by kinship-groups, the public spaces generated are small enough to permit social meanings and their interpretations to be contested and their import rewritten by persons in stable interaction with each other. Herein lies its strength: a vigorous civic society ensures that regeneration is more or less an ongoing process. Autonomy is protected by the fact that the boundaries between civic and civil society create a legitimate private realm, which, by virtue of its oppositional nature, engages in critical dialogue with the public (civil) realm. This interactional process generates systems and patterns to which social actions conform since it allows for convergence between different constructions and interpretations of meaning.

One way of explaining how convergence is possible is to view each individual contribution to socially organised meaning as a "network experience"[26]. The "network experience" idea is a useful explanatory model in societies which have a high degree of symmetry, i.e. reciprocity, in the construction of relationships, a characteristic which Akan culture strongly exhibits. Networks are social relationships in which the production of meaning and interpretations of systems of production take place. A "network experience" is an interactive context in which social meanings are produced and individuals' perspectives are shaped. A network of perspectives grows out of an exchange between perspectives, diffusing meaning from the local civic scene to civil society at large:

> Individuals' perspectives, then, come to consist of the conceptions which they have come to construct or appropriate for their own use, as it were, but also of their perspectives on other perspectives – their approximate mappings of other peoples' meanings. And culture as collective phenomenon becomes the network of such perspectives (Kuper 1992:43).

The cultural content of one network is brought to bear on how social meaning is managed in another network, a process which culminates in creating mechanisms for the collective management of meaning – mechanisms which transmit a culture's precepts and reconstruct and renegotiate its social meanings. These are mechanisms *internal* to a cultural structure. In Akan culture they are provided by a system of neighbourhood mutual help. This system is rooted in reciprocity between kin and close friends which forms networks of tightly knit interest groups and expands into a system of local community cooperation. Neighbourhood mutual help creates community through circles of reciprocity and a sense of empowerment which grows up in the wake of one significant spin-off of reciprocal relations – viz. confidence in sustainable regeneration.

Community created in this way has the power to resist and even subvert the normative hegemony of civil society. Though participation in kinship activities is not wholly voluntary, and though social roles are ascribed rather than "freely" chosen, the space created in the tension between civic and civil society maintains a balance between the autonomy of kinship groups and their interaction with civil society. This is space in which kinship-groups strive to obtain a moral equilibrium – moral because they seek to balance their autonomy against the need for constructive interaction with civil society – and, in the process, affective ties involving mutual respect and obligations are generated. Reciprocity is a crucial element in the attempt to (re)define a morally balanced relationship between autonomous groups and to (re)create a moral order and identity which includes all local communities. Ideally, such an order is the shared realm of social life which civil society should or ought to offer.

3.3.3 *Community as reference point*

The picture so far presented is one of an ethnic perspectival model of morality. This model does not proceed from any self-evident point of view. Rather, an ideology of its own – viz. the value of kinship relations – participates in the construction of the model itself. In other moralities highest value is accorded to autonomous individuals rather than kinship relations, or kinshipgroups. Should we recognise this ascription of value to autonomous individuals as ideological, i.e. as specific to a particular kind of society or, more narrowly, to a particular society? If so, it must take its place as one perspective or point of view among many. Or, do we accord it the status of universal value? This is to ask whether we regard it as setting up a foundational truth in the search for knowledge about the nature of the moral.

If "autonomous individual" is not defined sociologically the very idea of a society tends to disappear. Society becomes simply a collection of autonomous individuals. Morality must then do with a different grounding if it is to erect a system which accords moral agency to individuals regarded as standing in mere interrelationship with one another. One consequence, if not the most significant consequence, of treating the individual as the locus of deontology is that we must construct moralities for strangers as the primary object of our moral concerns. We then end up reducing the alien feel of alien social dimensions to the alien feel of the otherness of a single person, thus neglecting justification with reference to social relationships in favour of self-referential explanations. Individual self-reference leads to either nihilism or omnipotent subjectivity. If similarly atomised, the communal social dimension relativises moral truth to a function of a particular social ideology. But these truths need not be mere relativisms. Consider how Wiredu approaches the issue of relativism:

> It seems to me that at present there are not enough philosophically analytical studies of the traditional thought of the various peoples of Africa to support any very responsible or illuminating generalisations. The times, then, seem to call for ethnically specific studies. My own hope is that such inquiries would disclose a variety of philosophies, similar in some important respects, but distinct, nevertheless. It would be exceedingly useful, for example, to know from a philosophical elucidation of Yoruba or Mende or Luo or Banyonwardan conceptions of mind, as distinct from unanalytical narratives about their beliefs on the subject, *how the thought of other African peoples compares with that of Akans on the same matter* (Kwame 1995:125).

What could the value of such comparisons be? Wiredu's advocacy of particularist studies in philosophy points to a way of arriving at generalisations and discovering what is distinctive about philosophies in Africa. The basic idea comes to this: what is shared and has value attributed to it in a society is best understood as distinctive, not only of the society in question, but also of the philosophy to whose creation it contributes when compared with what is shared and valued in other societies, for in comparing we see differences, and, indeed, which differences should be compared and generalised over the specifics of social structures. Ultimately, moral truth is understood in the context of a "parts-to-whole" paradigm, and is thus comprehended through the relations between (social) systems. Wiredu offers such a relational universal[27] for morality, conceived of as a "certain minimum of harmonization of interests" which serves a social end: this is to construct a "tolerable form of human social existence" (Oladipo 1995:7).

4. PARTICULARITY AND EMPOWERMENT

The proper role of particularity in morals may be described as one of empowerment. The desire for empowerment is a response to a lacuna and a way of unmasking the vacuity of a criticism. The lacuna appears when we consider that there is no way of knowing the correct background assumptions by which to identify, describe, and resolve moral controversies in the absence of the content-full contexts which social structures provide. But solutions based on the assumptions drawn from the specifics of social structures are not, as is standardly claimed, full-blown relativisms which fail to transcend their own particularity and so fail to bring critical comment to bear on the very specifics from which the background assumptions are drawn. Social structures are not monolithic in the sense in which the criticism requires.

The desire for empowerment can be satisfied in many ways. Firstly, we are morally empowered to the extent that we find that a given set of social ends are reasons to prize things like harmony and kinship relations. This desire for empowerment can be addressed by an agent only in his/her capacity to recognise the moral relevance of a set of factors, but this skill is formed and acquired in community, i.e. in a context which supplies exposure to phenomena like power differentials and gender discrimination, and which treats such phenomena (in their appropriate contexts) as interpretations of social criticism. Non-contextualised accounts of moral agency alienate agents from their autonomy because they alienate them from the conditions that enable them to claim their lives as their own and to comprehend moral situations through their own self-understanding.

Particularity addresses the issue of empowerment through its concern for the applicability of moral precepts to a given constituency. Wiredu's (in Oladipo 1995) conception of the moral terrain as a diverse set of relevant conditions, which makes space for customary rights to be understood as rights (because custom is included in morality), opens the door to a "skills" interpretation of the task of moral education: education is development in competence for discerning the settings in which moral precepts apply. Given the appropriateness of the "parts-whole" paradigm referred to earlier on, what begins as a moral dilemma for some individuals is, in that paradigm, reconceived through interaction with others, and redescribed in terms which reveal the conditions that need to be identified for resolution to become possible.

The identification of particularity with a distinct community, formed by traditions and constituted by narratives, governs Wiredu's interpretation of the role of particularity in morality. It is, however, wrong to think of the public dialogue which our picture has presented as foundational in the modernist sense in which it operates under the constraints of neutrality, i.e. under a set of criteria neutral enough in its language to state *all* moral commitments. Public dialogue comes into existence whenever civic societies engage in debate, i.e. whenever they evaluate the validity of the social and political norms by which they live. There may be as many civic societies as there are public dialogues, but no debate abstracts so radically from the recognition of differences, that parties to the debate are compelled by their language to consent to moral truths *they* do not hold or share. Dialogue, then, serves pragmatic ends – to identify the norms *they* think reasonable to abide by.

Secondly, generating agreement through the contested dialogue of a public debate has a significant spin-off which aids empowerment. Conceptions of the good life are privatised before being pushed out onto the agenda of the public dialogue, where they compete for validation. No belief to which anyone may be deeply committed – such as the belief that a sexual division of labour is morally wrong because it oppresses women and hinders their attainment of personhood – can be excluded, and so no-one is prevented from seeking the widest possible forum to arrive at a consensus. The contested dialogue of a public debate renegotiates and redefines the boundary between "private" and "public" since it helps to define the nature of the issues that get pushed onto the agenda of the public dialogue, and since parties discover what their deepest disagreements or agreements are only once the process of public dialogue has run its course. It is appropriate to note that struggles to off-set the effects of power differentials in any context begin with a redefinition of what had previously been considered "private" and therefore as not matters of public concern (i.e. not matters for debate on a public agenda). The "bottom-up" strategy of renewal referred to earlier ensures that the boundary between "private" and "public" cannot be redrawn in such a way that it limits the reach of the moral particularity of civic society into civil society, which means that the boundary cannot prevent privately held values from becoming public shared norms, and therefore that it cannot limit civic autonomy. Indeed, where the boundary is drawn is a matter for negotiation which rests on mutual consent arrived at by exploiting the relations of egalitarian reciprocity, which is so characteristic of Akan culture.

The third point elaborates on the moral perspectives that arise from self-"Other" relations within interactional social structures. Since kinship is the source of these relations, and hence the source of all moral perspectives, the self is morally required to view the "Other" as a concrete individual with a particular history, identity and constitution. We might say that the self is morally required to abstract from the commonality – which manifests at the level of civil society – and to focus on the individuality of the "Other" – as this manifests itself in the interactional civic structures made possible by kinship relations. Kinship structures are governed by relations of mutual (or complementary) reciprocity: each individual expects from the other forms of behaviour which grant recognition and confirmation of their concreteness and individuality. Differences do not separate – rather, they are both complementary and definitional, for they are bound by kinship ties which fashion the circumstances of one individual's life in relation to the circumstances of another's as a coherent narrative.

Finally, we need to return to a point raised earlier about the possibility of creating a commonality from a multiplicity of civic perspectives. Individuating character- istics are ascribed by kinship relations making possible coherent distinctions between individuals: they enter the moral arena in an undifferentiated condition, to become distinct and differentiated with respect to their identities and their interests. In their forum of actual contested dialogue they operate without any alien epistemic restrictions on their form of moral reasoning, i.e. restrictions on knowledge of themselves, their history, the specifics of their (civic) community, its structures and their places within it. This forum privileges no-one and no subject matter. As pointed out in an earlier section, practical reason requires that there be a willingness to participate and a willingness to suspend disagreement (making possible agreed actions without necessarily agreed notions). Besides the need to agree (in the sense just given) there is no privileged subject matter in contested dialogue: social goods and the desire for them are equally subjects of dispute. Insofar as the willingness to participate and suspend disagreement forms part of the social conditions which make contested dialogue possible, and insofar as these conditions act as constraints under which dialogue takes place and can be evaluated for fairness, they are privileged, though this, in itself, does not close any level of reflexivity to any agent. Such social conditions form the backdrop of a fixed system of agreements within which contested dialogue becomes possible, and so help to link civic and civil society, bringing about a greater convergence of "different flows of meaning" (Kuper 1992:43). Under these conditions the underlying conceptions of the good life in contested dialogue become visible in a way not possible in moral systems requiring strict neutrality with respect to conceptions of the good life in the systems of reasoning employed. One might say that Akan conceptions are related to a specific understanding of the nature of human association, and so are embedded in the concrete world.

5. CONCLUSION

In Akan culture the public sphere of social life is diffused with particularistic considerations of kinship relations. The structure of these relations forms the ground of an ethic which grows from the precepts generated in a civic forum of actual debate into the norms of civil society, through a process of consensus. This "bottom-up" generation of norms ensures that the value of kinship relations remains the most significant social bond. This bond is the ground of a shared understanding of the value of belonging to Akan society itself. As a social bond kinship relations produces a sense of moral agency at a level of sociability (family and other sibling institutions) which ensures optimal efficacy for moral agency by virtue of a custom of complementary reciprocity. The social bond itself, and the conceptions of the good life which regulate civic institutions, are visible and comprehensible. Role-identification and a system of rejuvenating tradition through forms of practical reasoning embedded in the specifics of social structure, and born of the self-understanding of a particular people, enables individuals to develop a coherent sense of self and of community.

NOTES

1. This "resource"-view of culture derives from R. Thornton, "Culture: a contemporary definition", in E. Boonzaier & J. Sharp (1988:17–28).
2. I am using the word "moral" in its generic sense, to connote all normative endeavours, including natural science and epistemology.
3. I borrow this idea, its formulation, and the definition which follows from Walzer (1983: 31–63).
4. I owe this insight to Walzer (1983:3–30). Wiredu, I am sure, will agree with me on its appropriateness in describing interactive relations based on kinship ties in a communitarian theory.
5. This idea derives from Kymlicka (1989:162–181). Again, I think Wiredu will agree with me that it is appropriate in describing self-other relations in communitarian theory. See, for example, Wiredu's conception of the self in this section (2).
6. MacIntyre (1981 & 1989) suggests this definition.
7. This, again, derives from Walzer (1983:312–321). Wiredu defends much the same view. See, for example, Wiredu's conception of morality in section 2 of this article.
8. Wiredu (1992b), in effect, defends this insight.
9. This is one of Wiredu's theses (see 1992b).

10. This thesis is defended by Wiredu (1995g): "The need for conceptual decolonization in African philosophy" (in Oladipo 1995:22–32).
11. This, too, is Wiredu's thesis (see 1992a & 1992b).
12. This insight is derived from Wiredu (1992b).
13. I am indebted to Wiredu (1992b & 1995e).
14. I am indebted to Wiredu (1992b & 1995a).
15. I am indebted to Wiredu (1992b & 1992c).
16. See Wiredu (1992a).
17. I am here interpreting Wiredu (see Wiredu 1990 & 1992a).
18. I am here interpreting Wiredu (1990 & 1992a).
19. Here again I am interpreting Wiredu (1990 & 1995d).
20. See Wiredu (1992b).
21. I am here interpreting Wiredu (1980:2–50 & 1993:450–476).
22. See Wiredu: "Custom and morality" (in Oladipo 1995:33–52).
23. I am here interpreting Wiredu's "Custom and morality" (in Oladipo 1995:33–52).
24. Again, see Wiredu (1992a & 1992a).
25. Here again I am interpreting Wiredu (1992b & 1992c). My distinction departs from the traditional view as presented by Hann (see Hann & Dunn 1996:79–98).
26. Here I am interpreting Wiredu with reference to Hannerz: "The global ecumene as a network of networks" (see Kuper 1992:34–56).
27. This term is from de Coppet's "Comparison, a universal for anthropology" (Kuper 1992:73).

Readings

INDIVIDUALITY, COMMUNITY, AND THE MORAL ORDER

SEGUN GBADEGESIN

Two issues are of particular interest to us in this chapter. Firstly, what is the relationship between individuality and the community in traditional African thought systems? Included in this question are the value placed on individuality *vis-à-vis* community, the expectations the community has of its members, and the humanist foundations of communalism. Secondly, the philosophical basis of traditional moral values will be explored. There have been controversies over the alleged religious basis of morality in Africa, and this needs to be clarified. In the process, we will discuss some of these moral values in the hope that this will throw some light on their foundation.

To better understand the meaning of the individual in relation to the community, it is useful to trace our steps back to the coming-to-being of the new member of the family and community. The new baby arrives into the waiting hands of the elders of the household. Experienced elderly wives in the household serve as mid-wives, they see to it that the new baby is delivered safely and the mother is in no danger after delivery. They introduce the baby into the family with cheerfulness, joy, and prayers: *Ayò abara tíntín* (This is a little thing of great joy). From then on, the new mother may not touch the child except for breast feeding. The baby is safe in the hands of others: co-wives, husband's mother, step-mothers, and a whole lot of others, including senior sisters, nieces, and cousins.

On the seventh or eighth day, the baby is given his/her names, a ceremony performed by the adult members of the household. Before the actual naming ceremony, the most elderly male member – usually the baby's grandfather – consults the *Ifá*-divination oracle to find out the child's portion, the chosen profession, and *òrìsà*. The appropriate names that will be given to the baby are then decided upon by looking at a combination of factors, including the household profession (e.g. a hunting family will give a name reflecting this – *Odéwálé*), the household *òrìsà* (e.g. *Sàngó* devotees will give a name after *Sàngó* – *Sàngó – fúnmikê*), the day of birth (*Bósèdê*), the significance of the birth (e.g. a reincarnation or a symbol of a recently deceased member of the family – *Babáwálé* or *Iyábòdé* – or a symbol of victory over a recent crisis – *Olúségun*). In all these, the importance of the new arrival as a unique individual is reconciled with his or her belonging to an existing family which not only decides his/her name but also has a duty to see his/her birth as a significant episode in its existence. The Yoruba say *Ilé ni à nwò, kí á tó so omo lóríuko* (We look back at the family traditions before we give names to a new baby). The meaning of this is that the child, as an extension of the family tree, should be given a name that reflects his/her membership thereof, and it is expected that the name so given will guide and control the child by being a constant reminder to him/her of his/her membership of the family and the circumstance of his/her birth.

The process of socialisation begins right from birth. The mother constantly communicates with the baby by tracing the family tree from the beginning, reminding him/her of the nobility of his/her birth and the uniqueness of the family. Co-wives (step-mothers) are on hand to tease the growing child, chanting the family praise-names and demanding gratification in return. All these raise the consciousness of the child as a member of a family and he/she begins to internalise its norms.

The structure of the family compound makes the process easy. Members of the extended household of several related extended families belonging to a common ancestor occupy a large compound called *agbo-ilé*. The compound is usually in the form of a circle with one or two main entrances. The various extended families have their own houses joined together (to form the compound or household) and each family member has apartments within the house, with each wife having a room. There is a large covered corridor into which all the wives' rooms lead and there they all sit, play, and eat in the daytime with their children, and at night they retire to their rooms. Inside each apartment, the children of co-wives and other elderly members play together and are overseen by the elders. A child who misbehaves is corrected immediately and may be punished by the elders. This is the first exposure to socialisation. Then, in the larger compound, all the children play together, and again, any of them may be punished by any older member of the household for misbehaving. Where there is a misunderstanding among the co-wives, the elderly male or female members intervene, and if they do not succeed, the matter is taken to the head of the compound – *Baálé,* assisted by other male members. In this kind of environment, growing children are able to see themselves as a part of a household and not as atoms. They see their intrinsic relation to others and see the interdependent existence of their lives with others. Here is the limit of individualism. Not that the community forces itself on an unyielding individual, rather the individual, through socialisation and the love and concern which the household and community have extended to him/her, *cannot* now see himself or herself as anything apart from his/her community. Interest in his/her success is shown by members of the extended family who regard him/her as their "blood", and the community are also able to trace their origin to a common, even if mythical, ancestor. There is, therefore, a feeling of solidarity among its members and this is neither forced nor solicited. It develops naturally as a result of the experience of love and concern which the growing child has been exposed to.

The process of socialisation that begins in the family apartment and the household compound finally enters the larger community where the child is further exposed to the virtues of communal life. Here children of the community are exposed to the display of selfless efforts by others to uplift the community. They gain first-hand experience of how adults contribute to the welfare of children, how women and men work on the farms, and how the warriors risk their lives to save the community. Building on the initial exposure in the family compound they now see themselves as those who should carry the banner and, having been prepared for the task, they, severally and collectively, cannot but shut out individualism. This is the meaning of the common reference to the typical African as saying, "I am because we are: I exist because the community exists." From what we have discussed above, this is the simple truth.

It follows that the usual rendering of this to the effect that the individual in traditional African societies is crushed by the almighty presence of the community is not the whole truth. Of course, individuals are valued in themselves and as potential contributors to communal survival. For, why should the new baby be so immersed in love and affection? Further, it is known that many individuals have the wisdom to guide the community and such people are well respected. Emphasis is placed on usefulness for self and community and not on wealth or strength. If individual uniqueness were not recognised, how could such powerful figures as *Kúrunmí*, *Látóòsà*, *Obòkun*, and *Móremí* become charismatic leaders?

The example of *Móremí is* worth recounting here. A native of Ile-Ife, *Móremí* was a woman of great strength, power, and communal feeling. At a time when Igbo invaders were troubling the Ife kingdom, *Móremí* decided to do something. She went to ask for permission from the *Oòni*, the king of Ife, to be allowed to pursue the invaders. After some hesitation occasioned by surprise, the king allowed her. She then sought help from the Ifá oracle about how she could accomplish the task. She was advised to perform some sacrifice to the Esinmirin river. She did this and a spirit appeared to her with information on the Igbo and how to capture them. Specifically, she was informed that they disguised themselves in grass costumes which made them look like spirits and she should prepare fire to burn them. Armed with this information she went back and prepared the warriors against the invaders who came as usual and were routed.

Now, before this information was given to *Móremí,* she had promised the spirit of *Esìnmirìn* river anything it would take if she could succeed in her mission. The spirit demanded the sacrifice of her only son, *Olúorogbo,* in return for the favour. *Móremí* could not go back on her words. She sacrificed her only son for the sake of her community. This is an example *par excellence* of the spirit of community, the voluntary submission of individual happiness to the community. There are common examples like this in African social history. Such cases exemplify the possibility of individuals foregoing their own interests when the interest of the community is at stake, and so the idea of individual right does not, for traditional people, defeat the claim of the community. A high premium is placed on the practical demonstration of oneness and solidarity among the members of a community. Every member is expected to consider him/herself an integral part of the whole and to play an appropriate role towards achieving the good of all. Cooperation is voluntarily given and is institutionalised in several ways. Wives of the family (co-wives, wives of brothers, wives of cousins, etc.) know that they are expected to cooperate in raising their children as full members of the family. They are free to borrow household items from one another, they feel free to baby-sit for one another, they advise one another, and settle any dispute between themselves and their children. A person who watches while children fight or when tension mounts between two adults is not a good person. Also, properties left outside are taken care of by other members in case there is rain or a storm. Everyone is expected to be the keeper and protector of the interests of others which are, by extension, their own too.

All the above point to the value that traditional Yoruba place on community and communal existence, with all its emphasis on fellow-feeling, solidarity, and selflessness. This leads directly to the social order of communalism. The structure of traditional African society is communal. This means that the organisation of socio-economic life is based on the principle of common ownership of land, which is the major means of production in a non-industrial, agrarian subsistence economy. Ownership of land is vested in the community which gives out portions for individual use as required from time to time. Such land reverts to the community when it is no longer needed by the individual. Some scholars have identified this social practice as an outgrowth of the principles of solidarity and selflessness which pervade the traditional society. However, this is only partially so. More important is the fact that in traditional society a man is not able to accumulate and appropriate a large area of land because he does not have the machinery and expertise to operate it. So the reasonable thing is to have some portion earmarked for each adult. This is with respect to the distribution of land and its communal ownership.

On the other hand, however, the indigenous values of fellow-feeling, solidarity and cooperation feature prominently in the economic activities of individuals. Thus, there is the system of *òwè*, a cooperative endeavour in which people help one another on a specific task; for instance, building a new house or clearing a forest for farmland requires help from others. Such is freely given on the basis of reciprocity. Sometimes a male adult with married female children may seize this opportunity to call on his sons-in-law to help with the task. They are only too willing to do this. There is another kind of mutual cooperation known as *àró* in the form of a standing cooperative association. A member may call upon the group to help him harvest or plant or clear the weeds. He only has to feed the participants and later on he may also be called upon to help. In this kind of situation, where commercial labour is not available and not encouraged, it becomes clear that individuality is helped by communality. "I am because we are" becomes an understandable and reasonable expression of dependence which does not entail suppression. For even here, the sky is the limit for an enterprising person.

The picture presented thus far should not be interpreted as meaning that there are no conflicts at all in traditional Yoruba societies. Any human society is bound to have cases of conflicts involving individuals who either refuse to conform or who feel somehow offended. In such instances of conflict, there are avenues for resolution in the traditional system: elders intervene to reconcile the disputing parties on the basis of the community's accepted moral principles. For instance, a man may be blamed for mistreating his wife and not considering her interests as a human being. The point here is that appeals are made in such cases to certain moral principles or standards which also occur in Western societies. However, in the case in which survival of the community is pitched against an individual's will, it is clear that the community's welfare is emphasised. The reason for this is not far-fetched. As observed earlier, the individual involved also understands and appreciates the meaning of community: "I am because we are." From this it follows that there need not be any tension between individuality and community since it is possible for an individual freely to give up his/her own perceived interest for the survival of the community. But in giving up one's interest thus, one is also sure that the community will not disown one and that one's well-being will be its concern. It is a life of give and take. The idea of individual rights, based on a conception of individuals as atoms, is therefore bound to be foreign to this system.

For the community is founded on notions of an intrinsic and enduring relationship among its members.

This same theme of individuality-in-community is prominent in other African social thought. For instance, K.A. Busia says of the Akan that

> [t]here is, everywhere, the heavy accent on family – the blood relatives, the group of kinsfolk held together by a common origin and a common obligation to its members, to those who are living and those who are dead. . . . The individual is brought up to think of himself in relation to this group and to behave always in such a way as to bring honour and not disgrace to its members. The ideal set before him is that of mutual helpfulness and cooperation within the group of kinsfolk (1962a:33).

Furthermore,

> [c]ooperation and mutual helpfulness are virtues enjoined as essential; without them, the kingroup cannot long endure. Its survival depends on its solidarity (Busia 1962b:34).

And Gyekye (1987:155) recalls an Akan proverb on the same theme: "The prosperity (or well-being) of man depends upon his fellow-man." Such proverbs are numerous in African social thought and they help to point up the wisdom of traditional thinkers concerning matters pertaining to the good of the community.

FOUNDATIONS OF MORALITY

What is the basis of morality in traditional African thought? There are two opposing views on this question. On the one hand there is the view held by Mbiti and Idowu that religion is the source and foundation of morality. On the other hand, Wiredu (1983:13) is in the forefront of those who oppose this view with his claim that at least for the Akan of Ghana, the moral outlook is "logically independent of religion". The same position (modified in a sense) is held by Gyekye (1987: 129–153).

Idowu (1962:144) starts off by questioning the positions of two schools of thought regarding the foundation of morality: the social school and the common sense school. The first traces morality to society: "it is essentially a social phenomenon. Society must keep itself alive and its machinery smooth-running, and to this end it evolves a system of self-preservation." Conscience in this hypothesis is nothing more than "a complex of residual habits, which society implants in him as if it brings him up" (1962:144). The second school of thought sees morality as "a product of common sense" (1962:144). In order to live, people must adapt themselves to their environments. Experience soon teaches people what can be done and what must be avoided. A steady accumulation of this experience over a long period results in a very strong sense of what has popularly come to be known as "right" and "wrong".

Idowu (1962:144) rejects both hypotheses on the grounds that they are partial explanations. They "have conveniently overlooked two vital questions. The first school still has to make it explicit why this 'mass' which is called society should be so keen on its own preservation." Idowu's point is that were society a soulless machine, it would not bother about its own breakdown. So, someone must be responsible for giving society its sense of its own value. Obviously, the notion of God is needed as a basis for society's concern for morality. On the other hand, the second school of thought has not made its case. For it has yet to tell us, Idowu

(1962:145) argues, "what it is that puts so much 'common sense' in man. Why is it that, like the candle-drawn moth, he does not fly into the flame and be burnt."

I find these arguments interesting but not convincing. But before raising my objection, let us note that Idowu has not here given an account of the Yoruba view of morality. Thus far, it is his own view about the foundation of morality. This view may or may not agree with the Yoruba account and one may disagree with the view without thereby denying that it is one held by the Yoruba.

Now, the problem with this view is simply that the way Idowu puts it does not help his case. If one says that society creates morality to avoid its own self-destruction, why is this not enough as a reason? Why must we assume that there is some other being responsible for putting the soul in the human person to think of his/her survival? This would seem to deny the independent rationality of human beings. The second objection is even less helpful. The denial of the sufficiency of common sense experience as a basis for correction is something I find rather interesting. So we are being asked to agree with the view that if a child puts his/her finger in the fire a first time, the child cannot on the basis of this experience refrain from fire next time, unless we assume that something other than the pain of the first experience intervenes to convince him/her to refrain. Then, what prevents a wicked person from claiming that God has not intervened to guide him in his actions? Idowu's view is that

> morality is basically the fruit of religion and . . . to begin with, it was dependent upon it. Man's concept of the Deity has everything to do with what is taken to be the norm of morality. God made man, and it is He who implants in him the sense of right and wrong. This is a fact the validity of which does not depend upon whether man realizes and acknowledges it or not (1962:145).

Perhaps one point may be granted here – that human beings are created by the Deity and that the creator endows them with reasoning ability as well as the conscience as source of moral reasoning. However, it does not then follow that, given this reasoning ability, human beings cannot, on their own, make moral choices and determine their ideas of moral rightness and wrongness. The Euthyphro Question (cf. Flew 1979:107) is pertinent here.

But as I have observed, this is Idowu's view and we are concerned here with a traditional Yoruba account of moral values. On this too, however, Idowu has argued as follows:

> With the Yoruba, morality is certainly the fruit of religion. They do not make any attempt to separate the two; and it is impossible for them to do so without disastrous consequences (1962:146).

Idowu (1962:146) then goes on to observe that:
1. The Yoruba belief in taboo (*èèwò* – what ought not to be done) took its origin from the people's discernment of certain things that were morally approved or disapproved by the Deity.
2. Some scholars have misunderstood Yoruba religion and morality in their assessment of the cruelty of certain Yoruba practices as emanating from their religion.
3. But they are wrong because such practices they attack, e.g. human sacrifice, do not originate from religion but rather from the desire of the Yoruba to fulfil an imperative, what they understand as a sacred duty.

4. But they (i.e. the Yoruba who sacrifice human beings) are wrong because the Deity's demand is not for physical sacrifice but for one's heart, and his demands are purely clinical and spiritual.

What is interesting here is that one would expect Idowu to follow through his original claim that, as God is the source of our conscience and therefore of notions of right and wrong, everything is traceable to God. But if, in fact, humans can discern on their own what is good (even to please God) then the identification of morality with religion is not as tight as first assumed. In other words, since the people are credited with discerning what is good or bad (as in the concept of *eewo*) they should also be credited with an independent arrival at notions of right and wrong, using their reasoning ability which is granted to be God-given. This is clear especially if we examine Idowu's claims (3) and (4) above.

Again, this seems to be borne out more clearly in Idowu's (1962:149) treatment of covenants in Yoruba ethics. "Person-to-person, and divinity-to-person relations," Idowu observes, "have their basis in covenants." In person-to-person covenants, the parties bind themselves to each other by bilateral obligations. It is like a contract. But while the divinities are called in as witnesses to the covenant in most cases (e.g. the Earth or *Ogún* divinities) to give it more force, the essence and purpose of a covenant is to assure the parties of the sincerity of each party. And, as Idowu goes on to suggest (rightly, I think):

> Although every covenant has a ritualistic basis, nevertheless, the obligations which are its outcome are ethical. It would seem that the Yoruba have found it necessary in an imperfect society to introduce this element of subtle "coercion" in order to strengthen their weak will in the performance of ethical duties (1962:150).

This suggests that we have a distinction between rituals and ethics and that therefore the Yoruba may have an independent basis for their ethical duties but bring in the Deity for enforcing such duties in the minds of not-so-trusted fellow human beings.

Theologians are not the only ones who defend the idea of a religious foundation for morality in Africa; philosophers also do so. Thus, Moses Makinde (1988:1–27) has recently attempted to defend the religious foundation of an African system of morality and to show that this position is reasonably defensible, in spite of the views of some contemporary Africans to the contrary.

Makinde's (1988:2) position is that "whatever else anybody may say, religion is surely a competing foundational theory of morals in African societies". In defence of this position, which appears to be a modest one, he advances some arguments and appeals to the authority of Kant, Mill, and Awolowo. I must unfortunately say, however, that the defence does not succeed because the considerations brought in support of it are too weak for the realisation of the objective. I would like to examine here six arguments which I have been able to dig out from the clusters of considerations that Makinde has urged us to accept.

The first argument is based on the authority of Mbiti who has asserted that Africans live in a religious universe. Makinde's (1988:2) argument, based on this, may be reconstructed as follows:

1. Africans live in a religious universe (as confirmed by Mbiti and others).
2. Religion plays a great role in the lives of African people (this is another way of stating the first premise).

3. All their activities must be influenced by one religion or the other (this is yet another way of stating the first premise).
4. Therefore an African system of morality, based on African cultural beliefs, must have a religious foundation.

Stated in this way, it seems obvious that the conclusion does not follow. Even if we grant that premise 1 is true, and that premises 2 and 3 are just other ways of stating premise 1, premise 4 still does not follow. Religion may influence peoples' activities and play a great role in their lives. This is still a long way from the conclusion that therefore morality must have a religious foundation. At best, we may conclude that religion may (even must) have an influence on their morality. But from this, it still does not follow that it is the foundation. To say it is the foundation or must be the foundation is to suggest that without religion, the people cannot have any conception of what is good or bad. Perhaps this is what Makinde wants to establish, but this argument is too weak to accomplish that task.

In his second argument, it seems to me that Makinde's purpose is to establish the meaning of the claim that Africans live in a religious universe by connecting it with their belief in God's existence. However, the argument here seems to me to be even less successful. Makinde (1988:3) notes that:

1. Some religions are based on a belief in God, Jesus Christ, Prophet Mohammed, and in lesser deities.
2. The existence of God cannot be established empirically, neither can it be established by a priori reasoning.
3. Nonetheless, Africans, like people in the rest of the world, do believe in the existence of God and do attempt to establish God's existence a priori.
4. But the existence of God can be established a priori only if that existence is completely independent of experience.
5. If African systems of morality depend on the existence of the Deity, then perhaps morality can be established a priori too, since it will be completely independent of what exists.
6. African morality is prescriptive and a priori, not descriptive or empirical.
7. Therefore, because the African system of morality is prescriptive and a priori, the idea of (the will) of God (which is also established a priori) comes in as a ready foundation for it.

The problem with this argument seems easy to identify. To establish that an African system of morality can be established a priori, Makinde ties it in with the existence of the Deity in premise 3. But premise 7 now uses the same premise that African morality is a priori to conclude that therefore it has a religious foundation. In other words, Makinde (1988:3) is urging on us the following:

1. If the African system of morality depends on the existence of the Deity, then morality can be established a priori.
2. The African system of morality can be established a priori.
3. Therefore, because it is a priori and prescriptive, it depends on the existence of the Deity. (This can be the only meaning of "the will of God comes in as a ready foundation" in this context.)

Spelt out in this way, the problem with the argument seems obvious.

The third argument is an appeal to the authority of Idowu and others. If my argument against Idowu's position is sound, Makinde's appeal to it falls with that position. Besides, it is important to note that the idea of taboo among a people is not an adequate proof of their having a religious foundation for their moral system. The wise people of a community have their own well-tried ways of motivating their less cooperative members to perform. If there is an appeal to God or religion, as in some taboos, it is only to influence behaviour. But surely the concept of support should not be confused with that of foundation. Consider the following. A building has a foundation. When, however, the foundation becomes weak, there is a danger of its collapse. Then the owner is advised either to demolish it and rebuild or to provide a support for it. In our traditional villages, it is a common practice to prop up buildings with columns or beams. Furthermore, it cannot be true that the idea of "things not to be eaten" (taboo) is never understood except in connection with religion (Makinde 1988:4). And even if it is, it is not quite clear how this could help the case of a religious foundation for morality.

Obàtálá, the Yoruba deity of creativity, hates palm wine. His devotees are therefore forbidden to take it – perhaps a clear case of a taboo from religion. But *Orúnmìlà*, the deity of wisdom, has no such taboo for his devotees. From Makinde's showing, drinking palm wine (against *Obàtálá's* injunction) must also be an offence against *Olódùmarè* since any offence against the lesser deities is also an offence against the supreme deity. But are the devotees of *Orúnmìlà* who drink palm wine also committing an offence against *Olódùmarè?* Perhaps not. For we may say that since they are devotees of different deities, what is morally wrong for one *(Obàtálá)* is not so for the other *(Orúnmìlà)*. What is not clear is how this helps the case of a religious foundation for morality. For we now have a relativity of morals in which what is right is determined by particular *òrìsà's*. Since people serve different gods, how they are expected to organise their social life from a moral perspective is not clear if we deny them an independent source of morality.

There is, fourthly, an appeal to the authority of Kant which may be reconstructed as follows:
1. Though Kant argues against our need for God in a moral law, he nevertheless bases his moral law on the Golden Rule (do unto others as you would wish them do unto you).
2. This is a corollary of the biblical injunction: love thy neighbour as thyself.
3. Since Kant's statement is in every sense similar to that of the Bible, there is the possibility that he actually derived his Categorical Imperative from the same source and later claimed that morality did not depend, or is not based, on religion (Makinde 1988:6).

There seems to me to be a problem with this argument. Kant insists that the Categorical Imperative is a principle of reason. Even if there is reference to the Golden Rule in Kant's theory, does this make it the foundation of the theory? Is there no difference between the Golden Rule and the Categorical Imperative even in terms of their logic? Notice that the Golden Rule takes its cue from what "you would wish others do unto you". Thus if you would wish other people to steal from you, you would presumably be free to steal from them, following the Golden Rule. But the Categorical Imperative does not depend on any prior desire, at least in Kant's various formulations of it. It is a formula of reason. Kant's theory, of course, has its problems. But a motive of basing that theory on religion or God is hardly an adequate criticism of it.

Makinde also takes Mill's reference to the Golden Rule as evidence that he derives it from the Bible. Mill's point is that *even* Jesus of Nazareth lived by and preached the ideas that make up the content of utilitarian morality. In other words, Mill would say that more than anything else, Jesus was a utilitarian. Which is to say that utilitarian ethics was the *basis* of Jesus' injunction as contained in the Golden Rule. Since there was an historical Jesus, Mill's point is that he (Jesus) understood and utilised the insights that inform the utilitarian theory. Recall here, again, the Euthyphro Question. We may well ask why Jesus recommended the Golden Rule. The answer, for Mill, is because he knows that the general consequence of following that principle is good.

Regarding the appeal to the authority of Chief Awolowo who, according to Makinde (1988:6) "is convinced that virtually all systems of good morality spring from the Bible", we can only infer that, contrary to what Makinde has deduced from this claim, it must be Awolowo's view that traditional Yoruba, like other Africans, had no (good) morality until the Bible was introduced to them. I am not sure, however, that this view could be attributed to Awolowo. But let us assume that it is a view that Awolowo may in fact be willing to have attributed to himself. This fact alone does not make the view correct. For there are a number of other people who hold quite contrary views, and we need to weigh the reasons for each of the views. Tai Solarin, for instance, comes from the same home town as Awolowo and he would certainly deny that view. I am sure that if we looked closely enough there would be at least a few Tai Solarins in the traditional society. Are we to say that such people cannot behave in a morally responsible way? Or that in the traditional society they are not given due respect if they so behave?

A fifth argument (Makinde 1988:10) is supposedly derived from the Yoruba understanding of the dialectics of good and evil as necessary for a meaningful experience of reality. The following is a reconstruction of a very obscure passage.
1. Moral principles only make sense when we can distinguish between moral and immoral acts, between good and evil.
2. The concept of good and evil *(ire* and *ibi)* are necessary for our understanding of moral concepts and moral principles.
3. God's will is the source of good and evil in man's behaviour and without which we would never have had the concept of morality.
4. Therefore God must be the source of our concept of morality.
5. Therefore God is the source of our moral ideas.

This reconstruction of Makinde's argument should reveal the problem with it: premise 3, which seems to be the crucial one for the conclusion, is asserted without any argument.

Finally, I would like to comment briefly on Makinde's use of the *Ifá* literary corpus. Put simply, I do not think that it advances his case. It is true that the most important religious and moral ideas of the Yoruba are contained in the *Ifá* corpus. But, as is clear even to traditionalists, *Ifá* is not only a religion. It is, as Abimbola (1975b:32) puts it, also "a literary and philosophical system". Furthermore, it is "the store-house of Yoruba culture inside which the Yoruba comprehension of their own historical experiences and understanding of their environment can always be found" (1975b:32). Makinde (1988:12) himself refers to it as "the ancient wisdom" of the Yoruba. The *Odù's* make use of parables to teach moral ideas, in most cases without reference to *Olódùmarè* or the other deities. Makinde also provides a clear illustration of such cases in his first example which deals with the ethic of respect for elders and the consequences of breaking it as a moral law:

> Don't you know that prosperity ever eludes those who assault a *Babaláwo* of high repute, long life will not be within the reach of those who beat up reputable herbalists. Surely a young man who physically assaults a Mallam at his prayer is courting premature death (in Abimbola 1975b:32).

The point of this *Odù* is to emphasise the undesirable consequence (in this world) of disrespect for elders, not just for experts. Besides, Yoruba proverbs, regarded as signposts in Yoruba ethics, also feature numerous cautionary notes of good behaviour and respect for elders. Thus, they say *Omo tó mó ìyá ré lójú, òsi ni yóó ta omo náà pa* (A child who makes an abusive face at his mother will die in abject penury). Or *Omo tí kò gbó ti ìyá, tí kò gbó ti baba, òde níí lé 'mo wálé* (A child who habitually disobeys his mother and pays no heed to his father's admonitions, will need to seek refuge with the same parents, when chased – from outside – by malevolent strangers) (Oladeji 1988:49). These make no reference to oracles or religion. It is clear from the foregoing that Makinde has not succeeded in making a case for the idea of a religious foundation for morality in Yoruba thought.

It is one thing to claim that religion influences peoples' approach to moral behaviour, but another thing entirely to argue that religion *must* be the foundation of their morality. To say that religion is the foundation of a people's morality is to say that without it they could not behave in a morally responsible manner. But the question remains, which comes first, religion or morality? Indeed, is it not plausible to suggest that it is the concern that people have about their moral and social relationships that force religious concerns on them? Secondly, is it really the case that we do not have people who are not bothered about spiritual issues among the traditional Yoruba? I have myself argued elsewhere (Gbadegesin 1986:227–244) that there is evidence for the view that some moral values have a religious *influence* for virtually all Nigerian traditional thinkers, but that this does not mean that morality is founded on religion or that a further ultimate source cannot be found for their moral ideas. I referred to the belief common among the Yoruba that a person who is morally good, who is generous in giving, or respectful to elders, or chaste in words and deeds would find favour with the gods and, barring the evil machinations of the people of the world, he or she would prosper. I then observed that from this last point, it appears that morality is also justified by reference to its consequences for the individual. It seems now the answer to the question, "Why be morally good?" is the prudential one: "It will pay you." This appears to be the ultimate appeal for moral goodness in traditional Nigerian world-views (Gbadegesin 1986:242).

As a Yoruba saying puts it: *Enití ó se oore, ó seé fún ara rè, enití ó se ikà, ó seé fún ara rè. Ati oore àti ikà, òkan kìí gbé. Ojó àtisùn l'ó sòro* (The person who performs good deeds does so for him/herself. The person who performs wicked acts does so for him/herself. Neither good deeds nor wicked acts will go unrewarded. The time of death is the hard fact that should be born in mind). Of course, this is not to say that the Yoruba therefore emphasise selfish considerations in moral matters. The question why should I be morally good is not posed by everyone. It is posed by those who have inclinations to do otherwise. They are the selfish ones who need to be motivated for reasons that appeal to themselves.

The point, therefore, is that for those who may, for selfish reasons, not be motivated to do what is right, there are considerations in the system to help them. The important thing is to get people to do what is right. There is much evidence for this contention. In the Yoruba world-view, a person is expected to show hospitality and generosity to others since he/she may sometimes be in a position in which he/she would need the hospitality of others, and if he/she has denied it to others sometimes, he/she cannot expect to have it from anyone. For, "the calabash which contains poison does not break easily" (*Igbá oró kì í fó*), meaning "Whatever one sows, one will reap"; or, on the positive side, "Kindness begets kindness" *(Oore loore í wó tò)*. Even when it cannot be guaranteed that one will reap the fruits of one's character in one's life-time, moral goodness is still enjoined by appeal to one's moment of death – so that it may be a peaceful one.

A wealthy and powerful person who thinks he/she can afford to be selfish and arrogant should think twice, then. On the one hand, no one knows what tomorrow may bring. Today's powerful human being may be the most underprivileged tomorrow. A wise person would therefore be open handed and respectful of others, however poor and wretched they may be. Even when people are sure that they will not themselves need help from anyone, they should think of their children's fate. For their own seeds of selfishness or, indeed, real wickedness, the Yoruba believe, will be reaped by their children. On the other hand, one of the most valued things in life is a peaceful moment of death. For this is generally regarded as an indication of a pleasant life in the land of the dead. A wicked person, it is believed, starts paying for his or her deeds on the death-bed by suffering an unusual agony that will be their future lot. Far from having a religious foundation, then, we have here a system of morality which, while it makes use of religion as a motivating factor, is clearly pragmatic and "this-worldly" to the core.

IWÀ: THE PRIMACY OF EXISTENCE AND CHARACTER

Iwà is, for the Yoruba, perhaps the most important moral concept. A person is morally evaluated according to his/her *ìwà* – whether good or bad. A miser (*ahun*) is an *oníwà-burúkú*; a generous person *(òlàwó)* is an *oníwà-rere*. A gentle person is an *oníwà-pèlé*; a short-tempered, aggressive person (*onínú fùfù*) is an *oníwà-líle*. It is interesting, though, that each of these evaluations has an adjective attached, suggesting that *ìwà* may be good or bad, gentle or tough, generous or stingy. *Iwà* as character needs further elaboration.

That elaboration has been provided by Wande Abimbola (1975b) and Roland Abiodùn (1983). According to Abimbola (1975b:393), the original meaning of *Iwà* is "the fact of being, living or existing". So *ìwà* means existence. *Iwà* as character is therefore a derivative from this original. In its original meaning, the perfect ideal of *ìwà* is *àìkú* (immortality). Hence the saying *Aikú parí ìwà* (Immortality completes existence or immortality is perfect existence) (Abimbola 1975b:393). However, *ìwà* (as character) and *ìwà* (as existence) do not just have a homophonous relationship; they are also related by etymology and one appears to be a derivation of the other (Abiodun 1983:14).

Iwà as existence has a strong connection with *ìwà* as character. According to a myth recorded in the Ifa literary corpus, *iwà*, the daughter of *Sùúrù* – the first child of *Olódùmarè* – was married to *Orúnmìlà*. *Iwà* was extremely beautiful, but lacked good behaviour and character. When *Orúnmìlà* could no longer accommodate her bad disposition, he sent her packing. However, he later experienced a terrible plunge in his fortunes which had been made possible by *Iwà's* presence. He therefore decided to seek out *Iwà* again, even if it meant selling all his property. He eventually went looking for *Iwà*, singing the praise names of *Iwà* along the way: "*Iwà, Iwà l'à nwá, Iwà. Kámúrágbá tarágbàá, Iwà; Iwà, l'à nwá, Iwà*", etc. He got her back finally; but he (not *Iwà* and her misbehaviour) was blamed. The moral is that he is expected to be tolerant, to understand *Iwà* for what she is: "*Mo Iwà fún oníwà.*"

As Abiodun (1983:14) has rightly said, it is noteworthy that *Iwà* (as the one with bad character) is not blamed, but *Orúnmìlà* (who cannot tolerate her) is blamed. This should point to another element in the emphasis on individuality in the tradition. *Iwà* is the handiwork of the Deity, the originator of existence, and her beauty as well as her character are expressions of her existence as an individual being. The fact of existence which *Iwà* illustrates is an endowment of the Deity. Her beauty is consistent with that endowment and so *Orúnmìlà* is expected to treat her as an individual expression of *Olódùmarè's* creativity. Existence is primary, then, and character is derivative, based as it is on human ideas of morality. Each creature of *Olódùmarè* is thought of as having its beauty (*Iwà l'ewà*) by the fact of its existence, and it is not to be undermined by human valuation. Thus, among the Yoruba there are admirers and devotees of such historical figures and deities as *Sàngó* (in spite of his recognition as a strict disciplinarian), *Esù* (trickster god, in spite of his unpredictability), *Sònpònná* (god of smallpox). All these manifest characters which may be inadequate in human terms (Abiodun 1983:15). And physically deformed persons are also expected to be appreciated and respected by virtue of their special relationship to *Orìsà-nlá*, the creation divinity who is supposed to have made them specially as his devotees. Thus, they deserve special protection: *òwò òrìsà làá fìí wo àfin*.

Yet *iwà* as character is given its own place too. Individuality is symbolised by the appeal to *Iwà* (as existence), the wife of *Orúnmìlà*. On the other hand, paradoxically, it is *Sùúrù* (the father of *Iwà*) that symbolises the idea of *iwà* as character. *Sùúrù* means patience. Patience is therefore symbolically the father (we may say master) of *Iwà* (in both senses). *Iwà* (as existence), wife of *Orúnmìlà*, who lacks good character, needs patience to understand her, deal with her, and if possible, transform her. On the other hand, *Iwà* (as character) is a child of *Sùúrù* (patience) in the sense that patience is the overall embodiment of good character – *Agbà t'ó ní sùúrù, ohun gbogbo l'óní* (The elder who has *sùúrù* has everything). *Sùúrù* is the source of gentle character (or *iwà pèlé*) and good character (*iwà rere*). A demonstration of *iwà pèlé* is to be mindful of the individuality of others, to treat them gently, to be tolerant and accommodating of the peculiarity of others' existence. The Yoruba expression *Iwà l'ewà* depicts their understanding of existence itself as constituting beauty, while the cognate expression *Iwà rere l'èsó èniyàn* (Good character – good existence – is the adornment of a human being) depicts the significance attached to good character.

An existence, by virtue of its source in the Deity, is good and to be appreciated. It is good to exist. Existence itself is beautiful. But however beautiful a thing is, there is always room for improvement. There are degrees of beauty. Thus an original beauty of existence could be improved upon by adorning it with character. The difference between one form of existence and another would then be located in the quality of its adornment, that is, the quality of its character. This is the meaning of *ìwà rere l'èsó èniyàn*. But *èsó* (cosmetic) is fleeting; it could fade. Does this mean that *ìwà* (character) could fade too? It would appear so. It is not unusual to find a person who has been known to be a very good model of excellent character *(omolúwàbí)* suddenly turn bad. This may be due to several factors: a downturn in fortunes, the sudden and shocking loss of a loved one, etc. The case of *Efúnsetán Aníwúrà, Iyálóde Ibadan* comes readily to mind here. In the play written by Akinwumi Isola, Efunsetan is presented as a very cheerful and generous woman. Then something happens. Her only daughter dies during childbirth and suddenly Efunsetan turns monstrous, committing all kinds of atrocities. The point that needs to be noted in this is that even in such cases, when the cosmetic of existence suddenly disappears, there still remains the core of existence and its original beauty. The moral that appears to come out of this, therefore, is that to avoid this sudden degeneration of *ìwà* (character), there is a need for character training from the beginning so that the cosmetic of *ìwà* (character) may have time to sink into the core of *ìwà* (existence) very early in life. This is what the socialisation process is all about, though the limits on how far it can go are also very well appreciated in the pragmatic approach of the people to moral education. Both concepts of *ìwà* are therefore important for our understanding of Yoruba moral ideas, and attention is normally paid to them in traditional patterns of moral education.

Children are appreciated for what they are. Though they are encouraged to be the best they could be, when, for some reason, they do not conform, they are not thrown out because, as they say, *A kì í fi omo burúkú fún ekùn pa je* (We do not throw a child to the tiger just because he/she is bad). Indeed, it is recognised, in various idioms, that a child cannot be altogether bad; he/she must have certain traits of goodness or virtues. Even if all the child's traits are bad, he/she must have certain useful features even in his/her badness: *Omo burúkú ní ojó tirè* (A bad child has his/her day of usefulness), and also *Nítorí wèrè ti ìta láá fìí ní wèrè ti ilé* (Since there are rascals outside, we should not mind the rascality of our own kids – because they can stand up to defend us if the rascals from outside should attempt to attack us). These sayings show that the Yoruba have a more or less pragmatic approach to the moral upbringing of children and an attitude of tolerance to adult behaviour. While they do not encourage immoral behaviour, they know that once in a while people may behave immorally when they are out of sight (*Kò sí eniti kìí hu ìwà ibàjé bí ilè bá dá tán; eniti Olódúmarè pa tirè mó ní èniyàn rere*).

It may be argued by advocates of the claim that religion is the foundation for Yoruba morality that the foregoing reference to *ìwà* as the primacy of existence and character supports their position and contradicts the point I have made concerning the pragmatic nature of Yoruba ethics. However, this would be a misconception. As I observed above, *Ifá* is not just a religion. It is a source of Yoruba collective wisdom. It is generally acknowledged that *Orúnmìlà* speaks in parables and when traditional thinkers need to drive home a point, they have easy recourse to what appears to be the age-old tradition of speaking in parables. It should also be noted that in the story, *Orúnmìlà*, the oracle himself is blamed for maltreating his wife. This should strike a note: not even the oracle is spared as far as the moral judgement of actions is concerned. And for a devotee of the *Ifá* oracle, the morality of the society appears to provide a yardstick for judging the conduct of the oracle. It follows therefore that the Yoruba are very pragmatic in their approach to morality, and though religion may serve them as a motivating force, it is not the ultimate appeal in moral matters.

THE MORAL FOUNDATIONS OF AN AFRICAN CULTURE

KWASI WIREDU

INTRODUCTION

Morality in the strictest sense is universal to human culture. Indeed, it is *essential* to all human culture. Any society without a modicum of morality must collapse. But what is morality in this sense? It is, simply, the observance of rules for the harmonious adjustment of the interests of the individual to those of others in society. This, of course, is a minimal concept of morality. A richer concept of morality, even more pertinent to human growth, will have an essential reference to that special kind of motivation called the sense of duty. Morality in this sense involves not just the *de facto* conformity to the requirements of the harmony of interests, but also that conformity to those requirements which is inspired by an imaginative and sympathetic identification with the interests of others even at the cost of a possible curtailment of one's own interests. This is not a demand for a supererogatory altruism. But a certain minimum of altruism is absolutely essential to the moral motivation. In this sense, too, morality is probably universal to all human societies, though most certainly not to all known individuals.

The foregoing reflection still does not exclude the possibility of a legitimate basis for differentiating the morals of the various peoples of the world. This is so for at least three reasons. First of all, although morality in both of the senses just discriminated is the same wherever and whenever it is practised, different peoples, groups, and individuals have different understandings of it. The contrasting moral standpoints of humanism and supernaturalism, for example, illustrate this diversity. Secondly, the concrete cultural context in which a moral principle is applied may give it a distinctive colouring. Lastly, but most importantly, there is a broad concept of morals closely contiguous to the narrow one – which is what the two concepts of morality noted earlier on together amount to – in regard to which the contingencies of space, time, and clime may play quite a constitutive role. This appertains to the domain that, speaking very broadly, may be called custom. What is pertinent here are such things as the prescriptions and proscriptions operative in a community regarding life and death, work and leisure, reward and retribution, aspirations and aversions, pleasure and pain, and the relationships between the sexes, the generations, and other social categories and classes. The combined impact of such norms of life and thought in a society should give a distinctive impression of its morals.

AKAN HUMANISM

But let me start with the matter of conceiving morals. African conceptions of morals would seem generally to be of a humanistic orientation. Anthropological studies need substantial support for this claim. Nevertheless, the accounts are not always philosophically inquisitive, and I prefer, in elaborating on this characterisation, to rely on my own native knowledge of the life and thought of the Akans of Ghana. On this basis, I can affirm the humanism in question with less inhibition. The commonest formulation of this outlook is in the saying, which almost any Akan adult or even young hopeful will proffer on the slightest provocation, that it is a human being that has value: *Onipa na ohia*. The English translation just given of the Akan saying, though pertinent, needs supplementation, for the crucial term here has a double connotation. The word *(o)hia* in this context means both that which is of value and that which is needed. Through the first meaning the message is imparted that all value derives from human interests, and through the second that human fellowship is the most important of human needs. When this last thought is uppermost in his or her consciousness an Akan would be likely to add to the maxim under discussion an elucidation to the effect that one might have all the gold in the world and the best stocked wardrobe, but if one were to appeal to these in the hour of need they would not respond; only a human being will. (*Onipa ne asem: mefre sika a, sika nnye so; mefre ntama a, ntama nmye so; onipa ne asem.*) What is already beginning to emerge is the great stress on human sociality in Akan thought, but before pursuing this angle of the subject, let me tarry a while on the significance of Akan humanism.

One important implication of the founding of value on human interests is the independence of morality from religion in the Akan outlook: what is good in general is what promotes human interests. Correspondingly, what is good in the more narrowly ethical sense is, by definition, what is conducive to the harmonisation of those interests. Thus, the will of God, not to talk of that of any other extra-human being, is logically incapable of defining the good. On the Akan understanding of things, indeed, God is good in the highest; but his goodness is conceptually of a type with the goodness of a just and benevolent ancestor, only in his case quality and scale are assumed to be limitless. The prospect of punishment from God or some lesser being may concentrate the mind on the narrow path of virtue, but it is not this that creates the sense of moral obligation. Similarly, the probability of police intervention might conceivably give pause to a would-be safe-breaker, though if he or she had any sense of morals at all it would not be thanks to the collective will of the police or even the state.

This conceptual separation of morals from religion is, most likely, responsible in some measure for the remarkable fact that there is no such thing as an institutional religion in Akan culture. The procedures associated with the belief in sundry extra-human beings of varying powers and inclinations, so often given pride of place in accounts of African religions, are in fact practical utilitarian programs for tapping the resources of this world. The idea, in a nutshell, is that God invested the cosmos with all sorts of potentialities, physical and quasi-physical, personal and quasi-personal, which human beings may bend to their purposes, if they learn how. Naturally, in dealing with beings and powers believed to be of a quasi-personal character, certain aspects of behaviour patterns will manifest important analogies to the canons of ordinary human interactions. For example, if you wanted something from a being of superhuman repute who is open to persuasion mixed with praise, pragmatic common sense alone would recommend an attitude of demonstrative respect and circumspection and a language of laudatory circumlocution reminiscent of worship, but the calculative and utilitarian purpose would belie any attribution of a specifically religious motivation. In fact, the Akans are known to be sharply contemptuous of "gods" who fail to deliver; continued respect is conditional on a high percentage of scoring by the Akan reckoning.

In total contrast to the foregoing is the Akan attitude to the supreme being, which is one of unconditional reverence and absolute trust. Absent here is any notion that so perfect a being requires or welcomes institutions for singing or reciting his praises. Nor, relatedly, are any such institutions felt to be necessary for the dissemination of moral education or the reinforcement of the will to virtue. The theatre of moral upbringing is the home, at parents' feet and within range of kinsmen's inputs. The mechanism is precept, example, and correction. The temporal span of the process is lifelong, for, although upbringing belongs to the beginning of our earthly careers, the need for correction is an unending contingency in the lives of mortals. In adulthood, of course, as opposed to earlier stages in life, moral correction involves discourses of a higher level and may entail, besides, the imposition of compensatory obligations (of which more later); but, at all stages, verbal lessons in morality are grounded in conceptual and empirical considerations about human well-being. All this is why the term "humanistic" is so very apt as a characterisation of Akan moral thinking. At least in part, this is why it is correct to describe that ethic as non-supernaturalistic in spite of the sincere belief in a supreme being.

Insofar, then, as the concept of religion is applicable to the Akan outlook on life and reality, it can refer only to the belief and trust in a supreme being. In this respect, Akan religion is purely intellectual. In this respect, too, it is purely personal, being just a level of an individual's voluntary metaphysic, devoid of social entanglements. In truth, most Akans espouse that metaphysic as a matter of course. Akan conventional wisdom actually holds that the existence of God is so obvious that it does not need to be taught even to a child *(Obi nkyere akwadaa Nyame)*. Nevertheless, sceptics are not unknown in Akan society, and a time-honoured policy of peaceful *laissez faire* extends to them as to all others in matters of private persuasion.

DEFINING MORALITY

Morality, too, is intellectual, by Akan lights. Concrete moral situations in real life are frequently highly composite tangles of imponderables, and perceiving them in their true lineaments is a cognitive accomplishment in itself. So, too, is the sure grasping of first principles and their judicious application to the particulars of conduct. Morality is also personal, for in the final analysis the individual must take responsibility for his or her own actions. But surely morality is neither purely intellectual, for it has an irreducible passional ingredient, nor is it purely personal, for it is quintessentially social.

All these insights are encapsulated in various Akan maxims and turns of phrase. Recognition of the intellectual dimension of right conduct is evidenced in the Akan description of a person of ethical maturity as an *obadwenma*. This word means "one possessed of high thinking powers". Literally, it means "child, thinking child", in other words, a thinking child of the species. The Akans are no less emphatic in their articulation of their sense of individual responsibility. According to a very popular proverb, it is because God dislikes injustice that he gave everyone their own name (thereby forestalling any misattribution of responsibility). Along with this clear sense of individual responsibility goes an equally strong sense of the social reverberations of an individual's conduct. The primary responsibility for an action, positive or negative, rests with the doer, but a non-trivial secondary responsibility extends to the individual's family and, in some cases, to the surrounding community. This brings us to the social orientation of the Akan concept of a person. We will not be able to elaborate it fully in the present discussion, but a crucial consideration will be adduced here. It is that, for the Akans, a person is social not only because he/she lives in a community, which is the only context in which full development, or indeed any sort of human development is possible, but also because, by his/her original constitution, a human being is part of a social whole.

The underlying doctrine is this. A person consists of three elements. One of these comes *directly* from God and is, in fact, a speck of the divine substance. This is the life principle. By virtue of this constituent all human beings are one; they are all members of the universal family of humankind whose head and spring is God (*Nipa nyinaa ye Nyame mma: obiara nnye asaase ba*). Literally, all human beings are the children of God; none is a child of the earth. The two remaining elements are more mundane in origin. There is what might be called the blood principle which derives from the mother and, somewhat more specifically, there is what might be called the charisma principle which comes from the father. The blood from the mother is what principally gives rise to a person's body. The biological input from the father is responsible for the degree of personal presence that each individual develops at the appropriate stage (i.e. the individual's degree of charisma). The ontological classification of these elements is not exactly straightforward. Suffice it to say that the physical/spiritual dichotomy is unlikely to be a source of light in this connection. In any case, our interest here is in the social significance of those components.

Both the maternal and paternal contributions to the make-up of a person are the basis of membership in specific social units. The Akans being a matrilineal group, it is the blood principle that situates a person in the most important kinship unit, namely, the lineage, or, more extensively, the clan. Through the charisma principle one is a member of a grouping on the father's side which, although largely ceremonial, is nevertheless the framework of a lot of goodwill.

The point now is that, on this Akan showing, a person has a well structured social identity even before birth. Thus, when an Akan maxim points out that when a human being descends from on high he/she alights in a town (*se onipa siane fi soro a obesi kuro mu*), the idea is that one comes into a community in which one already has well defined social affiliations. But society presupposes rules, and moral rules are the most essential of these. Since all rules have their rationale, a question that challenges the ethical imagination, especially one thoroughly impregnated with visions of the ineluctable sociality of human existence, is: what is the rationale of moral rules? Among the Akans some of the most profound philosophic conceptions are expressed by way of art motifs, and a celebrated answer to this question is offered in one such construct of fine art: a crocodile with one stomach and two heads locked in combat. The lessons are:

1. Although human beings have a core of common interests, they also have conflicting interests that precipitate real struggles.
2. The aim of morality, as also derivatively of statesmanship, is to harmonise those warring interests through systematic adjustment and adaptation. The single stomach symbolises not only the commonality of interests, but also a natural basis for the possibility of a solution to the existential antinomy.

Two levels of solution are distinguishable, corresponding to a distinction foreshadowed in our opening paragraph. There is the level of prudence or enlightened self-interest, and there is that of pure moral motivation. Both species of thought and intention may be equally adapted to securing the social good, the first through cool and calm ratiocination, the second through both rational reflection and human sympathy. But they evoke different appraisals from people of goodwill. There will always be something distasteful about correctness of conduct bereft of passion. A Ghanaian comedian puts it even more strongly. Speaking with a deliberately unidiomatic bombast, he opines: "Ability without sentimentality is nothing short of barbarity." Nevertheless, it appears that teachers of morals everywhere have tended to find prudential considerations more psychologically efficacious in moral persuasion than abstract appeals to goodwill. Certainly, Akan ethical reflection does not stay immobile at this level of ethics, but Akan discourse abounds in prudential maxims, for example:

1. If you do not allow your neighbour to reach nine you will never reach ten. *(Woamma wo yonko antwa nkrong a worentwa edu.)*
2. Somebody's troubles have arrived; those of another are on the way. *(Obi de aba; obi de nam kwan so.)*
3. It is a fool that says, "My neighbour is the butt of the attack, not me." *(Kwasea na ose, "Ye de meyonko, yenne me.")*
4. The stick that was used to beat Takyi is the same that will be used to beat Nyankomago. *(Abaa a yede boo Takyi no aa na ye de bebo Nyankomago.)*
5. One person's path will intersect with another's before too long. *(Obi kwan nkye na asi obi de mu.)*

That Akan ethics transcends this level of moral understanding is evident from other parts of their corpus of moral sayings. I will comment here on one particularly instructive form of moral expostulation. To a person whose conduct betrays obliviousness to the interests of others, it is said, "Sticking into your neighbour's flesh, it might just as well be sticking into a piece of wood" *(Etua woyonko ho a etua dua mu)*, than which there can scarcely be a lower rating for a person's moral stature. On this reading of morals, the ultimate moral inadequacy consists in that lack of feeling which is the root of all selfishness. The implied imperative is: "In all inter-personal situations put yourself into the skin of the other and see if you can contemplate the consequences of your proposed action with equanimity." If we call the recommended frame of mind sympathetic impartiality, we may elicit from the Akan maxim under discussion the view that sympathetic impartiality is the first principle of all morals. This principle is the logical basis of the Golden Rule, or the obverse of it that is frequently heard in Akan ethical talk, namely, "Do not do unto others what you would not that they do unto you" *(Nea wo yonko de ye wo a erenye wo de no mfa nye no)*. Or, more literally, what you would not find acceptable if it were done to you by another, do not do to him or her. To be sure, this does not sound, even in our vernacular, as epigrammatic as the normal run of Akan apothegms, but it provides, nonetheless, a solid foundation for the definition of moral worth in its most edifying sense.

ETHICS AND PRACTICE

The foregoing account of the Akan perspective on moral first principles, however brief, must form the basis of our next question, which is: "In what basic ways do the

Akans endeavour to translate their ethical understanding into practical fact?" In this regard the single most important consideration concerns the depth of the Akan sense of what we have called the sociality of human existence. Morality is, of course, necessarily social. Hence any group of humans that can be credited with any sense of morals at all – surely, a minimal species credential – will have some sense of human sociality. But in the consciousness of moral humankind there is a finely graduated continuum of the intensity of this feeling which ranges, in an ascending order, from the austerely delimited social sympathies of rigorous individualism to the pervasive commitment to social involvement characteristic of communalism. It is a commonplace of anthropological wisdom that African social organisation manifests the latter type of outlook. Akan society is eminently true to this typology.

What this means, more amply, is that Akan society is of a type in which the greatest value is attached to communal belonging. And the way in which a sense of communal belonging is fostered in the individual is through the concentrated stress on kinship identity already adumbrated in our earlier allusions to the Akan concept of a person. Not only is there what might perhaps be called an ontological basis for this identity in terms of the constituents of personhood, but there is also a distinct normative layer of a profound social significance in that concept. Thus conceived, a human person is essentially the centre of a thick set of concentric circles of obligations and responsibilities matched by rights and privileges revolving round levels of relationships irradiating from the consanguinity of household kith and kin, through the "blood" ties of lineage and clan, to the wider circumference of human familyhood based on the common possession of the divine spark.

In consequence of this character of the Akan concept of a person, habitual default in duties and responsibilities could lead to a diminution in one's status as a person in the eyes of the community. Not, of course, that becoming less and less of a person implies being thought more and more unworthy of human rights. On the contrary, there is a strong sense of the irreducibility of human dignity in Akan thought. However socially inept an individual may be, he/she still remains a being begotten of a direct gift of God incarnated through the intimacy of man and woman. He/she remains, in other words, a human being, and as such is deserving of a certain basic respect and sympathy. Indeed, as soon as confirmed social futility begins to look pathologically chronic, animadversion quickly turns into solicitude, and any previous efforts in hortatory correction or in the application of more concrete sanctions are redirected towards rehabilitation, usually with the aid of indigenous specialists in bodily and mental health.

Nevertheless, any Akan steeped in the culture, or even just sensitive to surrounding social norms, constantly watches and prays lest he/she be overtaken by the spectre of loss of personhood (in any degree). More positively and also more optimistically, every cultivated Akan *(Okaniba)* sees life as a scenario of continual striving after personhood in ever increasing dimensions. The details of this life mission, so to speak, will also be the details of the Akan vision of the ethical life. We must here content ourselves with only broad outlines. But before going on, let us note that our focus has been on ethics or morals in the sense in which morality is a matter of *mores* rather than of the Categorical Imperative or even of the less hallowed canons of prudence.

What, then, in its social bearings, is the Akan ideal of personhood? It is the conception of an individual who, through mature reflection and steady motivation, is able to carve out a reasonably ample livelihood for self, "family", and a potentially wide group of kin dependants, besides making substantial contributions to the well-being of society at large. The communalistic orientation of the society in question means that an individual's image will depend rather crucially upon the extent to which his/her actions benefit others rather than him/herself, not, of course, by accident or coincidence, but by design. The implied counsel, though, is not one of unrelieved self-denial, for the Akans are well aware that charity further afield must start at home. More pertinently, they are apt to point out that one cannot blow a horn on an empty stomach (*Yede ayaase na ehyen aben*). Still, an individual who remained content with self-regarding successes would be viewed as so circumscribed in outlook as not to merit the title of a real person.

Opportunities for other-regarding exertions in Akan society were legion in the past and remain so even now. By the very nature of the traditional economy, which was predominantly agricultural and based on individual self-employment, public works had, as a rule, to be done by voluntary communal labour. Habitual absences or malingering or half-hearted participation marked an individual down as a useless person (*onipa hunu*) or, by an easily deduced Akan equation, a non-person (*onye onipa*). In contemporary Ghana (and Ivory Coast), where the Akans live, many of the public works are financed out of mandatory taxes and carried out by professionals with hired labour. Nevertheless, in the villages and small towns a significant portion of such work is still done by way of voluntary communal labour, and a good proportion also through voluntary contributions of money and materials.

SOME CONTEMPORARY PROBLEMS

What follows is a contemporary complication: with the growth of commerce and industry, including the industry of modern politics, a non-negligible number of Akans have become very rich. In the Akan manner, they make voluntary contributions of unprecedented magnitude to their communities; and the communities, for their part, reciprocate in fine eulogistic style and lionise them in other ways too, as is traditional. So far, so good, except for the following circumstance. Some of these rich people are known to have come by their assets through dubious techniques of acquisition. The unfortunate effects of this situation on the ideals of the young constitute some of the more intractable problems generated by the impact of industrialisation on the Akan traditional ethic.

Another aspect of Akan communalism imperilled by modern conditions, through atrophy rather than adulteration, is the practice of neighbourhood mutual aid. This practice has its foundations deep in the Akan conception of values. It is relevant here to recall the Akan adage, *Onipa na ohyia*, quoted earlier in this discussion. It was interpreted as affirming, through the semantic fecundity of the word *hyia*, both that human interest is the basis of all value and that human fellowship is the most important of human needs. The concept of *hyia* in the context of that adage is, in fact, a veritable mine of ethical meanings. In that context it also bears the seeds of another fundamental thought in the Akan philosophy of life which is made explicit in the maxim, *Onipa hia moa*, meaning, by way of first approximation, "A human being needs help." The intent of the maxim, however, is not just to observe a fact, but also to prescribe a line of conduct. The imperative here is carried by the word *hia,* which in this context also has a connotation of entitlement: a human being deserves, ought, to be helped.

This imperative is born of an acute sense of the essential dependency of the human condition. The idea of dependency may even be taken as a component of the Akan conception of a person. "A human being," says a noted Akan proverb, "is not a palm tree so as to be self-sufficient" (*Onipa nye abe na ne ho ahyia ne ho*). Indeed, at birth a human being is not only not self-sufficient but also radically self-insufficient, if one may be permitted the expression: he/she is totally dependent on others. In due course, through growth and acculturation, acquired skills and abilities will reduce this dependency but will never eliminate it completely. Self-reliance is, of course, understood and recommended by the Akans, but its very possibility is predicated upon this ineliminable residue of human dependency. Human beings, therefore, at all times, in one way or another, directly or indirectly, need the help of their kind.

One very standard situation in Akan life in which this truth was continually illustrated was in traditional agriculture. As hinted earlier, this was generally based on smallholdings worked by individual farmers and their households. In such a mode of production recurrent stages were easily foreseeable where the resources of any one farmer would be insufficient to accomplish a necessary task efficiently – be it the initial clearing of the ground or the scooping out of, say, cocoa beans from great heaps of pods. At such moments, all that was necessary was for one to send word to one's neighbours indicating the time, place, and the nature of the help needed. Very much as day follows night, the people would assemble at the right time at the indicated place with their own implements of work and together help get the job done speedily and with almost festive enthusiasm, in full and warranted conviction that when their turn came the same gesture would be returned in exactly the same spirit. Anybody who availed himself of the benefits of this system and yet dragged his feet when the call came from others was liable to be convicted, at the bar of public opinion, of such fathomless degeneracy as to be branded a social outcast. The type of mutual aid here discussed probably occurs in varying intensities in rural communities all over the world, but in traditional Akan society it was so much and so palpably a part of working experience that the Akans actually came to think of life *(obra)* as one continuous drama of mutual aid *(nnoboa)*. *Obra ye nnoboa:* "Life is mutual aid", according to an Akan saying.

In recent times, however, amidst the exigencies of urbanisation and the increasing – if not as yet preponderant – commercialisation of agriculture, the ideology of mutual aid is losing some of its hold; and the spirit of neighbourhood solidarity, though by no means extinguished, is finding fewer avenues of expression. It has not escaped some leaders of opinion that the traditional ethos of mutual aid might profitably be channelled into a strong movement of modern cooperatives, but as yet, organised effort in this direction is halting in momentum and paltry in results.

Nevertheless, in countless small ways the sense of human solidarity continues to manifest itself quite pervasively in the daily life of the Akans and of the peoples of Ghana generally, of whom these moral characterisations remain true, if not to the letter, then at least to the syllable. Happily, too, the threat of individualism posed by urbanisation has not as yet proved unduly deleterious to the Akan's national trait. Thus, even now, whether in the countryside or in a large city, a Ghanaian coming upon another human being, Ghanaian or foreigner, who is in difficulty, will go out of his/her way to help. As far as he/she is concerned, the bad person is exactly the one who would walk off on the excuse of some pressing business. Of course, if urbanisation and other apparent concomitants of modernisation are not controlled with conscious and rational planning based on the humane sensitivities of the communalistic ethic, then this fund of automatic good will dry up and African life will experience increasingly the Hobbesian rigours of a single-minded commercialism.

KINSHIP AND MORALITY

The allusion to foreigners in the last paragraph prompts a further observation. The sense of human solidarity which we have been discussing works particularly to the advantage of foreigners, who, in the deeply felt opinion of the Akans, are doubly deserving of sympathy; this is on the grounds, firstly, of their common humanity, and, secondly, of their vulnerability as individuals cut off for the time being, at any rate, from the emotional and material support of their kinship environment. Accordingly, when, some time ago, an Akan guitarist and lyricist, Kwabena Onyina, sang *Akwantu ma sem: akwantufo ye mmobo* (Think of the woes of travel: the plight of a traveller is rueful) he struck a sympathetic chord in the deepest reaches of the Akan consciousness. Gratified visitors to Ghana have often been quick to acknowledge the benefits accruing to them.

Again, to pursue an allusion in the preceding paragraph: the notion of kinship support just mentioned is of the highest importance in the Akan communal set-up, for it is the basis of the sense of belonging which gives the individual much of his/her psychological stability (this, incidentally, is why a traveller bereft of it strikes the Akan so forcefully as a sad case). It is also, conversely, the basis of a good proportion of the obligations in terms of which the individual's moral standing is assessed. The smallest and most intimate Akan kinship unit is the matrilineal household. This includes a person's mother and his/her mother's children, his/her mother's sisters and brothers, the children of the mother's sisters, and, at the top, the grandmother. It is instructive to observe that the English words aunt and cousin fail to capture the depth of kinship feelings corresponding to the relations of mother's sister and mother's sister's children respectively, in spite of their mechanical correctness as translations. In the Akan language the words for mother and mother's children are the same as for mother's sister and mother's sister's children. Since the relationships noted already comprehend quite a sizeable community, especially if the grandmother concerned has been even averagely fertile, this guarantees that in a traditional setting an Akan child begins life with quite a large sense of belonging and a broad sweep of sympathies.

The next extension of the circle of the kinship relations just described brings us to the level of the lineage. Here the *basic* unit consists of a person's grandmother and her children and grandchildren, together with the grandmother's brothers and sisters and the children and grandchildren of her sisters. This unit quickly swells with the culturally legitimate addition of a grandmother's maternal "cousins" and their descendants. From the point of view of a person's civic existence, this is the most significant circle of relations, for it was through the head of the lineage that, in traditional times, a person had his/her political representation. The lineage, as can easily be imagined, is a quite considerable group of people, but it is small in comparison with the maximal limit of kinship grouping, which is the set of all the people descending from one woman. The latter is the clan. For a quick idea of magnitude, consider that the Akans, now numbering in the region of seven million, trace their collective ancestry to seven women. Patently, individual Akans will never know all their relatives, but they can rest assured that they have a million of them.

For many practical purposes, however, it is the household and (basic) lineage circles of relations that have the most significance in terms of informal rights and obligations. Two illustrations must suffice here. Adult members of the lineage may be called upon to make financial contributions to rescue one of the fold fallen on hard times, say, with threatening insolvency. In view of the group's numbers, this does not necessarily take a heavy toll on individual pockets. Moreover, it is not lost upon the reflective individual that he/she might conceivably have been the beneficiary.

The next illustration has to do with somewhat lugubrious subject matter. Bereavement is one of the severest trials of the human psyche; unfortunately, it is recurrent. By both precept and practice Akan traditional culture engages itself, pre-eminently one might say, with finding ways to soothe lacerated emotions in such crises. The lineage system incorporates in its arrangements just such a mechanism. In full operation, everyone in the lineage is expected to play his/her part by word, song, dance, and material resource. Nor does the culture leave this to the lineage alone. Friends, neighbours, and even indirect acquaintances can always be counted upon to help in various ways to lighten the burden of sorrows. The framework for all this is the elaborate system of the Akan funeral. In spite of the excesses to which this institution has become subject through the rising tide of commercialism and egotistical exhibitionism, it remains an avenue for the expression of human solidarity at its most heartfelt. Proper participation therein is, in Akan eyes, contributory proof of real personhood.

CONCLUSION

It is clear from the foregoing that socialisation in the broad context of the lineage can be a veritable school for morality in its Akan acceptation. It is through the kinship channels of the lineage set-up that the Akan sense of the sociality of human beings finds its most natural expression. Moral life in the wider community is only an extension of a pattern of conduct inculcated at the lineage level. The fundamental values, some of which we have already outlined above, are the same on the two planes, and may briefly be summarised. A communalistic orientation will naturally prize social harmony. A characteristic Akan, and, it seems, African way of pursuing this ideal is through decision-making by consensus rather than by majority opinion. In politics – traditional African politics, not the modern travesties rampant on the continent – this leads to a form of democracy very different from the Western variety.

A thoroughgoing consensual approach to social issues can be expected to lead to corresponding procedures in other areas of social life too. A particularly interesting case relates to the Akan reaction to wrongdoing. Though the retributive spirit is not totally absent from reactions, especially at the state level, with some forms of wrongdoing the predominant tendency is to seek compensation or reconciliation or, in cases where extra-human forces are thought to be estranged, purification. I abstain advisedly from using the word "punishment" in this context, for, given this last remark, it may well be that there is no unproblematic rendition of this notion in the Akan conceptual framework. I am unable, however, to pursue this question here.

A well-known feature of Akan morals is respect for age. This is intelligible not only from the fact that we are dealing with a society strongly based on kinship relations which are naturally patterned into hierarchies based on age, but also because in traditional societies, which in part Akan society still remains, age is associated with knowledge, experience, and wisdom.

Akan moral thinking with regard to sex and marriage also deserves special mention. Here the humanistic and communalistic aspects of the Akan outlook come into play with interesting results. Because only empirical considerations bearing on human interests are admitted in moral evaluation, such unconditional proscriptions of pre-marital sex as are found in Christian teaching are absent from the moral rules of the Akans. From their point of view, it would be irrational to stop a prospective couple from seeking full knowledge of each other, moral, psychological, sexual, and so on. There is, of course, no sexual free-for-all; but still, a non-furtive relationship between an unmarried man and an unmarried woman need not be restricted to hugging. The only proviso is that it should be above board. On the other hand, the high value placed on reproductive fertility in a communalistic society based on single family unit agriculture will predictably lead to great emphasis being placed on the desirability of marriage and procreation. So much is this the case that being married with children well raised is part of the necessary conditions for personhood in the normative sense. A non-marrying, non-procreative person, however normal otherwise – not to talk of a Casanova counterpart – can permanently forget any prospect of this type of recognition in traditional Akan society. The only conceivable exceptions will be ones based on the noblest of alternative life commitments.

To understand all these facts about the Akan conception of morals is not necessarily to understand the culture in its entirety, but it is to have some sense of its foundations.

PERSON AND COMMUNITY IN AFRICAN THOUGHT

KWAME GYEKYE

INTRODUCTION

The existence of a social structure is an outstanding, indeed a necessary feature, of every human society. A social structure is evolved not only to give effect to certain conceptions of human nature, but also to provide a framework for both the realisation of the potential, goals, and hopes of the individual members of society, and the continuous existence and survival of society. The type of social structure or arrangement evolved by a particular society seems to reflect – and be influenced by – the public conceptions of personhood held in the society. These conceptions are articulated in the critical analyses and arguments of its intellectuals.

Questions raised by the intellectuals, especially the moral and political philosophers among them, relate, in this connection, to the metaphysical and moral status of a person (or self). The metaphysical question is whether a person, even though he/she lives in a human society, is a self-sufficient atomic individual who does not depend on his/her relationships with others for the realisation of his/her ends and who has ontological priority over the community, or whether the person is by nature a communal (or communitarian) being, having natural and essential relationships with others. Moral questions which may, in some sense, be said to be linked to, or engendered by, metaphysical conceptions of the person, relate to:

1. The status of the rights of the individual – whether these are so fundamental that they may not be overridden in any circumstances.
2. The place of duties – how the individual sees his/her socio-ethical roles in relation to the interests and welfare of others.
3. The existence and appreciation of a sense of common life or common (collective) good.

Moral or normative matters may be expressed in sophisticated and elaborate conceptual formulations; but as practical matters they have their best and least ambiguous articulation or translation in the actual way of life of a people – in the way individuals are expected or not expected to respond to one another in times of need, to spontaneously care for one another, and so on.

My intention in this paper is to explore the above questions which bear on personhood and community; how the two concepts feature and are understood in African culture will be my point of departure. In "An essay on African philosophical thought: The Akan conceptual scheme" (1987) I discussed the concepts of individuality and communalism as they are understood in Akan philosophy in the traditional setting. I shall now, however, focus my attention mainly on the normative aspects of personhood and community.

COMMUNITARIANISM IN AFRICAN SOCIO-ETHICAL THOUGHT

The communal or communitarian (I use the two words interchangeably) aspects of African socio-ethical thought are reflected in the communitarian features of the social structures of African societies. As remarked by many scholars and researchers on the cultures of Africa, these features are not only the outstanding, but the defining characteristics of those cultures. The sense of community that characterises social relations among individuals is a direct consequence of the communitarian social arrangements. This sense of community, according to Dickson, is a

> characteristic of African life to which attention has been drawn again and again by both African and non-African writers on Africa. Indeed, to many this characteristic defines Africanness (1977:4).

According to Senghor,

> Negro-African society puts more stress on the group than on the individuals, more on solidarity than on the activity and needs of the individual, more on the communion of persons than on their autonomy. Ours is a community society (1964:93–94).

Kenyatta makes the following observation with regard to traditional life in Kenya:

> According to Gikuyu ways of thinking, nobody is an isolated individual. Or rather, his uniqueness is a secondary fact about him; first and foremost he is several people's relative and several people's contemporary (1965:297).

Elsewhere, he observes the following:

> Individualism and self-seeking were ruled out. . . . The personal pronoun "I" was used very rarely in public assemblies. The spirit of collectivism was . . . [so] ingrained in the mind of the people (Kenyatta 1965:180).

The communitarian ethos of African culture is also echoed in the works of some African novelists. Clearly, then, African social structures with their underlying socio-ethical philosophy were, and still are, very communitarian.

Now, what would be the conception of personhood held in such a communitarian socio-ethical philosophy? The question is appropriate and would need to be explored, for it is possible for people to assume that with its emphasis on communal values, collective good, and shared ends, communitarianism invariably conceives of the individual person as *wholly* constituted by social relationships; that it tends to whittle down the moral autonomy of the person; that it makes the being and life of the individual person totally dependent on the activities, values, projects, practices, and ends of the community; and, consequently, that it diminishes his/her freedom and capability to choose or question or revaluate the shared values of the community.

The communitarian conception of the individual person needs to be critically and thoroughly examined before making a final judgement on those assumptions. In making the communitarian self – as variously understood in African culture – my point of departure, I shall examine the views expressed in an interesting paper published by Menkiti (1984).

Making Mbiti's (1970:141) understanding or assessment of the status of the person in African culture (expressed in the statement "I am, because we are; and since we are, therefore I am") the basis for his analysis, Menkiti maintains that the African view asserts the ontological primacy, and hence the ontological independence, of the community. He says that

> as far as Africans are concerned, the reality of the communal world takes precedence over the reality of the individual life histories, whatever these may be. (Menkiti 1984:171).

From this assumption, Menkiti infers the following:

1. That in the African view, in contrast with the Western one, "it is the community which defines the person as person, not some isolated static quality of rationality, will or memory" (1984:172).
2. That the African view supports "the notion of personhood as acquired" (1984:174, 178–179); that "personhood is something which has to be achieved, and is not given simply because one is born of human seed" (1984:172).
3. That "as far as African societies are concerned, personhood is something at which individuals could fail" (1984:173).

Menkiti (1984:173) infers the notion of acquisition of personhood also from the use of the pronoun *it* "in many languages, English included" to refer to "children and new borns". I take issue with the views or conclusions expressed in (1) to (3), for they do not necessarily follow from the notion of the priority of the community. Menkiti's views on the metaphysical status of the community *vis-à-vis* that of the person, and his account of personhood in African moral, social, and political philosophy are, in my opinion, overstated and not entirely correct, and require some amendments or refinements. I will, during the course of my argument, justify my criticisms of his views.

However, I should perhaps point out here that the metaphysical construal of personhood in African thought such as Menkiti's, which gives the community priority over the individual person, has a parallel in the conceptions of the social status of the person held by some scholars, both African and non-African. Their position is grounded in the ideological choice of socialism – African socialism – made by most African political leaders in the early days of political independence. Or, is it the case that the social conception of the individual's status is a logical consequence of the metaphysical? The social conception holds a view of communitarianism which may be either radical and unrestricted or moderate and restricted, with either extreme or moderate socio-political consequences for the individual person. Thus, the advocates of the ideology of African socialism, such as Nkrumah, Senghor, and Nyerere, in their anxiety to find anchorage for their ideological choice in the traditional African ideas about society, argued that socialism was foreshadowed in the African traditional idea and practice of communalism (communitarianism). Thus, Nkrumah observed:

> If one seeks the socio political ancestor of socialism, one must go to communalism . . . in socialism, the principles underlying communalism are given expression in modern circumstances (1964:73).

And Senghor also opined that

> Negro-African society is collectivist or, more exactly communal, because it is rather a communion of souls than an aggregate of individuals (1964:49).

These statements clearly suggest the conviction of these African leaders or scholars that the African social order, in its traditional setting, was communitarian and would, for that reason, easily translate into modern socialism. Hence the euphoric and unrelenting pursuit of socialism by most African political leaders for more than two decades following the attainment of political independence. But, inasmuch as they do not appear to have allowed room for the exercise of individual rights, the view of communitarianism held by them may be said to be radical, excessive, and unrestricted – a view of communitarianism I find insupportable.

Communitarianism immediately sees the human person as an inherently (intrinsically) communal being, embedded in a context of social relationships and interdependence, and never as an isolated, atomic individual. Consequently it sees the community not as a mere association of individual persons whose interests and ends are contingently congruent, but as a group of persons linked by interpersonal bonds, biological and/or non biological, who consider themselves primarily as members of the group and who have common interests, goals, and values. The notion of common interests and values is crucial to an adequate conception of community; that notion in fact defines the community. It is the notion of common interests, goals, and values that differentiates a community from a mere association of individual persons. Members of a community share goals and values. They have intellectual and ideological, as well as emotional, attachments to those goals and values; as long as they cherish them, they are ready to pursue and defend them.

It is an obvious fact, of course, that an individual human being is born into an existing human society and, therefore, into a human culture, the latter being a product of the former. As an Akan maxim has it, when a person descends from heaven, he/she descends into a human society *(Onipa firi soro besi a, obesi onipa kurom)*. The fact that a person is born into an existing community must suggest a conception of the person as a communitarian being by nature, even though some people insist on the individuality of the person. The communitarian conception of the person has the following implications:

1. The human person does not voluntarily choose to enter into human community, that is, community life is not optional for any individual person.
2. The human person is at once a cultural being.
3. The human person cannot – perhaps must not – live in isolation from other persons.
4. The human person is naturally oriented toward other persons and must have relationships with them.
5. Social relationships are not contingent but necessary.
6. Following from (4) and (5), the person is constituted, but only partly (see below), by social relationships in which he/she necessarily finds him/ herself.

The fundamentally relational character of the person and the interdependence of human individuals arising out of their natural sociality are thus clear. It is the necessary relationships which complete the being of the individual person who, prior to entering into those relationships, would not be self-complete for, as we are reminded by an Akan maxim, a person is not a palm tree that he or she should be self-complete or self-sufficient *(Onipa nnye abe na ne ho ahyia ne ho)*. It is evidently true that in the social context, in terms of functioning or flourishing in a human community, the individual person is not self-sufficient; his/her capacities, talents, and dispositions are not adequate for the realisation of his/her potential and basic needs. What accrues to a person's natural sociality – and hence natural rationality – provides the buttress indispensable to the actualisation of his/her possibilities.

All this presupposes the priority of the cultural community in which the individual person finds him/herself. Yet, it might be supposed that if a community crucially consists of persons sharing interests and values in some sense, this fact would establish the priority of the individual rather than that of the community, and that therefore the community existentially derives from individuals and the relationships that would exist between them. We may here turn briefly, but critically, to the Akan maxim that one tree does not make or constitute a forest (*Duo baako nnye kwae*). This means that for there to be a forest there should be a number of individual trees; the reality of the forest derives from the individual trees. In the context of the relationship between the individual and the community, the analogical meaning of the maxim is that one individual person does not constitute a community. Just as we would not speak of a forest where there is only one tree, so we would not – cannot – speak of a community where there is only one person. Even though communities are of varying sizes, yet not even the smallest one is constituted by one individual person. According to the maxim, a community emerges, that is, comes into existence, with the congregation of individual persons: the priority of the individual *vis-à-vis* the derivativeness of the community appears implicit in the maxim.

The analogy the maxim seeks to establish between forest and community, however, is a defective one, even though the notion of the metaphysical priority of the individual person implicit in the explanation of the maxim I have provided may be found attractive by some people. The analogy is defective in that whereas the individual tree can grow in a lonely place in isolation from other trees and, thus, without any relationship with them or assistance from them, an individual human person cannot develop and achieve the fullness of his/her potential without the concrete act of relating to other individual persons. Also, whereas the individual person is born into an existing community, not into a solitary wilderness, and is naturally oriented toward other persons, the individual tree can sprout from, or be planted, in a lonely place. But it would be pointless to strain the analogy of the maxim whose intention is to establish that the whole is a function of its parts, and hence to establish the ontological derivativeness of the community.

The ontological derivativeness of the community cannot, however, be upheld. The reason is that the view of the priority of the individual, logically implied by the notion of the ontological derivativeness of the community, makes relationships between persons merely contingent, voluntary, and optional. That conclusion may not lead to the emergence of a community, which, however, is necessary as a basis, not only for defining and articulating the values and goals shared by individual persons, but also for realising the nature or possibilities of the individual person. The community alone constitutes the context, the social or cultural space, in which the actualisation of the possibilities of the individual person can take place, providing the individual person with the opportunity to express his/her individuality, to acquire and develop personality, and to become the kind of person he/she wants to be, i.e. to attain status, goals, expectations, etc. The system of values which the person inherits as he/she enters into the cultural community, and the range of goals in life from which he/she can choose – these are not anterior to a cultural structure, but a function of the structure itself: they are therefore posterior to – indeed the products of – the culture, i.e. the community. Thus, insofar as the cultural community constitutes the context or medium in which the individual person works out and chooses goals and life plans – activities through which the person ultimately becomes what he/she wants to be and acquires the sort of status he/she desires – the cultural community must be held as prior to the individual.

COMMUNAL STRUCTURE AND PERSONHOOD

The articulation of the ontological primacy of the community, the natural sociality of the human person, the organic character of the relations between individual persons, and the all-importance of the community for the total well-being or complete realisation of the nature of the individual person – all this as explicated in the foregoing section certainly can give rise to a hyperbolic and extreme view of the functional and normative status of the community. The characterisations of the nature and status of the community just provided may be true; in fact they are true, to my mind. Yet one could err in at least some of the conclusions one might draw from them by overlooking the logic or relevance of attributes that can be delineated as belonging essentially to the human person *qua* person. A consideration of other aspects of human nature would certainly be appropriate: a person is, of course, by nature a social (communal) being; but he/she is by nature other things as well (i.e. he/she possesses other essential attributes). Failure to recognise this may result in pushing the significance and implications of a person's communal nature beyond their limits, an act that would in turn result in investing the community with an all-engulfing moral authority to determine everything in the life of the individual person. One might thus easily succumb to the temptation of exaggerating the normative status and power of the cultural community in relation to those of the person, thus obfuscating our understanding of the real nature of the person. It seems to me that Menkiti succumbs to this temptation.

Menkiti deploys arguments to prove that African thought considers personhood as something defined or conferred by the community and as something that must be acquired by the individual. In my critical examination of his paper I shall start with arguments that emerge out of his understanding of African cultural practices or beliefs and his attribution to African thought of an analysis of a characteristic of English grammar.

Menkiti, as I have already mentioned, infers the notion of acquisition of personhood from the use of the neuter pronoun "it" in many languages, including English, to refer to children and new borns but not to adults. The point he wants to make is that the use of the neuter pronoun for children and new borns means that they are not yet persons – the community has not yet conferred personhood on them. They are now going through the "process" of becoming persons. The inference Menkiti draws would most probably be incorrect for a number of African languages. It is, indeed, surprising that an inference based on the characteristics of a non-African language is regarded as having serious implications for African thought.

It would have been more instructive and appropriate for him to examine how the neuter pronoun "it" functions in some African languages, and whether it functions in the same way in African languages as it does in English. What he says about the pronoun "it" does not apply at all to the Akan language; for example, the neuter pronoun "it" does not exist in this language for animate things. Thus, "He is in the room" is translated in Akan as *Ówó dan no mu*; "She is in the room" as *Ówó dan no mu*; and "It (referring, for example, to a dog) is in the room" also as *Ówó dan no mu*. However, "it" is used for inanimate things. Thus, the answer to one question, "Where is the book?" will be *Éwo dan no mu*, that is, "It is in the room." Thus *"e" is* used as the neuter pronoun only for inanimate objects. Children and newly borns are of course not inanimate objects. Since the Akan neuter pronoun "ó" applies to all three genders (though strictly only to a part, i.e. the animate part of the neuter gender), it would follow on Menkiti's showing that not even the adult or oldest person can strictly be referred to as a person. For, the answer to the question, "Where is the old man?" (if we want to use a pronoun) in Akan will be *ówó dan no mu*, that is, "He/it is in the room."

In Ga-Dangme languages, also in Ghana, the pronoun *"e"* is used to refer to everything – stones, trees, dogs and human beings (of both the masculine and feminine genders). The pronoun *"e"* (he/she/it) is thus gender-neutral, encompassing all the genders: masculine, feminine, and neuter. In this group of languages there is no pronoun used solely for inanimate objects, as there is in Akan, since the pronoun *"e"* is used for both animate and inanimate objects. Clearly, then, neither the neuter pronoun for animate things in the Akan language, nor the gender-neutral pronoun in Ga-Dangme languages, gives an indication as to the real nature of its designatum. The argument that "it" used of new borns and children (in the English language) implies that they are not yet persons therefore collapses when examined in the context of these languages, for "it" in Akan and Ga-Dangme languages is, as we have observed, used to refer to adults and older people as well as to children and new borns. Are older people persons or have they yet to acquire their personhood? The semantics of the neuter pronoun in the African languages I have examined does not in any way lead to the view of a non-person. Thus, Menkiti errs.

Menkiti also argues that the relative absence of ritualised grief over the death of a child in African societies, in contrast to the elaborate burial ceremony and ritualised grief in the event of the death of an older person, also supports his point about the conferment by the community of personhood status. It is not true that every older person who dies in an African community is given an elaborate burial. The type of burial and the nature and extent of the grief expressed over the death of an older person depend on the community's assessment, not of his/her personhood as such, but of the dead person's achievements in life, his/her contribution to the welfare of the community, and the respect he/she commanded in the community. Older persons who do not satisfy such criteria may in fact be given simple and poor funerals and attenuated forms of grief expressions. As to the absence of ritualised grief on the death of a child, this has no connection whatsoever with the African view of personhood as such, as alleged by Menkiti. It stems rather from beliefs about the possible consequences, for the mother of the dead child, of showing excessive grief. One belief, among the Akan people, is that excessive demonstration of grief in the event of the death of a child will make the mother infertile, as it will make her reach her menopause prematurely; another belief is that the excessive show of grief over the death of a child will drive the dead child too "far away" for it to reincarnate, and so be reborn; and so on. These beliefs are of course superstitious, but that is beside the point.

Thus, no distinctions as to personhood can be made on the basis of the nature and extent of ritualised grief over the death of a child or of an older person. A human person is a person whatever his/her age or social status. Personhood may reach its full realisation in a community, but it is not acquired or achieved as one goes along in society. What a person acquires is status, habits, and personality or character traits: the person, *qua* person, thus becomes the *subject* of the acquisition, and being thus prior to the acquisition process, cannot be defined by what he/she acquires. One is a person because of what one is, not because of what one has acquired. Thus, the contrast Menkiti wants to establish between the African and the Western views of the nature of personhood by describing the former as "processual" (1984:172) or "some sort of ontological progression" (1984:173), and the latter as grounded on "some isolated static quality" (1984:172) is, in my opinion, misguided.

However, there are some expressions in the Akan language, and judgements or evaluations made about the life and conduct of people, which give the impression that it is the community that defines and confers personhood. When an individual appears in his/her conduct to be wicked, bad, ungenerous, cruel or selfish, the Akan would say of that individual, "He is not a human person" *(Onnye 'nipa)*. Implicit in this judgement is the assumption that there are certain basic norms and ideals to which the behaviour of a person, *if* he/she is a person, ought to conform, and that there are moral virtues that the human person is capable of displaying in his/her conduct. And because the person is thought to be capable of displaying those virtues, it is expected that he/she would, when the situation arises, display them in his/her conduct and act in conformity with the accepted moral values and standards. Considering the situations in which that judgement is made about persons, these norms, ideals, and moral virtues can be said to include generosity, kindness, compassion, benevolence, respect, and concern for others; in short, any action or behaviour that is conducive to the promotion of the welfare of others. And the reason for the judgement, "He is not a human person" being made of an individual is that the individual's actions and conduct are considered as falling short of the standards and ideals of personhood.

In Akan cultures, then, much is expected of a person in terms of the display of moral virtue. The pursuit or practice of moral virtue is held as intrinsic to the conception of a person. The position here may thus be schematised as follows: for any p, if p is a person, then p ought to display in his/her conduct the norms and ideals of personhood. Thus when a person fails to exhibit the expected moral virtues in his/her conduct, he/she is said not to be a person *(Onnye 'nipa)*. The evaluative judgement opposite to the one we have been considering is, "He is a person" *(Oye 'nipa)*. The judgement here is not a descriptive one at all, though it can be used descriptively, for instance, to distinguish a human being from a tree. A descriptive use of that judgement would be obvious. It is, however, the normative form of the judgement that I am concerned to point out:

> "he is a person", used normatively, means, "he has good character", "he is peaceful – not troublesome", "he is kind", "he has respect for others", "he is humble" (Ahene-Affoh 1976:51).

The Akan, fully satisfied with, and profoundly appreciative of, the high standards of the morality of a person's conduct, would say of such a person: "He/she is a real (human) person" *(ōye onipa paa)*.

Now, the moral significance of "denying" personhood to a human being on the grounds that his/her actions are dissonant with certain fundamental norms and ideals of personhood, or that he/she fails to exhibit certain virtues in his/her behaviour is extremely interesting and is worth noting. It means that human nature is considered in Akan culture to be essentially good, not depraved or warped by some original sin; that the human person is basically good, can and should do good, and should in turn have good done to him/her. It means, further, that the human person is considered to possess an innate capacity for virtue, for performing morally right actions, and therefore should be treated as a morally responsible agent. I will here refer to the Akan maxim or belief that "God created every man (to be) good" *(Onyame bòò obiara yie)*. But the meaning of the statement that "God created every man good" is ambiguous. It is ambiguous with regard to a person's actually doing good, that is, actually behaving virtuously, and being capable of moral choice, that is, having the moral sense to distinguish between good and evil or right and wrong. In other words, it is not clear whether the statement means that a person is determined to do good, to pursue virtues, or that he/she is merely endowed with a sense of right and wrong. How do we interpret the meaning of the statement, then? In view of the human person's evil and unethical actions, the first interpretation cannot be accepted as the correct meaning of the statement: the first alternative is plainly contradicted by the human person's moral experience. The correct interpretation of the view that the human person was created a moral being, then, might be that he/she is a being endowed with moral sense and capable of making moral judgements. The human person can then be held as a moral agent, a moral subject – not that his/her virtuous character is a settled matter, but that he/she is capable of virtue.

The foregoing discussion of some morally significant expressions in the Akan language or judgements made about the conduct of persons suggests a conception of moral personhood; a person is defined in terms of moral qualities or capacities: a human person is a being who has a moral sense and is capable of making moral judgements. This conception of a person, however, must not be considered as eliminating or writing off children or infants as persons even though they are not (yet) considered as moral agents, as capable of exercising moral sense. The reason is that even though children are not actually morally capable, they are potentially so. Unlike the colt, which will never come to possess a moral sense even though it will eventually grow into an adult (horse), children do grow to become *moral* agents on reaching adolescence: at this stage they are capable of exercising their moral sense and thus of making moral judgements. Menkiti in fact accepts the characterisation or definition of personhood in terms of moral capacities when he says:

> The various societies found in traditional Africa routinely accept this fact that personhood is the sort of thing which has to be attained, and is attained in direct proportion as one participates in communal life through the discharge of the various obligations defined by one's stations. It is the carrying out of these obligations that transforms one from the it-status of early childhood, *marked by an absence of moral functions, into the person-status of later years, marked by a widened maturity of ethical sense – an ethical maturity without which personhood is conceived as eluding one* (1984:176).

This passage surely commits Menkiti to saying that a person is defined in terms of "some isolated static quality" – the quality of moral sense or capacity in the African case – which he thought was a characteristic of Western conceptions of personhood.

Yet to explicate personhood in terms of moral capacities is not to imply by any means that it is the community that fully defines or confers personhood, even though it can be admitted that through such activities as moral instruction, advice, admonition and the imposition of sanctions, the community can be said to play some role in a person's moral life. Moral capacities as such cannot be said to be implanted or catered for or conferred by the community.

Now, I wish to turn briefly to other forms of judgements made about persons which are not particularly moral in nature. In the communal setting of the African life, an individual's social status is measured in terms of:

1. A person's sense of responsibility, expressed, in turn, through his/her responsiveness and sensitivity to the needs and demands of the group.
2. What a person has been able to achieve through his/her own exertions – physical, intellectual, and moral.
3. The extent to which a person fulfils certain social norms, such as having a marital life and bringing up children.

Faced with such social demands and requirements, an individual would strive in several ways to demonstrate a sense of personal responsibility, to achieve some measure of success in life, and to have a family (that is, an immediate family). All these strivings are aimed at attaining some social status. The individual may fail in his/her strivings and, in the Akan community, for example, may consequently be judged a "useless person" *(onipa hun)*, an opprobrious term. But it must be noted that what the individual would be striving for in all these exertions is social status, not personhood. The strivings are in fact part of the individual's self-expression, an exercise of a capacity he/she has *as a person*. And even if at the end of the day he/she fails to attain the expected status, his/her personhood would not for that reason diminish, even though he/she might lose social respect in the eyes of the members of the community. So it is in terms of social status, not personhood, that individuals could fail. Menkiti is thus mistaken in thinking that individuals could fail at personhood.

The foregoing arguments I have deployed are intended to prove that the view, as held by Menkiti, that personhood is defined or conferred by the communal structure, cannot be wholly true. This is so despite the natural sociality of the human person which at once places him/her in a system of shared values and practices and a range of goals – which, in short, places the person in a cultural structure. I have made the observation that, besides being a communitarian being by nature, the human person is also by nature other things as well. By "other things", I have in mind such essential attributes of the person as rationality, having a capacity for virtue and for evaluating and making moral judgements, and hence being capable of choice. It is not the community that creates these attributes; the community discovers and nurtures them. So that if these attributes play any seminal roles in the execution of the individual person's lifestyle and projects, as indeed they do, then it cannot be persuasively argued that personhood is *fully* defined by the communal structure or social relationships.

It is true that the whole gamut of values and practices in which the individual is necessarily embedded is a creation of the cultural community and is part of its history. For this reason, it can be said that some of our goals are set by the communal structure. Yet the following questions may be asked:

1. Is it possible for the communal structure to set the whole or a seamless complex of the values, practices, and ends of the individual that will perfectly reflect the complexity of human nature, values, and practices – at least some of which, we know, do change and so cannot be considered monolithic?
2. Does the communal, and therefore cultural, character of the self really imply that the self is ineluctably and permanently held in thrall by that structure?
3. Does the ethos of the communal structure pre-empt or permanently nip in the bud a possibly radical perspective on communal values and practices that may be adopted by the self?

All of these questions can be answered in the negative. The reason is that individual persons, as participants in shared values and practices, and enmeshed in the web of communal relationships, may find that aspects of those cultural givens are inelegant, undignifying or unenlightening and can be questioned and evaluated. The evaluation may result in the individual's affirming or amending or refining existing communal goals, values, and practices; but it may or could also result in the individual's total rejection of them. The possibility of re-evaluation means, surely, that the person cannot be absorbed by the communal or cultural apparatus, but can to some extent wriggle out of it, distance him/herself from it, and thus be in a position to take another look at it; it means, also, that the communal structure cannot foreclose the meaningfulness and reality of the quality of self-assertiveness which the person can demonstrate in his/her actions. The development of human, i.e. communal culture results from the exercise by individual persons of this capacity for self-assertion; it is this capacity which makes possible the intelligibility of autonomous individual choice of goals and life plans. The fact that changes do occur in the existing communal values – for some new values are evolved as some of the pristine ones fall into obsolescence – this fact is undoubtedly the result of the evaluative activities and choices of some autonomous, self-assertive individual persons.

The capacity for self-assertion which the individual can exercise presupposes, and in fact derives from, the autonomous nature of the person. By autonomy, I do not mean self-completeness, but the having of a will, a rational will of one's own, that enables one to determine at least some of one's own goals and to pursue them. (The word "autonomy" consists of two Greek words – "autos" (self) and "nomos" (rule); thus, it means self-governing, self-directing). The actions and choice of goals of the individual person emanate from his/her rational will. Thus, the self-determining is also self-assertive. The communitarian self, then, cannot be held as a cramped or shackled self acting robotically at the beck and call of the communal structure. That structure is never to be conceived as, or likened to, the Medusa head the sight of which reduces a person to inactivity and supineness – in this case, cultural or rational or intellectual supineness.

In concluding this section, then, I wish to say again that even though the communitarian self, such as is held in African moral and political philosophy, is not permanently detached from its contingent communal features, and though the individual is fully embedded or implicated in the life of his/her community, nevertheless the self, by virtue of – or by exploiting – other natural attributes (besides the natural attribute of being communal) essential to its metaphysical constitution, can from time to time take a distanced view of its communal values and practices and reassess or revise them. This possibility implies that the self can set some of its own goals and, in this way, participate in the determination or definition of its own identity. The upshot is that personhood can only partly, and never completely, be defined by one's membership of the community. The most that can be said, in my view, is that the person is only partly constituted by the community. This view constitutes an amendment to Menkiti's position, put forward without any qualifications, that the community fully defines personhood:

> in the African understanding human community plays a crucial role in the individual's acquisition of full personhood (1984:179).

Menkiti's view of communitarianism, which appears to have support in the writings of African political leaders (whose view I adumbrated in my introductory remarks), appears to coincide with unrestricted or radical or excessive communitarianism. This view differs from the one I am putting forward which is that of a restricted or moderate communitarianism. It seems to me that restricted communitarianism offers a more appropriate and adequate account of the self than the unrestricted or radical account, in that the former addresses the dual features of the self: a communal being and an autonomous, self-determining, self-assertive being with a capacity for evaluation and choice. There are, to be sure, other reasons for preferring restricted or moderate communitarianism over unrestricted or radical communitarianism, which I discuss in the section that follows.

RIGHTS, DUTIES, AND THE COMMUNAL STRUCTURE

It might be supposed that communitarianism, with its emphasis on and concern for communal values, will have no truck with the doctrine of rights, for that doctrine is necessarily an individualistic doctrine. Rights belong primarily and irreducibly to individuals; a right is the right of some individual. Yet the supposition that communitarianism has little if any place for rights is false both in theory and in practice, especially in the case of restricted or moderate communitarianism.

Communitarianism is not necessarily antithetical to the doctrine of rights, for several reasons. In the first place, communitarianism cannot disallow arguments about rights which may in fact form part of the activity of a self-determining autonomous individual possessed of the capacity for evaluating or re-evaluating the entire practice of his/her community. Some such evaluations may touch on matters of rights, the exercise of which a self-determining individual may see as conducive to the fulfilment of human potential, and against the denial of which he/she may raise some objections.

Secondly, respect for human dignity, a natural or fundamental attribute of the human person which cannot, as such, be set at nought by the communal structure, generates regard for personal rights. The reason is that the individual person's natural membership of a community cannot rob him/her of dignity or worth, a fundamental and inalienable attribute he/she possesses as a person. Some conceptions of human dignity are anchored in theism, in the conviction that the dignity of the person is a natural endowment by God, the creator of humankind. One maxim of an African people whose social structure is communal has it that "All persons are children of God; no one is a child of the earth" (*Nnipa nyinaa ye Onyame mma; obiara nnye asase ba*). The insistent claim that is made in the maxim that every person is a child of God does seem to have some moral overtones or relevance, grounded, as it must be, in the belief that there must be something intrinsically valuable in God. A person, being a child of God, presumably by reason of his/her having been created by God and regarded as possessing a divine spark called soul *(okra)*, must be held as having intrinsic value, as an end in him/herself, worthy of dignity and respect. It is possible to derive a theory of individual rights from theistic conceptions of the intrinsic worth of persons. One conception of rights famously known to be grounded in an act of God is in the Preamble of the American Declaration of Independence (1776): "We hold these truths to be self-evident, that all men are created equal, that they are *endowed by their Creator with certain inalienable rights."*

However, it is possible to derive a conception of human dignity and hence individual rights, not from theism, but from reflecting on human nature, particularly on the qualities that dispose the human being to function at his/her best in human society and to realise his/her full potential as a person. Thus, the eighteenth-century German philosopher, Immanuel Kant, on the basis of his rational analysis, grounds the notion of human dignity or intrinsic worth in the capacity of the person for moral autonomy, i.e. rational freedom. Thus conceived, argues Kant, the person ought to be treated as an end in himself:

> Now I say that man, and in general every rational being, exists as an end in himself, not merely as means for arbitrary use by this or that will: he must in all his actions, whether they are directed to himself or to other rational beings, always be viewed at the same time as an end (1965:95).

Kant thus formulates his famous Categorical Imperative, considered by him as the supreme principle of morality, as: "Act in such a way that you always treat humanity, in your own person or in the person of any other, never simply as a means but at the same time as an end" (1965:95). This leads Kant to a notion of moral rights which he refers to as "innate rights", but which belong to everyone by nature and so could be called natural rights, which are our fundamental ethical end. Thus a conception of human dignity and moral or natural (human) rights which concomitantly flow from it can be reached through purely rational reflection on human nature. But howsoever the conception of human dignity or rights is derived, whether from theistic considerations or from sources independent of God, that conception is linked with, and in fact compels, the recognition of rights, not only in an individualistic but also in a communitarian situation. In other words, the derivation of individual rights from naturalism (humanism) or supernaturalism cannot be confined to an individualistic framework; the derivation is not an activity or a characteristic or a possibility solely of an individualistic social ambience.

Thirdly, at both the theoretical (conceptual) and the practical level, communitarianism cannot set its face against individual rights. For, implicit in communitarianism's recognition of the dual features of the self as an autonomous, self-determining entity capable of evaluation and choice, and as a communal being, is a commitment to the acknowledgement of the intrinsic worth of the self and to the moral rights which may be said to be necessarily due to it. The recognition by communitarian political morality of individual rights is a conceptual requirement. At the practical level communitarianism must realise that allowing free rein for the exercise of individual rights – which obviously includes the exercise of the unique qualities, talents, and disposition of the individual – will enhance the cultural development and success of the community. If communitarianism were to shrug off individual rights, it would not only reveal itself as an inconsistent moral and political theory, but in practical terms would also saw off the branch on which it was going to sit.

However, it can be said that restricted or moderate communitarianism is a consistent and viable theory, one that is not opposed to individual rights, even though it may, for a reason to be stated presently, consciously and purposively give greater attention to other communal values of the community. The foregoing discussion has, I hope, clearly shown the falsity of the view that communitarianism has little or no room for individual rights.

Having said all this, however, it must be granted that communitarianism cannot be expected to make a fetish of rights; thus, talk about rights is not likely to be brought to the forefront of its concerns and preoccupations. The reason is not hard to find; it may be derived from the logic of the communitarian theory itself: it assumes an overwhelming concern for communal values, for the good of the wider society as such. Even so, the absorbing interest in the common good, in the provision for the social conditions which enable each individual person to function satisfactorily in a human society, does not – indeed should not – result in the subversion of individual rights. The reason is that even though rights belong primarily to individuals, as we said, nevertheless, insofar as their exercise will often either directly or indirectly be valuable to the larger society, their status and role must be recognised by communitarian theory. But the theory will disallow the separation of rights from the common values of the community and the conferring on them of a pre-eminent status. It must be noted that in any scheme of value ranking occurs or is resorted to when situations require that preferences for some values be made over other values. This is so whether the system of ethics is deontological (i.e. moderately deontological) or teleological. Thus, in the communitarian political morality, priority will not be given to rights if doing so will stand in the way of attaining a more highly ranked value or a more preferable goal of the community. Rights would not, therefore, be held as absolute in the communitarian theory, even though I think they will – in fact they should – have some place in that theory.

However, although it is conceivable, as has already been explained, that the communal structure will allow the exercise of individual rights, yet it can be expected that communitarianism will not suggest to individuals that they should incessantly insist on their rights. The reason, I suppose, is the assumption that rights, i.e. political, economic, and social rights, are built into the ethos and practices of the cultural community. Thus, the economic, political, and social needs of the individual members, which are the concern of most individual rights, would be expected to have been recognised, if not catered for, to some degree of adequacy by the communitarian structure. Individuals would not have a penchant for, or an obsession with, insisting on their rights, knowing that insistence on their rights could divert attention to duties they, as members of the communal society, strongly feel towards other members of the community. Rights and duties are not polar concepts, even though they could be: if I insist on my right to all my possessions or to all that has resulted from the exercise of my endowments, I may not be able to show sensitivity to the needs and welfare of others, even though showing sensitivity to the needs of others is an important plank in the ethical platform of communitarianism. The danger or possibility of slipping down the slope of selfishness when one is totally obsessed with the idea of individual rights is, thus, quite real. In a social situation that as a matter of ethical testament stresses social relations, concern and compassion for others, and other communal values, insistence on (some) rights may not be necessary.

However, while the communitarian structure would not have a fetishistic attitude to individual rights, it would certainly have one toward duties that individual members have or ought to have toward other – perhaps the least advantaged – members of the community. The communitarian theory will most likely give priority to duties rather than rights. Concerned as it is with the common good or the communal welfare, the welfare of each and every member of the community, communitarianism will undoubtedly consider duty as the moral tone, as the supreme principle of morality. By "duty" I mean a task, service, conduct or function that a person feels morally obligated to perform in respect of another person or other persons. The duties which some members of the community feel they owe others by reason of a common humanity and should demonstrate in practice, are such as the duty to help others in distress, the duty not to harm others, and so on. Duties to the community as a whole or to some members of the community would not derive from a social contract between individuals. The contract theory is a contrivance for voluntary, not natural, membership of the community, regarded by some people as a mere association of individuals. In a communitarian framework, however, there would be no place for the contract theory to set forth the duties and rights of individuals who are to inhabit a society that is being contemplated.

Even though such duties as caring for one another and concern for the welfare and needs of others may not be said to be idiosyncratic to the communitarian system alone, and though an individualistic system can also evince or practice them, it seems to me that the pursuit of those duties in the latter system will be less spontaneous and less successful because of its obsession with individual rights. And it appears that some of the American philosopher Rawls's notions fit better into a communitarian framework than the individualistic one which he makes the basis of his arguments. Rawls makes the following statements:

> The difference principle represents, in effect, an agreement to regard the distribution of natural talents as a *common asset* (1971:101).
>
> In justice as fairness men agree to *share* one another's fate. In designing institutions they undertake to avail themselves of the accidents of nature and social circumstance only when doing so is for the *common benefit* (1971:102).
>
> The two principles are equivalent . . . to an undertaking to regard the distribution of natural abilities as a *collective asset* so that the more fortunate are to benefit only in ways that help those who have lost out (1971:179).
>
> The members of a community *participate in one another's nature;* we appreciate what others do as things we might have done but which they do for us (1971:565).

Rawls's language resonates with communitarian expressions, meanings, and content.

The notions of "sharing one another's fate", "common assets", "collective assets", "common benefit", "participating in one another's nature" – these notions and others related to them in Rawls's scheme will surely find a more ready embrace in the communitarian home than in the home artificially and instrumentally constructed by individuals in pursuit of their own egoistic advantages or ends.

These notions are, it seems to me, appropriate rather than idealistic in a communitarian political culture, where they elicit greater significance and understanding and less philosophical controversy or resistance than in a system, like Rawls's, which seeks to give priority to individual rights rather than to duties. The point I am at pains to make, in other words, is that Rawls's essentially individualistic framework, determinedly poised to secure and cordon off individual rights, can hardly provide an effective support for those "communitarian notions" he so well articulates, let alone bring them to practical realisation.

The question may be raised as to the justification for giving priority to duties over rights in the communitarian political morality. The priority is, I think, based on, and is most probably required by, the demands of the relational character of the person in the wake of his/her natural sociality. The sociality of the person immediately makes him/her naturally oriented to other persons in relation with whom he/she must live. Living in relation with others directly involves a person in social and moral roles, duties, obligations, and commitments which the individual person must fulfil. The natural relationality of the person thus immediately plunges him/her into a moral universe, making morality an essentially social and trans-individual phenomenon focused on the well-being of *others*. Our natural sociality then prescribes or mandates a morality that, clearly, should be weighted on the side of duty, i.e. on that which one has to do for others.

The success that must accrue to communal or corporative living depends very much on each member of the community demonstrating a high degree of moral responsiveness and sensitivity in relation to the needs and well-being of other members. This should manifest itself in each member's pursuit of his/her duties. Also, the common good, which is an outstanding goal of the communitarian moral and political philosophy, requires that each individual should work for the good of all. The social and ethical values of social well-being – solidarity, interdependence, cooperation, compassion, and reciprocity – which can be said to characterise the communitarian morality, primarily impose on the individual a duty to the community and its members. It is all these considerations that elevate the notion of duty to a priority status in the total enterprise of communitarian life.

It is often said that rights are correlated with duties, that if there are rights, then there must be corresponding duties, and vice versa. This hackneyed statement seems to me to be not wholly true, certainly in aspects of moral relationships between individuals, or in cases where individuals feel they owe their community some duty or duties. It is true that if I have a right to education, then it is the duty of someone, a parent or a local authority or the state, to provide what is necessary for my education; similarly, if I have the right to work it is the duty of the state to make jobs available to me. In such cases, where rights are asserted against the state or against some persons in specific roles or positions, the correspondence or correlation between rights and duties will clearly be on track. However, it is possible for a person to carry out a duty to someone else without our having to say that the duty was carried out because of the right of this other person, that is, the person for whose sake the duty was done. Here I am not thinking of what is called an act of supererogation – an act that a person does not have to do – even though it would be morally commendable if he/she did it. I am thinking, rather, of an act that a person morally feels he/she should do, and does it. It seems to me that communitarian ethics will rightly obliterate the distinction between duties and so-called supererogatory acts or acts of charity, and consider all of them as our moral duties. If I carry out a duty to help someone in distress, I would not be doing so because I think that person has a right against me, a right I should help fulfil. I would be carrying out that duty because I consider that person as worthy of some moral consideration by me, as someone to whose plight I ought to be morally sensitive. (I am here not referring to duties enjoined upon persons by reason of certain specific social roles, positions or statuses they occupy in society.)

When we want to carry out certain duties, especially of a positive kind such as providing aid to someone in distress or looking after aged parents, in conferring benefits we do not first ask ourselves whether the persons to whom we owe those duties have any rights against us and whether we should perform those duties because of their rights. People in societies in which the concept of rights has not gained (much) currency in their moral or political vocabulary would carry out their duties to their fellow human beings, yet without the conviction that the latter have rights against them. Our positive duties toward others, then, are not based on their rights: it is not so much a consciousness of the rights of others as our moral responsiveness to their particular situations that impinges on our decision to carry out our duties toward them. This, I think, is generally true, and would be very much so in a social structure like the communitarian one, which does not lay any particular stress on rights. A rider is, however, required here: negative duties, such as the duty not to harm others, and to refrain from killing or robbing others, do have corresponding rights. For, one's right not to be harmed imposes a duty on others not to harm one. Even so, it can be concluded that the correlation between rights and positive duties collapses and becomes a one-way, asymmetric relation, for, as I have explained, there are duties without corresponding rights as far as the individual moral agent is concerned. The upshot of the foregoing discussion is that it is possible for communitarian ethics to hold the moral status of duties in high esteem without this being mandated or induced by a consciousness of rights.

Yet, in stressing duties to the community and its members rather than the rights of the individual members of the community, the communitarian political and moral theory does not imply, by any means, that rights are not important; neither does it deny duties to the self. As pointed out earlier in this section, communitarianism acknowledges the intrinsic value of the person and the moral rights that this acknowledgement can be said to entail.

Individual rights, such as the right to equal treatment, to property, to freely associate with others, to free speech, etc. would be recognised by communitarianism, especially of the restricted or moderate type. However, in the light of the overwhelming emphasis on duties within the communitarian moral framework, rights would not be given priority over the values of duty and so would not be considered inviolable or indefeasible: it might, on this showing, be appropriate occasionally to override some individual rights for the sake of protecting the good of the community itself. As an autonomous, self-determining being, the individual person must, within limits, care for his/her well-being or needs just as he/she cares for the needs of others. Altruistic duties cannot obliterate duties to oneself. This is because the pursuit of altruistic duties does not lead to the dissolution of the self. The individual person has a life to live, and so must have plans for his/her life and must see to the realisation of those plans. The attainment of the goal imposes on the self the responsibility or duty to develop one's natural abilities. Therefore, the duty one has toward the community and its members does not – and should not – enjoin one to give over one's whole life and be oblivious to one's personal well-being.

What the communitarian ethic will enjoin, then, is dual responsibility, a proposal – or better, an imperative – which will be consistent in every way with the *dual* features of the human being I referred to earlier. The successful pursuit of dual responsibility requires that, through the development of his/her capacities and through personal exertion and striving, and hence through self-attention, the individual person should attain some appropriate status socially, economically, intellectually, and so on. One is not saying that all the needs or interests of the individual person should be taken care of before he/she embarks on duties and commitments to others. Yet it is surely a necessary requirement that the individual be in a position to do so – hence the need to carry out duties to him/herself. If the notion of duties to oneself, if self-attention makes sense even in a communitarian context, as I maintain, so does the notion of individual rights, which, as a reflexive notion, must be conceptually linked to that of self-interest or, as I prefer to say, self-attention.

CONCLUSION

Communitarian ethical and political theory which considers the community as a fundamental human good advocates a life lived in harmony and cooperation with others, a life of mutual consideration and aid and of interdependence, a life in which one shares in the fate of the other – each bearing the other up – a life which provides a viable framework for the fulfilment of the individual's nature or potential, a life in which the products of the exercise of an individual's talents or endowments are (nevertheless) regarded as the assets of the community as such, a life free from hostility and confrontation: such a life, according to the theory, is most rewarding and fulfilling.

It is the moderate or restricted version of communitarianism that, to my mind, is defensible and which I support and have argued for in this paper. It is not too clear which of the two versions, if any, is espoused in African cultural traditions. But the position I have taken generally appears to run counter to that of those African political leaders whose writings in the period following the attainment of political independence suggest a radical or extreme type of communitarianism which is traced to African cultural traditions.

Moderate or restricted communitarianism gives accommodation, as has been shown, to communal values as well as to values of individuality, to social commitments as well as to duties of self-attention. Even though in its basic thrust and concerns it gives prominence to duties toward the community and its members, it does not – indeed it cannot – do so to the detriment of individual rights whose existence and value it recognises, or should recognise, and for a good reason. I believe strongly that an ethical and political theory that combines an appreciation of, as well as a commitment to, the community as a fundamental value, *and* an understanding of, as well as a commitment to, the idea of individual rights, would be the most reasonable theory to support. Guided by assumptions about the dual features of the self with its implied dual responsibility, it should be possible to deflate any serious tension between the self and its community.

REFERENCES

Abimbola, W. 1975a. *Sixteen great poems of Ifa.* Niamey: Centre d'Études Linguistique et Historique pour Tradition Orale. Niamey: Unesco.

Abimbola, W. 1975b. "*Iwapele*: The concept of good character", in W. Abimbola (ed.), *Yoruba oral tradition: Ife African languages and literatures series.* No. 1. 1975.

Abiodun, R. 1983. "Identity and the artistic process in the Yoruba aesthetic concept of *Ìwa.*" *Journal of Cultures and Ideas,* 1(1):13–30.

Ahene-Affoh. 1976. *Twi Kasakoa ne Kasatome Ahorow Bi.* Accra: Ghana Publishing Corporation.

Boonzaier, E. & Sharp, J. (eds) 1988. *South African keywords: The uses and abuses of political concepts.* Cape Town: David Philip.

Busia, K.A. 1962a. *The position of the chief in the modern political system of the Ashanti.* London: Frank Cass.

Busia, K.A. 1962b. *The challenge of Africa.* New York: Praeger.

Dickson, K.A. 1977. *Aspects of religion and life in Africa.* Accra: Ghana Academy of Arts and Sciences. The J.B. Danquah Memorial lectures: series 10.

Flack, H.E. & Pellegrino, E.D. (eds) 1992. *African-American perspectives on biomedical ethics.* Georgetown: Georgetown University Press.

Flew, A. (ed.) 1979. *A dictionary of philosophy.* London: Macmillan.

Gbadegesin, S. 1986. "World-view", in T. Falola & A. Adediran (eds), *A new history of Nigeria for colleges.* Lagos: John West, 1986:227–244.

Gbadgesin, S. 1991. "Individuality, community and the moral order," in S. Gabadegesin, *African philosophy: traditional Yoruba philosophy and contemporary realities.* New York: Peter Lang. 1991:61–82.

Gyekye, K. 1987. *An essay on African philosophical thought: The Akan conceptual scheme.* New York: Cambridge University Press.

Gyeke, K. 1992. "Person and community in Akan thought", in K. Wiredu and K. Gyekye (eds), *Person and community: Ghanaian philosophy studies,* Vol. 1. 1992:101–122. The Council for research in values and philosophy: CIPSH/Unesco.

Hann, C. & Dunn, E. 1996. *Civil society.* New York: Routledge.

Idowu, B. 1962. *Olódùmarè: God in Yoruba belief.* Lagos: Longman.

Kant, I. 1965. *Groundwork of the metaphysic of morals.* Tr. H.J. Paton. London: Hutchinson University Library.

Kenyatta, J. 1965. *Facing Mount Kenya.* New York: Vintage.

Kuper, A. 1992. *Conceptualizing society.* New York: Routledge.

Kwame, S. (ed.) 1995. *Readings in African philosophy.* Lanham: University Press of America.

Kymlicka, W. 1989. *Liberalism, community, and culture.* Oxford: Clarendon.

MacIntyre, A. 1981. *After virtue.* London: Duckworth.

MacIntyre, A. 1989. *Whose justice? Which rationality?* Notre Dame: University of Notre Dame Press.

Makinde, M.A. 1988. "African culture and moral systems: A philosophical study." *Second Order,* 1(2):1–27.

Mbiti, J.S. 1970. *African religions and philosophy.* New York: Doubleday.

Menkiti, I.A. 1984. "Person and community in African traditional thought", in R.A. Wright (ed.), *African philosophy: An introduction.* Lanham: University Press of America, 1984:171–182.

Nkrumah, K. 1964. *Consciencism: Philosophy and ideology for decolonization and development with particular reference to the African revolution.* London: Heinemann.

Oladeji, N. 1988. "Proverbs as language signposts in Yoruba pragmatic ethics." *Second Order,* 1(2):44–57.

Oladipo, O. (ed.) 1995. *Conceptual decolonization in African philosophy.* Ibadan: Hope.

Oruka, H.O. and Masolo, D.A. (eds). 1983. *Philosophy and cultures.* Nairobi: Bookwise.

Rawls, J. 1971. *A theory of justice.* Cambridge, Mass.: Belknap.

Senghor, L.S. 1964. *On African socialism.* Tr. M. Cook. New York: Praeger.

Thornton, R. 1988. "Culture: A contemporary definition", in E. Boonzaier & J. Sharp (eds), 1988:17–28.

Walzer, M. 1983. *Spheres of justice: A defence of pluralism and equality*. Oxford: Martin Robertson.

Wiredu, K. 1980. *Philosophy and an African culture*. Cambridge: Cambridge University Press.

Wiredu, K. 1983. "Morality and religion in Akan thought", in H.O. Oruka & D.A. Masolo (eds), 1983.

Wiredu, K. 1990. "An Akan perspective on human rights", in A.A. An-Naim & F.M. Deng (eds), *Human rights in Africa: Cross-cultural perspectives*. Washington: Brookings Institute, 1990:243–260.

Wiredu, K. 1992a. "The African concept of personhood", in H.E. Flack & E.D. Pellegrino (eds), 1992:104–117.

Wiredu, K. 1992b. "The moral foundations of an African culture", in H.E. Flack & E.D. Pellegrino (eds), 1992:80–93.

Wiredu, K. 1992c. "Problems in Africa's self-definition in the contemporary world", in K. Wiredu & K. Gyekye (eds), *Person and community*. Washington: The Council for Research in Values and Philosophy, 1992:59–70.

Wiredu, K. 1992. "The moral foundations of an African culture", in *Person and community*. CIPSH/Unesco. 1992:193–206.

Wiredu, K. 1993. "Canons of conceptualization." *The Monist*, 1(4):450–476.

Wiredu, K. 1995a. "Are there cultural universals?" *The Monist*, 78(1):52–64.

Wiredu, K. 1995b. "The concept of mind with particular reference to the language and thought of the Akans", in S. Kwame (ed.) 1995:123–151.

Wiredu, K. 1995c. "The concept of truth in the Akan language", in S. Kwame (ed.) 1995:185–191.

Wiredu, K. 1995d. "Democracy and consensus in African traditional politics: A plea for a non-party polity", in O. Oladipo (ed.) 1995:53–63.

Wiredu, K. 1995e. "Custom and morality: A comparative analysis of some African and Western conceptions of morals", in O. Oladipo (ed.) 1995:33–52.

Wiredu, K. 1995f. "On decolonizing African religions", in J.G. Malherbe (ed.), *Decolonizing the mind: Proceedings of the 2nd colloquium on African philosophy held at the University of South Africa, October 1995*. Pretoria: Unisa Press, 1995:178–193.

Wiredu, K. 1995g. "Particularist studies of African philosophies as an aid to decolonization", in J.G. Malherbe (ed.), *Decolonizing the mind: Proceedings of the 2nd colloquium on African philosophy held at the University of South Africa, October 1995*. Pretoria: Unisa Press, 1995:169–177.

CHAPTER SEVEN

The Problem of Political Self-Definition in South Africa: Marxism and Pluralism[1]

PIETER H. COETZEE

1. OVERVIEW

In addressing the problem of political self-definition in South Africa I shall attempt to trace and explain the rise of political consciousness among the black people of South Africa and to show that the rise of political consciousness was expressed in two attempts at political self-definition, namely, Marxism and Pluralism. Both attempts have conceptual connections with communitarian politics which explain why they were so easily accepted by black people. In the end Pluralism prevailed because Black Consciousness had to make room for a wider political consciousness which included the political consciousness of whites.

2. THE PROBLEM OF POLITICAL SELF-DEFINITION IN SOUTH AFRICA

How a community understands itself underpins its own cultural bias. The contemporary understanding of culture is that it is an open-ended resource, built up through history, upon which members of a community draw to mediate the exigencies of their everyday lives. Accordingly, at any given time in a community's history – the bedrock of its cultural capital – a community's self-understanding provides at once:

1. An interpretative framework for the generation of social meaning (especially as this relates to the generation of a political identity, a matter which we will take up shortly).
2. A marker for the boundaries of individual and social identity.
3. A conception of the social processes by which social and cultural goods are produced and distributed.

We call the integrated sum of these things a community's self-understanding. The latter forms the bedrock of its social and political identity. A community's social identity is its characteristic way of life which its members have sustained over a considerable period of time as an integrated cultural whole, and to which individual members stand in a dialogical relation, i.e. one which supplies an interactive context in and through which they actualise their identities. A community's political identity is expressed in its characteristic forms of institutional organisation; these characteristic forms of organisation reflect its cultural bias, and so provide distinctive avenues through which power (and particularly coercive power) is attained and exercised.

Ideally, a community's political identity should grow out of its social identity. A community can be said to enjoy a coherent and stable social life if its political life is embedded in customary norms and practices, which means that its social and political life can be viewed simply as institutionalised culture. This view of a dependence relation between social and political identity poses some problems for culturally diverse and heterogeneous states like South Africa and, indeed, for most African states. The problem here is that diverse cultural communities which do not inhabit the same world of shared social meanings and understandings co-exist within single political communities. So, the question arises, if they do not inhabit the same world of shared understandings, how do we conceive of the relation between social and political identity? African philosophers and politicians have responded to this problem with genuine ingenuity and skill. Briefly, the communal form of social life which is so characteristic of Africa works largely on the idea of "decisions by consensus", giving rise to forms of non-party politics and the idea of "consensual democracy". The basic structure of these forms of social and political organisation can relatively easily be adapted to the "multi-cultural community" phenomenon to create political structures which all cultural communities inhabiting a single political union may recognise as expressing (something) of their cultural bias.

3.   THE BACKGROUND TO WHITE SUPREMACY

In South Africa the problem of working out an acceptable political structure for diverse cultural communities was delayed by the apartheid system. Let us pause here briefly to consider some of the major impediments. For better or worse, the growth of a black culture of resistance – and with it a philosophy of liberation – was formatively linked to the search for an inclusive idea of political identity, one suited to a culturally heterogeneous South Africa.

Various forms of hegemony of white over black – institutional as well as ideological – bequeathed a socio-economic landscape divided between a dominant white centre and a subordinate black periphery. This feature of white centre pitted against black periphery played a major role in legitimising the fragmentation of our society along racial and ethnic lines. The reduction of the black periphery to a marginalised area of social life became a legitimate process by virtue of the self-legitimising authority of the dominant consensus of the centre. This is a typical feature of societies containing marginalised groups: in such societies the centre is usually the source of legitimisation.

It is a truism to say that the social and political identities constructed in the centre were ones conforming to white conceptions. For "whiteness" colonised the public sphere in which the common life of our society is lived. White hegemony of the centre and white control of public space enabled the white middle-class to construct a picture of the universality and objectivity of its values, and through this claim to universality and objectivity, to project a false view of the nature of difference. Briefly, for difference to be recognised as *significant* difference requires that the claim to difference be offered in a specific social and/or historical context which is generally acknowledged or recognised as authoritative with respect to the alleged significance of the claim. For instance, the claim (often made in the journals of the Dutch Trekkers) that they, as whites, were the carriers of a superior civilisation, has significance as marking a (perceived) difference between them and the indigenous peoples of Southern Africa. The significance of the claim as a marker of difference derives from a nineteenth-century milieu in which it was offered as a justification for aggressive European expansion. Today we recognise the social and historical situatedness of the claim, and can deal with it as such. To recognise that the significance of the claim rests on its embeddedness in social and historical circumstances is to see it as one should – as a claim which has status as a marker of difference between white and black, but one which can be challenged simply because it has a place in a specific social and historical milieu. As a marker of difference it has no status outside this milieu.

Now, in South African society the nineteenth-century world-view of an expansionist Europe continued to prevail. Accordingly, difference was seen to be a natural given, conforming to the order of nature. In this context difference marked different essences (it is of the essence of being white to be superior, and of the essence of being black to be inferior), and essences were naturalised (the essential difference between black and white is a natural one, occurring as a matter of fact in nature), so it seemed that the social and racial stratification of our society conformed to the natural order of things. As a marker of difference, then, the idea of "white superiority" was removed from the social and historical setting in which such ideas usually gain meaning, and so (correctly) ceased to be a social and historical construction, becoming instead merely a tool of oppression.

This process of social and racial stratification based on the interpretation of difference as "naturalised essence" had a counterpart in linguistic stratification. No black language ever became an official language. The delegitimisation of black languages as languages of the public domain had two major consequences: it denied to black cultural groups a place in the articulation of our society's self-understanding and it undermined the role of black languages as purveyors of culture. It is not difficult to see why these consequences obtained. Language is one carrier of the cultural symbols and meanings of groups and so plays a crucial role in constructing social identities. To the extent that black languages were marginalised as languages of the public domain, their potential as rallying points of resistance to social and racial rank ordering was diminished, with the result that black cultural symbols, and the meanings associated with those symbols, failed to become part of the forms of social and political life which were articulated and constructed in the centre.

The point at issue here runs much deeper. A language maintains its role as the medium through which conceptions of social and political organisation are articulated in a way which expresses a people's cultural bias if its speakers are able to sustain their society as an integrated cultural whole over a long period of time. If not, a language loses its role as purveyor of culture. In South Africa the construal of difference as "naturalised essence" formed part of a racist discourse through which black languages lost this status. In a milieu of discrimination and oppression it is easy to lose sight of the proper status of difference as a social and historical construction and to accept a stratification of racial and linguistic differences as part of the natural order. It is not difficult to see that this stratification had the effect of elevating "whiteness" to a norm-setting position, above the social and historical situatedness which the authority of such positions usually have. It is, then, no accident that the common life of our society was driven by standards of excellence and achievement which derived from the cultural capital of the white middle class.

The idea of an acultural, ahistorical position for the authority of norm-setters, and the talk of "naturalised essences" which became part of their (hegemonic) forms of discourse, involve epistemological errors, and are good examples of how "truth" functions as a politicised commodity in repressive societies. It is largely through the role language plays in the construction of meaning and identity that the centre was able to manufacture a picture of its asocial and ahistorical situatedness, and to project an image of its standards as universal. For the white centre this privileged position had a significant spin-off. It became possible, by the same means, to construct images for others which they were persuaded to accept as constitutive of their self-image. Hence many blacks absorbed the idea of their essential incompetence. The alleged essentialist nature of differences between groups became the source and justification of a division of labour – for whites positions of responsibility, for blacks the lower ranks of the job market. Also, the alleged universalism of the standards of the centre profited by identifying the achievements of *European* culture with the achievements of *human* civilisation. The failure to see that these things are not co-extensive was part of the failure to criticise forms of discourse which give little or no recognition to the specific and distinctive values which other cultures have to offer, and which undermine their roles as the context in and through which *other* people actualise their humanity.

All and all, black groups were reduced to the status of "add-ons" to the centre. We have said that difference can be a marker of rank. *Qua* "difference" then, "add-ons" signify a representation from the centre of groups "accretively" joined to a nucleus but which do not form an integral part of it. This notion of an "accretive addition" is best explained by considering the picture of public space that it generates: a public space is any locus of "action-in-concert", the site at which common action is co-ordinated through argument and persuasion. In this space the topic of conversation – of what gets included in the agenda – is usually something over which competing groups (including the "add-ons") struggle. Participation in this struggle is a push for justice (a push for a public debate on some issue of unfairness). For instance, various feminist movements went public over the question of women's rights, and forced a redrawing of the boundary between the "private" sphere and the "public" sphere, pushing the question of the status of women from the former to the latter in order that it might become a question for debate within the realm of justice. Similarly, pressure from the periphery over the question of civil and political rights for black people was an attempt to go public and to let justice be done by challenging the centre's monopoly of power. The kind of pressure which was exerted clearly showed the limits of the white model of public space: it could maintain itself only by a highly questionable delimitation of social spheres, some of which were recognised as legitimate spheres of public debate, while others were not. So, for instance, "labour" never figured as an item on the public agenda because this sphere of social life had become a centre of black resistance to white power. It became part of the public conversation only once the basis of its exclusion – the philosophy underlying the division of labour – had been challenged and overthrown. It is to this struggle – in essence a struggle over the question of black political identity – that we now turn.

4. THE QUEST FOR POLITICAL SELF-DEFINITION

The black resistance movements understood their task in a certain way: they took themselves to be opposing a racist *ideology*, one which claimed that whites are – as a matter of fact, as a given of nature – superior to blacks .

In very general terms ideology is commonly described as a science of ideas which raises questions about the basis and validity of our most fundamental ideas – ideas like the proper ordering of social life, the nature of justice, the moral requirements of interpersonal relations, and so on. Ideological discourse is often contrasted with scientific discourse which, according to the preferred conception of the latter, is not value-laden (as ideological discourse is claimed to be), not dependent on any world-view or perspective (as ideological discourse is claimed to be), and aims at truth (which ideological discourse cannot do since it has no claims to objectivity or universality in all the senses of these terms). This latter point is particularly interesting since it encapsulates many of Marx's ideas on ideology, as formulated by J.B. Thompson. According to Thompson's Marx,

> ideology is a system of representations which serves to sustain existing relations of class domination by orientating individuals towards the past rather than the future, or towards images and ideals which conceal class relations and detract from the collective pursuit of social change (Thompson 1990:41).

In other words, ideology masks truth by propagating untruths. As Thompson asserts:

> ideology . . . is a theoretical doctrine and activity which erroneously regards ideas as autonomous and efficacious and which fails to grasp the real conditions and characteristics of social-historical life (1990:35).

There are at least two critical themes which we must take note of that are implicit in Thompson's formulation of Marx's approach to ideology. We have already touched on them. They are:

1. The erroneous asocial, ahistorical treatment of the notion of difference through which whites aspired to dominate blacks, and the false asocial, ahistorical position of the authority of the white norm-setters through which the values of Western culture aspired to universal status.

2. The inequitable and unfair division of labour which has thrived on the false propositions mentioned in (1).

Let us examine each in turn in the light of Thompson's formulation of Marx's approach to ideology. The point to note about (1) is the falsity of racism, especially in its institutionalised forms. According to Marx all systems of thought and ideas are always embedded in and determined by social and historical conditions, especially in the material conditions of social life. On his assumption of the social determination of human consciousness there can be no system of thought or ideas which has a claim to truth outside a social and historical context. This pushes white claims to a natural superiority back into a social and historical context where these claims can be exposed as the orthodoxy of a group that was intent on maintaining its power. The significant point about (2) follows directly from this. A division of labour between "mental" and "manual" has thrived on a false sociology and produced a class division between blacks and whites, the former becoming a labour class, the latter an entrepreneurial class with control over the means of production. Once established, this class division itself became the source of false doctrines in philosophy, doctrines aspiring to a truth unconditioned by the material conditions of social life and the history of production.

Marxism offers a particular view of the nature of society. According to Marx, society is constructed from the way in which humans respond to their material needs (for food, shelter, work, leisure time, and so on). Since these needs are satisfied through labour, Marx recognises labour as the fundamental human activity, and holds that the only valid social science is one which accepts labour as its starting point in theorising about society. So all social practices must be explained with reference to labour, and this includes the division of labour which obtains in any society since the division of labour determines all social and economic arrangements. According to Marx, this starting point in labour secures for Marxism the only possible "correct view" of society, and as such it generates useful critique: in any society in which an uneven distribution of power and resources obtains, an ideology can be found that masks perceptions of a "true account" of its proper social and economic organisation. So, in South Africa, a racist ideology created the illusion that the division of labour between "mental" and "manual", and the concomitant unequal distribution of power and resources were glimpses of a true reality in which whites were the "natural" leaders. What makes these racist ideas ideology (and hence false) is their distortion of the fact that at bottom the conflict in South Africa is a class conflict. The way out of ideology lies in acknowledging this fact and understanding that justice requires a reorganisation of social and economic relations between the classes with a view to a redistribution of social and economic power.

We have said that a racist ideology falsely portrayed South African society as cohesive rather than conflictual (as it in fact is), and falsely attempted to justify an unequal distribution of power and resources with reference to a "natural order of things". If we look beyond ideology we will see that South African society is indeed conflictual in nature, and that this conflict is due to two factors:

1. The division of labour between "mental" and "manual" which empowered only whites, placing them in positions of economic and political ascendancy.
2. The creation of an open market economy and a community in which individuals motivated by self-interest compete with one another, with the

concomitant loss of traditional communal social organisation in which the interests of the individual coincide with those of the community.

Point (2) is an unwanted consequence of (1). The exploitation inherent in the relations between the white capitalist class and the black labour class was conceded by the illusion of a free society based on the free exchange of commodities. The kind of community which developed was the very antithesis of what (in Marx's view) community is all about. Marx, of course, has a communitarian conception in mind, one in which the pursuit of self-interest is tied to the pursuit of the good of the community as a whole. Marxism presents a negative picture of a class-divided society like South Africa:

1. The better-off class (the whites) was also the ruling class, i.e. its interests were served by the major political institutions; all available instruments of coercion were used in favour of the privileged class at the expense of the labouring class (the blacks).
2. Since (1) is true, it follows that the social arrangements acceptable to the better-off class would never be acceptable to the labouring class, and hence that a state of conflict obtained.
3. In this state of conflict unequal distributions remained in force while the better-off class maintained its privileged position.

We have said that what makes ideas ideological is that they mask the true nature of society, creating the illusion that an unequal distribution of social and economic resources is symptomatic of the proper ordering of relations between the classes. In other words, free exchange in a capitalist economy was simply a cover for a distribution in which one class (the whites) exploited another class (the blacks).

4.1 The first attempt at political self-definition: Marxism

Black resistance to white oppression developed into a quest for political self-definition. The first attempt at political self-definition was modelled on a Marxist conception of a just political order. Consider the following view:

> Examining Black Consciousness as an ideology capable of challenging the cultural hegemony of the white supremacist regime entails understanding the movement as the ethico-political weapon of an oppressed class struggling to reaffirm its humanity. . . . It would be wrong to equate the Black Consciousness movement with a mere cultural renaissance; it was indeed more than that. Black Consciousness recognised the centrality of the material conditions of existence and it was precisely because of these that it rejected collaboration with whites . . . (Falton 1986:57–58).

The agenda for the creation of a Marxist political state began with the identification of the black existential condition as that of
1. a labouring class, and hence
2. a socially exploited group, intent on
3. ending its exploitation by rising to political self-definition and power.

We are primarily interested in (3). What form did the initial attempts at self-definition take? The Black Consciousness Movement (henceforth the Movement) recognised that since colour determined the privileged position of whites, there could be no alliance between black and white workers. White workers could not be regarded as genuine workers – members of an oppressed and exploited class – as long as they enjoyed white privileges (job reservation, higher wages, recognition of trade unions, etc.). The Movement determined that all participants in white privilege were accomplices in oppression on the grounds that to participate was to fail to prevent crimes being committed against humanity. This meant that not even liberal whites could be included in the Movement.

Liberal whites had to be watched lest they arrested and blunted the edge of black revolutionary zeal, for their "mosaic multi-racialism" (Nengwekhulu quoted in Falton 1986:84) was simply a cover for the maintenance of white power and privilege. The goal of racial integration propounded by these whites was a futile political gesture as long as white norms in culture, economics, and morality remained in force. The critical point to note here is that liberal white norms represent the individualism of the privileged class which was opposed to the communal outlook characteristic of African society. Falton expresses the point as follows:

> It [the Movement] condemned the conditions of everyday life, the capitalistic-induced erosion of communual solidarity, and African corporate personality (1986:86).

The Movement had to exploit the solidarity of African culture, and African cultural groups had to coalesce into a solid power block to bring down the white power structure. This meant, in effect, reviving the "consensual foundations" (cf. Falton 1986:86) of African culture. We now turn to the initial conception of the pre-conditions of social solidarity.

4.1.1 *The social thesis*

We begin with the idea that choice, and especially moral choice, is something that can properly be exercised only within a social context. An individual's choice of a way of life is constrained by the community's pursuit of shared ends which derive from the community's self-understanding. We call this kind of pursuit of common ends "the politics of the common good". The common good fits the patterns of preferences and conceptions of the good prevalent in the community, and rests on a consensus about what that good is. The common good is a substantive conception since it defines the community's way of life – substantive in the sense that specific norms, mores, and moral precepts are derived from it; it provides a standard against which all norms and precepts are evaluated, and forms the basis of a public ranking of alternative conceptions which individuals may have, and the weight to be accorded to those conceptions. The good life for an individual person is usually conceived as coinciding with the good of the community, and is highly or lowly ranked according to the extent to which it contributes to or detracts from the common good. The pursuit of shared ends, which defines the community's good, and hence its way of life, always takes precedence over the pursuit of other ends which do not contribute to the common good. This is something which individuals cannot veto because shared ends have much greater weight in the life of the community than other ends.

One way of understanding the social thesis is to look at it as *encouraging* the growth of a certain way of life in order to ensure the growth of a political culture of the right kind – one which works on the basis of commitment to the common life – and as *discouraging* other forms of life. We may note two points regarding the idea of a political culture of the right kind:

1. In the right sort of political culture the continuance and growth of the common life would be regarded by all members as a good in its own right and not just as a good which serves their individually chosen goods.
2. The community is the context in which essential interests are actualised.

The first point touches on the status of the community as the locus of deontology. The community is the focus of moral identification, and collective decisions always have overriding moral authority. Collective decisions cannot be trumped by individual decisions because identification with the common good as the focus of allegiance remains paramount. Our point works on an interesting assumption relating to a question of constraints. What is it that constrains members to acknowledge the common good as their individual good? The assumption is that they are likely to respect the (rights) claims of others, just as they require others to respect their (rights) claims, if they are bound by shared conceptions of the good and a common life. The call for mutual respect is clearly recognisable as a command of justice, in particular a claim to equal consideration.

With regard to (2) above: in the previous chapter we said that egalitarian reciprocity is a good in Akan culture. In practice this means equal rights to participate in the communal life, and equal rights of access to opportunity. Equal access to opportunity assumes free choice. One criterion of a good political community is that it helps individuals to expand the range of their choices, especially their choice of a way of life. Note that if we acknowledge that our capacity for choice can only be developed in a certain kind of society, and we accept the necessity of sustaining it, we have *eo ipso* accepted a politics of the common good. If we accept this, we may ask whether it is better to live in a community which offers us a whole choice of life plans than one which limits choice as to modes of life, i.e. whether more choice is necessarily better than less choice. The point of sustaining a society which makes available a context of choice is to protect the avenues through which we arrive at self-understanding. But attempts to sustain the political forms which these understandings require lead to limitations in our choice of forms of the good life. This seems unavoidable: the goods available to us are all goods *internal* to cultural structures, and these goods are constitutive of our identities. A choice between such goods is a choice limited by the cultural structures in which we grow up and achieve fulfilment.

4.1.2 The Marxist thesis

The social thesis forms part and parcel of the idea of a community oriented polity, and of the African picture of values. This picture, however, has been significantly modified by input from Marxist ideology as a consequence of the racial stratification of society in South Africa. In this section we shall take a critical look at the Marxist overlay in an attempt to see what the lure of Marxism added to black attempts at political self-definition.

The infiltration of Marxist ideology into traditional black conceptions of social and economic life had a significant consequence: black intellectuals identified an open market economy as the backbone of the apartheid system. Falton makes the point as follows:

> It is precisely because racism was such an active ideological force encroaching on the material base of society, that the South African political economy developed as a Volkskapitalisme. . . .

Volkskapitalisme is a social system in which a racially determined hegemonic core, controlling the state, drains the economic surplus from a racially determined subordinate periphery (1986:45).

Marx identified two main areas in which modes of production failed to treat the worker as human:

1. Regarding relations of production, Marx believed that the worker was dehumanised in his/her position as a worker in some production processes, reduced to a cog in a machine with no control over the system which needed his/her labour.
2. Regarding relations of exchange, Marx believed that the open market served only the interests of the governing classes, i.e. it was the arena in which the labour of the worker advanced the needs of others (non-workers).

According to Marx the open market economy denies individuals their true or essential nature as social beings in three ways:

1. It separates persons from the individuating functions of their social roles in a system of mass production, making it easy for them to be exploited as a labouring class. Relations of production become exploitative in the sense that the individual is unable to discover his/her good in his/her social role and so becomes a means to the fulfilment of someone else's good.
2. It alienates (separates) the worker from the products of his/her labour, from him/herself insofar as the individuating function of a social role is denied the worker, and from society insofar as he/she has no voice in the articulation of the community's self-understanding.
3. It divides the worker's life into a "private" and a "public" sphere, the latter becoming the domain of the governing classes, and public institutions instruments of class rule. The governing classes silence the political will of the working class by their control over the public sphere.

The remedy is the creation of a certain kind of community, one in which the goods internal to communal relations (especially economic relations) are also personal goods. According to Marx the working classes can be freed, and equality restored, by freeing people from alienation, which means restoring the identity-defining function of their social roles and gaining a voice for them in the articulation of the community's self-understanding – in effect organising the labour classes into a political force.

What kind of society would be needed to implement Marx's vision of the just social order? Marx is concerned with the question of what follows for social and economic life from supposing that the interests of everyone in a specific community matter equally. What are the conditions that need to be fulfilled to secure for individuals an equal right in pursuing a life that is (in their view) good? An open market economy fails to treat people as equals in two areas of social life, and creates social interactions which subvert the requirements of moral equality, namely, equal concern and respect. Marx accepts the need for an equality principle, i.e. one suitably qualified in terms of the familiar distinction between an equality of regard and an equality of outcome. Everyone is entitled to equal consideration regarding the satisfaction of individual needs and desires, but this does not mean that everyone's desires and needs should be equally fulfilled, as an equality of outcome requires. Marx favours the idea of an equality of respect since it makes provision for unequal talents and unequal needs, which demand an unequal distribution of the products of labour. If you have greater talents than others, then a greater effort and a greater labour output is required of you, and if you have greater needs then you are entitled to a greater share of the total labour output, irrespective of whether you or someone else produced the products of labour. For Marx unequal talents and unequal needs are relevant moral differences between persons, which must be acknowledged in the distributive patterns of social institutions. So, in Marx's good society, the following principle of distribution is the right one: "From each according to his ability, to each according to his needs."

Marx is not a classical rights theorist. Problems of distributive justice are not central to his thinking. Marx thinks that a system of equal rights necessarily has unequal outcomes or effects, and that therefore there is no point in constructing such systems. The latter invariably need the *ad hoc* input of "back-up" systems (like the ones made available under policies of affirmative action) to bring about the desired equality of regard (not to mention equality of outcome). Moreover, systems of equal rights wrongly concentrate on problems of distribution rather than on problems of "production" and "exchange". The former are merely an ineffective remedy for the evils of the open market – ineffective because the preoccupation with redistributing wealth or productive assets from those who have them to those who don't reinforces (rather than remedies) the exploitation of the labouring classes by the governing classes, making social conflict inescapable. As long as problems of *distributive* justice sit at the centre of our thinking, communities will be divided, and sectarian interests will prevail. Public life is merely an arena in which persons act from motives of self-interest in competition with others, rather than the arena in which members accept responsibility for fellow members in cooperative pursuit of the common interest. The good community will have no need for appeals to (distributive) justice because members will make no (conflicting) claims to resources they regard as exclusively *theirs*.

A communist community will be one in which the communal interest remains paramount because members are bound by an identity of interests. The real evil that attaches to conflictual relations is that they are unchosen: workers find themselves in competitive relations with other workers, which require that they regard others as the means of the satisfaction of their interests, and this breaks down a sense of community in that an individual's development and growth can be bought only at the expense of others. Such conflictual relations must be replaced by a sense of sociality based on productive work for the sake of the community. Marx offers a picture of the emergence of the social individual as the foundation of the good society. The social individual is intended to replace the competitive individual which the open market creates in two areas of social interaction: "relations of production" and "relations of exchange". The creation of the social individual will eliminate conflict since the social individual works (produces) for the community (i.e. asserts no exclusive rights-claims to the common wealth). Note Marx's claim in this regard: relations of "production" and relations of "exchange" are social processes in which affective ties between individuals will eliminate unchosen conflicts. In the communist state a social identity is a precondition of informed choice. Social interaction in the labour field would be governed by such choice, and would accordingly be harmonious (and not conflictual), because no one would choose ends which are in conflict with the common interest.

Earlier on, when discussing the social thesis, we raised a question about the nature of *free* choice and supplied a tentative answer. We said that the goods available to us are all internal to cultural structures and that these goods are constitutive of our identities. A choice between such goods is a choice limited by the cultural structures in which we grow up and achieve fulfilment. According to this view of what constitutes free choice, we cannot go outside society to evaluate and revise our projects; our ability to question the value of our projects is a consequence of being subject to social interaction. One way of showing what this entails is as follows: if we try to stand outside the roles and expectations of society to arrive at a perspective or yardstick from which to judge the value of a particular choice (of way of life), we run into emptiness. The instruction to choose a way of life freely gives no direction for choice, for such "freedom" offers no determinable criterion of what way of life is good. We will not know that our choices are worth pursuing. This is because our idea of what it means to lead a valuable life is a consequence of our doing things directed at specific ends within a social context which provides criteria of worth and value. Free choice understood as something which has inherent worth or value is something we arrive at as a consequence of actions directed at or dedicated to other socially determined ends. In a Marxist society, geared as it is towards self-realisation, no one is concerned with self-realisation as an end which can be isolated and pursued for itself; people are rather concerned with their work – achieving or realising the goods internal to their roles in labour – as the means to freedom and self-realisation. Freedom (or free choice) and self-realisation come about as a consequence of the achievement or realisation of their roles or purposes in the social fabric – specifically in the context of labour.

Now, Marx's social individual cannot be a person whose freely chosen projects deny his/her social nature. This is because, in the communist state, choice is informed by social identity. In the communist state the worker sees his/her work as satisfying his/her most important wants and needs, and hence as his/her most important project. This makes for a cooperative way of life. If Marx is right, cooperation would outstrip competition because no one has any advantage over anyone else with regard to control over the instruments of social and political power. Indeed, control would strictly be unnecessary because in the communist state the administration of (distributive) justice is not only superfluous (there is no competition for limited resources) but also undesirable (competition for limited resources is dysfunctional).

4.2 The second attempt at political self-definition: pluralism

An account of the nature of a consensual democracy (the preferred form of democracy in Africa) needs some preparatory work, which involves sketching briefly the ideological framework of a consensual democracy, as well as the social precondition of the typical form which a consensual democracy takes, viz. pluralism.

4.2.1 Ideology

Marx operates on the assumption that all thought is socially determined: there can be no system of thought and ideas which has a claim to truth outside the social/

historical context in which thought and ideas arise. So, if this is true, Marx's so-called correct view of society – the whole picture of understanding social arrangements in terms of labour, production, and distribution – must be ideological too. Marx does not draw a clear distinction between the idea of socially determined thought and ideology insofar as he does not clearly show what kind of social determination produces ideology. Marx can clearly not accept the view that all socially determined thought must be ideological, for this view turns his correct view of society into ideological thoughts as well. Yet Marx continues to call all systems of thought which perpetuate relations of domination (of ruling class over labouring class) ideological, which he contrasts with his correct view, and which he considers the only correct (socialist) view. The view that all socially and existentially determined thought qualifies as ideological thought implies that an ideology can be found in any attempt to reconstruct the world-view or way of life of any cultural group.

We begin, then, with the idea that in every culture there exists a set of general principles which regulate social and economic life, which legitimises the attainment and exercise of political power, and which enjoys general acceptance within a cultural group. The general acceptance of such a set of principles within a group is called a *consensus*. The principles themselves constitute an ideology.

Now, legitimating principles underlie the life of a society. They give it the forms it takes. We may distinguish three kinds of theory offering different principles (ideologies) of social organisation:

1. The theory of a power elite (oligarchy, theocracy, technocracy), which makes all major political decisions without accountability to the governed. The basis of power may vary. Power may be based on religion (theocracy), entrepreneurial skills (technocracy), or property (oligarchy).
2. The theory of classical democracy, which requires that the elected be accountable to the electorate. Power is based on voting strength in a system of universal franchise. Majorities have decision-making power.
3. The theory of pluralism, which advocates a political position midway between (1) and (2). Power is based on consensus, but the basis of power may vary. Power may be based on wealth, skill or religious/cultural/agrarian/urban groups (to mention but a few). The idea here is that power has to be competed for by different groups having different power bases. No one group has or can have a monopoly of political power. So political decisions are not made by an elite, or by majorities, but rather by arriving at a consensus.

What are the ideological undertones of consensus forms of government? Consider the following:

1. Preferences for consensus reflect a distrust of elitism and majoritarianism. Consensus places organised minorities (acting in concert on specific issues) in power, which means that even the smallest group can expect to have its point of view considered by those making the decisions. In this respect, consensus is more open and representative than elitism or majoritarianism.

But is this really so? Consider that if we accept a certain account of ideology (Habermas 1970), we might argue as follows:

2. Since pluralism sometimes falls victim to the idea of an underlying (not transparent) consensus on political issues, consensus may in effect rely on

established elites to maintain the values of democracy (openness, representativeness, transparency, playing by the rules, etc). But this devalues one crucial
feature of democratic governments, viz. popular participation. In this respect
pluralism moves closer to elitism.

We are interested in the contrast between (1) and (2); (1) would seem to be mere
appearance while (2) states the reality. The underlying consensus operative in
pluralism may amount to an undemocratic rule by elites, rather than by majorities.
How might such an ideological bias be exposed?

Elitism, even in disguised forms, works against the emancipatory interests of
democratic institutions. One crucial interest of the institutions of democracy is to
safeguard the autonomy of the individual, irrespective of whether the individual
is seen as the basic unit of social interaction independently of his/her
membership of a group, or whether membership is seen to be the basic factor.
The theory of classical democracy assumes that everyone is able to know and
articulate his/her interests, a view which pluralism (in its disguised form) denies:
people may not be aware of their own interests, or may misconceive them; so
majoritarianism is untrustworthy as a protector of true democratic values. It is up
to informed elites to articulate the requirements of autonomy and to design
institutions to protect them. In this respect a pluralist ideology performs an
emancipatory function.

The German philosopher Habermas offers us a view of the emancipatory goals
of ideology. Habermas thinks that all points of view are ideological, and that it is
sometimes necessary to dig below surface appearance to expose ideological bias.
Like Marx, he thinks that the material conditions of social life have a powerful
influence on the design of social structures, but he thinks our ideological concerns
extend beyond this. We also have an interest in communicating with each other, so
the forms of social organisation we create must facilitate communication.

How does ideology link with these concerns? Habermas sees the link in
language. Language provides the key to a study of society. Habermas thinks that
language not only constitutes social phenomena, but that it is also constituted and
distorted by social phenomena. A good example of distortion emerges from the
contrast drawn between (1) and (2) above: (1) is mere appearance; (2) states the
reality. We articulate pluralism in terms of (1). But this is a distortion (a falsehood)
because (1) covers a less acceptable reality, as articulated in (2). We have to dig
below surface appearance to understand the reality of our political lives. It is in this
sense of uncovering a legitimating ideology that the study of ideology is a study of
systematically distorted communication. This is the emancipatory function which
Habermas believes ideology has.

Now, one ideology may supersede another if the superseding ideology is better
adapted at serving our interest in emancipation. Such an ideology would be one
which has mastered distorted communication and put in its place the "ideal speech
(communicative) situation". This ideal situation would be one in which all
distortion is uncovered, and so everything that is said would be
- transparent, and so comprehensible for what it is;
- true;
- legitimate (in the context in which it is offered);
- sincerely meant.

The kind of society which meets the standards of the ideal speech situation would have to be one in which everyone is included in the public forum of debate, and has, in this forum, an equal chance to participate in the discussions. An emancipatory ideology would require social evolution to bring everyone to the required level of communicative competence, i.e. to the level where each person can free him/herself from manipulation (distortion) and domination (elitism).

4.2.2 Contextualism

At the outset we took note of the relationship between a community's social and political identity. We said that ideally a community's political identity should grow out of its social identity, and we noted that in Africa diverse cultural communities co-exist within single political communities, and that this creates a problem since these diverse cultural communities do not inhabit the same world of social meanings and shared understandings. The problem that arises is how to understand the relationship between social and political identity in culturally heterogeneous societies. This is a problem facing South Africa. How might we approach the problem?

The specific history of a cultural group – the history of its institutions and practices – as well as the shape of its social identity and the norms which obtain at any particular time, combine to form standards which give expression to political life; these standards form the bottom line against which we evaluate and justify political actions. Political life plays off against a background of established practices. In our discussion of community we have seen that any practice which is a practice of politics must serve basic needs (jobs, housing, health care) and goals (security, justice). Any institution that counts as political must try to meet these basic needs and goals. But, by themselves, basic needs and goals are not enough to define a cultural or historical community's political life – for political life is richer than this. Political life also embraces cultural connections with the community and the values to be attained from cultural structures.

If this is so, what sense does it make to talk of a single political identity for culturally heterogeneous societies? What form might each cultural group's attempt at articulating a common political identity take? Is there a neutral language in terms of which they might articulate their respective interests and arrive at a common political self-definition? Consider what happens if members of just two groups differ on values. A judgement by members of one community that others are wrong about what is important in their culture, is a serious matter. This is because the values to which people freely subscribe carry great weight with them, and form a crucial part of how they understand their moral experience. Moreover, values are key elements of the cultural context in which political judgements are made. For those values to be overridden requires an interpretation of the culture which shows not only that the values in question are wrong, but also why other values implicit in the practices of the culture are right.

What is at issue here is that in cases of conflict within a culture we can reasonably expect to arrive at a solution by appeal to the culture's central or core values. But in cases of conflict between cultures, we need an interpretation of value which shows why appeal to core values may be overridden. Resolution is commonly achieved with reference to the necessity for association between cultures. In cases in which different cultures have to live with each other (the grounds may be historical necessity, as in South Africa), and create common political institutions, mere appeal to values lying at the centre of the different cultures will not be enough. We need to appeal to values associated with or generated by the necessity for association – those associated with actual participation in the (creation of) common structures. The call for *participation* generates a range of values associated with participation.

4.2.2.1 The need for transparency

It is essential that all legitimating ideologies be transparent to ensure that the political structures created perform their desired emancipatory function, i.e. that they work for the preservation of autonomy and against asymmetrical power relations among the various communities. To meet this end it is necessary to ensure that all persons have an equal chance to participate in the conversation and that they enjoy the desired level of communicative competence, which will in turn ensure that they are free from manipulation (distortion) and domination (elitism).

4.2.2.2 The need for a secure context of choice

It is essential also that all cultures be granted a juridical equality, i.e. an equality of treatment, though in fact different cultural communities may be unequal relative to each other with respect to their different social endowments and circumstances. The issue about equality is serious: different communities need to be given the same status, one consistent with guaranteeing equal access for their members to opportunities and resources. *Qua* members of a historical or cultural community, it is easy enough to guarantee equality of membership, but *qua* citizens of the broader political community there is likely to be equality only in name – access to resources and opportunity is likely to be monopolised by communities who control various power bases, e.g. the means of production. This may mean that other communities could be outbid on matters crucial to their survival as cultural communities. They may be outbid

1. For important resources like land;
2. For a voice on important policy decisions like the official languages of public administration; or
3. For a say in the design of work patterns, an issue connected with people's conceptions of themselves (especially under conditions of oppression made possible by the migrant labour system, which became a monument to white *baasskap*).

It is important to secure equality of access to resources and opportunity in the broader political community because it is in this context that choice is translated into outcome. Differences in resources which affect people's choices are differences which arise from people's circumstances – e.g. which cultural community they are born into, the cultural and material circumstances of their cultures, the disadvantaged status (if any) in the wider political community regarding their ability to participate freely, etc. Unequal circumstances which may inhibit and even penalise participation in the wider political community constitute an area of illegitimate inequality. How might this be addressed?

If all cultural groups are to be treated equally in the political domain, the particular interests of different cultural communities have to be equally protected, either institutionally or constitutionally. If special political rights protecting the cultural heritage of people were entrenched constitutionally, no community would have to pay to secure something valuable to their cultural heritage and survival, thus leaving them with fewer resources to pursue other cultural projects. Minority cultures in particular would be vulnerable. This is so particularly in cases involving language rights. If, for argument's sake, a minority culture does not have its language recognised as an official language, and children must attend public schools in which the medium of instruction is in some other language, speakers of the minority language would have to build their own schools and train their own teachers if they wish to survive as an integrated cultural whole. This is costly and places a drain on the resources they need for survival. They have to spend their resources on securing mere survival, a problem which members of the dominant cultures do not face, and, indeed obtain gratis.

What is so important about ensuring that cultural structures survive? We have emphasised that cultural structures are significant in that they provide the contexts (of choice and for the growth of identity) in which people actualise their humanity. Access to a secure cultural structure is a necessity, for this is the context within which we choose or pose ends, decide on their value, and fulfil our essential interest in leading a good life. Should some people have to pay to obtain these things when others – members of the dominant cultures – obtain them gratis by virtue of their control of the wider political arena?

We have here briefly raised the problem of fairness which originates with unequal social endowments or circumstances. Part of what it means to recognise differences concerns the recognition of the inequality of social endowments and the disadvantage that this creates for small cultures in the pursuit of their collective life. Should state funds be used to protect the collective life of cultures disadvantaged by their circumstances? The reasons for respecting a principle of state supported assistance for disadvantaged cultures are also the reasons for respecting a principle affirming the significance of cultural membership. No person should be hindered from interpreting his/her cultural experiences in his/her own way. But this requires that cultural structures, especially smaller structures, be protected from the disintegrating effects of decisions made by people outside their structures. The fact of the matter is that the members of disadvantaged cultures would – in the field of opportunity – be outbid and even outvoted on matters crucial to their survival as cultural communities. Since this is an inequality – one which is the product of circumstances and not choices – we need to respond with some kind of compensatory arrangement, one likely to keep participation as an option for disadvantaged cultures.

Compensation for the loss of a cultural context is something we are not, as a rule, willing to make the subject of a trade-off. The best way to compensate for unequal social endowments or circumstances is to institute special political status for minority/disadvantaged cultures. How far should we go? It should be borne in mind that the idea is to facilitate participation by all cultures as equal parties in the wider political arena. We therefore suggest that special measures for cultural protection is the best possible guarantee of political equality. Two points should be noted:

1. Adopting a principle affirming the importance of cultural membership affirms the *equal* rights of individual members of different cultural groups in the wider

political arena. The principle at issue here is strictly procedural: it does nothing more than allow communities space to open the door (to participation) as wide as they wish.

2. But if communities are to compete successfully for power, whether singly or in alliance with other communities, something more substantial is needed as an insurance against domination and the erosion of collective life. Protecting a cultural context is tantamount to protecting a context of choice. The unequal social endowments or disadvantaged circumstances of any community makes their context of choice less secure. Inequalities in the context of choice must be addressed before political choice in the wider arena can meaningfully be exercised. We need therefore to see the protection of a context of choice as a source of rights designed specifically to protect cultural integrity in the wider political arena. These would be group rights that guarantee communities' recognition of their dues (e.g. as disadvantaged people).

4.2.2.3 The need for recognition

It is essential that differences be recognised and affirmed, because recognition of differences in the public (political) forum has an impact on the formation of identity.

What does it mean to receive equal recognition in the public arena of political life? There are two main lines of thought which need briefly to be discussed here. The first line of thought begins with the idea that all members of a political community are equally entitled to respect because they are all members of the human race. Sometimes this entitlement is defended as something grounded in our status as rational agents, and sometimes as grounded in our status as culture creating beings. The second line of thought does not reject the ideal of our entitlement to an equality of respect (or dignity), but treats this as itself insufficient. Entitlement needs to be amplified by a (public) recognition of differences. We are asked to recognise distinct identities, particularly cultural identities, as morally significant categories. What is at issue here? Moral identities are formed by recognition. Misrecognition counts as a harm because it deforms identity (women, people of colour, and even people who prefer to live in primitive technologies, are victims of misrecognition). Marginalised groups tend to internalise deformed images of themselves, making deformity a constitutive part of their self-expression.

The first line of thought – let us call it *the line of equal dignity* – champions non-discrimination and advocates difference-blindness: given any case, no one is entitled to differential treatment unless there are good (publicly defended and accepted) reasons why some particular individual should be treated differently. The second line of thought – let us call it *the line of unique identity* – argues that in order to attain a political community in which non-discrimination is the norm, we need to make distinctions between different cultural communities – distinctions which call for differential treatment as morally justified.

The line of unique identity identifies two main areas in which the recognition of difference is necessary and differential treatment justified. Firstly, in some political communities (e.g. South Africa), a great many cultural communities have been handicapped by poverty which has reduced their citizen rights to second and even third class status. It does not help to offer these people citizenship rights without social programmes designed to alleviate their poverty and upgrade the status of their citizenship. Inherited poverty traps are difficult to overcome and they mark a difference which citizen rights cannot eliminate. The mere awarding of citizenship is difference-blind in the wrong sense in that it perpetuates a social order in which asymmetrical power relations between rich and poor remain in force. In such communities social measures affording people from disadvantaged groups a competitive advantage for jobs, social security, housing, health care, etc. are necessary to grant them *worth* of citizenship.

There is, of course, a problem with social programmes designed to alleviate the social conditions of historically disadvantaged groups. Such programmes tend to assimilate disadvantaged groups to the cultural identity of the communities who dominate the political life of the society at large, a fact which tends to reinforce the "inferior" status of disadvantaged cultures. Their identities are suppressed, which is highly discriminatory and non-egalitarian. This brings me to the second point.

At the beginning of this article we attempted to explain the hegemonic success of white culture in South Africa. We suggested that values deriving from the cultural capital of white culture were falsely presented as universal values. Prior to the demise of apartheid the allegedly universalist status of white values was used as a divisive tool. There is in this a lesson to be learnt for the post-apartheid era. The difference-blind value structures which have gained ascendancy in the current political life of South Africa also claim to be universalist insofar as the capacity for moral action is recognised as a capacity all humans share. It is by virtue of this capacity that all humans are regarded as deserving of equal respect and dignity. This is the right sense of difference-blind values. But we must take care that the wrong sense does not override the right sense, which is associated with the values of particularity, especially those connected with our need to be recognised for who we are and where we come from. This capacity for defining identity as constituted by the identity of a cultural community must likewise be respected equally in everyone. We must guard against the idea that some cultures are more valuable than others, for in entertaining this possibility we deny human equality.

A politics of equal recognition will be one hospitable to difference because it not only insists on uniform entitlements, but also looks at the *worth* of these entitlements; also, it takes the collective goals of cultural communities seriously, which means making space in the public (political) forum for these goals in the attempt to construct a common political identity.

It may, of course, be argued that the claim that all cultures have a claim to an equality of worth is presumptuous. Do all cultures have something valuable to say to all human beings? Political structures are seldom neutral regarding those who value remaining true to their cultural heritage and those who do not. So it is important that such structures be designed against a backdrop in which valuation from one cultural background can be situated alongside valuation from another cultural background. The guiding principle of valuation must be that non-recognition or misrecognition denies equality, which denial has harmful consequences for people's identity. Recognition and equality must then be treated as moral imperatives for all – irrespective of whether we find anything of personal value in other cultures.

5.   CONSENSUS

5.1 The case of the Ashanti of Ghana

How does consensus work in African society? For an account of this we turn to Kwasi Wiredu. According to Wiredu, the habit of making decisions in politics by consensus was cultivated by even the most centralised of ethnic groups in Africa, the Zulus and the Ashanti. Wiredu offers a view of how consensus operates in Ashanti communities. The Ashanti are a matrilineal group, and so the lineage is their basic political unit. Every lineage (which consists of a number of kin groups) has a head, and every head is, by virtue of headship of the lineage, a member of a council which is the governing body of every Ashanti community. Headship, however, is not hereditary – the qualifications are "[s]eniority, age, wisdom, a sense of civic responsibility and logical persuasiveness" (Wiredu 1995a:55). "Appointment" to a headship follows a specific route: through "[p]rolonged and painstaking consultations and discussions aimed at consensus" (Wiredu 1995a:55). An act of "voting" is not carried out. (According to Wiredu there is no long-standing word for "voting" in the Ashanti language.) Consensus is arrived at by a different route: "[t]he elders sit under the big trees, and talk until they agree" (Wiredu 1995a:53). The point at which the head of a lineage is "appointed" is the point at which the elders *agree*, i.e. the point at which they reach *consensus*. This procedure is followed for all "appointments" to political office.

The first point to note about consensus is that it involves *agreement*. The potential for agreement lies in the idea that ultimately the interests of the members of a community are the same, though their perceptions may differ regarding their place in the overall scheme of things. Wiredu expresses this point very neatly:

> This thought [of agreement] is given expression in an art motif depicting a crocodile with one stomach and two heads locked in struggle over food. If they could but see that the food was, in any case, destined for the same stomach, the irrationality of the conflict [the disagreement over who gets what share] would be manifest to them. But is there a chance of it? The Ashanti answer is "Yes, human beings have the ability eventually to cut through their differences to the rock bottom identity of interests" (1995a:57).

Agreement, however, is not *unanimity*, i.e. it does not necessarily involve a complete identity of opinions. If this is the case, how does political decision-making work? It is, according to Wiredu (1995a:57), important to keep the dialogue open because even minority opinion must retain the right of representation. The object of an open dialogue is to achieve a "suspension of disagreement". Wiredu (1995a:54) says the point is to achieve "[w]illing suspension of disagreement, *making possible agreed actions without necessarily agreed notions*", (emphasis added).

This means that at some point the elders may agree to disagree, but that the fact of participation in political structures compels them to go forward and implement a decision. Participation is the key to recognition of political differences in the political constituency as a whole. Non-participation is dysfunctional because it removes a constituency of opinion from the public arena in which its identity is affirmed, thus undermining its significance as a context in which identity is actualised and choices are posed. As long as participation remains the key virtue of political or civic life, no one loses or appropriates power. As Wiredu argues:

None of the groups . . . organised themselves for the purpose of gaining power in a way which entailed others not being in power, or worse, being out of it. For all concerned, the system [of consensus] was set up for participation in power not its appropriation (1995a:59).

A government is formed not by a majority party, but rather by the consensus of representatives, i.e. a government by coalition of all constituencies, which entails, as Wiredu puts it, a "coalition of citizens". Wiredu argues for the significance of this as follows:

If the community is to go forward, a particular line of action must be taken . . . the majority [consensus] prevails not over, but upon, the minority [consensus] – they prevail upon them to accept the proposal in question, not just to live with it, which latter is the basic plight of minorities under majoritarian democracy. In a consensus system the voluntary acquiescence of the minority with respect to a given issue would normally be necessary for the adoption of a decision (1995a:62).

5.2 Consensus in culturally heterogeneous societies

We are now moving to our main objective, which is to come to grips with consensus in culturally heterogeneous societies. The idea of consensus, understood as an *agreement* to cooperate in society, i.e. to carry out a particular line of action, though all parties to the agreement do not agree that the particular line of action is the best, has been emphasised. This idea is known as *common action by agreement without substantial agreement*. The most important principle which a culturally heterogeneous society would have to recognise and emphasise is the equal value of a system of liberties which is available to all. But this does not mean that participation in the wider political arena deprives individuals of membership of a cultural group. The point at issue here is one of emphasis. There exists a multiplicity of incommensurable social and cultural viewpoints, each demanding its own political form – one that conforms to its own cultural bias. Membership of groups is fully recognised and affirmed in the system of liberties available to all as citizens of the wider political arena. But their participation in this arena is *qua* individuals rather than *qua* groups, for on this depends the working of the mechanism of consensus, i.e. of going forward in a particular line of action without all groups agreeing that it is the best or most appropriate.

What guarantee have we that particular individuals will participate when their group(s) oppose the common line? All we can do here is fall back on the assumption that each cultural group recognises, as part of its political culture, general ideas about freedom and equality, ideas which specific individuals might offer as reasonable grounds for cooperation with other individuals. Rawls (1987) makes a case for reasonableness:

1. Reasonable people can be expected to put forward fair terms for cooperation, *terms which they expect other reasonable people to abide by, as diligently as they abide by those terms themselves.*
2. Since political power is partly coercive power – the power to make people do things which they may not want to do – those who have power must be prepared to accept its burdens when using it. This is of critical importance when seen together with (1) above. Political power should be used only when there is *a shared basis of justification* for its use, i.e. only if there is a consensus that its use is justified. Specifically, those who hold power may not use it to suppress opposing views of a minority consensus. Why not? The answer is simple.

Precedents of this kind would entitle anyone who holds power, and believes his/her views (or choice of way of life) to be the right one, to impose his/her choice on anyone else who might reasonably reject those choices.

3. The idea of *cooperation among individuals for mutual advantage* implies ideas of reciprocity and of benefit to each along with benefit for others, benefit which each singly, in competition with others, might not gain. The basic idea here is that individuals cooperate to maximise the sum or total benefit available to each, and that each person's share of the gross product would be greater than if each had attempted to maximise only those benefits accruing to him/herself. There is one condition which all must meet. In a cooperative social world any individual can appeal, and should limit him/herself to appealing only to arguments and principles of justice which others can reasonably be expected to accept, for otherwise the cost of cooperation will outweigh the benefits. For instance, one might appeal to the state use of coercive power only if one could appeal to arguments that others accept in support of the state use of coercive power (for some case in question), for otherwise the use of power would be counter-productive, i.e. the costs (of using power) would outweigh the benefits (of using power). And this assumes a consensus about the proper use of the state's coercive power.

An issue like the proper use of the state's coercive power demands that there be a strong consensus – any concession to the power of competing groups on this issue is likely to render the whole of society unstable. Much the same applies in the case of consensus about principles of justice: if (unfair) concession is made to powerful groups in disregard of an established consensus, patterns of distribution in the society are likely to break down and the cost of cooperation is likely to outweigh the benefit. The argument over a public policy concerning the issue of power runs together with an argument over the limits of public reason – of what is included or is left out of the political agenda, and what considerations we may or may not appeal to when advancing particular arguments.

5.3 The idea of an "overlapping" consensus

An "overlapping" consensus (Rawls 1987) is, in the sense we require, a basis for agreement to go forward on a common line of (political) action without there being substantial agreement. The possibility of such a consensus assumes that the conception of justice which will in the end prevail, will be one tailored to the particular society it has to serve. This means that this conception of justice

1. cannot be one containing only the moral and political concepts of one or two of the groups competing in the wider political arena; rather, it has to contain only fundamental intuitive ideas inherent in the political cultures of groups, ideas like the equal value to all of a system of liberties;

2. must be one designed to fit the basic structure of the particular society in question; it cannot be a general and comprehensive view of justice developed outside the framework of the historical, social, and cultural contingencies of the contracting groups; and it

3. must allow for a plurality of conceptions of the good – an issue touching on two basic needs: the need for a secure context of choice and the need for recognition of difference.

It is important to stress that, regarding (3), all conceptions of the good are equally permissible provided they respect the constraints of the overlapping consensus. The fact that people participate from within their own cultural milieu and bias, and hence operate with different premises and grounds, does not affect their affirmation of the authority of the overriding consensus. This authority has special priority, for it affects all measures pertaining to the common good of the society as a whole. Affirmation of this priority is part of the commitment to the idea of free public reason, i.e. to the idea that the considerations appealed to in debate have to be ones which others are likely to endorse or accept, rather than considerations which appeal only to the cultural bias of particular groups. Finally, it is important to stress that regarding (1) and (2), a conception of justice fitting heterogeneous societies will have to be "home grown" in the sense that it develops from intuitive ideas about fairness implicit in the public lives of each cultural group. Within the scope allowed by (1) and (2), cultural communities can pursue their ways of life on fair terms with each other and with mutual respect in the non-public arena of the wider political platform.

NOTE

1. A version of this paper was read at the Third Colloquium on African Philosophy at the University of South Africa, Pretoria, in October 1996. A different version was first published in *Koers* 62(4). 1997:423–446.

Readings

THE DEFINITION OF BLACK CONSCIOUSNESS
STEVE BIKO

We have in our policy manifesto defined blacks as those who are by law or tradition politically, economically, and socially discriminated against as a group in South African society, and identify themselves as a unit in the struggle towards the realisation of their aspirations. This definition illustrates to us a number of things:

1. Being black is not a matter of pigmentation – being black is a reflection of a mental attitude.
2. Merely by describing yourself as black you have started on a road towards emancipation, you have committed yourself to fight against all forces that seek to use your blackness as a stamp that marks you out as a subservient being.

From the above observations, therefore, we can see that the term black is not necessarily all-inclusive, i.e. the fact we are all *not white* does not necessarily mean that we are all *black*. Non-whites do exist and will continue to exist and will continue to exist for quite a long time. If one's aspiration is whiteness but pigmentation makes attainment of this impossible, then that person is a non-white. Any man who calls a white man "Baas", any man who serves in the police force or Security Branch is *ipso facto* a non-white. Black people – real black people – are those who manage to hold their heads high in defiance rather than willingly surrender their souls to the white man.

Briefly defined, therefore, Black Consciousness is in essence the realisation by the black man of the need to rally together with his brothers around the cause of their operation – the blackness of their skin – and to operate as a group in order to rid themselves of the shackles that bind them to perpetual servitude. It seeks to demonstrate the lie that black is an aberration from the "normal" which is white. It is a manifestation of a new realisation that by seeking to run away from themselves and to emulate the white man, blacks are insulting the intelligence of whoever created them black. Black Consciousness, therefore, takes cognisance of the deliberateness of God's plan in creating black people black. It seeks to infuse the black community with a new-found pride in themselves, their efforts, their value systems, their culture, their religion and their outlook on life.

The interrelationship between the consciousness of the self and the emancipatory programme is of paramount importance. Blacks no longer seek to reform the system because so doing implies acceptance of the major points around which the system revolves.

Blacks are out to completely transform the system and to make of it what they wish. Such a major undertaking can only be realised in an atmosphere where people are convinced of the truth inherent in their stand. Liberation therefore is of paramount importance in the concept of Black Consciousness, for we cannot be conscious of ourselves and yet remain in bondage. We want to attain the envisioned self which is a free self.

The surge towards Black Consciousness is a phenomenon that has manifested itself throughout the so-called third world. There is no doubt that discrimination against the black man the world over fetches its origin from the exploitative attitude of the white man. Colonisation of white countries by whites has throughout history resulted in nothing more sinister than mere cultural or geographical fusion at worst, or language bastardisation at best. It is true that the history of weaker nations is shaped by bigger nations, but nowhere in the world today do we see whites exploiting whites on a scale even remotely similar to what is happening in South Africa. Hence, one is forced to conclude that it is not coincidence that black people are exploited. It was a deliberate plan which has culminated in even so-called black independent countries not attaining any real independence.

With this background in mind we are forced, therefore, to believe that it is a case of *haves* against *have-nots* where whites have deliberately been made *haves* and blacks *have-nots*. There is for instance no worker in the classical sense among whites in South Africa, for even the most downtrodden white worker still has a lot to lose if the system is changed. He is protected by several laws against competition at work from the majority. He has a vote and he uses it to return the Nationalist Government to power because he sees them as the only people who, through job reservation laws, are bent on looking after his interests against competition with the "Natives".

It should therefore be accepted that an analysis of our situation in terms of one's colour at once takes care of the greatest single determinant for political action – i.e. colour – while also validly describing the blacks as the only real workers in South Africa. It immediately kills all suggestions that there could ever be effective rapport between the real workers, i.e. blacks, and the privileged white workers, since we have shown that the latter are the greatest supporters of the system. True enough, the system has allowed so dangerous an anti-black attitude to build up among whites that it is taken as almost a sin to be black and hence the poor whites, who are economically nearest to the blacks, demonstrate the distance between themselves and the blacks by an exaggerated reactionary attitude towards blacks. Hence the greatest anti-black feeling is to be found amongst the very poor whites whom the class theory calls upon to be with black workers in the struggle for emancipation. This is the kind of twisted logic that the Black Consciousness approach seeks to eradicate.

In terms of the Black Consciousness approach we recognise the existence of one major force in South Africa. This is white racism. It is the one force against which all of us are pitted. It works with unnerving totality, featuring both on the offensive and in our defence. Its greatest ally to date has been the refusal by us to club together as blacks because we are told to do so would be racialist. So, while we progressively lose ourselves in a world of colourlessness and amorphous common humanity, whites are deriving pleasure and security in entrenching white racism and further exploiting the minds and bodies of the unsuspecting black masses. Their agents are ever present amongst us, telling us that it is immoral to withdraw into a cocoon, that dialogue is the answer to our problem and that it is unfortunate that there is white racism in some quarters but you must understand that things are changing. These in fact are the greatest racists for they refuse to credit us with any intelligence to know what we want. Their intentions are obvious; they want to be barometers by which the rest of the white society can measure feelings in the black world. This then is what makes us believe that white power presents itself as a totality not only provoking us but also controlling our response to the provocation. This is an important point to note because it is often missed by those who believe that there are a few good whites. Sure there are a few good whites just as much as there are a few bad blacks.

However, what we are concerned with here is group attitudes and group politics. The exception does not make a lie of the rule – it merely substantiates it.

The overall analysis therefore, based on the Hegelian theory of dialectic materialism, is as follows. That since the thesis is a white racism there can only be one valid antithesis, i.e. a solid black unity, to counterbalance the scale. If South Africa is to be a land where black and white live together in harmony without fear of group exploitation, it is only when these two opposites have interplayed and produced a viable synthesis of ideas and a *modus vivendi*. We can never wage any struggle without offering a strong counterpoint to the white races that permeate our society so effectively.

One must immediately dispel the thought that Black Consciousness is merely a methodology or a means towards an end. What Black Consciousness seeks to do is to produce at the output end of the process real black people who do not regard themselves as appendages to white society. This truth cannot be reversed. We do not need to apologise for this because it is true that the white systems have produced throughout the world a number of people who are not aware that they too are people. Our adherence to values that we set for ourselves can also not be reversed because it will always be a lie to accept white values as necessarily the best. The fact that a synthesis may be attained only relates to adherence to power politics. Someone somewhere along the line will be forced to accept the truth and here we believe that ours is the truth.

The future of South Africa in the case where blacks adopt Black Consciousness is the subject for concern especially among initiates. What do we do when we have attained our Consciousness? Do we propose to kick whites out? I believe personally that the answers to these questions ought to be found in the SASO Policy Manifesto and in our analysis of the situation in South Africa. We have defined what we mean by true integration and the very fact that such a definition exists does illustrate what our standpoint is. In any case we are much more concerned about what is happening now, than what will happen in the future. The future will always be shaped by the sequence of present-day events.

The importance of black solidarity to the various segments of the black community must not be understated. There have been in the past a lot of suggestions that there can be no viable unity amongst blacks because they hold each other in contempt. Coloureds despise Africans because they (the former), by their proximity to the Africans, may lose the chance of assimilation into the white world. Africans despise the Coloureds and Indians for a variety of reasons. Indians not only despise Africans but in many instances also exploit Africans in job and shop situations. All these stereotypical attitudes have led to mountainous intergroup suspicions amongst the blacks.

What we should at all times look at is the following:
1. We are all oppressed by the same system.
2. That we are oppressed to varying degrees is a deliberate design to stratify us not only socially but also in terms of aspirations.

3. Therefore it is to be expected that in terms of the enemy's plan there must be this suspicion and that if we are committed to the problem of emancipation to the same degree it is part of our duty to bring to the attention of the black people the deliberateness of the enemy's subjugation scheme.
4. We should go on with our programme, attracting to it only committed people and not just those eager to see an equitable distribution of groups amongst our ranks. This is a game common amongst liberals. The one criterion that must govern all our action is commitment.

Further implications of Black Consciousness are to do with correcting false images of ourselves in terms of culture, education, religion, and economics. The importance of this must not be understated. There is always an interplay between the history of a people, i.e. the past, and their faith in themselves and hopes for their future. We are aware of the terrible role played by our education and religion in creating amongst us a false understanding of ourselves. We must therefore work out schemes not only to correct this, but further to be our own authorities rather than wait to be interpreted by others. Whites can only see us from the outside and as such can never extract and analyse the ethos in the black community.

OUTLAWING RACISM IN PHILOSOPHY: ON RACE AND PHILOSOPHY

MABOGO P. MORE

INTRODUCTION

One of the salient and vexing problems facing today's liberal democratic nation-states is the tension between the individual citizen and group or collective rights. Liberal democracies, guided by their fundamental principles of individual autonomy, equality, freedom, and rights find themselves confronted by the emergence of profound, pervasive, and persistent diversity among their citizens and the consequent demand for the recognition of these group or collective differences and diversities. In attempts to articulate and find solutions to this problem, a number of different types of democratic liberalism have been suggested to address the problem of diversity. These include, among others, "comprehensive liberalism", "political liberalism", "radical liberalism", "national liberalism", and "cosmopolitan liberalism".

Recast in the light of new philosophical concerns the debate is about the tension between universalism and particularism or what has come to be called the "politics of sameness" *vis-à-vis* the "politics of difference", unity or diversity. The names attached to these positions and the suggested solutions have ranged from multi-culturalism, pluralism, liberalism of every kind, to unity in diversity. Though these are not substantially different, it is the latter position that I wish to examine because it expresses the basis underlying the political philosophy of the new South Africa, namely "rainbowism". Framed in the form of a question, the problem as Lucius Outlaw (1996:137) sees it amounts to this: is it possible to reduce tensions (between, for example, difference and sameness) while allowing for the recognition – even celebration and nurturing – of racial and/or ethnic difference?

This essay attempts to interrogate Outlaw's suggested resolution of this problem in his recent text *On race and philosophy* (1996), by contextualising it within the framework of a plural social formation such as South Africa which in many ways faces similar kinds of problematic issues to that which Outlaw attempts to address within the American context. As Derrida (in Gates 1986:369) says: "The problem of (post)apartheid is surely an American problem." I shall therefore attempt to address the following question: how helpful and sustainable can Outlaw's suggested solution be to South Africa?

A significant number of philosophers have recently advanced theories articulating political philosophies geared toward addressing this problem and its variations. Charles Taylor's *Multiculturalism* (1992), Will Kymlicka's *Liberalism, community, and culture* (1989), and Iris Marion Young's *Justice and the politics of difference* (1990), are some of the much debated texts currently articulating the recognition of diversity. But the problem itself is not actually of recent origin except that recent social, political, economic, and technological events have brought it into focus. Both the African-American philosopher W.E.B. Du Bois in *The conservation of races* (1897), and Jean-Paul Sartre in *Portrait of the anti-Semite* (1948), for example, anticipated the current debate over universalism and particularism. For them, however, this was more an individual and social problem rather than specifically a political dilemma.

As a short detour, a brief statement concerning Du Bois's and Sartre's articulation of the dilemma might be helpful. This is in order to contextualise Outlaw's articulation of particularism and universalism within the broader articulation anticipated by the other two philosophers. It is also because Outlaw, while to a large extent adhering to Du Bois's position, however goes beyond Sartre's solution to the tension between particularism and universalism, diversity and homogeneity.

THE DILEMMA

Long before this century, Plato problematised the dilemma generated by a universalism predicated on sameness and a particularism emanating from the recognition of difference. This he called the problem of "the one and the many" (cf. Plato 1961:par. 596A).

Writing in 1897 and anticipating current debates about citizenship and the individual, and mindful of the tensions associated with attempts to fashion racial identity within a universalistic nation-state such as America, Du Bois states:

> Here, then, is the dilemma, and it is a puzzling one, I admit. No Negro who has given earnest thought to the situation of his people in America has failed . . . to ask himself at some time: What, after all, am I? Am I an American or am I a Negro? Can I be both? Or is it my duty to cease to be a Negro as soon as possible and be an American? If I strive as a Negro, am I not perpetuating the very cleft that threatens and separates Black and White America?. . . . Does my black blood place upon me any more obligation to assert my nationality than German, or Irish or Italian blood would? (Foner 1970:25).

Almost over half a century later, in 1943, Sartre forcefully articulates the tension between the anti-Semite's particularism and the liberal democrat's humanistic universalism in relation to the Jew. The former, Sartre contends, denies the human being in the Jew while the latter refuses to recognise the Jew in the human being:

> The former wants to destroy him [the Jew] as man, so that only the Jew, the pariah, the untouchable will remain, the latter wants to destroy him as a Jew, in order to preserve in him only the man, the universal and abstract subject of the rights of man and of the citizen (1948:47).

For Sartre, the liberal democrat's humanistic universalism, because it is predicated on the concept of abstract human nature, requires the obliteration of concrete difference and the imposition of essential sameness and homogeneity. This essentialist position, Sartre argues, posits each individual as a particular example or incarnation of a universal conception of "human", thus denying the particularity of each person. Anti-Semitism, on the other hand, is predicated on the identification of the Jew, the "Other", as a member of a distinct group by virtue of a variety of biological and/or cultural traits, thus denying, a priori, sameness. Neither the anti-Semite's particularism nor the humanist's universalism, therefore, can resolve the Jew's problem.

In the face of such a double bind, how then should Jews – and by analogy blacks, women, gays, lesbians, and all excluded and oppressed groups – respond to both the liberal democrat's universalist social philosophy that denies their specificity, particularity or difference, and the anti-Semite's (racist, sexist, etc.) particularism that destroys their humanity?

OUTLAWING APPIAH: UNITY IN DIVERSITY

Anticipating later postmodernist critiques of universalism, Sartre demonstrates how the abstract humanism of the liberal democrat is not actually inclusive, as it purports to be, but is rather exclusive and oppressive. As Sartre (1982:752) would later declare, "Humanism is the counterpart of racism: it is a practice of exclusion." In line with Sartre, Outlaw also rejects the universalist liberal metanarrative. According to him, liberalism fails to take into serious account the concerns raised by raciality and ethnicity, an argument also articulated by Young (1990). Liberal political philosophy, requires that

> one look beyond what has been regarded as accidental "differences", including raciality, ethnicity, gender, and "national character", to the *essence* thought to be the definitive constitutive aspect of the human species shared by all humans that thus makes for the *essential* unity, oneness and identity of all persons, all other differences notwithstanding: *reason, a capacity* or *capability* defined by unique laws or principles (Outlaw 1996:148).

By virtue of this liberal principle of the essential sameness of individuals, Outlaw continues, all human beings are taken as essentially identical. Unfortunately, by excluding racial and gender differences, liberal universalism degenerates into nothing more than ethnocentrism, a universalised particularism.

What about Sartre's implicit appeal to a socialist solution of the problem? While Sartre accuses liberal democrats of a fraudulent universalism that is not only exclusionary but also oppressive, and suggests socialism as a solution, Outlaw, echoing Frantz Fanon, also rejects Marxism for failing to handle problems of racial, ethnic, and sexual oppression adequately, either theoretically or practically. Ultimately, the problem with both liberal democratic humanistic and Marxist metanarratives is that they are in fact particularisms parading as universalism – false universalism, as Outlaw (1996) calls it. This means therefore that the problem is not exactly between particularism and universalism as such, but among particularisms.

How then can the black person (or member of any other oppressed group) respond to this exclusionary false universalism? Outlaw takes the path of the Sartrean authentic Jew, that is, the one who demands recognition for what he/she is. Authenticity involves the re-appropriation of the self imposed on one, as a positive value. Hence, following on Du Bois, Outlaw (1996:136) calls for "the need to conserve 'race' and 'ethnie' (and 'ethnicity') as vital components of a philosophical anthropology . . . in racially and ethnically complex societies". What Outlaw calls for is a particularism grounded in the valorisation of difference. His project therefore is to work out conceptions of raciality and ethnicity that could help articulate a political philosophy appropriate to a modern liberal democratic society in which diversities – including those of race and ethnicity – are normal and important features.

In his introduction to *On race and philosophy*, and in his essay, "Against the grain of modernity: The politics of difference and the conservation of race", Outlaw predictably interrogates Kwame Anthony Appiah's contention that there are no "races". Rather than a reality, race is for Appiah nothing more than an illusion, at best a social construction. The socially constructed is, accordingly, that which is fictive, imaginative, not natural – and therefore not real. According to Appiah (1986) the term "race" – *pace* Du Bois's insistence that it must be conserved – should be discarded because it is now loaded with centuries of pernicious valorizations accumulated from dehumanizing mobilizations of sentiments and practices ranging from the merely impolite to the genocidal (quoted in Outlaw 1996:9).

Furthermore, Appiah argues, the term lacks "scientific" validity. Besides, even if races really do exist, in racially complex nation-states such as America there are no pure races. Therefore, identifying persons and groups as races cannot be accomplished with precision, and is at best arbitrary. This is interesting because it resonates with the ideas of certain nineteenth-century proponents of racial superiority who abandoned the notion of "purity of blood" as differentiating races, and replaced it with culture as a distinguishing category.

Supposing Appiah is correct, why, then, Outlaw inquires, would one continue to justify talk about "race" and "ethnicity" philosophically and thus contribute to the dangerous politics of identity and difference? Why "endow raciality and ethnicity with highly honorific philosophical significance?" (Outlaw 1996:10). Why even attempt to conserve "race" and "ethnicity"? Outlaw's (1996:10) emphatic answer is: "because we must". Our hopes to the contrary notwithstanding, physical and cultural differences among groups of people in terms of which they continue to identify themselves and be identified, still exist. For Outlaw, a mixture of social ontology and philosophical anthropology, informed by the best empirical work of biologists, geneticists, physical and cultural palaeo-anthropologists, as well as everyday social life, should convince philosophers of the truth that racial and ethnic differences will not disappear simply because of the "lexical surgery" that removes "race" from usage, replacing it instead with notions such as "communities of meanings", as Appiah (in Outlaw 1996:11) suggests.

Humans, according to Outlaw (1996:12), are not only biological beings, they are also social beings. For this reason, "human populations . . . are better understood as social-natural kinds". Because humans are part of the natural world, they are conditioned but not "strictly *determined* by processes in the natural, but socially influenced world" (1996:138). Outlaw is obviously careful not to define "race" in essentialist terms, that is, as a term for identifying only a natural kind. He connects the natural with the social conjunctively such that each element separately becomes necessary and both are jointly sufficient. Given this conception of a human being, it follows that to privilege the social construction aspect only, as Appiah and other social constructionists do, is to elide the equally important *natural* element and thus to indulge in reductionism.

What then? Are the relations between universalism and particularism simply relations of mutual exclusion? Is the supposed chasm between the universal and the particular unbridgeable? Sartre, while advocating authenticity, that is the affirmation of who and what one is, however recognises (1948:116) that "the choice of authenticity is not a social solution to the Jewish problem: it is not even an individual solution". By affirming their Jewish particularity the Jews simultaneously fall into the trap of acquiescing and complying with the demands of, and reproducing the beliefs and attitudes of, the anti-Semite or racist. On the other hand Humanism deliberately excludes gender, race, and other categories of oppressed groups. It not only excludes but also relegates the "Other" to the status of the subhuman.

In the first place it is these constructed binary oppositions between modernism and postmodernism, universalism and particularism, sameness and difference, that Outlaw seems to be contesting. For, while modernity with its false universalism is unacceptable because it does not take race and gender into account, the notion that we are in "a new historical era that is *beyond* modernity, an era of 'post-modernity' . . . is to go too far" (Outlaw 1996:151). The assertion of pure particularism independent of any content or of the appeal to a universality, is mistaken. Again, it is not universalism *qua* universalism that is put into question; it is particularism parading as universalism that is problematic. Subjecting a false universalism to immanent critique to render it truly universal and therefore inclusive is thus, for Outlaw, important both as strategy and ideal. The future, therefore, lies in a world of "unity in diversity", a world in which

> we can share a larger, more encompassing life-world . . . by agreeing to public political principles that have sufficient overlap with the various life-world orienting doctrines to which we may be committed to provide a basis for a shared life, one which leaves each race and ethnie almost – though not quite – as they were and wish to be (Outlaw 1996:21).

This is, of course, the old but recurrent problem of trying to achieve unity while preserving diversity.

Outlaw's *On race and philosophy* is therefore an attempt to work out a conception of a social and political philosophy that is capable of transcending the shortcomings of modern liberal individualism by taking seriously "racial and ethnic groups in order to be a resource for praxes that might help us to realise social peace and harmony with justice" (1996:8). This social and political philosophy attempts what Outlaw characterises as the treacherous "third path" between racism and anti-racism. This third path involves the conservation and nurturing of collectivities referred to as "races" and "ethnies" without concern for rank ordering, exploitation or invidious discrimination (Outlaw 1996:4).

How then can this project be realised? In other words, "how might we work to conserve coloured populations and subgroupings (and white is a colour, as well), races and ethnies, without making it easier for racialism and ethnocentrism" (Outlaw 1996:21) to degenerate into racism and invidious ethnocentrism? Outlaw envisages as a solution a world of "unity in diversity" constituted by people of different racial, ethnic and/or cultural practices coming together under democratic circumstances bound by a common interest in securing the well-being of others as well as themselves to work for principles of universality by which all are bound.

In this way we can share a larger, more encompassing life-world, perhaps by agreeing to public political principles that have sufficient overlap with the various life-world doctrines to which we may be committed to provide a basis for a shared life, one which leaves each race and ethnic group almost – though not quite – as it would wish to be (Outlaw 1996:21).

THE RAINBOW NATION AND THE NEW CONSTITUTION

Outlaw's social and political philosophy of "unity in diversity" may have a familiar and striking resonance to South African ears. Nothing could be closer to Outlaw's articulation than the "rainbow" metaphor used to characterise the newly-constituted South African nation. South Africa is a multi-racial, multi-ethnic, multi-cultural, and plural society emerging from a previously separatist apartheid regime that exploited these differences to construct, constitute, and enforce racial and ethnic divisions and differences for purposes of domination. Outlaw's questions referred to above become even more pertinent and assume a sharper immediacy and urgency in the South African context:

> Is it possible to reduce the tensions [between national unity and ethnic particularism] and thereby substantially reduce the threats to social order by achieving and maintaining social order, harmony and justice while allowing for the recognition . . . of racial and/or ethnic differences? (1996:138–9).

At a more practical level, Outlaw asks:

> Given human variety and the differences such variety entails . . . on what terms (by which rules or *principles*) might different racial and ethnic groups live together in the same community, or in communities in close proximity to each other, in ways that are sufficiently ordered so as to provide social peace and mutual benefit in accord with shared notions of justice? (1996:138–9).

Recognising the already well-entrenched particularistic ethnic consciousness of the apartheid era, but simultaneously eliding invidious racist ethnocentrism, the new Constitution of the "rainbow nation" seeks to achieve a balance between universalism and particularism, between liberal individualism (citizenship) and group or collective rights, between the "politics of sameness" and the "politics of difference". This balance is symbolised by the metaphor of the "rainbow". "Rainbowism" is essentially pluralistic, emphasising ethnicity, cultural difference, and diversity as defining experiences of all South African citizens. The founding principle of "rainbowism" is thus expressed in the notion of "unity in diversity" which in turn is predicated on the principles of non-racism and non-sexism.

Reminiscent of the Freedom Charter of 1955, the Preamble of the newly-promulgated Constitution of the Republic of South Africa, in accordance with "rainbowism" and a political and social philosophy similar to the one articulated by Outlaw, states:

> We, the people of South Africa . . . believe that South Africa belongs to all who live in it, united in our *diversity* (emphasis added).

We have here, contained in the Constitution, neither radical universalism nor pure particularism. The former holds that cultural and ethnic differences are absolutely irrelevant as grounds for a just, unitary, democratic, and non-racial nation. The latter maintains that, based on cultural and ethnic diversities and particularities, justice would require self-determining ethno-national "balkan" states as an imperative for lasting peace. What the Constitution instead reflects are the particular interests of different groups within the unity of a single nation – a rainbow nation bound together by a Hegelian higher synthesis of opposite moments, a "unity in diversity".

Outlaw's insistence on the conservation of "race" is, obviously, antithetical to Article 1(b) of the Constitution which states that the Republic of South Africa is founded on non-racism and non-sexism. This clause – evidently a spin-off from the liberal oriented Constitutional Guidelines of the ANC which states, *inter alia*, that "a Bill of Rights shall guarantee the fundamental human rights of all citizens irrespective of race, colour, sex or creed" – is a consequence of the concern to avoid the racism projected by the deeply racialised principles of apartheid. The non-racism and non-sexism clause is thus grounded on universalistic principles of equality applicable to all citizens of a united and democratic South African nation

("*Simunye*-ism"). In accordance with liberal political philosophy, the Constitution therefore requires that one look beyond what has been regarded as accidental differences such as race and gender

> to the essence thought to be the definitive constitutive aspect of the human species shared by all humans that thus makes for the essential unity, oneness, and identity of all persons, all other differences notwithstanding (Outlaw 1996:148).

Within this universalistic paradigm, however, the Constitution allows for cultural, religious, linguistic, and ethnic differences and particularity in an implicit acceptance of the National Party's insistence on concepts such as "own affairs" and "group rights" or "ways of life". Article 31 (1) states that cultural, religious, and linguistic communities have the right "to enjoy their culture, practise their religion and use their language. Sensitivity to linguistic differences is expressed, for example, through the proclamation of eleven official languages and the establishment of the Pan-South African Language Board to "create conditions for . . . the development and use of", and to "promote and ensure respect for", among others, languages such as Khoi, Nama, San, German, Greek, Gujerati, Hindi, etc.

Except, as we have noted, for Outlaw's insistence on the conservation of "races", the Constitution seems to approximate very closely what he articulates. However, a closer look at the Constitution reveals that it is more of a liberal democratic document founded on liberal principles of individual autonomy, rights, equality, etc. than a true synthesis of opposing moments. For example, there are strict conditions laid down for the exercise of cultural, religious, and linguistic group rights. These group rights "may not be exercised in a manner inconsistent with any provision of the Bill of Rights" (Article 31 (2)). This makes it clear that group rights and policies are subsidiary to the general individual rights enjoyed by all. It means therefore that individual universalistic rights override particular group rights in the event of conflict. That is, despite its accommodation of diversities and its pretensions to synthesis, the Constitution remains an expression of liberal universalism.

CRITIQUE OF NON-RACISM

It is no accident that Outlaw confronts both Appiah and liberalism simultaneously. For both enunciate the same principle that discounts race as a category. Since in many respects the Constitution expresses liberal principles such as a strong commitment to individual rights, freedom, and equality before the law, irrespective of "accidental" differences, including race, gender, and national character, one might say that Appiah's rejection and transcendence of "race" is in harmony with the sentiments and beliefs enshrined in the Constitution with regard to race. Indeed, as Goldberg (1993:74) correctly points out, Appiah gives a sophisticated reading of the liberal interpretation of race as a morally irrelevant category. In short, the Constitution resembles liberal democratic political and social philosophy as depicted by Sartre. Just as the liberal democrat wishes to annihilate the Jew in order to preserve in the Jew only the individual – "the universal and abstract subject of the rights of man and of the citizen" (Sartre 1948:47) – so, too, the non-racism enunciated in the Constitution seeks to destroy race as a reality in order to preserve among races only individuals – abstract and universal subjects of the rights of the citizen of South Africa.

A liberal democratic constitution of this sort is precisely the kind Outlaw seriously objects to; it is one that does not take into *serious* account racial and gender differences, and is hence an expression of a false universalism. By privileging the individual over the collective, liberalism asserts the moral primacy of the person against the claims of race. Through its universalistic principle it affirms the moral unity of the human species and accords only secondary importance to the specific historic associations of categories such as race. But, as Outlaw argues, human beings are not merely individuals, they are also social beings who belong to certain groups and collectives in terms of which they are judged in society. To ignore race, as Appiah insists we should, is to ignore one of the aspects of human reality.

Non-racism, as enshrined in the Constitution, is the rejection of the concept of race or an attempt to transcend particular races or a refusal to privilege racial identity. It therefore refuses to acknowledge and confront the exclusionary practices and concerns – whether cultural, religious or linguistic – that in a variety of ways continue to be racialised by social subjects, though less formally now than before. For example, non-racism is bound to reach an impasse as soon as it is confronted by neo-racism, what is variously called "new racism", "differentialist racism", and "racism without race" by Paul Gilroy and Stuart Hall in Britain, and Etienne Balibar and Pierre-André Taguieff in France. The articulation of this neo-racism is often in terms of culture, tradition, way of life or religion; it deploys a vocabulary of particularistic specificities or group identities, especially where these intersect with race, as is largely the case in a society such as South Africa. This kind of racism grants that races do not exist, but populations and cultures do; a politics of difference emphasising "culture" can, indeed, masquerade as racism. Racism does not need the word "race" in order for it to be a problem, a point succinctly pointed out by Paul Gilroy:

> the frequent absence of any overt reference to "race" or hierarchy is an important characteristic of the new types of racism with which we have to deal. This kind of coded language has created further . . . problems for anti-racism (in Donald & Rattansi 1992:53).

To deny that "race" exists, as both Appiah and the Constitution do, offers "only the frail reassurance that there shouldn't be a problem" (Donald & Rattansi 1992:1). Yet there is a problem, and it cannot be ignored or simply wished away by declaring its non-existence; it needs to be confronted as a part of South African and world reality. Race is a problem when African children are terrorised in schools previously designated as white, "coloured", or Indian schools. Race is a problem when a white or Indian woman, on noticing an African man in a lift, decides not to get in the lift because she thinks the African man will rape or kill her. Race is definitely a problem when it "tends toward opening up or shutting down job prospects, career possibilities, available places to live, potential friends and lovers . . . and [results in] presumptions by one's students" (Alcoff 1996:6). Finally, and without belabouring the point, race in South Africa is a problem as was demonstrated by the racial nature of the 1994 election where the voting pattern had the characteristics of a "racial census". Johnson (1994:6) notes "how racially polarised the election [was] and how signally unsuccessful black and white multiracialism [was] in the election".

The irony of the South African situation is, however, that while the Constitution entrenches non-racism, it simultaneously recognises the very races whose existence it attempts to deny. The equality clause, Article 9 (3) of the Constitution, states, for example:

> The state may not discriminate directly or indirectly against anyone on one or more grounds, including race, gender, sex, pregnancy, material status, ethnic or social origin, colour, sexual orientation, age, disability, religion.

When the law, for instance, says "regardless of race, sex, religion, sexual orientation" etc., it definitely promotes an ideal of individual freedom and equality. But this same law simultaneously asserts that there are different races, sexes, religions, people of different sexual orientation, colour, social origin, etc. Similarly, by mentioning race, sex, gender, etc., the Constitution tacitly posits and recognises their reality. It also says that different races, sexes, colours, etc. are equal and should be treated equally.

Restitution programmes such as affirmative action, for example, can therefore only make sense within a framework of racial and gender categories. If, however, a liberal constitution such as ours outlaws matters of race (South Africa is one sovereign democratic state founded on non-racism and non-sexism), then the implementation of affirmative action programmes is doomed to failure because the latter ostensibly infringe on the rights of citizens not to be discriminated against on the basis of race or sex. Given the historical material, intellectual, and economic imbalances, challenges to affirmative action programmes by white males condemns blacks and women to perpetual servitude.

But, it could be argued, lynching may be nothing more than murder, irrespective of its racial nature. However, this characterisation misses, as Goldberg (1995:12–13) indicates, the terror against the racial group, in light of which its members may feel especially terrified. Moreover, it is often as a member of a race and not as an individual that one is judged and treated in a race conscious society.

Outlaw's call for the conservation of race, its nurturing and even its celebration, is at once dangerous and politically correct, capable of producing opposite consequences. On the one hand, there is the danger that such a call may be used by conservatives to reinforce, entrench, and reproduce racial stereotypes which perpetuate racism. On the other hand, it is the unifying principle of race that enables groups to win certain political concessions and victories. While race is a social construction, it is also a social reality.

It is, indeed, as a member of a race and not as an individual that one is judged and discriminated against in a race conscious society. The same goes for the valorisation of ethnic (or cultural or linguistic or religious) group identities. It may function as an effective critique of existing power relations and as a project of minority group self-empowerment.

POWER-RELATIONS

A surprising feature of Outlaw's text is that while he makes considerable use of Michel Foucault's genealogical and archaeological methods, he practically ignores one of the most potent Foucauldian concepts applicable to racism and ethnicity, namely, the concept of power. His "unity in diversity" ("rainbowism") solution to racial and ethnic problems presupposes the existence of a balance of power among racially and ethnically different groups, constitutional guarantees and safeguards notwithstanding.

Theoretically useful as the "rainbow" metaphor may be, it is, however, misleading. Colours constituting the rainbow differ in terms of brightness and visibility. Some are brighter than others and are therefore more visible to the naked eye. In other words, some colours are more powerful than others. Similarly, we know that in a racist multi-ethnic society the relations between groups are necessarily constituted as relations of power. The dominant hegemonic group invariably excludes and subordinates other groups as was, and still is, the case in South Africa, "rainbow nation" notwithstanding. Indeed, black people who wish to point out that power relations remain much as they were in pre-1994 South Africa will often wryly remark on the rainbow metaphor, "There ain't no black in the rainbow." Power, as Goldberg (1995:13) argues, "is exercised in the promotion and execution of the exclusions, whether intended or not".

Outlaw's philosophical solution of "unity in diversity" may have correlates both in education and constitutional politics. Is multi-culturalism in education not a recognition of cultural differences within a pedagogical context? At the constitutional political level, is federalism not a political analogue of "unity in diversity"? If so, why would both the Constitution of South Africa and particularly that of the ANC reject federalism while espousing "rainbowism" at the cultural and group level? Is federalism not a political recognition of difference, self-determination, and state autonomy within a wider national unity? Is multi-culturalism in education not similarly sensitive to cultural differences within a single and united educational system?

It seems to me that Outlaw has valuable advice for South Africa by insisting not so much on the conservation of race, but on the importance of racial identity. Why reduce race not just to an epiphenomenon but to a non-existent phenomenon? A race conscious society cannot just dismiss or ignore race in a liberal democracy. Even though race may be nothing more than a social construction, it is nevertheless a social reality, and every aspect of social transformation must constitutionally come to terms with it.

Why stop at cultural, linguistic or religious identity without taking into serious account racial identity – the very identity upon which the fabric of South African society is based? Why ignore the intersection between culture and race, particularly in the South African context? As Heribert Adam acutely observes, despite the fact that apartheid imposed racial categories which were rejected, yet

> the historical racial and ethnic perceptions of difference – partially invented, reinforced and entrenched by apartheid, but, above all underscored by material inequalities – did not psychologically homogenise the population, the ideology of colour-blind non-racialism notwithstanding. This legacy of apartheid lives on in everyday racial and ethnic consciousness (1995:468).

DEMOCRACY AND CONSENSUS IN AFRICAN TRADITIONAL POLITICS: A PLEA FOR A NON-PARTY POLITY

KWASI WIREDU

It is often remarked that decision-making in traditional African life and governance was, as a rule, by consensus. Like all generalisations about complex subjects, it may be legitimate to take this with a pinch of prudence. But there is considerable evidence that decision by consensus was often the order in African deliberations, and was so on principle. Thus it was not just an exercise in hyperbole when Kenneth Kaunda (Rohio and Mutiso 1975:A76), the (democratically) displaced President of Zambia, said, "In our original societies we operated by consensus. An issue was talked out in solemn conclave until such time as agreement could be achieved", or when Julius Nyerere (Rohio and Mutiso 1975:A78), retired President of Tanzania, similarly said, ". . . in African society the traditional method of conducting affairs is by free discussion," and went on to quote Guy Clutton-Brock with approval: "The elders sit under the big trees, and talk until they agree."

Ironically, both pronouncements were made in the course of a defence of the one-party system. Of this I will have more to say below. But for now, let us note an important fact about the role of consensus in African life. It is that the reliance on consensus is not a peculiarly political phenomenon. Where consensus characterises political decision-making in Africa it is a manifestation of an immanent approach to social interaction. Generally, in interpersonal relations among adults, consensus as a basis of joint action was taken as axiomatic. This is not to say that it was always attained. Nowhere was African society a realm of unbroken harmony. On the contrary, conflict (including mortal ones) among lineages and ethnic groups and also within them were not infrequent. The remarkable thing, however, is that if and when a resolution of the issues was negotiated, the point of it was seen in the attainment of reconciliation rather than the mere abstention from further recriminations or collisions.

It is, however, important to note that disputes can be settled without the achievement of reconciliation. Reconciliation is, in fact, a form of consensus. It is a restoration of goodwill through a reappraisal of the importance and significance of the initial bones of contention. It does not necessarily involve a complete identity of moral or cognitive opinions. It suffices that all parties are able to feel that adequate account has been taken of their points of view in any proposed scheme of future action or coexistence. Similarly, consensus does not in a general way entail total agreement. To begin with, consensus usually presupposes an original position of diversity. Because issues do not always polarise opinion on lines of strict contradictoriness, dialogue can function – by means, for example, of the smoothing of edges – to produce compromises that are agreeable to all or, at least, not obnoxious to any. Furthermore, where there is the will to consensus, dialogue can lead to a willing suspension of disagreement, making possible agreed actions without necessarily agreed notions. This is important because certain situations do, indeed, precipitate exhaustive disjunctions which no dialogic accommodations can mediate. For example, either we are to go to war or we are not. The problem then is how a group without unanimity may settle on one option rather than the other without alienating anyone. This is the severest challenge of consensus, and it can only be met by a willing suspension of disbelief in the prevailing option on the part of the residual minority. The feasibility of this depends not only on the patience and persuasiveness of the right people, but also on the fact that African traditional systems of the consensual type were not such as to place any one group of persons consistently in the position of a minority. Of this, too, more below.

But first, let us see how faith in consensus worked in one concrete example of an African traditional system of politics. It may be well to note, as a preliminary, that African political systems of the past displayed considerable variety. There is a basic distinction between those systems with a centralised authority exercised through the machinery of government, and those without any such authority in which social life was not regulated at any level by the sort of machinery that might be called a government. Fortes and Evans-Pritchard (1940:5) classify the Zulu (of South Africa), the Ngwato (also of South Africa), the Bemba (of Zambia), the Banyankole (of Uganda) and the Kede (of Northern Nigeria) under the first category, and the Logoli (of Western Kenya), the Tallensi (of Northern Ghana), and the Nuer (of Southern Sudan) under the second.

It is, or should be, a matter of substantial interest to political thinkers that societies of the second description, that is, anarchistic societies, existed and functioned in an orderly manner, or at least not with any less order than the more centralised ones. It is also, perhaps, easier in the context of the less centralised social orders to appreciate the necessity of consensus. Where the exercise of authority (as, for example, in the settlement of disputes) rested purely on moral and, perhaps, metaphysical prestige, it is obvious that decision by the preponderance of numbers would be likely to be dysfunctional. But it is more interesting to observe that the habit of decision by consensus in politics was studiously cultivated in some of the most centralised and, if it comes to it, warlike ethnic groups of Africa, such as the Zulu and the Ashanti. By a somewhat paradoxical contrast, the authorities in some of the comparatively less militaristic of the centralised societies, such as the Bemba or the Banyankole, seem to have manifested less enthusiasm for consensus in political decision-making than the Ashanti or the Zulu. In what immediately follows I propose to take advantage of the elaborate description and analysis of the Ashanti traditional system of politics in K.A. Busia's *The position of the chief in the modern political system of Ashanti* (1951) and my own personal experience to trace the course of consensus in the Ashanti political example.

The lineage is the basic political unit among the Ashanti. Because they are a matrilineal group this unit consists of all the people in a town or village having a common female ancestor, which, as a rule, is quite a considerable body of persons. Every such unit has a head, and every such head is automatically a member of the council which is the governing body of the town or village. The qualifications for lineage headship are seniority in age, wisdom, a sense of civic responsibility, and logical persuasiveness. All these qualities are often united in the most senior (but non-senile) member of the lineage. In that case, election is almost routine. But where these qualities do not seem to converge in one person, election may entail prolonged and painstaking consultations and discussions aimed at consensus. There is never an act of formal voting. Indeed, there is no long-standing word for voting in the language of the Ashanti. The expression which is currently used for that process (*aba to*) is an obvious modern coinage for a modern cultural import or, shall we say, imposition.

The point, then, at which the head of a lineage is elected is the point at which consensus first makes itself felt in the Ashanti political process. This office, when conferred on a person, is for life unless moral, intellectual, or physical degeneration sets in. As the representative of the lineage in the governing council of a town, he – or, in rare cases, she – is duty bound to hold consultations with the adult members of the lineage regarding municipal matters. In any matter of particular significance consensus is always the watchword. It is also the watchword at the level of the municipal council which, as indicated, consists of the lineage heads. This council is presided over by the "natural ruler" of the town, called a chief. This word, though tainted with colonial condescension, has remained in general use even in the post-independence era by dint of terminological inertia. The "natural" aspect of this position lies in its basic hereditary status: normally, a chief can only come from the royal lineage. But it is only basically hereditary, for, a lineage being a quite substantial kinship group, there is at any one time a fair number of qualified candidates. The choice, which is proposed by the "queen mother" (the mother or aunt or maternal sister or cousin of the chief), has to be approved by the council and endorsed by the populace through an organisation called, in literal translation, "the young people's association" in order to become final.

Contrary to a deliberately fostered impression, the personal word of the chief was not law. His official word, on the other hand, is the consensus of his council, and it is only in this capacity that it may be law; which is why the Akans have the saying that there are no bad kings, only bad councillors. Of course, an especially opinionated chief, if he had the temerity, might try – sometimes with success – to impose his will on a council. But a chief of such habits was as likely as not to be eventually deposed. In truth, as Abraham (1962:77), also speaking of the Akans, points out in *The mind of Africa*, "kingship was more a sacred office than a political one". The office was "sacred" because a chief was supposed to be the link between the living population and their departed ancestors, who were supposed to supervise human interests from their post-mortem vantage point. Insofar as it was political, the office bore substantial analogies to the status of a constitutional monarch. The chief was the symbol of the unity of his kingdom and, in the nominal course of his duties, fulfilled a variety of ceremonial functions. But he was unlike a constitutional monarch in being a member (at least as a lineage personage) of the ruling council and in being in a position to exercise legitimate influence on its deliberations by virtue, not of any supposed divine inspiration, but rather of whatever intrinsic persuasiveness his ideas might have.

If these facts are borne in mind it becomes apparent that the council was strongly representative with respect both to the nature of its composition and the content of its decisions. This representativeness was duplicated at all levels of authority in the Ashanti state. The town or city councils were the most basic theatre of political authority. Representatives from these councils constituted divisional councils presided over by "paramount" chiefs. These latter units also sent representatives to the national council presided over by the "Asantehene", the king of the Ashanti, at the highest level of traditional government. It is at this stage needless to say that decision-making was by consensus at all these levels.

Now, this adherence to the principle of consensus was a premeditated option. It was based on the belief that *ultimately* the interests of all members of society are the same, although their immediate perceptions of those interests may be different. This thought is given expression in an art motif depicting a crocodile with one stomach and two heads locked in struggle over food. If they could but see that the food is, in any case, destined for the same stomach, the irrationality of the conflict would be manifest to each. But could such a perception arise? The Ashanti answer is, "Yes, human beings have the ability eventually to cut through their differences to the rock bottom identity of interests." And, according to this view, the means to that objective is simply rational discussion. With regard to the capabilities of such means, the Ashanti are explicit: "There is no problem of human relations that cannot be resolved by dialogue." Dialogue, of course, presupposes not just (a minimum of) two parties, but also two conflicting positions: "One head does not hold council." Nor was any suggestion that one voice might be entitled to be heard to the exclusion of others countenanced for one moment: "Two heads are better than one", says another maxim. Indeed, so much did the Ashanti (and the Akan in general) prize rational discussion as an avenue to consensus among adults that the capacity for elegant and persuasive discourse was made one of the most crucial qualifications for high office.

I would like to emphasise that the pursuit of consensus was a deliberate effort to go beyond decision by majority opinion. It is easier to secure majority agreement than to achieve consensus. And the fact was not lost upon the Ashanti. But they spurned the line of least resistance. To them, majority opinion is not in itself a good enough basis for decision making, for it deprives the minority of the right to have their will reflected in the given decision. Or, to put it in terms of the concept of representation, it deprives the minority of the right of representation in the decision in question. Two concepts of representation are involved in these considerations. There is the representation of a given constituency in council, and there is the representation of the will of a representative in the making of a given decision. Let us call the first formal, and the second substantive, representation. Then, it is obvious that you can have formal representation without its substantive correlate. Yet, the formal is there for the sake of the substantive. In the Ashanti view, substantive representation is a matter of a fundamental human right. Each human being has the right to be represented not only in council but also in counsel in any matter relevant to his/her interests or those of their groups. This is why consensus is so important.

Nor are pragmatic reasons for consensus lacking. Formal representation without substance is apt to induce disaffection. If the system in use is such as to cause some groups periodically to be in substantively unrepresented minorities, then seasonal disaffection becomes institutionalised. The results are the well known inclemencies of adversarial politics. From the Ashanti standpoint consensus is the antidote. But, again, can consensus always be had? As already noted, the Ashanti seem to have thought that it could – at least in principle. But suppose this were not the case. Even so, it can always be aimed at, and the point is that any system of politics that is seriously dedicated to this aim must be institutionally different from a system based on the sway of the majority, however hedged around with "checks and balances".

What is the bearing of these considerations on democracy? Current forms of democracy are generally systems based on the majority principle. The party that wins the majority of seats or the greatest proportion of the votes, if the system in force is one of proportional representation, is invested with governmental power. Parties under this scheme are organisations of people of similar tendencies and aspirations with the sole aim of gaining power for the implementation of their policies. Let us call such systems majoritarian democracies. Then, those based on consensus may be called consensual democracies. The Ashanti system was a consensual democracy. It was a democracy because government was by the consent, and subject to the control of, the people as expressed through their representatives. It was consensual because at least as a rule, that consent was negotiated on the principle of consensus. (By contrast, the majoritarian system might be said to be, in principle, based on consent without consensus.)

The Ashanti system, furthermore, was not a party system in the sense of the word "party" noted in the last paragraph, which is basic to majoritarian democracy. But in a broad lexical sense there were parties. The lineages were parties to the project of good government. Moreover, in every Ashanti town the youth constituted themselves into an organised party under a recognised leader who was entitled to make representations directly (though not as a member) to the relevant council on all matters of public interest. The sense in which the system in question did not feature parties is that none of the groups mentioned organised themselves for the purpose of gaining power in a way which entailed others not being in power, or worse, being out of it entirely. For all concerned, the system was set up for participation in power, not its appropriation, and the underlying philosophy was one of cooperation, not confrontation.

This is the aspect of the traditional system to which the advocates of the one-party system appealed in their attempts to prove its African ancestry and authenticity. The illusory analogy was this: in a one-party system there is no conflict of parties. No party loses because the party wins. But the comparison is faulty for the following reason. In the traditional set-up no party lost because all the parties were natural partners in power or, more strictly, because there were no parties. In the one-party situation the reason why no party loses is because murdered parties don't compete. (If these last remarks should occasion any sense of inconsistency, a careful disambiguation of the term "party" in this context should dissipate it.)

The disappearance of the one-party system from the African scene is, and should remain, unlamented. But my reason for mentioning that subject is not to flog a dead horse; it is, in fact, to point out the good parts of a bad case. One valid point which was made again and again by the one-party persuaders is that there is no necessary connection between democracy and the multi-party system. An associated insight was that indigenous African systems of politics, at least in some well-known instances, offered examples of democracy without a multi-party mechanism. But although the traditional systems in question avoided this mechanism, it should constantly be borne in mind that, as already noted, it had room for parties in the broad sense. This is important because these parties provided the centres of independent thought presupposed by the very idea of meaningful dialogue in the process of political decision-making – those conditions of rational interaction that the one-party system was so efficient in destroying.

In the drive towards democracy that occurred in Africa in the past half decade or so, African dictators, both civilian and military, were under sustained Western pressure to adopt the multi-party way of life. This proved politically fatal to some of them, though others eventually discovered tricks for surviving multi-party elections. There is no denying, of course, that some gains in freedom have accrued to African populations. But how substantial have these been, and to what extent have these developments built on the strengths of the indigenous institutions of politics in Africa? It is hard to be convinced that this question has as yet attracted enough attention.

The cause of this relative neglect of the question may conceivably be connected with its difficulty. The conditions of traditional political life were surely less complicated than those of the present. The kinship networks that provided the mainstay of the consensual politics of traditional times are simply incapable of serving the same purpose in modern Africa. This is especially so in urban areas where industrialisation, albeit paltry in many parts of Africa, has created conditions, such as sharp socio-economic cleavages, which carry all or many of the ingredients of ideological politics. In these circumstances it may well seem a trifle too utopian to envisage the possibility of a non-party approach to politics.

It might seem, furthermore, that the account of traditional politics given above essentially involves exaggerations of harmony in traditional life. In fact, even if consensus did prevail in the politics of certain ethnic groups in Africa, historically, inter-ethnic relations involving those same groups have *by nature* been marked, or, more strictly, marred by frequent wars, the most extreme negations of consensus. The point is not just that there have been ethnic wars from time to time, as was conceded early on, but more seriously that the ethnic orientation of the various groups, by their own inward fixations, have tended to generate conflict in their external relations. Of this the contemporary world has unspeakably tragic illustrations. It might seem, therefore, that neither in the past nor in the present nor in any foreseeable future can consensus be seen to have been, or to promise, a realistic basis for politics in any African state that is a composite of distinct ethnic units. On the contrary, so it might appear, the more pluralistic approach of a multi-party system, provided it incorporates reasonable safeguards against the tyranny of the majority, offers the more practical option.

The premises of both objections may be granted, quite readily in the first case and with a qualification in the second. But the conclusions in favour of the multi-party system in both cases are *non-sequiturs*. As regards the premises, it is true that any suggestion that the kinship basis of traditional politics could be a model for contemporary African politics can be dismissed as an anachronistic nostalgia. But, in the matter of conflict among the ethnic groups, it should be noted that African history furnishes examples not only of conflict but also of cooperation among them. Still, the history of inter-ethnic conflict and the problem of its contemporary reverberations ought not to be minimised. Interestingly, this is precisely why the idea of a consensual non-party system ought to be taken especially seriously in Africa.

One of the most persistent causes of political instability in Africa derives from the fact that in many contemporary African states certain ethnic groups find themselves in the minority both numerically and politically. Under a system of majoritarian democracy this means that, even with all the safeguards, they consistently find themselves outside the corridors of power. The resultant frustrations and disaffections, with their disruptive consequences for the polity, should not take anybody by surprise.

Consider the non-party alternative. Imagine a dispensation under which governments are not formed by parties but by the consensus of elected representatives. Government, in other words, becomes a kind of coalition – a coalition not, as in the common acceptation, of parties, but of citizens. There is no impediment whatsoever to the formation of political associations to propagate preferred ideologies. But in councils of state, affiliation with any such association does not necessarily determine the chances of selection for a position of responsibility. Two things can be expected. Firstly, political associations will be avenues for channelling all desirable pluralisms, but they will be without the Hobbesian proclivities of political parties, as they are known under majoritarian politics. And secondly, without the constraints of membership in parties relentlessly dedicated to wresting power or retaining it, representatives will be more likely to be actuated by the objective merits of given proposals than by ulterior considerations. In such an environment willingness to compromise, and with it the prospect of consensus, will be enhanced.

Consensus is not just an optional bonus. As can be inferred from our earlier remarks, it is essential for securing substantive, or what might also be called decisional representation for representatives and, through them, for the citizens at large. This is nothing short of a matter of fundamental human rights. Consensus as a political decision-making procedure requires in principle that each representative should be persuaded, if not of the optimality of each decision, at least of its practical necessity, all things considered. If discussion has been even moderately rational and the spirit has been one of respectful accommodation on all sides, surviving reservations on the part of a momentary minority will not prevent the recognition that, if the community is to go forward, a particular line of action must be taken. This should not be confused with decision-making on the principle of the supreme right of the majority. In the case under discussion the majority prevails not over, but upon the minority – they prevail upon them to accept the proposal in question, not just to live with it, which latter is the basic plight of minorities under majoritarian democracy. In a consensus system the voluntary acquiescence of the minority with respect to a given issue would normally be necessary for the adoption of a decision. In the rare case of an intractable division a majority vote might be used to break the impasse. But the success of the system must be judged by the rarity of such predicaments in the workings of the decision-making bodies of the state. A less unwelcome use of majorities might occur in the election of representatives. Here choice may have to be determined by superior numbers in terms of votes. But even here the representatives will be under obligation to consult with all the tendencies of opinion in their constituencies and work out, as much as possible, a consensual basis of representation.

Further points of detail and even of principle remain to be spelled out but these indications must make it plausible to suppose that in the consensual non-party system no one group, ethnic or ideological, will be afflicted with the sense of being permanent outsiders to state power. That alone should suffice to forestall some, at least, of the unhappy conflicts that have in the past bedevilled African life and continue to do so. Thus, far from the complexities of contemporary African life making the consensual, non-party precedents of traditional African politics unusable today, they in fact make them indispensable. For this reason, if for none other, the exploration of that alternative to multi-party politics should commend itself to the urgent attention of contemporary African philosophers and political scientists.

But there is nothing peculiarly African about the idea itself. If it is valid, especially with respect to its human rights dimension, it ought to be a concern for our whole species.

REFERENCES

Abraham, W.E. 1962. *The mind of Africa*. Chicago. University of Chicago Press.

Adam, H. 1995. "The politics of ethnic identity: Comparing South Africa." *Ethnic and Racial Studies*, 18(3):459–468.

Alcoff, L.M. 1996. "Philosophy and racial identity." *Radical Philosophy*, 75:5–14.

Appiah, A.K. 1986. "The uncompleted argument: Du Bois and the illusion of race", in H.L. Gates Jr (ed.), 1986:21–37.

Appiah, A.K. 1992. *In my father's house: Africa in the philosophy of culture*. New York: Oxford University Press.

Biko, S. 1984. "The definition of black consciousness." *Frank Talk*, 1(1):3–9.

Busia, K.A. 1968 (1951). *The position of the chief in the modern political system of Ashanti*. London: New Impression.

Constitution of the Republic of South Africa, The. 1996.

Donald, J. & Rattansi, A. 1992. *Race, culture and difference*. London: Sage.

Du Bois, W.E.B. 1897. "The conservation of races", in P.S. Foner (ed.), 1970.

Engels, F. 1954. *Anti-Dühring*. Moscow: Progress.

Falton, R. 1986. *Black consciousness in South Africa*. Albany: State University of New York Press.

Fanon, F. 1963. *The wretched of the earth*. New York: Grove.

Foner, P.S. (ed.) 1970. *W.E.B. du Bois speaks: Speeches and addresses 1890–1919*. New York: Pathfinder.

Fortes, M. & Evans-Pritchard, E.E. (eds) 1940. *African political systems*. Oxford: Oxford University Press.

Gates Jr, H.L. (ed.) 1986. *"Race," writing, and difference*. Chicago: University of Chicago Press.

Goldberg, D.T. 1993. *Racist culture: Philosophy and the politics of meaning*. Oxford: Blackwell.

Goldberg, D.T. 1995. "Hate or power." *APA Newsletter on Philosophy and the Black Experience*, 94(2):12–14.

Habermas, J. 1970. *Towards a rational society*. London: Heinemann.

Johnson, R.W. 1994. "South Africa on the eve." *London Review of Books*, 16(8):3–6.

Kaunda, K. 1973. "The challenge of the future." *Addresses to the National Council of the United National Independence Party at Mulungushi Hall, Lusaka, 5–7 June 1973*. Lusaka: Zambia Information Service, 1973:1–35.

Kymlicka, W. 1989. *Liberalism, community, and culture*. Oxford: Clarendon.

McLellan, D. 1986. *Ideology*. Milton Keynes: Open University Press.

Nyerere, J. 1975. *Nyerere on socialism*. Dar-es-Salaam: Oxford University Press.

Outlaw, L. 1992. "Against the grain of modernity: The politics of difference and the conservation of race." *Man World*, 25(3–4):443–468.

Outlaw, L. 1995. "On race and philosophy." *Graduate Faculty of Philosophy Journal*, 18(2):175–199.

Outlaw, L. 1996. *On race and philosophy*. New York: Routledge.

Plato. 1961. "The Republic", tr. P. Shorey, in E. Hamilton & H.H. Cairns (eds), *The collected dialogues of Plato, including the letters*. Princeton: Princeton University Press, 1961:575–844.

Rawls, J. 1987. "The idea of an overlapping consensus." *Oxford Journal of Legal Studies*, VII(1):1–25.

Rohio, S.W. and Mutiso, G.C.M. (eds). 1975. *Readings in African political thought*. London: Heineman.

Ruch, E.A. & Anyanwu, K.C. 1981. *African philosophy: An introduction to the main philosophical trends in contemporary Africa*. Rome: Catholic Book Agency.

Sartre, J-P. 1948. *Portrait of the anti-Semite*. London: Secker & Warburg.

Sartre, J-P. 1982. *Critique of dialectical reason*. Vol. 1. London: Verso.

Taylor, C.W. 1992. *Multiculturalism and the politics of recognition: An essay*. Princeton: Princeton University Press.

Taylor, C.W. 1995. *The politics of recognition*. Oxford. Oxford University Press.

Thompson, J.B. 1990. *Ideology and modern culture*. Cambridge: Blackwell.

Wiredu, K. 1995a. "Democracy and consensus in African traditional politics: A plea for a non-party polity", *The Centennial Review*, 39(1), 1995:53–63.

Wiredu, K. 1995b. "The need for conceptual decolonization in African philosophy", in O. Oladipo (ed.), *Conceptual decolonization in African philosophy*. Ibadan: Hope, 1995:22–32.

Young, I.M. 1990. *Justice and the politics of difference*. Princeton, N.J.: Princeton University Press.

CHAPTER EIGHT

Using and Abusing African Art

JENNIFER R. WILKINSON

There is a concept of art – that art and works of art deserve the title art by virtue of being products and activities serving no purpose beyond their contemplation – which we, as post-Kantians, have more or less come to accept, even if we use it as a guide rather than as entailing strict conditions for what does and does not count as art. But this concept is under siege both internally and externally. While some artists challenge its boundaries from within by deliberately making works that do not fit the definition, many artefacts, especially those from Africa and other so-called primitive societies, stretch its limits for other reasons. Africa is a continent often presumed not to have, or at least not to have had, a notion of art. And yet, paradoxically, although masks, cloths, and other objects with aesthetic appeal are made to be used, we also have the widely acknowledged category of African art which is applied to those very functional artefacts. One consequence of this is that in South Africa, where art is often seen as an elitist notion, boundary disputes about art help to keep old racial prejudices alive.

Clarification of what is and what is not art has therefore become not merely a matter of academic interest but part of the confusing and tumultuous changes that are presently taking place. Given the often painful process of transformation towards a full democracy and a culture of cooperation and understanding, and the move away from a racially divided nation, the place of art and the importance ascribed to it has been elevated beyond mere academic quibbling. This is why the concept of art as described and as used must be urgently revisited. However, this needs to include more than an examination of what it means to have a category such as African art. I want to argue that many of the problems at the heart of the very idea of African art are not merely about the content that we give to the concept, but are symptomatic of a wider process of conceptual manipulation and colonisation.

Since the concepts which any society has depend on the concerns and practices of that society, it follows that if a society does not have the concept of art it cannot produce art. The evidence is that African and other primitive societies do not make objects for the sole purpose of aesthetic contemplation, and therefore it must follow that there cannot be African art. But as there are many objects from traditional African societies which are labelled "art" – indeed the recent massive *Africa: art of a continent* exhibition in the United Kingdom was held as a celebration of African art – we are faced with what clearly seems to be a conceptual problem. If we have art from African cultures which have no concept of art, then either the concept is incorrectly applied or there is no African art. Philosophers have addressed this issue in various ways but nearly always as a conceptual one. Although there have been philosophical efforts to include "African art" into the fold as art, most of these have concentrated on producing wider definitions and criteria of art. These, however, have tended to be paradigmatic.[1]

The result is that African art, its status still unclear because it does not fully fit the requirements for art, hovers as a hybrid at the edges, with the art of Western countries continuing to occupy centre stage. African art therefore is seen as something less than the other "pure" art, a sort of poorer cousin as it were. Understandably, there have been and continue to be reactions to what is perceived as the marginalisation of "African art" and therefore of African culture. In South Africa, where there was (and still is) a situation in which art, like many other concepts, was measured according to the perceived uncritical assimilation of foreign criteria, there have been calls for the conceptual decolonisation of art as part of the overall transformation process. The plea throughout Africa is, as Wiredu (1995b:22) has phrased it, to avoid the imposition of "categories of thought embedded in foreign languages or philosophical traditions which have exercised considerable influence on African thought and meaning" and rather to "exploit the resources of our indigenous conceptual schemes".

The flipside to this view is that since all concepts must be governed by at least theoretically discoverable criteria and therefore cannot be used at will, if what is made in Africa does not fulfil the logical requirements for art, it follows that there cannot be African art. At best, broadened definitions will allow, not for its absorption, but only for its uncomfortable and compromised accommodation where it does not truly belong. While the academic debate continues, curatorial and other decisions, with far-reaching and often unhappy consequences, continue to be made with neither clear guidelines nor consensus.

It is tempting for a philosopher to see these issues as purely conceptual. As the category "African art" has already gained acceptance, further analysis of the concept (although possibly leading to stretched boundaries and loosened criteria) should justify the use of this label – rather like the (perhaps reluctant) opening up of an exclusive club to new members by relaxing the conditions for membership. But this is not genuine reconciliation, even though it is interpreted as a gesture of generosity by those who think they can still afford to be generous. Aided by the wisdom of hindsight and the advantage of geographic location, I wish to propose a different diagnosis of the tensions inherent in the term "African art" and, armed with a fresh view of what is wrong, to indicate how some fresh insights might show where the appropriate logical space for African art can be found. At the same time I do not see that it follows that if there is indeed art which is African, such art must be accommodated at the outer borders of the concept. Nor does it follow that the concept as it is used in the non-African world must be jettisoned in Africa.

Quite simply, I think that the problem of African art has not been resolved because the concentration has been too narrow (because of inherited and imposed conceptual presuppositions), and also misguided (because the lure of the exotic and the desire to be politically correct have provided too many red herrings). In other words, trying to apply the conceptual scheme of one culture to that of a very different one is only part of the misunderstanding. The assumption has been that since the conceptual scheme of the more sophisticated West must be superior, Africa should be interpreted only in those terms – in fact it would be to the continent's advantage if these imported notions were to be adopted. So, since art is one of these concepts, I propose that we look beyond how we think "art" *should* (logically) be used, to how art and "art" *have* in fact (empirically) been used – and abused – in Africa, specifically in South Africa. In this way I think we might avoid confusing two categorically different issues and so make some headway in the struggle for the recognition of African art as art, and at the same time repair some of the rifts that have resulted from its resultant conceptual marginalisation – or at least avoid deepening them. This entails not confining ourselves to examining whether or not the concept "art" can be applied in Africa, but involves broadening the scope of the enquiry to see how both art and "art" have become mechanisms within complex shifting power relations on the continent. Only then shall we be able to understand why – conceptually restricted and caught up in political struggles as we are – we have, by limiting the scope of African art, missed not only the very point of the problem but also some of the actual processes and examples that can without difficulty justify the application of the term "African *art*".

Since part of my reasoning is that changing the definition of art has so far simply worsened the situation, we will, at least for the sake of the argument (and in agreement with certain current thinking as described above), adhere to the prevailing definition and accept that art includes only objects and activities whose aim is aesthetic contemplation, where this need mean nothing other than that their main purpose is exhausted by that contemplation. This has, of course, in the past led to functional artefacts being excluded and to the establishment of the neat distinction between art and craft. But not everything that is now unequivocally part of the canon of what we call art was made for this purpose. Examination of the accepted history of art reveals not a continuous development within the concept of art as we now understand it, but a progression from artefacts whose main purpose is functional but with some aesthetic features – however conceived – towards those whose main or even sole purpose is aesthetic. Art for art's sake is but a relatively recent innovation. And if we agree that the history of art has been a process of taking and making, and if it is art that has taught artists to see, then we must also agree that this progression is logical.[2]

But even if the history of art is a matter of logic, the history of it that we *do* have need not be the history of art that we *must* logically have. This history could have been different. Contingent factors have also influenced the choices and the preservations shaping the recorded progress of art, our interpretation of it, and what will merit inclusion in this record in the future. These choices will in turn shape further choices, and so the process will continue. What we leave out and what we keep at the margins will therefore not have a part in setting out the path that art's recorded history will take. And it does not follow that the history of art with which we are familiar, namely that which moves through prehistoric to Greek,

Roman, Byzantine, and early Christian, taking in the Renaissance, Mannerism, and the Baroque on its development to the present variety of modernist and even post-modern movements, is the only history of art there has been. We also tend to ignore the fact that it is not a history of artefacts made only for aesthetic contemplation.

However, when we look beyond the geographical, social (including gendered), and conceptual confines of Europe and America towards Africa, this familiar history is missing because here we have not seen a similar process of taking and making from artefacts – with some aesthetic features but whose main purpose is functional – to artefacts whose main purpose is aesthetic.[3] Whatever progress there might have been in Africa, we are unable to recognise a pinnacle of creativity as reached in the fine art so treasured in the West. But it does not mean that if we have not seen it there has been no such process. I suggest that it is not because there has been no such history of art, but because there has been a predilection to interpret Africa as not only savage but also as outside known history. As a result, what has come out of Africa has looked strange and exotic to the writers of history and of the history of art, and we, in turn, have not seen art. We have, however, been mistaken, I think.

The story of Africa which gives credence to the belief that there is no real art in Africa is well known. When the Europeans "discovered" Africa they found a strange and seemingly static culture producing artefacts which were made and used for tribal purposes. These, being of archaeological appeal, were taken as evidence of the primitivism of the peoples of Africa rather than as treasured booty to Europe where they were displayed in ethnic museums together with elephant tusks and peacock feathers. Later, having been moved to cultural museums, they were shown and contextualised with beadwork and weapons. However, after Picasso and others had recognised and used the formal qualities of these relics, they found their way into art galleries and exhibitions – although still displayed within a social and cultural context and not as autonomous objects of aesthetic creativity. Yet even Picasso, credited for opening the eyes of the art-going public to their aesthetic appeal, was forced, in acknowledging that recognition, to confront his own feelings of ambiguity about these objects – feelings not unlike those still prevailing among art lovers who are not from and who do not understand Africa. Picasso is reported to have expressed his perplexity in the following way:

> When I became interested, forty years ago, in Negro art and I made what they referred to as my Negro period in my painting it was because at the time I was against what was called beauty in the museum. At that time for most people, a Negro mask was an ethnographic object. . . . Men had made those masks and other objects for a sacred purpose, a magic purpose, a kind of mediation between themselves and the unknown hostile forces that surround them, in order to overcome their fear and horror by giving it a form and image. At that moment I realised what painting was all about. Painting isn't an aesthetic operation; it's a form of magic designed to be a mediator between this strange hostile world and us, a way of seizing the power by giving form to our terrors as well as our desires. When I came to that realisation I knew I had found my way. Then people began looking at those objects in terms of aesthetics (reputed discussion with Francoise Gilot, in Phillips 1995:29).

The colonisation of Africa and the romantic views about the dark continent combined to foster and nurture the perception that what was produced in Africa and incorporated into the art of Picasso and his contemporaries was fetishist, influenced by the spirits and used for magico-religious practices, and, although not really art, was worth looking at all the same.

Colonisation itself was largely a process of domination by invaders who, on the assumption of their own natural superiority, imposed their values and their concepts on the indigenous people in the name of progress. But, ironically, it reveals as much about the colonisers as about the colonised. Because there was nothing that conformed with the idea of art, no art institutions and no recognisable artists, the presumption was that there *was* no art, and that the artefacts produced in Africa, although often visually and aesthetically interesting, were only magical and/ or religious and therefore of no value beyond quaintness. Therefore they were treated as curiosities – hence the term "curio". And yet, thanks to artists like Picasso, Vlaminck, Matisse, and Derain who used aspects of them in their own work, perceptions of these objects changed – they were looked at in terms of aesthetics – and they were taken out of their natural habitat and placed alongside accepted art in galleries. As a result, many were eventually uncomfortably reclassified as art. This led to the situation where objects, made for non-aesthetic purposes and within a culture taken to be without the concept of art, are called not just "art" but specifically "African art", and hence the accumulation of confusions.

This story, however, like many others about Africa, can be retold. In this retelling, if the factual inaccuracies are corrected, at least some of the conceptual confusion can be removed. Contrary to the popular view, when the white man came to Africa he did not find, as he thought he had, a culture caught in a time-warp; what he in fact found was a multicultural continent at only one moment in a long and dynamic process of adjustment and adaptation. This was, however, not an innocent mistake. The misperceived idea of Africa without a history has, by perniciously depriving people of their roots, also imposed and ensured physical, political, and conceptual domination, with well-known consequences.

The point is that once we cease to think of Africa as a continent without a history, we may begin to realise that it is also a continent with a history of art. Increasing evidence shows that a centuries-old tradition of making objects *with* aesthetic appeal developed gradually into making objects *for* aesthetic appeal, all the while following the same logical pattern as Western art even if the concept of art as it was used in the so-called developed countries was unknown. From pre-3000 BC votive figures, to functional and religious artefacts with some aesthetic features, production has moved towards artefacts which, although useful, are primarily of aesthetic interest.[4] But since nothing comparable to the *Mona Lisa*, a Shakespearean sonnet, or a Mozart sonata was found in Africa, and since there were no recognisable art institutions, this process went unnoticed by the colonisers, and so art as a universal concept was taken not to apply in Africa. Furthermore, not only did the objects themselves not resemble art, and consequently were not treated as art – no recognisable artists could be found.

But in Africa, social, cultural and religious circumstances did not exclude the making of art, as was thought; they merely precluded the making of art in the Western mould. At the risk of generalising and over-simplifying the complexities of the continent, African society, being communitarian and collective, instead of embracing individualism, builds itself around the community and the extended family. Hence, private acts of individual creation as are to be found in Europe and the West are replaced by cooperative ventures between the maker and the client. Since the client often, accordingly, dictates the look and even the shape of the work, the maker assumes the status of what to Western eyes is considered to be that of an artisan rather than an artist. Materials, too, because dependent on local availability, have been different and have not traditionally included paint on canvas or other conventional Western media. Even when, after contact with Europe and European media, these were used, their role was changed: colour, for instance, was applied not for expressive purposes but rather to emphasise form. Hence the conclusion was reached that there is in Africa no art, only craft of varying aesthetic merit. However, it was also assumed that if the natives could be taught, they might possibly produce artefacts within the overall umbrella of the concept – although, lacking the required historical and cultural background, these would, of course, be different (i.e. inferior) to those of the mainstream. This assumption was strengthened by evidence of other only partially successful attempts to imbue the indigenous folk with features of European civilisation.

And yet, although what was found in Africa defied precise categorisation, it was both interesting and exotic to the newcomers. Picasso, in the same conversation already referred to, describes his horrified fascination with the objects he first encountered at the Trocadera exhibition of 1907, and how, although he was so depressed that he wanted to leave immediately, he could not bring himself to do so (reputed conversation with Francoise Gilot, in Phillips 1995:29). Unfortunately, together with this interest in the exotic went a tendency to read an innate Africanness into it, so encouraging a systematic primitivisation of the cultures from which the objects came and preventing an open assessment of their merits; this persists to the present day, as can be seen in the marketing of "African art" which is often dependent on the creation of an "out of Africa" context, as masks, beadwork, and batik cloths are juxtaposed with safari clothes and pith helmets. The romanticised and patronising assumption that Africa is – and should remain – pure and unadulterated is at the root of the further assumption that later African artefacts (and therefore Africa's "art") have not developed. Instead, as the latter have increasingly included new features as a result of more contact with Europe and America, they are interpreted as having been corrupted by the influence of the West.

But, contrary to what was thought, the story of Africa is also about change and adaptation, and African artists, like artists elsewhere, have absorbed and assimilated for their own particular purposes. It is interesting that even an insightful critic like Ivor Powell, who in his recent *Ndebele: A people and their art* (1995) recognises these advances, yet voices his regret that this type of progress will lead to the adaptation of tribal culture to the point where it will no longer exist, as its art becomes more Westernised; this regret reveals Powell's own lingering romanticism about Africa:

> African tribal cultures, like any others, have always been dynamic, responding to and incorporating historical events as much as natural cataclysms and human interactions. Like all forms of knowledge, all world views and mythologies, African tribal usages are in the end a means to understanding, ordering and controlling the world. Events of overwhelming significance will be appropriated within the overriding belief structure, interpreted in terms of its assumptions, brought into line with the ever expanding body of lore that informs the life of the society and finds articulation in its ritual and material culture. If, however, transformation, adaptation and change represent one pole of the way that knowledge functions in tribal societies, the other is that of continuity. . . . But now, in the 1990s, this characteristic balance is in jeopardy. The precariousness of the cultural moment is particularly poignantly noted in the

fact that though the majority of rural Ndebele continue to make some form of "traditional" beadwork, it is stylistically so changed that it no longer possesses any ritual efficacy; the ancestors, so older informants told us, neither recognize nor acknowledge the so-called "party-style" appurtenances (1995:10).

However, the fact of people's adjusting rather than nostalgically lamenting should instead be taken as an illustration of the ongoing process of looking and learning. Ironically, though, what was seen in Picasso as innovative and exciting, namely his use of African elements, continues, when taken in reverse (i.e. when it becomes the adaptation by Africans of Western elements and the African use of modern technology and other foreign features), to be interpreted in Africa as proof of the slide towards decadence and inauthenticity. On the one hand, therefore, there is the assumption that there has been no development in Africa and hence that what is classified as art is not really art but only fetishist and magico-religious objects; and on the other hand there is the denial of the authenticity and integrity of works whose creators have detached themselves from tribal and other constraints, so opening themselves to wider aesthetic choices. Art created and judged under these conditions cannot but be inferior.

Colonial disruption and imposition upon the social fabric of African life, all in the name of development, was a double-edged sword. It not only wrecked the old conceptual frameworks of the people who lived there but also distorted those that survived. In South Africa this process was brutally carried out and, indeed, legalised. Apartheid was a shameful and deliberate attempt to alienate Africans from all forms of cultural stimulation which, as a result and as planned, undermined self-confidence and will. Art and "art" inevitably became part of this process.

After colonisation and during the period of apartheid, white artists and those involved in the art institutions (mainly white liberals), in spite of their increasing isolation as a result of their reaction to racial laws and practices, did manage to travel abroad; their black counterparts, however, with one or two exceptions such as Gerard Sekhoto who lived and worked in Paris for many years, remained separated from both international and national influences. But, motivated partly by guilt, partly by defiance of the system, and partly by altruism and curiosity, many liberal white gallery owners in particular initiated the move to expose the work of black artists in local galleries. For similar reasons beadwork and other cultural objects found their way onto exhibitions. But since this was always within a cultural and social context, these well-meant efforts paradoxically and unintentionally entrenched prevailing attitudes and differences. Instead of encouraging an interest in Africans' art as art, there was a greater awareness and appreciation of these works as being made by "others" – those who had been deprived, disadvantaged, and from whom "we" remained separated by law.

Together with this growing awareness of difference was a feeling of guilt tempered by the knowledge that, despite the prevailing restrictions, ways were being found to bypass the system without having to suffer the consequences – apart from the ever-present danger of censorship and the righteous indignation that could be expressed as a result. Given the repressive laws of the time it was also inevitable that white South Africans, educated separately from their black counterparts, should think of themselves not as Africans but as European transplants, and that they interpreted their own environment through European eyes and within a largely European conceptual framework. The resultant unavoidable inability to see beyond these conceptual constraints is aptly illustrated by Esmé Berman's well researched and well respected *Art and artists in South Africa* (1983) which lists only those black artists who had had one-person exhibitions, even though most of the work of these artists and other black colleagues was displayed in mixed groups.

At the same time, and underlying these well-meant attempts to encourage black artistic endeavours, there were also several less altruistic hidden agendas which had far-reaching effects. On the one hand there was the encouragement of remaining vestiges of primitivisation (given impetus by the government's retribalising efforts including the creation of separate "homelands" for blacks) and with it expectations of a recognisable African animus; on the other hand, however, there was the adoption of Western practices which were seen to legitimise art as universal (as encouraged by white artists, curators, and teachers), so allowing it to be subsumed into the Western category.[5] It is therefore not surprising that tensions between the two widely disparate cultures increased. One of the consequences has been the understandable temptation to black artists of financial reward: the reproduction of "traditional" art in order to supply an ever-increasing curio industry (but at the cost of authenticity). So, while the production of "traditional" art was given an impetus by market demands, if Africans were to earn the title "artist" they were encouraged to conform to what was seen as an imported idea of what was expected of them. Another result, fuelled by the resultant insecurity, has been the manipulation of the marketability of black artists which is often justified on the grounds that it is in their own interests, but which has in many cases ironically resulted in fluctuating popularity and fortunes.[6]

Democratisation, with its radical shift in political – though not yet economic – power, instead of bringing consensus on the matter, has created even more confusion by further muddying the conceptual waters. This is nowhere more evident than in the saga of the Cape Town Triennial (1982–1991), which serves to illustrate the clash between democracy on the one hand, and the Western emphasis on individualism and excellence on the other (du Plessis 1993:47). Instead of furthering its goals, the Triennial, which set out to attract the best artists and judges, finally foundered precisely because of these differences. Competitiveness, individual gain, and honour – worthy goals for some – directly conflicted with the new demands for democratic inclusiveness and group participation. Agreement could not be reached on the criteria for selection and awards, based as they were on mutually exclusive world-views. The resultant arguments and threatened boycotts eventually led to the withdrawal of the sponsor who did not want to be seen as supporting a platform for political differences.[7]

However, an interesting picture emerges if the various recognisable movements which resulted from these events are reappraised without the inherited burden of earlier conceptual and political frameworks. This revisiting of the story of African art can hopefully bridge some of the unfortunate gaps which misperception has widened. Given the complex social and cultural context of the continent and the many and varied influences, there will always be a multitude of directions for creative efforts to take – especially in a multicultural and rapidly changing environment. Each identifiable "movement" could have developed otherwise than it subsequently has, had other choices been made – just as each could have been interpreted otherwise from within alternative conceptual frameworks. Furthermore, each of these deserves detailed research in its own right and each could and should be seen as a *bona fide* artistic movement.

My concern, though, is not to retell the history of art in Africa or even in South Africa; it is to argue that this history of art has not only been misconceived, but there has been a failure to recognise that there is a history of art at all. Instead, serving both benign and malicious purposes, art has found itself playing the role of a pawn within larger political manipulations. This power game, founded on and fed by conceptual blindness, has in turn perpetuated the misuse and the abuse of art on the continent. Unfortunately, present preconceptions continue to mitigate against fair and reasonable assessment of the African art scene, while at the same time they mistakenly promote only certain dubious practices as passing for art. As in all cultures, though, art in Africa – and especially in South Africa – has taken a number of different directions. This in itself is nothing surprising, but where it has become problematic is that each of these, when taken in isolation, has been touted as the paradigm of what is being made in Africa under the rubric of a sort of boundary art. This is a distortion that has served to reinforce prevailing attitudes about the inferiority of art in Africa, and which continues to marginalise it.

One of these movements has been artistic Negritude. Deliberately and overtly political, its aim was in line with the general programme of decolonisation and assertion of the Africanness of Africa, and therefore it tried to decolonise art by freeing it from the shackles of what was seen as one of many unwelcome imported Western notions. Its roots lay in the ideas of Léopold Senghor who argued for a "negro style of sculpture, a negro style of painting and even a negro style of philosophy" (El Hadji 1995:84). If my argument is taken seriously, however, there will be no need – whatever its merits and in spite of the recent and urgent demands for the removal of Shakespeare, ballet, and opera from the repertoires of those cultural bodies who receive state subsidisation in a newly democratic South Africa – to resuscitate artistic Negritude as part of the process of Africanisation. A reaction to what is taken to be an exclusively imposed concept, artistic Negritude, while it did succeed in other African states, has in any case never flourished in South Africa. This is not because there was no need, but rather because of the success of the harsh separatist policies which managed to triumph even over the rising tide of Black Consciousness.

At the same time, because of the lure of the strange and exotic as it has been thought to exist in Africa, and the consequent saleability of what are presented as "magico-religious" artefacts, there has been the encouragement of primitivisation to continue for its own sake. This has had the effect, particularly in view of the new accessibility and novelty of post-apartheid South Africa, of leading to an ever-burgeoning tourist market with a demand for goods which, because in general they do not actually express the values of the maker, tend to be boringly repetitive. Recognising the marketability of their Africanness as perceived by foreigners, makers and dealers also mystify many of these objects by conveniently providing stories about their origin. The purchaser is satisfied by buying "authentic" African art, the maker has satisfied the client's expectations, and everyone is happy. Although tourist art is an interesting phenomenon, and although much of it is becoming worthy of attention, its acceptance because of its popularity and ready availability as being what constitutes African art merely adds, however, to the multitude of misconceptions. But this form of art will continue to thrive as long as there is one more tourist, and although it provides employment opportunities for many who would otherwise be denied them, it should not be assumed to be the paradigm of what is made in Africa as art simply because of its assumed authenticity and wide accessibility.[8]

In addition, although conceived with worthwhile intentions, the many efforts to encourage and train black artists have had some unfortunate results. One of these was the establishment (mainly in the 1950s, 1960s, and 1970s) of numerous art centres of which a well-known example is the Polly Street Art Centre in Johannesburg which became a gathering place for black artists and their white mentors to discuss and exchange ideas. One of the aims was to introduce black artists to the media of European art while at the same time allowing the content and style to reflect the artists' own cultures. Although it provided a much needed forum for black artists to meet and share knowledge and expertise, there has been a downside to this initiative. Run originally by whites to provide art instruction as close to the townships as safety and the law permitted, these centres have gradually proliferated into a number of Community Arts Centres. However, given the negative connotations that the notion of community had in the context of apartheid (with its "own affairs" ideology and its separate communities), these Community Arts Centres have ironically served to marginalise black artists rather than promote them internationally and nationally. Although many artists were given a platform for their creativity, and although some good work is still being produced in these centres, the volume of objects of dubious aesthetic merit has also increased. Many of the works coming from these and other centres which have recently come to be known as "transitional art" because they exist in the gap between European art and traditional artefacts, have been politicised by the underlying implications of illegitimacy, temporality, and inferiority.

Then there has been the often naively patronising over-eagerness of some would-be politically correct white curators to redress past wrongs for the purpose of promoting acceptance. They have been guilty of displaying many artefacts, regardless of merit, provided only that these are made by black artists. The result has been an acceptance by many of the more gullible members of the gallery-frequenting public of what is recognised (but not openly acknowledged) to be inferior art. But honest and astute critics have exposed and challenged this patent vestige of colonialism, exposing it for what it is. Kendall Geers, for example, has queried a fashionable Johannesburg gallery's choice of exhibition.[9] He both accuses the gallery owners of contributing to the fluctuation in the fortunes of black artists and points to the dangers inherent in such manipulation. In a review of the exhibition where he is critical of the artist's lack of skill he says:

> Affirmative action is a very useful political strategy to redress certain political imbalances. In art, however, it is very destructive and is harming some of this country's most talented black artists. Instead of being encouraged to grow and develop, [these artists] are encouraged to settle into easy fashionable solutions that the market eventually grows tired of and then abandons altogether (Geers 1996).

Hopefully, informed market and other forces will eventually act as correcting mechanisms.

While these events reflect art's role as a political football and add to the conceptual confusion, another movement has simultaneously developed from a multiplicity of influences, one which has until recently gone almost unrecognised because of the veil of conceptual prejudice and disorder. Despite both the destructive interference of apartheid policies and the misbegotten, though usually benign, blunders of their white colleagues, some black artists, often with little or no formal training, have been assimilating and absorbing the influences of other cultures – including European, American, and Islamic – into inherited African traits. This has not been because of coercion, or because there has been no choice, or for any other reason except the desire to create, and it has been a deliberate effort to extend and develop their repertoires through experimentation and the creation of new forms. Although originally mainly political and hence first known as "resistance art", this art has developed into a vibrant, mainly urban art form.

Eventually recognised in an exhibition entitled *The neglected art* held at the Johannesburg Art Gallery in 1988, this new art form has been described as "realist, incisive and honest" (Williamson 1989:10). Typical examples include Tommy Motswai's painting, *The tea-party* (1987), a parody of the white middle-class lifestyle as perceived through black eyes; Toto Zungu's ballpoint drawings first done on envelopes and sold to migrant labourers to send letters home to their wives and families for less than the price of a picture postcard; and Titus Moteyane's buses, cars, and aeroplanes made out of old cans, bits of wire, and whatever else he can find. Recent work can be seen at numerous metropolitan galleries such as the Goodman Gallery's exhibition of Sam Nhlengethwa paintings entitled *Mine trip* and, at the same venue, Austin Hleza's ceramics. The process has also now become reciprocal in that many white artists have learned from the ingenuity of the materials used. Though some of these black artists have received formal training, many have not, and their work remains largely unrecognised except by those who have refused to be blinded by fashion, dubious interests, and political pressure. If we are able to stand back from the power struggles and are prepared to reassess our interpretations of art and "art" in Africa, then I believe we may come to recognise the importance of this flourishing though hidden stream which is only now receiving the acknowledgement it deserves.

Unlike the trends which have been identified as supposedly constituting African art – an identification that serves to confirm the prejudices whose roots are in the colonial mentality – the objects of these trends fit without discomfort into the logical space occupied by a universally conceived notion of art. This art is made for no other reason than to be looked at and contemplated. Its history, like that of all histories of art, has been a logical progression of taking and making as the art has taught the artists to see. Much of it is still informed by earlier African influences, while some has moved almost aggressively towards contemporary Western forms – including the incorporation of technological and commercial images. This movement, only loosely coordinated more by happenstance than design, and despite the fact that it still bears the ideologically loaded name of "township art" and is subject to ongoing pressures for retribalisation, is one of the genuine attempts to assimilate and utilise day to day experience in contemporary South Africa in all its bewildering variety. It deserves to be called art in every sense of the term. But because of the context within which it has developed, the works produced have often been interpreted as the inauthentic borrowings of Western features and materials and are still frequently dismissed as decadent and inferior, thus denying this art the opportunity of being assessed on its own merits.

My point is that while we quibble because of incompatible ideological positions which have developed from our differing conceptual schemes, thinking all the while that our concern is conceptual, the history of art in Africa which fits the universal notion has not been absent, but has in fact been missed because of misplaced and ill-conceived expectations – at least partly as a result of the manipulation of art within political and concomitant power struggles. These misconceptions, far from being nothing but the innocent lack of understanding of a strange culture, have been the source of the misuse of art in Africa. A further reason for – as well as result of – this is, I propose, that the tensions within the term African art, when seen as inherently and exclusively conceptual, have been misdiagnosed. The lament that Africa is losing its roots and traditions also perpetuates the myth that the only true African art is traditional and tribal (the originals of which in any case are only to be found in the museums and galleries of Europe and America), and which, since it was made within a culture believed to have been devoid of the concept of art, cannot therefore really be said to be art. And yet, ironically, all art depending on principles based on experience and practice is traditional in at least one sense, so even this inconsistency in African art is probably only apparent.[10]

Furthermore, to think that the concept of art in its only true sense requires *l'art pour l'art* is to overlook the history of the concept and to distort its meaning. If this is indeed what it involves then we would have to reclassify much that is proclaimed as the pinnacle of art in the West. With its roots in Kantianism and Romanticism and the then cult of the beautiful, this notion of art is only of relatively recent origin – as late as the nineteenth century. So, to elevate it to its present universal prominence is in itself to ignore its context and its history. It is *we* who have kept the concept of art in quarantine, as it were, and by giving it a false history we have forced it to live an artificially isolated life by keeping it embedded in foreign soil, so depriving it of contact with the richness and diversity of African and other cultures. But ironically, even if we do want to maintain such a universal notion, at least one contemporary movement shows that the very concept of art, which has excluded African art because its perceived empirical use has misled us, has in fact been quite at home in Africa.

Consequently, although the conceptual debates will continue, and perhaps contrary to much prevailing opinion, I do not think that there is any proven evidence either from South Africa or from the rest of Africa to suggest that the concept of art is not universal. Although the concept may be impoverished and may seem strange to many Africans, there are grounds for accepting that there is "African art" that must be accepted as "art". Moreover, I do not think that, being perceived as exclusively Western and therefore as imposed, the concept needs to be rejected as part of the process of decolonisation. On the contrary, in spite of confusion about its past and its subsequent abuse, there seems every reason to think that art in Africa has always been, and continues to remain, alive and well.

NOTES

1. See for example Kamber (1993) and Hanfling (1995).
2. Gombrich's (1977) argument shows that the reason art has a history is a matter of logic.
3. This would, of course, also apply to other so-called primitive societies. However, given the uniqueness of the South African political situation, my general argument is unlikely to be relevant to them.
4. This is discussed frequently and in different contexts in several chapters of Vogel's *Africa explores: 20th century African art.*
5. See van Roebbroeck (1993:50). This topic has also been the subject of many personal conversations with her.
6. A good example is Jackson Hlongwane who, having once been fêted, now lives and works in relative obscurity, arguably because of the vested interests of gallery owners.
7. The Johannesburg Biennale (1995) is also beset by ongoing tensions. It failed in its attempt to be a showcase for international art, partly as a result of diametrically opposing views about art.
8. Interesting research on tourist art by Antoinette du Plessis (Department of History of Art, University of South Africa) and others is presently being documented.
9. The exhibition in question was of the works of Velaphi Mzimba curated by the Everard Read Gallery.
10. The Shorter Oxford Dictionary includes, *inter alia*, "a custom, opinion, or belief handed down to posterity" in its definition of "traditional". Neither of these definitions need apply exclusively to African artefacts or art.

Readings

TRADITIONAL AFRICAN AESTHETICS: A PHILOSOPHICAL PERSPECTIVE

INNOCENT C. ONYEWUENYI

This paper is an attempt to think differently to the way in which Western aestheticians think. It will try to show that African aesthetic standards are different from the "accepted" standards of uniqueness and individuality; that African works of art, be they visual, musical, kinetic, or poetic are created as an answer to a problem and serve some practical end. It will also delineate the philosophical foundation for such differences, and finally propose a theory of African art as Africans see it.

IS THERE AN AFRICAN AESTHETICS?

Before delving into the problem, we will first of all attempt to establish whether there is an African aesthetics or not. By way of definition, we are told that aesthetics is that branch of philosophy which has tried to answer such questions as "What is art?" and "What is beauty?". Dagobert Runes (1966:6) defines aesthetics in a traditional way as the branch of philosophy dealing with beauty or the beautiful, especially in art, and with taste and standards of value in judging art. Accepting the above definition as universal, there is an intellectual temptation to take the position that it is unnecessary and even futile to ask about the existence of an African aesthetics. If aesthetics is universal, it is as ridiculous to talk of African aesthetics as it is to talk of African physics or African chemistry. The question may even be regarded as racially and nationally loaded, an attempt to narrow the discipline of aesthetics in order to satisfy some racial or national whim.

A similar problem arose in my paper, "Is there an African philosophy?" (1976/77), where I argued that philosophising is a universal experience and that

> [w]hat is generally agreed about philosophy is that it seeks to establish order among the various phenomena of the surrounding world and it traces their unity by reducing them to their simplest elements . . . that while these phenomena are the same in all cultures and societies, each culture traces the unity of these, synthesizes, or organizes them into a totality based on each culture's concept of life. . . . Hence it is that the order or unity that the people of a culture establish is their own order, relative to their own conception of life in which everything around them becomes meaningful (Onyewuenyi 1976/77:513).

If the above is accepted as true, then we have the basis for calling a philosophy (and by extension, an aesthetics) European, Indian, American, or African. We can and should talk of African aesthetics because African culture has its own "standards of value in judging art"; its own "general principles" in explaining the value of any work of art. Africa has its own view of life, which Dilthey regarded as the starting point of philosophy. Georg Misch summarises Dilthey thus:

> Dilthey regarded life as the starting point of philosophy; life as actually lived and embodied or "objectified" in the spiritual world we live in. . . . Our knowledge of life is above all, contained in certain cultural and personal views of the world – which play a prominent part in philosophy as well as in religion and poetry (Misch 1950:47).

That the philosophy of art is universal does not mean that all aestheticians should employ similar standards of value in judging art, or similar general principles of explaining the value of any work of art. Neither does it mean that all the rationally warrantable or objectively granted principles or methods must be identical or that they must establish similar truths. Two separate aesthetic standards of value or general principles – both rational – can be opposed to one another.

Hegel underscores the cultural and relative aspect of philosophy when he says:

> But men do not at certain epochs merely philosophize in general. For there is a definite philosophy which arises among a people and the definite character which permeates all the other historical sides of the Spirit of the people, which is most intimately related to them, and which constitutes their foundation. The particular form of a philosophy is thus contemporaneous with a particular constitution of the people amongst whom it makes its appearance, with their institutions and forms of government, their morality, their social life and their capabilities, customs and enjoyments of the same (Hegel 1975:53).

From the foregoing one may safely suggest that the general principles or standards of value of aesthetics, which is a branch of philosophy, are bound up intimately with a people's spirit and constitution, and are a factor in their life history, subject to the conditions of race, culture, and civilisation.

One function of the arts is to make explicit the images by which a society recognises its own *values,* and thus to offer a means by which the members of a community may express and evaluate new elements in their lives. Furthermore, the arts afford a perspective on human experience as they are created to channel or express the powers of the super-human world – a world upon which people recognise their dependence. Europeans/Americans and Africans evidently have different views of life here and in the hereafter: they have different conceptions of the powers of the super-human world to which they may owe their existence, different ethical and moral values, different social institutions and forms of government – in short, different ideas of life and reality. Since works of art – be they visual, musical, kinetic, or poetic – are used "to convey the unfamiliar in the familiar, the abstract in the concrete, the discursive in the intuitive and the spiritual in the physical; in general to communicate the nonsensory through the sensory" (Berndtson 1969:36), it follows that the symbols must be culturally invested with the contents of their referents. Victor Uchendu may be quoted to round off these arguments in support of the issue of aesthetic relativity. He advises:

> To know how a people view the world around them is to understand how they evaluate life, and a people's evaluation of life, both temporal and non-temporal, provides them with a "charter" of action, a guide to behaviour (Uchendu 1965:12).

A BRIEF SURVEY OF AFRICAN ONTOLOGY

An adequate understanding of African ontology, especially in its conception of the nature of "reality" or "being" as dynamic, is fundamentally important to our discussion of African art appreciation. The essence of anything is conceived by the African as force: "There is no idea among the Bantu of 'being' divorced from the idea of 'force' " (Tempels 1959:37). Without the element of force, being cannot be conceived. Force is the nature of being; force is being; being is force. The concept of force or dynamism cancels out the idea of separate beings or substances which exist side by side, independently of one another, and which we have shown in our discussion of Western ontology to be responsible for individuality and uniqueness being standards or regarded as the essence of art. Existence-in-relation, communalism, and being-for-self-and-others sum up the African conception of life and reality:

> The African thought holds that created beings preserve a bond one with another, an intimate ontological relationship. There is an interaction of being with being. . . . This is more so among rational beings, known as Muntu which includes the living and the dead, Orishas and God (Tempels 1959:104).

Because of this ontological relationship among beings, the African knows and feels that he/she is in intimate and personal relationship with other forces acting above and below him/her in the hierarchy of forces.

A corollary to this relationship is the traditional African view of the world as one of extraordinary harmony, which Adebayo Adesanya explains as

> not simply a coherence of fact and faith, nor of reason and traditional beliefs, nor of reason and contingent facts, but a coherence of compatibility among all disciplines. A medical theory, e.g., which contradicted a theological conclusion was rejected as absurd and *vice versa*. . . . Philosophy, theology, politics, social theory, land law, medicine, psychology, birth and burial, all find themselves logically concatenated in a system so tight that to subtract one item from the whole is to paralyze the structure of the whole (cited in Jahn 1961:96).

INFLUENCES ON AFRICAN AESTHETICS

Traditional African aesthetics, or the interpretation and appreciation of works of art as a discipline in the body of African reality, cannot but fall in line with other theories and disciplines which "all find themselves logically concatenated" (Adesanya cited in Jahn 1961:97) in the tight system of the African world-view; otherwise it would paralyse the whole structure of African life and being. Works of art, as expressions of ritual and religion, as clues to the temperament of the tribe and society, as language in a culture without writing, must do all these in service to the community whose ritual and religion they express, whose temperament they reveal, the being of whose ancestors they participate in. Its theory or standard of evaluation must conform to the theories of its sister disciplines and stem from identical metaphysical foundations. Hence African art is functional, community-oriented, depersonalised, contextualised, and embedded.

By functional and community-oriented we mean that African arts – visual, musical, kinetic, and poetic – are designed to serve practical, meaningful purposes, and that beauty of appearance is secondary. All the same, functional beauty can also be regarded as beauty, says Janheinz Jahn (1961:174). A carving, for example, is aesthetically beautiful according to the African standard if it functions well as a stimulus in the worship of the deity – the community of worshippers being the judges. A mask, despite its "ugly" appearance, is judged beautiful and good if used correctly in the movement of the dance to depict the divine power with which it is imbued through the rhythmic incantations and sacrificial rites of the communal ceremonies: "Through his dance Efe has the power to please the witches and so turn their malevolent self-seeking power into a generous benevolence towards the community" (Harper 1981:3).

If a sculpture of an ancestor were to be scarified for purposes of worship in an Igbo society and endowed with all the paraphernalia that combine to make a work aesthetically good, it would not be accepted by the Igbo and would have no aesthetic recognition simply because it is neither true nor meaningful to them. Such a sculpture would not fulfil the function which an Igbo society expects of it. For, the Igbos do not scarify their bodies, and the Muntu-face represented in such a sculpture does not command their respect for a revered ancestor. Yet the same scarified Muntu-face may be aesthetically beautiful to the Yoruba or other tribes who culturally scarify their bodies. Harper makes the following observation:

> The various African peoples have coined various basic forms for the "Muntu-face" but they all express the Muntu-face. Within one people the Muntu face is constant, for it is derived from their common ancestor, that *muzimu* who formed the physiognomy of his people. Thus the artist is not free to think out a Muntu-face for himself, according to his own conception. The Muntu to be represented must belong to his own people (cited in Jahn 1961:162).

When we say that African art is depersonalised we mean that the artist's concern is not to express his/her own individual ideas and feelings. The African artist works from a background diametrically opposed to the Nietzschean expressionist influence about which Ben Gottfried (quoted in Jahn 1961:148) writes: "Our background was Nietzsche: his drive to tear apart ones's inner nature with words, to express oneself, to formulate, to dazzle, to sparkle at any risk and without regard for the results." He/she performs rather in such a way as to fulfil the ritual and social purposes of a community for whom the arts are meant to regulate the spiritual, political, and social forces within the community.

Speaking specifically about African poets, Jahn testifies as follows:

> In reality, the neo-African poet is not primarily concerned about his own ego. He is Muntu-man who speaks and through the word conquers the world of things. His word is the more powerful the more he speaks in the name of his people living as well as dead. As a poet he is the representative, he is the representative of all, and as a representative he is a poet (1961:142).

Whether it be in music, dancing, painting, or poetry, the artist cannot express his/her own motifs, themes, and obsessions in such art. The needs of the community determine the artist's production. This art is never "art for art's sake". The artist is responsible to society. Hence, African artists are

> held in high esteem by the society because they supply those design needs as are vital to their spiritual and physical well-being. They are not as a rule separated or differentiated from the generality of their kindred people for whom they fashion tools and objects of belief (Okeke 1982:62).

The foregoing emphasis on the depersonalisation of the artist does not, however, rule out every professional freedom. While the artist is bound to adhere to the basic forms recognisable by the people, "the determinant of the first degree, the Muntu face for man, or the animal shape for beasts", he/she does have some freedom with "the determinants of the second degree" (Jahn 1961:163). Thus, the artist may indicate a chief by a particular coiffure, by a crown, by a type of dress, or by setting the figure on a horse – the artist may even depict foreign European insignia and medals that are proper to kings.

CONCLUSION

An attempt has been made in this paper to show the philosophical foundation of traditional African aesthetics *vis-à-vis* Western aesthetics, and thereby to demonstrate the cultural relativity of the interpretation of works of art. Indeed, uniqueness and individuality are not, and need not be, the only basis for theories of aesthetics; African works of art are functional, community-oriented, and depersonalised, unlike Western art which is arbitrary, representative merely of the values and emotions of the artist without reference to the cultural environment and the historical reality of the people. I therefore suggest that the misinterpretation of African works of art by Western scholars of aesthetics is due to ignorance of cultural differences.

MORALITY, ART, AND AFRICAN PHILOSOPHY: A RESPONSE TO WIREDU

PARKER ENGLISH and NANCY STEELE-HAMME

ART HISTORY AND TRADITIONAL AFRICAN PHILOSOPHY

In a series of six recent works, the distinguished Akan philosopher, Kwasi Wiredu, argues that technological progress is apt to outstrip moral insight:

> Accordingly, the philosophical thought of a traditional [i.e. preliterate and non-industrialised] society may hold some lessons of moral significance for a more industrialized society (1991:98).

One surprising lesson Wiredu derives from his examination of traditional African culture is that Western moral thought is more supernaturalistic and less humanistic than that of traditional Akans. Western moral thought is more supernaturalistic in that Westerners tend to justify their moral principles with what they suppose to be the will of God, especially as expressed in the Ten Commandments. In contrast, traditional Akans go so far as to deny that moral principles must accord with the will of God. Instead, "traditional Akans regard the harmonization of interests as the means, and the securing of human well being as the end of all moral endeavour" (Wiredu 1995a:36–37). There is a "necessary" connection between moral principles and human interests. This approach to moral principles is humanistic in that it emphasises an even-handed securing of human welfare together with a sympathetic appreciation of another's interests:

> Akan ethics is a humanistic ethics in the precise sense that it is founded exclusively on considerations having to do with human well-being and, contrary to widespread reports, has nothing to do, except very extrinsically, with religion (Wiredu 1992/93:51).

Wiredu is concerned with protecting this Akan tradition. His primary reason is that the Western/supernaturalistic alternative tends to be authoritarian. A person who takes the supernaturalistic approach to moral thought easily gains a sense of "infallibility" by virtue of conceiving his/her own viewpoint from a "divine perspective". Too often this leads to unjustifiably overriding the will of one or more other people.

Wiredu's argument that Western moral thought is more supernaturalistic and authoritarian than traditional Akan moral thought is significant in that it reverses the view of traditional Africa popularised by writers such as John Mbiti:

> But precisely because religion became so deeply entrenched and institutionalized in all the different forms of (traditional) African life, it lost its ability to continue exercising supreme control and holding a position of absolute authority once new challenges came upon African societies (1969:266).

Nonetheless, it is notoriously difficult to make cross-cultural comparisons of concepts such as supernaturalism, humanism, and authoritarianism. As Appiah states:

> If I am reluctant to use the term *religion* without qualification, it is because religion in the contemporary West is, by and large, so different from what it is in traditional life that to report it in Western categories is as much to invite misunderstanding as to offer insight (1992:108).

In the limited space provided by this essay, we focus exclusively on traditional Akan moral thought. We hope to show that there are very significant ways in which traditional Akan moral thought was indeed both supernaturalistic and authoritarian.

Of course, there is a major obstacle to investigating traditional Akan moral thought: there is no extensive written record of Akan moral principles during the pre-colonial period when traditional thought flourished relatively purely. Nonetheless, there is an extensive record. It exists in the art objects that traditional Akans treated as integral to moral education and enforcement.

Art is a category term that originated in the cultural traditions of the West, expressing exclusively Western ideas. In a broader sense, however, art has come to mean something less Western-specific. Art, as we shall use the term, is to be regarded as "culturally significant meaning, skilfully encoded in an affecting sensuous medium" (Anderson 1990:238). It constitutes one of the ways in which the resources of the material environment are employed in the lives of people as social and communicative beings. The arts are also a collection of describable activities (and responses to these activities) based on the proclivity to "make special".

In traditional oral societies art was also used to facilitate or make palatable socially important behaviour. This is especially true of ceremonies in which group values are expressed and transmitted. An oral tradition comprises a memorised body of information considered important for the perpetuation of the group. This includes the group's history, social organisation, technical skills, and moral principles. As the only repository of important information, an oral tradition must be easily memorisable. Hence, it is taught by a system of indoctrination that emphasises obedience and de-emphasises the individuality of teachers, their instruments, and their students. Within an oral tradition, art is an adaptive necessity for this system of indoctrination. It is used as an encoding and mnemonic instrument to make important information more easily and accurately assimilable. As a result, even in the absence of written texts essential aspects of culture are not lost, ignored or dismissed. Instead, coded in non-literate ways, they are integrated and expressed in socially shared symbols.

Traditional Akan art, a body of material objects extant from the traditional cultures of the Akan, is a residue of events whose purpose was to impose on social individuals unforgettable patterns of essential knowledge and explanation. Functional objects such as robes, sandals, jewellery, staffs, swords, and umbrellas, for example, were elaborated to serve as regalia identifying the rank and function of their owner. In addition, traditional Akan artworks expressed ideas about political and moral relationships, especially as the latter related to the rank and function of the ruler. Traditional artworks were also used to invoke messages from and actions by spiritual entities. This was not moral philosophy in the sense of a peer-reviewed sequence of written arguments deriving moral conclusions from moral laws. Rather, it was moral philosophy as a way of accommodating one's neighbours-for-life when they demanded certain actions and prohibited others under conditions that were highly flexible and subject to incompatible interpretations. Art expressed moral philosophy for traditional Akans who were not constrained by the precise implications of writing, but who were nonetheless constrained by an evolving group consensus based on proverbs and myths. Often a traditional art motif might refer directly to certain proverbs explicitly taught in association with this motif. Such motifs existed as enduring, material evidence not only of the proverbs themselves but also of the ways in which these proverbs were used.

Contemporary art history studies such motifs by using not only the literature of history and art criticism but also that of anthropology, economics, agronomy, sociology, religious studies, and other disciplines as needed. Art history situates a functional artefact within a specific cultural practice. It identifies significant events in the development and use of specific artefacts. It elucidates constraints on and conditions for the production of the beliefs associated with art-artefacts as these beliefs were created, circulated, and renegotiated within different historical moments.

In the next section, we take the approach of art history to identify how the most important traditional Akan art-artefacts display moral principles as these were related to supernaturalistic authoritarianism. We attempt to address the following questions:

1. To what extent did traditional Akans use beliefs about supernatural entities in teaching and enforcing their moral principles?
2. To what extent were priests and other specialists regarded as having unique access to knowledge about the socially relevant action of supernatural entities?
3. To what extent did specialists about supernatural entities serve as secular, political powers who could override the wills of other people?

TRADITIONAL AKAN ART AS MORAL PHILOSOPHY

Akan society and its attendant culture were, in the most literal sense, hacked out of nature. Throughout the sixteenth and early seventeenth centuries, in a recalcitrant tropical forest environment, a protracted investment of labour transformed the dominant mode of production from hunting and gathering to crop agriculture. Sustainable crop agriculture was established through unremitting land clearing of the most difficult order which, to be successful, had to be carried on throughout several generations. This labour required vastly more social cooperation than did the previous economic labour of hunting and gathering. In particular, it divided labour into categories that had to be regulated by principles to which most people were voluntarily compliant: land clearing, land cultivation, livestock husbandry, structure building, tool making, container making, apparel making, administration, defence, and trade. This social cooperation required that an individual's thought be disciplined by relatively unquestioning obedience to certain permissions and prohibitions controlling behaviour within a social context. The development of an agricultural economy was thus the most significant determinant event in Akan history, at least before extensive trade with distant Africans and with Europeans. It also produced the indispensable base of food production on which a more formally structured social order would later be enlarged. This more formally structured social order itself evolved into the expansionistic eighteenth-century state, as a strong and centralised authority became necessary for efficient interaction with traders from the rest of Africa and from Europe.

As McCaskie (1989:421) points out, "[c]ulture, society and polity were brittle artifacts, inserted with enormous effort into the constantly encroaching anarchy of nature." Consequently, traditional Akan societies evolved various instruments to profoundly condition an individual's understanding of the group's hard-won and fragile mastery over the environment. Traditional Akans were taught to believe that order within society was a concern that affected all. It required everyone's committed participation, as had the communal creation of agriculture. In particular, traditional Akans were taught to believe that a person's sense of peace with the invisible world of spirits could be achieved only by cooperation and harmony with other members of human society. Thus, supernatural beliefs were an essential element in traditional Akan moral and social philosophy.

For traditional Akans, reality was a divine cosmic order fashioned by the high god *Nyame* "by the very law of his own being" (Wiredu 1992/93:42). Within this cosmic order was a set of subordinate orders comprising one comprehensive universe. The natural order regulated physical, chemical, and biological events; the moral order regulated the conduct of human beings in society; the actions of entities within the supernatural order could be tapped and used by priests and other specialists for benefit or harm. All social rules were directed to an individual's maintaining harmony with each of the subordinate orders of which human beings were a part: "Religion for the Akan is a quest for harmony. . . . When this harmony is maintained things go well, otherwise there is chaos" (Opuku 1982:63). It was through sacrifices, offerings, prayer, and other social rituals, including those concerned with punishments, that this harmony was maintained, especially when a prohibition had been violated. Speaking specifically of the Asante, McCaskie remarks that until scholars

> are prepared to accept anxiety as a "cultural" fact – and one not obfuscated by something called religion – they will never be able to comprehend the indigenous reading of the fragility of history, or of the need for totemic devices to defuse irruptive disorder (1986:329–30).

How did the most important art objects function in traditional Akan cultures? Stools provide the best example. A stool served several functions for traditional Akans. It was sometimes used as a utilitarian object of rest; it was sometimes associated with rites of passage; it was sometimes viewed as a sacred object imbued with the *sunsum* of its owner. (*Sunsum* is the activating principle of the person and is responsible for thought or ratiocination.) A stool was also sacred when used in ancestor veneration. In particular, contact with the ancestors was established and maintained through ceremonies involving the blackened stools of deceased chiefs, especially that of the *Asantehene*, paramount ruler of all traditional Asantes during the Asante ascendancy. Consequently, a royal stool was also a political symbol. As successor of the royal ancestors, only a chief could successfully perform the various rites associated with the stool that were essential for spiritual entities to support the welfare of all in his community.

The political authority of all Akan chiefs rested on their being viewed as successors of those ancestors who had been the principal actors in establishing Akan societies. The *Asantehene*, however, held supreme authority by virtue of holding the Golden Stool, the sacred shrine that housed the *sunsum* of the nation. Thus, any words of abuse uttered against the *Asantehene* reflected on the most important of the principal ancestors. This offence was punishable by death. So were adultery with any of the chief's wives, invoking a curse on the chief, theft of stool property, and assaults attempted by the chief's council against the chief. These were religious offences that angered and threatened to estrange the ancestral spirits and gods from the community, thereby putting at grave risk both spiritual harmony and societal well-being. As Busia (1968:96) observes, "The Asante do not like to even speak of the *Asantehene*, still less to be questioned about him. When they have to talk about him, they do so in low tones, modulating gradually into whispers."

The Golden Stool was understood by traditional Akans to be of spiritual provenance. According to Asante oral traditions, the Golden Stool first appeared near the end of the seventeenth century. Osei Tutu, chief of Kumase (traditional capital of the Asante), successfully led an alliance of small states against the kingdom of Denkyira to whom they were subject. Osei Tutu thereby became the supreme ruler, the *Asantehene*, of the newly unified Akan nation whose spiritual centre was the Golden Stool. According to Asante oral traditions, Osei Tutu's success resulted at least in part from the powerful magic of his priest, Komfo Anokye. Later, on a Friday, a great gathering was held at Kumase. There, Komfo Anokye brought down from the sky, "with darkness and in thunder, and in a thick cloud of white dust" (Ward 1948:119), a stool of solid gold, which floated to earth, alighting gently on Osei Tutu's knees. Komfo Anokye announced that all the strength and bravery of the Asante nation depended on the safety of the stool.

As a precondition to producing the Golden Stool, however, Komfo Anokye had demanded that the blackened ancestral stools and the royal regalia of all the Akan member states be surrendered to him so that they could be buried in the Bantama River. This ensured that no item of regalia in the new kingdom could have a longer history than the Golden Stool and therefore take precedence over it. Komfo Anokye declared the stool must be fed at regular intervals so that it might not sicken and die, causing the Akan nation to perish also. Komfo Anokye then organised the military structure of Akan power and presented a formal constitution that outlined a code of seventy-seven laws to be observed by all. These laws are regarded as the basis for traditional Akan moral thought.

In sum, traditional Akans, led by the Asante, constructed their social order and the moral code that supported it in response to their understanding of existence as fragile. By the time Osei Tutu was implementing Akan expansionist policies, the moral code had been given divine sanction and was embodied in a tangible visual symbol, the Golden Stool. This moral code was upheld, protected, and passed on through those who held the sacred office of *Asantehene*. The authority of *Asantehenes* was legitimated by their superhuman ability to mediate between the world of spirits and that of humans so as to protect the entire nation. The Golden Stool was not only the object that contained the sacred essence of the Asante nation but also a metaphor for the sacred office that administered and supported it.

Royal regalia such as robes, sandals, jewellery, staffs, swords, and umbrellas are further excellent examples of how important art objects functioned in traditional Akan cultures. A considerable body of such regalia arrived in the eighteenth and nineteenth centuries with the growth of a central government for the Akan. Each object obtained its own history, use, and significance. By aggrandising and validating the chief's position of leadership, these objects helped to run an empire without a large literate class. The royal regalia were not merely symbols of office, however. By virtue of their art motifs, they also served as the chronicles of history and as evidence of traditional religion, cosmology, and social organisation.

One of the most distinctive characteristics of royal regalia, and of virtually all traditional Akan visual arts, was the presentation of symbols, objects, or scenes directly related to traditional sayings and proverbs. Indeed, the relationship between art motifs and their verbal equivalents is often cited as one of the cornerstones of Akan aesthetics. While not exclusively an Akan phenomenon, in West Africa it is among the traditional Akan that this verbal-visual nexus was most highly developed. One such motif appearing frequently on royal regalia deals with the continuity of the ruling matrilineage. It depicts one bird nesting and another bird resting above. The proverb is, "When the kite is away, the hawk rests on its eggs." For the Akan, the birds are admired predators and are believed to come from the same family. The principal message here is that when the chief dies, there will be someone else from his matrilineage to take his place and guard the state.

In numerous external and internal accounts of traditional Akan-land, death and the mortuary rituals that surround it figure prominently. Social anthropologists have demonstrated a general connection between beliefs about death and attendant funerary practices, on the one hand, and beliefs about sexuality and reproduction, on the other. This is particularly true concerning the deaths of traditional *Asantehenes*. Such deaths led to reflection on higher-order social abstractions concerning increase, the fertility of the land, and that of its people. In turn, these reflections necessitated the introduction of measures to affirm and to renew the latter as goals. It should be clear that the initial and recurrent mortuary rituals for deceased *Asantehenes* functioned as expressive representations of basic beliefs within Asante experience.

The performance of funeral rites for a traditional *Asantehene* was complex, demanding, and prolonged because of the traditional Asante conception of afterlife. Traditional Asantes conceived of afterlife as an extension or mirror of the prevailing hierarchies of lived existence. Thus, a deceased *Asantehene* was still an *Asantehene*. In afterlife he had the same status and role, together with the same needs and requirements – wives, servants, clothes, gold, food – as he had in his biological existence. Providing these needs involved killing prisoners, slaves, subjects, and wives. The most important thing to bear in mind here is that any error or oversight, neglect or failure in the intricate performance of the royal funeral rites constituted a grave offence against the departed *Asantehene*. Without proper observance, he could not be fully incorporated into the world of spirits in a manner appropriate to him. If left with a lesser, ambiguous, or uncertain status, "he could withdraw his protective cooperation from society and instead remonstrate with it for its injurious abandonment and willful insult of him" (McCaskie 1989:428).

A short paper such as this can do no more than present an overview of answers to the three questions we are using to explore supernaturalistic authoritarianism. As far as we can tell, however, both Akan and Western scholars are in broad agreement about the general thrust of these answers concerning traditional Akans:

1. Traditional Akans used beliefs about the authority and action of spiritual entities to an overwhelming extent in teaching and enforcing their moral principles. Those beliefs were designed to influence people who typically viewed environmental order as fragile. The beliefs were meant to shape an individual's thought so that he/she could feel at peace with ever-present spiritual entities only if he/she cooperated in maintaining social harmony. This meant obedience to extant moral principles.
2. As successors to departed leaders, traditional chiefs (especially the *Asantehene*) were regarded as the living humans most able to intercede with spiritual entities

for general social welfare. This was a primary source for the secular, political power of traditional chiefs.

3. By virtue of his apparent success in contacting spiritual entities, Komfo Anokye had the secular power to destroy the most important symbols of political authority in the Akan member states, their royal regalia. Likewise, he had the authority to present the seventy-seven laws that served as the basis of traditional Akan moral thought. Perhaps the most dramatic proof that specialists on supernatural entities held authoritarian control over traditional Akan societies, however, concerns the ritual killing involved in royal funerals. By virtue of their unique relationship with departed ancestors and other supernatural entities, chiefs literally had the power of life and death in secular matters. Because of their power in the world of supernatural entities, immediately deceased chiefs (especially the *Asantehene*) were regarded as still having immense power concerning life and death in their human communities. Consequently, royal princes and priests were licensed to ritually kill thousands of people during the extended funerals for chiefs and *Asantehenes*. If this does not count as overriding the welfare of individuals for spiritualistic purposes, then Wiredu needs to explain what would count as such.

Wiredu thinks the supernaturalistic type of moral thought imported into contemporary Akanland involves a self-validating notion of absolute truth about moral principles that has been appropriated by self-interested leaders:

> [O]n the African continent there are everywhere groups privileged with direct access to *the* Truth, social and political; and woe betide those, who, not having eyes to see, do not at the very least stay silent (Wiredu 1980:96).

Such leaders reinforce the traditional Akan respect for leadership so as to facilitate dogmatism in their followers. The leaders then develop authoritarian power to the point of stifling opponents by imprisoning them.

Our research so far indicates that there is very little doubt that traditional Akan thought was much more supernaturalistic than contemporary Akan thought when this is measured by the three questions raised above. Whether or not traditional Akan thought was also more authoritarian in purely secular terms is, however, more subject to debate, though the bulk of available evidence indicates it was. Space prevents our exploring more fully why Wiredu might think contemporary Akans are actually more supernaturalistically authoritarian than were traditional Akans. One point is worth noting in brief, however. Wiredu is surely right that Westerners, during their colonisation of Akanland, often claimed universalism and superiority for their own moral principles. Missionaries in particular often justified these claims by appealing to the authority of God as interpreted in accordance with their own self-validating opinions about the Bible. At the same time, however, Akans were encountering quite a different kind of Western authoritarianism in the persons of colonial bureaucrats. When facing Akan opposition, the bureaucrats relatively quickly dominated Akans by using economic, political, and military force. Consequently, many Akans perceived the colonial bureaucracy as concerned more with domination than with legitimation:

> The formal agencies transferred to African hands were . . . alien in derivation, functionally conceived, bureaucratically designed, authoritarian in nature and primarily concerned with issues of domination rather than legitimacy (Appiah 1992:164).

The significance of this point, however, is that supernaturalistic thought played no important role in the bureaucratic type of authoritarianism – this, even though the colonial bureaucracy was clearly self-serving. In contrast, the authoritarianism displayed by missionaries obviously did involve supernaturalistic thought. This was the authoritarianism of demanding that traditional beliefs about spiritual entities and the moral principles they endorsed be assimilated to Christian ones, rather than vice versa. But few traditional Akans viewed the missionaries as self-serving in ways that were significant and malignant. At worst, they viewed a few missionaries as patronising or as inflexible concerning charitable endeavours sponsored by missionary societies.

Finally, a reasonably complete challenge to Wiredu's view of supernaturalism and authoritarianism would contrast contemporary African moral thought with contemporary Western moral thought, following Wiredu's well-known suggestion that traditional African thought be compared with traditional Western thought (Wiredu 1984:150–157). We might find that supernaturalistic authoritarianism in Western moral thought has evolved in roughly the way this feature is now evolving in Akan moral thought.

IS PRIMITIVE ART "ART"?

GENE BLOCKER

A gratifying recent development in American education is the desire (and demand) for greater multicultural education, including multicultural art education. For too long, it has been argued, we have acted as though the only significant contributions to art, science, law, morality, and literature have come from Europeans (and mainly dead, male Europeans), thus ignoring the cultural contributions of other traditions, ethnic groups, and the other half of the human race, as divided by gender. This omission is all the more troubling when it occurs in a pluralistic, multicultural, multi-ethnic country like the United States of America where the students we are trying to educate are of African, Hispanic, Amerindian, Asian, as well as European origin. Insofar as one of the goals of education is to help our students find a viable sense of self-identity, the emphasis on European models as the only or the most worthwhile exemplars is frustrating and self-defeating for many of our students – and thereby for their teachers as well. The solution would seem to call for the expansion of the curriculum to include a study of diverse cultural heritages. The problem is how best to accomplish that worthwhile goal.

One response, widely lauded, is to encourage African Americans to study African culture, Native Americans to study Amerindian culture, Hispanic students to study Hispanic culture, and so on. But this actually *defeats,* rather than encourages, *multi*cultural understanding, for by adopting this scheme no one is studying any culture but their own. This would, therefore, seem to be more a *unicultural* approach, in which each student studies but *one* culture, the one with which he/she identifies in terms of ethnic origin. It is multicultural only in the sense that many different cultures are studied within the school system, though only one per student. When we think of the goal of multicultural studies as fostering mutual understanding and communication across cultural boundaries, this notion of multicultural education appears far from adequate. But the notion of multi-culturalism as educating students to appreciate cultures other than their own is cross-cultural, and that introduces enormous problems of its own. How can the members of one cultural group ever hope to understand another culture? If we inevitably look at everything from our own cultural point of view, how can we investigate another culture except in a hopelessly ethnocentric manner?

In this article I want to discuss the example of so-called primitive art – that is, the traditional arts of black Africa, pre-Columbian meso-American Amerindian art, and the art of the South Seas. But the very term primitive art indicates the problem involved in any cross-cultural study – that is, the problem of using *our* concepts to study *their* culture. It is a Western cultural perspective to suppose there is an evolution of cultures from "primitive" to "advanced", and the concept of "art" in the sense of "fine art" is equally a Western designation and concept. In other words, we are studying their culture in our own terms, and since these are the only terms we have, we seem to have no choice but to be ethnocentric and therefore inaccurate and unfair. The central question of primitive art is therefore whether primitive art is "primitive" and whether it is "art". That is, what do we mean when we say this kind of art is "primitive", and what do we mean when we say it is "art"? More generally, what right do we have to impose these Eurocentric labels on non-

European cultures? More important, do we have any choice – is there any alternative?

In what follows we will look at the second of these two questions: is primitive art *art*? Primitive art is only now beginning to be investigated as art. Until recently most serious, professional study of primitive artworks has been conducted piecemeal by treating the objects as accessories to various nonaesthetic, nonartistic societal functions. For the most part the study of primitive art is not carried out in art schools but in anthropological studies of social organisation, religious practices, secret societies, initiation rites, and so on. On the other hand, those who have been excited about primitive art as art are primarily Western artists from 1905 onward, whose comments have been admittedly personal and highly subjective reactions to art forms that they frankly knew little or nothing about. The anthropologists accuse the artists of ignorance of the scientific, factual basis on which such artefacts rest, and the artists blame the anthropologists for their lack of concern for these objects as works of fine art.

Thus the discussion of primitive art has from the beginning been pervaded by a curious dilemma – you can approach primitive art from an aesthetic point of view but subjectively, or you can approach primitive art from a more objective basis but not aesthetically. What has not occurred in the case of primitive art, as has occurred with practically every other art form, is an approach that is both aesthetic *and* objective. When we study the art of the Italian Renaissance, or the Ming Dynasty, for example, we study it scientifically as *art*.

Why has there been so little aesthetics, art history or art criticism of primitive art? The answer has to do with the very special nature of primitive art. The fact is that, in a curious way, primitive art becomes art, not through the primitive peoples who made and continue to make such objects, but through Europeans who buy and collect it. It is not art because those who make and use it say it is, but, ironically, because we say it is. It is art by alien decree. But somehow objects designated as art only by alien decree, by outsiders only and not also by insiders, are considered art only half-heartedly and perhaps even hypocritically.

It has often been said that traditional tribal art is not produced from within an "aesthetic" perspective as "fine art", as these terms are usually understood. It is often pointed out that, unlike Western art, primitive art is not made to be appreciated aesthetically, or at least not primarily aesthetically, from which it would seem to follow that such objects are not produced as works of art. And this, in turn, is what I am suggesting leads to *our* reluctance to treat primitive art as *art*.

But this merely introduces the question I want to raise in this article, "Is primitive art 'art' "? Should we look at primitive artefacts as works of fine art, or as religious paraphernalia, or in some other way? My approach is to reject the subjective point of view of the enthusiastic Western artist in favour of the more objective standpoint of the anthropologist, but to deny the anthropologist's conclusion that there is no aesthetic dimension within the perspective of the indigenous peoples who produce and use primitive art. Thus, the anthropologists were right in their approach but wrong in their conclusions, while the opposite is true of the Western artists who were correct in their assessment of the artistic character of primitive art, but wrong in their reasons for making those assessments.

The problem we face is not one that is peculiar to primitive art, but a general problem affecting any cross-cultural study. Whenever group A uses A's concepts to describe group B's activities, problems of meaning arise: do we mean that this is how B looks at it or only A, or both? Until we make it clear that *our* description of *his/her* behaviour must incorporate not only our understanding of that description but his/her perception of the situation as well, problems of ambiguity will inevitably arise. And since descriptive terms can seldom be adequately translated cross-culturally, especially if the two societies are very different, we always seem to be caught in something of a dilemma – either we use terms of our own language, in which case our descriptions are apt to be unfair and misleading in their implications, or else we do not use terms of our own language, in which case it is difficult to see how we can make ourselves understood to the group we are addressing (the group, that is, which speaks our language).

At first, the solution might seem fairly obvious. Since it is clearly unfair to describe their behaviour in *our* terms, why not describe their behaviour in *their* terms? To avoid the errors of ethnocentrism, why not describe the alien society from within their own perspective and point of view? But this will prove to be impossible for the simple and obvious reason that, as human beings, we can never escape entirely from our own point of view.

The conclusion, then, is inevitable – a cross-cultural *comparison* is unavoidable in any cross-cultural *description*; the concept must be ours while the behaviour and beliefs are theirs. But how can that possibly be fair? How can any anthropological description hope to achieve the barest minimum of objectivity? Only, as we will see, if the concepts by which we describe their society and the concepts by which they describe the same things in their society are synonymous (or at least similar) in meaning.

Suppose I am an early missionary to West Africa. I see people making what appear to be "sacrifices" and "offerings" and "prayers" to carved wooden figures which they call by what I have been told are the names of their "gods". Hence I am led to believe that they worship these idols, and so I write in my next report home that the natives worship pieces of wood, that these carvings are idols worshipped as gods. But this claim or interpretation of mine clearly assumes that these people themselves believe that as well. Let us say that they come to my mission school and begin to learn English, and, after some years, they inform me that they do not consider the carving itself to be the god, but only to represent it, or to be the temporary abode of the god who can occasionally enter and occupy it. Then, assuming I believe what my informants are now telling me, I would have to admit that I had been wrong in my earlier report and to deny now that the practices I had observed in connection with the wood carvings were instances of idolatry.

But now if we analyse this situation, we see that it very clearly lays down as necessary conditions for correct translation of their practices into our language the following: the meaning of the term which I use to describe their activity must be one which they share in the terms of their language with which they describe this same activity. If I say they worship idols, I quite clearly imply that they believe that these bits of wood are gods. But now it becomes an empirical, factual question whether this is or is not their belief. If it is not, then "idol" is not the right word to use in describing their activities.

Suppose now that having been in this West African village for many years I become very attracted to the aesthetic qualities of these wooden carvings, especially as friends back home inform me that they are becoming quite valuable as artworks. If I now change my opinion as to what these objects are, rejecting the idea that they are idols and embracing now the idea that they are works of art, then precisely the same problem confronts me once more. By calling them works of art I imply that the people who make and use these objects have the same or very similar attitudes and beliefs to those involved in the English meaning of "work of art". I imply, for example, that the people in this community enjoy looking at them, that they "use" them more for just looking at than for some more utilitarian end, that they grade and rank them according to critical standards, that they regard the objects as expressing the attitude or world view of the carver, that they respect the carver as a person of vision and originality, that they respect creativity and originality in the carving in its own right, and so on.

But now I may learn that I was mistaken once again in my assumptions about the beliefs and attitudes of these people. It may turn out, for example, that they have no idea and don't care who made the pieces or that anyone and everyone makes them, that each is considered just as good as every other, that they never take the objects out just to look at them, that when they have finished with them in a religious ceremony they just throw them away, that they reject any innovation and have no conception of the carvers expressing themselves or their view of things in producing the objects, and so on. In that case I will have to conclude that they are not works of art either.

But notice what I would mean by this. I do not mean that they fail to have the visible marks and features which qualify objects in my society to be artworks or that they are not good enough to be works of art. I simply mean that the people who make and use such objects do not themselves regard them in ways that are sufficiently similar to the ways in which native English speakers indicate they regard them by calling them works of art. My refusal to call them works of art casts reflection more on the traditions and institutions of the people than it does on the objects themselves.

To summarise, we have identified three criteria for a good cross-cultural description. To apply a concept P correctly to X from group A to group B, it must be the case that

1. X is correctly classified as P by A;
2. X is correctly classified as Q by B;
3. P and Q are synonymous (or at least similar in meaning).

Since the ambiguity obviously turns on the cross-cultural aspect of the situation (one culture talking about another) rather than the descriptive terms themselves, our claim is not that there is an ambiguity in *words* like "worshipping" or "gods", though there may well be ambiguities in these words which we are not here concerned with, but that the ambiguity arises from their cross-cultural application.

But clearly, not all descriptive terms applied cross-culturally are ambiguous in this sense, or at least, if it turns out to be a matter of degree, all are not equally so ambiguous. If I say, as an American anthropologist observing a South American tribe, "They wear no shoes", or "They eat cooked fish", or "Their houses are built of bamboo and palm thatch", there is not the same ambiguity, or at least not the same degree of ambiguity, as when I say, "They worship many gods", or "They express their innermost thoughts in creating works of art", or "They perform plays and other theatrical dramas."

What is the difference between these two types of cross-cultural description? We might begin by noting that the less ambiguous seem to be more factual and empirical, while the more ambiguous appear more interpretative and non-empirical. Secondly, the non-empirical component or aspect is an "intentional" one in the sense that the truth or falsity of its application depends on the intentions (i.e. the point of view, attitude, etc.) of the indigenous agents being referred to. If I say, "They eat cooked fish", it is difficult to see how the point of view, purposes or whatever of those referred to could affect the truth or falsity of the claim. Whereas if I say, "They worship many gods", I stand to be corrected, whatever the immediate empirical evidence of ritualised behaviour I have observed, by improved knowledge of the intentions, points of view, and so forth, of the agents. If it turns out later that this is not what they meant or intended, then my claim is defeated. In fact, ideally, controversies inevitably arising out of the interpretative character of the more ambiguous descriptions are settled by appeal to the representative native speakers who have learned our language. Only they are able to tell us whether our word captures what they intend in performing certain acts: "No, this is not a 'drama' or 'theatrical play' in your sense of the words, but something resembling more what you call 'religious ritual', as when your priest traces the 'stations of the cross'."

But, of course, we are not here talking about the personal intentions of a particular individual, but the collective intentions of a certain group. We are speaking, in other words, of institutionalised attitudes, forms of behaviour, and patterns of perception as generated and regulated by a particular culture. Thus, in a cross-cultural description, ambiguity occurs where the accuracy of the description depends on the institutional character of the indigenous culture. If there is an institutionalised set of theatrical conventions in their society of which this behaviour is a part, then it will be true and apt to say of this behaviour, "They are performing a theatrical drama." And if not, not. These institutional conventions will be assumed to govern the individual intentions of particular members of that society and to be reflected in the objects and behaviour that they produce. So, when we speak of "the man's intentions" or "what is meant by sprinkling blood on the stone effigy", we are referring indirectly to the cultural conventions and institutions that govern those sorts of activities.

Now, to test our analysis, let us consider three possible objections that might be raised against our claims, somewhat like Plato's "three waves" in *The Republic*. The first wave is the objection that it doesn't matter what we call objects, so long as we all know what it is we are referring to. But this certainly won't do, since our entire theoretical and practical approach to such objects depends on what we call them. As noted earlier, the first Europeans described primitive artefacts as idols and for that reason proceeded to destroy as many of them as they could. In the nineteenth century these same objects were described as curiosities and treated accordingly, and it was only in the twentieth century that Western artists began to call these objects works of art and to treat them accordingly, that is, displaying them in art museums, collecting and discussing them artistically, and so on.

The second wave, or objection, is that since we are free, especially in scientific discourse, to define words as we like, we ought to eschew ethnocentrism and simply redefine our concepts in line with what we know to be the attitudes and beliefs of the people we are describing: "For them art is inseparable from life;

everything they do is done with a style and grace which to them are art" or "To them art is not perceived as something to be appreciated in some way apart from their appreciation of its religious function; to them art need not be appreciated aesthetically." But this approach can only add to the existing confusion. Since these words of ours (e.g. art) already have well-established meanings, using them in new ways will only create new confusions. All we can possibly mean thereby is that what we regard in one way, they regard in another way; that what we regard as art, for example, they do *not* regard as art. If our concept resembles theirs, then we can extend our concept to apply to their practices and artefacts. But if their concept is known to be different from ours, then why use this particular concept of ours? Such an approach does not subsume two subconcepts under one larger concept, unless both are subconcepts of our concept.

If, for example, our concept of a god included both immortal but otherwise human entities (such as Greek gods) as well as more spiritually abstract beings such as Allah, who have no physical characteristics or human foibles, then it would make sense to say of an alien culture, "Their gods are not like ours, high and mighty, pure spiritual beings, morally perfect, but are very energetic, often wicked, anthropomorphic beings." But it would not make sense to say, "They do not worship any gods in our sense of the word; their gods are simply individual bits of matter, such as small pebbles and twigs uninhabited by unseen forces of any kind, which they use to soften leather or to clean their teeth." This would simply be a misuse of language as odd as one who tried to prove the existence of God by displaying a small pebble which he had named "God". After all, it is we who select from among our own concepts the one we think most appropriate in a given situation. But why choose one concept over another? Surely it can only be on the basis of some perceived resemblance between their meaning and ours. If we know the meanings are different, this is a perfect reason to reject that concept of ours in favour of another ("These small pebbles and twigs are not gods at all but rather household tools").

Thus, it is nonsense to claim, as is often claimed today, that different groups can and do have their own concept of "philosophy", "art", or "god". Indeed, it is widely held that within our own culture such important concepts can be redefined at will. Of course, concepts can and do change, and one of the reasons new meanings are often suggested as replacements for old, established meanings of the same word is to try to bring about that change. They are, as C.L. Stevenson called them, "persuasive definitions". But even so, as a factual claim about the actual meaning of the word, such definitions are quite false and mistaken. Secondly, it is up to us to accept or reject them as persuasive definitions – if enough of us are persuaded to use the terms in this new way, then the terms will gradually change in meaning, but if not, then the attempt at persuasion has failed. In neither case can the meaning of a word be changed simply by fiat, as the innovators would have us believe. What we can and should allow, however, are subconcepts within our own concepts, along with the possibility that the group we are investigating may have a greater affinity for a different subconcept than the subconcept that defines our own current interests.

If someone calls God the "big bang" with which the physical universe is said to have begun, we will object that this is stretching it a bit; but if someone calls a Yoruba *Orisha*, such as Shango, a god, we will certainly not object since, although

Shango little resembles the God of the Judaeo-Christian tradition in its sublime transcendent omniscience and moral perfection, Shango does most certainly resemble our own subcategory of gods of the ilk of Zeus, Odin, and Shiva.

And the same principle would seem to operate in the case of art. True, our current preferred sense concerns a notion of (more or less) art for art's sake for purely or largely aesthetic interests, with emphasis on formal, symbolic content, and so on, in comparison with which primitive art stands out in fairly sharp contrast. But we also have other subconcepts of religious art from the Graeco-Roman era, as well as European art prior to the Renaissance, as well as the subcategory of art as a skill or craft, with which we can find far greater similarity with primitive art.

The final "wave" is the objection that our insistence upon using our concepts in describing alien cultures amounts to a form of intellectual imperialism, especially as this results so often in belittling comparisons of their culture in relation to our own. But this objection rests on a confusion. The fact that the concept must be our concept implies no imperialistic superiority whatever, but springs simply and only from the fact that *we* are the speakers. If *they* are speaking about us, exactly the same principle applies. It is purely the logical or conceptual point that when speaker A attributes some description to an alien group B, it is A's concept which determines the meaning of that description, whoever A is. If an African were to say (in his/her language here adequately translated), "Americans in their burial practices have insulted their ancestors and rejected their legitimate needs and wants", his/her remark would be equally misleading and false. Since we do not have quite the same concept of, much less belief in, the living-dead ancestor (which is not the same as either a ghost or a god), the claim makes no sense, or else is simply false. To reject our ancestors we would have to set out intentionally – knowing what they are, believing in them, and knowing about their needs – to refuse their demands, which we cannot do if we do not believe in, or even have the concept of, such ancestors.

Nonetheless, it is hard to remove the evaluative element in any cross-cultural description, and even though describing alien cultures in our terms is not necessarily ethnocentric in itself, there is always that tendency. Because any cross-cultural description involves an implied comparison between our culture and theirs, cross-cultural descriptions always involve the "politics" of commendatory or derogatory comparisons. Implied in any such comparison is always the unspoken idea that their practices or beliefs will or will not match up to our own most praiseworthy concepts or that they will or will not sink to the level of our own most scorned concepts. Obviously, many of our concepts imply that cultural values have a written language, or a science, or a complex social organisation, or a developed art form, or a system of formal education all these things are not just facts about some societies, but terms of praise for those who possess them and terms of shame for those who do not.

Now, having thoroughly politicised the entire discussion, it becomes virtually impossible to avoid this evaluative ranking and simply describe these cultures in a scientific, objective manner. For now, despite one's own intentions, whatever one says will inevitably be interpreted as praising or slighting the societies under investigation.

The difficulty of partial compliance is especially troublesome in the case of primitive art. Suppose we find that, on balance, it is mistaken to call such objects works of art, that upon closer investigation we find that, despite our own interest in such objects aesthetically and our willingness to treat them as artworks, it is simply false (or more nearly false than true) to attribute such attitudes to the people who made and used them – what then? Must we now take them out of the museums, galleries, art books, and art journals? Not at all. We must simply make it clear that we are shifting to a partial and therefore weaker sense of "work of art" in which we, the aesthetic audience and consumer, determine the aesthetic context that qualifies the objects as works of art, rather than their makers. This would meet the first of our three criteria for a good cross-cultural description, but not the other two. In the *full* sense of the word, all three criteria must be met, but the term can also be used in a partial sense involving only the first of the three criteria.

This is not, of course, an entirely novel sense. We are already familiar with it in describing as art certain kinds of furniture, storage jars, eating utensils, driftwood, ordinary manufactured objects in Found and Dada art, such as hat racks, bicycle wheels, and so on. But what we must in that case reject is the idea that the makers of these objects are artists. So, even though we could continue to enjoy and discuss and collect such objects as artworks in this weakened sense, the conclusion would nonetheless have serious ramifications in the sense that it would deny to the vast majority of our fellow human beings any aesthetic appreciation, artistic production or critical sensibilities as regards art. It would also have the effect noted earlier of not taking seriously the claim that these are works of art. As we saw, whenever objects are designated art by alien decree they tend to be considered art only half-heartedly and somewhat hypocritically.

But now, having laid out in painstaking detail the truly awesome dimensions of the problem, let us at least suggest a solution. Is it appropriate to call African wood carvings and other examples of primitive artefacts works of art in the full sense?

We have argued for a modified objectivist approach to cross-cultural studies, embodying the three criteria outlined earlier, and rejecting both the purely subjectivist approach and the purely objectivist approach. We reject subjectivist accounts which describe *their* culture from *our* point of view without regard to their point of view, ones, that is, which meet only the first of the above three criteria. But neither can we accept the purely objectivist approach of describing the matter entirely in their terms, especially when the description is being offered in our language. Thus, we must reject descriptions based on the second criterion alone (where Q is an expression in B's language and the description is in A's language), since this will be either unintelligible or uninteresting or both to the speakers of A's language in which the description is offered.

In the modified objectivist approach embodied in the three criteria above, we attempt so far as possible to translate their conceptual terminology into our conceptual terminology. This involves the two-step process of finding out empirically how the indigenous society regards the phenomenon in question and then *conceptually* deciding which of our concepts is the best translation into our language and conceptual framework. If I say that the carver is an artist creating an artwork, I imply, among other things, that within his/her society some creativity is involved in such projects, that the object will be appreciated for itself, for its beauty, that it will have some aesthetic value apart from its immediate use, and so on, because this is what the expression "work of art" means in my language (and since I am the speaker). Whether these implications are true is a matter of fact that must be determined by empirical investigation in the field.

But this gives us a practical way of answering difficult cross-cultural questions, such as, "Is primitive art really art?" First we define our own concept of art as clearly as we can in terms of empirically observable traits (e.g. the carver is respected for his/her originality), and then we look to see if those empirically observable traits obtain (e.g. whether the indigenous people praise the carver in terms of his/her originality, inventiveness, or not). And that brings us at last into an empirical realm where issues can be more or less decided. Having defined our own concepts in terms of various beliefs and behavioural attitudes and dispositions, our problem becomes one of looking to see if the group we are describing does or does not share the concepts in question judging by their beliefs and behavioural attitudes and dispositions. Only by moving in this way back and forth between the armchair and the field can we hope to answer the question, "Is primitive art art?"

I hope it is clear by now how my discussion of the study of so-called primitive art illustrates what I suggested at the beginning concerning recommendations for multicultural art education. First, and most important, despite all its admitted problems, we must not give up the attempt to encourage our students to try to understand cultures other than our own, especially those that have had major influences on American culture, though not limited to these. Put another way, we must not allow ourselves to be so overwhelmed by the enormous difficulties of cross-cultural understanding that we retreat into divisive and self-serving unicultural studies of Hispanic culture by Hispanic-American students, Asian studies by Asian-American students, African studies by African-American students, and so on. My proposal is to face squarely the challenges of any cross-cultural study, admitting the unavoidable comparative nature of any cross-cultural study, with its inevitable and ever-present risk of ethnocentric bias, and finally to embrace what hermeneutics explains as the mutual give and take in any cross-cultural studies, whereby we open ourselves as far as possible to an alien culture which we nonetheless realise, despite our best intentions and efforts to the contrary, we are inevitably interpreting according to our own cultural bias. It is not, after all, unlike getting to know another person: we try to understand the other person from his or her unique standpoint though we know we can do this only by understanding the other person in terms of our own experience. Do we ever really know another person? Perhaps not, at least not completely; but would we want to give up the effort? In the end, what, really, is the alternative?

ON THE DISTINCTION BETWEEN MODERN AND TRADITIONAL AFRICAN AESTHETICS

GENE BLOCKER

The tradition of the "aesthetic attitude", or "aesthetic experience", beginning in the eighteenth century and continuing through the first half of the twentieth century, has been called into question from many sides by analytic philosophers such as George Dickie, who doubt the very existence of a peculiarly aesthetic experience, by neo-Marxist and other political theorists who accept the existence of traditional aesthetic experience but reject its apolitical pretence as a dishonest politics supporting the dominance of the *status quo*, and by postmodernists, including deconstructionists, who reject the pretence of artworks, aesthetically experienced, to symbolically interpret the world for us. In my own recent work considering the aesthetic experience of so-called primitive peoples (those who made and used traditional African wood carvings and pre-Columbian meso-American ceramic objects, for example), and its contrast with the aesthetic experience appropriate to modern nation-states of the so-called developed world, I have come to see new, more compelling ways to defend the aesthetic attitude in a broader cultural context as a socially instituted kind of experience of works of art and objects of natural beauty that is peculiarly appropriate to a particular developmental stage of modernist culture. My approach is therefore developmental and evolutionary, urging that modern cultures arise from more primitive ones and that, correspondingly, the modern aesthetic experience evolves from a more primitive aesthetics.

Let us first look briefly at some of the more important implications of aesthetic experience for modern culture. The immediate consequence of the impersonal and non-utilitarian posture of the aesthetic attitude was to isolate the object of this aesthetic attention from its mundane, physical surroundings, transforming it into a self-contained whole, unconnected with the rest of the world, except, as we shall see shortly, symbolically. This is what Sartre calls the "unrealising" function of aesthetic experience and what is often referred to as the "willing suspension of disbelief". To experience a novel, painting or play aesthetically, one must realise that the events represented in these artworks are fictional, that is, they are not contiguous with ordinary space-time physical reality. The unrealising function of aesthetic experience is closely related to its disinterestedness. To say that aesthetic perception is not concerned with practical consequences is just to say that in aesthetic experience we do not perceive the object as a real object with real consequences for us. It is the function of the arena, the picture frame, and the pedestal to transform and elevate the object from its ordinary space-time, which also ensures the adoption of the aesthetic attitude on the part of the audience, who may interact with and participate in the aesthetic fiction or semblance, but only in aesthetically appropriate ways, whether as mere spectators, passively contemplating the aesthetic object, or more actively participating but within carefully defined aesthetic boundaries, separating fiction from reality. One may hiss and boo the villain, but one must not rush onto the stage to disarm him/her; one may weep for the hero's mortal wounds, but one must not call the doctor.

As a result of this attitude of detachment and disinterestedness, the aesthetic attitude is generally more reflective or contemplative in orientation, and as a result of that, the object of aesthetic attention is generally understood symbolically to refer to meanings and significant content of a quite general though undefined sort. When I look at a tree, for example, from a pragmatic point of view, to see how much firewood it will yield, I see that object simply as an instance of the category *tree*. It is just a particular instance of a tree. But when I disengage myself from such practical concerns and look at the tree for its own sake, then, as Schopenhauer points out, my attention may be drawn to the general symbolic significance of the tree – as the link, for example, between heaven and earth, or the monumentality, quiet dignity, strength, and stability of the tree, or its protective aspect. It is no longer simply a member of the category *tree,* but an object that seems to partake of quite general and far-ranging meaning and significance.

Only by the unrealising act of psychic distance, in which beliefs are temporarily suspended, can one object come to represent something that it is not, especially where the object is concrete and what it represents is something quite general, such as rebirth and renewal, or the dialectical tension between creative and destructive forces. The epistemological paradox of the aesthetic attitude is that one is simultaneously aware of both the symbol and of what it symbolises. The aesthetic attitude is composed of two contradictory states of mind held together in a dynamic tension: consciousness of the art object as existing in its own right and also as fused with and participating in what it symbolises. The mystery of representation and impersonation is this simultaneous belief and disbelief in their identity and distinction. Those lines on paper become a generalised human face, but only if I know full well that they are not a face but only lines drawn on paper. The actor becomes Hamlet only if I know he is an actor playing the part of Hamlet.

The emotional interest in an object at this symbolic level can be very intense, indeed, especially because it involves an ordering of experience that is quite impossible in the chaos and confusion of everyday life. This symbolic meaning also transcends the concerns of a particular regional or ethnic group. Although we no longer worship Dionysus, we can still enjoy the plays of Sophocles and Euripides, which were once a part of that worship. We continue to appreciate the tragedy because our aesthetic attitude has detached it from its religious context and thereby transformed it into a potent, cross-cultural symbol that it was not for the original audience.

In precisely the same way, potent symbols in Soyinka's plays of Obatala and Ogun – Yoruba gods of creation and of war – transcend the ethnic borders of Yorubaland and become available on an aesthetic level to all Nigerians, whether Ibo, Tiv, Ishan or Hausa, as well as to non-Nigerians around the world. Furthermore, once the aesthetic dimension has emerged as an independent entity, it becomes possible to deliberately, self-consciously *create* symbolic meaning in art. Once we see that from within the gaze of the aesthetic attitude ordinary physical objects from everyday life take on symbolic meaning, it becomes possible to isolate, select, reorganise, and manipulate such symbolic content in deliberately constructed patterns; and these patterns will possess greater aesthetic intensity than objects of natural beauty because they are more tightly organised and unified. Thus, artists can create symbols that express and represent their society if they are able to disengage themselves from that society and look on it from a detached perspective.

Of course, the problem with the experience of aesthetic distance is that it appears excessively narrow and elitist, excluding any appreciation of art and beauty in most of the world's cultures – and even in European culture before the eighteenth century, or, at the earliest, the Renaissance. The reason most societies are excluded from this definition is that their interest in art is submerged in various nonaesthetic concerns, including religious, ceremonial, military, agricultural concerns, and so on. The Chiwara antelope carvings of the ancient Bambara of Ivory Coast, for example, which today are so highly prized as art by European and contemporary collectors, were originally made to be used in ritual masquerade dances in the fields each year just before planting in celebration of the original ancestor spirits who taught the Bambara the arts of farming. Here the aesthetic dimension of sculpture, music, and dance is submerged within a predominantly religious and agricultural concern.

But, of course, to say that something is not exclusively or predominantly aesthetic is not to say that it is not aesthetic at all. If the aesthetic is a dimension of human experience, then we would expect to find it mixed in varying degrees with many other sorts of activities. It is true that in *our* society the mixture of nonaesthetic elements in the enjoyment of works of art is regarded as an inappropriate distraction not sanctioned by our collective aesthetic institutions and conventions, as opposed to primitive societies, where such mixture is the approved norm. Nonetheless, it does not follow that the aesthetic is entirely absent from the primitive perception: nor that it is entirely disapproved within the primitive society. Nor does it follow from the fact that the aesthetic is *different* from the religious or moral or ceremonial that it is necessarily or usually *opposed* to them. Obviously, in many cases the aesthetic quality of the accompanying music, dance, and plastic sculpture will *enhance* the religious import.

Many conceptual confusions and pitfalls surrounding the relationship of functional and aesthetic elements need to be clearly sorted out. Once these confusions are sorted out, I think it will be clear, as John Dewey said, that the aesthetic is a dimension in all human experience, present in varying forms and degrees in all peoples and in all societies, and that, as such, aesthetic experience is not the exclusive prerogative of Western or European cultures. At the same time, I think it will also become clear that in the degree of its mixture with nonaesthetic elements, different *types* of aesthetics are possible. In this sense we will try to define the nature of a primitive aesthetics as a significantly different subset within the broader category or genus of aesthetics proper.

As we have seen, primitive artefacts are not made aesthetically *as* works of art. From this widely accepted fact, many writers on primitive art have concluded that traditional Africans and other primitive peoples have no aesthetic sense, no critical standards of taste, and no sense of the artistic worth of their own art. In my view this conclusion is unwarranted and represents a serious misunderstanding both of the nature of primitive art and also of our own aesthetic experience. In this article, I argue that having an aesthetic sense is not synonymous with, and does not require the socially accepted institution, which we know, of adopting in art contexts that degree of aesthetic perception that defines the modern aesthetic attitude, and that, while primitive peoples do not possess the latter, they most certainly do have aesthetic sensibilities. Similarly, I will argue that possessing critical standards for judging works of art is not synonymous with, and does not require, a theory of art criticism, and that while primitive peoples do not possess the latter, they do have and use critical standards in judging artworks.

These different types of aesthetic expression represent stages in a hierarchy in the sense that the latter presupposes the former, but not the reverse. There can be no verbalisation of preference without some initial preference to start with. Nor can there be any institutionalised isolation of aesthetic experience from other types of experience unless there first exists some aesthetic experience to start with. Nor can social institutions select among preferences, channelling preferences into socially approved "good taste", unless there are first preferences from which to accept and reject. And until there is verbalisation, there can be no judgemental standards or criteria, and until standards appear, there can be no attempt to reconcile and order them, an effort that eventually leads to theories of art.

The fact that one level of aesthetic awareness is not present does not imply that none are present. The attempt to define the aesthetic attitude, as we have seen, is the attempt to locate that part of any experience that is aesthetic and discover what makes it so. It is not the discovery of a totally new kind of experience that is always and exclusively aesthetic and nothing else. Most aesthetic experience with artworks and objects of natural beauty is mixed with other elements and concerns. In Western aesthetic history, it is true that certain institutions surrounding the notion of fine art have indeed developed that foster the relatively sharper focusing on, and therefore greater concentration of, the aesthetic element as the accepted norm in the enjoyment of works of art. Nonetheless, as anyone with an interest in art surely knows, most encounters with works of art of whatever kind are always mixed, and the socially accepted norm is generally just that – an idealised norm.

It does not follow, therefore, that experiences that are not *primarily* aesthetic contain *no* aesthetic elements. Aesthetic and nonaesthetic elements need not be contradictory in every case but may often complement and enhance one another. Both a crucifix and a fragment of a saint's thigh bone are objects of religious worship, but the former requires an aesthetic character, which the latter does not. To convey its religious message, the crucifix must be carved or rendered to *look* a certain way, whereas a fragment of the saint's skeletal remains of any shape, size or colour whatever will serve equally well. Consequently, the crucifix may fail in a way the bone cannot through its visual appearance. As a result, the crucifix becomes a better candidate for becoming an art object within the perspective of the aesthetic attitude because it already *has* an aesthetic aspect, which the bone fragment does not, to be abstracted for aesthetic contemplation. Similarly, the music of the mass must *sound* solemn and profound if it is to accomplish its religious and devotional function.

This same principle seems to apply, at least in some cases, in primitive art. Certainly, there is evidence that it operates in much, though not all, West African art. Masks and figures worn atop the head, paraded or carried in ritual dances, will often only work if they have been fashioned to look the part. The top portion of a Yoruba Gelede mask, for example, is designed to entertain and thus pacify evil witches, but if the masks are not visually entertaining, they can hardly be expected to do the job. This aesthetically subservient function would not be present or required, for example, in a stone fetish – that is, an ordinary stone covered with a thick patina of blood, oil, and other "medicines", which can have any shape or colour whatever and indeed is usually not seen at all but, like the fragment of the saint's thigh bone, is enclosed in a shrine or other ritual container. In many, though not all, cases of religious art, then, an aesthetic role is present, and while it may be *secondary* to a religious function, it is nonetheless *necessary* to that predominantly religious function.

Finally, granted an underlying root-aesthetic concept common to both primitive aesthetics and our own aesthetic point of view, what differences exist between the two, and what are the strengths and weaknesses of each? In general, the main difference between the modern aesthetic attitude of the West and the aesthetic sense of primitive cultures concerns the *relative* ability and desire of separating aesthetic and nonaesthetic elements originally joined together, and detaching the aesthetic more or less from the rest as one element having a character and value of its own. This relative separation is what makes it possible for the Buddhist to appreciate the crucifix; the atheist, the B Minor Mass, and the European, the awe, terror, and dignity of a tribal African mask. In addition to the ability of the aesthetic point of view to transform the object from a piece of religious paraphernalia into a symbol of far-ranging meaning to be contemplated and reflected on, the other great advantage of the modern aesthetic point of view is that it is not limited to a particular sociopolitical, tribal-religious setting. As Europeans increasingly begin to admire African art aesthetically, Africans' ritual participation in their own art is steadily declining. At the same time, however, with increasing education, Africans themselves are more and more adopting the modern aesthetic attitude toward their own art, with the result that *aesthetic* interest in their own art is gathering considerable momentum, especially in the ongoing search for "roots". In the rush to modernise, the tightly knit fabric of traditional tribal life disintegrates. Because the art is inseparable at that level from the religious and social pattern, the ritualistic art succumbs to the overall pattern of tribal life. Thus, the strength of the primitive aesthetic – its holistic integrity – proves to be its greatest weakness.

Yet other factors are at work in West Africa and other centres of primitive art in New Guinea, Northwest America, and the South Sea islands, which encourage the development of aesthetic consciousness, that in turn gives primitive art a new hold on life – albeit in the museum and on the stage rather than around the communal fire. The weakness of primitive aesthetics is precisely the strength of the modern aesthetic attitude. And it is this aesthetic attitude, both in the West and among the educated elite in developing countries, which ironically ensures the survival of primitive art. As Africans, for example, relinquish their tribal identities in search of a new national identity, they turn increasingly to the university-trained young artists, such as Olayinka, Bruomah, Fakeye, and Twins Seven Seven, to inspire them with a new sense of national unity. Much of the new art in West African cities tries to recapture and preserve motifs of the tribal past, but self-consciously, deliberately, selecting and abstracting from the ritual practices of different secret societies and, indeed, from different tribes, which are then mixed and woven together into a new entertaining "art" product, self-consciously projecting a new, positive sense of national unity and regional pride.

In short, the new art can only succeed *as art* within a modern aesthetic consciousness, and primitive art survives only when it ceases to be the art of a primitive society. In much the same way, recently independent countries are making an effort to collect representative examples of the tribal art of their past for display in newly constructed art museums in the larger cities. The art is displayed to be viewed aesthetically, and its audiences come to view these pieces, in the museum and in the theatre, much as Western spectators do, as symbols of generalised aspects of their past to be contemplated aesthetically as sources of national and regional pride. The same carving can go through various stages from a predominantly religious icon to a work of art. The Egungun mask, for example, was once used as part of a sacred funerary ritual in which the spirit of the deceased spoke to surviving members of his/her family. Years later, the family converted to Christianity, and the mask was demoted to the status of a false idol, removed in shame, and hidden from view. At this point, the object could have been sold through a Muslim trader to a foreign art collector, or even destroyed as an act of faith in the new religion. But in this particular case, the piece remained in the family, largely forgotten, much as our grandparents' possessions often moulder away in our attics and basements, ignored and forgotten for decades until they are rediscovered, often quite by accident. Many years later, after the country has become independent, a new emphasis by the Ministry of Culture is begun that changes the status of the mask once more, this time elevating it to the rank of a work of art and a national treasure as part of the programme of nation-building to instil feelings of pride and nationality in the people. And so the mask is dusted off and taken to the regional museum, where it is proudly placed on display for the enjoyment and education of museum-goers.

As we have indicated, the result of the impact of European civilisation on primitive societies was, among other things, to undermine the very fragile basis of primitive culture, including, of course, primitive art, interlocked as it was in the total fabric of family, agricultural, military, political, and religious aspects of primitive society. But as religious interest in primitive art by the indigenous peoples declined, two interesting things happened. Firstly, as we have already pointed out, these same primitive peoples began to take a more aesthetic interest in their own art and to plan for its protection from exportation, and for exhibition in newly constructed museums in the emerging independent nations formerly under colonial rule.

But the other thing that happened was equally interesting. Under the impact of European culture, some of these primitive peoples began to evolve new art forms within a newly emerging modern aesthetic point of view. Newly colonialised primitive peoples began to respond to the interest that their European masters were taking in their primitive, indigenous traditional crafts. As a result, in many cases, instead of declining, as might have been expected, modern versions of traditional art thrived under colonial administrations. By the turn of the present century, native Navaho blanket making had become a dying art. It was cheaper and easier for Native Americans to purchase brightly printed wool blankets from local "Anglo" traders than it was to spin, dye, and weave the wool – all by hand – into the traditional blankets. But at this critical moment, American tourists, settlers, and collectors expressed a great interest in these increasingly rare blankets as works of "primitive art", and what is probably more important, expressed their willingness to pay considerable sums (though seemingly small by today's standards) for the older blankets. Older tribal members who still remembered how to make such blankets were sought out and encouraged to re-enter the manufacture of the blankets in the traditional manner, but this time for export trade to tourists and "Anglo" collectors. Similarly, New Mexico traditional Amerindian pottery was rescued from a total replacement by cheaper metal and later plastic pots by an enthusiastic tourist market willing to pay the price for authentic "Indian-made" articles. Similarly, in

Africa, carvers were encouraged to produce more and more wood carvings, not for their declining religious and ceremonial use in the indigenous society, but for export to the lucrative European market.

In many cases, this resulted in what was effectively new art forms. Despite the insistence of the European market on "authenticity", European preferences for some kinds of native art and for some individual pieces over others inevitably acted as a filter, influencing carvers and potters to produce more of what was wanted and less of what was being rejected. Eventually, a stable style developed within each of these transformed primitive art styles. It is only by comparing the expensive but beautiful New Mexican Amerindian blankets and pottery today with those made a hundred years ago that we can see this gradual evolution toward a steady and flourishing contemporary Indian tourist market.

In the early 1950s, a British missionary to Nigeria, Father Carroll, became concerned with what he correctly perceived were clear signs of the imminent demise of traditional Yoruba wood carving. Feeling some responsibility for the missionaries' role in this decline, Father Carroll sought to reverse the trend by re-establishing traditional carving centres in Nigeria. Under his direction, Lamidi Fakeye brought his nephews, Joseph and Ganiyu Fakeye, into the carving workshop, and their work, especially that of Lamidi Fakeye, now teaching in the School of Art at the University of Ife, became internationally well-known. Retaining key elements of the traditional Yoruba style, they expanded the traditional repertoire to include such utilitarian objects as bas relief doors, chests, tables, wall hangings, and to work in beautiful West African woods, such as Iroko and African mahogany, whose fine grain is not covered with vegetable dyes, as were the older sacred carvings, but, like modern European wood sculptures, preserved as part of the total aesthetic effect. Unlike the older, sacred carvings, the newer works are more concerned with secular, even anecdotal subjects depicting typical everyday scenes of village life. The carving has also become more polished and commercially more refined. Nonetheless, the style remains broadly and recognisably Yoruba. These works are not only sold to a growing tourist market abroad but are seen prominently displayed throughout Nigeria in hospitals, banks, universities, and government buildings.

In other cases, totally new artistic crafts have been introduced by Europeans, both to preserve local art and craft traditions and also to provide a means of economic support for the indigenous communities: thorn carvings in Nigeria, stone carvings among the Eskimo, silver and turquoise jewellery introduced by the Spanish in Mexico in the sixteenth century (as well as various lacquered wood and glazed ceramic styles introduced by Spanish missionaries throughout central Mexico and the Southwestern United States), and glass bead weaving introduced by the French missionaries among the Native North Americans, to name only a few. Sometimes this was more a matter of substituting new materials for older materials but also frequently introducing completely new art forms. Soon each became a stable art style entirely naturalised within that particular group of people and an expected source of income. In some cases, as with the slate carving among the Haida of North America, the new art was developed entirely for a foreign tourist trade. In other cases, as with the glass bead art of the Plains Indians and the silver and turquoise jewellery among the Indians of Mexico and the American Southwest, the new art became a source and a symbol of family wealth among the indigenous peoples themselves. Or, in the case of the lacquer and ceramic styles introduced by the Spanish missionaries in the sixteenth century, the new art forms became a permanent part of the everyday culture of the local people.

Thus, we can distinguish the relatively more integrated aesthetics of primitive cultures from the relatively more detached and abstracted and self-conscious aesthetics of the modern aesthetic attitude that evolves out of the former. Each has opposing strengths and weakness. The strength of the primitive aesthetics lies in its greater contextual integrity and audience involvement and participation, whereas the strength of the modern aesthetic attitude rests on its more contemplative and hence universalising, non-parochial, symbolic nature. Contemporary West African countries provide interesting case studies of the transformation of the one into the other, with all the negative and positive connotations which that transformation inevitably involves.

Certainly, it does not follow that the greater the isolation of the aesthetic, the better. My interest has been to trace the development or emergence of the relatively more aesthetic from the relatively more functional, but this does not necessarily imply progress. Indeed, we have just distinguished between a relatively pure aesthetics and a relatively mixed aesthetics with opposing strengths and weaknesses. Where the aesthetic element is more thoroughly mixed with non-aesthetic concerns, as in the more traditional societies of West Africa a hundred years ago, there is a much greater sense of social and cultural integration and participation of the individual in the total cultural milieu than in the relatively pure aesthetic contexts, such as Europe since the eighteenth century, whose culture is more fragmented, disjointed, and the individual is relatively more alienated than in the former.

The isolation of the aesthetic also results in a semantic depletion of the religious beliefs, which tend to be taken less literally and seriously and more symbolically as the aesthetic dimension gains the upper hand. The religiously potent crucifix of Ibeji now merely decorates a study or museum shelf. On the other hand, the greater the aesthetic purity, the greater the possibilities for deliberately creating universal, cross-cultural symbolic meaning. Here, there is less literal belief but greater scope for self-conscious reflection and conscious manipulation of symbols.

Thus, the modern aesthetic attitude is more suited to pluralistic societies of the modern type in which individual freedom of expression, religion, and life-style is encouraged, and ethnic and tribal integrities give way to national objectives. In other words, whereas the more integrative, participatory aesthetics of the mixed mode is ideally suited to the tribal setting, a relatively pure aesthetic attitude is needed to forge national symbols of identity and aspiration in modern developing nation states.

Finally, one must be careful not to exaggerate the differences between traditional African and modern European aesthetic attitudes, as if they marked mutually exclusive domains. It is frequently claimed, for example, that Western aesthetics is a cerebrally detached concern with art for art's sake, whereas African aesthetics involves total participation and immersion. Both sides of the comparison are mistaken; the differences, as we have tried to show, are not categorical but a matter of degree. It would be as serious a mistake to ignore the element of aesthetic distance present in African traditional aesthetics as it would be to ignore the existence of audience participation in modern European aesthetics.

REFERENCES

Anderson, R. 1990. *Calliope's sisters: A comparative study of philosophies of art.* Englewood Cliffs: Prentice Hall.

Appiah, K.A. 1992. *In my father's house: Africa in the philosophy of culture.* New York: Oxford University Press.

Berman, E. 1983. *Art and artists in South Africa.* Cape Town: Balkema.

Berndtson, A. 1969. *Art, expression and beauty.* New York: Holt, Rinehart & Wilson.

Blocker, H.G. 1991. "Is primitive art art?" *The Journal of Aesthetic education,* 24(4):87–89.

Blocker, H.G. 1995. "On the distinction between modern and traditional African aesthetics", in A.G. Mosley (ed.), *African philosophy: selected readings.* Englewood Cliffs, N.J.: Prentice Hall, 1994:428–438.

Busia, K.A. 1968 (1951). *The position of the chief in the modern political system of Ashanti.* London: New Impression.

Du Plessis, A. 1993: "The Cape Town Triennial: What price democracy?" in *Revised frameworks and extended boundaries in research and education: Proceedings of the 8th Annual Conference of the South African Association of Art Historians.* Pretoria: Unisa Press, 1993: 45–49.

El Hadji, S. 1995. "Objects of performance", in J. Havell (ed.), *Seven stories about modern art in Africa.* Whitechapel: Flammarion.

Geers, K. 1996. *The Star,* July 1, 1996.

Gombrich, E.H. 1977. *Art and illusion: A study in the psychology of pictorial representation.* London: Phaidon.

Hanfling, O. 1995. "Art, artifact and function." *Philosophical Investigations,* 18(1):31–48.

Harper, P. 1981. "The inter-relation of the arts in the performance of masquerades as an expression of oral tradition in Nigeria." *Black Orpheus,* 4(1):1–6.

Hegel, G. 1975 (1968). *Lectures on the history of world philosophy.* Vol. 1. London: Cambridge University Press.

Jahn, J. 1961 (1958). *Muntu: An outline of the new African culture.* New York: Grove Press.

Kamber, R. 1993. "A modest proposal for defining a work of art." *British Journal of Aesthetics,* 33(4):313–320.

Mbiti, J.S. 1969. *African religions and philosophy.* London: Heinemann.

McCaskie, T. C. 1986. "Komfo Anokye of Asante: Meaning and history in an African society." *Journal of African History,* 27:319–346.

McCaskie, T. C. 1989. "Death and the Asantehene: A historical meditation." *Journal of African History,* 30(3):417–444.

Misch, G. 1950. *The dawn of philosophy.* London: Bern Francke.

Okeke, U. 1982 (1933). *Art in development: A Nigerian perspective.* Nimo: Nigerian Documentation Centre, Asele Institute.

Onyewuenyi, I.C. 1976/77. "Is there an African philosophy?" *Journal of African Studies,* 3:513–528.

Onyewuenyi, I.C. 1984. "Traditional African aesthetics." *International philosophical quarterly,* September 1984:237–244.

Opuku, K.A. 1982. "The world view of the Akan." *Tarikh,* 7(2):48–73.

Parker, E. and Steele-Hamme, N. 1995. "Morality, art and African philosophy: a response to Wiredu", in A.G. Mosley (ed.), *African philosophy: selected readings.* Englewood Cliffs, N.J.: Prentice Hall. 1995:407–420.

Phillips, T. 1995. *Africa: The art of a continent.* London: The Royal Academy of Arts.

Powell, I. 1995. *Ndebele: A people and their art.* Cape Town: Hirst & Carter.

Runes, D.D. 1966. *Dictionary of philosophy.* Littlefield: Adams.

Senghor, L.S. 1963. "Negritude and African socialism", in K. Kirkwood (ed.), *St Anthony's papers,* no. 15, Oxford, 9–22.

Tempels, P. 1959. *Bantu philosophy.* Paris: Présence Africaine.

Uchendu, V. 1965. *The Igbo of southeast Nigeria.* New York: Holt.

Van Roebbroeck, L. 1993. "Urban 'black art' in South African literature: A discourse of otherness." *Revised frameworks and extended boundaries in research and education: Proceedings of the 8th Annual Conference of the South African Association of Art Historians.* Pretoria: Unisa Press, 1993:50–64.

Vogel, S. 1991. *Africa explores: 20th-century African art.* New York: New York Center for African Art.

Ward, W.E.F. 1948. *A history of Ghana.* London: Allen & Unwin.

Williamson, S. 1989. *Resistance art in South Africa.* Cape Town: David Philip.

Wiredu, K. 1980. *Philosophy and an African culture.* Cambridge: Cambridge University Press.

Wiredu, K. 1984. "How not to compare African thought with Western thought", in R.A. Wright (ed.), *African philosophy.* Lanham: University Press of America, 1984:150–157.

Wiredu, K. 1991. "On defining African philosophy", in T. Serequeberhan (ed.), *African Philosophy.* New York: Paragon, 1991:87–110.

Wiredu, K. 1992/93. "African philosophical tradition: A case study of the Akan." *Philosophical Forum,* 24(1–3):35–62.

Wiredu, K. 1995a. "Custom and morality: A comparative analysis of some African and Western conceptions of morals", in O. Oladipo (ed.), *Conceptual decolonization in African philosophy.* Ibadan: Hope, 1995:33–52.

Wiredu, K. 1995b. "The need for conceptual decolonization in African philosophy", in O. Oladipo (ed.), *Conceptual decolonization in African philosophy.* Ibadan: Hope, 1995:22–32.

CHAPTER NINE

African and European Philosophising: Senghor's "Civilization of the Universal"

AUGUSTINE SHUTTE

1. INTRODUCTION

I have become convinced that African insights into our humanity can serve as an important corrective to the dominant forms of contemporary European philosophy. This implies on the one hand that African insights should be introduced into so-called European philosophical debates and discussions, and on the other that methodological problems facing such inter-cultural discussion should be addressed. One such attempt at philosophising across cultural borders is that of Léopold Senghor of Senegal who uses the European philosophy in which he has been trained (French in his case) to give contemporary expression to insights inherited from his African past which he considers to have a universal value. I have found this attempt particularly instructive and take it as something of a model. It seems to me that the history of Africa makes linking African and European philosophy unavoidable; therefore, we cannot attend to African philosophy without attending to this link and how it can be developed. I shall here consider an approach of creative interpenetration.

2. LÉOPOLD SENGHOR: A PIONEER

Senghor's thought develops against the background of French colonialism in Africa. That situation determines the ultimate aims of his intellectual life. He wishes most of all to overcome the loss of identity suffered by Africans due to a history of slavery, colonialism, and racism. And so he argues first of all for political independence. But this is only a first step towards a more comprehensive freedom of spirit which he wants for himself and his fellow Africans. The second step is to initiate a cultural rebellion against the French policy of cultural assimilation of their colonies to metropolitan France. To this end his main intellectual work is to define and foster the idea of Negritude which he defines as

> the whole complex of civilised values – cultural, economic, social and political – which characterise the black peoples, or, more precisely, the Negro-African world (Senghor 1963:11).

What these values are we shall presently see. Here it is important to note Senghor's reasons for going to work in this way.

His main reason is his conviction that traditional African culture has something of great and unique value to offer to a future "Civilization of the Universal" (Senghor 1963:9) which he recognises as a necessity if there is to be peace between nations and the gap between developed and undeveloped nations is to be overcome. Though deeply indebted to it, Senghor is, as we shall see, extremely critical of contemporary European culture, and feels that it needs the help that Africa can give. This Negritude is able to supply, as a kind of complement to European ideas and values; it will make up something that is presently lacking. On the other hand, Senghor is quite clear that Africa needs what Europe has to offer – not only in the realm of science and technology and the organisation of society. New developments in European scientific thinking and philosophy provide precisely the intellectual tools suitable for developing the idea of Negritude in a systematic and detailed way. Negritude is not simply an archaeology of ancient values but a new creation out of traditional materials; thus it needs modern tools.

I now propose to explain briefly Senghor's main criticisms of European culture and thought, before setting out in some detail how he uses particular developments in European philosophy and science, especially the work of Teilhard de Chardin, to articulate his conception of Negritude to the full. In the course of this I hope to give a clear idea of the characteristics of Negritude as well as a more specific idea of how Senghor thinks this will help towards the creation of a "Civilization of the Universal".

3. SENGHOR'S CRITIQUE OF EUROPE

Senghor's chief criticism of European culture is directed at its materialism. This is present in both capitalism and communism and makes a true understanding of persons and a truly human society impossible. Theoretical and practical materialism is born of the application of scientific reason to every aspect of life. Science is incapable of understanding even matter properly; it is quite inadequate for dealing with humanity. Marxism, though praised for its (limited) use of a new dialectical method, comes in for special criticism for its determinism and atheism, as also for its idea of class struggle. For Senghor the chief economic problem is

> not to eliminate classes by a class struggle within the nation; it is to bridge the gap between developed and undeveloped nations (1965:143).

The full force of Senghor's criticism of European culture appears, oddly enough, in connection with his account of that part of European culture, of European thought in particular, which he feels is indispensable for the development of Negritude, the way of thinking he calls "dialectical" (Senghor 1963:12ff.). We will now consider this in some detail.

Dialectics, in Senghor's terminology, is contrasted with the naive realism and positivism in philosophy that grew up in connection with the natural sciences, and reigned supreme as a theory of knowledge until mid-way through the nineteenth century. It produces a general attitude to reality that is the opposite of the mechanistic and deterministic materialism that it supplants:

> This new method . . . is born of the new scientific revolutions: relativity, wave mechanics, quantum theory, para-Euclidean geometry, theories of the discontinuous and undetermined. And also from the new philosophical revolutions: phenomenology, existentialism, Teilhardism (Senghor 1965:70).

In spite of this indication of the origins of the dialectical method, which admittedly does communicate the character of the method in its contemporary setting, Senghor usually locates its origin in the dialectics of Hegel. He then praises Marx and Engels for taking over the method, but criticises them for failing to grasp its full import and so remaining materialists. Indeed, it is precisely the scientific discoveries listed above that reveal the inadequacies of materialism:

> the discoveries since Engels's death – of relativity, quantum mechanics, wave mechanics, relations of uncertainty – have upset the materialist and determinist metaphysics of Marx and Engels (Senghor 1965:133).

Senghor (1965:72) quotes Bachelard with approval when he asserts that the "qualities of the scientific real are thus, primarily, the functions of our rational methods", understanding this to imply that scientists "suspect that the most minute particles of matter – photons, protons and electrons – have no reality outside of our thinking". He concludes that

> dialectics and consequently knowledge is essentially an *elan* of the mind. . . . How far we now are from the "reflection", from the "copy"! This is a dialectical turn that almost rehabilitates Hegel (Senghor 1965:150).

In general, dialectics, for Senghor, is any method of knowledge that involves the creative engagement of the subject with the object of his/her study. Speaking of a "knowledge by confrontation and intuition", Senghor (1965:72) states the following:

> It is essentially in the confrontation of the subject and the object – and *vice versa* – that one finds dialectical logic, the act of knowledge, which is at once theory and practice. By *theory* I mean the "categories" of understanding, and, by *practice*, the methods and techniques of the subject (Senghor 1965:150).

He stresses the active, creative character of knowing; it is a practical activity, not merely a contemplative gaze:

> to know an object, it no longer suffices to see it, to dissect it, to weigh it, even if one has the most perfect precision instruments. One must also touch it, penetrate it from the inside – so to speak – and finger it (Senghor 1965:71).

This understanding of knowledge is especially relevant to the knowledge of humanity and the human sciences:

> To know a human fact, psychological or social, no longer means to investigate it with the aid of statistics and graphs, but to live it: like the white man who, to understand the situation of Negro Americans, blackened his skin with a chemical product and worked as a Negro shoe-shine boy. This is what phenomenological or existential thought reveals, as it follows the path of Marxism and exceeds it while integrating it. In this school of thought, the real coincides with thought, the content of a statement coincides with the form in which it is expressed, philosophy blends with science, as art merges with existence, with life (Senghor 1965:71).

Understanding knowledge in this way clearly has implications of a metaphysical kind. The fact that one cannot separate the knower from the known entails that one cannot make a distinction between two kinds of reality, one purely mental, the other merely material. Similarly, the undermining of mechanism and determinism makes the world appear as "a discontinuous and perhaps undetermined reality" (Senghor 1965:70), the work and the home of freedom. The world as a whole, including humanity, is dynamic, developing – and human freedom is part of this dynamism of development.

For Senghor it is the discovery of this dialectical method for acquiring knowledge of ourselves and the world that has shown up the true inadequacies of European scientific-technological culture. On the other hand it is precisely this new way of thinking that makes a bridge between European culture and Negritude possible and provides the necessary intellectual tool for expressing the insights of traditional African thought in a systematic way.

Senghor goes on to argue that, on closer scrutiny

> this knowledge by confrontation and intuition is Negro-African knowledge. . . . From our ancestors we have inherited our own method of knowledge. Why should we change it when Europeans now tell us it is the very method of the twentieth century – and the most fruitful method? (1965:73).

Senghor then proceeds to describe the traditional African method of knowing in some detail:

> In contrast to the classic European, the Negro African does not draw a line between himself and the object; he does not hold it at a distance, nor does he merely look at it and analyse it. . . . He touches it, feels it, smells it. . . . Subjectively, at the tips of his sensory organs, his insect antennas, he discovers the Other. Immediately he is moved, going centrifugally from subject to object on the waves of the Other. . . . Thus the Negro African "sympathizes", feels with, abandons his personality to become identified with the Other, dies to be reborn in the Other. He does not assimilate; he is assimilated. He lives a common life with the Other; he lives in a symbiosis. . . . Subject and object are dialectically face to face in the very act of knowledge (1965:73–74).

To the objection that he is reducing knowledge to emotion and denying the role of reason, he replies as follows:

> However paradoxical it may seem, the vital force of the Negro African, his surrender to the object, is animated by reason. Let us understand each other clearly; it is not the reasoning-eye of Europe, it is the reason of the touch, better still, the reasoning-embrace, the sympathetic reason, more closely related to the Greek *logos* than to the Latin *ratio*. . . . European reasoning is analytical, discursive by utilization; Negro African reasoning is intuitive by participation (Senghor 1965:74).

Such descriptions echo, in a more poetic way, everything he has had to say about European dialectic. In his desire to provide a contemporary systematic philosophical account of the insights and values of Negritude, he therefore seizes on dialectic as the most suitable intellectual tool. Method of knowledge and conception of reality hang together; dialectic ought therefore to be capable of giving a contemporary account of the traditional African vision of the world and the values of human life. Of all European thinkers who use this method, Teilhard de Chardin, Senghor feels, comes closest to establishing a philosophical system that incorporates African insights.

4.   TRADITIONAL AFRICAN THOUGHT

Before I give an account of how Senghor uses de Chardin I will briefly enumerate what Senghor takes to be the important characteristics of traditional African thought that must be retained in any contemporary system of Negritude.

Like all African philosophers, he recognises certain ideas as fundamental to traditional African wisdom: that reality is force and the world a process of interplay between forces, that humanity is part of this universal field of force, that at bottom all force is alive, spiritual rather than material, that the individual's life and fulfilment are only to be found in community with others (a community that does not end at death), that morality is the development of natural tendencies to fuller being and more abundant life, and finally that all human life and world process is directed and empowered by a transcendent origin of life and force. The following two quotations give us an idea of Senghor's own attachment to this vision:

> Far back as one may go into his past, from the Northern Sudanese to the Southern Bantu, the African has always and everywhere presented a concept of the world which is diametrically opposed to the traditional philosophy of Europe. The latter is essentially static, objective, dichotomous; it is, in fact, dualistic, in that it makes an absolute distinction between body and soul, matter and spirit. It is founded on separation and opposition, on analysis and conflict. The African, on the other hand, conceives the world, beyond the diversity of its forms, as a fundamentally mobile yet unique reality that seeks synthesis. . . . This reality is being in the ontological sense of the word, and it is life force. For the African, matter in the sense the Europeans understand it, is only a system of signs which translates the single reality of the universe: being, which is spirit, which is life force. Thus, the whole universe appears as an infinitely small, and at the same time infinitely large, network of life forces which emanate from God and end in God, who is the source of all life forces. It is He who vitalizes and devitalizes all other beings, all the other life forces (1966:4).
>
> Negritude . . . as a complex of civilized values, is traditionally socialist in character. . . . It is a community based society . . . communal, not collectivist. We are concerned here, not with a mere collection of individuals, but with people conspiring together, *con-spiring* in the basic Latin sense, united among themselves even to the very centre of their being, communing through their ancestors with God, who is the Centre of all centres (1963:16).

There is nothing new in this inventory of the characteristics of Negritude. What is new in Senghor's contemporary synthesis, however, is his application of the traditional wisdom far beyond the traditional situation to take in the whole international scene, and the future as well as the present.

Combining the African ideas, especially those of community, of morality, as the drive to fuller being, and God as the source and goal of all life force, Senghor develops a theory of the tendency of all peoples to communicate, to merge, and eventually to become a universal community. This is what he understands by African socialism; he calls it "the Civilization of the Universal":

> The means of socialism transcend mere physical comfort, even on the national level; they are already personal *values*, values of the fuller being. . . . Today, ships and railways, aeroplanes and rockets, books and newspapers, radio and television, are all more than means to an international economy, they are *values* of the Civilization of the Universal (Senghor 1963:21).

Because of this, Senghor continues, Africa has a special part to play in the construction of this international community – a moral part:

> Beyond the objective of material well-being, Man aspires to fuller being, which is his end; beyond the satisfaction of his material needs, to that of his spiritual needs. Especially in black Africa and in the underdeveloped countries. Their peoples hunger not so much after American or Russian surpluses, as after independence, dignity, science and culture: after *Love-in-Union*. Try to imagine a world without love: between man and wife, in the family, in the nation, on the whole planet. Without this Love-in-Union, which is made real in God, through religion and art, the world would be ice-bound; we would be powerless to prevent the *taedium vitae* taking possession of our souls (1963:20–21).

The insights of traditional African thought into the human need for community and the values it entails are precisely what are needed to direct the world-wide process of socialisation.

This is the culmination of Senghor's theory of Negritude and his conception of the role that Africa can play in the future:

> I would like to emphasize at this point how much these characteristics of Negritude enable it to find its place in contemporary humanism, thereby permitting black Africa to make its contribution to the "Civilization of the Universal" which is so necessary in our divided but interdependent world of the second half of the 20th century. A contribution, first of all, to international co-operation, which must be and shall be the cornerstone of that civilization. It is through these virtues of Negritude that decolonization has been accomplished without too much bloodshed or hatred and that a positive form of co-operation based on "dialogue and reciprocity" has been established between former colonizers and colonized. It is through these virtues that there has been a new spirit at the United Nations, where the "no" and the bang of the fist on the table are no longer signs of strength. It is through these virtues that peace through co-operation could extend to South Africa, Rhodesia and the Portuguese colonies, if only the dualistic spirit of the Whites would open itself to dialogue (1966:5).

The "Civilization of the Universal" will not result from the extension of European culture across the globe, though that is certainly inevitable, but from what Senghor calls, in a striking phrase, "biological and psychic miscegenation", a process of entering into personal communion that African thought so well understands and values:

> The Civilization of the Universal, which will be the culmination of socialization, will not be European civilization – in either its Eastern or Western form – imposed by force, but a biological and psychic miscegenation, a *symbiosis* of the different civilizations (1963:22).

5. A SYNTHESIS: SENGHOR AND TEILHARD DE CHARDIN

We are now in a position to see how the work of Teilhard de Chardin enabled Senghor to gather the insights of traditional African thought into a coherent system and, what is more, to bring those insights to bear on the post-colonial predicament of Africa – and the world itself as well.

We have already become acquainted with Senghor's notion of dialectic as a method of knowledge more consonant with the scientific advances of the twentieth century. In his eyes Teilhard de Chardin, both as a scientist and as a philosopher, clearly exemplifies this method:

> It was on the basis of these discoveries, through a combination of logical coherence and amazing intuition, of scientific experiment and inner experience, that Pierre Teilhard de Chardin was able to transcend the traditional dichotomies with a new dialectic, to reveal to us the living throbbing unity of the universe (Senghor 1966:3).

In *The Phenomenon of man* Teilhard de Chardin describes the situation of modern scientists who are

> now beginning to realise that even the most objective of their observations are steeped in the conventions they adopted at the outset and by forms or habits of thought developed in the course of the growth of research . . . at the same time they realise that as the result of their discoveries, they are caught body and soul to the network of relationships they thought to cast upon things from outside: in fact they are caught in their own net. . . . Object and subject marry and mutually transform each other in the act of knowledge; and from now on man willy nilly finds his own image stamped on all he looks at (1959:32).

This does not however mean that we are locked up in our own subjectivity so that true knowledge is impossible. Teilhard de Chardin believes that the human viewpoint on reality is uniquely privileged. Our subjective viewpoint happens to coincide with the centre-point of the way things are in fact arranged so that we see them as they are:

> It is peculiar to man to occupy a position in nature at which the convergent lines are not only visual but structural. . . . By virtue of the quality and the biological properties of thought, we find ourselves situated at a singular point, at a ganglion which commands the whole fraction of the cosmos that is at present within reach of our experience. Man, the centre of perspective, is at the same time the centre of construction of the universe. And by expediency no less than by necessity, all science must be referred back to him (Teilhard de Chardin 1959:33).

The foundation of Teilhard de Chardin's work, for Senghor, was his overcoming of dualism and materialism through his theory of a single basic energy with two complementary aspects, both involved to a greater or lesser degree in every event in world process. Senghor argues as follows:

> On the basis then of the new discoveries, Teilhard de Chardin transcends the old dualism of the philosophers and the scientists, which Marx and Engels had perpetuated by giving matter precedence over the spirit. He advanced the theory that the stuff of the universe is not composed of two realities, but of a single reality in the shape of two phenomena; that there is not matter and energy, not even matter and spirit, but spirit-matter, just as there is space-time. Matter and spirit become a "network of relations", as the French philosopher, Bachelard, called it: energy, defined as a network of forces. In matter-spirit there is, therefore, only one energy, which has two aspects (1966:3).

Teilhard de Chardin called these two aspects of energy "radial" and "tangential" energy. These aspects are derived by him from analysing the process he calls "complexification". This is the process whereby over vast periods of time and through the effect of the interplay of large numbers, reality becomes more complex: basic elements are organised into atoms, which combine to become molecules, mega-molecules eventually being organised into cells, and so on through the ever increasing forms of biological life. For this process to occur there must be two distinct forms of energy, one of which is the principle of organisation within the unit, the other being the principle of interaction between units. The energy that organises, giving the organism a unity and centre, a "within", Teilhard de Chardin calls radial, visualising the organism as a sphere. The energy that merely relates and connects things to each other in a sheer aggregated plurality he calls tangential. Of the two the radial is the more fundamental, since the direction of world process is towards ever greater complexification; both are nevertheless necessary. In Teilhard de Chardin's own words,

> essentially, all energy is psychic in nature; but add that in each particular element this fundamental energy is divided into two distinct components: a tangential energy which links the element with all others of the same order (that is to say, of the same complexity and the same centricity) as itself in the universe; and a radial energy which draws it towards ever greater complexity and centricity – in other words forwards (1959:64).

The notion that all energy is fundamentally "psychic" sounds very odd, but becomes more intelligible when other aspects of Teilhard de Chardin's thought are taken into account, in particular the connection he postulates between complexity and consciousness in his so-called "Law of complexity-consciousness". According to this law, the more complex, the more organised, a thing is, the more "centred" it will be, (the more distinct will be its "within"), and hence, beyond a certain level of complexity, the more conscious. Thus, from the beginning, the energy of the universe contains within it "psychic" potential. As Teilhard de Chardin states,

> [t]he degree of concentration of a consciousness varies in inverse ratio to the simplicity of the material compound lined by it. . . . Spiritual perfection (or conscious "centreity") and material synthesis (or complexity) are but the two aspects or connected parts of one and the same phenomenon (1959:60).

It is not difficult to see the way in which Teilhard de Chardin's theory of all energy being in the last resort "psychic" could be used to articulate the traditional African idea of force. Senghor uses it precisely for this purpose, delighted to find a scientific and philosophical vindication of his anti-materialist position. One has to admit that the parallels between Teilhard de Chardin's system and the world-view of traditional African thought are, in this respect, striking.

One of the consequences of this unified metaphysical vision which is most apt for Senghor's purpose of systematising traditional African ideas, is the complete unity between humankind and the rest of the world that it entails. Everything that eventually appears in human nature is present in a less developed form throughout the universe; in the course of evolution the elements combine and a unique combination is produced. But there is no break in the web of relationships of force that combine to produce humanity out of simpler forms of life, and continue to support and develop human life into the ever newer social forms it takes in the future.

There is another consequence of the law of complexity-consciousness which fits in well with Senghor's ultimate aim in constructing his system of Negritude. This is the fact of there being a direction, and hence a centre, to world-process and evolution. The direction is towards ever greater complexity of organisation, and therefore towards ever greater "centring" and unity. This accounts for the special position of humankind, and the reason why our perspective on the world is a privileged one: we are the centre of the process, humanity is simply evolution become [*sic*] conscious of itself. In the words of Teilhard de Chardin (1959:61), the law of complexity-consciousness is one "that itself implies a psychically convergent structure and curvature of the world".

This complexifying and centring continues even after the production of humanity, in human culture and labour and the construction of ever new forms of civilisation and society. This is the realm of what Teilhard de Chardin calls the noosphere. Again, this aspect of Teilhard de Chardin's thought fits Senghor's purpose well. Summarising Teilhard de Chardin, he writes:

> But what is socialization-civilization? It is, the scientist answers, the organization of human relations, the re-construction of the earth – of nature, Marx and Engels would say – for the promotion of a new *human* society. By "human society" we mean not one nation, one race, one continent, but all men without exception in a common effort of organization and reconstruction, of co-reflection (Senghor 1965:137).

Teilhard de Chardin's theory of convergence is the perfect foundation for Senghor's idea of the "Civilization of the Universal" and the "psychic miscegenation" (1963:22), that goes with it. The "human tendency to merge", as Senghor (1963:21) puts it, to synthesise their cultural products, is the conceptual foundation for the idea of the complementarity of cultures which is such an important element in Negritude.

Finally, there is the moral element, the element of human value in the whole Teilhardian scheme. The complexifying and centring goes on, as has been said, even once the human level has been reached. But here the radial energy that is its principal dynamism wears a truly personal face; it is the energy we know as love. Teilhard de Chardin defines love as energy by taking the Thomist definition (the affinity of being with being) and re-expressing it in terms of his evolutionary world-view:

> Love in all its subtleties is nothing more, and nothing less, than the more or less direct trace marked on the heart of the element by the psychical convergence of the universe upon itself (Teilhard de Chardin 1959:265).

The importance of love as an energy of socialisation, for Teilhard de Chardin, is that it is the only moral force that is capable of "personalizing" (1959:265) the developing order. We do not here have the space to spell out fully why Teilhard de Chardin thinks this is so. A couple of quotations, by way of illuminating this crucial point, must suffice:

> Love alone is capable of uniting living beings in such a way as to complete and fulfil them, for it alone takes them and joins them by what is deepest in themselves. This is a fact of daily experience. At what moment do lovers come into the most complete possession of themselves if not when they say they are lost in each other? In truth, does not love every instant achieve all around us, in the couple or the team, the magic feat, the feat reputed to be contradictory, of "personalising" by totalising? And if that is what it can achieve daily on a small scale, why should it not repeat this one day on world-wide dimensions? (Teilhard de Chardin 1959:265).

This phenomenon finds its explanation in a general principle of Teilhardian biology: union differentiates. Thus,

> [i]n any domain – whether it be the cells of a body, the members of a society or the elements of a spiritual synthesis – *union differentiates*. In every organised whole, the parts perfect

themselves and fulfil themselves. Through neglect of this universal rule many a system of pantheism has led us astray to the cult of a great All in which individuals were supposed to be merged like a drop in the ocean or like a dissolving grain of salt. Applied to the case of the summation of consciousnesses, the law of union rids us of this perilous and recurrent illusion. No, following the confluent orbits of their centres, the grains of consciousness do not tend to lose their outlines and blend, but, on the contrary, to accentuate the depth and incommunicability of their egos. The more "other" they become in conjunction, the more they find themselves as "self" (Teilhard de Chardin 1959:262).

When the union in question is a strictly personal one then it can only be achieved by means of love:

For the human particles to become really personalised under the creative influence of union – according to the preceding analysis – not every kind of union will do. Since it is a question of achieving a synthesis of centres, it is centre to centre that they must make contact and not otherwise. Thus, amongst the various forms of psychic interactivity animating the noosphere, the energies we must identify, harness and develop before all others are those of an "intercentric" nature, if we want to give effective help to the progress of evolution in ourselves. Which brings us to the problem of love (Teilhard de Chardin 1959:263).

Clearly, this way of thinking is very sympathetic to what we have seen of traditional African thought and Senghor's understanding of it. Senghor's (1963:22) idea of "love-in-union" in particular seems to be a derivative of Teilhard de Chardin's. Senghor uses it in an explicitly political context to define the conditions of a truly human society. As such it is the basis of his criticism of all other social systems:

Although all present political regimes – democracy, socialism, Communism – have as their goal totalization and socialization without depersonalization, they fail in the attempt. This is because they sacrifice the part to the whole, the person to the collectivity. Since a materialist postulate underlies this, and since the collectivity is conceived solely as a technical organization, it does not attract; to push the individuals towards it, one must resort to constraint and violence. This is the reason for the failures. But if one conceives of the collectivity as human convergence cemented by liberty, equality, fraternity – terms that Marx scorned – and if one places love of the Super-Person above human love, there will naturally be a powerful attraction to group individuals without constraint. For, once again, "union differentiates", love personalizes (Senghor 1965:147).

6. CONCLUSION

Senghor's use of Teilhard de Chardin, though copious and acknowledged, is not really systematic. Negritude appears as a collection of insights, each bearing a certain relation to the others deriving from their common origin, rather than as a systematic philosophy embracing a metaphysics, an ethics, and a theory of the human person. Senghor is content to use Teilhard de Chardin's concepts; he does not develop them or shape them in his own way. In spite of that I find his attempt impressive. He sees what needs to be done, and he gives us an example of how European and African thought can come together. In addition to that there is, I think, substantial truth in what he has produced, and he has applied his thought creatively to tackle the problems of post-colonial Africa.

Reading

NEGRITUDE AND AFRICAN SOCIALISM[1]
LÉOPOLD S. SENGHOR

You in Britain have been criticised in the past for not having a sense of universality, for your refusal to assimilate native populations. Today, you are praised for having emphasised points of difference rather than of similarity. You must agree that the *Civilisation of the Universal* will be brought about by the fusion of "differing civilisations" (Teilhard de Chardin 1959). And that to achieve this, the peoples who until now "had hardly any life beyond the surface of themselves" (Teilhard de Chardin 1959) must, in the words of Teilhard de Chardin, arouse the "world of energy" which "still slumbers within them". But all these peoples and races must first re-discover the profundity of life; they must not only know it but, as the French word "*con-naître*" suggests, be reborn with it. The University of Oxford, through its chairs devoted to overseas studies, continues to teach the knowledge of these hidden springs of life.

This brings me to the theory of Negritude. A few months ago, in Nairobi, a friendly journalist from that much-respected paper, *The Times,* put on a show of naivety and asked whether the concept of Negritude was not, in the final analysis, a new form of racialism. I must admit that it was, indeed, in its early days "an anti-racial racialism", as Jean-Paul Sartre calls it in his *Orphée Noir*.

Now, try to put on a black skin for five minutes. I know you find this hard to do, but there is no other way to get the living feel of our situation. Go back in time some thirty years, to the years between the two world wars. We black students in the Latin Quarter were filled with pride, passion, and also the naive ignorance of youth.

We had been taught, by our French masters at the *Lycée,* that we had no civilisation, having been left off the list of guests at the Banquet of the Universal. We were *tabula rasa*, or, better still, a lump of soft wax which the fingers of the white demiurge would mould into shape. The only hope of salvation you could hold out to us was to *let ourselves be assimilated.*

This is what you taught, and we followed your precepts meekly – because we despaired of ourselves. I say "you". I mean, of course, the Latin peoples.

Yet, about the same time, ethnology began to be taught in France. But it was confined to specialised institutes, such as the *École Coloniale,* where I long taught myself. In the University of Oxford this new science of Negro-African ethnology held a place of honour long before its triumphal entry into the Sorbonne. That is the first point I wished to make, and for which I wanted to praise you, the University of Oxford, who so promptly invited the black man to take his seat at your Banquet.

"Yes, but in the kitchen," I can hear the disgruntled say. And they go on to quote the lines of the American Negro poet, Langston Hughes:

I am the darker brother.
They send me to eat in the Kitchen
When company comes.
But I laugh
And eat well
And grow strong.

"No, not in the kitchen," I would reply; at the bottom of the table, perhaps. What matters is that we were invited, and we did come. Is there any people, any nation, which does not consider itself superior, and the holder of a unique message? I repeat, what matters is that the black man was present among you, and that you treated him like a brother, who might be the youngest member of the family, but had something worthwhile to say. What matters is that, through its most famous university, Great Britain recognised the *Negro-African personality,* and considered it *digna amari,* worthy of fostering. A fact to which the United Kingdom had for a long time given expression through its policy of *indirect government.*

"But what do you mean by Negritude?" you may ask, in company with the friendly journalist from the much-respected *Times.* To answer your question, may I again recall my student days in the Latin Quarter? Paradoxically, it was the French who first forced us to seek its essence, and who then showed us where it lay.

The French forced us to seek the essence of Negritude when they enforced their policy of assimilation and thus deepened our despair. It almost drove the West Indian poet, Aimé Césaire, who had become a Negro-African in spirit, to insanity. Early on, we had become aware with ourselves that assimilation was a failure; we could assimilate mathematics or the French language, but we could never strip off our black skins nor root out our black souls. And so we set out on a fervent quest for the Holy Grail, which was our *Collective Soul.* And we came upon it. It was not revealed to us by the "official France" of the politicians who, out of self-interest and political conviction, defended the policy of assimilation. Its whereabouts was pointed out to us by that handful of free-lance thinkers – writers, artists, ethnologists, and pre-historians – who bring about cultural revolutions in France. It was, to be quite precise, our teachers of ethnology who introduced us to the considerable body of work already achieved in the understanding of Africa by the University of Oxford.

What did we learn from all those writers, artists, and teachers? They taught us that the early years of colonisation and especially, even before colonisation, the *slave-trade,* had ravaged black Africa like a bush fire, wiping out images and values in one vast carnage. That negroid civilisation had flourished in the Upper Palaeolithic Age, and that the Neolithic Revolution could not be explained without them. That their roots retained their vigour, and would one day produce new grass and green branches. That mere discursive reason, the *reason which only sees,* was inadequate to "comprehend" the world, to gather it up and transform it. That it needed the help of intuitive reason, *the reason which comes to grips,* which delves beneath the surface of facts and things. I must admit that this revelation went to our heads, and set us well on the way to racialism. Soldiers in the cause of Negritude, the Senegalese light infantry, we unsheathed our native knives and stormed the values of Europe, which we summed up in the threefold expression: discursive reason, technical skill, and a trading economy. In other words, *capitalism.*

I ought at this point, you may think, to define Negritude. Well, Negritude is *the whole complex of civilised values – cultural, economic, social, and political – which characterise the black peoples,* or, more precisely, the Negro-African world. All these values are essentially informed by intuitive reason. Because this sentient reason, the reason which comes to grips, expresses itself emotionally, through that self-surrender, that coalescence of subject and object; through myths, by which I mean the archetypal images of the Collective Soul; above all, through primordial rhythms, synchronised with those of the cosmos. In other words, the sense of communion, the gift of myth-making, the gift of rhythm, such are the essential elements of Negritude, which you will find indelibly stamped on all the works and activities of the black man.

As I said when discussing our revelation, we were as harshly uncompromising as neophytes, and our attitude was reinforced by all the resentment stirred in us by the colonial regime. We refused to cooperate; we took pleasure in a root and branch opposition to Western civilisation. "But," notes Cheikh Anta Diop, "the word Negritude has a whole history of its own. The historical circumstances which attended its birth seem fully to justify it. Nevertheless, we must draw attention to the fact that its content has been enriched with the passing of time, and has been renewed as circumstances have altered." Like life, the concept of Negritude has become historical and *dialectical.* I should now like to trace the stages of this evolution for you as briefly as possible.

In opposition to European racialism, of which the Nazis were the symbol, we set up an "anti-racial racialism". The very excesses of Nazism, and the catastrophes it engendered, were soon to bring us to our senses. Such hatred, such violence, ah! above all, such weeping and such shedding of blood produced a feeling of revulsion – it was so foreign to our continent's genius: *our need to love.* And then the anthropologists taught us that there is no such thing as a pure race: scientifically speaking, races do not exist. They went one better and forecast that, with a mere two hundred million people, we would in the end disappear as a "black race" through miscegenation. At the same time they did offer us some consolation. "The focal points of human development," wrote Teilhard de Chardin, in 1939, "always seem to coincide with the points of contact and anastomosis of several nerve paths," that is, in the ordinary man's language, with the meeting points of several races. If, then, we were justified in fostering the values of Negritude, and arousing the energy slumbering within us, it must be in order to pour them into the mainstream of cultural miscegenation (the biological process taking place spontaneously). They must flow towards the meeting point of all humanity; they must be our contribution to the Civilisation of the Universal.

Biological miscegenation, then, takes place spontaneously, provoked by the very laws which govern life, and in the face of all policies of apartheid. It is a different matter in the realm of culture. Here, we remain wholly free to cooperate or not, to provoke or prevent the synthesis of cultures. This is an important point. For, as certain biologists point out, the psychological mutations brought about by education are incorporated in our genes, and are then transmitted by heredity. Hence the major role played by *culture.* We Negro-Africans and you Europeans thus have a common interest in fostering our specifically native values, whilst remaining open to the values of the *Others.* Do we not agree, then, that culture, far from rooting us in materially determining factors – geography, ethnology, and history – is in the end a means of transcending them?

Seen within this prospect of the Civilisation of the Universal, the colonial policies of Great Britain and France have proved successful complements to each other, and black Africa has benefited. The policies of the former tended to reinforce the traditional native civilisation. As for France's policy, although we have often reviled it in the past, it too ended with a credit balance, through forcing us actively to assimilate European civilisation. This fertilised our sense of Negritude. Today, our Negritude no longer expresses itself as opposition to European values, but as a *complement* to them. Henceforth, its militants will be concerned, as I have often said, *not to be assimilated, but to assimilate*. They will use European values to arouse the slumbering values of Negritude, which they will bring as their contribution to the Civilisation of the Universal.

Nevertheless, we still disagree with Europe: not with its values any longer, with the exception of capitalism, to which I will return, but with its theory of the Civilisation of the Universal, as formulated by the Society for European Culture. This theory has been very precisely defined by Humberto Campagnolo, and more aggressively, but, fortunately, less narrowly defined by Denis de Rougemont. We had this matter out at the Rome conference, in February 1960, at a joint meeting of the Society for European Culture and the Society for African Culture. In the eyes of the Europeans, the "exotic civilisations" are static in character, being content to live by means of archetypal images, which they repeat indefinitely. The most serious criticism is that they have no idea of the *pre-eminent dignity of the human person*. My reply is this. Just as much as black Africa – taking this as an example – Europe and its North American offspring live by means of archetypal images. For what are free enterprise, the American way of life, democracy, communism, but myths, around which hundreds of millions of men and women organise their lives? Negritude itself is a myth (I am not using the word in any pejorative sense), but a living, dynamic one, which evolves with its circumstances into a form of Humanism. Actually, our criticism of the thesis advanced by the Society for European Culture is that it is monstrously anti-Humanist. For if European civilisation were to be imposed, unmodified, on all peoples and continents, it could only be by force. That is its first disadvantage. A more serious one is that it would not be *humanistic*, for it would cut itself off from the complementary values of the greater part of humanity. As I have said elsewhere, it would be a universal civilisation; it would not be the Civilisation of the Universal.

Whereas our revised Negritude is humanistic, I repeat, it welcomes the complementary values of Europe and the white man, and indeed, of all other races and continents. But it welcomes them in order to fertilise and reinvigorate its own values, which it then offers for the construction of a civilisation which shall embrace all mankind. The *neo-Humanism* of the twentieth century stands at the point where the paths of all nations, races, and continents cross, where the four winds of the spirit blow.

THE AFRICAN MODE OF SOCIALISM

I said, a few moments ago, that, among the values of Europe, we had no intention, we still have no intention, of retaining capitalism, not in its nineteenth-century form at least. Of course, private capitalism was, in its early days, one of the factors of progress, just as feudalism was in its time, and even colonisation. For the backwardness of black Africa, for example, has been caused less by colonisation than by the slave trade, which in three centuries carried off some two hundred million victims, *black hosts*. Capitalism, then, thanks to the accumulation of financial resources and its development of the means of production, was a factor of progress for Europe and also for Africa.

Today it is an out-of-date social and economic system – like federalism, like colonisation. And, I would add, like the imperialism in which it found its expression. Why? Because if, with its specialisations, the collectivisation of work constitutes a critical step towards *socialisation*, the defence or, more exactly, the extension of private property does not lead in this direction. Just as serious is the alienation, in the material realm and the realm of the spirit, of which capitalism is guilty, because capitalism works only for the well-being of a minority. Because, whenever state intervention and working-class pressure have forced it to reform itself, it has conceded only the minimum standard of living, when no less than the maximum would do. Because it holds out no prospect of a *fuller being* beyond *material well-being*. That is why, under the capitalist system, the political, cultural, and spiritual liberties, which are so often quoted, are enjoyed only in theory: on the surface. They are not *lived*. Under this system the word is not bound up with the idea, the act is not linked with the word; there is, in short, a gap between practice and theory, between life and ethics. The result is the theoretical contradictions of free enterprise, with its doctrines of *laissez-faire* and *laissez-aller,* and the anarchy of its practical application. There can be no concrete freedoms – political, cultural or spiritual – without economic freedom. Now, we can hardly define economic freedom as the freedom granted to a minority to exploit the majority. "Freedom," writes Teilhard de Chardin, "means the opportunity offered to each and every man (by suppressing the obstacles in his path and equipping him with the appropriate means) of transcending his human state by extending himself to the limits of his being." Private capitalism does not offer each man this opportunity of attaining the fuller being which lies beyond well-being.

It is because private capitalism finds it repugnant – or, more precisely, finds it impossible – to transcend its material bounds, it is because of its transformation into colonialist imperialism, that we were converted, after much hesitation, to socialism. As a matter of fact the general reasons I have just exposed were reinforced by more specific reasons arising from our colonial situation. It is undeniable that the principal motive of European overseas expansion was financial profit. I am not saying it was the sole motive. Trade opened the way to soldiers, missionaries, administrators, teachers. But private capitalism's aim has always been to sell the products of European industry to native populations, at the highest price possible, and to buy from them, at the lowest possible price, their raw materials. This is still the situation today after the granting of independence, and it goes some way to nullify the effects of the New Deal for underdeveloped countries: the European and American policy of *gifts*.

But our socialism is not that of Europe. It is neither atheistic communism nor, quite, the democratic socialism of the Second International of the Labour Party, for example. We have modestly called it the "African mode of socialism". Why? I should now like to explain our reasons as briefly as possible.

Mr Potekhin, the Director of the African Institute in Moscow, in his book entitled *Africa looks ahead,* gives the following definition of "the fundamental traits of the socialist society":

> The State's power is vested in the workers. All means of production are collective property, there are no exploiting classes, nor does one man exploit his fellow; the economy is planned, and its essential aim is to afford the maximum satisfaction of man's material and spiritual needs.

Obviously we cannot withhold our support from this ideal society, this earthly paradise. But it has still to come about, the exploitation of man by his fellow has yet to be stamped out in reality, the satisfaction of the spiritual needs which transcend our material needs has to be achieved. This has not yet happened in any European or American form of civilisation: neither in the West nor the East. For this reason we are forced to seek our own original mode, a Negro-African mode, of attaining these objectives, paying special attention to the two elements I have just stressed: *economic democracy* and *spiritual freedom.*

With this prospect before us, we have decided to borrow from the socialist experiments – both theoretical and practical – only certain elements, certain scientific and technical values, which we have grafted like scions on to the wild stock of Negritude. For this latter, as a complex of civilised values, is traditionally *socialist* in character. In this sense, our Negro-African society is a classless society, which is not the same as saying that it has no hierarchy or division of labour. It is a *community-based society,* in which the hierarchy – and therefore power – is founded on spiritual and democratic values: on the law of primogeniture and election; in which decisions of all kinds are deliberated in a *palaver,* after the ancestral gods have been consulted, in which work is shared out among the sexes and among technico-professional groups based on religion. This is a community-based society, *communal,* not collectivist. We are concerned, here, not with a mere collection of individuals', but with people conspiring together, *con-spiring* in the basic Latin sense, united among themselves even to the very centre of their being, communing through their ancestors with God, who is the centre of all centres.

Thus, in the working out of our "African mode of socialism", the problem is not how to put an end to the exploitation of man by his fellow, but to prevent its ever happening, by bringing political and economic democracy back to life; our problem is not how to satisfy spiritual, that is, cultural needs, but how to keep the fervour of the black soul alive. It is a question, once again, of modernising our values by borrowing from European socialism its science and technical skill, above all its spirit of progress.

The theory of historical and dialectical materialism justifies us in thrusting our roots deep into Negritude, seen as the historical situation of a group of actual men at a point in time, informed by a set of precise determining factors: geographical, ethnological, economic, social, cultural, and political. I am aware that many Europeans of all political creeds dislike both the name and the theory of Negritude. I can only see in this the expression of a superiority complex: the cultural imperialism of Europe.

Scientific research, cooperation, syndicalism, and planning represent so many contributions to serve as a working model. We must use them to fertilise the concept of Negritude and turn it into a *twentieth century socialism,* by means of which our countries can attain full economic and social development. They must help us to ensure the well-being of each individual.

Syndicalism represents the negative aspect of socialism. Even today, after some sixty years of colonial rule, no economic bourgeoisie is to be found in the majority of the Negro-African states promoted to independence. As for feudalism, it collapsed in the former "French colonies", and was turned into a showpiece in the former "British colonies". The specific object of African socialism, after the Second World War, was to fight against foreign capitalism and its slave economy; to do away, not with the inequality resulting from the domination of one class by another, but with the inequality resulting from the European conquest, from the domination of one people by another, of one race by another.

Marx nowhere deals with this form of inequality, this domination, and the struggle for freedom which they were to provoke. That was one of his omissions, which we had to repair by starting from our own situation, extrapolating, nevertheless, from his analyses and his theory, pressing them home to the very last of their logical implications and of their practical implications. For the celebrated *solidarity of the world proletariat* has remained purely theoretical, even among Marx's disciples. In hard fact, as we must have the clear sight – and the courage – to admit, the rise in the standard of living of the European worker has been effected, through a colonial slave economy, to the detriment of the masses of Asia and Africa. Hence the difficulties of decolonisation. I do not seek to deny, in this process of decolonisation, the disinterested action of certain noble minds, of intellectuals, of teachers, of philosophers, spurred on by a high ideal of brotherhood. These men and women have saved Europe's honour, and made possible the cooperation between Africa and Europe which exists today. But I would say that they were not in the majority, that decolonisation, as General de Gaulle admits in his plain-speaking magnanimity, now suits the needs of Europe and the conditions imposed by the Cold War.

And so scientific research, planning, and cooperation have as their first objective to ensure the well-being of each member of a given society, on an area of the world's surface which is shrinking as the population grows; the problem is to ensure that the earth – its soil, sub-soil and the air above it – is so treated that its resources are exploited with maximum efficiency, by modernising our agricultural, industrial, and commercial methods. But a prior condition of this modernisation is scientific research; we must first make a survey of our riches, our potentialities, and our shortcomings: not only our material riches, potentialities, and shortcomings, but also technical and human ones. The Plan for Social and Economic Development is then drawn up on the basis of this survey. This is a working hypothesis; it is, above all, the harmonious organisation of financial and technical inter-relationships, and even cultural and social ones, all of which have as their primary objective, I repeat, the satisfaction of material needs: housing, food, clothing, transport, etc. At this level, cooperation is the positive aspect of syndicalism. Here it is not only a matter of suppressing private capitalism, it is a question of replacing it, by organising work on a collective basis for the benefit of the workers. The workers in field and factory must take over the means of production and organise them more rationally, that is, more efficiently, thanks to help from the state, and the new hope roused in them by their re-won freedom, of which they now have a *living experience*.

Scientific research, planning, and cooperation sum up exactly the programme which my country, Senegal, has just put into action, the moving force being Monsieur Mamadou Dia, the Prime Minister. Our first Four-Year Plan has been under way since April 1961 with its research institutes, its state banks, its state enterprises, its office for the commercialisation of agriculture, and its cooperatives, which now comprise 80% of the peasants, who themselves form 70% of the total population. All this was preceded by a Social and Economic Survey, which took more than eighteen months to complete, and which is summed up in some two thousand pages.

And yet we have not legally suppressed private capitalism, which is foreign to our country; we have not even nationalised anything; above all, we have not shed a single drop of blood to obtain our independence or to get our Four-Year Plan under way. Why? Because we began by analysing our situation as an under-developed and colonised country. The essential task in the years following the war was to win back our national independence. Next we had to eliminate the flaws of colonial rule while preserving its positive contributions, such as the economic and technical infrastructure and the teaching of the French language; in spite of everything, the balance sheet of colonisation is positive rather than negative. Finally, these positive contributions had to be rooted in Negritude by a series of comparisons between existing systems. When private capitalism comes into peaceful competition with socialism, the latter must, I feel sure, emerge triumphant, provided that it transcends the goal of mere well-being, and does not secrete hatred. In the meantime, we need capital, even from private sources. Our aim is to fit it into the Development Plan, by controlling its use, as we do.

At this point we part company with the socialist experiments of Eastern Europe, with *communist* experiments, whilst taking over their positive achievements, when it is necessary. I spoke earlier of the *living experience* of a re-won freedom. To the list of needs which the plan must satisfy, I might have added *leisure*. This is how research, planning, and cooperation transcend, in their essence, the objective of material well-being. Science, by which I mean the quest for truth, is already a spiritual need. As is that rapture of the heart, of the soul, which *art* expresses, art which itself is only the expression of *love*. These spiritual needs, which weigh so heavy in Negro-African hearts, were touched on by Marx, as by Mr Potekhin; but Marx did not stress them, nor did he fully define them.

For, Marx's world-view, although that of a genius, remained too narrow; it was neither sufficiently *retrospective,* nor sufficiently *prospective,* as the Senegalese philosopher Gaston Berger (who was Director of Higher Education in France) would have said. We can hardly blame Marx for this, for, in the middle of the nineteenth century, theories, like relativity and the quantum theory, which have since revolutionised science, had not yet been advanced. History was scarce come to manhood; biology, geology, anthropology, and linguistics were still in their infancy. Prehistory had not yet been conceived. With the revolutions brought about in physics and chemistry, now that those sciences I mentioned have solidly established their methods, we can form a new world-vision which takes in the whole of matter and life: a *Weltanschauung* deeper and more complete than Marx's, and therefore more human. That is what Pierre Teilhard de Chardin tried to achieve. Henceforth, it is to this neo-Humanism that we must refer, not to refute the old scientific socialism, but to *revise* it, just as we revised our Negritude: by plugging the holes in it, and by opening up its blind alleys.

In this new world-view, historical and dialectical materialism remains fertile, to the extent that we extract all its consequences. But matter, "Holy Matter" as Teilhard de Chardin has called it, is no longer the indefinable thing it used to be. On analysis, it appears, through a bold reversal in the dialectical process, to be subtended by a *radial* energy of a psychic nature. And this, paradoxically, is how Negro-Africans have always thought of matter. History, in this new vision of the world, is no longer restricted to man or to the West; it plunges, way back beyond prehistory, into geology.

In this *retrospective-prospective vision,* in this total history, which is founded on evolution, man loses his position of domination, only to rediscover it on the farthest edge of the biological and cosmic drift, equipped with its irreducible idiosyncrasies. His essential idiosyncrasy is the tendency for all peoples, nations, and races to merge, whereas other animals are dispersed through the development of species.

Now, seen from this new and total view, the class struggle, the cornerstone of Marxist theory, is set in its true place. It becomes simply one aspect among many of the conflicts which set social groups, nations, and continents one against the other. In Europe – and in America – classes are being transformed into technico-professional groups, and the conflict between them is gradually resolved in balanced syntheses, following the human tendency to merge. It has already been pointed out that the American and Soviet social systems are growing more like each other, even though they are enemies.

For,now the great conflicts of history take place between nations – we call them the Cold War and decolonisation. They are only the exterior signs of the painful labour from which will be born the world of the future, with all divisions healed.

Why and how this reconciliation? For whom and by whom? Now we come to the problem of ultimate goals and methods, of *ends* and *values.* This is an aspect which Marx, in his excessively apocalyptic and determined vision, failed to stress sufficiently, forgetting that, as he progressed, man remained free to choose; he could accept or reject progress, depending on whether he found the goal attractive or not.

Let me remind you of our first objective – material well-being, *comfort* – and the means I described of achieving it. At the same time I suggested its limitations. As a syndicalist of the East German Democratic Republic put it, "Now I could do with reading some good literature." And you know that religious vocations are more numerous in the America of plenty than in the America of poverty in the South. Beyond the objective of material well-being, man aspires to fuller being, which is his end; beyond the satisfaction of his material needs, to that of his spiritual needs, especially in black Africa and in the underdeveloped countries. Their peoples hunger not so much after American or Russian surpluses, as after independence, dignity, science, and culture: after *Love-in-Union.* Try to imagine a world without love: between man and wife, in the family, in the nation, on the whole planet. Without this Love-in-Union, which is made real in God through religion and art, the world would be ice-bound; we would be powerless to prevent the *taedium vitae* taking possession of our souls.

For that rapture of the heart, that Love-in-Union which is Man's true end, to come into being, a minimum of material well-being is obviously necessary. On this scale, the means of socialism, which I listed above, may be considered as *values,* especially if we elevate them from the national to the international level. In any case, an economy which is restricted to the frontiers of a nation is not viable, as Francois Perroux has affirmed. Marx had already suggested that this was so.

Thus, the means of socialism transcend mere physical comfort, even on the national level; they are already personal *values,* values of the fuller being. Research, planning, and cooperation almost always allot large sums of money to family welfare, education, culture, leisure, and sometimes, as with us, to religious communities, to the satisfaction of spiritual needs. But the major phenomenon of the century in which we live is the development of international relations. The United Nations Organisation has taken the place of the League of Nations. What is the role of the UNO, but to organise on a rational basis, and to perfect, the interrelationships which have already been woven between peoples and nations, covering the surface of the globe with an ever-tighter network of material, cultural, and moral communications? Today, ships and railways, aeroplanes and rockets, books and newspapers, radio and television, are all much more than the means to an international economy, they are *values* of the Civilisation of the Universal. With an ever-growing awareness of the part these means can play, the United Nations Organisation proposes to coordinate and develop them through its specialised agencies, so that they lead us to the meeting point of all humanity.

Now, about the major role of UNESCO, which is to help build the Civilisation of the Universal by bringing the different civilisations together in discussion. It has started to show that the concept of race is a false myth; that each civilisation is a complex of material, technical, cultural, and spiritual values, the fruits of geography, history, and a mingling of ethnic characteristics; that the great civilisations of antiquity – Egypt, Sumeria, India, China, Greece – were born at the meeting points of the world's roads, and the world's races. Finally – last but not least – that the Civilisation of the Universal, which will be the culmination of *socialisation,* will not be European civilisation – in either its Eastern or Western form – imposed by force, but a biological and psychic miscegenation, a *symbiosis* of the different civilisations.

From now on, our duty as Negro-Africans is plain. We remain free to travel with the current, or to row against it. I say "our duty". I should say "our easily appreciable interests", which lie in the direction of the Civilisation of the Universal, of a socialism revised as socialisation, in which body and soul shall be fulfilled, and know the ineffable rapture of Love-in-Union. That Civilisation of the Universal, to which we shall contribute, when all is said and done, by pouring into it the burning lava of our Negritude, those values of our civilisation which I have defined above. If we were missing, civilisation would lack the rhythm section of its orchestra, the bass voices of its choir. Henceforth, *revised socialism* will have as its counterpart *revised Negritude,* which, let me repeat, is a form of *Humanism.*

Such are the thoughts (far too long, I know) that the University inspires in me. Black Africa and the whole world are deeply in its debt. Oxford is one of the peaks of the Civilisation of the Universal.

NOTE

1. Lecture delivered at St. Anthony's College, Oxford, 26 October 1961.

REFERENCES

Senghor, L.S. 1963. "Negritude and African socialism", in K. Kirkwood (ed.), *St Anthony's papers*, no. 15, Oxford, 9–22.

Senghor, L.S. 1965. *On African socialism*. Stanford: Pall Mall.

Senghor, L.S. 1966. "Negritude." *Optima*, 16:1–8.

Senghor, L.S. 1971. "Negritude and African socialism", in *Liberté II*, Paris: Editions du Seuil

Teilhard de Chardin, P. 1959. *The phenomenon of man*. London: Collins.

Glossary

Alienation: the state of being estranged. A person can be alienated from his/her own essence, nature, values, and beliefs, feeling unable to understand or accept him/herself (self-alienation). One can also be alienated from society (a feeling of being isolated or powerless in relation to society).

Baas/Baasskap: The Afrikaans word *baas* means master, and connotes the natural, God-given right of the white man to dominate black people on the basis of his racial superiority. The system of *baasskap* or masterdom underpinned the policy of apartheid and facilitated the oppression of black people in South Africa.

C^4: Contemporary Confluence of Cultures on the Continent of Africa. This is a post-colonial phenomenon where different cultures meet and mingle to form new, hybrid forms.

Causality (reasons and causes): causality is a relation between things or events, as when one (the cause) necessarily precedes and produces or alters the other (the effect). Sometimes a distinction is drawn between reasons and causes; one view is that there is a logical relation between an action and its reason – an action gets its identity from its place in an intentional plan of the agent; another view is that a reason is only a mental event, and unless the reason is causally linked to the action or event, we cannot say that it is the reason for the action or event.

Communitarianism: a social model of organisation which stresses ties of affection, kinship, and a sense of common purpose (as opposed to a morality of contractual ties entered into between individuals).

Community of mutuality: a community with a distinctive set of social meanings (shared understandings and interpretations) as well as a shared geographical location and shared memories; such a community includes various psychological communities.

Consensus: by harmonising the interests of the individual with those of others in the group or society by means of rational argument, common action is enabled. In the process, the considered judgement of the collective is reflected, the communal good is served, and the moral identity of the group is affirmed.

Dialectic: the process of overcoming the contradiction between thesis and antithesis by means of synthesis (the building up of separate elements into a connected whole), which in turn becomes contradicted; this process (a historical force) repeats itself until perfection is reached. Dialectical materialists confirm the primacy of matter over consciousness.

Dualism: the theory that reality is composed of two different, irreducible "substances" or two sorts of entities (which cannot be reduced to one another); spirit and matter, mind and body are often designated as such opposing realities.

Epistemology: the theory of knowledge; an enquiry into the nature and grounds of experience, belief and knowledge, justification and truth.

Ethnophilosophy: an African philosophical trend focusing on the documentation of the mythical concepts, ritual practices, proverbs, and institutions of the different African ethnic groups.

Freedom Charter: drawn up in 1955 at the instigation of the African National Congress in South Africa, this vision of the future embraces non-racialism. While recognising difference, its central tenets (e.g. "South Africa belongs to all who live in it, black and white", "All national groups shall have equal rights", "The people shall govern") constitute a vision of equality and democracy.

Holism/holistic: the theory that the fundamental principle of the universe is the creation of wholes. A whole is seen as built up of parts – but it is always more than the mere sum of its parts. Any doctrine emphasising the priority of a whole over its parts.

Ideology: any wide-ranging system of beliefs or ways of thought directing political and social action; a conceptual scheme with a practical application.

Metaphysics: the study of ultimate reality; the term "metaphysics" is derived from the Greek *metaphysika* which literally means "those things which lie behind physical phenomena". Traditionally, the metaphysician is expected to ontologise, i.e. to assert the existence of non-visible things behind the visible world on purely conceptual considerations; the existence of these non-visible entities is deemed necessary for a proper understanding of the visible world.

Modus ponens: a rule of logic/inference which applies to conditional statements. Given a conditional statement, if the antecedent of that conditional is also given, the rule allows that the consequent of that conditional follows necessarily. The traditional formulation of *modus ponens* is: {(p.q).p}⊃q. The conjunctive connective is commutative.

Nationalistic-ideological trend: an African philosophical trend developed as a reaction to the experience of colonialism; an African resistance and liberation philosophy.

Negritude: a term originating in the 1940s in the prose and poetry of Aimé Césaire, Léopold Senghor, and Léon Damas; it covers the totality of the black experience – the culture, values, and especially the spirit of black African civilisation.

Noncontradiction: the rule/principle of noncontradiction or excluded middle states that no statement may be both asserted and denied, either explicitly or implicitly, in the same context. In any given context a statement is either true or false; it cannot be both true *and* false.

Ontology: the branch of metaphysics that concerns itself with what exists, with what there is in the world.

"Other", the: the minor term in the binary opposition Self/Other, a hierarchically organised relationship in which the Self is what rules, names, and defines. The process of othering reduces the human person to a nobody, to the position of "Other", thus relegating traditionally oppressed groups of people (e.g. blacks, women, gays) to social and political margins. When identity is constructed as "Other", i.e. inferior, oppression or disempowerment is legitimated (cf. the phrase "the West and the rest").

Principle of charity: normative rather than intellectual, this principle encourages one to judge the truth-status of beliefs outside one's culture in a charitable way. A belief-claim coming from a culture one does not understand should be assumed to accord with the standards of one's own culture and, furthermore, to be consistent and correct.

Professional philosophy: a universalist and critical African philosophical trend, favouring second-order evaluation of first-order claims about the African cultural heritage and world-view.

Rainbowism: a post-apartheid South African notion of national unity that transcends difference and historic divisions. The putative "Rainbow nation" is constituted of people from diverse racial, ethnic, and cultural backgrounds who are united around a common purpose of forging a new, democratic nation.

Sagacity, philosophical: a critical analysis of African cultural belief systems, wisdom, practices, i.e. of the generally accepted ideas and beliefs in African communities.

Sage: a man or woman regarded as profoundly wise and knowledgeable regarding the traditional customs and wisdom of his or her culture. A philosophic sage has a critical, second-order approach and is capable of critical reflection on established views. The sage frequently favours change so that contemporary needs may be met.

SASO (South African Students' Organisation): an exclusively black (i.e. African, Indian, and "Coloured") organisation born of the experience of black students that their interests could not be defended by a white liberal organisation such as the National Union of South African Students (NUSAS). SASO was founded in 1969 by, among others, Steve Biko, who was also one of the founders of the Black Consciousness Movement (BCM) in South Africa. Both SASO and the BCM redefined "blackness" as an inclusive and positive concept of identity that discredits demeaning colonial/apartheid terms such as "non-white" and "non-European".

Sociality: this is the state of being interdependent, part of a kinship, lineage, community structure. The relational character of the individual person is paramount; it is within a shared system of values, a cultural structure, that the human person is actualised.

Simunye: this Zulu word means "we are one". It is a rallying cry of the new South African government in its attempt to build national unity founded on universalistic principles of equality and democracy.

Ubuntu: closely related to African Humanism, *Ubuntu* incorporates notions of an African collective consciousness and the universal brotherhood of Africans. Its values include sharing, treating other people as humans, empathy, warmth, sensitivity, understanding, care, respect, patience, reciprocation, and communication. Related to communalism, it perhaps finds its clearest expression in the saying that a person is a person because of other people.

Index

Biko, S.
and Black Consciousness 78
Black Consciousness (Movement) 78,
343–344
definition of 360–363
and liberation 360
Blanshard, B.
wisdom 243
Boas, F. 4
culture-embeddedness of the person 59
Bodunrin, P.
and Lansana Keita 102–103
nationalistic-ideological philosophy 95–98
philosophic sagacity 93, 107
professional philosophy 80
Buber, M.
demythologisation of religion 252
Busia, K.
African deity 197–198
Akan communalism 296

C⁴ (cross-culturation) 208–209, 211, 216

C^4 (cross-culturation) 208–209, 211, 216
Capitalism 25, 27, 53, 58
appropriation of culture in 20
instrumentalisation of reason in 65
Senghor's critique of 429, 439, 441–445
Categorical Imperative 37–38, 300, 311, 329
Catholicism
and authority 267, 270
and degenerationalism 57
and mysticism 120–121
Causality 139, 144, 261
Akan view of 197
Western vs. African view of 139
Causation 110, 188
in African thought 177–185
law of universal 189
primary theory and secondary theory
177–185
Césaire, A. 119
and African essence 75, 116
on Tempels 76, 128
Chafe, W.
on language production 8
Chain of being 138
Character
and existence 303–305
Chewa
culture 170–174
epistemology 240–244
personhood 175
notion of truth 240–241

Choice
and identity 277
secure context of 352–354
and self-realisation 348
Christian(ity) 10, 19, 25, 119, 192–194,
251–253, 257
and ancestors 271
the Bible 301
ethics 38
concept of God 194–196, 199, 201
influences 122
metaphysics 188
and religiosity 116
notion of the soul 57, 159
theodicy 261
tradition 261
See also Missionaries.
Civic and civil society 285–286
Civilisation of the Universal 428–437
Class theory
and white workers 361
Coevalness, theory of 53–54, 70, 79
Collectivism 45–46
Colonialism 1, 21, 429
British and French models 4, 438–439
Colonisation 30, 383–384, 386–387, 389
conceptual 190–191
Common good, the 317, 332
politics of 344–345
Common sense 217–218
Communalism 28, 127
and being 398
and belonging 311
and familyhood 96
and the individual 173
and land ownership 295
and mutuality 278
politics of 315
selflessness 295
solidarity 294–295
thesis 170, 172
threats to 312–314
in traditional societies 196
See also Communitarianism.
Communism
Senghor's critique of 429, 437
Communitarianism 148, 443
in African socio-ethical thought 317–322
and the contract theory 331
and human dignity 328
"left" and "right" theories of 276
and personhood 312, 320